VETERAN AND VINTAGE AIRCRAFT
Fourth Revised Edition

Where are the world's aeronautical museums and collections — and the veteran and vintage machines, military and civil, of the two World Wars and the era between the wars? Also the rare 'one-offs' — prototypes and record-breakers — like Alcock and Brown's *Atlantic Vimy,* Lindbergh's *Spirit of St. Louis,* Amy Mollison's *Gipsy Moth,* and the world's only Wellington bomber and Hawker Typhoon fighter?

This Fourth Edition of the internationally famous reference guide, again considerably expanded and up-dated, gives the answers. Leslie Hunt shows where some 9000 of the world's oldest, rarest and most fascinating aircraft and other flying machines, from the Wright Brothers' original 1903 Flyer to the British Aircraft Corporation's TSR 2, are flown or preserved. More than 2000 different types, illustrated by over 900 photographs, are listed in more than 90 countries.

The history of civil and military aviation is recorded in a unique and exciting way through *Veteran and Vintage Aircraft.* This is now a 'must' for all enthusiasts whether they are occasional air display visitors, museum browsers, current fliers, former aviators, youngsters, airline passengers or spacecraft trackers.

Leslie Hunt was born in Nottingham in 1911, is married, with two sons and four grandchildren, and lives in Leigh-on-Sea, Essex, England. He published his first newspaper article when he was at school, and this Fourth Edition of *Veteran and Vintage Aircraft* is his eighth book; he has written hundreds of articles for newspapers and journals mainly about aircraft and aviation. Leslie Hunt retired from the Royal Air Force in 1959. He has visited 60 countries since he was seventeen, and this book reflects his first-hand experience of aircraft and their present world-wide locations. His most recent book is *Twenty-One Squadrons: A History of the Royal Auxiliary Air Force, 1925-1957.* He devotes his spare time to the charity Muscular Dystrophy.

veteran and vintage aircraft

Fourth Revised Edition
Compiled by Leslie Hunt

Foreword by
Marshal of the Royal Air Force,
Sir John Grandy G.C.B., K.B.E., D.S.O.

Over 900 illustrations

Erwin Dean Hirtle
111 Penny Ln
Gahanna Ohio
43230

Charles Scribner's Sons • New York

Printed in Great Britain
Library of Congress Catalog
Card Number 74-29025
ISBN 0-684-14895-1

CONTENTS

FOREWORD by MARSHAL OF THE ROYAL AIR FORCE SIR JOHN GRANDY G.C.B., K.B.E., D.S.O.

The preservation and restoration of vintage and veteran aircraft was for many years the exclusive province of museums or bands of enthusiasts in various parts of the world. Until the appearance of the first edition of this book the existence and location of these aircraft was comparatively unknown. It is a measure of the popular demand for information on the remaining examples of our heritage of aviation history that "Veteran and Vintage Aircraft" - which started as a small scale venture - now emerges in a much enlarged fourth edition, well established as a unique and authoritative work of reference.

Flight Lieutenant Leslie Hunt RAF (Retd) has devoted a great deal of time, talent and sheer painstaking research to the production of this comprehensive coverage of a fascinating subject. In the three years which have passed since the publication of the third edition he has discovered and recorded the existence of over 4000 additional examples. There are now 136 collections in 39 countries, and airworthy vintage types of aircraft are in existence in 55 other countries. No less than 9000 machines have been listed.

In addition to the valuable contribution made by this book as a record of aviation history, its sale has the praiseworthy object of raising funds for the Muscular Dystrophy Group of Great Britain; both the historian and the humanitarian owe the author a great debt.

John Grandy

Marshal of the Royal Air Force

INTRODUCTION

Those who have purchased the earlier editions will know that I make no claim to expertise in the sphere of aircraft—my aim has always been to record the locations of veteran and vintage machines, flying or static, and, where possible, to encourage preservation of those threatened with destruction. Success has not always followed pleas to owners but once again V. and V. can claim a hand (in the moves of the Ju 52 from Portugal to England, the Mosquito from Speke to Salisbury Hall, the setting-up of the museum at Southend and with aid for the Torbay Museum). There are many other ways in which items shown in earlier editions have been saved for posterity by purchase, loan or donation and it is earnestly requested that any reader with knowledge of a rarity facing the scrapyard, sends details to the compiler who will pass them to the appropriate source. Too often, alas, unique machines are still being destroyed—the only-flown TSR.2 at Foulness, and the last Hermes, are but two recent cases; let us all try to keep to a minimum such acts of vandalism on the part of authority where, regrettably, limited vision sometimes seems to go cap-in-hand with a highly-paid post.

Since the third edition we have seen the opening of the RAF Museum and any who have not yet visited should place it high on their lists. This also applies to the new USAF Museum and to all museums listed in V. and V. for the first time, as well as to old and dear friends like the Shuttleworth Collection, the Fleet Air Arm Museum, Cole Palen's fabulous aircraft and, of course, the Canadian National Aeronautical Collection in and around Ottawa.

In the last edition I suggested that the time had probably come to divide the airworthy and static machines into two separate volumes. This has proved impracticable if only on the score of cost and if any feel I have included, this time, far too many Piper Cubs, Tiger Moths, Stearman Kaydets, or Harvards, may I mention that *more than three thousand* readers have corresponded with me since V. and V. Mk III and although I may not have answered (yet) every letter, I have thought it only fair to list many of the machines owned and flown by these kind helpers. It was my ambition to record every machine of WW.I and WW.II which still exists but there are so very many in USA that I can only try again if there is a demand for a 5th edition, by which time one imagines a few of the Dakotas may have left the air.

May I add here that I do not compile this book from registers but only from personal observation and the reports I receive. Unfortunately one or two have proved "red herrings" in that in one instance my enthusiasm led to an immediate call to the RAF Museum to secure a rarity reported in an overseas airmail. Signals flashed across the oceans only to reveal that the machine had been scrapped *twenty years* ago. Would kind friends please always give the date of their sighting and as much detail as possible of the condition of the a/c to avoid costly journeys, telephone calls, and, most valuable of all, the time and effort of many busy people. My reward—and that goes for all my good-hearted helpers—is in the locating and securing for preservation a machine not yet preserved or, if preserved, in such limited numbers as to warrant duplication. Because of the many moves which have taken place during the printing of this volume it is proposed to have an "Amendments" page, as up-to-date as possible when the page-proofs are finally checked. Readers can then decide whether to ink-in the relevant details or snip-out and paste-in on the proper page. It is impossible to be absolutely correct, especially with privately-owned veterans, and it may here be worth remarking that some years ago the compiler was asked to find a Spitfire for an "enthusiast" in England. As it happened one was available and was traded for a vintage car, only for the aircraft to depart these shores for USA—a donation for £5.00 being given by the "trader" to the Trueloves School—not over-generous, I thought! I was furious that the machine had left England but, happily, it is now back, allegedly at a cost of 100,000 dollars to its new owner. This for a Spitfire sold for only £100.00 by the RAF when in the markings of the Air Chief Marshal who had flown it and although sold as not airworthy, it was borrowed some long time afterwards from the garage where it stood, by the nearest RAF station and, without hesitation, was started and flown!! This long-winded tale is included to inform all and sundry that I am NOT in the buying and selling game, as some callers (especially from USA) seem to think, and I have learned that many who claim to be preservationists are dealers. I have been "used" for the last time! Genuine preservationists only please! In closing may I hope that you will find something of interest in these pages. If you have time or a little spare cash, join one of the Societies, or support your nearest museum by donation.

Leslie Hunt

ADDITIONS & AMENDMENTS TO 4TH EDITION

During the printing of this edition the following movements have taken place. Readers can decide whether or not to alter the pages:—**LONDON AREA. RAF MUSEUM.** *Handley Page Halifax II* W1048 "S" 35 Sqdn, landed on ice-covered Lake Hoklingen, Norway, April, 1942, after flak damage during attack on "Tirpitz". Sank as ice melted into 90ft of water. Discovered 1968 by Norwegian enthusiasts and recovered by RAF diving team 1973. To be restored, probably at Bicester, Oxfordshire. **MIDDLESEX. UXBRIDGE. RAF.** *Spitfire XVI* RW382 on display, from Leconfield. **BEDFORDSHIRE. BEDFORD.** Reported that the *Handley Page HP.115* and *BAC.221* are earmarked for RAF Museum. **CRANFIELD.** The *Boulton Paul P.111A* is to go to Boulton Paul's Factory, Wolverhampton, Staffs. **HENLOW. RAF.** *Catalina* not now coming. See Colerne. **LUTON.** *Mitchell* now at Prestwick—for disposal? **BUCKINGHAMSHIRE. BOOKER.** Wycombe Air Park. *Fiat G-46* I-AEHU ex MM52801 c/n 44—from Italy. *Rapide* G-AKIF (back from Norway). **CAMBRIDGESHIRE. DUXFORD.** *Douglas DC-3* G-ANAF for IWM Store; from Leavesden. *Vampire T.11* XD590, from Hawker Siddeley (hereafter, H.S.). **CHESHIRE. BRAMHALL.** Comprehensive School. *Vampire T.11* WZ505 from H.S. **CHEADLE HULME.** Cheadle Hulme School. *Vampire T.11* XD534 from H.S. **HAZEL GROVE.** Girls Secondary School. *Vampire T.11* XK627 from H.S. **STOCKPORT.** Northern A/c Preservation Society. *Vampire T.11* XD435 (loaned to 1832 Sqdn, ATC) *T.11* XD535 (loaned to Royal Umpire Museum, Croston, Lancs.) both from H.S. **WOODFORD.** Apprentice School. *Vampire T.11* XE998. **DERBYSHIRE. BOLSOVER.** *Viscount* XR802, to be Cafe—from Boscombe Down, Wilts. **DEVONSHIRE. HIGHER BLAGDON.** Torbay A/c Museum. *DH. Vampire T.11* XE995 from H.S. **ESSEX. SOUTHEND-on-SEA.** Historic A/c Museum. *DH. Puss Moth* G-AEOA, for Tony Haig-Thomas's Moth Collection; from King's Somborne, Hants. *DH. Vampire T.11* XK625, from H.S. *DH. 89A Rapide* G-AIUL, for display. *Sea Fury* CF-OHB from Cold Lake, Alberta, also *T-33s* CF-EHB, CF-IHB, all owned by O. Haydon-Baillie, airworthy. *Republic F-84F* FU-6 ex 52-7133, donated by Belgian AF. **GLOUCESTERSHIRE. STAVERTON.** Skyfame Museum *Messenger* G-AIEK airworthy; painted RG333 (Monty's WWII a/c.) *DH. Vampire T.11* WZ515 from H.S. **HAMPSHIRE. KING'S SOMBORNE.** *Puss Moth* moved to Southend. **LASHAM.** *DH. Comet* 4G-APDB preserved by Dan-Air. **HERTFORDSHIRE. LEAVESDEN.**

DH.Puss Moth (Southend)

Javelin FAW.8 (West Raynham)

Fieseler Storch (St. Athan)

Spitfire XVI (Leavesden)

DH.Comet 1A (Colerne)

Spitfire XVI G-BAUP ex SL721 N8R from St. Charles, Illinois. Also here, Doug Arnold's *Harvards* G-AZKI and G-AZSC, from Fairoaks, Surrey. **REDBOURN.** *Seafire F.46* LA564 from Newark, Notts; with Peter Arnold. **LANCASHIRE. BARTON.** *DH. Vampire T.11* XD434 (Manchester University) from H.S. **CHADDERTON.** Apprentices School, *DH. Vampire T.11* XD395 from H.S. **MOSTON.** Technical College. *DH. Vampire T.11* XK623 from H.S. **LIVERPOOL.** Speke. *Vampire* with Merseyside Aviation Society is WZ553 c/n 15112 ex 202 AFS/7 FTS/4 FTS. from H.S. *Boeing Stearman PT-17 Kaydet* 4X-AIH c/n 3250-1405 and 4X-AMT c/n 3250-2606, from Israel are to fly at Speke. **SQUIRE'S GATE.** *Lancaster* to RAF Scampton. **LINCOLNSHIRE. SCAMPTON. RAF.** *Lancaster* VII NX611 from Blackpool. **TATTERSHALL.** *DH. Vampire T.11* XD477 from H.S. **NORFOLK. NEATISHEAD. NORWICH.** *Avro Anson* G-AWSA with Norfolk & Suffolk Aviation Society. **WEST RAYNHAM. RAF.** *Gloster Javelin FAW.8* XH980 from Stafford. **NOTTINGHAMSHIRE. NEWARK.** Air Museum *Vampire T.11* is XD593 from H.S. *Seafire F.XVII* SX336, Neville Franklin. **SHIREBROOK.** *Viscount* XR801 from Boscombe Down, in garden—see **EDWINSTOWE**—is this the same movement? **OXFORDSHIRE. BENSON.** *Spitfire XIX* PM651 from Bicester. Has TE311 gone to 71 MU? **SHROPSHIRE. SHAWBURY.** *Comet* and *Javelin* moved to Colerne, Wilts. **TERNHILL. RAF.** *Bristol Sycamore HR.14* XJ385 "SJ", on display. **SOMERSET. YEOVILTON.** Add *Gannet AEW.3* XL503. **STAFFORDSHIRE. COSFORD.** The stored RAF Museum a/c from Topcliffe. **SUFFOLK. HONINGTON. RAF.** On display *Blackburn Buccaneer S.1* XK531 ex 700Z, 809 and 736 Sqdns. **SURREY. EWELL.** *Vampire* moved to 71 MU, Bicester—possibly for scrapping. **FAIROAKS.** *Pup* (replica) G-APUP. **GODALMING.** At RFD Ltd (from Cranfield) *English Electric Canberra T.4* WH657 and *Westland Whirlwind HAS.7* XK906 reported on display. **SUSSEX. FLIMWELL.** Add *NA. Texan* G-AZJD ex 41-33931, EX958, H-9, Belg. AF., F-BJBF. **WARWICKSHIRE. COVENTRY.** Midlands A/c Preservation Society. Add:— *DH. Vampire T.11* XE872 ex H.S. (displayed at Blue Lias Inn, Stockton, Nr Rugby.) *Gloster Meteor F.4* EE531, from Lasham, Hants, used for gunnery trials and folding-wing experiments etc. *Hawker Sea Hawk FB.3* from Cranfield (held by MAPS member in Swansea.) **YORKSHIRE. LEEMING. RAF.** *Javelin* XA634 from Colerne. **PAULL** *Beverley* XB259 *Me 101* from Henlow. *Bf 109* (replica) and *Spitfire* (replica) painted N3313 BO-D, ex Madame Tussauds) both owned by John Berkeley, MAPS chairman. *Slingsby Cadet* is being rebuilt to fly with University of Aston-in-Birmingham Gliding Club as a MAPS a/c. **WILTSHIRE. COLERNE.** *DH. Comet 1A* XM823 and *Gloster Javelin FAW.9* XH982 from Shawbury. *Dakota* KN645 from Northolt; *Catalina* L-866, from Denmark. **SCOTLAND. STRATHALLAN.** *Scion* from Bankstown, NSW. **GLAMORGAN. ST. ATHAN.** *Storch* from Coltishall. **BELGIUM. BRUSSELS.** *Vampire T11* XH289 to museum from H.S. **FRANCE. PARIS.** *Aerospatiale-BAC Concorde* prototype 001 for museum. **NETHERLANDS. LEIDEN.** *Fieseler 103/RE* (piloted V1). **RHODESIA. THORNHILL. GWELO.** *Vampire FB.9* RII2; *Tiger Moth* SR26; *Vampire T11* R4201. **SALISBURY.** Museum. *Vampire T11* (serial ?) *Harvard* SR48. **JAPAN. TOKYO.** "Zero" CF-GVT from Carman, Manitoba. **CANADA. MANITOBA.** St. James' Assinboine Park *T-33C* 21232 on pedestal. **USA. LANCASTER,** Cal. Western Aerospace Museum defunct. **SAGINAW,** Michigan. Military Museum defunct. All a/c from USAFM to be re-allocated. **BRAZIL. SAO PAULO.** Marte Airport. *Viscount* PP-SRN c/n 62 ex G-ANHG preserved.

ACKNOWLEDGEMENTS
AND THANKS

As mentioned in the Introduction, I have received letters from over three thousand readers since the 3rd edition appeared and of these about a thousand are my "backbone" helpers, some having co-operated with me since before the first pocket-version, issued in 1965 to pay for the extension to Trueloves School. You will understand, I know, that I cannot mention here every single name but I hope to atone for this as I clear the backlog of correspondence which has accumulated during the typing of this edition. May I say now, a very warm thank-you to all who have, in any way, assisted to make this a more-detailed volume. It will largely depend upon you whether or not we try again with a fifth edition; for it is your encouraging letters which keep me going, especially on days when I learn that yet another valuable machine has been reduced to scrap.

For the gift or loan of blocks from which the illustrations have been made, my gratitude again to David Dorrell of Air Pictorial, Chris Wren of Esso Air World, Ron Moulton of Scale Models, John W. Taylor and Lance Jackson of Air BP, Bruce Quarrie of Airfix Magazine, Leslie Bichener of Essex Countryside and to the kind photographers—Ron Cranham, Stuart Howe, Philip Birtles, Brian Stainer and his associates of Aviation Photo News, Ken Smy, Miss Nancy Woodall, NA Magazine, Norway, Harry McDougall, John Wegg, Arni Gudmundsson, Bryan Philpott, Henry, Carter and Lindsay Peacock, Brian M. Service, Harry S. Gann of Douglas A/c, Walt Boyne, Vic Kondra, J. M. Kucera, Captain Keith Sissons, Mal Sketchley, S. G. Richards, Clive Moggridge, Air Portraits, Tom Dunstall, and Art Schoeni of Vought Aeronautics, for allowing use of their copyright photos without fee to keep down the cost of this edition.

For the continuing flow of information I am grateful to many old friends, notably Neville Franklin, Peter Arnold (Spitfire specialist) A. J. "Jack" Jackson, David Welch, Roy Bonser, A. C. Harold (VAG) Allan Hall, Roderick Simpson, Bernard Martin, Flt Lt Russ Snadden, RAF, S/Ldr Beeton, ATC, Chris Wills, Peter Berry, P. G. Lysley, Peter Schofield of MAPS, John Dawe, Flt Lt Jock Manson, RAF, Ian McConnell "Airdata", Peter Bish, Dr. Paul Haig, Roger Smith, D. Johnson, L. Hitchings, John Havers, Bob Ogden, George Jones and "Flypast", John Tanner, Jack Bruce and Bill Randle of the RAF Museum; Les Cox, FAA Museum; Keith Fordyce and his associates at Torbay; Willie Roberts and Dick Richardson at Strathallan; Capt. J. C. Kelly-Rogers in Dublin; John Berkeley of MAPS, J. D. Storer in Edinburgh, Flt Lt Frapwell of Colerne; David Ogilvy of Shuttleworth; Doug Bianchi and Philip Mann of Wycombe Air Park; G. W. B. Lacey, Science Museum; Walter Goldsmith, Mosquito Appeal Fund Museum; Philip Jarrett, George Pennick, and not least Mike Ramsden of Flight International for so kindly allowing my many letters to appear in his columns. My overseas helpers have greatly increased and I can, alas, only mention a comparative few:—in Belgium, Lt-General (Aviation) Baron Michael Donnet and Colonel Mike Terlinden; France, Lt-Colonel Jean Reveilhac and A. Picollet; Denmark, Hans Kofoed; Sweden, Benny Karlsson; Italy, Jerome Geeson, Roberto Gentilli; Germany, Roland Poehlmann, Andreas Weise, Flt Lt M. P. Keitch, RAF, Christian Emrich, Karl Kramer; Netherlands, Fred Roos; Norway, Flt Lt Jeremy Collins, RAF, Bjorn Olsen, Miss Smith of RAFA, Oslo and the R.No.A.F. HQs; Poland, Ray Draper and John Beales; Finland, Romania and Yugoslavia, John Wegg and T. G. W. Potts; South Africa, Andy Heape and Dave Becker; India, Pushpinder Chopra; Australia, W. A. Lancaster and S. C. Gladwin of the Australian War Memorial; Gp Cpt Keith Isaacs, RAAF, Ian McArthur, Major Charlie Miller, Ralph Bullock, Pearce Dunn of Warbirds. In Canada, New Zealand and USA I have so many kind friends that pages would be required to include all of them. I must start, though, with Wg Cdr Ralph Manning of CanadianWar Museum,

Walter Henry of C.A.H.S., Bob Bradford of the Canadian National Aeronautical Collection and Wg Cdr Markham; plus "Bunny" d'Arby, of Auckland. Royal D. Frey of USAF Museum has been, as ever, a constant source of information and illustrations, as has Bob Snyder. Roger Baker and Lloyd Nolen of CAF have kept me well-furnished with data and Colonels Rhodes Arnold and "Pancho" Morse have helped enormously, with Pima County Museum and many other snippets. Max Heinz, John Tiley, John Allen-Price, Bill Carmody, David Menard, Bill Larkins, Ed Maloney, Robert F. Pauley, Quinnie N. D. Elliott, Gary Battson, Robert Mikesh (NASM), Barret Tillman Leonard Opdycke and Neil Rose have been towers of real strength with all parts of USA. In South America, D. W. Robinson (RAF) with Paulo Rezende, Ronaldo S. Olive and Alex Reinhard of Swissair have kept me supplied with information, though there is much more I'd like to know about vintage types, flying and static here and in Central America and West Indies. Please, though, do give the dates of your photographs and sightings. Once again it is not possible to show the names of photographers under illustrations partly to keep down captions and secondly because many prints have come of some aircraft, often taken at the same time and identical. We (the compiler and publisher) hope that the note of thanks above will satisfy those whose pictures are used in this edition and that you will all continue to contribute them to enable us to keep the cost of the book within reason.

Finally; may I express warm thanks to Malcolm P. Fillmore, who has speeded-up production by checking the typescript and proofs, and to Michael Balfour and all at Garnstone Press for their faith in yet another volume. My wife, as usual, has kept me going with ample refreshment and has endured the endless telephone calls and my "days of depression", with commendable patience.

January 1974   L.H.

USEFUL ADDRESSES

The Air League, 142 Sloane St, London SW1X 9BJ (01-730 9285) For all interested in British and Commonwealth Aviation. "Air Pictorial" same address.

Air Britain, 208 Stock Rd, Billericay, Essex (Registrar). The International Society of Aviation Historians.

British Aircraft Preservation Council, 42 Dorridge Rd, Dorridge, Solihull, Warwickshire.

Cambridge Aircraft Preservation Society, 49 Edinburgh Rd, Chesterton, Cambridge C4B 1QR.

East Anglian Aviation Society, Rutland House, 9 Hay St, Steeple Morden, Royston, Herts.

Lincolnshire Aviation Enthusiasts, Tumby Woodside, Mareham-le-Fen, Boston, Lincs.

Merseyside Society of Aviation Enthusiasts, 43 Ashdale Rd, Mossley Hill, Liverpool L18 1LU

Northern Aircraft Preservation Society, 36 Harlech Drive, Hazel Grove, Stockport, Cheshire.

The Southern Aircraft Preservation Group, 300 Coulsdon Rd, Old Coulsdon Surrey CR3 1EB.

The South Wales Historical Aircraft Preservation Society, 5 Four Acres, Llantwit Major, Glam. CF6 9XN.

York Aircraft Preservation Group, 22 Brecksfield, Skelton, York.

American Aviation Historical Society (British Chapter) Hon. Sec:— Gerry Bevan, 18 Portland St, Leamington Spa, Warwickshire.

"Control Column", the monthly magazine for all interested in aircraft preservation is edited by Neville Franklin, 127 Hawton Rd, Newark, Notts.

THE WORLD'S MAJOR AVIATION COLLECTIONS

ENGLAND
LONDON. RAF Museum, Hendon.
Imperial War Museum, Lambeth.
Science Museum, Kensington.
BEDFORDSHIRE. Shuttleworth Collection, Old Warden.
BUCKINGHAMSHIRE. Wycombe Air Park, Marlow.
CAMBRIDGESHIRE, IWM Store, Duxford. Limited viewing.
DEVONSHIRE. Torbay Aircraft Museum, Higher Blagdon.
ESSEX. Historic Aircraft Museum, Southend Airport.
GLOUCESTERSHIRE. Skyfame Museum, Staverton Airport.
HAMPSHIRE. Army Air Corps Museum, Middle Wallop.
HERTFORDSHIRE. Mosquito Appeal Fund Museum, London Colney.
NORFOLK. Battle of Britain Flight, Coltishall.
NOTTINGHAMSHIRE. Newark Air Museum, Winthorpe.
SOMERSET. Fleet Air Arm Museum, Yeovilton.
STAFFORDSHIRE. Historic A/c Hangar, Cosford.
SURREY. The Tiger Club, Redhill Airfield.
WARWICKSHIRE. Midlands A/c Society —watch for new site.
WILTSHIRE. Station Museum, RAF, Colerne, Chippenham.
YORKSHIRE. Vintage A/c Club, RAF, Finningley. Limited viewing.

SCOTLAND
Auchterader. Strathallan Collection. By appointment.
East Fortune. Royal Scottish Museum Store. Not yet viewable.

WALES (SOUTH)
RAF St. Athan—Open Days or by appointment.

REPUBLIC OF IRELAND
Irish Aviation Museum, Dublin. Check before visiting.

AUSTRIA
Military,& Technical Museums, Vienna.

BULGARIA
SOFIA. Central Army Museum.

CZECHOSLOVAKIA
PRAGUE. Military and Technical Museums.

DENMARK
COPENHAGEN. Tojhusmuseet.
ELSINORE. Technical Museum.
FUENEN. Egeskov Veteranmuseum.

FINLAND
TAMPERE. Technical Museum.
VESIVEHMAA. By appointment only.

FRANCE
LA FERTE ALAIS. Jean Salis Collection. By prior appointment.
PARIS. Musee de l'Air.

GERMANY (EAST)
DRESDEN. Verkehrsmuseum.

GERMANY (WEST)
BERLIN. Berliner Verkehrsmuseum.
BUCKEBURG. Hubschraubermuseum.
GOPPINGEN-BETZGENRIED. Fritz Ulmer Collection.
MUNICH. Deutches Museum.
UETERSEN. Luftwaffenmuseum.

HUNGARY
BUDAPEST. Kozlekedesi Museum.

ITALY
MILAN. Museo Nazionale Della Scienza E Della Tecnica.
TURIN. Museo del Volo.
VENEGONO SUPERIORE. Museo Aeronautica Caproni di Taliedo.
VIGNA-di-VALLI. Museo del Volo store—by appointment only.

NETHERLANDS
AMSTERDAM. Aviodome, Schiphol.
SOESTERBERG. R.Neth.A.F. Museum

NORWAY
OSLO. Norsk Teknisk Museum.
VAERNES. R.No.A.F. Store—by appointment only.

POLAND
KRAKOW. National Air Museum.
WARSAW. Army Museum.

PORTUGAL
ALVERCA. The Air Museum.
LISBON. Naval Museum.

ROMANIA
BUCHAREST. Aviation Museum.

SWEDEN
MALMEN. R. Swedish A.F. Museum.
STOCKHOLM. Technical Museum, also Arlanda Civil Air Museum.

SWITZERLAND
DUBENDORF. Swiss A.F. Museum, by C.O.'s permission only.
LUCERNE. Swiss Transport Museum Air & Space Hall.

TURKEY
CUMAOVASIR. Turkish Air Museum.

U.S.S.R.
MONINO. Air Forces' Red Banner Academy.
MOSCOW. Central House of Aviation & Cosmonauts.

YUGOSLAVIA
BELGRADE. Museum Store—by appointment only.
ZAGREB. Technicki Muzej.

SOUTH AFRICA
JOHANNESBURG. National War Museum.

CHINA
PEKING. War Museum.

INDIA
PALAM (New Delhi). Indian A.F. Museum.

PHILLIPINES
LIPA CITY. Air Force Museum.

THAILAND
BANGKOK. Royal Thai A.F. Museum.

AUSTRALIA
CANBERRA. Australian War Memorial.
BANKSTOWN NSW. Marshall Airways
CAMDEN NSW. Museum of Aviation.
BERWICK. Vic. Vintage A/c Club.
MILDURA. Vic. Warbirds (due to open 1973).
MOORABBIN. Vic. Australian A/c Restoration Group.
POINT COOK. Vic. RAAF Museum.
WODONGA. Drage's Historical A/c Museum.
JANDAKOT. W.A. Air Force Association.

NEW ZEALAND
AUCKLAND. Museum of Transport & Technology.

CANADA
CALGARY. Alberta. Centennial Planetarium.
WETASKIWIN. Alberta. Pioneer Museum.
CARMAN. Manitoba. Diermert Collection.
ROCKCLIFFE & OTTAWA. Ontario. The Canadian National Aeronautical Collection.

UNITED STATES OF AMERICA
FORT RUCKER. Alabama. U.S. Army Aviation Museum.
ANCHORAGE. Alaska. Transport Museum.
TUCSON. Arizona. Pima County Air Museum.
BUENA PARK. California. Planes of Fame.
CHINA LAKE. Calif. U.S. Naval Weapons Center.
CHINO. Calif. Yesterday's Air Force.
LANCASTER. Calif. Western Aerospace Museum.
MORGAN HILL. Calif. Jan & Irving Perlitch Transportation Museum.
OAKLAND. Calif. American Air Museum.
SAN DIEGO. Calif. Aerospace Museum.
SANTA ANA. Calif. Movieland of the Air.

WINDSOR LOCKS. Connecticut. Air Museum of Connecticut Aeronautical Historical Association.
WASHINGTON D.C. National Air & Space Museum.
CAPE KENNEDY. Florida. Air Force Space Museum.
PENSACOLA. Florida. Naval Aviation Museum.
CHICAGO. Illinois. Museum of Science & Industry.
MUNDELEIN (Ivanhoe). Ill. Victory Air Museum.
RANTOUL. Chanute AFB. Limited viewing.
BLAKESBURG. Iowa. The Airpower Museum.
LOUISVILLE. Kentucky. Aircraft Industries Museum.
ABERDEEN. Maryland. U.S. Army Ordnance Center.
MARLBOROUGH. Massachusetts. The Marlborough Antiquers.
DEARBORN. Michigan. The Ford Museum.
MINNESOTA. Minneapolis. Minnesota A/c Museum.
MINDEN. Nebraska. Harold Warp Pioneer Village.
OFFUTT. Nebraska. Nebraska Aerospace Museum.
RENO. Nevada. Harrah's Automobile (and A/c) Collection.
HOLLOMAN. New Mexico. Air Force Missile Center.
WHITE SANDS. New Mexico. Missile Park.
HAMMONDSPORT. New York. Glenn H. Curtiss Museum.
RHINEBECK. New York. The Cole Palen Collection.
CLEVELAND. Ohio. Auto-Aviation Museum of Western Reserve.
DAYTON. Ohio. USAF Museum, Wright-Patterson AFB.
PHILADELPHIA. Pennsylvania. The Franklin Institute.
TOUGHKENAMON. Pennsylvania. Colonial Flying Corps Museum.
WILLOW GROVE. Pennsylvania. Naval Air Station A/c.
FLORENCE. South Carolina. Florence Air & Missile Museum.
SANTEE. South Carolina. Wings & Wheels Exhibition.
FORT WORTH. Texas. Pate Museum of Transportation.
HARLINGEN. Texas. The Confederate Air Force "Ghost Squadron" & Museum.
LACKLAND. Texas. Air Force Base Collection—limited viewing only.
BEALETON. Virginia. Flying Circus Aerodrome.
FORT EUSTIS. Virginia. U.S. Army Transportation Museum.
HAMPTON. Virginia. Aerospace Park.
QUANTICO. Virginia. United States Marine Corps Museum.
SEATTLE CENTER. Washington. Pacific Northwest Aviation Museum.
HALES CORNERS. Wisconsin. The EAA Air Museum.

CENTRAL AMERICA. MEXICO
MEXICO CITY. Museo de Talleres de la Fuerza Aerea Mexicana.

SOUTH AMERICA
ARGENTINA
BUENOS AIRES. Museo Nacional de Aeronautica.

BRAZIL
SAO PAULO. Museum of Aeronautics of São Paulo.

CHILE
SANTIAGO. Museo Aeronautio.

COLOMBIA
BOGOTA. Museum of the Air Force (being established).

NOTES ON ABBREVIATIONS AND SYMBOLS USED

A and AEE	Aeroplane and Armament Experimental Establishment
AAF	Auxiliary Air Force (to 15 Dec. 1947. See RAuxAF)
AAHS	American Aviation Historical Society
ADC	Air Defence Command, Canada
AEW	Airborne Early Warning
AFB	Air Force Base, USA
AMB	Air Material Base, Canada
ANG	Air National Guard, USA
ANS	Air Navigational School
AOP	Air Observation Post
ARW	Air Refuelling Wing, USA
AS	Anti-submarine
ATA	Air Transport Auxiliary
ATC	Air Training Corps, UK Air Training Centre or Command, Canada/ USA
BAPC	British Aircraft Preservation Council
BCATP	British Commonwealth Air Training Plan
Bf	Bayerische Flugzeugwerke; Messerschmitt factory until 1944
BGS	Bombing and Gunnery School
Bu	Bureau of Aeronautics, USA
CAACU	Civilian Anti-Aircraft Co-operation Unit
CAF	Canadian Armed Forces
CATCS	Central Air Traffic Controller School
CAW	College of Air Warfare, UK
CEPE	Central Experimental and Proving Establishment, Canada
CFS	Central Flying School
CJATC	Canadian Joint Air Training Centre
COD	Carrier On-board Delivery
CONAC	Continental Air Command, USAF
DOT	Department of Transport, Canada
EAA	Experimental Aircraft Association, USA
EAC	Eastern Air Command, Canada
EFTS	Elementary Flying Training School
ERFTS	Elementary and Reserve Flying Training School
FAW	Fighter All Weather
FIS	Fighter Interception Squadron, USA
FGA	Fighter Ground Attack
FRS	Fighter Refresher School
FRU	Fleet Requirements Unit
FTS	Flying Training School
FTW	Flying Training Wing, USA

FWS	Fighter Weapons Squadron, USA
HAR/HAS/HR	Helicopter, Air Rescue; Air Search; Helicopter Rescue
HTE	Helicopter Trainer Elementary
IBM	Intercontinental Ballistic Missile
JATP	Joint Air Training Plan
JASDF/GSDF	Japanese Air Self Defence Force; Ground Self Defence Force
JRV	Jugoslav Air Force
MAC/MAW	Military Airlift Command; Military Airlift Wing, USAF
MCAS	Marine Corps Air Station, USA
MH	Medal of Honor, USA
MLD	Marine Luchtvaart Dienst (R. Netherlands Naval Air Service)
MOS	Ministry of Supply
MOT	Ministry of Technology
NAS	Naval Air Station, USA
NAHA	Norwegian Aviation Historical Society
NAPS	Northern A/c Preservation Society
NASA	National Aeronautics & Space Administration, USA
NF	Night Fighter
NOTS	Naval Ordnance Test Station, USA
OCU	Operational Conversion Unit
OTU	Operational Training Unit
RAE	Royal Aircraft Establishment
RAuxAF	Royal Auxiliary Air Force (from 16 Dec. 1947—see AAF)
RD	Repair Depot, Canada
RLS	Rijks Luchvaart School (Dutch Govt Aviation School)
RNAS	Royal Naval Air Station (before 1 April 1918 was RN Air Service)
SAC	Strategic Air Command, USAF
SAW	Strategic Aerospace Wing
SFTS	Service Flying Training School, Canada
S of TT	School of Technical Training
SR	Stored or Serviceable Reserve, Canada
SRW	Strategic Reconnaissance Wing, USAF
TC	Training Command, Canada
TCW	Troop Carrier Wing, USAF
TTS	Technical Training School, Canada
UAS	University Air Squadron, UK

USAF/USAFE	United States Air Force; United States Air Forces, Europe
USMC	United States Marine Corps
USN	United States Navy
V1	Vergeltungswaffe (retaliation weapon No. 1)
V-1	Versuchmuster (German experimental a/c or prototype)
WAC	Western Air Command Canada
WR	Workshop Reserve, Canada

THE BRITISH ISLES

LONDON AREA

RAF Museum, Hendon

RAF badge

HENDON. Royal Air Force Museum. Nearest underground station, Colindale (10 mins), or by road from London via A5, seven miles, turn into Colindale Avenue, then Aerodrome Road. From the North or Midlands, leave M1 at Watford Way (A41), turning west after one mile. Opened by The Queen 15 November, 1972, public admission Mon-Sat 1000-1800; Sunday 1400-1800. Free at present, charge may be levied later. Two of Hendon's original hangars linked by a new hall

Bleriot and Vickers Gunbus—replica (RAF Museum)

dedicated to Sir Sydney Camm provide the aircraft hall and alongside are galleries on two levels covering aviation exhibits from 1900 to 1970 with a Lord Trenchard Gallery, Personalia Gallery, V.C. and G.C. Gallery, lecture theatre/cinema, art gallery, refreshment room, shop. On the second floor are aviation records and library. Entering the aircraft hall the 1973 display is, in sequence:— *Bleriot XI* serial possibly 164, on loan from R.Ae.S. *Morane-Saulnier Type BB* serial A301 (fuselage only) (c/n MS.16). *Vickers F.B.5 Gunbus* (replica) 2345 ex G-ATVP, donated by Vintage Aircraft Flying Association, Weybridge. *R.A/c Factory S.E.5a* F938 ex G-EBIC, loaned by R.Ae.S. *Avro 504K* E449 ex G-EBJE/EBKN, loaned by R.Ae.S. *Caudron G III* 3066, ex OO-ELA, allotted G-AETA but never used (c/n 7487). Was at 1936 Hendon Pageant. Loaned by R.Ae.S. *Sopwith Triplane* N5912, formerly displayed Biggin Hill/ Yeovilton. Used by Aerial Gunnery School, Marske, Yorks, until Armistice. *Sopwith Camel F.1* as F6314 "B" 65 Sqdn; loaned by R.Ae.S. *Gloster Gladiator II* K8042 (c/n 40468) ex No1 ASU, 1937; then Boscombe Down, Ternhill, Marshall's School, Biggin Hill. Restored as 87 Sqdn machine. *DH Tiger Moth* T6296 donated Royal Navy, was 7 EFTS (1942-1946). *Vickers Vimy* (replica) painted F8614 ex G-AWAU; damaged by fire Manchester after construction and flight by Vintage Aircraft Flying Assn to mark Alcock & Brown 50th anniversary. Donated to RAF Museum and fully restored to static condition only. *Westland Lysander III* R9125 "LX-L" of 225 (Army Co-op) 1940/1 and 161 (Special Duties) Sqdns 1944/5. Turning slightly right to view the Camm Memorial Hall:— *Hawker Hart Trainer* K4972, built Armstrong Whitworth with Kestrel X; found in barn by Solway Group of Aviation Enthusiasts. Had been 1764M with 1546 Sqdn ATC. Restored RAF St. Athan. Known to have been 2 FTS, Digby 1935, Brize Norton 1937, then MUs 1938-43. *Hawker Hart* J9941 ex G-ABMR/ J9933, 57 Sqdn markings, from Hawker Siddeley, Dunsfold and airworthy until presented. *Hawker Hunter F.5* WP185 formerly 208 and 1 Sqdns; 7583M. *Hawker Hurricane I* P2617 of 607 (County of Durham) Sqdn in France, 1940. Was painted AF-T when exhibited by

S.E.5a and Avro 504K (RAF Museum)

71 MU. Will be re-lettered when 1940 details are confirmed. *Hawker Tempest V* NV778, composite a/c,
previously painted as SN219 of 56 Sqdn. Displayed
33 Sqdn as SR-F, Middleton St. George. *Hawker
Typhoon IB* MN235 built Gloster A/c. To USA 1944
given test number T-2/491. Presented by Smithsonian
Institution (National Air & Space Museum) Washington
in exchange for a Hurricane. Restored 27 MU, Shawbury.
Last example. *Hawker Cygnet* G-EBMB, Sydney Camm's
first design for Hawker Aircraft. Winner of 1926 Lympne
competitions. With 1100 cc Anzani for 1924 competition,
re-engined with 32 hp Bristol Cherub for 1926; flown by
Flt Lt Bulman, max speed 65 mph sea level. *Hawker
P.1127* XP831 VTOL experimental aircraft; from Royal
Aircraft Establishment, Thurleigh, Bedford. Prototype
for Harrier. *Hawker Hind* unserialled; one of 20 supplied
to R.Afghan Air Force in 1938, restored and presented
by them in 1968. Now continue along left-hand side of
the aircraft hall:— *Gloster Gladiator* N5628, front fuselage
only, as salvaged from Lake Lesjakog, Norway by RAF
Team from Cranwell and Wyton in 1970. One of number
operated by 263 Squadron off the frozen lake in the

Sopwith Triplane (RAF Museum)

Vickers Vimy—replica (RAF Museum)

Westland Lysander III (RAF Museum)

Hawker Hart J9941 in flight (now RAF Museum)

brief defence of Norway in April 1940. It is believed that the Germans bombed the ice. *Miles Magister* T9707 ex Hawk Trainer 3 G-AKKR, formerly painted as T9967 and displayed at Gaydon and Abingdon. In reality T9708 (c/n 1995). *Boulton Paul Defiant I* N1671 in night-fighter markings of 307 (Polish) Sqdn; modified Mk II 1942, with 285 (Anti Aircraft) Sqdn. *Vickers Wellington X* MF628 of May, 1944 but not issued until 1949 to 1 ANS Hullavington. Bought back by Vickers then to R.Ae.S. who have loaned it. Formerly kept at Biggin Hill. Last survivor of 11,461 built. *Supermarine Stranraer* serialled 920 coded "QN" of RCAF. Served with 5BR and 7BR Squadrons RCAF; later Queen Charlotte Airlines of Vancouver BC as CF-BXO. Last example. *Avro Lancaster I* R5868, was OL-Q of 83 Sqdn, then PO-S of 467 (RAAF). Actually flew 125 confirmed sorties 8th July, 1942-23rd April, 1945. Was at RAF Scampton, Lincs, as gate guardian. *Bristol Belvedere H.C.1* XG474 ex 66 Sqdn, Far East Air Force. *Sikorsky Hoverfly I* KK995 ex 43-46558 coded E and earlier painted as KL110. First type of helicopter used by RAF; British version of Sikorsky VS-316 (R-4 in USAAF). Entered service Helicopter Training School, Andover, early 1945. *Hawker Sea Fury FB.11* VX653, ex RNAS Lossiemouth. Really a part of the Camm Hall but displayed with the two types above at opening. *Bristol Beaufighter TFX* RD253, no RAF history. Sold to Portugal, donated from Lisbon Technical College as BF-13. Restored by St. Athan with original engines and propellers, with instructional airframe serial 7931M. *DH Mosquito T.III* TW117 once "Z" of 3 Civilian Anti-Aircraft Co-operation Unit.

Hawker Typhoon IB (RAF Museum)

Hawker Cygnet in flight (now RAF Museum)

Camm Memorial Hall aircraft (RAF Museum)

Gloster Gladiator front fuselage (RAF Museum)

Boulton Paul Defiant I (RAF Museum)

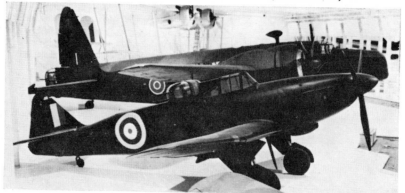

Defiant and Vickers Wellington X (RAF Museum)

Supermarine Stranraer (RAF Museum)

Bristol Beaufighter TFX (RAF Museum)

English Electric Lightning and Canberra (RAF Museum)

Cody Man Lifting Kite (RAF Museum)

Short Sunderland V (RAF Museum)

Post-war aircraft, built in July 1951. Then continue beyond Camm Hall to:— *Supermarine Spitfire I* K9942 the oldest surviving example, coded SD-V of 72 Sqdn, the original markings when the late Wg Cdr J. B. Nicolson flew it before going to 249 and gaining Fighter Command's only V.C. It was earlier coded RN-V, the wartime 72 Sqdn code. *Spitfire F.24* PK724 once RAF Norton, only flown 7 hours, later 7288 M and at Gaydon (and Henlow for B. of B. film but did not fly). *English Electric Canberra P.R.3* WE139; winner 1953 race to New Zealand 11,792 miles in 23 hrs 52 mins (Flt Lts R. L. Burton and D. H. Gannon). Later 231 OCU, Bassingbourn. *Gloster Meteor Mk IV Special* EE549 Group Captain E. M. Donaldson's record-breaking aircraft— world air speed record 615.81 mph, 7 September 1946. Later at RAF Innsworth but now back to High Speed Flight condition with high speed canopy. *English Electric P.1B Lightning* prototype XA847, the first British aircraft to fly at Mach 2.0, November 25, 1958, with Wg Cdr "Roly" Beamont as pilot. Later used for arrester trials at Farnborough. *Hawker Siddeley Dynamics Blue Steel* strategic rocket-propelled air-to-surface cruise missile with thermonuclear warhead. Became operational with Vulcan B.2s of 617 Sqdn, February 1963. Powered by 20,000 lb thrust Bristol Siddeley Stentor rocket engine, has range of about 200 miles, speed Mach 1.6 at high altitude. Length 35 ft, wing span 13 ft. Incorporated in gallery displays—present or to arrive:— *Cody Man Lifting Kite. Bristol F.2B fuselage. Bristol Beaufighter* nose portion. *Bleriot XXVII* serial 433, in Gordon Bennett Race 1914, USA. On loan from R.Ae.S. was at RAF Lyneham for restoration. Outside main building:— *Blackburn Beverley C.1* XH124, flown in after Royal Review, RAF Abingdon, 1968. At present in the Grahame-White hangar for restoration is *Short Sunderland V* ML824 A-Z of 201 Sqdn, later with 330 (Norge) then Flotille 27F, French Aeronvale. Donated from France to Short Sunderland Trust, Pembroke Dock, Wales, thanks to Peter Thomas (Skyfame Museum, Staverton, Glos.). Moved by road to Hendon and will form part of a maritime section with Catalina etc. As only one-fifth of the RAF Museum's aircraft can at present go on exhibition at Hendon, changes will take place from time to time using those now at Colerne, Wilts; Cosford, Staffs; Topcliffe, and Finningley, Yorks; St. Athan, Glamorgan; and possibly machines still in service as this is compiled. Whatever the changes you can be certain of a memorable day when you visit this great museum. Also at Hendon, with No 120 ATC Sqdn, *DH Vampire FB5* VX461/7646M which was to have been repainted as WA346, 98 Sqdn. *DH Venom NF3* WX905/7458M ex 23 Sqdn and RAF Yatesbury, once with the ATC, may now be restored for RAF Museum.

Avro Lancaster I (RAF Museum)

Sikorsky Hoverfly I (RAF Museum)

DH. Mosquito T.III (RAF Museum)

DH. Venom NF.3 (RAF Museum)

Supermarine Spitfire F.24 (RAF Museum)

LAMBETH. Imperial War Museum, Lambeth Road, SE.1. Lambeth North or Elephant and Castle stations or by frequent buses. Open 1000-1800 weekdays, 1400-1800 Sundays (earlier in summer, please verify). Closed Good Friday and Christmas. Admission free. Aircraft displayed 1973:— *R.A/c Factory BE2c* 2699. First log missing but 398 hours in second with pilots Captain Sowrey, Lt Drummond, Major Brandon. It served with 50, 51, 192 Sqdns. *Bristol F.2B Fighter* E2581, 38 Sqdn RFC, No 1 Com Sqdn, RAF. Pilots Major (AV-M) Marix and others. *Sopwith Camel 2F.1* N6812 flown by Lt (Gp Cpt) D. S. Culley when he shot down Zeppelin L.53, 11 August 1918. *R.A/c Factory R.E.8* (Daimler-built) F3556, flown only 30 minutes, France, 31 Oct 1918, then crated and stored. *Supermarine Spitfire I* R6915, possibly the most operational in existence. With 609 (West Riding) Sqdn. Battle of Britain, then 602 (City of Glasgow) Sqdn. during which time 10 enemy aircraft either destroyed or damaged. Later 61/57 OTUs, until 1947. *Fairey Swordfish II* (Blackburn built) NF370—no known history. *Focke Wulf Fw 190 A-8/R6* 733682 ex Air Min. 75, formerly Biggin Hill. On long loan from Ministry of Defence. *DH Mosquito TIII* TV959 ex 266 Sqdn. HQs Home Cmd, 3 CAACU. *Gloster Meteor F8* WK991 ex 46/56 Sqdns. Cockpit only on show but remainder stored for eventual restoration. *Heinkel He 162 A-1* 120235 ex Air Min. 63. *Messerschmitt Me 163 B-1* 191160 ex VF241, AM evaluation. *Avro Lancaster I* DV372 ex 467 (RAAF) Sqdn.—front fuselage only. *Mitsubishi Zero*—cockpit only. *Hawker Typhoon*—cockpit. *Fieseler Fi 103 Flying bomb* (V1) 477663 and *V2 rocket* displayed. *Short 184* serial 8359 (Westland-built) awaiting restoration. See also Duxford, Cambs, for other IWM aircraft.

R.A/c Factory B.E.2c and Sopwith Camel (Imperial War Museum)

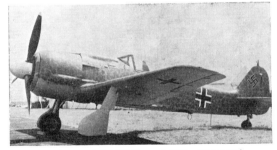

Focke Wulf Fw 190 A-8/R6 (Imperial War Museum)

Fairey Swordfish II (Imperial War Museum)

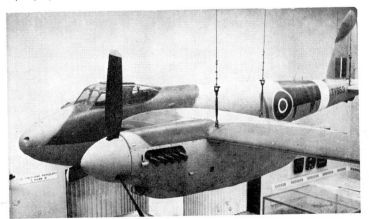

DH. Mosquito T.III (Imperial War Museum)

R.A/c Factory R.E.8 (Imperial War Museum)

R.A/c Factory S.E.5a (Science Museum)

SOUTH KENSINGTON. Science Museum Aircraft Gallery SW7 2DD. Hours similar to IWM but telephone 589-6371 to confirm. Underground to South Kensington or by frequent buses. *Lilienthal Glider* of 1895, built and flown by Otto Lilienthal, killed testing later version. *Pilcher Hawk Glider* (replica) original in Edinburgh. *Wright Flyer 1903* (replica) built by de Havilland apprentices when original returned to Smithsonian. *Roe No 1 Triplane* of 1909, second of two built and flown by A. V. Roe, making first powered flight by British aeroplane in Great Britain 13 July 1909. *Levasseur Antoinette monoplane* of 1910, brought to England by Hubert Latham, later used by Robert Blackburn and may have influenced his 1910 monoplane design. *J.A.P./Harding*

1910 Bleriot-type based on Bleriot XI, built by J. A. Prestwich for H. J. Harding. Flown first at Tottenham 10 April 1910. *Cody biplane* 1912 serial 304. Cody, then American citizen, made first sustained powered flight in Great Britain 16 October 1908. This was first of two biplanes ordered for RFC following success of Cody's earlier machine in August 1912 trials. *Fokker monoplane (Type E III)* of 1916 believed 210/15, employed wing-warping control and interrupter gear for two machine guns to fire through arc of propeller. *Avro 504K* of 1918 D7560, type on which Prince Albert (Geo VI) taught to fly, over 8,000 constructed after 1913 prototype. *R.A/c Factory S.E.5A*, F939 of 1918, later G-EBIB, one of several used by Major J. C. Savage for sky-

Wright Flyer—replica (Science Museum)

Cierva C.30A (Science Museum)

Roe No. 1 Triplane (Science Museum)

Supermarine Spitfire IA (Science Museum)

Vickers Vimy (Alcock and Brown) (Science Museum)

Westland-Hill Pterodactyl (Science Museum)

Amy Johnson's Moth (Science Museum)

writing. *Vickers Vimy* (two Rolls-Royce Eagle) flown by Captain J. Alcock and Lt. A. Whitten-Brown St. John's Newfoundland-Clifden, Co Galway, in 16 hrs 12 mins (coast-to-coast 15 hrs 57 mins) 14 June 1919; the first non-stop air crossing of Atlantic. Both knighted and Vimy stayed in RAF service as bomber until 1929. *Westland-Hill Pterodactyl* of 1928 J8067, powered version of 1924 glider with 34 hp Bristol Cherub engine, rotating wingtips. *de Havilland DH60G Gipsy Moth* G-AAAH c/n 804 "Jason" flown to Australia by Miss Amy Johnson, Croydon-Darwin May 1930, taking 19 days. Amy lost her life with ATA January 1941. *Supermarine S6.B* of 1931 S1595 flown by Flt Lt (later A/M Sir) John Boothman to win Schneider Trophy outright at 340.08 mph 13 September 1931. Powered by Rolls-Royce "R" engine 2,350 hp, later developed to produce war-winning Merlin. The floats of the seaplane contained fuel and the wing surfaces, portions of the floats and fuselage sides, formed water-filled radiators to dissipate the heat generated by engine. *Cierva C.30A* of 1934 AP507 ex G-ACWP c/n 728. Into RAF 1940 for 529 Sqdn, Halton, later restored by No 1 S. of T.T., under Chief Technician J. and brother Corporal E. Hanby. Flown wartime by Flt Lt Norman Hill, Halton, later from Duxford as "Rota". *Hawker Hurricane I* L1592 ex 56 Sqdn then 615 (County of Surrey "Churchill's Own") in Battle of Britain as KW-Z. Piloted by P/O D. J. Looker was crash-landed near Croydon 18 August 1940. *Supermarine Spitfire IA* 1940 P9444 "RN-D", to RAE then 72 Sqdn; was crash-landed by Deacon Elliott 3 July, 1940, near Acklington, after he had flown above 15,000 ft without oxygen. Later went to 52,58,61 OTUs. *Gloster E.28/39* of 1941 W4041/G, first British jet to fly, 15 May 1941 with P. E. G. Sayer as pilot. Powered by Whittle W.1, the "G" suffix indicating that armed guard must always be provided for a secret aircraft. *Focke Achgelis Fa 330* of 1943 Werk-Nr 100509, rotating-wing kite towed by U.boat. *Fuji Ohka 11 Baka* of 1944 serial 15-1585,

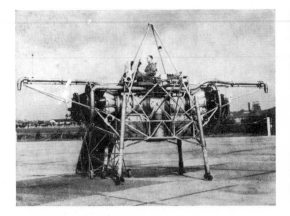

Rolls-Royce "Flying Bedstead" (Science Museum)

Gloster E.28/39 (Science Museum)

Pou-du-Ciel (Science Museum)

rocket-powered suicide aircraft launched from Jap "Betty" bomber. *Messerschmitt Me 163 B-1* of 1944 191316, 600 mph rocket interceptor, 3,750 lbs thrust; jettisonable undercarriage. *Fieseler Fi 103 flying bomb* (V1) of 1944 serialled 442795. *Rolls Royce "Flying Bedstead"* of 1944 XJ314, flying test-rig built to investigate vertical take-off techniques. Two R-R Nene jet engines supplying thrust principally in the vertical direction but also to auxiliary gas jets for lateral and fore-and-aft control. The following cockpits/baskets/mock-ups also exhibited:—*Short Bros. balloon basket* of 1900. *Beta airship car* 1910, Farnborough. *Piccard's balloon gondola* of 1932, the $10\frac{1}{2}$ mile record ascent. *Vickers Vimy cockpit* (reproduction) *Gloster Meteor 3 cockpit*, EE416. *English Electric Canberra B5 cockpit*, VX185. *Hunter Mk6 cockpit. Vickers Vanguard* (T.C.A. mock-up).

Aircraft in store and not available for public viewing:— *Clarke T.W.K. biplane glider* of 1910 built for R.Aero Club. *Handley Page HP39 "Gugnunc"* 1929 G-AACN, runner-up in the Guggenheim Safe Aircraft competition. Later K1908, RAF; under restoration. *Pou-du-Ciel* (Flying Flea) G-AEHM, "Blue Finch" built by H. J. Dolman, Bristol. *Cierva C.26 autogiro* of 1931 G-ABLM, a 2-seater produced by de Havilland's, under overhaul when last reported, at Stag Lane. *Weir W.2* of 1934,

Handley Page HP39 "Gugnunc" (Science Museum)

painted W-2, with original engine, the tail is the mock-up for the proposed W.3, Glasgow-built. *Westland SR-N1 G-12-4*, the world's first hovercraft, designed & built by Christopher Cockerell 1959, presented by B.A.C. formerly exhibited at Beaulieu. *Short SC.1* of 1957 XG900, the first British aircraft to combine vertical take-off by jet lift with forward propulsion, the pioneer of lift-thrust propulsion. Presented by the Royal Aircraft Establishment 22 June 1971 and displayed for three months before going into store at Hayes, Middlesex, with the other machines which, we hope, will be exhibited in the not-too-distant future, in Kensington or on loan to other collections in the country.

Weir W.2 (Science Museum)

Westland SR-N1 (Science Museum)

Aeronca 100 G-AETG (Hanwell)

DULWICH. Townley Rd, Alleyn's School Combined Cadet Force, *Westland WS-51 Dragonfly HR.3* WG752 coded "901".

MIDDLESEX DISTRICTS

HANWELL. R. W. Mills & Partners and D. S. Everall and others (stored) *Fairchild 24W Argus* G-AIZE c/n 565 ex 43-14601, N9996F. *Aeronca 100* G-AETG AB110 (PFA No. 34 Group) *Aeronca 100* G-AEXD c/n AB124 (D. C. Everall).

Aeronca 100 G-AEXD (Hanwell)

HESTON. Combined Cadet Force. *Auster AOP9* XN435.

HOUNSLOW. ATC Sqdn reported to have *Tiger Moth* EM697/6940M.

LALEHAM. *Demoiselle (replica)* PPS/DEM/3 from "Magnificent Men" film with Captain Ronnie Jude, airline pilot, probably to fly again.

NORTHOLT. RAF. *Douglas Dakota 4* KN645, Field Marshal Montgomery's wartime machine, later C.in.C Allied Forces, Norway, stored for RAF Museum. *Spitfire XVI* TE476/7451M ex Biggin Hill, North Weald, 1957 Royal Tournament Horsham St. Faith, Coltishall, Neatishead.

RUISLIP. ATC HQs. *Auster AOP9* XK419/8058M.

SOUTHALL. Technical College. *Provost T.1* XF898 ex CFS, 27 MU. *DH. Sea Vampire* XG775. *Saro Skeeter AOP.12* XL763.

Hawker Hurricane IID (Stanmore)

STANMORE. HQs No 11(F) Group, RAF. *Hurricane IID* LF751/5466M composite with parts of PG593/Z3687, ex 1681 Bomb Disposal Flt, 24 OTU, Waterbeach Coded FB-B of 24 OTU. *Spitfire XVI* SL574 ex Manby,

CGS, 102 FRS, B.of B. Flt. Force-landed 20 Sept. 1959, Oxo Sports Ground, Bromley, Kent, ending flying over London of Hurricanes & Spitfires during B. of B. ceremonies. The cricket stumps hit by the Spitfire were presented to MOD for exhibition. Re-coded as 234 Sqdn. AZ-B to honour B. of B. pilot serving at Stanmore 1970s.

STANMORE PARK. RAF HQs Unit. *Gloster Javelin F(AW)1* XA553/7470M.

BEDFORDSHIRE

CARDINGTON. RAF. *ML Utility Mk 1* XK776, inflatable wing a/c.

CRANFIELD. Institute of Technology (Aviation Hangar) open on special occasions or by prior appointment. Some a/c up for disposal but following listed when going to press:— *Avro CF-100* serial 18393 (RCAF). *Boulton Paul P.111A* serial VT935, high-speed research a/c. *English Electric TSR.2* XR222 (the 4th aircraft). *English Electric Canberra T.4* WH 657. *Fairey Rotodyne* XE521, dismantled and possibly only some parts remain. Experimental VTOL transport. Project abandoned February 1961. *Fairey Ultra Light* helicopter G-APJJ. *Flettner Fl 282 Kolibri* WNo 28368. *Focke Achgelis Fa 330* Werk-Nr 100406. *Hawker P1121. Hawker Hunter T.7* WV383, converted from F.4 by Armstrong Whitworth— from RAE Instrumentation Test Flight. *Hawker Sea Hawk FB.3* WM994 built by Armstrong Whitworth. *Messerschmitt Me 163 B* 191659 (AM215). *Morane Saulnier MS760 Paris* G-APRU, ex F-WJAC, G-36-2. *Tipsy B. Sers 1* G-AISB c/n 18; Cranfield Flying Group.

English Electric TSR.2 (Cranfield)

Messerschmitt Me 163B (Cranfield)

DUNSTABLE. London Gliding Club. Following reported:— *Schemp Hirth Minimoa Goppingen 3* of 1936/39; one of last airworthy (two may be in USA). This example, modified to 1939 standards, imported by air from Holland in good shape. *Schemp Hirth Goevier 1936*, Fokker-built. The world's first side-by-side two-seater. *Abbott Baynes Scud 2 of 1931*, BGA231 owner John Jefferies, to be restored. Previously G-ALOT. Unique. *Carden Baynes Scud 3 of 1935*, no longer motorized but one of the world's first motorized gliders. Now being restored. *Kite 1 prototype of 1935*—also two *Kite 1's of 1935*, examples of the first Slingsby gliders in series production; 25 built and possibly 7 now exist. *D.F.S. Grunau 2b of 1939. J. S. Weihe 1939 model*, built 1943; the only German-built Weihe in England. Best flights Redhill-Brussels, over 200 miles, by Lorne Welch, and 29,600 ft by J. Williamson. Undergoing C. of A. *Eon Olympia, 1947*, 2 examples. *DH.82A Tiger Moth* G-ANFC c/n 85385 ex DE363; G-AOCV c/n 3974, ex N6670; G-AOEL c/n 82537, ex N9510, all London Gliding Club tugs.

English Electric P.1A Lightning (Henlow)

HENLOW. RAF. On the parade ground the first prototype *English Electric P.1A Lightning* WG760/7755M. Achieved Mach 1 second flight by Wg Cdr Beamont. Later at Weeton and St. Athan. Hangars nicknamed "The Pickle Factory" house some of the RAF Museum reserve machines and magnificent restoration continues. Some are displayed, usually on Spring Holiday Monday, in aid of charities but otherwise can only be viewed by appointment:— *Avro Anson CXIX.* TX214 ex Staff College Com Flt, 31 Sqdn, Reserve Cmd and Metropolitan Sector. *Avro 504K* H2311 (G-ABAA) loaned from RAeS—serial may be changed as not authentic. *Bristol Belvedere HC.1* XG454 from 66 Sqdn, Far East. *Bleriot XXVII* serial 433, on loan from RAeS— may go to Hendon. *Bristol Bolingbroke* 10001, donated by Canadian Armed Forces, to be restored as Blenheim IV for Hendon. *Bristol Type 173* XF785 ex G-ALBN, c/n 12871, used for Naval trials 1953. *English Electric Canberra B.2* WJ573/7656M, thought flown by Wg Cdr K. Bazarnik AFC, Institute of Aviation Medicine on "Operation Swifter". *DH. Comet C.2* XK699/7971M from 216 Sqdn. Lyneham, VIP a/c. *Airspeed Consul* G-AJLR ex R6029, for restoration as Oxford. *DH. Dragon Rapide* G-AHED c/n 6944, donated Hunting Surveys, to be restored as Dominie RL962. *English Electric P.1A Lightning* WG763/7816M, second prototype, from RAE, Farnborough. *Focke Achgelis Fa 330* Werk-Nr 60.00012. *Fokker D.VII* 2319/18 (earlier displayed as OAW 8417/18) "Death's Head" insignia of Jagdstaffel 71; loaned RAeS. *Junkers Ju 88 C-6* PJ876 Werk-Nr 360043, surrendered a/c. *Farman F.40* F-HMFI original prototype 1913, per-

Avro 504K H2311 (Henlow)

Supermarine Spitfire I (Henlow)

Bristol Belvedere HC.1 (Henlow)

Gloster Meteor F.8 WH301 (Henlow)

Avro Shackleton MR.3 (Henlow)

Miles Hawk Major (Henlow)

sonal mount of designer-constructor Henri Farman. Acquired by Mr. Nash 1936 when 1,040 hrs flown. F-FARB applied for the 1936 Hendon Pageant. Later at RAF Benson; on loan from RAeS. *Gloster Meteor F.8* WH301/7930M from Flying College, Manby, earlier with CFE, 609 (West Riding) and 85 Sqdns; in 85's marks, "T". *Miles Hawk Major DG590* ex G-ADMW, c/n 177. *Scottish Aviation Prestwick Pioneer CC1.* XL703, from Far East. *Percival Provost T.1* XF690 from Queen's University Air Sqdn. *Bristol 171 Sycamore HC.12* WV783 ex G-ALSP, 7841M, and *HR.14* XL824. *Hafner Rotachute III—P.5. Fieseler V.1* flying bomb. *BAC TSR.2* XR220/7933M, second of four completed; not flown. *Scottish Aviation Twin Pioneer* XL993, Air Support Command markings. *Airspeed Oxford* G-AITB ex MP345, from Airwork, Perth, for restoring. *Vickers Valetta C.2* VX573 "Loreley" ex RAF Germany C. in C.'s a/c, flew 5,000 hrs, 1,000,000 miles for eight Commanders.

Saunders-Roe SR.53 XD145, Britain's first mixed-power interceptor (rocket/turbojet) from Rocket Research Establishment, span 25′ 1½″, length 45′, height 10′ 10″, Mach 2, Farnborough 1957, Viper jet plus rocket-motor; 5 minutes' endurance. *Supermarine Spitfire I* X4590 "PR-F" 609 (West Riding) AAF Sqdn, 1940, then 66 Sqdn, about fifty "Ops" known, with several successes. From 71 MU, Bicester, for long-term storage for RAF Museum. *Supermarine Spitfire XVI* TB382/7244M was "LO-X" 602 (Glasgow) Sqdn, from Middleton St.

V2 rocket (Henlow)

Consolidated PBY-6A Catalina (Henlow)

Messerschmitt Me 110 G-4 (Henlow)

George and RAF Hospital, Ely. Stored. *Miles Messenger 4A* G-ALAH ex RH377, loaned from N.A.P.S. *Avro Shackleton MR3* XF703, last operational Phase 3, MR3 in 18 Group, "J" of 42 Sqdn, earlier 203 Sqdn, flown in Sept, 1971. *Supermarine Southampton I* N9899 (fuselage) ex 210 Sqdn, used as houseboat at Felixstowe—for restoration. *Thor missile* 110. *R.A/c Factory RE.8 remains* found Coventry, donated by N.A.P.S. *Jap Ohka 11 Baka. V2 rocket* (ex Biggin Hill). *Westland WS.51 Dragonfly HR.1* VX595. *Consolidated PBY-6A Catalina* L-861 (with R-1830-90Cs from a Dakota) ex 721 Sqdn, R. Danish Air Force, used until recently in Greenland, will be flown in for RAF Museum. *Messerschmitt Me 110 G-4* 730301 "OL" formerly at Biggin Hill, May go., with other ex-Luftwaffe machines (see St. Athan etc) to Chilham Castle, Kent, for B. of B. Museum. The fuselage of *Hawker Tempest V* EJ693, donated from Holland. *Airspeed Oxford* G-AITF, from Airwork, Perth, to assist in restoration of G-AITB. *EoN Eton TX.1* WP270—

Primary glider. *Bristol F2B* restoration project; with parts from Shuttleworth. *DH Vampire T.11* XE920 "D" of CATCS, Shawbury, stored. *Fairey Swordfish*; expected from Canada for restoration. *Supermarine Seagull* VH-ALB ex RAAF's A2-4 and Barrier Reef Flying Services, to be restored as a Walrus—Spitfire XVI TE384/7207M ex 603 (City of Edinburgh) Sqn. and RAF Syerston, Notts, apparently given as part of the ex-change-deal.

Supermarine Seagull (Henlow)

LUTON. Airport. When compiled, *NA B-25 Mitchell* N7614C (ex 44-31171) was here, airworthy. *Miles Messenger* G-AJKL was for disposal.

OLD WARDEN. The Shuttleworth Collection, near Biggleswade, close to A.1/A.6001 and linked by B.658 to aerodrome. Telephone NORTHILL 288 for details of landing facilities if flying, or about special events. General Manager David Ogilvy ARAeS. This is the country's premier airworthy collection (perhaps the world's finest veteran flyables) endowed by the late Mrs. Frank Shuttleworth OBE in memory of her son, Richard Ormonde Shuttleworth, killed in the RAF, who started the Collection pre-war. Open, except for a few days at Christmas, daily throughout the year 1000-1700 (later on flying days, usually last Sunday of months March-October, subject to weather etc.) Charges, subject to VAT effects, 30p adults 15p children over five, free parking. Flying and Pageant occasions—see advertisements and booklets. Why not apply for membership of the Shuttleworth Veteran Aeroplane Society; to receive the magazine and associated benefits—you could not help a more worthy cause, Aircraft as at time of writing:—*Bleriot XI* No 14 of 1909 BAPC3 found in a garage at Ampthill in 1935 and thought to be one of the original complement of the Bleriot School

Bleriot XI (Shuttleworth Collection)

at Hendon, October, 1910. Rebuilt and re-covered at Old Warden it was flown by Richard Ormonde Shuttleworth in 1936's RAF Display and is thought to be the only one of its type in the world still flying. The engine is the 25 hp semi-radial Anzani, achieving speed of 40 mph. Cost, as exhibited in 1910, was £480. *Deperdussin* of 1910, BAPC4, No. 43 like the Bleriot found in 1935 at Ampthill, and it is known that a Mr. Grimmer bought it at a sale at Hendon in 1914, rebuilding and flying it from Bedford. Completely rebuilt and re-covered it was flown by R. O. Shuttleworth in 1937 and has since flown at most of this country's leading displays. The engine is the 35 hp radial "Y" type Anzani, giving speed of 55 mph. The "Popular" types, exhibited in Paris, 1911, gained great credit for design and workmanship and were priced at £920, £1,080 and £1,820, according to engine and whether single, two, or three-seat. In 1913 the Deperdussin moved into the records, gaining the Gordon-Bennet Trophy for France in a racing version with average speed over 124 mph. *Blackburn, single-seater Monoplane No 9 of 1912;* BAPC5 built for Mr. Cyril Foggin who learned to fly at the Blackburn School at Hendon. Later put into storage at Wittering in 1914 where it was found, partly covered by a haystack, in 1938. Restoration was completed 1946/7 and it now flies very well. The 50 hp Gnome was found in a dismantled state in a barrel! The gross weight is approximately 1,400 lbs and speed is 60 mph. *Avro 504K* of 1915, E 3404. This exhibit, as ac-

cepted for custody from the de Havilland Company was of the 504N type and rebuilding and restoration to "K" type was undertaken by the A. V. Roe Company as an exercise for their apprentices. The engine, 110 hp Rhone, is from a damaged Hanriot (see California) flown back from the Continent by R. O. Shuttleworth. Work of restoring the Avro was expedited so that it could appear in the classic Douglas Bader film "Reach for the Sky". *Sopwith Pup* of 1916 N 5180 ex G-EBKY. Taken over as a Sopwith Dove from a private owner in 1936 it was dismantled and converted back from two-seat to single-seater, finished in RFC colours and markings. The 80 hp Rhone was reconditioned and has given trouble-free service ever since. The original cost of the type was £1,390 and about 1,800 were reputedly built (and highly praised by Von Richtofen). *Bristol Fighter F2b* of 1917, D 8096 ex G-AEPH, found stored in a shed at Elstree in 1949, purchased about 1936 at a disposal sale by ex-RFC pilot Mr. C. P. B. Olgivie who intended but did not achieve restoration. Accepted by the Trust with spare engine and other parts, plus Hucks Starter the engines were overhauled by Rolls-Royce and the Bristol Aeroplane Company completed restoration in time for the King's visit to see the Brabazon airliner in 1950. Since then it has been in continuous use both home and abroad, completing many flying hours (the Rolls-Royce Falcon installed is the oldest R-R aero engine still running). A total of about 3,000 "Brisfits" had

Bleriot XI (Shuttleworth Collection)

Avro 504K (Shuttleworth Collection)

Deperdussin (Shuttleworth Collection)

Blackburn Monoplane (Shuttleworth Collection)

Avro 504K (Shuttleworth Collection)

Sopwith Pup (Shuttleworth Collection)

R.A/c Factory S.E.5a (Shuttleworth Collection)

Sopwith Pup (Shuttleworth Collection)

Sopwith Pup (Shuttleworth Collection)

Bristol Fighter F2b (Shuttleworth Collection)

R.A/c Factory S.E.5a (Shuttleworth Collection)

DH.53 Humming Bird (Shuttleworth Collection)

R.A/c Factory S.E.5a (Shuttleworth Collection)

DH. 53 Humming bird (Shuttleworth Collection)

English Electric Wren (Shuttleworth Collection)

DH. 60X Hermes Moth (Shuttleworth Collection)

Avro Tutor (Shuttleworth Collection)

been made by end of 1918, their cost—airframe without engine, instruments or guns £1,350. Rolls-Royce Falcon £1,210, Sunbeam Arab £1,210, Hispano-Suiza £1,017. *Royal Aircraft Factory S.E.5a* of 1917 G-EBIA, now re-serialled F 904 restored by the Royal Aircraft Establishment, Farnborough as D7000 and normally housed there, kept in immaculate trim for displays. Found, less engine, hanging from the roof of what was the Armstrong-Whitworth Aircraft factory, Baginton. A 200 hp Hispano-Suiza engine, water cooled, was found in Essex and a second one in USA. A total of about 5,025 S.E.5/5as was built, cost without engine £1,063. Hispano-Suiza 200 hp £1,004, 200 hp Wolseley Adder £946 (see Farnborough). *L.V.G. Type C-VI* of 1917 serial 1594. This is on loan from the Air Historical Branch, Ministry of Defence (RAF) and captured from the Germans in 1914-18 war. It was flown at the RAF Hendon Display, 1937 and with span of 45 ft, one of the biggest German reconnaissance and artillery observation 2-seaters of 1917—also used as short-range bomber. Fitted with 230 hp six cylinder vertical water-cooled Benz, maximum speed 110 mph at sea level. Weight 2,188 lbs, fuel tank capacity 522 gallons. Armament, Spandau machine gun bolted to fuselage and worked by pilot with Bowden wire control, plus one Parabellum or Mondraggen machine gun on movable mounting in rear cockpit. *de Havilland DH 53 Humming Bird* c/n 98 G-EBHX. Found by Sqdn Ldr Jackson in a shed belonging to a miner at Betteshanger Colliery, Kent, as a result of a casual bar conversation, it was without engine and tail unit. An ABC Scorpion 35 hp was available within the Collection and was overhauled by the manufacturers; de Havilland Technical School students reconditioned the aircraft structure. The aeroplane was built for the Air Ministry Competition of 1923, held at Lympne, and although it did not win, it was the only entrant to receive production orders. One was flown by Sir Alan Cobham to Brussels and the engine, then a Blackburn Tomtit inverted "V" motor cycle engine roaring away at 3,000 rpm, reputedly the reason for the nickname "Humming Bird". Span 30 ft, speed 72 mph. *English Electric Wren* of 1923, No 4 BAPC11, with parts of No 3 (G-EBNV). Donated to the Collection by Mr. R. H. Grant of Dumfries and restored by English Electric, using a similar machine, then on loan to the Science Museum. The completed aeroplane was flown at Warton by Mr. Peter Hillwood. Designed 1922 by Mr.

L.V.G. Type C-VI (Shuttleworth Collection)

DH.60X Hermes Moth (Shuttleworth Collection)

Hawker Tomtit (Shuttleworth Collection)

R.A/c Factory S.E.5a (Shuttleworth Collection)

Hawker Sea Hurricane and Spitfire XI (Shuttleworth Collection)

DH. 51 (Shuttleworth Collection)

Gloster Gladiator (Shuttleworth Collection)

W. O. Manning FRAeS, to meet Air Ministry specification for ultra-light trainer. The engine is a 3 hp overhead valve 398 cc flat twin ABC motor cycle type adapted for aeroplane. Maximum speed 50 mph but perfectly controllable at little more than 20 mph. One of these machines won the *Daily Mail* Light Aeroplane Contest, Lympne, 1923 when it flew 87.5 miles on a gallon of fuel —later over 100 miles was achieved per gallon and a height of 1,200 feet was reached. Span 37 feet, length 24 ft 3 inches. *DH 60X Hermes Moth* of 1925 G-EBWD c/n 552. Bought by Richard Shuttleworth from Brooklands 1931, originally with Cirrus II but fitted later with the 105 Hermes II. Designed by the late Sir Geoffrey de Havilland it became a standard trainer for light aeroplane clubs and popular choice for record flights such as Miss Amy Johnson's solo to Australia (see London Science Museum). The choice of the name "Moth" came from Sir Geoffrey's boyhood interest in moths and butterflies. Two-seater, maximum speed 90 mph. *DH 51* of 1925 G-EBIR c/n 102, ex VP-KAA "Miss Kenya". This type was an attempt to provide an aeroplane for the private owner. A 2/3 seater fitted with the 8-cyl Vee Airdisco Renault it did not sell but was a logical step to the 1925 Moth. *Hawker Tomtit* of 1929 K1786 ex G-AFTA, this machine was deposited with the Collection in September, 1959 having been flown at many rallies by Sqdn Ldr Neville Duke, then Hawker's chief test pilot. Designed as a trainer for the RAF with Armstrong Siddeley 150 hp 5 cylinder air-cooled radial, maximum sea level speed 124 mph. *Avro Tutor* of 1933 K 3215 ex G-AHSA. This exhibit, was being used in the film "Reach for the Sky" when it suffered a crankshaft failure and was bought from its owner for the Collection. A spare engine was found at College of Aeronautics

and was overhauled by Armstrong Siddeley. It is finished in the RAF colour scheme current during its period and is a very popular display aeroplane. The 205 hp Lynx air-cooled radial gives top speed of 122 mph and cruising of 105 mph. Ex RAF CFS, 1 FTS, 41 and 61 OTUs. *Percival Gull* of 1932 G-ADPR c/n D55, impressed as AX 866. This Percival P.3 Gull Six was placed in the custody of the Collection and endowed in 1961 by the Hunting Aircraft Co of Luton, having been placed in storage there by the then Percival Aircraft Ltd in 1955. In 1935 Miss Jean Batten flew it for her record breaking flight to Brazil and later for her solo flights to Australia and New Zealand—Miss Batten's epic flights are recorded on the Percival Gull which delights all who see it in the air and on the ground. The 3-seat monoplane with Gipsy 6 engine, cruises at 155 mph, top speed 176 mph. *DH 88 Comet* of 1934. G-ACSS "34" "Grosvenor House". This exhibit was the winner of the England-Australia International Air Race of 1934 to mark the centenary of the State of Victoria. Flown by C. W. A. Scott and Tom Campbell Black it arrived in Melbourne 70 hrs 54 minutes after leaving Mildenhall, Suffolk. It was then acquired by Air Ministry for tests, given the serial K 5084, reverting to G-ACSS in 1937. In 1938, flown by Clouston and Ricketts it broke several records between England and New Zealand then, in 1939, it was stored at Gravesend and in 1951, was retrieved and rebuilt by the de Havilland Technical School and exhibited at the Festival of Britain. Stored for a time at Leavesden it was donated to the Collection by Bristol Siddeley Engines and the de Havilland Company. Span 44 ft, length 29 ft, engines two Special Gipsy Six, In Line Inverted, Air Cooled. Speed on first official test 235 mph at 1,000 ft, 225 mph

DH. 88 Comet (Shuttleworth Collection)

Pou-du-Ciel G-AEBB (Shuttleworth Collection)

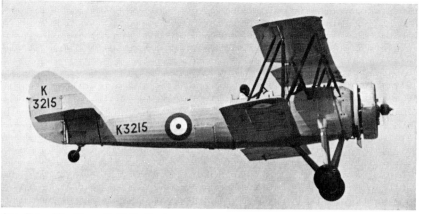

Avro Tutor (Shuttleworth Collection)

Percival Gull (Shuttleworth Collection)

Percival Gull (Shuttleworth Collection)

Percival Provost T.1 (Shuttleworth Collection)

Parnall Elf (Shuttleworth Collection)

Granger Archaeopteryx (Shuttleworth Collection)

Auster AOP.9 (Shuttleworth Collection)

Hawker Hind (Shuttleworth Collection)

Heath Parasol (Shuttleworth Collection)

Piper Cub (Shuttleworth Collection)

B.A. Swallow (Shuttleworth Collection)

Miles Hawk Speed Six (Shuttleworth Collection)

Miles Magister (Shuttleworth Collection)

Chilton DW.1A (Shuttleworth Collection)

Avro Triplane IV—replica (Shuttleworth Collection)

at 10,000 ft. *Gloster Gladiator* of 1934 K 8032 (from L 8032 and N 5903) ex G-AMRK. Acquired from Mr. V. H. Bellamy of Eastleigh and built up by the Gloster Aircraft Co, the enterprise activated by the enthusiasm of Wg Cdr R. F. Martin, then Gloster's Chief Test Pilot. Handed over and endowed by the Gloster Aircraft Company, 25th November, 1960. Engine Bristol Mercury IX (Static Radial) Air Cooled. Speed 253 mph maximum. *Hawker Sea Hurricane Mk Ib* of 1937 Z7015 (hook covered), built by the Canadian Car and Foundry Company and converted in England by fitting catapult spools and arrester gear. After the war used by Loughborough Technical College from where it was acquired on permanent loan It then reverted to Mk I standard, metal wings being exchanged with the Mk IV in Birmingham. *Supermarine Spitfire XI* of 1944 PL 983, ex N74138 of U.S. Air Attache who handed it back to Vickers Armstrong from whence it came to the Collection through the good offices of Mr. Jeffrey Quill who was the Chief Test Pilot. Speed of this version 415 mph maximum, 240 mph cruising. *Percival P.56 Provost T.1* XF 836, the RAF's last piston-engined Provost trainer, flown into Old Warden 1969. *Fieseler Fi-103 (V-1)* from "Operation Crossbow". *Mignet Pou-du-Ciel* G-AEBB, built by K. W. Owen at Southampton in 1936, has been donated by No 424 ATC Sqdn, Southampton and restored to taxying standard. *Parnall Elf* of 1929, G-AAIN c/n J6, the last type of a series designed by Mr. Harold Bolas and produced by George Parnall of Bristol. One was entered for the King's Cup Air Race of 1930 and came 5th out of a field of 88. It was priced around £880, with 105 hp Cirrus Hermes, giving speed of 116 mph maximum. *Southern Martlet* G-AAYX c/n 202. *Cierva C.30A* G-AHMJ ex K 4235. *A.N.E.C. 2* G-EBJO. *DH. Queen Bee* LF 858. *BAT Bantam* K123/G-EACN, earliest registered civilian a/c still existing c/n FK 23/15 ex F1654. *Blake Bluetit*, built by Lt-Cdr W. H. C. Blake from Simmonds Spartan G-AAGN/G-AAJB, with Avro 504K mainplanes and powered by 32 hp "Gnat" of 1914/18 vintage. Formerly stored near Winchester. *Granger Archaeopteryx* G-ABXL—(built Nottingham 1926-30). *Dixon Ornithopter*—BAPC8. *Southampton University Man Powered Aeroplane* BAPC7. *Miles M.14A Magister* P6382 c/n 2169 restored to flying; formerly Miles Hawk Tr3. G-AJDR. *Auster AOP 9* XR241, flown by Lt.Col Mike Somerton-Rayner in 1969 England-Australia Air Race as G-AXRR. Formerly 654 Sqdn, Germany. Handed over by Brigadier W. McNinch OBE, DFC, Army Aviation. *Slingsby T.38 Grasshopper TX1.* WZ821, from Royal Liberty School. *Hawker Hind*, collected from Afghanistan with Ford Ltd's help. To be restored to flying condition as world's only airworthy example. *Heath Parasol* G-AFZE c/n PA.1 ex Luton—for restoration to fly. *DHC Chipmunk T 10* G-AOTD, ex WB588, c/n C1/0040—for restoration to fly. *DH Tiger Moth* G-ANZU c/n 3583 ex L6938. With 14 EFTS, 17 EFTS and 28 EFTS during war. *DH Rapide* G-ALAX c/n 6930 ex RL948, with parts of others, may be restored here or by N.A.P.S. (see Stockport.) Replicas owned by the Collection are being generously loaned to other preservation organizations, along with certain aircraft which cannot at present be properly displayed at Old Warden. Still here:—*Avro Triplane IV* (replica) airworthy, from "Magnificent Men" BAPC1. *Bristol Boxkite* (replica) "Phoenix Flyer" airworthy from same film, BAPC2. Flying from Old Warden, privately owned: *B A Swallow 2* G-AFCL c/n 462 (A. M. Dowson). *Tipsy Belfair* G-APIE c/n 535 ex OO-TIE (G. S. Whitley). *Tiger Moth* G-ANKT c/n 85087 ex T6818 (Air Cdre A. H.

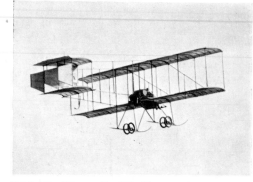

Bristol Boxkite—replica (Shuttleworth Collection)

Wheeler). *Tipsy Trainer 1* G-AFWT c/n 13, (A. G. Thelwall/P. R. Harris.) *DH 87B Hornet Moth* G-ADND c/n 8097 ex W9385 (Air Cdre Wheeler). *Miles M2L Hawk Speed Six* G-ADGP c/n 160 (D. A. Hood). *Piper J-3C-65 Cub* G-AXHR c/n 10892 ex 43-29601 F-BETI (Miles Motors). *Chilton DW.1A* G-AFSV c/n DW.1A/1 ("Manx" Kelly). *DH Tiger Moth* XL716, Royal Navy formerly with 2365 ATC, Brechin, said to be here, for rebuilding. ex G-AOIL T7363, c/n 83673.

Also many rare engines, plus the veteran cars and other historic material to make any visit a memorable occasion.

THURLEIGH. Royal Aircraft Establishment (Bedford) Only by prior approval or on a very rare Open Day:— *Auster 5* G-APBE c/n 3403, Thurleigh Flying Group. *Auster AOP 9* WZ672—Aero Flight. *BAC 221* WG774, formerly the Fairey FD.2 high speed research a/c which held world speed record 1,132 mph 10 March, 1956 (Peter Twiss) beating by over 300 mph the previous F-100 record of Col. Horace A. Hanes 20 August 1955. *DH Comet 2E* XV144 c/n 06033 ex G-AMXK of BOAC, now grounded after 3,200 hrs and 3,109 landings, the majority in the BLEU (blind landing experimental unit) programme now developed in the RAF's Belfasts and BEA's Tridents. This ought to be preserved for posterity. *Comet 3B* XP915 c/n 06100 formerly G-ANLO. Development aircraft for Comet 4, first flew 19 July 1954. *English Electric Lightning F.1* XG327, pre-production a/c. *F.2* XN725 *F.1* XG308. *Comet C 4* XV814, formerly BOAC's G-APDF, c/n 6407. *Armstrong Whitworth Meteor NF.11* WD686, *NF14* WS804. *Handley Page HP115* XP841—scaled-down supersonic research a/c, to test low speed handling. *Folland Gnat T.1* XP505. *Short SC.1* XG905 experimental VTOL. *Westland WS 55 Whirlwind HAR.1* XA864 with P. & W. Wasp 4001. *HAS.7* XK906 *English Electric Canberra PR.9* WH793, the PR.9 prototype.

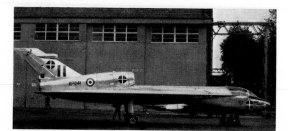

Handley Page HP115 (Thurleigh)

English Electric Canberra PR.9 (Thurleigh)

B.2 WD953. *Supermarine Scimitar F.1* XD228, of 1st production order. *Hawker P.1127 Kestrel FGA.1* XS688 formerly of tripartite squadron. *Hawker Hunter F.6* XG290. *T.7* XL612. *Handley Page Hastings C.2* WD480 (of Radio Flt, Farnborough). *Avro Shackleton MR3* WR972. *T.4* VP293 (last survivor of first production batch). *Vickers Varsity T.1* WF417 used by BLEU. *DH Sea Vixen FAW1.* XJ474. *Supermarine Spitfire V* G-AWII ex AR501 of 504 (County of Nottingham) Sqdn. of Shuttleworth Trust—flown in B. of B. film as N3314/3316/3320, coded AI-E, AI-G and DO-A, is kept here pending covered accommodation becoming available at Old Warden. Let us hope it appears one day in 504's markings.

TWINWOODS FARM. World War II airfield now used for light a/c:—*DH Tiger Moth* G-ANOO c/n 85409 ex DE401, RAE Bedford Aero Club. *DH Tiger Moth* T6274 rumoured here in original RAF livery. *EoN Primary glider* BGA580 ex G-ALPS c/n EoN/P/003.

WOBURN ABBEY. *Westland WS.51 Dragonfly* HR.3 WG661 said to be here.

BERKSHIRE

Supermarine Spitfire F.22 (Abingdon)

ABINGDON. RAF. By special permission of C.O. or on Open Days. *DH.Rapide 6* G-AGSH c/n 6884 ex NR808 EI-AJO; RAF Sport Parachute Association. *Supermarine Spitfire F.22* PK624 ex 614 (County of Glamorgan) Sqdn, North Weald, Uxbridge and Northolt.

ARBORFIELD. Army Apprentices College. *Auster AOP.9* WZ679/7822M (uses parts of XP244). WZ726.

READING. Brock Barracks, Oxford Rd. 381 ATC Sqdn. *Hawker Hunter F.1* WT684/7422M; ex MOD exhibition a/c. At the Presentation College, outskirts of Reading, with No. 2287 ATC Sqdn. *Vampire T.11* XD536/7734M ex RAF Oakington, 234 Sqdn, 5FTS, Geilenkirchen.

Hawker Hunter F.1 (Reading)

Vampire T.11 (Reading)

SUNNINGDALE. Private house. *British Klemm Swallow* of 1934 G-ACXE c/n 21—formerly Don Ellis. For rebuild, after storage since war.

THATCHAM. Airstrip. *Tiger Moth* G-AJHU ex T7471 c/n 83900.

WALLINGFORD. House. *Grunau 2 glider* being restored (Stan Johnstone).

WHITE WALTHAM. Airfield, Fairey Surveys Ltd have *Douglas Dakota 4* G-AHCT c/n 12308 ex 42-108846 KG313; G-AIWC c/n 13590 ex 42-93654 KG723; G-AMCA

Douglas Dakota 4 (White Waltham)

c/n 32966 ex 44-76634. *DH.87B Hornet Moth* G-AHBM c/n 8126 ex P6785 CF-BFJ and *DH.85 Leopard Moth* G-APKH c/n 7131 ex G-ACGS AX858 (Peter Franklin). *Auster 6A* G-APRO ex WJ370 (Air Cdre Allen Wheeler). He also owns *DH Tiger Moth* G-ADGV c/n 3340 ex BB694 from R. N. Yard Fleetlands. *DH. Tiger Moth* G-ANHK c/n 82442 ex N9372 F-BHIM (J. D. Iliffe). *Miles Gemini 1A* G-AKDK c/n 6469 (G. W Harben). *DHC Chipmunk T.10* WP861 believed still here with London University Air Sqdn, the machine on which Prince Philip trained.

DHC. Chipmunk (White Waltham)

WINKFIELD. House. *Tiger Moth* G-AKXS, 83512, ex T7105, being restored by owner.

WOODLEY. House/Garage. Bob Ogden, one-time chairman, British Aircraft Preservation Council, hopes to fly during 1973:—*BAC Drone* G-AEDB c/n 13, originally owned G. Scott Pearce at Perth, then H. R. Dimock, Ely. Modified pre-war to tricycle u/c; re-engined with Bristol Cherub III. Bought pre-war by D. C. Burgoyne of Knowle who fitted tailwheel u/c. Sold to R. Graham of Aspatria 1956 and then to Bob, who has spent several years re-building. *DH Moth Minor* G-AFOB c/n 94018 once X5117, being restored to fly by Bob, with parts of G-AFPT and G-AFRY. Barry Welford has here *DH Moth Minor Coupe* G-AFNI c/n 94035 for a restoration project.

BUCKINGHAMSHIRE

BOOKER. Wycombe Air Park near Marlow, Personal Plane Services (Doug Bianchi) Telephone High Wycombe 29432. Here are to be found many Bianchi-built or restored a/c and readers should watch the aviation press for date of the flying events here. Many aircraft are privately-owned, as indicated:—*Fokker E III* (replica) G-AVJO c/n PPS/FOK/6. *Morane Type N* (replica) MS.No 50 G-AWBU c/n PPS/Rep/7. *Dewoitine D.26* HB-RAA c/n 274 used for sailplane towing, Switzerland; stored. *Morane-Saulnier MS.500* G-AZMH

c/n 637 ex F-BJQG, EI-AUU (not used) owned by the Hon. Patrick Lindsay, who also has here *Morane-Saulnier MS.230* G-AVEB c/n 1076 ex F-BGJT. *Boeing A75N1 Stearman Kaydet* G-AZLE c/n 75/8543 ex CF-XRD, Bu 43449. *Currie Wot* G-APWT c/n HAC/4-Mr. and Mrs. Roy Mills. *Supermarine Spitfire Mk I* G-AIST ex AR213 of RAE, 57/53 OTUs, owned by Air Cdre Allen Wheeler, painted "QG-A", military marks. *Supermarine Spitfire IXB* G-ASJV, formerly MH434, SM-41, OO-ARA, flown by Wg Cdr Lardner-Burke 222 Sqdn, 74 "Ops" recorded, later R. Neth and Belg. A. F. Fitted long-range tanks by Tim Davies; now owned by Adrian Swire and sometimes flown by Sqdn Ldr Ray Hanna. *Yakovlev C.11* G-AYAK c/n 172701 ex OK-KIE, force-landed Cyprus when en route Middle East. Behind block of flats Famagusta until purchased by Philip Mann and restored to flying condition. *VIIMA II* G-BAAY ex OH-VIG (Finland) and Finnish Air Force VI-3, now owned by Philip Mann. 1938-built, presented to Finnish AF by NCOs of Finnish Army. On major overhaul for flying again. *Westland Lysander III* serial 1244—from Canada for restoration. *Percival Proctor 3* G-AOGE

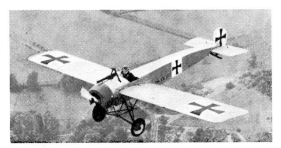

Fokker E III—replica (Booker)

Fokker E III—replica (Booker)

Morane Type N—replica (Booker)

Dewoitine D.26 (Booker)

Morane-Saulnier MS.500 (Booker)

Boeing Stearman Kaydet (Booker)

Boeing Stearman Kaydet (Booker)

Boeing Stearman Kaydet (Booker)

Yakovlev C.11 (Booker)

Supermarine Spitfire IXB (Booker)

VIIMA II (Booker)

DH. Rapide (Booker)

Bücker Bü 133 Jungmeister (Booker)

Miles Whitney Straight (Booker)

Miles Falcon (Booker)

c/n H.210 ex BV651—owner R. J. Sewell. *B.A. Swallow 2* G-ADPS c/n 410, P. R. Harris. *DH. Rapide* G-AHGD c/n 6862 ex NR786—Lowe & Oliver Ltd. *Bücker Bü 133 Jungmeister* G-AXIH c/n 11 ex U-64 Swiss AF, HB-MIP (R. E. Legg). G-AYSJ (*Dornier-Bucker 133*) c/n 38, ex U-91 Swiss AF and HB-MIW (S. B. Riley). *Miles M.11a Whitney Straight* G-AFGK c/n 509; W. S. Scott-Hill/ C. A. Herring. *Piper J-3C-65 Cub* G-ASPS c/n 22809 ex N3571N; A. J. Chalkley. *DH Tiger Moth* G-ANFM c/n 83604 ex T5888; Reading Flying Gp. G-AZZZ c/n 86307 ex NL864 F-BGJE owned by S. W. McKay also G-BABA c/n 86584 ex F-BGDT, PG687. Also here *Stampe SV-4C* G-AXAC c/n 616 ex F-BDFL (Major R. L. Gardner); *SV-4C* G-AWXZ c/n 360 ex F-BHMZ; *SV-4A* G-AZNK c/n 290 ex F-BKXF (Personal Plane Services) *SV-4C* G-AZGC c/n 120 ex F-BCGE (Hon. P. Lindsay); *SV-4C* G-AZGE c/n 576 ex F-BDDV (Mr. L. Astor). *Seafire FR47* VP441 being restored. *Messerschmitt Bf 109* (replica) from B. of B. film is here. *Military 1910 monoplane* (replica) is under PPS construction, 1973. *Miles M.3A Falcon* G-AEEG c/n 216 ex U-20, SE-AFN, Fv7001 (Philip Mann) *N.A. AT16 Harvard IIB* G-BAFM c/n 14A-868, ex 43-12569, FS728, B-104, RNethAF, PH-SKL, now owned by Hon. Patrick Lindsay. *Gull 1* (modified) last airworthy example of glider that first flew the English Channel.

DENHAM. Airfield. *DH. Moth Minor* G-AFPN c/n 94044 ex X9297 flown here by E. Harris. *Somers-Kendall SK.1* G-AOBG c/n 1 said to be stored here or nearby— information please for next edition.

Piper Cub (Booker)

DH. Moth Minor (Denham)

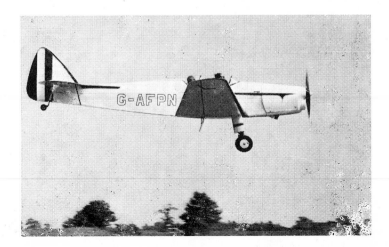

GERRARDS CROSS. House. *DH. Tiger Moth*
G-ACDJ c/n 3183 ex BB729—for restoration.

HALTON. No 1 S of TT RAF. Aircraft viewable only
on AOC's authority or on Open Days. At the entrance
gates is *Spitfire LF Mk XVI* RW386/6944M ex 604(County
of Middlesex) RAuxAF Sqdn; Technical College,
Lindholm; Debden. *Armstrong Whitworth Argosy* XP
409. *Avro Vulcan B.1A* XH479 "21" (7974M) *Bristol
Sycamore 3* WA576/7900M ex G-ALSS c/n 12887 pre-
production; WT933/7709M ex G-ALSW c/n 12891
(Middle East tropical tests). HC14 XG506/7852M,
XG515/8008M, XG518/8009M all ex CFS; S-P. S-F. *de
Havilland Sea Vixen FAW.1* XJ560/8142M, XJ571/8140M,
XJ526/8145M, XJ582/8139M, XJ604, XN658, XN688/
8141M, XN691/8143M, XN700/8138M, XN705, XN707/
8144M, XN699, XP919, XP921. *English Electric Canberra
B.2* WD999/7387M ex 9 & 103 Sqdns WK132/
7913M, WK134/7914M, *T4* WJ878/7636M "19" ex
231 OCU "U". *English Electric Lightning F.1*
XG336/8091M ex A & AEE. *Folland Gnat T.1* XM698/
8090M pre-production trials a/c. *Hawker Hunter F.4*
WV276/7847M, XF319/7849M. *Hawker (Armstrong Whit-
worth) Sea Hawk FGA.4* WV794/8152M, WV795/8151M,
WV797/8155M, WV903/8153M, WV908/8154M. *FGA.6*
XE339/8156M, XE369/A2580 ex FRU Hurn RNAS Arbroath now 8158M, XE390/8157M. *Hunting Jet Provost
T 3* XM351/8087M, XM367/8083M, XM369/8084M, XM386/
8076M, XM409/8082M, XM410/8054AM, XM417/8054BM,
XM467/8085M, XM468/8081M, XM480/8080M/69, XN492/
8079M, XN594/8077M. *T 4* XR669/8062M ex BAC. *Percival
Provost T.1* WV443/8035M, WV471/7952M, WV486/
7694M ex CFS and 6FTS WV492/7695M, WV493/7696M,
WV495/7697M, WV505/8036M, WV512/7613M, WV573/
7617M, WV618/7614M, WV686/7621M, WW397/8060M,
WW442/7618M, XF555/8037M, XF608/7954M, XF689/
8038M, XF841/8039M. Readers will understand that the
above are training airframes which are in use by the
apprentices. They are listed because, as the needs of
the RAF change, many will become available for museums, four Provosts going to Collections 1971/2.
Many Hunters listed previously have gone for refur-
bishing and sale and some machines have been
scrapped when museums could not afford to move them

HIGH WYCOMBE. House. *Sopwith Pup* (replica)
G-AVPA c/n CJW.1; C. J. Warrilow.

PINEWOOD. Film Studios. *Proctor-Stuka* W8-AE
reported here in poor shape but studios refuse to sell.
Before "conversion" for ground shots in Battle of
Britain film it was G-AIEY a Proctor I c/n K261 ex
P6227.

Supermarine Spitfire XVI (Halton)

WESTCOTT. Ministry of Technology Rocket Propulsion Establishment—view only by invitation: *Me 163B*
191614. *Fieseler Fi 103 (V1)* flying bomb, 418947. *V2*
rocket. *Fuji MXY-7 Ohka 11.*

CAMBRIDGESHIRE

BASSINGBOURN. John Howe's Farm. *Miles Magister* G-AKPF c/n 2228, ex V1075 with parts of N3788/
G-ANLT for restoration.

CAMBRIDGE. Airport. Cambridge A/c Preservation
Society own *Miles M.14A Magister* G-AIUA c/n 2035
ex T9768, built June 1940, at RAF Wyton, 15 FTS & FIS,
10 AGS. Struck off RAF charge November 1946. Flown
1950s by the late C. A. Nepean Bishop, then by S. M.
Aarons who won the Norton Griffiths Trophy and, in
1961, the Air Racing Championship. This a/c will be
restored using starboard wing of G-ANWO and prop
from G-AJDR and will be finished in 1940 Training
Command colours. Flying from Cambridge airport are
the following:—*DH. Tiger Moth* G-AHIZ c/n 86533 ex
PG624; D. Jackson/W. F. A. Ison. *DH. Tiger Moth*
G-ANFI c/n 85577 ex DE623; Cambridge University
Gliding Trust. *DH. Tiger Moth* G-AOEI c/n 82196 ex
N6946; Cambridge Private Flying Gp. *DH. Tiger Moth*
G-AZDY c/n 86559 ex PG650, F-BGDJ; B. A. Mills.

DUXFORD. Former RAF base. The Imperial War
Museum have a store and restoration centre here and
local enthusiasts are lending a willing hand, initially on
the Mustang which will be transferred to Lambeth when
restored to exhibition standard. Here, as at January,
1973:—*Beagle 206X* G-ARRM prototype c/n B001 and
Beagle Pup G-AVDF prototype c/n B121/001. (owned by
Sir Peter Masefield). *DH Sea Venom F.21* XG613. *DH Sea
Vampire T.22* XG743 coded BY/798. *DH. Sea Vixen FAW.2*
XS 576, "125-E". *English Electric Canberra B.2* WH 725.

Proctor-Stuka (Pinewood)

Auster AOP.9 XP281—from Middle Wallop. *Supermarine Scimitar* (expected) *Fairey Gannet AS.4* XG797 coded "766". *Avro Shackleton MR.3 Mk.3* XF708 "C" flown in from Kemble 22 Aug, 1972, by crew of No 8 Sqdn. *NA.P-51D-25-NA Mustang* RCAF 9246 ex 44-73979 USAAF, from St. John, Quebec where serialled "612". Donated by Canadian Armed Forces. *Avro Anson C.XIX* TX183, flown into Old Warden from Boscombe Down in 1968 is stored here pending more accommodation at Shuttleworths. It should be stressed that the public cannot visit the IWM store at present but it is hoped to make viewing facilities available in due course—watch the aviation press for details. *Junkers Ju 52/3m* is expected to arrive by sea from Portugal as a gift from the Portuguese Air Force. A Magister also expected—perhaps from Cambridge.

ELY. RAF Hospital. *Armstrong Whitworth Meteor NF(T)14* WS774, from Upwood.

LEVERINGTON COMMON. *Auster AOP.9* G-AVXY c/n B5/10/120 ex XK417, owned by R. J. Moody; formerly A. R. Else of Wisbech.

LITTLE GRANSDEN. Airstrip. *Tiger Moth* G-ADJJ c/n 3386 ex BB819, flown by L. B. Jefferies of Fullers Hill Farm.

CHESHIRE

CHESTER (Hawarden). Hawker Siddeley (Avro) airfield. *DH.80A Puss Moth*, G-AAZP c/n 2047 ex HL537, SU-AAC. HS Social Club. *DH. Mosquito T.III* RR299/ G-ASKH, ex RAF Aden, Benson, Fighter Cmd Com Flt, 3/4 CAACU. Flew in 633 Sqdn and Amiens Jail films as HK695 "HT-E" etc. *DH. Tiger Moth* G-ANTE c/n 84891 ex T6562, HS Sports & Social Club. *DH. Vampires T.11* XH330 ex Cranwell and XE852 believed at HS Apprentice Training School, though may be up for disposal.

DH. Mosquito T.III (Chester)

MACCLESFIELD. Technical College. *DH. Vampire T.11* XD624.

SEALAND. RAF. Officers Mess grounds ex 610 (County of Chester) *Supermarine Spitfire XVI* TD248/ 7246M "DW-A". *DH. Vampire T.11* XE890/7871M ex 233 OCU, 8/1 FTS and *Hawker Sea Hawk FB.3* WM913 "SAH.1" in use with Maintenance Unit Training School.

NA. Mustang (Duxford)

Avro Anson C.XIX (Duxford)

STOCKPORT. The Northern Aircraft Preservation Society. Although the Society's aircraft are located in various counties it is felt advisable to include all the *stored* machines under Stockport, with suitable annotations. Permission to view or to learn of displays should be addressed to Peter Schofield BSc, 8 Greenfield Avenue, Urmston, Manchester, M31 1XN, and offers of material should also be sent there. This Society was responsible, in 1967, for forming the British Aircraft Preservation Council and is affiliated to the Transport Trust and Popular Flying Association. *Avro 594 Avian IIIA* G-EBZM c/n R3/AV/160, registered May 1928, owned by Lady Heath for racing, rescued from Ringway Fire Section; 80 hp ADC Cirrus "C"—to be loaned to Torbay Aircraft Museum in 1973. *Slingsby T.7 Cadet TX.1* of 1943 from Woodford Gliding Club, being prepared for exhibition in Bradford Industrial Museum. *Avro Avian IV.M* of 1930 G-ABEE; spent war at RAF Bassingbourn, post-war Avian Syndicate, Denham (parts of G-ACKE used) fuselage from Selhurst Grammar School—remains stored at Irlam, following donation of parts to G-EBZM. *HM.14 Pou-du-Ciel* BAPC.12 (see Newcastle-upon-Tyne.) *B.A. Swallow 2* G-AEVZ c/n 475 of 1937 with 90 hp Cirrus Minor. Being prepared for Royal Scottish Museum, Edinburgh, at Peel Green, near Eccles. *HM.14 Pou-du-Ciel* BAPC.13 with 600cc.

DH. Mosquito T.III (Chester)

DH. Puss Moth (Chester)

Douglas "OE". From C. M. Barrington-Robinson 1965, owned by Peter Schofield, at Peel Green. *Addyman Standard Training Glider* of 1934, BAPC.14, under rebuild by Alder Grange School, Rawtenstall, for Bradford Industrial Museum. *Addyman S.T.G.* 1936-uncompleted, BAPC.15, stored at Irlam. *Addyman Ultra Light*, 1936, uncompleted, BAPC.16; stored Irlam. *Bristol F2B* of 1919, uncompleted, BAPC.19—bare frame from Weston-on-the-Green; in store at Irlam. *Miles Messenger 4A* G-ALAH (see RAF, Henlow). *Killick man-powered helicopter*, 1963, BAPC.18, from estate of late H. D. Killick, 1967; stored Irlam. *Slingsby T.7 Cadet TX.1* of 1943, RA848, from Lancs and Derbys Gliding Club; front fuselage converted into giant collecting-box. *Saro Skeeter AOP.12* XL811—(see Southend-on-Sea). *Woodhams Sprite*, 1966 uncompleted, BAPC.17; twin-boom low-wing pusher, designed by Society member; stored Irlam. *Focke Achgelis Fa 330 Bachtelge* of 1944 Werk-Nr 100502. On loan from RAE Aero Club. At Peel Green as mobile exhibit. *Chrislea Airguard* of 1938 G-AFIN c/n LC-1 new fuselage built Finningley, 1971 and now at Irlam awaiting completion. *DH.89 Dragon Rapide* of 1935 G-ADAH c/n 6278 two Gipsy Queen 3s; from Shuttleworth. At Peel Green for rebuild for R. Scottish Museum. Operated by Allied Airways throughout War. *Fairey Ultra Light helicopter* G-AOUJ c/n F9424 expected 1973. *Murray helicopter* of 1964, BAPC.60, with 36 hp JAP-99, at Irlam. *Bensen-Wallis Gyrocopter* of 1959, G-APUD, c/n 1 with 1600 cc. Volkswagen, for use as mobile exhibit, housed in Society's van. *Fairchild F.24W Argus* of 1943 G-AJOZ c/n 347 ex 42-32142, FK338, from Southend, now with member in Market Drayton for restoration. (Wing of G-AJPI). Nose section only of *Avro Anson C.XIX* VP519; stored Peel

Avro Avian IIIA (Stockport)

Green. The Society is to be congratulated on acquiring aircraft which would otherwise be scrapped and for loaning-out where possible. *Luton Minor* G-AFIU fuselage (drelict) is with a member, housed at Peel Green pro-tem pending decision on restoration. *DFS Kranich 2 glider,* from Christopher Wills, awaiting re-location.

WOODFORD. Avro Gliding Club. 5 miles SSW of Stockport. *DFS Kranich 1,* two-seater of 1936, Swedish-built in 1942/3.

CORNWALL

CULDROSE. HMS Seahawk, RNAS. Available only on Navy Days or by prior appointment. *Sea Hawk F.1* WF225 at entrance. *Douglas Skyraider AEWI* WV106

Armstrong Whitworth Sea Hawk (Culdrose)

stored for FAA Museum. At School of Aircraft Handling are the following:— *Hawker Sea Hawk (Armstrong-Whitworth) FB.5* WM 969/A2530/SAH-5. *FB.5* WM 983/A2511/SAH-6 (was SAH-9). *FGA.6* WV798/A2557/SAH-4 (was SAH-10). WV826/A2532/SAH-2; WV865/A2554/SAH-1 (was SAH-7 "038"). *FGA.6* XE368/A2555/SAH-3—wings from WM915. Also on ground duties here:—*DH. Sea Vixen FAW.2* XJ575/A2611 "713". *FAW.2* XN647/A2610 "707"; XN650/XN651/A2616 "705". *Fairey Gannet AS.6* WN464/A2540. *AS.6* XA459/A2608. *AS.6* XG831/A2539. *Blackburn Buccaneer 1* XN954/A2617. *Westland Wessex HAS.1* XL729—pre-production, from FAA Museum, to which it may return one day. The following aircraft have been relegated to rescue and fire-fighting:—*Sea Hawk FB.3* WF299/A2509; WM913/A2510; *FGA.4* WV909/A2549. *Fairey Gannet AS.1* WN346/A2493; XA363/A2528; XA342/A2471. *DH. Sea Venom F.21* XG616/A2492. *Westland Whirlwind HAR.1* XA869/A2451. *Supermarine 544* WT854/A2499. *Supermarine Scimitar F.1* XD215/A2573; XD332/A2574. *Supermarine 508* VX133/A2529. *DH.110 Naval prototype* XF828/A2500. *Wessex HAS.1* XP155 instructional a/c. Preservation organizations would do well to keep in touch with the Naval Department concerned with disposal of aircraft, but only those with finance available for purchase and—most important—transport should contact A/c Dept (Naval) M.O.D., Golden Cross

House, Duncannon St, London WC2N 4JG. Please inform compiler of (a) acquisitions and (b) of known *scrappings* at Culdrose (and elsewhere).

HAYLE. Carwin Garage on A.30. *Miles Messenger 2A* G-AJKK c/n 6366, now dismantled.

HELSTON. B. C. Peters. *Bristol Sycamore HR.14* XJ917 for display.

PERRANPORTH. Airfield. *Tiger Moth* G-ANFW c/n 3737, N5469; Dr. D. Wright. *Avia 40P*—last airworthy example of famous French pre-war sailplane.

ST. JUST. Airfield. *Rapide* G-AIYR c/n 6676, HG691; V. H. Bellamy for joy-flights. *Nord 1002 Pingouin* G-AVJS c/n 196, ex F-BFKA; F. R. Brown.

COUNTY DURHAM

MIDDLETON ST. GEORGE. Tees Side Airport (east of Darlington) *Tipsy Trainer 1* G-AFSC c/n 11; F. H. Greenwell.

USWORTH. Sunderland Airport. *Vickers Valetta C.2* VX577, owned Mr. Bambrough; static. *DH. Rapide* G-AJSL c/n 6801, ex NR713; Trent Valley Avn; ex Parachute Regt. *DH. Tiger Moth* G-AREH c/n 85287 ex DE241; Sunderland Flying Club Ltd.

CUMBERLAND

CARLISLE. Airport. Solway Aviation Society. *DH Vampire T.11* WZ507 "C" of CATCS, Shawbury. *Handley Page Hastings T.5* TG518 ex SCBS, Lindholme —at airport for non-destructive training & display. At No 14 M.U., on main highway—photography by C.O.'s permission:—*DH. Vampire FB.5* VZ304/7630M ex 249 Sqdn, 3/4 CAACU. *Hawker Hunter F.1* WT660/7421M ex DFLS, West Raynham, 229 OCU.

DH. Rapide (St. Just)

DH. Rapide (Usworth)

DH. Vampire T.11 (Carlisle)

Hawker Hunter F.1 (Carlisle)

HOLMROOK. Irton Hall School for Spastics. *Anson C.XIX* VV901, ex Silloth.

DERBYSHIRE

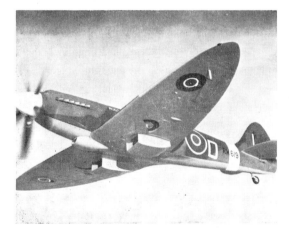

Supermarine Spitfire XIV (Castle Donington)

CASTLE DONINGTON. East Midlands Airport. (The *village* is in Leicestershire and it is possible a *DH. Comet* may be moved there to act as a cafe; for the sake of convenience it is recorded here). *Supermarine Spitfire XIVc* G-ALGT ex RM689 of 83 GSU, 350 (Belg) 443 (Can), in B. of B. film and repainted RM619 "AP-D" inaccurately. Owned by Rolls-Royce (1971) Ltd and kept airworthy. *Auster V* G-ANIH c/n 1779 ex TW449; C. R. Barker. *DH. Rapide* G-AKNN c/n 6598 ex X7456; G. H. Smale. *Douglas Dakota 4* G-AMYB c/n 16598 ex 44-

77014, KN652, SN-AAK, ST-AAK. *Dakota 4* G-AMZS c/n 26582 ex 43-49321, KK127, SN-AAI, ST-AAI; both of Field A/c Services.

GREAT HUCKLOW. Derby & Lancs Gliding Club. *Shenstone, Czerwinski, Harbinger,* two seater of 1947. Two built; one may exist in Canada. Although Shenstone is often given credit it is pointed out by experts that Czerwinski was Poland's best pre-war glider designer. The Harbinger is the last example of his work. *Zlin 24 Krajanek* of 1947; Czech intermediate sailplane.

DEVONSHIRE

DUNKESWELL. Airfield. Torbay Flying Club. D. N. Downton. *Percival Prentice 1* G-AOLP c/n B3/1A/PAC/ 314, ex VS385. *Auster V* G-AKXP c/n 1017 ex NJ633; F. Breeze & Ptrs.

EXETER. Airport. South-West Aviation Ltd. *Douglas Dakota 6* G-AMYJ c/n 15968/32716 ex 44-76384, KN353 XF747 (temporary trooping serial). *Dakota 4* G-APBC c/n 15675/27121 ex 43-49860, KN250. *Dakota 3* G-AMDB c/n 14987/26432 ex 43-49171, KJ993, G-37-2; F. H. Mann. *Miles Gemini 3B* G-AJTG c/n 6459; P. L. Ashworth. Near the By-pass at Bertram Arden's Farm, sometimes taxying:—*Surrey Flying Services AL.1* G-AALP; *DH Tiger Moth* G-ACDA (1st 82A, impressed as BB724, the oldest in existence). *BA Swallow* G-AFGC c/n 467 and G-AFGD c/n 469 (still painted as BK897) used as a glider at Farnborough, also G-AFHC c/n 486. *Taylorcraft Plus C2* G-AFTN, c/n 102 impressed as HL535. Let us hope these historic machines will be preserved for posterity.

Hafner Revoplane (Higher Blagdon)

HIGHER BLAGDON. Near Paignton. Torbay Aircraft Museum, owned by TV personality (and pilot) Keith Fordyce M.A. Now open daily from 1000-1800 (or longer in summer). Admission probably 30p, children 15p, reductions for parties. Refreshments in licensed cafeteria. Wheelchairs no problem. Parking unlimited. Overnight accommodation can be arranged, subject to availability and notice. *Desoutter Mk I monoplane* G-AAPZ c/n D25 ex National Flying Services *Percival Provost 1* WV605. "O-V" *EoN Primary glider* EON/P/063 (Sunderland Gliding Club) *Saunders-Roe Skeeter AOP.12* XN351. *Hafner R.11 Revoplane* of 1933, BAPC.10 one of the first helicopter designs to demonstrate the practicability of VTOL. Stored by Raoul Hafner at Yeovil until 1966, then donated to Shuttleworth who have loaned it, and the other four listed exhibits, to encourage Keith Fordyce with his project.

The following are owned by the museum or its helpers
—including Walter Ellis and Vernon Hillier and the
Devon & Cornwall A/c Preservation Society:—*DH
Tiger Moth* G-ANSM c/n 82909 ex R5014. *Percival
Proctor IV* G-ANYP. c/n H.591 ex NP 184. *Hurricane*
(replica) as L1592, 615 Sqdn. *Percival Provost T.1*
WV679/7615M, from 1 S. of T.T. ex 2 FTS "O-J".
DH. Sea Venom F.21 XG629 from RNAS Culdrose, ex
893/831 Sqdns. *Hawker (AW) Sea Hawk FB.3* WM961,
formerly 898/902 Sqdns and A2517/SAH.6 of School of
A/c Handling, Culdrose. *BAC Overdraft,* 1959 experi-
mental hovercraft. *Westland Whirlwind HAR.3* XJ393
(ex XD363) ex Portland and Royal Radar Estab. *DHC
Chipmunk T.10* WB758/7729M ex 14 RFS, Com Flt,
Andover, Oxford UAS, 2030 ATC Sqdn, Elmdon and
71 MU Exhibition Hangar. *Bristol Sycamore HC.14* XG544
(the RAF's last airworthy example) ex 275, 118, 225, 32
Sqdns and other units. Flown into museum from
Northolt via Upavon 11 August 1972. *Westland Dragonfly*
WN499 from Station Flt Culdrose coded "CU911".
BA. Swallow 2 G-AFGE c/n 470 ex BK894; loaned by
D. G. Ellis. *Focke Achgelis Fa 330* probably 160000/10
loaned by Sid Miles. *Miles Messenger 2A* G-AKEZ,
c/n 6707 to be repainted as Field Marshal Montgomerys'
aircraft. *Bf109* (replica) loaned by Doug Bianchi. There
is an English Electric Canberra cockpit and a magnificent
display of engines and other aviation items in a splendidly laid-out "Long Gallery"—converted animal sheds
which show up the exhibits to advantage. Further aircraft are expected; on loan and by purchase, to make
this one of the worthwhile air museums of England. Do
make a point of visiting when in the area.

HONITON (Near). Devon & Somerset Gliding Club.
DFS Weihe of 1939 Swedish-built 1942/3.

MANADON. HMS Thunderer. RN Engineering Col-
lege. Viewable by invitation only. *Blackburn Buccaneer
S.1* XK532. *Westland Whirlwind 3,* XJ402. *Fairey Gannet
T.2* XA408 *Westland Wessex* XS867. *Wasp* XV625.

DORSET

BLANDFORD FORUM. Garage & Caravan Sales,
A.354 Road. *Auster AOP9* XN412; XR236, XR267. Pre-
sume for sale.

Part of Torbay Aircraft Museum (Higher Blagdon)

Sycamore HC.14 flies in (Higher Blagdon)

BOVINGTON. Tank Museum. *Saunders-Roe Skeeter
AOP.12* XM564.

COMPTON ABBAS. Airfield. *DH. Moth Minor*
G-AFOZ c/n 94055, ex W7975; C. P. Burrell & W. G.
Watson. *Chrislea Super Ace* G-AKVF c/n 114 ex AP-
ADT. *Tipsy B series 1* G-AISC c/n 19, Wagtail Flying
Group. *Auster 5D* G-ANIJ c/n 1680 ex TJ672; G. W. B.
Donaldson/H. L. G. Melly. *Auster 6A* G-ARGB c/n
2593 ex VF635 (AOP.VI) now Dorset Flying Club. There
is also said to be a *1935 Kite glider* here.

Tipsy B (with Tipsy Belfair from Blackbushe, Surrey) (Compton Abbas)

DORCHESTER. Sam Fowler's Night Club, High West Street. *Auster AOP.9* believed XK421, from farmyard near Blandford.

TARRANT RUSHTON. Airfield. Flight Refuelling Ltd. *Meteor T.7* WF877 with PR nose and cutaway rear canopy; last used for Derwent engine and ejector trials. *Meteor F.8s* VZ462, VZ530, WA850, WA984, WE685, WE919 said here as airframes for drone contracts. *DH.60 Gipsy Moth* G-AAWO c/n 1235; J. F. W. Reid. *Auster 5-150* G-ALXZ c/n 1082 ex NJ689, PH-NER, D-EGOF; Dorset Gliding Club. *DFS Weihe glider,* built to 1939 design with wings built in Germany 1942/3 and fuselage in Sweden 1942/3. The bubble canopy is, however, different from the original design.

WIMBORNE. Ferndown Modern School. 2358 ATC Squadron. *DH. Vampire* XH318/7761M "68" ex Shawbury and Cranwell; well cared-for.

DH. Vampire T.11 (Ferndown)

ESSEX

ARDLEIGH. Strip. *Taylorcraft Plus D.* G-AHXE c/n 171, ex LB312 D. G. Stephenson.

BASILDON. Children's Playground. *Percival Prentice* G-AOPY ex VS633.

BELCHAMP WALTER. Strip. *DH Tiger Moth* G-AIRK c/n 82336 ex N9241; C. R. Boreham, R. C. Treverson, R. W. Marshall.

BURNHAM ON CROUCH. House. *DH. Rapides* G-AEMH c/n 6336 ex X7387 and G-AKRN c/n 6513 ex X7340 owned by Ian Jones, son of Sqdn Ldr R. J. Jones AFC; for possible restoration.

CHELMSFORD. Waterhouse Lane, 276 ATC Sqdn HQs. *Gloster Meteor T.7* WH132/7906m "J" ex 207 AFS, 8FTS, Manby, CFS.

DEBDEN. RAF. Thaxted Road gate. *Hawker Hunter F.1* WT694/7510M ex "Y" 54 Sqdn. May go to Southend when station closes.

NAVESTOCK. Strip. *DH. Moth Minor* G-AFOJ c/n 9407, ex E.1, E-0236; R. M. Long, also *Tipsy Tr 1.* G-AFJR c/n 2. *Bücker Bü131 Jungmann* G-ASLI c/n 20 ex HB-EVA; D. H. Reay. *Jungmann* G-ATJX c/n 36 ex HB-AFE, D-EDMI; R. Fautley. *Piper J3C-65 Cub* G-AXGP c/n 9542 ex 43-28251, F-BDTM, F-BGPS; R. M. Long.

NORTH WEALD. Airfield. Essex Gliding Club. *DFS Weihe* of 1939, Swedish-built for American Paul McReady to participate in the 1950 world championships; he came 2nd. Silver Wings Restaurant. *Westland Dragonfly* WG720 "920 BY".

SOUTHEND-on-SEA. Historic Aircraft Museum, Aviation Way, Cherry Orchard Lane; reached from A127, turning off at Kent Elms Corner into Eastwoodbury Lane, or from airport via Eastwoodbury Lane. Open 1000-1900 (summer) 1000-1700 winter. Cafeteria etc. The complex includes motel, restaurant, discotheque and filling station. Opened 26 May 1972 by Air Marshal Sir Harry Burton KCB, CBE, DSO, RAF, the following are displayed as this is written (Jan 1973):— *Hawker Sea Fury FB.11* WJ288 coded "029" ex Donibristle, Anthorn, Hurn and Lossiemouth. SOC 1962 with 1193 hrs since last repair. *Hawker Sea Hawk FGA.6* XE489 (painted as XE 364:J/485 to represent a/c of 899 Sqdn HMS Eagle during Suez campaign). Actually to Abbotsinch 1956, then Hal Far (Malta), Lossiemouth, Brawdy, Abbotsinch, Fleetlands, FRU Hurn. Disposed out of service with 1402 recorded hours. *Pou-du-Ciel* (Flying Flea) G-ADXS with Scott A2S, loaned by the widow of the late Chris Story who flew this machine on 19 Jan, 1936. *Saunders-*

Hunter F.1 (Debden)

Roe Skeeter AOP.12 XL811 "157" ex 9/11 Hussars; loaned from N.A.P.S. *Mignet HM.293* G-AXPG "Modern Flea" c/n PFA 1333; loaned from W. H. Cole. *Roe Triplane 1* (replica) BAPC.6, of Shuttleworth Collection, loaned from NAPS. *Fieseler Storch* D-EKMU c/n 110094 built Prague 1943 as Fi.156-C3; to Sweden June 1943 as 3812 RSwedAF, then OE-ADR. Bought airworthy from Dianaflug, Hamburg where it was banner-towing. Repainted as Luftwaffe a/c. *DH.84 Dragon 1* G-ACIT c/n 6039 "Orcadian" to Aberdeen Airways 1933, flown by Captain Fresson OBE and others who pioneered Orkney/Shetlands schedules. This machine to be kept airworthy for air displays. *Miles Gemini 1A* G-AKGD

c/n 6492, donated by "Dizzie" Addicott, pilot of the Vickers Gunbus and Vimy replicas (now in RAF Museum). Anthony Haig-Thomas of Ipswich is at present loaning his "Moth Collection":— *DH. Moth Minor* G-AFNG c/n 94014 ex AW112. *DH. Fox Moth* G-ACEJ c/n 4069. *DH Hornet Moth* G-ADLY c/n 8020 ex W9388, once owned by Marquis of Londonderry, Sir Lindsay Everard MP, Viscountess Mairi Bury, V. H. Bellamy and other famous pilots. Later Straight Corporation, Western Airways and Fredair Ltd. *DH. Gipsy Moth* G-ATBL c/n 1917 ex CH-353, HB-OBA. *DH. Tiger Moth* G-AGYU c/n c/n 85265, DE208 (may be away, flying). *Supermarine Spitfire XVI* TB863 "FB-Y" ex

Fieseler Storch (since painted camouflage) (Southend)

DH. 84 Dragon (Southend)

Pou-du-Ciel (Southend)

DH. Fox Moth (Southend)

DH. Gipsy Moth (Southend)

453 (RAAF) 183, 567, 691, 17 Sqdns, 3 CAACU, "Reach for the Sky" film, owned by Bill Francis, currently being restored here (but may be moving to a garage at Southam, Warwickshire). *Humber-Bleriot* (replica) BAPC9. Built for a Royal Tournament 1950s, then in "Magnificent Men" film, given by Shuttleworth to MAPS on indefinite loan and loaned by them. Now restored to depict Humber Monoplane built Coventry 1909, fitted with original Humber-built Anzani. *Fiat G.46-4* coded "FHE" serial awaited—from Italian Air Force at a very nominal charge. *Proctor IV* G-ANZJ c/n H687 and restored as NP303 of RAF. *Percival Provost T.1* WV483/7693M c/n 46, from No 1 S of TT, earlier with 6 FTS and 4 S. of TT.

Outdoors (though changes possible as a/c are rotated). *Blackburn Beverley C.1* XB261, flown in from A. & AEE, Boscombe Down. *Avro Lincoln B.II* G-29-1 ex RF342 G-APRJ, repainted as Napier Icing Research a/c, flown into Southend from Cranfield. *NA B-25J Mitchell* N9089Z painted as HD368 "VO-A" to honour No 98 (RAF) Sqdn, No 2 (B) Group. Actually c/n 34136 44-30861, from which a/c it is said "The War Lover" and "633 Squadron" were filmed. *Avro Anson 19 sers 2* G-AGPG c/n 1212, formerly EKCO Avionics and retaining radar nose; earlier with Skyways. Still airworthy. *DHA Drover* G-APXX c/n 5014 formerly VH-EAS, restored as Royal Flying Doctor a/c VH-FDT. *CASA. 2111* (Spanish-built Heinkel He 111) painted "6J-PR" and flown in "Battle of Britain" film, registered G-AWHB. ex B2-137 c/n 167, but a/c plate reads He.111-H16 c/n 049 built 3 December 1951. *Gloster Meteor T.7* VZ638 ex 25, 54, 85, 501 Sqdns, 8 FTS "X" of CAW. *SAAB J-29F* 29640, donated R.Swedish AF and restored to former colours of F.20 Wing, code "08" and "20". Was flown into Southend from Sweden. *Hurricane* (replica) on loan from B. of B. Museum. *Gloster Javelin FAW9* XH768/7299M ex 25 and 11 Sqdns and restored as E" of 25 Sqdn. From Cranwell by road. *Noorduyn AT. 16 Harvard II* LN-BNM c/n 14a/639 ex 44-12392, FE905 and RDanAF 329, by sea from Norway, 1972. Nose section of Viscount G-AVHE (ex Channel Airways). In open-air storage *Sea Fury FB.11* WJ244 (may be exchanged for Fairchild Cornell). *Westland Dragonfly HR.3* WG670 (damaged by fire—may become children's cabin-exhibit). Stored in hangars for restoration and possible future exhibition:— *DH. Vampire T.11* XD527 (ex Aviation Traders (Engineering) Ltd). *DH Tiger Moth* G-APMM c/n 85427 ex DE419—from Boscombe Down. *DH.*

Last flight of Lincoln—into Southend (Southend)

NA. Mitchell (Southend)

Avro Anson 19 (Southend)

Harvard (since repainted USAF marks) (Southend)

DHA. Drover (Southend)

CASA 2111 (Southend)

Tiger Moth F-BHAT c/n 83738 ex T7397, for restoration as G-ANPE. *Stampe SV-4C* G-AYHV c/n 609 ex F-BDFE. *Stampe SV-4C* G-AYLK c/n 673 ex F-BDNR, damaged in Ireland, may become a static exhibit in the museum. The remains of *Short Scion* G-AEZF c/n PA 1008 are owned by Anglian Aviation Group. *Gadfly A/c Co's Gadfly H.D.W.1* autogiro G-AVKE is due at the museum on loan. *Bf109 (replica)* from B. of B. film also here on loan but may move to Kent. In Aviation Traders (Engineering) hangars—not available to public:— *Percival Proctor III* G-ANPP c/n H264 ex HM354; *Proctor IV* G-ANXR c/n H803 ex RM221; *Proctor V.* G-AKIU c/n Ae129 and former Rolls-Royce hack.—all owned by R. J. "Bob" Batt, director-pilot (AKIU may be restored or used as spares). *Percival Prentice I* G-AOKL c/n PAC/208 ex VS610 and G-APIT c/n PAC/016 ex VR192 also here, the former flown by Bob Batt, the latter owned by NAPS, but may be restored and displayed at Southend for a time. *Douglas Dakota 3* G-AMPO c/n 33186/16438 ex 44-76854, KN566, LN-RTO, flies from Southend,

Bf 109—replica (Southend)

owned by Macedonian Aviation. *Auster 5* G-APAH c/n 3402 is also likely to fly in Ladi Marmol's ownership by the time this edition appears. *Vampire T.11* WZ458/7728M, "31" ex North Weald is with 1312 ATC Sqdn, on the airport.

Avro Lincoln B.II (Southend)

Meteor T.7 (Little Rissington)

Vampire T.11 (Little Rissington)

STANSTED. Airport. Near Bishop's Stortford. *Douglas Dakota 3* G-AJRY c/n 13331 ex 42-93421, KG600, 601B/RCAF, N96U, CU-P-702, N702S, G-ASDX; T. D. Keegan. Named "Executive Jet"! There are often interesting types in the Fire and Rescue Section—some of which ought to be preserved for posterity, but usually are not. Recent losses include a Comet I and a former BOAC Canadair Argonaut.

STAPLEFORD. Airfield. N. of Romford, NE of Woodford. *DH. Hornet Moth* G-AEZG c/n 8131, ex BK830: Mrs M. K. Wilberforce. *Tiger Moth* G-ANDE c/n 85957 ex EM726, R. Sanders. *Messenger 2A* G-AKIM c/n 6724; B. J. Clack.

UPMINSTER. Damyns Hall strip. Mr G. R. French. *DH. Tiger Moth* G-AZGH c/n 86489 ex NM181, F-BGCF, also *G-BACK* c/n 85879 ex DF130, F-BDOB.

GLOUCESTERSHIRE

ASTON DOWN. Airfield. Cotswolds Gliding Club. *Schleicher Rhönbussard* 1933 built by Alexander Schleicher 1937, believed the last airworthy. *Hutter H.17* of 1936 design, diminutive training sailplane, built in Britain 1946.

BRISTOL. City Museum. *Bristol Boxkite* (replica) from "Magnificent Men". *Sycamore* XL829 (may not be exhibited yet). *DH. Tiger Moth* 6787M said to be with 2146 ATC Sqdn; Formerly DF204. *Percival Provost T.1* XF603 "H" Coll of A. W., *Varsity T.1* WF410 at Tech. College on A.38.

INNSWORTH. RAF. *Gloster Javelin FAW 9* (was FAW7). XH903/7938M, though repainted as XM903; from 29, 33 and 5 Sqdns.

KEMBLE. RAF. No 5 M.U. Many aircraft here in store or for instructional training, of which the following reported:— at gate—*Gloster Meteor F.8* WH634 in 601 Sqdn colours, although "U" 85 Sqdn. *Meteor F.8* WF654 "Z", *Meteor T.7* WA591/7917M, AW *Meteor TT20* WM151. *DH. Sea Vampire T.22* XA165. *Percival Pembroke C.1* XF798. *Vickers Valetta T3/T4.* WJ476/7919M. *Vickers Varsity T.1* WL684 "B".

LITTLE RISSINGTON. Central Flying School, RAF. *Spitfire XVI* TE356/6709M ex 695, 34 Sqdns, a CAACU, and Kemble. *Harvard IIB* FS890/7554M c/n 14A-1030, ex 43-12731, was with 21 FTS, 600 Sqdn, 2 FTS, 1 FTS, Nottingham, Birmingham, Manchester UAS. Last flown 1957 when 1,650 hrs recorded, from RAF Hullavington; restored by 71 MU for CFS Jubilee. *Gloster Meteor T.7* WA669 and *DH. Vampire T.11* XH304, maintained by Kemble, are flown now at RAF and other displays by CFS pilots.

MORETON-in-MARSH. Airfield. *DFS Grunau 2* glider; Eric Rolfe.

NEWENT. House. *Flying Flea* BAPC.46; Alan McKechnie.

NYMPSFIELD. Airfield. Bristol Gliding Club & Trust. *Abbott-Baynes Scud 3* BGA283 of 1935 and formerly G-ALJR being restored. No longer motorized; one of two remaining examples of the world's first motor gliders. *Auster 6A* G-ASIP c/n 2549 ex VF608, and parts from VF600.

QUEDGELEY. RAF M.U. *Meteor T.7* WF784/7895M, displayed. *Auster AOP.9* XR243/8057M with 2419 ATC on 3 Site.

STAVERTON. Airport. Between Cheltenham-Gloucester-Tewkesbury on A.38 and A.40 roads. Skyfame Museum. Now open daily. 1100-1700 (1800 on Sundays, Holidays) Admission 20p. Exhibited 1973:— *Avro Anson I* N4877, G-AMDA, believed the oldest WW II a/c to fly, but now, from 1972, grounded. Joined RAF 1938, then No 2 Ferry Pilots' Pool, Filton; ATA White Waltham, later Derby Aviation & London School of Flying, coded "VX-F" honouring 206 Sqdn and all who flew the versatile "Annie". *Cierva C.30A* autogiro G-ACUU c/n 726, of 1934. With RAF as HM580 1448 Flt and 529 Sqdn; loaned by Mr. G. S. Baker. *Airspeed Oxford I* V3388 G-AHTW, built Hatfield, 1940 c/n 3083; With Boulton-Paul A/c for 14 years. Restored to repre-

Cierva C.30A (Staverton)

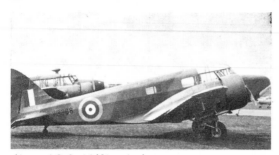

Airspeed Oxford I (Staverton)

Miles Magister (Staverton)

sent the machine in which Desmond Thomas (brother of Peter Thomas, museum director), who lost his life flying Wellingtons 1941, gained his wings at Brize Norton. *Miles Magister* G-AFBS c/n 539, ex BB661; impressed 1940 at 8 E & RFTS, Woodley, "FDT-A". Sold to BOAC 1948; then Denham Flying Club. Oldest "Maggie" in U.K. *Fairey Firefly 1* G-ASTL ex Z2033, SE-BRD, c/n F.5607, flown in from Sweden, and donated by a most generous supporter of "Skyfame". *Mosquito 35* TA719 G-ASKC flown as HJ898 "HT-G" in 633 Sqdn film, later painted "SY-G" to honour AV-M Bob Bateson, 613 Sqdn. Damaged; but partially restored for static display. *Hawker Tempest II* LA607—from College of Aeronautics, no "Ops". *Percival Proctor III* LZ766 ex G-ALCK c/n H536; loaned by Tamworth ROC. *Saunders-Roe SR.A1* TG263 ex G-12-1, the world's first jet-powered flying boat fighter conception, flown 16 July 1947. From College of Aeronautics, Cranfield. *Handley Page Hastings C.1* TG528, ex 24 Sqdn, RAF Transport Command. *DH. Sea Venom NF.21* WM571, coded "VL/742" flown in from Yeovilton 30 April 1969. *Chilton DW.1* G-AFGI c/n DW1/3—on loan. *Bristol Sycamore 3* G 48-1 ex G-ALSX. On permanent loan from Westland Helicopters to Elfan ap Rees and re-loaned by him: 1,233 hrs flown. First flown 20 April 1951, later VR-TBS, Tanganyika; restored BAC Dec 1959. *Short Sherpa G-36-1*—fuselage; from Bristol Tech. College. Nose only of *Halifax VII* PN323—presented by Graham Trant.

Fairey Firefly I (Staverton)

Hawker Tempest II (Staverton)

Saunders-Roe SR.A1 (Staverton)

Handley Page Hastings C.1 (Staverton)

Chilton DW.1 (Staverton)

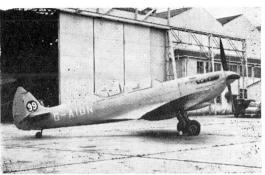

Spitfire Tr VIII (Andover)

STROUD. Tech. College. *Vampire T.11* XD599 "A" CATCS. Shawbury.

WHITESHILL. Mr. Cyril Pugh, re-building *DH Tiger Moth* G-ANEH ex Defford.

WITNEY. Tech. College. *Vampire T.11* XK590 "V". CATCS.

HAMPSHIRE AND THE ISLE OF WIGHT

ALDERSHOT. Browning Barracks, Airborne Forces Museum. *Dakota IV* KP208 in "D" Day markings, formerly C-47B-35-DK 44-77087, once Coastal Command Com Sqdn, then Aldergrove.

ANDOVER. RAF. *Supermarine Spitfire Tr VIII* G-AIDN c/n 6S/729058, ex MT818, N-32, owned by John Fairey and Tim Davies, who also have *Spitfire IXTr* G-ASOZ ex MJ627, IAC 158 (MJ772 wings) as spares for the 2-seater which delights so many at air displays. *Percival*

Provost T.1 G-AWPH c/n PAC/F/003 ex WV420, also here, owned by J. A. D. Bradshaw, the King's Cup winner with this a/c. At Red Post Bridge, RAF Andover, 1213 ATC Sqdn have *Percival Pembroke C.1* WV742/8111M, ex St. Athan. Portway Junior School, between airfield and town, houses *Avro Anson XIX* TX235 "The Portway Penguin" for the children. Mr Johnson of Weyhill Rd (by appointment only) has *DH. Rapides* G-ALAX c/n 6930, ex RL948 (from Old Warden) with parts of G-AFRK, G-AHGC, G-AHJS, and G-ASRJ, for a rebuild of one or more for The Dumey Aeronautical Collection.

BLACKBUSHE. Airfield. Home of many vintage types including:—*Miles Monarch* G-AFLW c/n 792; J. E. Randall, who also owns:— *Tipsy Belfair* G-AOXO c/n 537, ex OO-TIG. Rex Coates now has *Miles M.18 sers 2* G-AHKY c/n 4426 ex HM545, U-0224, U.8. *Taylorcraft Plus D.* G-AHUG c/n 153 ex LB282; R. L. Venning. *DH Leopard Moth* G-AIYS c/n 7089 ex YI-ABI, SU-ABM; B. Gardner. *DH. Tiger Moth* G-AXBW c/n 83595 ex T5879/6854M; R. L. Venning. *DH. Hornet Moth* G-AMZO

Dakota IV (Aldershot)

Spitfire Tr VIII (Andover)

c/n 8040 ex VR-RAI, OY-DEZ, SE-ALD; L. C. Webb. *Hornet Moth* G-ADNE c/n 8089, ex X9325; C. B. L. Harding. *Proctor I* P6237 G-AJLS being restored by Blackbushe Avn Group and *DH. Tiger Moth* G-APJP c/n 82869 ex R4961, also said under restoration at Blackbushe. *Piper J-3C-65 Cub* G-ATKI c/n 17545 ex N70536, believed now owned by Cliff Lovell, here. *Avro Triplane IV (replica)* one of those used in "Magnificent Men" reported here with John Habin of Hants Aero Club.

FAREHAM. Tech. College. *Sea Hawk (AW) FGA.4* WV831 "032".

FARNBOROUGH. Royal Aircraft Establishment. On occasional Open Days or by appointment only. Some aircraft may be seen flying at Bedford, Boscombe Down, or Pershore. *DH Comet 2E* XN453, was G-AMXD c/n 06026 (believed grounded). *Comet C.2E* XV144 (ex BLEU.) was G-AMXK, grounded. *Handley Page Hastings C.2* WD480. *Gloster Meteor T7* XF274; WL375 (F.8 tail, FR.9 nose). *Hawker (Siddeley) P.1127* XP964. *Blackburn Buccaneer S.1* XK530—development a/c. *Hawker Hunter F.6* XG210—from College of Aeronautics. *T.12* XE531. *Percival Provost T.1* XF844. *Auster AOP.9* XP277 ex 651 Sqdn. *Supermarine Scimitar F.1* XD231. *Westland Wessex HAS.1* XM330. *HC.2* XL728. *Westland Scout AH.1* XP 166 ex G-APVL, with Wasp parts, ex ETPS *Avro Shackleton MR.3* WR972. *DH. Sea Vixen FAW 2* XN652 "122/E", XS577 "137/E" ex 899 Sqdn. *DH. Devon C.2* XG496 "K" (was Dove G-ANDX) c/n 04435. XM223 "J" VP959 "L" and VP975 "M" of RAE Transport Flight. Said to be up for disposal (or scrapping) are:— *Gloster Meteor T.7* WL405; *Meteor F.4* EE531 (at Lasham). Owned and flown by RAE members are some vintage gliders plus *DH. Hornet Moth* G-AESE c/n 8108 ex W5775; H. J. Shaw. *DH. Tiger Moth* G-AJHS c/n 82121 ex N6866; RAE Aero Club *Aeronca C.3* G-ADYS c/n A.600 also reported with the Club, in storage since 1946. *Auster AOP.9* XP250/7823M is with 457 ATC Sqdn, Farnborough, ex Borden. RAE machines are being grounded and changed at this time and no guarantee can be given that all the above are likely to be seen if and when there is a public viewing day.

GOSPORT. Royal Navy Air Yard, Fleetlands. *Whirlwind I* XA862 c/n WA/A/1, ex G-AMJT.

HURN. Airport. *Miles Whitney Straight* G-AEUJ c/n 313; C. H. Parker. *Percival Prentice 1* G-APJB ex VR259; D. P. Golding. *Messerschmitt Bf.109 E-3* Werk-Nr 1190 which crashed near Eastbourne 30 Sept 1940 piloted by Unteroffizier Horst Perez of 4./JG.26, shipped to USA 1941 for "Bundles for Britain" campaign and later purchased in Ottawa by the German Aviation Research Group of "Air Britain", is here for restoration—future location as yet unspecified. *Cessna 170A* G-ABLE c/n 19903 ex N1327D, VR-NAH, said here for rebuild. *Saunders-Roe Skeeter 8* prototype G-APOI c/n S2/5081; B. G. Heron.

KING'S SOMBORNE, Hampshire. Private Strip of John Fairey, Bossington House (see Andover). *DH.80A Puss Moth* G-AEOA c/n 2184 ex ES921, owned and flown by Dr John Urmston of Botley, one of the machines purchased by Sqdn Ldr Jack Jones, AFC, to start East Anglian Flying Services and, in fact, the very first

aircraft to start his civilian operations from a field at Herne Bay, Kent, on 16th August, 1946, prior to moving into Southend Airport. Now beautifully restored, G-AEOA is to be seen at other Hampshire fields. *Currie Wot 1* G-ARZW c/n 1, is also flown and owned by Dr Urmston. A/C *NOT* viewable.

LARKHILL. Garrison playground. *Percival Pembroke C.1* WV734.

LASHAM. Airfield. *Avro York* G-ANTK ex MW232 of RAF on Berlin Airlift. Later Dan-Air and equivalent of 99 round-world flights on runs to Woomera rocket range. Now Boy Scouts' bunkhouse. *Gloster Meteor F.4* EE531/7090M used for wing-folding tests (see Farnborough). *Airspeed Ambassador 2* G-ALZO c/n 5226 ex 108 Royal Jordanian Air Force. Flew the last scheduled service by this type Jersey-Gatwick 26 Sept 1971. Now to be preserved by Dan-Air. *Douglas Dakota 3* G-AMPP c/n 15272/26717 ex 43-49456, KK135, XF756 (temporary RAF trooping serial post-war). Painted as G-AMSU (KP246) and preserved. *DH. Comet 4* G-APDE c/n 6406 ex 5Y-ALF, 9V-BAU, 9M-AOE; cabin trainer. *Beechcraft D.18S* N15750 c/n A-850 ex G-ATUM, D-IANA, N20S with *Beechcraft D18S* G-AXWL c/n CA.167 ex N6685, 1567/RCAF and G-AYAH c/n CA-159 ex N6123, 1559/RCAF. The Lasham Gliding Society, which embraces several clubs, offers:— *Schempp Hirth Minimoa* of 1936-39, now being restored by Ken Fripp to 1939 standards. *Cayley glider replica.*

Swordfish III (Lee-on-Solent)

Sea Hawk FGA.6 (Lee-on-Solent)

LEE-on-SOLENT. RNAS HMS Daedalus. Open Day or by appointment. *Fairey Swordfish III* NF389 coded "5B". (Blackburn built). *Blackburn Buccaneer S.1* XN934; *Gloster Meteor T.7* WS103. *DH. Sea Vixen FAW 1* XJ482;

Auster AOP.9 (Middle Wallop)

FAW.2 XJ521, XN706. *Hawker (AW) Sea Hawk FGA.6* WV828, *FGA.4* WV911 (*FGA.6* XE340 for FAA Museum). *Westland Whirlwind HAR.1* XA870, XA866, XA868; *HAR.3* XG574, XG577, XJ399; *HAR.7* XN314, XN305, XN944, XK911, XN259, XN308. *Wessex HAS.1* XM329, XT256, XP116, *HAS.5* XT457. *Supermarine Scimitar F.1* XD200 (XD220 for FAA Museum). Also Wasp and various Wessex for instructional purposes, not necessarily viewable.

Auster AOP.9 (Middle Wallop)

MIDDLE WALLOP. Army Air Corps. Museum understood to be closed (1973) so prior approval should be sought for visits. *Auster AOP.9* WZ670—on main gate, together with *Saro Skeeter AOP.12* XL769 ex 652 Sqdn *DHC.2 Beaver* XP812/7735M, *Beaver* XP770 also here. *Auster AOP.9* WZ721 and *Saunders-Roe Skeeter AOP.12* XL813, *Bristol Sycamore 14* XG502 ex 225/118/32 Sqdns and Wroughton, plus parts of Horsa glider all dismantled and stored for museum. *Auster AOP.9* XP242 ex 653 L.A. Sqdn Aden, RMCS Shrivenham, and XR244 with Advanced Fixed Wing Flight—due to be phased-out in 1973—preservation groups to note! *Sopwith Camel*

(replica) G-AWYY c/n 1701, is said to be here. Built by Slingsby's for film purposes. *Skeeter AOP.12* XL814 flies here. *Auster AOP.9* G-AVHT, ex WZ711 and *Skeeter AOP.12* XM553 G-AWSV c/n S2/5107, are owned and flown by Lt-Col Mike Somerton-Rayner (Ret'd) who still delights crowds at air displays throughout the country, when not providing a charter facility. *Aeronca 100* G-AEVS c/n AB114 is said to be here for restoration.

NEW MILTON. Airfield. *DH. Tiger Moths* G-ALUC c/n 83094 ex R5219 and G-ANOD ex T6121 and c/n 84588 dismantled. *DH. Hornet Moth* G-ADKK c/n 8033 ex W5749; B. G. Heron; and G-ADKM c/n 8037 ex W5751, King's Cup winner 1968; F. R. E. Hayter.

ODIHAM. RAF. *Gloster Meteor F.8* WK968 of 64, 63, 56, 46, CAW, Manby, on gate. *Slingsby Kite 2 glider* of 1947 said to be here with Army Gliding Club.

OVERTON. Strip *Watkinson Dingbat* G-AFJA c/n DB100: A. J. Christian.

PORTSMOUTH. Airport. *Auster V* G-ANFU c/n 1748 ex TW385 of Electricity Flying Group. *Percival Prentice 1* G-AOMF c/n B3/1A/PAC252 ex VS316; W. B. Wilkinson.

SOUTHAMPTON. Near Civic Centre 424 Sqdn, ATC. *Fairey Jet Gyrodyne* XJ389 ex G-AJJP, 2nd prototype (for disposal). *Supermarine S6B* S1596 (once at Royal Pier) currently stored by RAF for Mitchell Memorial, along with *Spitfire F.24* PK683, once at Changi, flown by Singapore Auxiliary Air Force. Watch aviation journals for details of the Mitchell Memorial progress. *DH. Hornet Moth* G-ADMT c/n 8093 is said to be nearby with Colin Clarke.

Spitfire F.24 (for Southampton)

Fairey Jet Gyrodyne (Southampton)

Britten-Norman BN-1F (Bembridge)

THRUXTON. Airfield. *DH. Tiger Moth* G-AMIU c/n 83228 ex T5495 said here with Southern Sailplanes. Kemps Aerial Surveys have:— *Reid & Sigrist Desford Tr.* G-AGOS c/n 3 ex VZ728 (believed to be earmarked for Leicester Museum when no longer airworthy). *Auster III* G-AREI c/n 518 ex MT438, VR-SCJ, VR-RBM, 9M-ALB; P. J. Pearce. *DH. Tiger Moth* G-ALNA c/n 85061, ex T6774; Wessex F/Group. G-ANFY c/n 86349 ex NL906; M. F. Ogilvie-Forbes.

Desford Tr. (Thruxton)

ISLE OF WIGHT. BEMBRIDGE. The Yacht Club. *Britten-Norman BN-1F* of 1950 G-ALZE c/n 1, rebuilt with dorsal fin, rudder of increased chord and inset ailerons. Stored. Let us hope this unique locally-built machine is exhibited.

SANDOWN. Airport. *DH. Tiger Moth* G-ANEZ c/n 84218 ex T7849; Isle of Wight Gliding Club.

HEREFORDSHIRE

HEREFORD. Credenhill. RAF. *Spitfire XVI* TE392/7000M, ex 126, 65, 595, 695, 34 Sqdns, 2 CAACU. Church Lawford, Wellesbourne Mountford and Waterbeach gates. *Hawker Hunter F.1* WT651/7532M and WT612/7496M. *DH. Vampire T.11* XE982/7564M ex RAF College, St. Athan, MOD exhibition a/c. now with 124 ATC Sqdn at 26 Eign Road. *DH. Vampire T.11* WZ550/7902M "R" ex 202 AFS, 7FTS, CFS, is with HQs 22 S.A.S.

SHOBDON. Airfield. *Miles Gemini 3C* G-AKGE c/n 6488 ex EI-ALM, J. M. Bisco. *Gemini 1A* G-AKKH c/n 6479 ex OO-CDO; Shobdon Aviation.

UPPERHILL. "The Spitfire" pub, formerly "Red Lion". *Spitfire XVI* TD135/6798M "NG-U" ex 604 (County of Middlesex) and ATC, Newcastle. Partially restored and now used as fund-raiser for Leominster Pensioners, a coin in a slot starting the propeller. *Supermarine Swift FR4* WK275 ex Hawker Siddeley Hatfield.

HERTFORDSHIRE

ALLEN GREEN. Between A.11/A.119. "The Queen's Head". *Hurricane* (*replica*) from Battle of Britain film; publican here is a former Hurricane fighter pilot.

ELSTREE. Airfield. *Hornet Moth* G-ADUR c/n 8085; Brian Kay. *Miles Messenger 2A* G-AKBN c/n 6377, ex EI-AFM; E. A. Shapero. *Messenger 2A* G-AJFF c/n

Spitfire XVI (Hereford)

DH. Hornet Moth (Elstree)

6363, formerly Airscooters Ltd, said displayed at Glowworm Petrol Station on the A.411. The "first" gull-wing version, due to wing spar failure! *Nord 1002 Pingouin* G-ASTG c/n 183 ex F-BGKI: Nipper F/Gp.

DH. Cirrus Moth (Hatfield)

HATFIELD. Hawker Siddeley (de Havilland) Airfield/Factory. *DH.60 Cirrus Moth* G-EBLV c/n 188, the 1928 prototype, airworthy.

LEAVESDEN. Airfield. *Dakota 4* G-ANAF c/n 16688/33436 ex 44-77104, KP220; G-AVPW c/n 12476 ex 42-92652 KG441; *Dakota 6* G-ANTC c/n 14666/26111 ex 43-48850 KJ938; all Hunting Surveys Ltd. *McKinnon (Grumman) G-21C Hybrid Turbo-Goose* G-ASXG c/n 1083 ex 926/RCAF, CF-BZY, N36992, N3692; Grosvenor Estates.

LONDON COLNEY. Salisbury Hall on A.6, also Green Line and London Transport buses and coaches. Open mid-April to end September on Sundays 1400-1800, Bank Holidays 1030-1730 or by appointment—Bowmansgreen 3274 (check new dialling codes). Admission fees, less expenses, to RAF Benevolent Fund and over £1,000.00 raised in 1972 season. Organized parties at reduced rates on Tuesday, Wednesday, Thursday 1030-1730 and, July-September, public welcomed on Thursdays from 1400. Light refreshments, free car park. No dogs. Full meals available nearby. Salisbury Hall is an ancient moated manor house with 15th century bridge and is said to accommodate the ghost of Nell Gwynne. Also residence of Winston Churchill 1905. In 1939 de Havilland's took over and in 1940 there emerged on to the meadow at rear the *prototype Mosquito* W4050, first of 7,780 "Wooden Wonder" machines

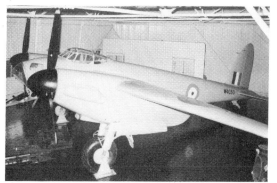

Prototype Mosquito (London Colney)

Mosquito B/TT.35 (London Colney)

which turned the scales in allied favour. The first prototype is now back in its own little hangar here (the second actually being flown by the late Geoffrey de Havilland from the field here, into Hatfeld). Also on display here:— *Mosquito B35/TT35* TA634 G-AWJV, built Hatfield April 1945, served with APS Sylt, 3/4 CAACU, then Aldergrove. Purchased by Liverpool Corporation and donated by them to Salisbury Hall. Painted now as "EG-F" HX922 of Gp Cpt "F" for Freddie Pickard who lost his life on the Amiens Jail raid, flying from nearby Hunsdon in a 487 (RNZAF) Sqdn Mosquito. Was HJ614 coded HT-B and HT-G in films. *DH. Vampire T.11* XD452 of 1 FTS, 7FTS, 3FTS, "The Clockwork Mouse". *DH. Venom NF.3* WX853/7443M ex 23 Sqdn and Debden. *Folland Gnat T.1* XM694 pre-production, from BAC, Filton may come here. Other machines are being sought (including a Sea Hornet) and may be on display —please inform Walter Goldsmith of anything suitable for this unique collection.

Vampire and Venom (London Colney)

PANSHANGER. Airfield. *Auster V* G-AOCU c/n 986 ex MT 349: R. & S. Precision Engineering; *Tiger Moth* G-ALTW c/n 84177 ex N7799; C. J. Musk. *Miles Messenger 2A* G-AILL c/n 6341; H. Best-Devereux. *Messenger 2A* G-AIDK c/n 6355; J. M. Lovett and S. W. Ward. *Messenger 2A* G-AJYZ c/n HPR/146 ex EI-AGU; Wasp Flying Group.

RUSH GREEN. Farm Aviation. *Tiger Moth* G-AMTO c/n 84655 ex T6229, possibly near here.

ST. ALBAN'S. Technical College. *Vampire T.11* XE956 "N", XH313 "E", and WZ584 "U" from CATCS, Shawbury, and Hatfield.

HUNTINGDONSHIRE

BRAMPTON. HQs RAF Training Command. By appointment only. *Armstrong Whitworth Meteor NF.14* WS760/7964M, ex North Luffenham, Duxford, Stradishall, Upwood; 959 hrs flown. *Hunting Jet Provost T3/4* XN602, ex Acklington and 27 M.U. 1961/68.

UPWOOD. RAF By appointment only. *English Electric Canberra B2/T4* WH723/7628M formerly of 231 OCU, RAF, and Upwood, but painted as WJ642 of 61/35 Sqdns. (The real WJ642 went to the Fire School, Catterick, December 1970.) *Hawker Hunter 5* WP190/7582M ex 1 Sqdn and *DH. Vampire T.11* XH278/7866M ex Cranwell, are here for instructional uses.

English Electric Canberra (Upwood)

KENT

BIGGIN HILL. RAF. Ask at Guardroom about photography. *Hawker Hurricane IIC* LF738/5405M ex 22 OTU, 1682 BD Flt. *Spitfire LFXVI* SL674 ex 501 (County of Gloucester) and 612 (County of Aberdeen) Sqdns, 17 OTU. At Battle of Britain Chapel. On the civil airport side many vintage aircraft including:—*GAL.42 Cygnet 2* G-AGBN c/n 111 ex ES915; J. and T. Robinson Ltd. Last Cygnet in existence. *Hornet Moth* G-AELO c/n 8105 ex AW118; J. A. C. Miles. *Percival Prentice 1* G-AOKH c/n B3/PAC/212 ex VS251 of 2 FTS, CFS, 3 FTS, Aviation Traders, Bob Batt; now owned by P. H. Louks. *Prentice 1* G-APPL c/n PAC/013 ex VR189; Miss S. J. Saggers. *Auster 5* G-APRF c/n 3412 ex VR-LAF; E. Drake. *Auster 5D* G-AOCR c/n 1060 ex NJ673, EI-AJS; G. W. Johnson. *Isaacs Fury 2* c/n 1 G-ASCM, smaller-than-normal replica of the famous Hawker Fury, in military markings; M. Raper. *Tiger Moth* G-AHMN c/n 82223 ex N6985; Vendair Ltd. G-ANCX c/n 83719 ex T7229; D. R. Wood; G-AOBO c/n 3810, N6473; D. J. Ronayne Ptr. G-AYVY c/n 86526, PG617, F-BGCZ; C. M. Jones; G-AOES c/n 84547 ex T6056,

GAL. Cygnet 2 (Biggin Hill)

Hurricane IIC (Biggin Hill)

R. F. D. Vickers and D. R. Wood. *Miles Messenger 2A* G-AHZT c/n 6334; E. Pratt (oldest extant?). *Messenger 4B* G-AKVZ c/n 6352 ex RH427; P. H. Louks. *Piper J-3C-65 Cub* G-AXHP c/n 12932 ex 44-80636 F-BETT; W. F. Barnes and R. W. Griffin. *Nord 1101 Noralpha* G-ATDB c/n 186 ex NATO Flying Club F-OTAN-6; A. G. H. Longbottom Ptrs. *Percival Prince 2A* G-ALWH c/n P50/10 ex YV-P-AEQ; Decca Navigator Co.

Isaacs Fury 2 (Biggin Hill)

CHATTENDEN. Joint Services Bomb Disposal Headquarters. *Fuji Ohka 11* "Cherry Blossom" ex RAF Cranwell and Cottesmore.

CHILHAM. Chilham Castle, home of Viscount Massereene. Enthusiasts Mike Llewellyn, Dick Windrow, Dick Mills, Frank Mason and others are opening a Battle of Britain Museum in June, 1973 to house the many pieces of historic wreckage recovered from the County. Also to be exhibited when covered accommodation available, the *Spitfire* (replica) *Hurricane* (replica) formerly at Langley, together with the *Bf109* (replica) both listed at Southend. It is hoped, later, to have on loan some authentic ex-Luftwaffe machines and this venture is to be praised and supported. It is planned to open daily; watch the press.

LYDD (Near). With Captain K. R. Sissons ARAeS, vintage enthusiast. (*Sea*) *Tiger Moth* G-AIVW c/n 83135 ex T5370. Winner of King's Cup, 1958, pilot, J. H. Denyer. Now owned by Norman Jones of "Tiger Club" fame and on floats from Aeronca Sedan for many years, delighting enthusiasts everywhere and "starring" in films. Long may she touch-down on the water. *Dakota 3* G-AMFV c/n 10105 ex 42-24243 ex FL522, 6810/SAAF ZS-DEF, at airport.

LYMPNE. Ashford Airport. *Auster 5D* G-ANHX c/n 2064, ex TW519; C. B. Lloyd and R. S. G. Kelly. *Dakota 4* G-AGYZ c/n 12278 ex 42-108843 FZ681; G-AMSM c/n 15764/27209 ex 43-49948 KN274; G-AMWW c/n 16262/33010 ex 44-76678, KN492, EI-ARP; are with Air Freight Ltd. *Tiger Moth* G-AHVV c/n 86116, ex EM929 is said to be here for restoration, following accident.

MANSTON. RAF. *Spitfire XVI* TB752/7256M ex 66 and 403 (Can), 3/5 CAACU RAF Sandwich, Middle Wallop and Hawarden gates, displayed in aid of RAF Benevolent Fund, to which over £1,000.00 already donated. *Gloster Javelin FAW.9* XH764 "C" 29 Sqdn *Gloster Meteor T.7* WF816. *English Electric Canberra PR.3* WE168. *Vickers Valetta C.2* VX572, may also be displayed. In the Fire and Rescue Section the following remained undamaged when last viewed but changes are always probable—*Hawker Hunter 4* WV268/7701M "P" of 26 Sqdn. *DH. Vampire T.11* XD388 ex 4/5/1 FTS. *Canberra B.2* WF908 ex 9/18 Sqdns. On the civil side the Vikings, alas, have been destroyed and *Miles Gemini 1A* G-AJZO c/n 6446 of E. C. Brace and *Tiger Moth* G-AHLT c/n 82247 ex N9128 of Thanet Flying Club may be the only vintage types; but a visit may be rewarding.

ROCHESTER. Fort Clarence. *Fieseler Fi103* (*V1*) from B. D. HQs, Horsham—NOT a piloted version but "faked" with car-seat. At the airport many vintage aircraft and unique gliders:— *Manuel Willow Wren*

Ohka 11 (Chattenden)

(Sea) Tiger painted for Chichester film (Lydd)

glider of 1931, BGA162 owned by Norman Jones. *Auster III* G-AHLK c/n 700 ex NJ889; H. Polhill. *Tiger Moth* G-ANJD c/n 84652 ex T6226; Strabor A/c Ltd. G-AOBX c/n 83653 ex T7187; N. H. Jones. G-AXAN c/n 85951 ex EM720 F-BDMM; A. J. Cheshire. G-AMTK c/n 3982 ex N6709 is dismantled but for possible rebuild.

SEVENOAKS. Home of C. C. Russell-Vick for restoration. *Klemm L25* G-AAXK c/n 182, 40 hp 9 cyl Salmson AD.9.

LANCASHIRE

ASHTON-in-MAKERFIELD. Nr Wigan. Lowbank Rd Garage. *Auster AOP.9* G-AXWA c/n B5/10/133 ex XN437; for sale 1973.

ASHTON-under-LYNE. *Spartan Arrow* G-ABWP c/n 78; R. E. Blain.

BARTON. Airfield. *DH.83C Fox Moth* G-AOJH c/n FM.42 ex AP-ABO built Canada 1947, shipped Pakistan, then to UK 1956. Used for pleasure flying Southport and Speke; owner J. S. Lowery.

BLACKPOOL. Squire's Gate Airport. As this is compiled *Avro Lancaster B.VII* G-ASXX ex NX611 WU-

15 of Aeronavale; flown from Australia by generous donors, for the defunct Historic Aircraft Preservation Society, Biggin Hill, is now owned by Lord Lilford but its future location and status is unknown. *Canadair Sabre 4* (F-86E) G-ATBF ex 19607/RCAF, XB733, MM19607 Italian Air Force, then HAPS/Reflectaire, now with private owner nearby but believed not for restoration.

LANCASTER. *Westland Dragonfly HC.3.* WG667 Code CU/901, ex Blackbushe, reported here for the proposed "Moby Dick" replica. News would be appreciated on this, the Lancaster and Sabre.

LIVERPOOL. Speke Airport. No 1 hangar. *Vampire T11* and *Fa330* Werk-Nr 100549 of Merseyside Aviation Society. Viscount Preservation Trust has *Viscount 701* G-ALWF c/n 5 ex Cambrian etc, the second production machine of 3 Dec 1952, flown here to be preserved and exhibited after the valiant efforts of a group of enthusiasts. *Miles Messenger 2A* G-AJWB c/n 6699; W. F. and M. R. Higgins.

LIVERPOOL. Planetarium. *Black Knight X* (on loan from Science Museum). Built early 60s, one of 15 for Black Arrow satellite launch vehicle, 30-ft long, 3-ft diameter.

Spartan Arrow (Ashton-under-Lyne)

Viscount (Liverpool)

Jet Provost and Hunter (Loughborough)

LYTHAM ST. ANNES. The Motive Power Museum. On Preston-Lytham-Blackpool A.584. Turn left at first traffic lights, after Warton. *Vampire T.11* XK624 flown from CFS, Little Rissington via Blackpool. *Provost T.1* WW421/7689M, tail code P2, ex Halton, formerly P-B/Q-H 3 FTS, B/CNCS (believed now wings of WW450/7688M, P-A of 2 FTS.) Also a well-kept collection of steam engines, carriages etc.

MOSTON. Tech. College. *Meteor T.7* WL332 ex FRU, Hurn.

ROYTON. Park Lane. 1855 ATC Sqdn. (near Oldham). *Armstrong Whitworth Meteor NF.14.* WS726/7960M ex 25 Sqdn, 2/1 ANS, ex 5 MU, Kemble in June, 1967.

WARTON. Airfield. British A/c Corporation. *Canberra B.2* WE121—bought back from MOD—may become available (with others) for preservation, in due course.

LEICESTERSHIRE

BILLESDON. Airstrip. *Tiger Moth* G-AOXN c/n 85958 ex EM727; D. W. Mickleburgh.

BITTESWELL. Airfield. *DH. Vampire T.11* XD626 ex "Q" CATCS Shawbury, and *Percival P.56 Provost T.1* WW444 ex Manby & Shawbury; for apprentice training.

HUSBANDS BOSWORTH. Airfield. Coventry Gliding Club. *1936 Schempp Hirth Govier*, German-built glider, being restored. *1938 Scott Viking I*, last survivor of 4 built *1938 Slingsby Petrel I*, one of three built, this and one, believed in Eire (with fixed tailplane) remain. *Tiger Moth* G-ALBD c/n 84130 ex T7748; Drive Lease Ltd, also G-ALWW c/n 86375 ex NL932.

LEICESTER. Museum of Technology. Proposed Aircraft Gallery. *Auster J/1 Autocrat* G-AGOH c/n 1442—the first J/1 built as new (G-AFWM was a rebuild) is presently flying from Leicester East but owned by and earmarked for a new branch of the museum for which Keeper Brian Waters (who flies the Autocrat) is responsible. It is hoped to add the Desford (see Hampshire) when grounded, plus others of local interest. The Abbey Pumping Station will be the site for the East Midlands Museum.

LOUGHBOROUGH. University (formerly Technical College). *Hunting Percival Jet Provost* G-AOBU c/n HPAL.6 ex G-42-1—loaned by Shuttleworth—the a/c from the first batch of Jet Provost T.I.s. Became RAF's standard basic trainer. *Hawker Hunter F.4* XE677 "Q" of 93 Sqdn, RS-8 of 299 OCU, then 4 and 118 Squadrons.

SIBSON. Airfield. *Tiger Moth* G-AYDI c/n 85910 ex DF174, F-BDOE; owned by M. J. Coburn and C. C. G. Hughes. *Auster AOP.9* G-AYUA ex XK416/7855M owned by A. D. Heath/M. D. N. Fisher (may be exchanged for WZ662, Sth Wales).

LINCOLNSHIRE

BARDNEY. Strip. Lincs Gliding Club. *DFS Weihe 1939*, Swedish-built 1942/3.

BINBROOK. RAF. *Meteor (AW) NF.14* WS797/7966M. *Spitfire F.22* PK664 ex 5466M/7759M of 615 (County of Surrey "Churchill's Own) and Waterbeach.

CRANWELL. RAF College. By appointment only or Open Days. Aircraft subject to constant changes as machines made redundant and available to preservationists—or scrap-merchants. *DH. Tiger Moth* G-ANEF c/n 83226 ex T5493; College Flying Club. *DHC.1 Chipmunk T.10* WP912—formerly flown by Prince Philip—perhaps for preservation? *Armstrong Whitworth Meteor NF12* WS692/7605M, ex 72 Sqdn "C", Henlow. *Percival Provost T.1* WV562/7606M, ex 1 FTS and Henlow. *Bristol Sycamore HC.10* WV781/7839M, ex Trials

Batch, Coastal Cmd. *Gloster Javelin FAW.8* XH991 ex "Q" of 85 Sqdn. *DH. Sea Vixen FAW.1* XJ607 (701/VL) and XN685 (703/VL) from 890 (HQs) Sqdn, RNAS Yeovilton.

CUXWOLD. Strip. *Provost T.1* G-AWVF c/n 375 ex XF877; J. R. Walgate.

DIGBY. RAF. *Gloster Meteor T.7* WH166.

HEMSWELL. Airfield. *Chilton DW.1* G-AFGH c/n DW1/2; J. T. Hayes/J. West. *Taylorcraft Plus D.* G-AHGW c/n 222 ex LB375: Lincoln A/Club. *Auster V* G-AOCP c/n 1800 ex TW462; RAF College F/Club.

Taylorcraft Plus D. (Hemswell)

IRBY-on-HUMBER. Strip. *Auster 5D* G-ALYG c/n 835 ex MS968; M. Lockwood.

STROXTON LODGE. Strip. *Auster V.* G-ALBK c/n 1273 ex RT644; V. G. Manton *Auster V.* G-AOVW c/n 894 ex MT119; B. Marriott.

SUTTON BRIDGE. Airfield. *Nord 1002 Pingouin* G-ATBG c/n 121 ex F-BGVX, F-OTAN-5; now L. M. Walton.

TATTERSHALL. Old Station Yard. Lincs Aviation Museum. Open Sundays Easter-September 1100-1800 or by appointment. *Percival Proctor IV* NP294 (never civilanized) ex Wilts School of Flying; from NAPS. *Miles Gemini 1A* G-AKER c/n 6491—for restoration. *Vampire T.11* WZ549—last flight Shawbury-Coningsby 19 Dec 1970. *DH. Dove* G-AHRI c/n 04008 ex 4X-ARI, 9th production a/c. *Flying Flea* BAPC.22 painted G-AEOF, with Scott engine, built by W. Miller, and found by Kent Branch "Air Britain". Not a "flown" example. On

Provost T.1 (Cuxwold)

Lancaster I (Waddington)

loan (see Newark) *Currie Wot* 2/3rds-scale (replica) BAPC.24. *Ward Gnome* G-AXEI c/n P.45. *BE.2D* remains serial 5778 from Lincolnshire shed.

Miles Gemini 1A (Tattershall)

WADDINGTON RAF. (See also Coltishall, Norfolk.) *Avro Lancaster I* PA 474, built as a PR 1 by Vickers-Armstrongs of Chester for use with Tiger Force against the Japanese. Due to the sudden ending of the war it was used instead by 82 Sqdn for extensive photo-surveys of Africa and West Germany until 1951. In 1952 it was loaned to Flight Refuelling for trials and then moved to Cranfield for use by Handley Page for laminar-flow investigations. In October 1963 it was adopted by Air Historical Branch of Air Ministry and flown to Wroughton to be repainted in wartime colours. It was used in several films and then flown into Henlow for RAF Museum—remaining out in the open as the hangars could not take so large a machine. C.O. No. 44 Sqdn (Wg Cdr D'Arcy) requested transfer of the Lancaster to the first squadron to operate the type. It is now painted as KM-B, 44 Sqdn, the code of the late Wg Cdr J. D. Nettleton VC who led the low-level daylight raid on Augsburg's M.A.N. factory. It

delights crowds at air displays and is to be hangared for part of the year with the Battle of Britain Flight at Coltishall so that it is advisable to make enquiries before journeying to Waddington.

WELLINGORE. *Flying Flea* BAPC.43, built by L. C. Troop, Scott engine. *Auster V* G-ALBJ c/n 1831 ex TW501; R. H. Elkington. *Auster V* G-ALFA c/n 826 ex MS958; J. Kilby.

WOODHALL SPA. Children's garden. *Westland Dragonfly* WG749 "757".

WYBERTON. Airfield. *Auster V* G-AKWS c/n 1237 ex RT610; Links A/T. Gp. *Tipsy Trainer 1* G-AFVN c/n 12; W. Callow, D. H. Harris, E. Lingard.

MONMOUTH

CALDICOT 2012 ATC Sqdn, *Auster AOP.9* XK421 ex Motorama Garages. Presented by Messrs Peachey and Brain of Newport.

NORFOLK

COLTISHALL. RAF. On B.1150 from Norwich. Open Days or appointment. The aircraft of the Battle of Britain Flight are popular at many air displays throughout Europe and intending visitors should choose Battle of Britain Day or verify in advance that permission can be given for these historic machines to be viewed. *Hawker Hurricane IIC* PZ865 "Last of the Many", formerly G-AMAU, donated by Hawker Siddeley and painted as DT-A of 257 "Burma" Sqdn; Sqdn Ldr R. Stanford-Tuck's machine 1940. *Hurricane IIC* LF363 LE-D, served with Nos 63, 309 (Polish) and 26 Sqdns, 65OTU, then Middle Wallop, Waterbeach, 61 Group Com Flt, Kenley, B. of B. Flt at Biggin Hill, North Weald, Martlesham Heath (name changed to Historic A/c Flt) Horsham St. Faith then to Coltishall 1963. Painted as Douglas Bader's 242 Sqdn a/c at Coltishall,

Battle of Britain Flight (Coltishall)

Hurricane IIC (Coltishall)

DH.Mosquito B/TT35 (for Coltishall)

1940. Present engine Merlin 502 from Argonaut. Max speed 330 mph, range 530 miles, climb to 20,000 ft 8½ mins, span 40 ft, wing area 257 sq ft, weight empty 5559 lbs, operationally loaded 7397 lbs. Max speed now during displays only 225/275 mph. *Spitfire IIA* P7350 ZH-T of 266 (Rhodesia) Sqdn, also with 66, 603 (City of Edinburgh) 616 (South Yorkshire). Bought as scrap by John Dale Ltd who generously presented it back. Battle of Britain film as N3310/12/16/17, N3321. Various codings used including AI-A/E, BO-H, CD-G/M, DO-M EI-C, also registered G-AWIJ. Transferred from Colerne to become airworthy here. *Spitfire VB* AB910, G-AISU, once MD-E of 130 (Eagle) Sqdn, later 53 OTU, Hibaldstow, Lincs where, February 1945 WAAF mechanic Margaret Horton, clinging to the tail during taxying in strong wind, suddenly found herself airborne. Pilot Jock Stevens, labouring round the circuit, realised something was amiss and, on landing, elevator almost useless, discovered, for the first time, that he'd had an involuntary passenger. Margaret later became the first WAAF member to fly in an RAF jet (Meteor) and is often to be seen where AB910 is displayed. BAC presented the Spitfire after test pilot Jeffrey Quill, OBE, AFC, had flown it for many years. Maximum speed 375 mph and recent engine from a Sea Balliol. Was in B. of B. film as N3318/19/21, N3313, AI-J/M, CD-D/K, DO-M. Now painted as SO-T of 145 Sqdn. *Spitfire PR XIX* PM631 AD-C ex 203 AFS, 206 OCU, Buckeburg, Woodvale and Hooton Park Met Flts, B. of B. Flt, Biggin Hill, North Weald, Martlesham Heath. B. of B. film N3316 and 3320., coded AI-L, DO-G. Range 1,550 miles, power plant 2050 hp Griffon 65/66. Loaded weight 9,000 lb. max speed 460 mph, ceiling 43,000 ft, no armament. *Spitfire PRXIX* PS853 (painted ZP-A of 74 "Tiger" Sqdn) was with 16/268, Sqdns 34 Wing Benson, CFE, Met Flt Woodvale (the last Spitfire to make an "Ops" sortie from U.K.). Then at West Raynham and Binbrook. In B. of B. film as N3314/19/21, AI-E/M, EI-K. *DH. Mosquito B35/TT35* TA639 ex Brooklands, Ballykelly, Aldergrove, 3 CAACU, Little Rissington CFS and "633 Sqdn" film, is reported to be coming here as an airworthy addition to the Flight. *Lancaster 1* PA474 (see Waddington, Lincs) to be used here for the season of display flying. *Spitfire XVI* SL542 ex 595/695 Sqdns, Duxford, Horsham St. Faith, is on a pylon as station "gate guardian". *Fieseler Fi 156 C-2 Storch* VP546, captured Luftwaffe a/c, Werk-Nr 475061 believed still here. *Meteor III* EE419 scrapped—why?

Spitfire IIA (Coltishall)

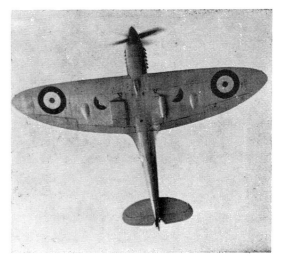

Spitfire VB (Coltishall)

Spitfire XVI (Coltishall)

FELTHORPE. Airfield *Tiger Moth* G-ANOH c/n 86040 ex EM838; M. M. Carr.

GORLESTON. Shrubland Youth and Adult Centre, 221 ATC Sqdn. *DH. Vampire T.11* XD511/7814M ex 206 AFS, 5FTS and Cranwell.

Spitfire PRXIX (Coltishall)

LITTLE SNORING. Airfield. McAully Flying Group. *Piper L-4H Cub* G-AKAA c/n 10780 ex 43-29489; D. S. Kirkham. *DH. Tiger Moth* G-ANRF c/n 83748 ex T5850; B. Tempest Ptnrs.

MARHAM. RAF. *Vickers Valiant B1* XD818 of 49 Sqdn, the aircraft which dropped the first British "H" bomb in 1957. First of the RAF's three types of "V" bombers, the *Valiant* entered service 1955 and equipped Nos 49, 7, 138, 207, 214, and 543 Sqdns. Destined for RAF Museum.

Vickers Valiant B1 (Marham)

NORWICH. Airport. Horsham St. Faith. The Air Scouts have *Vickers Valetta C2* VX580 ex Malta Com Sqdn, 114 Sqdn, Aden Com Flt, HQs NEAF, Metropolitan Com Sqdn. *Douglas Dakota 3* G-AMPZ c/n 16124/32872 ex 44-76540, KN442, OD-AEQ, PH-RIC, TF-AIV; now Rig-Air. *Dakota 4* G-ANTD c/n 14969/26414 ex 43-49153, TJ-ACF; *G-AOBN* c/n 11711 ex 42-68784 ex SE-BAU, F-OAIF; Air Anglia. *Benes-Mraz M.1C Sokol* G-AIXN c/n 6676 ex OK-BHA; G. Priest.

Vickers Valetta C2 (Norwich)

SCRATBY. 2356 Sqdn ATC Duncan Hall School. Confirmation required of *DH. Vampire T.11* XH298/7760M ex RAF College, 8 FTS.

SHIPDHAM. Airfield *Rapide* G-AKRS c/n 6952, RL981; Toftwood Avn. *Miles M.17 Monarch* G-AIDE c/n 793 ex W6463, G-AFRZ reported static here. *Auster AOP.9* G-AZBU ex WZ675/7826M and *XN441*; Arrow Air Services.

Miles M.17 Monarch (Shipdham)

STOKE FERRY. Wretham Rd *DH. Hornet Moth* G-ADOT c/n 8027 formerly X9326, was here for children, but has probably been moved for a rebuild. Possibly to C. C. Lovell at Southampton.

SWANTON MORLEY. RAF and civil aviation. *AW Meteor TT20* WM224, ex 3 CAACU, Woodvale. *Tiger Moth* G-AODT c/n 83109 ex R5250; N. A. Brett/A. H. Warminger. *Tiger* G-ANMV c/n 83745 ex T7404 F-BHAZ; Norfolk and Norwich A/Club—believed restored using wings of G-ADGT and G-APSS. *Miles Gemini 1A* G-AKHW c/n 6524; Mrs. J. A. and R. H. Cooper.

THETFORD. G. Eastell. *BAC. Drone* G-AEJR c/n 22 and G-ADPJ c/n 7. For rebuild as one, with spares from G-AEKU.

WATTON. RAF. Eastern Radar. *Meteor NF.14* WS807/7973M "J" 1 ANS.

NORTHAMPTONSHIRE

PETERBOROUGH. 115 ATC Sqdn (confirmation wanted.) *DH. Vampire T.11* XE887/7824M "115" 4 and 7 FTS, RAF College, 3 CAACU, 27 M.U.

SYWELL. Airfield. Midland Tiger Flying Group. *DH. Tiger Moth* G-ADIA c/n 3368 ex BB747; J. Beaty. G-ANOR c/n 85635 DE694; A. J. Cheshire. G-AOEG c/n 83547 ex T7120 D. C. Leatherland and Ptnrs. *Miles Messenger 2A* G-AKIN c/n 6728; A . J. Spiller.

Spitfire F.21 (Wittering)

WITTERING. RAF. No 1(F) Sqdn Flight Line Museum. *Spitfire F.21* LA255, of No 1(F) Sqdn, ex Cardington/West Raynham.

NORTHUMBERLAND

WOOLSINGTON. Newcastle Airport. *Viscount 701* G-AMOE c/n 17 ex BEA and Cambrian Airways, now cabin-staff trainer for Northeast Airlines.

NOTTINGHAMSHIRE

EDWINSTOWE. The old railway goods yard. Understood a *Viscount* ex ETPS, Boscombe Down, will be sited here as restaurant. Details of regn/serial please.

NEWTON. RAF. Viewable only Open Days or appointment as aircraft are for instructional purposes. *Avro Vulcan B.1* XA905/7857M. *Avro Shackleton T.4* WB849. *Shackleton MR.3* WR990/M8107 "N" 120 Sqdn. *MR.2* WB869. *English Electric Lightning 1A* XM187. *Canberra B(1)8* XM271. *Gloster Javelin FAW.8* XJ116/7832M, XJ 117/7833M, XH972/7834M. *Hunting Jet Provost T.3* XM402/ MC8055A/M. XM404/MC8055B/M. *Hawker Hunter F.2* WN 904/7544M. *F.4* WV265/7684M. *Vickers Varsity T.1* WL637/ M8105 ex 2 ANS.

A Missile Museum is also established here displaying Luftwaffe *X4* wire guided bomb. *STV1* RAE Test Vehicle. *Fairey Fireflash* Air/Air. *Hawker Siddeley Firestreak* Air-Air. *Hawker-Siddeley Red Top* Infra-red Homing Missile. *BAC Bloodhound Mk2. BAC Thunderbird* Surface-Air. *Hawker Siddeley Blue Steel* Air-Surface cruise missile with thermonuclear warhead. *Henschel HS293* radio controlled bomb. *Ruhrstal 5D1400* radio controlled missile. *Douglas Skybolt* Air-Ground bomb. *H. S. Dynamics Tail Dog* Air/Air missile. *Vickers Armstrongs Red Dean* Air/Air missile.

STAPLEFORD. Cliff Hill Avenue. 1360 ATC Sqdn. *DH. Vampire T.11* XD463/8023M ex St. Athan Sept, 1972.

TOLLERTON. Airport. Maid Marian Flying Group. *Taylorcraft Plus D.* G-AHGZ c/n 214 ex LB367—King's Cup winner 1952, also G-AIXA c/n 134 ex LB264; N. Gisby.

WINTHORPE. Old airfield now County Show Ground. The Newark (Notts & Lincs) Air Museum, opened 14 April 1973. Admission to public probably weekends/ holidays. Ring Newark 4976. Some of the aircraft are still undergoing restoration but the display will be from the following:— *Avro Anson C.19* VL348 ex G-AVVO ex Com Flts 62 Gp, 81 Gp, 24 Gp, 22 Gp, etc; obtained from Historic A/c Museum, Southend when *Anson XI* G-ALIH destroyed by vandals. *Gloster Meteor FR.9* VZ608 ex Moreton Vallance and Rolls-Royce. *Percival Provost T.1* WV606 P-B from 1 STT, Halton. *Percival Prentice T.1* G-APIY ex VR249, flown into Winthorpe 8 July 1967, ex Laarbruch Flying Club. *Miles Magister T.1* G-AKAT c/n 2005 ex T9738, formerly 15 and 24 EFTS, obtained from Leicester East. *Auster J/5F Aiglet Trainer* G-AMUJ c/n 2791, from farm at Ancaster 1966, after it had collided with vegetation in 1960. *GAL Monospar ST.12* VH-UTH—only example in U.K., built 1935 and shipped to Australia, this a/c was flown back to England with a view to re-registration but costs proved too high and it was acquired for the museum by Doug Revell. *Percival*

Missile Museum (Newton)

Proctor I BV631 c/n H.170 was G-AHMP, originally RNAS Worthy Down with 756 Sqdn (Lt. Cdr. Blake) later donated to Bristol Grammar School, then moved to G. C. Taylor's home near Exeter; loaned by Mr. Taylor/Lt. Cdr. Blake. *Pou-du-Ciel BAPC.22* painted G-AEOF (see Tattershall, Lincs) will return to Winthorpe by arrangement, after loan. *Supermarine Swift F.4/FR.5* WK277 ex N of 2 Sqdn, owned by Norman Pratlett—on indefinite loan. *Thruxton Jackaroo* BAPC.21 —the "lost" un-registered Jackaroo, not yet positively identified. *Westland Wallace II* K6038 c/n WA2417G, ex Electrical and Wireless School, Cranwell and wreckage obtained (with parts of two others) in 1965, with official permission. Will be restored probably as a Mk I to honour both 503 (County of Lincoln) and 504 (County of Nottingham) Sqdns, AAF. Only Wallace in existence. *Lee Richards Annular Biplane* (replica) from "Magnificent Men" film, from Doug Bianchi (who has loaned the quarter-scale replica used for aerial shots during the filming.) *R.A/c Factory S.E.5* (half-scale replica) BAPC.23 built by John Baker of Nottingham over 3 years; painted as Captain Albert Ball VC's machine and taken to displays by road. *DH. Vampire T.11* (possibly XE979 which served at Cranwell) is being sought from Hawker Siddeley, Woodford (Feb 1973.) Other aircraft will be obtained as funds allow and there are great hopes that *Seafire F.46 LA564* (owned by Peter Arnold & Neville Franklin) will be completely restored and displayed at the museum. The cockpit of a Harvard, nose of a Horsa, many engines, models and other fascinating material should attract visitors from a wide area. Air Commodore David Bonham Carter CB, DFC, who commanded Wigsley and Waddington, flying with Nos 463 and 467 (RAAF) Sqdns, and who flew 198 types of a/c between 1921-1950, has become President of Newark Museum; taking a practical interest in its progress.

OXFORDSHIRE

ARDLEY END. J. W. Benson. *DH85 Leopard Moth* G-ATFU c/n 7007 ex CH-366 HB-OTA.

BENSON. RAF. *Spitfire XVI* TE311/7741M ex ECFS Handling Sqdn and 1689 FPTF, Tangmere. In B. of B. film as AI-M and DO-. Serialled N3321 and N3324. *DHC Chipmunk T.10* WP903 is here, formerly flown by HRH Prince Charles.

BICESTER. RAF. No 71 MU—by appointment or Open Day, *Spitfire IX* MK732 ex 34 Wing, RAF, presented to No 14 Sqdn by R. Neth. A. F. Was at St. Athan. *Spitfire XVI* SM411/7242M ex 421 (Can) Sqdn, 83 GSU, Binbrook, 102/103 FRS, 2/3CAACU, Wattisham gate, Henlow. In B. of B. film taxying as N3310/11 N3329; AI-B, AI-A, AI-S. Now "AU-Y" *Buccaneer S.1* XN962 "635/LM" *Spitfire XIX* PM651 ex RAF Hucknall, Andover, Benson, PRU-blue. *Hawker Hunter F.4* XF946, ex 234 and 3 Sqdns. *Sycamore HC.14* XG540, restored for travelling displays. *Folland Gnat T.1* XM693/7891M— pre-production. *Gnat F.1* XK740—in "Red Arrows" markings. *A. W. Meteor TT20* WD785, converted from NF.11, ex R. Navy. Please note that aircraft are often out on exhibition and changes constantly taking pace— watch preservation journals. Flying from Bicester *Auster 6A* G-ASIF c/n 2556 ex VF615, with RAF Gliding and Soaring Association with *Primary EoN glider*

Meteor FR.9 (Winthorpe)

Proctor I (Winthorpe)

Spitfire XVI (Benson)

Spitfire IX (Bicester)

(S.G.38 Schulgleiter). *Auster 6A* G-ASTI c/n 3745 ex WJ359 here with Air Tows.

Avro York (Brize Norton)

BRIZE NORTON. RAF. *Avro York* G-AGNV c/n 1223 "Moville" BOAC, later Skyways, at Skyfame Museum as LV633 of 24 Sqdn, RAF. Held here for RAF Museum.

CHALGROVE. Airfield. Martin-Baker Engineering. *Dakota 6* G-APML c/n 14175/25620 ex 43-48359 KJ836 *Meteors* "7½" WA634, WA638, WL419—converted for ejector seat trials from T.7s—leading to the saving of very many lives. WA634 painted as "MBA634".

ENSTONE. Airfield. *Tiger Moth* G-AYKC c/n 85729 ex DE831 F-BGEO; G. Freeman. *Kite 1 glider* of 1935.

LOWER HEYFORD. Strip. *Piper L-4H Cub* G-AIIH c/n 11945 ex 44-79649 (rebuilt 1965) owner Bill Knapton.

KIDLINGTON. Oxford Airport. *Miles Magister* Quoted as G-AKUA (unlikely) restoration? *NA Harvard IIIA* EZ259 ex R. Navy and Skylines, Sandhurst scrapyard said to be hereabouts with D. G. Elvidge for restoration

WESTON-on-the-GREEN. Airfield. Oxford Gliding Club and RAFSPA. *DFS Grunau 2* of 1933 being rebuilt. *1939 Gull 3*, the last high performance sailplane designed and built by Slingsby before WW II. Only one built and was owned 1945/46 by Siamese racing driver Prince Bira. *DH. Rapides* G-ASIA (NF847 c/n 6718) and G-ASFC, formerly HG694, c/n 6679 constructed Brush Coachworks, Loughborough, then 781 and 782 Sqdns, FAA, Lee-on-Solent, Donibristle until bought by RAF Sport Parachute Club. First live descent 28 August 1963, by Sqdn Ldr M. C. Stamford. Now used for ground training and spares.

RUTLAND

COTTESMORE. RAF. *Canberra PR7* WH791/8187M ex 81 Sqdn, at gate.

Meteor NF14 (North Luffenham)

NORTH LUFFENHAM. RAF. *Armstrong Whitworth Meteor NF14* WS770 "Z" ex 25, 85, 92 Sqdns and 228 OCU. Also at the entrance *Bristol Bloodhound* radar homing surface-to-air missile.

SHROPSHIRE

SHAWBURY. RAF. View by prior appointment only. *DH. Vampire T.11* XD382 from 208/208 AFS, 5 FTS, RAF College, CATCS, mounted at entrance. XE920/8196M "D" CATCS, earmarked for RAF Museum and may be moving to Henlow. *Airspeed Oxford* G-AITB, stored for RAF Museum—may be at Henlow. *Gloster Javelin FAW.9* XH892 "B" of 29 Sqdn—for RAF Museum. *Handley Page Hastings C.1* TG516 ex 48 Sqdn—for RAF Museum? *DH. Comet 1A* XM823 c/n 06022 ex F-BGNZ of Air France, G-APAS and G-5-23, flown from Hatfield on being presented to RAF by Ministry of Technology—supposedly for RAF Museum?

SOMERSET

CONGRESBURY. Holders Garage. *Auster AOP.9* XK406

HENSTRIDGE. Airfield. *Taylorcraft Plus D.* G-AHSD c/n 182 ex LB323 and G-AHWJ c/n 165 ex LB294; A. Tucker. *DH. Tiger Moth* G-APCC c/n 86549 ex PG-640; R. J. Moody. *Tiger Moth* G-ARAZ c/n 82867 ex R4959; J. H. U. Mead.

LOCKING. RAF. Open Days or by appointment only. *Spitfire F.21* LA198 ex 1,602 (City of Glasgow) Sqdns, 3 CAACU, 187 ATC Sqdn, B. of B. film as N3316/17, AI-G, BO-C. Now "JX-C" of 1 Sqdn again. *Gloster Meteor T.7* WL360 "G" ex 153 Sqdn, silver with dayglow panels.

Spitfire F.21 (Locking)

YEOVIL. Chilton Cantelo School. Sea Cadets. *DH. Sea Venom FAW.22* XG691 ex RNAS Yeovilton.

YEOVILTON. The Fleet Air Arm Museum, RNAS Station A.303 East of Ilchester. Entrance free. Open Easter to 31st October. Weekdays 1030-1700; Sundays 1400-1700. Telephone Ilchester 551 extension 528. Lt-Cdr L. A. Cox, Curator. On display, in Hangar No 11, for 1973 season are:—*Sopwith Baby* serialled N2078 but built from 8214/8215. *Supermarine Walrus I* L2301 (hull of L2302, wings L2301). Three Walrus I's part of a Fleet Air Arm order, went instead to the Irish Air Corps, L2301 becoming N18. They took off for Ireland but bad weather caused the formation to break, one returning to Pembroke Dock, one landing in Dublin

Bay, and N18 putting down on the sea near Wexford, with engine trouble. The crew successfully beached the Walrus and in 1942 the aircraft re-crossed the Irish Sea in unusual circumstances when an officer under open arrest flew it to Cornwall, his crew unaware that the flight was not authorized. The aircraft and crew were returned and in 1945 N18 became EI-ACC of Aer Lingus. In 1947, No 615 (County of Surrey) Sqdn, seeking to recruit ground personnel, bought the Walrus to give airmen air experience flights. It cost £150.00 to buy but became expensive when, putting down on the sea during East Coast summer camps, the well-meaning public alerted the lifeboats—involving donations to the RNLI funds for the trouble caused! Sqdn Ldr (now AV-M) Freddie Sowrey, and Wg Cdr R. G. Kellett, adjutant and C. O. respectively, gave many Spitfire pilots "amphibian hours" for their logbooks. After 2 years G-AIZG as it then was, was sold for scrap and, in 1963, was found derelict in a field at Thame, Oxon, and recovered by the then Historic Aircraft Preservation Society who informed the FAA Museum curator. The wreck was taken to RNAS Arbroath and beautifully restored with components coming from as far away as Australia. It will remind many of "The Salvation Navy" which picked up airmen of allied forces from the sea during World War II. *Fairey Swordfish II* HS618 built, by Blackburn A/c and was repainted to honour the late Lt Cdr Esmonde VC DSC, whose Swordfish V6105 led the formation attacking "Scharnhorst" and "Gneisenau" in 1942. Now wears serial W5984 "5H". Presented by Royal Naval Engineering College, Manadon. *DH. Sea Vampire* LZ551/G, second of two prototypes (with LZ548) built by English Electric and hooked for deck trials. The first jet a/c to fly from a carrier—HMS "Ocean" 3 Dec 1945, pilot Lt Cdr E. M. Brown. On loan from Science Museum. *Grumman Martlet I* AL246. Little known of this particular a/c but was one of the original batch for Royal Navy 1940, destined for France and diverted. Claimed by some that AL246 and AL259 had the distinction of being the first US-built a/c serving with the FAA to shoot down a German a/c—a Ju 88 attempting to bomb Scapa Flow 25 Dec 1940 when 840 Sqdn intervened. AL246 has fixed wings and came from Loughborough College. *Vought Corsair IV* KD431—coded "E2-M", fighter-bomber version, built as FG-1 by Goodyear at Akron, Ohio, c/n 1871. Sent to Aircraft Holding Unit, Coimbatore late 1944, issued to 731 Sqdn, RNAS Easthaven, Scotland November 1945, later to 716 Sqdn. Delivered to Lossiemouth for destruction (most lease-lend a/c pushed into the sea) but this example was saved and sent to College of Aeronautics, Cranfield, December 1946. Acquired by H.A.P.S. 1963, loaned to FAA Museum but, it is believed, now purchased by them. *Grumman Hellcat II* KE209, produced as F6F-5, and transferred from Lossiemouth 1972. History would be appreciated. *Supermarine Seafire F.17* SX137, built by Westland Aircraft as F.XVII. Griffon Mk 6 40250/502068, delivered to RNAS Culham 25 September 1945. Later Henstridge, Fleetlands, Yeovilton, Anthorn, Stretton, 1831 Sqdn. To 759 Sqdn, Culdrose and written off charge 1955 with only 46 hrs 50 mins flown since last reconditioning of engine. To fly again?. *Hawker Sea Fury FB.11* WJ231. Last piston-engined type in frontline FAA service, this example was painted as WE726 in authentic Korean War markings, an 802 Sqdn machine with a MiG 15 jet to its credit. Now repainted

Sopwith Baby and Sea Hawk (Yeovilton)

Supermarine Walrus I (Yeovilton)

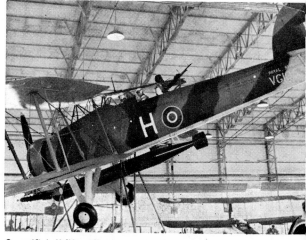

Swordfish II (Yeovilton)

with code "0/115". *Supermarine' Attacker F.1* WA473 fighter built by Vickers Armstrong, allocated to 800 Sqdn, Ford, re-allocated 702 Sqdn, Culdrose, then Lossiemouth for "Operation Soltaire". Mounted on plinth RNAS Abbotsinch, then to Brawdy for scrapping

DH.Sea Vampire (Yeovilton)

Grumman Hellcat II (Yeovilton)

Supermarine Seafire F.17 (Yeovilton)

Hawker Sea Fury FB.11 (Yeovilton)

Supermarine Attacker F.1 (Yeovilton)

Grumman Martlet I (Yeovilton)

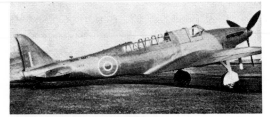

Fairey Fulmar N1854 (Yeovilton)

but saved for museum. Re-sprayed as Lt Cdr C. S. Casperd's a/c of 803 Sqdn, coded "146". *Hawker Sea Hawk FGA.4* WV856—built by Armstrong Whitworth. Coded "161". *Grumman Avenger AS.4* XB446, "992" ex-US Navy, supplied under Mutual Defence Aid Pact. Believed ex 815 Sqdn, 1953, then RNVR, formerly at Culdrose. *Fokker DR.1 Triplane (replica)* 5/8ths scale, built by A. R. Lowe and members of 209 Sqdn, RAF (originally 9 Sqdn RNAS) from the Lawrence Parasol monoplane (replica) RAF-built: constructed to commemorate 209 Sqdn's 50th anniversary and the shooting down of Richthofen—hence falling red eagle badge. *Hiller HTE-2* helicopter XB480—ex Mutual Defence Aid Pact. *Saro P531* (prototype Wasp) XN332 ex G-APNV, c/n S2/5268. From Manadon instructional airframe—A2579.

ON DISPLAY IN OPEN-AIR COMPOUND:—
Westland Wyvern TF.1 pre-production VR137, from College of Aeronautics; re-sprayed in normal service colours. *Percival Sea Prince C.1* WF137—from Culdrose. *Westland Dragonfly HR.3* WN493—from Culdrose. *Westland Whirlwind HAR.1* XA864. *DH. Sea Vampire T.22* XA129, from first production batch. *Fairey Gannet CO D.4* XA454 "H/264". *Gannet T.5* XG883. "BY/773" *Supermarine Scimitar F.1* XD317, from Airwork Hurn, in 807 Sqdn colours, coded "R/112". *DH. Sea Venom FAW.22* XG737. 819 Sqdn coded "B/438" *Meteor TT.20* WM292. "841". *Douglas Skyraider AEW.1* WT121, one of batch supplied 1951. Used operationally once—at Suez. Twelve sold to Sweden 1962 as target tugs. *Blackburn NA.39 Buccaneer S.1* XK488, of the pre-production batch. Former Mintech a/c, used mainly by Bristol Siddeley Engines, Filton and Hatfield. *Percival Sea Prince C.2* WJ350. *DH. Sea Vixen FAW.2* XS590. *Fairey Fulmar I* N1854, ex G-AIBE. First flew 4 Jan 1940. Donated by Fairey Aviation and formerly at Lossiemouth.

AIRCRAFT IN STORAGE, YEOVILTON, for MUSEUM:
Westland Dragonfly HR.3 WG718. *DH. Sea Venom FAW. 21* WW138. *DH. Sea Vixen FAW.1* XJ513. *Saro P.531* XN334. *DH. Tiger Moth* XL717—formerly glider-towing Lossiemouth. c/n 83805 ex T7291/G-AOXG.

AIRCRAFT PARTS WITH MUSEUM:
Sea Hawk F.1 WF 219/A2439 rear fuselage, tail and wings (sectioned) *Fairey IIIF*—fuselage and two wing frames (on loan). *Fairey Barracuda II* DP872, from Lough Enagh, Co Londonderry for possible rebuild. *DH. Sea Vampire T.22* forward fuselage, on display in Hangar No 11. *Gloster Sea Gladiator* N5903—on loan from Shuttleworth for restoration.

TYPES IN SERVICE REQUIRED FOR PRESERVATION:
Buccaneer S.2. Sea King HAS.1. Wasp HAS.1. Gannet AEW.3 Hunter T.8. Hunter GA.11. Phantom FG.1. Sea Devon C.20. Sea Heron C.20. Wessex HAS.3. HU.5., HAS.1

FLYING FROM YEOVILTON IN FAA MUSEUM VINTAGE FLIGHT:
Fairey Swordfish II LS326, Blackburn-built "5A". Formerly G-AJVH. *Fairey Firefly AS.5* WB271, the first Mk 5 delivered to FAA. With 814 Sqdn at Yeovilton, 1948. Saw service Korea and handed to Royal Australian Navy HMAS "Sydney" 1951 (hence "R" HMS "Glory" "K" HMAS "Sydney" on sides of a/c). After Korea the aircraft ended up as a target-tug and was put up for sale in 1966 at Bankstown, NSW where Lt-Cdr Michael Apps, C.O. of 814 Sqdn, flying Whirlwinds from HMS "Victorious" found it and organised a whip-round of RN/RAN to buy it for £160.00 Restored to Korean colours at RNAS Sembawang, Malaysia, it returned to U.K. in "Victorious" 1967 and, under supervision of CPO Gourlay and PO Chambers, has been restored to airworthiness for the new Historic Aircraft Flight. *Hawker Sea Fury FB.11* TF956, donated by Hawker Siddeley, Dunsfold (where much restoration work had been carried out) has been brought to airworthy standard and now delights crowds everywhere as the only Sea Fury flying in the British Isles. Now coded "T/123". *Tiger Moth* T8191 c/n 84483 is also flying with the Historic Aircraft Flight. *Aeronca C.3* G-AEFT c/n A.610 "Sea Duck" of the Buccaneer Flying Group is based and flown here by Cliff Humphrey and Ptnrs. Car parking here is free, refreshments are available and, with the added attraction of RNAS operational machines on occasions, this is a MUST for all enthusiasts and, for any in wheelchairs, the problems are minimal. There are models, dioramas etc, to make a journey from any part of Europe well worthwhile.

Fairey Fulmar—last flight (Yeovilton)

Fairey Firefly WB271 (Yeovilton)

Westland Wyvern TF.1 (Yeovilton)

Percival Sea Prince (Yeovilton)

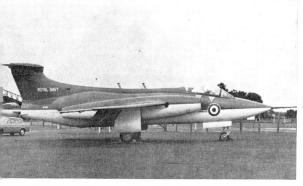

Blackburn Buccaneer (Yeovilton)

DH.Tiger Moth (Yeovilton)

Swordfish LS326 (Yeovilton)

Sea Fury TF956 (Yeovilton)

STAFFORDSHIRE

COSFORD. RAF. Wolverhampton WV7 3EX, Tel: Albrighton 2393 ext 458, Flt Lt G. Richmond, Historic Aircraft Hangar. Viewing only on Open Days or by prior approval. Some aircraft will move to Hendon eventually and (see Coltishall, Norfolk) the Mosquito may fly again. The following hangared here, 1973:— *Spitfire FRXIVe* MT847/6960M, once "UU-A" at Warton, later at Training Establishment, Freckleton. *Gloster Meteor prototype* DG202/G the F.9/40 "Rampage" with Rover W2B engines, flown by Gerry Sayers 10 July 1942 Newmarket Heath, by Michael Daunt 24 July at Barford St. John. First of initial seven, later to be called "Thunderbolt" and changed to "Meteor". because of our American allies' fighter. This machine was rotting at entrance to RAF Yatesbury when passing motorist (Dowty employee) recognised the unusual nose-wheel braking system and drew attention to this historic a/c. Two Roll-Royce Welland engines were found at Cosford and No 2 Radio School, Yatesbury—

personnel did a splendid restoration, to earn the R.Ae.S plaque for this machine. *Kawasaki Type 5 Model 1b* (Ki 100-1b) brought to England 1946 for trials. This machine may have served with 5th Fighter Sqdn Chofu or Yokkaichi for home defence—only 99 built before factory destroyed. *Messerschmitt Me 410 A-1/U2*, Werk-Nr 410478 or 470430. May have been AM72 also AMV.3. Once coded "PD+VO" was in the Balkans Campaign and believed coded "AK" and "CC" at different periods. *Fieseler* flying bomb (V1)—said to be two examples, all-black. *Avro Lincoln B.II* RF398 ex 151 Sqdn, flown from Watton to Henlow, then exhibited Royal Review, Abingdon 1968. *Armstrong Whitworth Meteor NF14* WS792 of 2/1 A.N.S. *Gloster Javelin FAW.1* XA564/7646M—cone removed to show radar scanner. *DH. Mosquito TT35* TA639—see Coltishall, Norfolk. Only 577 hrs flown. *Hawker Hunter F.1* WT555/7499M, from RAF Locking. 1st production aircraft. *Bristol T.188* XF926—stainless steel research aircraft—rescued from Foulness (where XF923 scrapped, unfortunately.) *Bristol Sycamore HR.14* XJ918, ex 32

Bristol T.188 (Cosford)

Spitfire FRXIVe (Cosford)

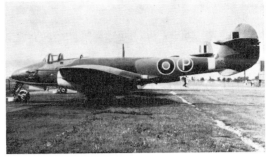

Meteor prototype (Cosford)

Kawasaki Type 5 (Cosford)

Messerschmitt Me 410 (Cosford)

Avro Lincoln B.II (Cosford)

Avro Shackleton T.4 (Cosford)

Sqdn. Now 8190M. In use here by the apprentice airmen are many instructional a/c only seen by civilians on Parents' Days or special appointments: *Avro-Shackleton MR2* WL798/8114M "Z". *MR.3* WR971/8118M "Q"; WR974 "K" 8117M; WR982/8106M "J"; WR985/8103M "H". *T.4* WB823/7885M "U" ex 22 and 206 Sqdns; WB 844 "R". *Avro Vulcan B.1* XA899/7812M, XA900/7896M ex 101 Sqdn and 230 OCU. RAE autoland trials. *Handley Page Victor B.1* XA923/7850M. ex Gaydon, Wyton, Cottesmore. *DH. Comet C.2* XK715/7905M "Columba" of 216 Sqdn. *English Electric Lightning F.1* XG337 of pre-production batch. *Vickers Valetta T.3* WJ488/7901M ex Cranwell. "N-B"—for fire? *Gloster Javelin FAW.5* XA699/7809M. *F(AW)8* XH992/7829M. *Bristol Belvedere HC.1* XG452—initial production. rotors off. *English Electric Canberra PR.3* WE145/7843M—dismantled. *Canberra PR.7* WT536/8063M. *B.15* WH984/8101M ex 32 Sqdn. *Hawker Hunter F.4* WV395/8001M. *Bristol Sycamore HR.14* XJ916 "S-P" of CFS. *DH. Vampire T.11*

XD613 ex CATS, Shawbury reported here. Preservationists should keep their ears to the ground in case surplus machines become available here.

HALFPENNY GREEN. Near Bobbington, Staffs, but on the borders of Shropshire. Airfield where many fascinating V. and V. types fly:—*Klemm L 25 a1 Swallow* G-AAHW c/n 152, owned by Roy Nerou, first flight since 1957 on 13 April 1972. *Comper CLA.7 Swift* G-ABUS c/n S.32/4 !K. Sedgwick. *Auster IV* G-ANHS c/n 737 ex MT197; J. N. West Ptnrs. *DH. Rapides* G-AGJG c/n 6617 ex X7344 (Aerial Enterprises) and G-AHAG c/n 6926 ex RL944 (for restoration or sale?) *Auster J/IN Alpha* G-AJRH c/n 2606 is flown here by J. P. Webster and though not strictly vintage, won the King's Cup Air Race 21 July 1956 piloted by J. H. Denyer at 124 mph. Let us hope it is preserved. *Avro Anson C.19* VM325 is reported here and *Proctor IV* G-AOBI c/n H729 ex NP358 (with Air Scouts.)

Klemm L 25 ai (Halfpenny Green)

Comper CLA.7 Swift (Halfpenny Green)

MILTON. Near Stoke. *Flying Flea* said to be owned by constructor J. Boulton—with Scott engine—details please.

STAFFORD. RAF. *Gloster Javelin FAW.2* XA801 ex "F" 46 Sqdn and *FAW.8* XH980, formerly 41 Sqdn— one said up for disposal. *DH. Vampire T.11* XD528/ 8159M from 27 M.U., now 395 Sqdn ATC.

STOKE ON TRENT. Mitchell Memorial. *Spitfire XVIe* RW388/6946M ex Benson and Colerne, Andover gate; used in Royal Tournament as Mk V. *Martin Monoplane* G-AEYY, last flown in 1938, is in Stoke with Mr. Ford and efforts are in hand to preserve it through BAPC. This aircraft, also known as the Luton Martin, was built in 1937 from parts of the Clarke Cheetah G-AAJK of 1929—in turn built from DH53 Humming Bird components.

TIPTON. Alexandra High School. ATC Sqdn restoring *Grunau Baby* glider.

WALSALL. ATC. *Proctor V.* G-AHTE, c/n Ae 58, from Wolverhampton.

WOLVERHAMPTON. ATC. Wharf St HQs. *Miles Messenger* G-AHUI c/n 6335 said to be under restoration. Confirmation and photo please.

SUFFOLK

BURY ST. EDMUNDS. Old County Grammar School, Northgate St. No 301 ATC Sqdn (by appointment through C.O. only.) *DH. Vampire FB.5* VV217/ 7233M—once flown by the late and great John Derry for

testing and racing; later with MOS, Boscombe Down, Farnborough and 5 FTS, Oakington. Let us hope care is taken to preserve this historic machine which, regrettably, was kept in the open when the compiler visited.

IPSWICH. Airfield. As this is compiled it is believed that *Auster V* G-ANHZ c/n 1753 ex TW384, formerly of Channel Airways is the only vintage machine based here. Details please, of any others.

LAKENHEATH RAF/USAF base. *Tiger Moth* N45TM c/n 86621 ex PG735, F-BGEG, G-AYVH. believed here.

WATTISHAM. RAF. *Spitfire V* EP120/5377M (with Mk 16 components) from RAF Boulmer and earlier with Nos 501 (County of Gloucester) 19, 402 (Can), then to St. Athan, Wilmslow, Bircham, Newton. Originally restored at Boulmer by Snr/Tech Ayling as a personal memorial to two brothers lost in the RAF and to all who flew Spitfires.

Spitfire V (Wattisham)

SURREY

CROYDON. Airfield. *Stampe SV4C* G-AZUL c/n 27 ex Belg.AF V-27; R. A. Seeley. Rollasons have a number of aircraft—Tigers and Stampes in store and under rebuild at any time. At the local ATC HQs a *Spitfire (replica)* from Battle of Britain film has been reported—confirmation and photo please.

EWELL. TA Centre, London Rd, 323 ATC Sqdn. *DH. Vampire FB.5* WA450/7634M ex Middle East Air Forces, 3 CAACU, St. Athan, Colerne and 1349 ATC, Woking. May go to RAF Chessington.

FAIROAKS. Airfield. Many interesting veteran and vintage types:—*Antoinette (replica)* from "Magnificent Men" E. Skinnley. *Piper J-2 Cub* G-AEXZ c/n 997; J. Turner. *Zaunkoenig V 2* G-ALUA c/n V.2 ex D-YBAR, VX190; D. Arnold. *Tipsy Junior* G-AMVP c/n J.III ex OO-ULA; A. Wershot. *Noorduyn AT.16 Harvard IIB* G-AZKI c/n 14A/1269 ex 43-12970, FT229, B-45 RNeth AF, PH-SKM; D. Arnold, who also owns G-AZSC c/n 14A/1363 ex 43-13064, PH-SKK. (AZKI painted FT239 which was scrapped 1957.) *DH. Tiger Moth* G-AIIZ c/n 84959 ex T6645; London Transport Flying Club. *Tiger Moth* G-AJOA c/n 83167 ex T5424; Universal Flying Services, also G-AOAC c/n 82216 ex N6978, but painted at one time as K4291 by owners Sqdn Ldr J. Burningham and Dick Blackburn to honour Wg Cdr C. E. F, Arthur, C.O. 18 ERFTS. *Tiger Moth* G-AXBZ c/n 86552 ex PG643 F-BGDF; same owners. *Chrislea CH.3 Super Ace 2* G-AKUW c/n 105; Fairoaks Avn Services.

Piper J-2 Cub (Fairoaks)

GATWICK. Airport. *Handley Page Hermes* G-ALDG c/n HP81/8 fuselage for British Caledonian cabin training. Formerly BOAC "Horsa" and last survivor of this type. Also flying:—*Dakota 6* G-AMHJ c/n 13468 ex 42-108962 ex KG651, ZS-BRW; *Dakota 6* G-AMRA c/n 152 90/26735ex 43-49474, KK151, XE280 and *G-AMSV* c/n 16072/32820 ex 44-76488 KN397; All operated by British Island Airways as Freighters.

GUILDFORD. Michael Alliott (with help from 261 ATC) building a *Sopwith Triplane (replica)* PFA/1539 with 125 Lycoming from Auster V.

OTTERSHAW. School Combined Cadet Force. On A.319 to Chobham. *Saro Skeeter AOP.12* XK482/7840M. *DH. Vampire T.11* XE950 *DH. Sea Venom FAW.22* WW217 "736".

Zaunkoenig V2 (Fairoaks)

Oldest Tiger Moth (Redhill)

Harvard IIB (Fairoaks)

Tiger Moth G-AOAA (Redhill)

Arrow Active 2 (Redhill)

Percival Q.6 (Redhill)

REDHILL. Airfield. Home of the world-famous Tiger Club. The following are registered to Norman Jones, pioneer "weekend" pilot and one of the early members of No 601 (County of London) Auxiliary Air Force Squadron, who, with others has ensured the success of the Tiger Club whose membership embraces airline captains, aviation writers, stage and screen stars, often to be seen at air displays. Currently:— *DH.Tiger Moth* G-ACDC c/n 3177 ex BB726, oldest Tiger airworthy. G-ANMZ c/n 85588 ex DE634 "The Canon", *G-ANZZ* c/n 85834 ex DE974 "The Archbishop"; *G-AOAA* c/n 85908 ex DF159. *G-ASKP* c/n 3889 ex N6588. *Arrow Active 2* G-ABVE c/n 2, also in the Norman Jones' stable. *DH.60G Gipsy Moth* G-ABYA c/n 1906; Dr. I. D. Hay. Being rebuilt following accident at Biggin Hill Air Fair. *DH. Tiger Moth* G-APMX c/n 85645 ex DE715; Rollason Flying Gp. *Percival Mew Gull* G-AEXF

c/n E22 ex ZS-AHM, winner of King's Cup 1938 and 1955. UK-Cape and back record etc; Restoration by M. Barraclough and Ptrs. Possibly at Hanwell, but will fly here when restored.
At the College of Aeronautical Engineering, Redhill:— *Percival Q.6* G-AFFD c/n Q.21 ex X9407—a "MUST" for preservation. *DH. Tiger Moth* G-AMNN c/n 86457 ex NM137. *Percival Proctor III* HM313. *Percival Prince* F-BJAJ c/n P50/8 ex G-ALRY "Survey Prince". *Percival Prentice* G-AOKZ ex VS623.

WEYBRIDGE. Brooklands Technical College. Aeronautical Dept. *DH. Vampire T.11* XE919 and XJ772 ex CATCS, flown in from Shawbury.

WOKING. Westfield Avenue, 1349 ATC Sqdn. *Folland Gnat T.1* XM697—pre-production, from B.A.C. Filton. Painted in Red Arrow colours.

DH.Gipsy Moth (Redhill)

Folland Gnat T.1 (Woking)

Oldest Tiger Moth (Redhill)

SUSSEX

CRAWLEY. Technical College. *Anson C.XIX* TX228 (may go to M.A.P.S.).

CROWBOROUGH. Beacon Rd, Crowborough Camp, 1414 ATC Sqdn. *DH. Sea Vampire T22* XA165 ex RN Brawdy, Lossiemouth, 5 MU.

FLIMWELL. W. J. D. Roberts *Spitfire XIV* NH904, stored, for restoration to airworthy state. Formerly 414 (Can) 610 (Chester) Sqdns. Belg AF as SG108 then Hoylake. Reserve a/c for B. of B. film (not used), Henlow. NH789 incorrectly attributed.

GOODWOOD. Airfield. *DH. 60G Gipsy Moth* G-ABAG, being restored. *DH. 80A Puss Moth* G-ABLS c/n 2164; J. D. Menzies, also *Comper CLA. 7 Swift* G-ABTC c/n S32/1; J. D. Menzies.

SHOREHAM. Airfield. *Auster IV* G-AJXY c/n 792 ex MT243; G. B. E. Pearce. *Auster V* G-AJGJ c/n 1147 ex RT486; J. J. McLaughlin Ptrs. *Auster V* G-ANHR c/n 759 ex MT192; M. F. Macey. *Auster V* G-ANRP c/n 1789 ex TW439; P. H. Jackson and J. D'Arcy. *Auster 5D* G-AGLK c/n 1137 ex RT475; W. C. E. Tazewell. *Taylorcraft Plus D.* G-AHNG c/n 200 ex LB341; D. J. Pratt. *DH. Tiger Moth* G-ANJA c/n 82459 ex N9389; J. J. Young. *G-AOZH* c/n 86449 ex NM129; V. B. and R. G. Wheele *Miles Gemini 1A* G-AKKB c/n 6537; Miles Avn & Transport. *Miles Messenger 2A* C-AKBO c/n 6378; J. R. Ramshaw. *Miles M100 Student 2* XS941 ex G-APLK; in Miles store, ex Ford.

Tiger Moth G-ANMZ (Redhill)

Comper CLA.7 Swift (Slinfold)

Robinson Redwing 2 (Slinfold)

SLINFOLD. Strip. *Comper CLA.7 Swift* G-ABUU c/n S32/5 and *Robinson Redwing 2* G-ABNX c/n 9; both owned by John Pothecary.

TANGMERE. RAF airfield. *Tiger Moth* G-ASXB c/n 3852 ex N6539/7152M; W. Verling/D. Wallis.

WADHURST. M. H. Reid. *Tiger Moth* G-AOZB c/n 3917 ex N6616.

WARWICKSHIRE

BAGINTON. Coventry Airport. Check viewing facilities first. *Avro Shackleton MR. 2c* WL751 "M" 204 Sqdn, ex 224 Sqdn, now with Shackleton Aviation for display. Same owners have *Auster III* G-AHLI c/n 540 ex NJ911. *Prentice 1* G-AOLU c/n PAC/108 ex VS356 EI-ASP. *Fairchild 24W Argus 2* G-AJPI c/n 851 ex 43-14887, HB614. *Prentice 1* G-AOKO c/n PAC/234 ex VS621 and *G-APIU* ex VR200; J. S. Coggins. *Comper CLA.7 Swift* G-ACTF c/n S32/9 ex VT-ADO; C. M. Woodhams. *DH. Hornet Moth* G-AHBL c/n 8135 ex CF-BFN, P6786; Dr. Ursula H. Hamilton. *DH.85 Leopard Moth* G-ACMA c/n 7042 ex BD148 and *DH. Rapide* G-AEML c/n 6337 ex X9450 (parts of G-AKOE in rebuild); J. P. Filhol Ltd. *DH. Hornet Moth* G-ADKC c/n 8064 ex X9445; E. J. Roe. *Miles Gemini 1A* G-AJTH c/n 6304 ex VP-UAY, VP-KFL; Lord Trefgarne. *Miles Gemini 3A* G-ALMU c/n WAL/C/1004; J. P. Snelling. *Miles Gemini 3C* G-ALZG

Leopard Moth (Baginton)

DH. Leopard Moth (Baginton)

Comper CLA.7 Swift (Baginton)

Leopard Moth (Baginton)

DH.Hornet Moth (Baginton)

c/n HPR/141; P. C. Blamire. *Miles Messenger 2A* G-AKKN c/n 6709; R. T. Knowles. *DH.85 Leopard Moth* G-ACLL c/n 7028 ex AW165; J. V. Skirrow. *DH.85 Leopard Moth* G-ACMN c/n 7050 ex X9381; J. J. Parkes.

BERKSWELL. Berkswell Forge. Ken Woolley—prior permission. *Foster Wikner Wicko GM.1* G-AFJB c/n 5 restored as DR613. Presented to Midland Aero Club 1938 by Wolverhampton Express & Star. With ATA during WW II as "Warferry". Post-war air-taxi, surviving ditching 1947 near Walney Island. Flew in 1951 Air Races and Hendon Pageant of Flying 1953.

In 1962 part-exchanged for car and acquired for preservation 1964. May fly again.

BIRMINGHAM. City Museum, Dept of Science & Industry, Newhall St. *Hawker Hurricane IV* KX829 (Merlin 20) ex 137, 286, 631 Sqdns, but painted as 6 Sqdn a/c of Desert Air Force "I". From Loughborough College, wings exchanged for Shuttleworth's Hurricane. *Supermarine Spitfire IX* ML427, Castle Bromwich-built, ex Rolls-Royce, Hucknall. RAF Millfield, 4 Sqdn and as 6457M at Castle Bromwich gate. Birmingham University Air Sqdn HQs, Edgbaston Park Rd has *DHC.1*

Foster Wikner Wicko (Berkswell)

No.

Hurricane IV (Birmingham)

Chipmunk T.10 WD303/7754M. 487 ATC Sqdn, Kingstanding Rd, Birmingham 22 display *Vampire T.11* XD377 ex 27 MU in July 1972. At Barrows Lane Sheldon, 2030 ATC is *AW Meteor TT20* WD646 "R" of 3 CAACU. At Birmingham Airport, Elmdon, Air Envoy Ltd operate *Douglas Dakota IV* G-AGJV c/n 12195 ex 42-92399, FZ638.

Spitfire IX (Birmingham)

COVENTRY. Carl Butler has *Mosscraft MA.1* G-AFHA c/n MA.1/2 and *MA.2* G-AFJV c/n MA.2/2 for rebuilding to fly. When completed they will virtually be new aircraft. The Midland Aircraft Preservation Society, 70 Eversleigh Rd, Coundon; telephone Keresley 4456 or Leamington Spa 29155 own numerous aircraft and although the collection is not currently available for viewing at one site, it is hoped to establish a Midlands Museum eventually. Meanwhile, some machines are loaned out (as Humber Monoplane at Southend) and others are in store or undergoing rebuild:— *Mignet HM Pou-du-Ciel "Flying Flea"* G-AEGV, built and flown by members of the East Midlands Flying Club, Sywell 1936. Douglas engine, new fuselage. Exhibited at air displays during summer. *Parnall Pixie III* G-EBJG, designed and built for the 1924 Daily Mail Lympne Light Aeroplane Trials. The remains of this sole-

surviving example were donated by MAPS member James Rowe. *DH. Vampire F.1* VF301 Debden gate until 1973, earlier 226 OCU 595 and 631 Sqdns "6D-Q" then 7060M. One of two Mk 1's in world. *DH.83 Fox Moth* G-ACCB c/n 4042—fuselage donated by Rollason A/c; to be restored with aid of Tiger Moth components. One of only three in U.K. *Bf 109 (replica)* from film, ex Solihull. *DH.89A Rapide* G-AJBJ c/n 6765 ex NF894; used by Air Navigation & Trading Ltd for joy-flights at Blackpool. To be restored using *G-ALAX. Wheeler Slymph* G-ABOI designed and built by Flt Lt (Air Cdre) Allen Wheeler in Iraq 1930/1 but never flown. On loan. *Crossley Tom Thumb* BAPC32 built in Banbury 1937 and currently stored pending restoration. *Miles Messenger 4A* VP-KJL ex G-ALAR, RH371. Built Woodley 1944; to be restored with parts of *G-AJKT.* Thought to be oldest example. *Slingsby Cadet T.8* BGA804 ex VW537 used at RAF St. Merryn, later Perranporth. This glider to be restored in original RAF training colours. *DFS Kranich* BGA964 c/n 087 ex SE-STF. Built Sweden 1940s, RSwedAF 8226, also Gliding Club of Technical University, Stockholm, then Stockholm Sailplane Club, subsequently RAF

DH.Vampire F.1 (Coventry)

Pou-du-Ciel (Coventry)

Farnborough 1960. Donated by Civil Service Aviation Association. *Nyborg glider* BAPC25. This unusual design, based on calculations of weights and wing areas of birds was built and flown near Worcester from 1936. *DFS Grunau Baby 2A* RAFGSA226 c/n 030795 ex VT921. Built 1944 this German design used by RAF and, at Benson, by RAFGSA. Donated by Southern Sailplanes Ltd; to be restored in colours of Hitler Youth Movement. Aircraft owned by individual members of MAPS include:— *Mignet HM14 Pou-du-Ciel* G-AEOH, built by R. C. Streather and now owned by Gordon Riley. *Pou-du-Ciel* BAPC27 owned by Mick Abbey. *Hawker Hurricane* (*replica*) painted H3426 from "Battle of Britain" film, being restored by MAPS chairman John Berkeley.

LAWFORD HEATH. Mr. Johansen reported to have *Hornet Moth, Tiger Moth,* and *Miles Gemini;* details and photos please.

RUGBY. Stanford Hall. *Pilcher Hawk glider* (*replica*) kept here by Lord Braye, whose father helped Pilcher in his 1895/99 experiments in these grounds. Replica was flown 1959 in the same grounds by Walter Neumark. Check before visiting (and see Edinburgh for original glider).

SHIRLEY. Haslucks Green Rd, 492 ATC Sqdn have pre-prodn *Bristol 171 Sycamore 3* 7718M/WA577 c/n 12888 ex G-ALST ex St. Athan.

SHOTTESWELL. *Auster VI* G-ARHM c/n 2515 ex VF557, owned and flown by the University of Aston Gliding Club.

SOUTHAM. Petrol Station. *Spitfire XVI* TB863 may come here—see Southend for details.

STRATFORD on AVON. James Rowe of MAPS has *Auster J/4* G-AIJK c/n 2067, ex Leics. Aero Club; the machine in which he learned to fly. This could be displayed or flown at MAPS' events.

SUTTON COLDFIELD. St. Bernard's Rd. ATC Sqdn has *Vampire T.11* XD602/7737M ex 125 Sqdn and Cranwell; formerly Smethwick ATC.

WESTMORLAND

APPLEBY. Grammar School. *Vampire T.11* WZ576/8174M with 2192 ATC, from 27 MU, formerly CATCS.

TARVER. W. J. Pennington said to have authentic *Flying Flea* with a Douglas engine. Details and photo please.

WILTSHIRE

BOSCOMBE DOWN. Aeroplane & Armament Experimental Establishment. Viewing only on very rare Open Days or by written approval. Some of the following are coming to the end of their service lives and may be up for disposal or scrapping—let us hope that any with histories will be preserved. (Nimrods/Harriers/Jaguars/Pumas etc not listed.) *Armstrong Whitworth Argosy C.1* XN817 of 1st production. *Armstrong Whitworth Meteor NF.13* WM367. *Avro Vulcan B2(a)* XH539. *Bristol Britannia 312F* XX367 c/n 13421 ex EC-BSY of Air Spain, G-AOVM of BOAC. *Blackburn Buccaneer S.2* XN974; *2A* XV352; *2B* XW329. *Blackburn Beverley C.1* XB259 once allotted G-AOAI—for disposal, possibly to Court Line of Luton. *Sea Vixen F(AW)1* XJ476, XJ481, XJ488. *DH. Tiger Moth* G-ALND c/n 82308 ex N9191; Bustard Flying Club. *English Electric Canberra B.2* WH734 (tanker), *WH876* nose-probe.

Harvard IIB (Boscombe Down)

Meteor NF.13 (Boscombe Down)

Handley Page Hastings (Boscombe Down)

WJ638—ejector seat development. *B(1)8* WV787 icing
trials *B.15* WT205; *TT.18* WH718. *English Electric
Lightning F2A* XN795; *T.4* XL629; *F.6* XP693. *Gloster
Javelin FAW.2* XA778; *FAW.9* XH897 (for disposal?)
Handley Page Hastings C.1A TG500; *C.2* WD496 (under-
wing tanks). *Hawker Hunter F.6* XF375 (ETPS); XE601
(with landing parachute). *T.7* XL564. *T7(a)* XL617.
Short SC.1 XG905 experimental VTOL (stored).
Scottish Aviation Twin Pioneer CC.2 XT610 (ETPS)
c/n 561 ex G-APRS. *Vickers Viscount 744* XR801 (ETPS),
745 XR802 (both ex Capitol Airlines USA) one fitted
with nose radar. Both for disposal. *Westland Whirlwind
HAS.7* XG589; *HAR.10* XJ398. *Westland Wessex HC.2*
XS679; *HAS.3* XT256. *North American AT-16 Harvard
IIB* KF183 c/n 14A-1884 ex 7(P)AFU, 7 SFTS, 3 SFTS,
ATDU. *KF314* c/n 14A-2014, stored 1944-49, then
A.A.E.E. FT375 c/n 14A-1415 ex 43-13116, to RCAF
1943, 1944 to 16 SFTS, to RAE and A.&A.E.E. 1946.
One of these earmarked for RAF Museum.

Hunter, Me 163, Meteor, He 162 and Javelin (Colerne)

Mosquito B35/TT35 (Colerne)

Hawker P1052 (Colerne)

A. and A.E.E. Harvards (Boscombe Down)

Hunter prototype (Colerne)

COLERNE. RAF. Station Museum. Near Chippenham.
By written appointment through Station Commander.
Telephone Hawthorn 810283 ext 417; Officer in Charge
Flt Lt J. Frapwell (Home telephone, Box 851). The
collection was started in 1964 with a twofold aim: first
a significant and practical attack on the problem of
preserving for posterity historic aircraft which might
otherwise be destroyed; second, to provide an interesting display for the numerous visitors to the Station,

Vampire F.3 (Colerne)

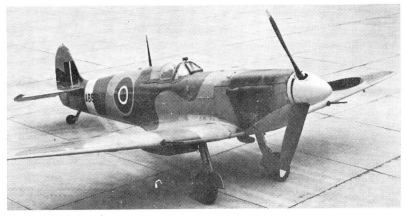

Spitfire VB (Colerne)

both service and civilian. From the original four aircraft which were residents, the collection has slowly but surely increased in size and variety achieving a world-wide reputation. As at 1st December, 1972 the following can be seen:— *Avro Anson C.XIX* TX226/7865M formerly VIP a/c of Air Attache, Copenhagen, later Bomber Command, Flying Training Command, to Colerne from 27 MU, Shawbury, 1964. Two Armstrong Siddeley Cheetah engines. *de Havilland Vampire F.3* VT812/7200M ex 32, 614 (Glamorgan) 602 (Glasgow) 601 (County of London) in whose colours it is displayed. From Cardington 1964 and destined for RAF Museum. Goblin 2 gas-turbine, four 20 mm Hispano, max speed 531 mph, range 1,145 miles. *Vampire T.11* XD542/7604M formerly "N" of Fighter Weapons School and Melksham. The first jet on which pilots qualified for wings. Type first flew November 1950, capable of 520 mph, two 20 mm cannon and could carry assorted

external stores. *English Electric Canberra B(I)8* WT346. *Canberra B.2* WJ676/7796M ex 35 and 50 Sqdns; from Tangmere. *de Havilland Mosquito B35/TT35* converted to *PR34* TJ138/7607M; ex 98(B) Sqdn, Brussels 1945, later 3CAACU, Exeter. Now in 98's colours, earmarked for RAF Museum. *Gloster Meteor F.4* VT229/715M ex 66,616 (South Yorkshire) 207/209 AFS, Northern Sector, Fighter Command. *Meteor F.8* WK935 converted by Armstrong Whitworth to a prone-position machine for investigation into the effects of high "g" loadings on pilots. This was the only one with extended nose, taking a couch, used by Farnborough's aviation medicine experts. *Meteor NF.14* WS838 built by Armstrorng Whitworth, from A.&A.E.E. Boscombe Down. *Gloster Javelin F(AW) 4/9* XA634/7641M, sixth production Mk IV, never flown by RAF but used by Flight Refuelling for trials at Tarrant Rushton; later Melksham ground instruction. Two Armstrong Siddeley Sapphire 6, capable of 730 mph, service ceiling over 50,000 ft. Armed with four 30mm Aden cannon and could carry external stores including missiles. *Hawker Sea Fury FB.11* VR930 ex 801 and 802 Sqdns RNAS Abbotsinch and Lossiemouth. Presented 1965 by Hawker Siddeley, engine by Staravia Ltd. *Hawker P1052* VX272/7174M. The link between P1040 Sea Hawk and P1067 Hunter. Two built (VX279) as research aircraft; first flew November, 1948 and force-landed Farnborough Sept 1949. Rear half of 279 then fitted to front half of 272, fuselage strengthened, arrester hook fitted and trials on HMS Eagle. Aircraft from Cardington via Abingdon 1964. *Hawker P1067 Hunter prototype* WB188/715M; first flown 1951 and converted from Mk 1 to Mk 3 in 1953, becoming holder of the world speed record of 727.6 mph, with

Heinkel He 162 (Colerne)

B.A.C. Drone (Colerne)

Squadron Leader Neville Duke as pilot, Engines used in development were various R-R Avons or Armstrong Siddeley Sapphire turbojets. This machine was statically displayed at Halton and Melksham and is earmarked for the RAF Museum as the one and only Mark 3. *Hunter Mk 2* WN907/7416M, the 20th production a/c and with 263 and 257 Sqdns (in whose colours it is today). From Melksham 1964. *Percival Provost T.1* XF690 from 4 S. of T.T. St Athan. *Supermarine 510* VV106/7175M "one-off" a/c (VV119 was a Type 535). Evolved from Spitfire F21/22 through the Spiteful and Attacker, an Attacker fuselage fitted with swept wings and tail surfaces. First flown as 510 December 1948. In November 1950 it became the first swept-wing a/c to operate from an aircraft carrier. Progression to the Swift via the 535, a modified 510, nose being lengthened. R-R Nene turbojet; was capable of about 670 but was only flown for 230 hrs 40 mins. From Cardington 1964. A kind of tribute to the late Mike Lithgow who flew the 510 and then set up world record of 737.7 mph in a Swift which, as this is written, still rots in a scrapyard, alas. *Supermarine Spitfire* VB BL614 ex 611 (West Lancs), 242, 222 (Natal), 64, 118 Sqdns; 6 S of TT, and Hereford as 4354M. B. of B. film as taxier, later Wattisham. Painted as AB871 in error by RAF Credenhill. *Vickers Valetta C. Mk 1* WD159/7858M. This example used in Far East during the Malayan Campaign and flown to Colerne 2 September 1964 to join the museum. *Westland WS.51 Dragonfly H.R.3* WG725/M7703 from St. Athan. *Heinkel He 162 A-3 Salamander* 120227 formerly AM.65/VH513. *Messerschmitt Me 163B Komet* 191904 formerly AM217. *Bristol (BAC) Bloodhound Mk 2* missile. *Mignet HM.14 Pou-du-Ciel* "Flying Flea" G-AEEH, original a/c at present minus engine. The following are on loan from Commander L. D. Goldsmith of Itchenor, Sussex:— *Bleriot XI* 225 now G-AVXV, restored by Shuttleworth Collection; 1912 original with 25 hp Anzani, said to be for sale at around £25,000.00. *Bensen B.8S Gyrocopter* G-ASPX (CA/204). *B.A.C. Drone* G-AEKV c/n 30 is owned by Wing Commander Macdonald at RAF Colerne and is not a part of the museum.

DEVIZES. Airstrip. *Auster 6A* G-ARXU c/n 2295 ex VF526, owned and flown by G. Mealing, D. W. Davis and R. Boor.

KEEVIL. Airstrip. *Auster V* G-AJXC c/n 1409 ex TJ343, formerly on the Devonair schedules to Lundy Island; now J. E. Graves.

LYNEHAM. RAF. At the Route Hotel. *Meteor T.7* WF825 "Z" with 2491 ATC, ex 603 and 33 Sqdns, CAW and 5 MU, Kemble. *Messerschmitt Bf 109 G-2*, Werk-Nr 10639 ex RN228 of 1426 Flt, now being restored once again to airworthiness by Flt Lt "Russ" Snadden, pilot and well-known preservationist. We wish him—and his associates—luck in their leisure-time endeavour.

MELKSHAM. Airfield. *Auster 5* G-APTU c/n 3413; B. G. F. King.

NETHERAVON. Army Air Corps. *Auster AOP.9* XK418/7976M and *Percival Provost T.1* WV544 reported at the entrance. *DH.89A Rapides* G-AGTM c/n 6746 ex NF875, JY-ACL, OD-ABP. *G-AIDL* c/n 6968 ex TX310. *Rapide 4* G-AJHO c/n 6835 ex NR747. It is reported that *Rapides* G-AHGC c/n 6583 ex X7442, *G-AHKU* c/n 6810 ex NR722 and *G-ASRJ* c/n 6959 ex TX301 are dismantled here and that *G-AHJS* c/n 6967 ex TX309 is in the training building as forward fuselage and cabin.

RUDLOE MANOR. RAF. *Provost T.1* WV541 from St. Athan.

SALISBURY. Ashley Rd 1010 ATC Sqdn. *Vampire T.11* XD453/7890M "64" from 19 MU.

Spitfire F.21 (South Marston)

SOUTH MARSTON. Vickers' Works. *Spitfire F.21* LA226/7119M ex 91, 41, 122 Sqdns, 3 CAACU, Cosford, then ATC Albrighton. Displayed CFS, Little Rissington, and with B. of B. film, Henlow etc.

WINTERBOURNE GUNNER. Porton Biological College. *Vampire T.11* XD375/7887M. *Meteor F.4* VT260 ex Flight Refuelling, 226 OCU, 12 FTS. *Whirlwind HAR 10* XR478.

Bf 109 G-2 (Lyneham)

WROUGHTON. RAF. *Whirlwind AS.7* XG594 and *Meteor T.7* WS103 stored for FAA Museum.

WORCESTERSHIRE

BICKMARSH. Worcester Gliding Club. *DFS Grunau 2b* of 1939. *Akaflieg (Aachen) FVA 10b Rheinland*—the last example of "an incredibly refined sailplane" says Chris Wills. Originally designed and built 1936/7 and extensively re-designed 1943. Now modified or rebuilt to 1943 standards.

HARTLEBURY. RAF MU. *Gloster Javelin FAW6* XA 821 "J" 29 Sqdn.

Gloster Javelin FAW6 (Hartlebury)

PERSHORE. Royal Radar Establishment. Viewing only by written approval and unlikely unless there is a Press Day. Seen flying:— *Armstrong Whitworth Meteor NF14* WS832. *NF.11* WD790. *Handley Page Hastings C.2* WD499. *Whirlwind HAR.10* XJ409. *Blackburn Buccaneer S.1* XN964 "LM-613" ex Thurleigh. *Fairey Gannet AEW.3* XL503. *Viscounts* XT661 (ex 9G-AAV) and XT575 (ex OE-LAG). Also several Canberras etc. In view of the regrettable scrapping of the world's last airworthy Handley Page Hermes here, preservationists may wish to keep eyes open for anything seemingly suitable for saving. *DH. Tiger Moth* G-ARTL c/n 83795 ex T7281; Defford Aero Club.

WORCESTER. Perdiswell. 187 ATC Sqdn. *Gloster Javelin FAW9* XH767/7955M ex 27 MU, earlier with 25 and 11 Sqdns, 228 OCU. *Chanute Hanging Glider* (*replica*) 15-ft span, 120 sq ft wing area, built and flown by Nick Upton of Redcliffe St, a glider-pilot who has achieved glides of 60 feet, heights up to 12 feet, after sprinting downhill to a platform from which he leaps. Latest news and photos please.

Blackburn B.2 (Brough)

YORKSHIRE

BARKSTON ASH. Tadcaster. St. Camillus School. *Vampire T.11* XD622/8160M ex 4 FTS and Jever Stn Flt. Now 2434 ATC Sqdn.

BROUGH. Hawker Siddeley (Blackburn Division) Airfield. *Blackburn B.2* G-AEBJ c/n 6300/8. Used for RAF Reserve training at E. & R. Hanworth FTS and elsewhere. Many now-famous pilots flew this machine. Said to be earmarked for RAF Museum.

CARLTON MOOR. S of Middlesborough. Newcastle & Teesside G.C. *DFS Kranich 2 glider* 2-seater of 1939, one of the last two airworthy in U.K.

CATTERICK. RAF. The Fire Fighting School here receives many machines for the vital training courses and it is not thought advisable to record them, since they are probably short-lived. The compiler will be delighted, though, to include in any future editions, any aircraft which remain intact here. Flying is *Tiger Moth* G-ANEL c/n 82333 ex N9238; W. P. Maynall.

CHURCH FENTON. RAF. *Armstrong Whitworth Meteor NF.14* WS739/7961M ex 1 ANS, painted as 85 Sqdn machine. *Spitfire VB* BM597/5718M ex 315/317 (Polish) Sqdns, 222 Sqdn, 58 OTU, St. Athan, Hednesford, Bridgnorth. Painted as 609 (West Riding) Sqdn RAuxAF aircraft.

Spitfire VB (Church Fenton)

DISHFORTH. RAF. RAF Gliding & Soaring Assn. *Auster 6A* G-ASOC c/n 2544 ex VF603; *Auster 7* G-AVCR ex WE572.

FINNINGLEY. RAF. The Vintage Aircraft Club was started here in 1966 by the then Wg Cdr Fennell and others and although some machines have moved to Topcliffe to be stored for Hendon, the following are believed to exist for Battle of Britain Days:— *Wright Flyer* (*replica*) constructed at Finningley 1960s. *Pou-du-Ciel (Flying Flea)* G-AEKR which was constructed by

Pou-du-Ciel, Wright—replica, Vampire (Finningley)

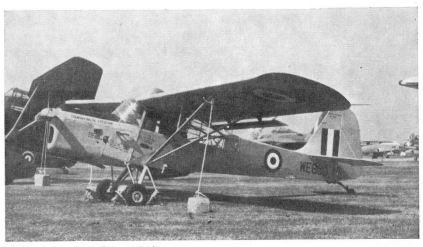

Auster Antarctic T.7 (Finningley)

Graham Claybourne's father in Doncaster 1936 with 30 hp Anzani, and loaned for some years to Finningley, was destroyed by fire 1970. A replica built at RAF Oakington, using the original engine has now replaced one of the best Fleas ever flown. *Blackburn Beverley* C.1 XL149/7988M ex 242 OCU, 84 and 30 Sqdns. *DH Vampire T.11* XD506/7983M ex 206 AFS, 5 FTS, CATCS. *Gloster Javelin FAW.1* XA726 (actually XA549/7717M from Swanton Morley). *Gloster Meteor F.8* WL168 (repainted as WH456 of 616 (South Yorkshire) Sqdn RAuxAF but actually from 111 and 604 Sqdns). *Handley Page Hastings C.1* TG605/7987M ex 24, 53/99, 114, 24/36 Sqdns. *Hawker Hunter F.4* XF309/7771M ex 112 Sqdn and Marham. *Percival Provost T.1* XF545/7957M ex 2 and 6 FTS "P-Z". *Auster Antarctic T.7* WE600/7602M non-standard for 1950 Trans-Antarctic Expedition fitted wheels/floats/skis, was formerly at Colerne. *Messerschmitt Me 262 A-1* Werk-Nr 112372 ex JG.7 and formerly AM51/VK893. At Cranwell Museum, Gaydon, and may go to RAF Museum eventually, direct or via Topcliffe.

Messerschmitt Me 262 (Finningley)

HOLME-on-SPALDING MOOR. HSA (Blackburn Division) Test Centre. *Buccaneer S.1* XK526 pre-production—may be for disposal.

HUDDERSFIELD. Drill Hall, St. Paul's St, 59 ATC Sqdn. *Vampire T.11* XE993/8161M ex 43 Sqdn and 27 M.U. At Polytechnic, *Vampire T.11* XD445.

HULL. TA Centre, Holderness Rd, 142 Sqdn ATC. *Auster AOP.9* XP286/8044M ex Leconfield.

Tiger Moth (Sherburn-in-Elmet)

LECONFIELD. RAF. *Spitfire XVI* RW382/7245M ex 604 (Middlesex) 3 CAACU and 609 Sqdn instructional airframe—once serialled (wrongly) RW729.

LEEMING. RAF. *Armstrong Whitworth Meteor NF.14* WS744/7962M ex "A" of 1 ANS and 5 MU, Kemble. *Fairey Battle III* L5343 ex 226 Sqdn, Iceland, for restoration.

LINDHOLME. RAF. *Hastings C.2* WD477 was at gate.

LINTHWAITE. Mr. K. Smith's family have *Avro Avian IIIA* G-ACGT but efforts to acquire this for museum display have not yet succeeded. This machine, c/n R3/CN/171 was EI-AAB.

LINTON-ON-OUSE. RAF. *Vampire T.11* XD515/7998M ex 206 AFS 5 FTS, 3 FTS.

MOOR MONKTON. Forway Garage on A.59. *Westland Dragonfly HR.3* WG664 "915/CU", and *WG724* "923/LM".

NETHERTHORPE. *Tiger Moth* G-APBI c/n 86097 ex EM903; J. N. Copley Ptnrs.

PATRINGTON. RAF. Radar. *Armstrong Whitworth Meteor NF.14* WS788/7967M ex "C" 1 and 2 ANS and "Z" 152 Sqdn.

PICKERING. Ian Stone's Restaurant. *Fieseler Fi 103 (V1)* captured by allies on Belgian/German border.

PONTEFRACT. Grammar School. *Scale* (replica) S.E.5a

Last flight of XG504 (Rotherham)

ROTHERHAM. (near) *Bristol Sycamore* XG504 with J. A. McArdle.

SHERBURN-in-ELMET. Airfield. East of Leeds. Flying Club. *DH. Tiger Moth* G-AODS c/n 82942 ex R5041 reported—confirmation? *Miles Messenger* 2A G-AJOC c/n 6370; S. B. Jolly & J. Don. *Miles Messenger* 2A G-AJOE c/n 6367; A. Townend.
Tiger Moth G-AXXE c/n 86635 ex PG626, F-BGDD; P. E. Scott.

Supermarine Swift FR.5 (Topcliffe)

TOPCLIFFE. RAF. Aircraft in store for RAF Museum. Only viewable with C.O.'s approval or on any Open Day. *Avro 707A* WZ736/7868M "Mini-Vulcan" delta-wing experimental a/c formerly at RAF Colerne. *Avro 707C* WZ 744/7932M, the only two-seater of the five built. First-flown July 1953 for converting pilots to delta-wing. Used continuously at Avro, Woodford, or at R.A.E. *Fairey FD.2* WG777/7986M, one of two high-speed a/c; the other, WG774 achieved world speed record 1,132 mph, flown by Peter Twiss, 10 March 1956. This became BAC-221 (see Thurleigh, Beds.) *Short SB.5* WG768/8005M experimental a/c for English Electric P.1. *Thor* missile. *Supermarine Swift FR.5* WK281 "S" of 79 Sqdn, ex 14(F) Sqdn ATC, Northolt and at Gaydon & Finningley. Also at Topcliffe for ground instructional training: *DH. Comet* XK671/7927M c/n 06029 ex G-AMXG from 216 Sqdn, Lyneham. *Avro Shackleton MR.2/3* WR981/8120M. *Armstrong Whitworth Argosy C.1* XN848 ex 70 Sqdn.

YORK. Yorks A/c Preservation Society 130 Jute Rd, Acomb. *DH. Tiger Moth* said under restoration—details from H. S. please. *Vampire T.11.*

SCOTLAND

ABBOTSINCH. Glasgow Airport. Airport Safety Services. *Douglas Dakota* G-ALYF c/n 19350 ex 42-100887 ex TS424 of RAF. Prototype "Pionair" for BEA, October

1950, later "Sir Francis Drake" of British Westpoint Airlines. Repainted and, we are told, unlikely to be scrapped during its useful rescue training work. *Beechcraft E.18S* G-ASUG c/n BA-111 ex N24R, N555CB, N575C; Loganair Ltd. *Vampire T.11* XD547—Aeronautics Dept, Glasgow University. ex "Z" of CATCS.

Dakota G-ALYF (Abbotsinch)

ABERDEEN. Air Scouts have *DFS Grunau Baby* BGA1079 c/n 105 ex SE-SDF for restoring?

ABOYNE. Deeside Gliding Club. *Miles Hawk Tr.3* G-AHUJ c/n 1900 ex R1914: J. N. Russell.

ARBROATH. No 45 Royal Marine Commando. *DH. Sea Vixen FAW.1* XJ477 coded AB/714 serial A2601.

AUCHTERADER. Strathallan Airfield. Perthshire PH3 1LA. The Strathallan Collection of Aircraft (W. J. D. Roberts) Telephone 076-46-2545 or write in advance to seek permission to view as aircraft not as yet on public show. At present:— *Hawker Hurricane X* c/n 42012 serial 5588 RCAF, built by Canadian Car & Foundry Co, later CF-SMI and brought to UK for B. of B. film (listed as G-AWLW Hurricane IIB). Flew as MI-A; still airworthy. *Westland Lysander IIIA* G-AZWT ex 2355 RCAF—being restored. *Fairey Battle* (serial/history wanted) ex Canada and Michigan; hopefully to be restored to flying condition. *Supermarine Spitfire IXTr* G-AVAV c/n CBAF/7269 ex MJ772 (fuselage) MJ627 (wings) and formerly Irish Air Corps 159. In B. of B. film as AI-D, CD-H/N, now "NL-R" *Spitfire IX* ML407 (IAC 162) and PV202 (IAC 161) stored. *DH. Mosquito TT.35* G-ASKB ex RS712 once 3 CAACU and in films as HT-N; from Gp Cpt Mahaddie, West Malling. Canadian-built *Bristol Bolingbroke* for restoration, serial? *Noorduyn AT-16 Harvard IIB* G-AZBN c/n 14A/1431, ex 43-13132 FT391, B-97 RNethAF, PH-HON. *Lockheed Hudson 4* c/n 6464 VH-AGJ ex VH-SMM; to be repainted as RAAF a/c. *Avro Anson 19 sers 2* G-AGWE c/n 1286 ex TX201. G-AHIC c/n 1313 ex Railway Air Services, BEA, College of Aeronautics.

Mosquito TT.35 G-ASKB (Auchterader)

G-AHKX c/n 1333 ex Smith Industries, Meridian Air Maps. G-APHV ex VM360 formerly BKS Air Surveys. G-AWRS ex TX213. G-AYWA c/n 1361 ex OO-CFA, OO-DFA, OO-VIT of Congolese Rlys etc. Believed 3 or 4 airworthy. All ex Kemps Aerial Surveys of Thruxton. Reported that an Avenger, Catalina and ex-Greek Bf 109 may be coming here to provide "Willie" Roberts with Europe's finest "Vintage Air Force." We look forward to it. *Tiger Moth* G-ANFV c/n 85904 ex DF155 here with Cirrus Aviation.

Lockheed Hudson 4 (Auchterader)

BLAIR ATHOLL. Airstrip. *Tiger Moth* G-AHUV c/n 3894 ex N6593; Flying Club. *DH. Tiger Moth* G-AFWI c/n 82187 ex BB814 reported here.

BROXBURN. West Lothian. TA Centre. 1756 ATC *Vampire T.11* XD444/7918M ex Nos 1 and 7 FTS, from Church Fenton.

CURRIE. Midlothian. Scottish A/c Preservation Group. *Auster* G-ALES (Proctor reg'n) ex Perth and Bathgate Tech College, for restoration.

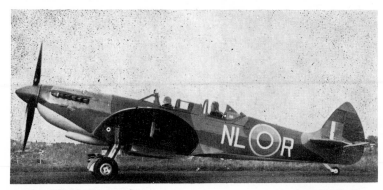

Spitfire IXTr (Auchterader)

EAST FORTUNE. Disused RAF airfield. Store for Royal Scottish Museum. *Spitfire XVI* TE462 ex No 1 Pilots Refresher Training Unit, and Ouston. *DH. Sea Vampire T.22* XA109. *Sea Venom FAW.22* WW145 *Hawker Sea Hawk FGA.1* WF259 (painted 171/A of 804 Sqdn.) *Blackburn Buccaneer S.1* XN967 (mainly from Lossiemouth RNAS.)

Pilcher Hawk glider (Edinburgh)

Kay Gyroplane (Glasgow)

EDINBURGH. Royal Scottish Museum, Chambers St, *The original Pilcher Hawk* glider (see Rugby, Science Museum & Glasgow). *Slingsby T.12 Gull glider* of 1939, plus engines and models. It is hoped to establish an aviation gallery here but, until that happy day, to make limited arrangements at East Fortune. Do NOT go, though, without prior written authority from Edinburgh.

EDINBURGH. George Watson's College CCF *Vampire T11* XD601/7878M. Fettes College CCF. *Vampire T11* WZ517/7889M—confirmation please.

GLASGOW. Museum of Transport. Pollockshields. *Pilcher Hawk* (replica) built by 2175 ATC Sqdn (Rolls-Royce Ltd.) *Kay Gyroplane Type 331* G-ACVA first flown 18 Feb 1935. Pobjoy 75 hp engine, normal autorotational RPM 285. Cruising 80 mph. Swept diameter of rotor 22-ft, all-up weight 920 lbs.

LEUCHARS. RAF. *Spitfire XVI* TB252 ex 340 "Ile de France" Sqdn, Odiham, Acklington. Now coded GW-H of 340 "Lucky Nine". Was 7527M. *Spitfire PR XIX* PS915, ex 2 Sqdn, Woodvale Met Flt, West Malling as 7548M, B. of B. Film as N3328 AI-R, now cocooned for RAF Museum.

Spitfire PR XIX (Leuchars)

PRESTWICK. Airport. *Klemm L 25* G-AAUP c/n 145; reconstructed by R. S. Russell.

PORTMOAK. Gliding Club. *Slingsby T21B* prototype BGA646, c/n 536 ex G-ALKS. *Skylark 2* prototype BGA733 c/n 926. *Swallow* BGA843 c/n 1043—second of type.

Spitfire XVI (Turnhouse)

Klemm L 25 (Prestwick)

Meteor NF.14 (Turnhouse)

TURNHOUSE. Airport. *Spitfire XVI* RW393/7293M, once personal aircraft of the late A. M. Sir William Elliot when AOC in C, Fighter Cmd. Later with 602 (City of Glasgow) instructional airframe. Now stands as memorial to men of 603 (City of Edinburgh) RAuxAF which formed Turnhouse 14 Oct 1925. *Armstrong Whitworth Meteor NF.14* G-ARCX, the prototype NF.14 WM261, flying here for Ferranti but said promised to R. Scottish Museum.

WEST FREUGH. Airfield. *Douglas Dakota III* TS423 ex C47 42-100884.

NORTH AND CENTRAL WALES

ABERPORTH. Royal Aircraft Establishment. Appointment only. *Bloodhound* at gate. *Hunter F.1* WT680/7533M ex RAF West Raynham and 8 STT Weeton. Now with 1429 ATC Sqdn. *GAF Jindivik* A92-255—which made 81 successful pilotless sorties is here, marked "81".

FLINT. Technical College, on A548. By appointment only. Changes in aircraft occur regularly and some may become available for preservationists from:—*Supermarine Swift F.7* XF114, ex College of Aeronautics. *Provost T.1* XF597 "G". *Provost T.1* XF914 ex London and Glasgow UAS, CFS, Flying Tg Cmd. *Fairey Gannet AS.4* XA460, from RNAS Brawdy, 768/BY. *Saro Skeeter AOP.12* 7979M/XM529, 7981M/XL769, 7870M/XM556, from Arborfield—*HS(DH)125* G-ARYA c/n 25001 from Hawarden.

HELDRE HILL. Montgomeryshire. Ultra Light Flying Club. *DH. Tiger Moth* G-ANJK c/n 84557 ex T6066.

LLANBEDR. Royal Aircraft Establishment. Appointment only. *Hawker Hunter F.6* WW598 from Aero Flight, Thurleigh. *DH. Devon C.2* XA880 ex RRE, Pershore. *Canberra PR.3* WE146 from RAE. Farnborough. *Armstrong Whitworth Meteor TT20* WM167 from Flight Refuelling. *GAF Jindivik* A92-999 (fictitious serial). *Avro Anson T.21* VS562/8012M ex RAE Llanbedr is with 2445 ATC Sqdn.

VALLEY. Anglesey. RAF, *Armstrong Whitworth Meteor TT20* WD702 ex 3 CAACU, Exeter; for use of 22 Sqdn winch-training NOT for fire.

SOUTH WALES

CARMARTHEN. G. O. Rees is still believed to be storing *Civilian Coupe* G-ABNT c/n 03 and the fuselage of G-ABFJ c/n 02.

Civilian Coupe (Carmarthen)

HAVERFORDWEST. Airfield. West Wales Gliding Centre. *Auster 6A* G-ASNB c/n 3725 ex VX118.

Watkins Monoplane (St. Athan)

KENFIG HILL. N. of Porthcawl. Pwll-Y-Garth St. 2117 ATC. *Hawker Hunter F.1* WT569/7491M ex 4 S. of TT, Melksham 1964.

Boulton Paul Sea Balliol (St. Athan)

Bristol Boxkite—replica (St. Athan)

Sopwith Camel—replica (St. Athan)

Junkers Ju 87 G (St. Athan)

Mitsubishi Dinah (St. Athan)

ST. ATHAN. Near Barry, Glamorgan. No. 4 S. of TT. RAF. Open Days or by prior approval of AOC only. Historic aircraft exhibited here on occasions or stored for RAF Museum:—*Watkins Monoplane* "Robin Goch" (Red Robin) BAPC 47 first aeroplane built & flown in Wales, loaned by Charles Watkins C.Ae.E. now almost 90 years of age. He constructed it 1908/9 at a cost of £300.00 and flew it mainly by night, his last flight 1918. Machine in excellent state and Mr. Watkins usually goes to St. Athan on public days to answer questions. Stored for years in Mr. Watkins' garage, Cardiff, the machine, with 40 hp engine, was moved into St. Athan some years ago for display. *Supermarine Spitfire IX* MK356/5690M originally 443 Sqdn. as 21-V of "D" Day coding, later Halton instructional then Hawkinge and Locking. In B. of B. film as N3328 AI-R. *Armstrong Whitworth Meteor NF14* WS843, ex 228 OCU, 1 ANS. *Saro Skeeter AOP.12* XN341/8022M ex 15 MU. *Bristol Scout* (replica) painted as A1742, constructed for and property of Royal Tournament committee, as also are the *R.A/c Factory BE2d* (replica) 6232. *Bristol Boxkite* (replica) *Sopwith Camel F.1* (replica). There is an *Avro 504K* (replica) built by the No 1 S. of TT apprentices, Halton, also for Royal Tournament and Edinburgh Tattoo. These are loaned to other stations on occasions and to RAF Assn. events. The following are earmarked for the RAF Museum and it is reported that the ex-Luftwaffe machines may one day go on show at the Battle of Britain Museum Chilham Castle, Kent:—*Boulton Paul Sea Balliol T.21* WL732 (to be restored as T.2?) *Hawker Hunter F.1* WT619/7525M (with plate "RAF Museum".) *Heinkel He 111H* Werk-Nr 701152 CW+HV, formerly Biggin Hill and at Henlow for B. of B. film, but not flown.

BE2d—replica (St. Athan)

Messerschmitt Bf 109 E-4 (St. Athan)

Fiat C.R.42 (St. Athan)

Junkers Ju 87 G 494083 marked RI+JK, at Henlow for B. of B. film but not flown. *Messerschmitt Bf 109 E-4* Werk-Nr 4101, built Erla factory, Leipzig, crash-landed Manston 27 Nov 1940 by Lt Teumer 2/JG51, allocated RAF DG200 and from Boscombe Down to 1426 Flt, Duxford. Engine transferred to a Bf 110 and the BF110 engine (Junkers Jumo) is still in the 109. Fuselage is original but wings and fin are from another E-4, the canopy believed from a G-9 or G-10. Code 12+GH. *Mitsubishi Ki-46-III Dinah Mk3* ex ETPS "29" *Fiat C.R.42 Falco (Falcon)* BT474 ex MM5701 c/n 326 shot down Orfordness, Nov 1940; ex Biggin Hill. *Focke Wulf Fw 190 A-8/U1* 584219 ex AM29 two-seater; from Henlow. With the cadets of No 30 Sqdn, ATC, in East Camp is *DH. Vampire FR.9* WL505/7705M ex 73 Sqdn and Ely Barracks, Cardiff. In use as this is compiled, are many instructional airframes, some of which may later be offered for preservation:—*Blackburn Buccaneer S.1* XN928/8179M, XN930/8180M, XN972/8181M, XN953/8182M. *English Electric Lightning F.1* XG327/8188M.

DH. Comet C.2 XK698/8031M ex G-AMXL c/n 06034 ex 216 Sqdn. *DH. Vampire T.11* XE849/7928M, XD896/7939M, *Armstrong Whitworth Argosy* XP408, ex Kemble. *DHC. Chipmunk T.10* WP905/7438M. *Westland Whirlwind HAR.3* XL111/8000M. *Hunting Jet Provost T.3* XM411, XN512, XN544. *Percival Pembroke C.1* WV703/8108M, WV704/8109M, WV741/8110M, WV743/8112M, WV753/8113M, XK862/8194M. *Hawker Hunter F.1* WT567/7489M. WW632/7516M, WW637/7518M, WW644/7521M. *F.4* WT746/7770M, XF972/7948M, XF974/7949M, XF975/7945M. Said to be in store here is *English Electric Canberra B.2* WD935, the seventh production a/c—perhaps for display at St. Athan? The South Wales Historical A/c Preservation Society own *Auster AOP.9* WZ662 and *Vampire T.11* WZ425. *Provost T.1* also being preserved at St. Athan. *Supermarine S6B* S1596 (world record 407.5 mph) stored.

Supermarine S6B S1596 (St. Athan)

SWANSEA. Blackpill. Peter Roberts has built here *Pou du Ciel* (Flying Flea) G-ADRY, a replica of splendid exhibition standard. *DH. Tiger Moth* G-ANFS, c/n 83569 ex T5812 also here for possible rebuild.

CHANNEL ISLANDS

GUERNSEY. Airport. *Anson C.19* TX192—to be preserved?

Focke-Wulf Fw 190 A-8/U1 (St. Athan)

JERSEY. Airport. *Dakota IV* G-AKNB c/n 9043 ex 42-32817 ex FD789, XY-ACN, and G-AMPY c/n 15124/ 26569 ex 43-49308, KK116, JY-ABE, TF-FIO, N15751. Intra Airways Ltd.

NORTHERN IRELAND

BELFAST. Aldergrove. RAF M.U. Said to be storing (for Transport Museum) *Spitfire LFXVI* TE184 ex 203 AFS/226OCU, 607 (instructional) 64 Reserve Centre, then 1855 ATC as 6850M FJT-A. At Finningley and used in "Darkie Pilbeam" TV programme, wrongly-painted.

Sea Hawk FGA.6 (Belfast)

BELFAST. RN Air Yard. *Sea Hawk FGA.6* XE327—displayed also *Sea Vixen FAW.2* XS583 At the Transport Museum's store, eventually planned to move into the Ulster Folk Museum, Holywood, Co Down, believed to be *Miles Whitney Straight* G-AERV c/n 307 ex EM999, loaned by Thompson Boys. *DH. Tiger Moth* G-AOUR c/n 86341, ex NL898 ex Ulster Flying Club. At Campbell College, CCF, *DH. Vampire T.11* XD525/7882M.

BISHOPSCOURT. Co. Down. RAF HQs. *Armstrong Whitworth Meteor NF14* WS840/7969M ex 264/64 Sqdns, 2 TAF Com Sqdn, 1 ANS.

Meteor NF.14 (Bishopscourt)

LONG KESH. Airfield. Ulster & Shorts Gliding Club. *Auster 6A* G-ARIH c/n 2463 ex TW591.

NEWTOWNARDS. Airfield. Ards Tiger Group. *DH. Tiger Moth* G-ANDP c/n 82868 ex R4960, N9920F, D-EBEC. G-ANON c/n 84270 ex T7909 owned R. Corry/ D. Harrison. G-AYIT c/n 86342, ex NL896, F-BGEZ; D. R. Wilcox. *Aeronca 7AC Champion* G-AOEH c/n 7AC-2144, ex OO-TWF, N79854; A. A. Alderdice. Let us hope that lasting peace soon comes to Northern

Ireland making it possible to open the long-awaited aircraft section of the Transport Museum—in which, surely, there must one day be an Avro Anson to perpetuate the magnificent record of the RAF's first Special Reserve Squadron—No 502 (Ulster) formed May 1925.

DH.84 Dragon (Dublin)

REPUBLIC OF IRELAND

DUBLIN AND DISTRICT. Dublin Airport. *DH.84 Dragon 2* EI-AFK c/n 6105 ex G-AECZ, AV982—repainted as EI-ABI "Iolar" of Aer Lingus, in Hangar 2, for projected Irish Aviation Museum (Hon Curator Captain J. C. Kelly-Rogers OBE, FRAeS). This collection is growing but still lacks accommodation for its larger exhibits and Capt Kelly-Rogers would be glad of offers to him at Spindrift, Shore Rd, Portmarnock Co Dublin. He has the promise of a *Vickers Viscount* ex Aer Lingus (regn not yet known) also of possible *Vampire, Provost, Chipmunk* from Department of Defence in due time. Meantime Capt Kelly-Rogers is at work on a *replica* of the machine designed and flown by Harry Ferguson on 31 December 1909. The engine and pilot's seat have been presented by the family for the replica. Hereabouts said also to be *Avro 631 Cadet* EI-ALU c/n 657 ex G-ACIH. At Terenure, being restored *Avro Cadet* EI-AGO, c/n 730 ex C-7, Irish Air Corps, EI-AFO (George Flood). Previously at Cloughjordan store. *Slingsby T.13 Petrel 1* EI-101 c/n 361 ex BGA651, G-ALPP, IGA 101 and *Slingsby T.26 Kite 2* IGA 102 ex IAC.102 to be preserved? *Vickers V803 Viscount* EI-AOL c/n 179 of Aer Lingus, in use as ground trainer; ex PH-VIH of KLM. Baldonnel, Casement Airfield. *Avro Anson 19* IAC 141 c/n 1313, of 1946, is used as instructional airframe and taxier. *M.14A Magister* IAC 34 ex N5392 c/n 1028, delivered Feb 1939, instructional 1952, being restored. This was earlier reported erroneously as the RAF's P6414. *DH. Vampire T.11* IAC 198 ex XE977 RAF, used for instruction, and delivered in August 1963 as non-flying airframe.

COUNTY KILDARE

WESTON. Aerodrome Leixlip. (10 miles west of Dublin City). Base for a collection of *replicas* which have been used for many films including "Blue Max", "Red Baron", "Darling Lily", "You can't win 'em all" and "Richthofen & Brown":—*Fokker D.VII/65* EI-APT, EI-APU, EI-APV, ex F-BNDF, F-BNDG and F-BNDH c/ns 01, 02, 03. All built by Rousseau Aviation 1965. *Fokker DR.1* EI-APW c/n 001 ex G-ATIY, built by Josef Bitz Flugzeugbau. *Pfalz D.III* EI-ARC, c/n PPS/PFLZ/1

Fokker D.VII—replica EI-APU (Weston)

Pfalz D.III—replica EI-ARC (Weston)

Caudron Luciole EI-ARF (Weston)

Morane-Saulnier MS.230 EI-ARG (Weston)

Ferguson Monoplane—replica (Dublin)

ex G-ATIF, built by Personal Plane Services at Booker.
EI-ARD c/n PT.16 ex G-ATIJ, built by Hampshire
Aeroplane Club; derelict. *SE.5 replica* EI-ARL c/n 1594
ex G-AVOX. *Caudron C.277 Luciole* EI-ARF c/n 7546/135
ex F-AQFB, G-ATIP, F-BNMB. The above all owned by
J. R. Maher. Lynn Garrison owns *SE.5 Replicas* EI-ARH
c/n 1590 ex G-AVOT and EI-ARM c/n 1595 ex G-AVOY.
These were built by Slingsby around Currie Wot air-
frames as type T.56. These two aircraft may be in the
US now. H. McGuinness owns *SE.5 Replica* EI-ARK
c/n 1593 ex G-AVOW. The Historic Aircraft Preservation
Group here own:—*Morane-Saulnier M.S.502 Criquet*
EI-AUY c/n 338 ex F-BCDG. *Morane-Saulnier M.S.230*
EI-ARG c/n 1049 ex F-BGMR is owned and flown by
H. Hutchinson and A. Wignall. *DH. Tiger Moth* EI-AUB
c/n 86509 ex NM201, F-BGCP; F. E. Biggar. *Taylorcraft
Plus D.* EI-AGD c/n 108 ex G-AFUB, HL534, and *EI-AMF*
c/n 157 ex LB286, G-AHUM, G-ARRK are with H. Wolf.
The latter is in use for spares. Other aircraft believed in
dismantled state here include *DH. Tiger Moth* EI-AGN
c/n 82943, ex R5042, G-ANEM; *Morane-Saulnier M.S.230*
F-BGJX c/n 1079.

COUNTY CORK

CORK. Airport. *Taylorcraft Plus D.* EI-ANA c/n 206 ex
LB347, G-AHCG is believed stored with Joyce Aviation
who operate *Percival Prentice 1* EI-ASP ex VS356,
G-AOLU. At Kilbrittain Castle *Miles M.75 Aries 1*
G-AOGA c/n 75/1007, EI-ANB, 2nd prototype, (damaged). *Miles Gemini 3C* G-ALCS c/n 6534 both owned
by R. E. Winn.

MALLOW. Rathcoole. *BA Swallow 2* EI-AFF c/n 406
ex G-ADMF with parts of *EI-AFN* c/n 485 ex G-AFGV;
being restored by Justin McCarthy & friend. *Piper
J3C-65 Cub* G-AXVV c/n 10863 ex 43-29572, F-BBQB
also here; J. Daniel.

COUNTY CAVAN

BALLYJAMESDUFF. Airfield. *Taylorcraft Plus D.*
EI-ALH c/n 106 ex G-AFTZ, HH987 G-AHLJ; N. Reilly.

COUNTY MEATH

CULMULLEN. Airfield. *DH. Tiger Moth* EI-AOP c/n
84320 ex T7967, G-AIBN; Dublin Tiger Group.

KELLS. Headfort Aerodrome. *DH. Tiger Moth*
G-APRA c/n 85347 ex DE313 reported dismantled, after
accident here 23 June 1963.

KILCOCK. In a cinema is said to be *DH. Tiger Moth* EI-
ANN c/n 83161 ex T5418, G-ANEE. This aircraft was
damaged 18 October 1964 at Culmullen. Confirmation
please of location.

COUNTY LAOIGHIS

PORTLAOIGHISE. Aldritt's Garage. The 1912
Aldritt monoplane believed still unrestored, although
wanted for display in Dublin. Aircraft never flew since
Mr. Aldritt died before completion, but the aircraft was
designed along Bleriot lines with an Aldritt 3 cylinder
engine. News please.

COUNTY LIMERICK

COONAGH. *Piper J-3C Cub* EI-AKM c/n 15810 ex
N88194 is with Shannon Flying Services. The *Pou-du-
Ciel* "Patrick", is still reported hereabouts unrestored
and engineless—up-dated news wanted. No connec-
tion with the 1936 registered EI-ABH, has been proved
but such link cannot be ruled out.

COUNTY WEXFORD

CASTLEBRIDGE. Airfield. *Avro 643 Cadet* EI-ALP
c/n 848 ex G-ADIE, rebuilt 1960 using parts of G-ACIH,
EI-AFO; J. C. O'Loughlin. NOTE:—No confirmation
has ever been received in respect of the ex-Irish Air
Corps *Hawker Hector* at CLOUGHJORDAN, but it
is thought the *Spartan Three-Seater* EI-ABU c/n 102
ex G-ABYN is still in the area, unrestored. Details and
photos please.

EUROPE

AUSTRIA

ASPERN. Airfield. *Vampire T.11* 5C-YD c/n 15180, A.A.F.

LINZ-HÖRCHING. *SAAB J29F* 29447 "B" ex AAF.

MAUTHAUSEN. Barn. *Austria A-9* owned by Herr Otto Palacro. Built 1924, registration A-5.

VIENNA. Military Museum. Outside, *SAAB J29* Tac No 0 ex Austrian Luftwaffe. Inside *Albatros B.1* 20.01 2-seater reconnaissance biplane of Austro-Hungarian A.F.
Technical Museum. Original *Lilienthal Glietflieger* 1892 glider. *Aviatik-Berg D.1* 101-37 locally-designed 1918 fighter, weight 800 kg. Built by Thöne and Fiala. *Etrich Taube* (Igo Etrich) of 1910. Dr. Ing Alfred von Pischof's *Autoplan* of 1910. *Wiener Automobile Klub Segelflugzeug* 1923 glider. On the Vienna-Styria road at the Auto-Metzker scrapyard were *Nord Norecrin* OE-DAU c/n 319 ex Vienna Flying School (on pole) *DH. 89A Rapide* OE-FAA c/n 6690 ex G-ALXI, HG705 (still there?)

Technical Museum aircraft (Vienna)

SAAB J29 (Vienna)

ZELTWEG. Air Force Base. *Fiat G.46-5B* coded 3A-BB at gate.

BELGIUM

AALST. Airfield. *Piper J-3C-65 Cub* OO-YOL c/n 12949 ex 44-80653 ex F-BCPD; G. Delbecq. *Piper L-4H Cub* OO-AJK c/n 12476 ex 44-80180; Aero Club.

ALKEN. Restaurant. *Fairchild UC-71 Argus* as advertisement.

ANTWERP. Deurne Airport, SE of city, 2 kilometres from centre. Vintage Dakotas of Delta Air Transport

Albatros B.1 (Vienna)

which (with airline's DC-6s) often have regn ending "VG"—Mr. Van Gaever being managing-director. *Douglas DC-3C* OO-AUX c/n 43088 ex 42-23800 (to be Sports Club). *Douglas DC-3C* OO-AUV c/n 43087 ex 42-24097. *OO-AVG* c/n 19458 ex 42-100995, RNoAF, LN-IAS, PH-SCC. *OO-DVG* c/n 43089 ex 42-23769, EC-BEC, OO-AUY. *OO-GVG* c/n 43090 ex 42-23798, EC-BED, OO-AUZ. *DC-3* OO-KVG c/n 4346 ex 41-7847, LN-RTW, OH-VKD, I-LUNA. *Douglas C-47* OO-VDF c/n 9410 ex 42-23548, FD864 (RAF), PH-TCY, PH-DAC, JZ-PDC. Sometimes seen in England with enthusiasts. *Douglas C-47* K-4 OT-CNB R.Belg.AF. as changing-room. *Piper L-4J Cub* OO-AVS c/n 12429 ex 44-80133; Royal Antwerp Aero Club. *J-3C-65 Cub* OO-SKY c/n 12893 ex 44-80597, HB-OWN, D-EGUH; also *OO-SKZ* c/n 12992 ex 44-80696 PH-NCV. *Percival Prentice* OO-LUC c/n 5840/18 ex VS398, G-AOLM; all Publi-Sky. *DH. Tiger Moth* OO-MOS c/n 86580 ex PG863, A-56 (RNethAF) P. Peeraer.

BALEN-NETE. Airfield. *L-4J Cub* OO-REX c/n 12416 ex 44-80120; Aeroclub de Keiheuval.

BANDE. Cafe. *Fairchild UC-61 Argus* OO-FAA c/n 949 ex 43-14985, HB 711—advertisement.

BEAUVECHAIN. Belgian Air Force base. In front of officers' mess. *Spitfire FR.XIVe* SG-31 ex RN201 of 349 (Belg) Sqdn and OTU. *Lockheed F-104G Starfighter* FR-34.

Spitfire and Starfighter (Beauvechain)

BIERSET. Airfield. *Tiger Moth* OO-BYL c/n 3882 ex G-AFNR, W7952, G-ANBU H. Vormezeele. *Piper L-4H Cub* OO-GEL c/n 12686 ex 44-80390; J. Van Der Keyden. *Republic RF-84F* FR-34 now at gate.

BRUSSELS. Melsbroek (Bruxelles-National) Airport. East on Autoroute. *Beech C-45G* OO-GEU c/n AF.55 ex USAF 51-11498 ex Cogea/Aviation Benelux, at cafe

R.A/c Factory R.E.8 (Brussels)

near airport. Vintage types believed based here:— *Douglas C-47A* OO-SBC c/n 13457 ex 42-93535, KG645 (RAF): B.I.A.S. *Douglas C-47* OO-SNC c/n 32664 ex 44-76332, K-28; Etat Belge. *Douglas C-47A* OO-UBT c/n 19536 ex 43-15070, OO-CBT: B.I.A.S. *Douglas C-47B* OO-AUW c/n 26297 ex 43-49036; *OO-CBX* c/n 33224 ex 44-76892, KN589, AP-ACV. *OO-CBY* c/n 11881 ex 42-92116, VT-CGE, AP-AAK: B.I.A.S. *Piper L-4H Cub* OO-AAT c/n 11529 ex 43-30238, OO-PAX; and OO-EAB c/n 12220 ex 44-79924; both Sabena.

At the *Musee de l'Armee et d'Historie Militaire* Parc du Cinquantenaire; some a/c on display, some seen only by appointment "Old" collection:—*Tipsy S.2* OO-TIP ex OO-ASB c/n 29, built 1937, became G-AFVH. Returned Belgium 1949. *Henri Farman F11-A2* unserialled, ex Stampe Flying School and Asch, 1919. with 80 hp Renault. *Halberstadt C.V* serial Halb CV3471/18 with 200

Sopwith Camel (Brussels)

hp Benz. Used by the Belgians for training purposes. *Hanriot HD.1* serial HD78 of 9 Sqdn and 4 Fighter Group, Shaffen. Rhone 9jb of 120 hp. *L.V.G. C.VI* serial 3141 with 200 hp Benz, used by 7th Training Group, Asch. Fuselage marked "Inter Danziger Luftreederei". *Nieuport 17C.1* N5024 "Abel de Neef" flight, No 1 Sqdn, B.A.F. 1917, later Asch FTS. *R.A/c Factory R.E.8* serial 8 with blue "Bee" of 6 Sqdn. Crashed 18 August 1918, crew Simonet and Piron; 180 hp Hispano-Suiza 8Aa. *Schreck FBA Type 4* serial 5,160 hp Lorraine-Dietrich. Based at Calais for North Sea patrols. *Sopwith Camel F.1* SC-11 Belgian AF built Clayton and Shuttleworth, Lincoln, ex B5747; 130 hp Clerget. *Sopwith 1A2*—French-built version of 1½-Strutter, serial 88; 120 hp Rohne. *SPAD XIII C.1* serial SP-49 ex 10 Sqdn; 200 hp Hispano-Suiza. *Kreit KL.2* OO-ANP, Anzani 35 hp, built by Belgian Air Force fighter pilot in 1934. *SABCA Poncelet Vivette glider* O-BAFH c/n 2 used in France 1925-27. *Spitfire FRXIVe* SG37 ex RM 860, 130 Sqdn RAF, struck off charge after colliding 14 January 1949 with SG46 and re-assembled at Koksyde with parts of SG46/SG55. This is NOT SG31/RN201 as previously thought and is one of 132 Spitfires delivered Belgium 1948. *Stampe SV.4B* OO-ATD c/n 4 flown to England (Thorpe-Le-Soken, Essex) on 5 July 1941 by Lts Donnet and Divoy (serialled J7777 a fictitious number, both pilots having been on No 77 Course BAF). It joined the Allied Flight in August 1942 and transferred 510 Sqdn, later 24 Sqdn as MX457 returning to Belgium 1945. Lt-Gen. Baron "Mike" Donnet, who commanded 64 and 350 (Belg) Sqdns, and the Hawkinge Spitfire Wing, is now the Belgian Air Force representat-

Belgian Air Force Hall (Brussels)

ive with NATO. The above fifteen machines, in the present Musée de L'Armée will eventually join a new and growing collection called "Les Amis du Musée de l'Air et de l'Espace" which began in the big adjoining hall and where there are, in 1973:—*Stampe SV.4B* V-28 c/n 1170, Belgian A.F. used by "Les Manchots" aerobatic team 1964-67; with *Stampe SV.4B* V-64 c/n 1206. To hang in "Mirror Formation" as a pair—the speciality of "Les Manchots". *Stampe SV.4B* V-56 c/n 1198, Belgian A.F. *NA Harvard IIA* H-21 Belgian A.F. c/n 88-15950 ex 42-84169, EZ256, SAAF in WW II. Belgian A.F. 1947/59. *NA Harvard IIA* H-39 c/n 88-9728 ex 41-33265 ex EX292— was stored at the Zellick Depot. *DH. (Canada) DHC.3 Otter* OO-SUD c/n 297, bought from US Navy 1968 for Belgian South Pole Expedition. *DH. Mosquito NF.30* MB-24 "ND-N" Belgian A.F. c/n 4597 ex RK952, formerly No 11 Sqdn, 1 Wing, Beauvechain. *Hawker Hurricane IIC* LF345 "ML-B" Belgian A.F. with Allied Flight, Metropolitan Com. Sqdn, Hendon. Then Belgian A.F. Advanced Flying School until 1947. *Percival Proctor IV* P-4 Belgian A.F. c/n H578 ex NP171 to Belgium 25.6.47 used by 367 Sqdn, 169 Wing, which became 21 Sqdn, 15

Wing, in 1948. *Percival Proctor V* OO-ARM ex G-AHZY c/n Ae84. *Airspeed Oxford I* O-16 Belgian A.F. c/n 936, to Belgium 3.9.47, used by 13 and 7 Wing, then OTU, Koksyde. *Piper L-18C Super Cub* OL-L87 Belgian Army, c/n 18-3149 ex 53-4749. *Spitfire LFIXC* SM-15, "MN-L" port wing from SM-13 (PT643) Formerly listed as MJ383, now known to be wrong. *Hawker Hunter F.4* ID-44 "O44" ex "Red Devils" team, formerly stored at Zellick Depot. *Hunter F.4* ID-46 "7J-F" Belgian A.F. built by Avions Fairey, ex 7 Sqdn, 7 Wing, Chievres, c/n AF/HOF 59. *Republic F-84G-21-RE Thunderjet* FZ132, was painted "YL-D" for Florennes Display but since removed. Thought ex 3 Sqdn's 51-10930. *Gloster Meteor F.8* (Avions Fairey built) EG224 "K5-K" built under licence from Gloster components. Ex 33 Sqdn, 13 Wing and 1 Fighter Wing and Fighter OTU. Additional aircraft received and mainly under restoration or repainting for display include:—*Fairchild UC-61K Argus III* OO-LUT c/n 951 ex 43-14987, HB713, ZS-BWM, ZS-BYN, F-OADB, F-BAMB. There are several Austers, some complete, from which it is planned to display two or three and, perhaps, to use some for exchanges with other collec-

Mosquito NF. 30 (Brussels)

Harvard IIA (Brussels)

Hurricane IIC (Brussels)

Spitfire LFIXC (Brussels)

Republic F-84G Thunderjet (Brussels)

Meteor F.8 (Brussels)

tions. Held in 1973:—*Auster J/1* OO-ABN c/n 2047—donated by SABENA. *Auster V* PH-NEO c/n 1802 ex TW464, G-AMFS. *Auster VI* OO-FDB c/n 2820, ex VT981, A-7, Belgian A.F. *Auster VI* OO-FDC c/n 2824, ex VT988, A-8, Belgian A.F. *Auster VI* OO-FDD c/n 2817, ex VT978, A-9, Belgian A.F. *Auster VI* OO-FDE c/n 2826, ex VT990, A-11, Belgian A.F. *Auster VI* OO-FDH c/n 2834, ex VT995, A-15, Belgian A.F. *Auster VI* OO-FDI c/n 2835, ex VT996, A-16, Belgian A.F. *Auster VI* OO-FDJ c/n 2832, ex VT993, A-17, Belgian A.F. *Auster VI* OO-FDL c/n 2836, ex VT997, A-22, Belgian A.F. *Auster VI* OO-FDA c/n 2818 ex VT979 and A-3 was registered to the museum as airworthy in 1972 and may still fly. *Avro CF-100 Canuck 5* 18534 ex RCAF, donated by Canada believed still crated, awaiting space for display. *Meteor F.8* EG-247 "B2-R" ex Koksyde target-tower. *Republic F-84F Thunderstreak* FU-30 ex 52-7169. *Republic RF-84F Thunderflash* FR-28 ex 51-1945. *Douglas C-47B Dakota* K-16 OT-CWG c/n 20823 ex 43-16357; from Koksyde, Bierset, and Melsbroek. *Morane MS500* (French-built Storch) F-BFCD c/n 374. *Jodel Bebe* OO-15 *Dassault Ouragan* (to come 1973). *Cessna 310* OO-SEL c/n 35524 (from SABENA). *Bristol Blenheim IV* and *Westland Lysander III* (due from Canada) *DH. Rapide* OO-CNP c/n 6458 ex R5922, G-AKNV, OO-AFG, believed earmarked for museum. *Fairchild C-119G Packet* also expected, ex Belgian A.F. *Percival Prentice* OO-OPO ex VS613, G-AOPO, for rebuild. *Miles Gemini* OO-RVE c/n 6525 ex G-AKHX—for complete restoration. *SPAD XIII* uncovered fuselage (unidentified as yet) *L.V.G. C.VI* 904/18 almost complete for restoration. Both above, found in garret of University, at Charleroi. Uncovered fuselage of prototype *1911 Cesar Bataille triplane* for restoration later. There are several gliders including:—two *SABCA Juniors* (one c/n 10). Four *Grunau Babys*, one OO-ZBA, one, PL-37 of Belgian AF; a Baby 3, c/n 82155. *Kassel 12* of 1931. *Schulgleiter SG.38* regn. PL-21. *V1* (replica). Also remains of a Rumpler C.V., wings of a Bleriot XI, wings of a Jan Olieslager aircraft, plus a hundred or more fabulous engines from Anzani to Sapphire. Eight balloons including "Belgica" which flew the Alps. All in all a magnificent prospect which will vie with Hendon, Chalais Meudon and many of the world's great collections. Colonel Michel Terlinden, at present commanding the Belgian Air Force Transport Wing, is the responsible officer; with M. Booten as curator of the "New" hall.

BRUSTEM. Belgian A.F. base. On display at gate, and in hangar. *Gloster (Fokker-built) Meteor F.8* EG-79. *Stampe V-46. Hawker Hunter* (SABCA-Fairey) at BAF Regiment Depot—serial please.

Stampe (Brusthem)

Spitfire FRXIV (Florennes)

CHIEVRES. BAF base. *Gloster (Fokker) Meteor F.8* EG-18 c/n 6339.

DIEST. Airfield. *DH. Tiger Moth* OO-EVA c/n 85873 ex DF124, T.1; CNVAV. *Piper L-4H Cub* OO-JAN c/n 11354 ex 43-30063; F. Hollanders. *L-4J Cub* OO-EIA c/n 12516 ex 44-80220; Diest Aero Club.

DINANT. Citadelle. *Gloster (Fokker) Meteor F.8* EG-162. Silver overall with red arrowhead each side of nose—plus "graffiti"! Reported in poor condition with panels missing (Oct. 1972)

FLORENNES. Belgian A.F. base. *Spitfire FRXIV* SG-57 ex RM921 "RL-D". Ex 2 Sqdn, 414 Sqdn RAF. *Miles Gemini 1A* OO-RLD c/n 6285 ex G-AISD, VP-KDH of Col. R. Lallemand DFC, who commanded 609 (W.R.) AAF Sqdn in WW.II.

GHENT. St. Denis Airport. North side Ghent-Brussels autoroute. *Miles Magister* OO-NIC c/n 1992 ex T9800, TMR-50, G.1; De Meulemeester. This is also quoted as ex-T9705? Motorized *Nord 1300* glider OO-39.

GOSSONCOURT. BAF Elementary Training School. Details wanted of *SV.4B* believed preserved here as tribute to "Mirror Aerobatic" team. On civil side are several vintage including *DH. Tiger Moth* OO-EVP c/n 86515 ex NM207, T.21; CNVAV.

GRIMBERGEN. Airfield. North of Brussels, near Vilvoorde. *Auster IV* OO-ISS c/n 891 ex MT165, G-AKYT, F-BECV: Laskiewicz. *Piper L-4H Cub* OO-ADJ c/n 12193

ex 44-79897; *OO-AGL* c/n 13211 ex 45-4471, PH-UCR; *OO-GEA* c/n 11768 ex 43-30477, HB-OGN; *OO-GEJ* c/n 12008 ex 44-79712. *L-4J* OO-ACB c/n 12468 ex 44-80172, OO-GEL, LX-ACL, LX-ACB; *OO-AED* c/n 12379 ex 44-80083, OO-LIL; *OO-AFI* c/n 12676 ex 44-80380, OO-GBA; *OO-RVA* c/n 12221 ex 44-79925, *OO-SOC* c/n 10418 ex 43-29127. Owned and flown by C. de Vleminck, Paulus, Limburgse Vleugels, Aeriennes Byl and Sabena.

KLEINE-BROGEL. BAF base. No 10 Fighter/Bomber Wing. *Republic F-84 Thunderjet* FS-2 coded "KB.1".

Hunter F.4 (Koksyde)

KOKSYDE. BAF Storage Base. On a pole at Military Hospital *Hawker Hunter F.4* (SABCA-Fairey built) ID-123 ex 7 Sqdn, 7 Wing. There are many post-war machines stored here for possible re-use or, one hopes, preservation in Belgium or elsewhere in Europe. Also

Douglas C-47 K-31 c/n 16064/32812 ex 44-74686, KN391, OT-CNR. *Piper L-4H* OO-RAZ c/n 11947 ex 44-79651 flies here; West Avn Club.

MAASTRIDIT. BAF. *Republic F-84F Thunderstreak* FU-108.

MAUBRAY. Airfield. *DH. Tiger Moth* OO-DLA c/n 85234 ex DE164, G-ANCY owned and flown by Delisse and Steyaert.

NAMUR. Airfield. *Piper L-4H* OO-CIN c/n 11818 ex 43-30527 HB-ODS, D-ECIN; J. Hollanders.

OSTEND. Airport. *Cessna UC-78* OO-TIN c/n 5253 ex HB-UEF 43-7733; R. Louage.

OVERBOELARE. Airfield. Many vintage machines flying here:—*Fairchild 24R-24/6A Argus* OO-EKE c/n 989 ex 43-15025 ex HB751 HB-AEC D-EKEQ; A. Coesens. *Stampe SV.4B* OO-LUK c/n 1183 ex V-71 RBAF; *OO-LYK* ex V-41; *OO-PAX* c/n 1147 ex V-5, BAF Gossoncourt. *Douglas DC-4 Skymaster* N90443 ex 42-72247 c/n 10352, American Airlines "Flagship Texas" then via Eastern Airlines to Aerovias Panama HP-298 in 1961. Impounded Basle 1962, illegally flown to Brussels as N2894C on 14th June 1963. Seized and eventually sold to M. Hanneschoert for 5,000 US dollars, to be used as restaurant. Left Melsbroek 5 July 1967 for new location, sometimes called Grammont.

TIENEN. Airstrip. *DH. Tiger Moth* OO-DPA c/n 85990, ex EM773, G-ANLD; owned by Le Milan Club.

SAFFRAENBERG. BAF. *Spitfire LFIX* SM-29 formerly MK912, B-1, H-59 "MN-P" (with the wings from SM-22).

VERVIERS. Airfield. *Piper L-4H Cub* OO-AJI c/n 11605 ex 43-30314; R. V. A. Verviers; also *Piper J-3C Cub* OO-VIL c/n 12005 ex 44-79709, OO-VVV.

WEVELGEM. Airfield. On the Courtrai-Muen road. *DH. Tiger Moth* OO-EVO c/n 86546 ex PG637, G-ANLH; CNVAV. What happened to Airspeed Oxford OO-DEC and OO-DUC?

ZELLICK. BAF Depot. *Hawker Hunter F.4* ID-26 at entrance. Said in store at Logistic Wing No 23:—*SV.4B* V-57.

ZWARTBERG (GENK) Airfield. *Stinson L-5B-VW Sentinel* OO-PBB c/n 76-3401 ex 44-17114, PH-PBB; Aeroplan. *Piper L-4H Cub* OO-RAM c/n 11990 ex 44-79694; Limburgse Vleugels. *Morane-Saulnier MS.732 Alcyon* OO-TYB c/n 1 ex F-WFDQ, the only one, now reported in local scrapyard—alas.

BULGARIA

SOFIA. Central Army Museum, 23 Boulevard Skobelev, open daily except Monday, 10 am to noon, 1.0 pm to 6.30 pm. Situated suburban south-central Sofia. *Tupolev Tu-2*, olive-green and blue, probably early post-war. *Yakovlev Yak-23*, Bulgaria's first jet, entered service 1953. (At entrance, unserialled). *Yakovlev Yak-3, Yakovlev Yak-9U. Ilyushin Il 2m3.* (Behind the museum. No serials visible). The Museum of Bulgarian-Soviet Friendship, 4

Boulevard Klement Gottwald, may be worth a visit as this is the Central Army Museum's annexe, and aircraft may go there.

VARNA. Naval Museum. *Arado Ar 196* of Bulgarian Naval Air Force.

Tupolev Tu-2 (Sofia)

Yak-23 (Sofia)

Yak-9U (Sofia)

Ilyushin Il-2m3 (Sofia)

Arado Ar 196 (Varna)

CZECHOSLOVAKIA

BRNO. Technical Museum. *MiG-15* (or S-102) 141194.

DUKLA. War Memorial. *Ilyushin Il-10* 5514, Czech A.F.

PRAGUE. Ruczyne Airport. Outside old terminal. *Li-2* OK-1962 ex 1801, Czech AF.

PRAGUE. Military Museum Kbely now open with:— *Super Aero 45* c/n 4911 OK-06 on one side, OK-DMO other. *Avia BH-11-C* c/n 18 L-BONK. *CS-199* serial 565 (2-seat Bf 109 built by Avia). *CS-104* (MiG-15) 722626. *C.104* (Bu Jungmann) A-27. *C-106* (Bu Bestmann) UA-264 c/n 64. *Ilyushin Il-10* 5502.B-33-502. *Ilyushin Il-2 M3* serial 38, USSR markings. *Lavochkin La-7* USSR markings 77. *K-65B (Storch)* 40-20, K65-475228. *Pou-du-Ciel* unmarked. *Zlin 26* UC-36 (C5-36). *HC-2 Helibaby* OK-09. *Spitfire IX* TE565 "NN-N" from RAF's Czech Fighter Wing. *Yakovlev Yak-11* (2nd generation Yak-9) 171727. *Yakovlev Yak-17* serial 30. *Yak-23* (S.101) 101101 "XH51". *BAK* 01. *VZ 10* (ToM-8) OK-08 28. *L-29 Delfin* 100010. *CZL L-60 Brigadyr* K160 c/n 150414, Czech A.F. *Praga E.114M* OK-BGL; *Mraz M-1C Sokol* OK-BHM c/n 127; *Yak 12R* OK-JEN c/n 14425: *CZL L-40 Meta-Sokol* OK-KHN c/n 150002: *L-60 Brigadyr* OK-KOS; *HC-2 Helibaby* OK-RVE and OK-RVY; *HC-3* OK O4; *Yak C-11* 1727 Czech A.F.; *CSS-13/PO-2* SP-BHA.
In the Prague Technical Museum are now displayed:— *Bleriot-type monoplane, Ing Kaspar*, Czech-built in 1910 No 65 with 65 hp Daimler Benz. *Anatra DS Anasalja* 11120 of 1917, 2-seat trainer wearing Czech post-WW.1 marks. *Avia BH-9* of 1924. *Avia 534*. *Avia BH-10* OK-AVO. *SPAD VII* serial 1918 (listed as XIII). *HC-2 Helibaby* OK-10. *Zlin 13* OK-TBZ. *Avia S 29* Me (262) the last Czech-built. *Kunkadio Monoplane* of 1925 L-BILG, homebuilt by Vaclov and Bohemel Simundk. *Knoller C.II* serial 119.15; Austro-Hungarian A.F. *Smolik SM.2* of 1921 with Mayback engine. *Sokol M.1C* OK-AHN c/n 118. *Thomas Morse L.W.F. Scout* 4 of 1917, USA markings. *Pou-du-Ciel* unmarked. It would appear that the machines missing from V. & V. 3rd edition are being restored, ie:—*Brandenburg D.1* floatplane fighter, 7139; *Omnipol Aero 145* OK-DMQ; *L-200 Morava* OK-MEE; *Mraz Cap* (Storch) OK-DPU; *Praga*

MiG-15 (Brno)

Spitfire IX (Prague)

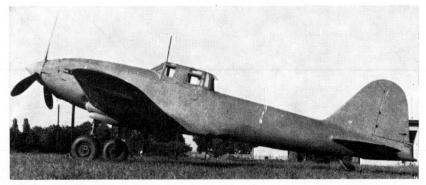

Ilyushin Il-10 (Dukla)

Lavochkin La-7 (Prague)

Avia S 29 (Prague)

Knoller C.II (Prague)

E-114 *Air Baby* OK-YIE; *PZL-11C* No 2 serial 883; *Zlin 26 Trener* OK-FRS c/n 611. *MiG-15* (*S102*) 225267. *Vetron Racek III* 1936 glider OK-8340. Can a reader kindly confirm whereabouts of non-exhibited aircraft and provide photos of the Military Museum a/c.

RUDNA. On the Prague-Pilzen road a *MiG-15 UTI* (CS 102) serial please.

STRIBO. On the Pilzen-Nuremburg road, *CS 102* (*MiG-15 UTI*) 722538—both aircraft in school yards.

VOIKOVICE. On the E.7 road from Poland, *MiG-15* serial 242508.

DENMARK

AALBORG. RDAF base. *Gloster Meteor F.8* RDAF 44-490 c/n G5/364 in children's playground. *Armstrong Whitworth Meteor NF.11* serial 504; *NA F-86D-21 Sabre* 51-8326 "F326" and *Republic F-84G-11-RE* 51-9996 "KR-A" reported displayed. Photos please.

ALLEROD. Airfield. *Auster J/1* OY-DPU c/n 2108; I/S. Midtjysk A.S.

BRODESKOV. Airfield. *Tiger Moth* OY-DGH c/n 85939 ex DF203, D-EDAS; Karsten Falkentoft.

COPENHAGEN. Royal Danish Arsenal Museum (Tojhusmuseet) Frederiksholms Kanal 29. *Berg & Storm B.S.III Monoplane* of 1910, used 1912 by newly-formed Danish Air Force as first machine. Engine 30 hp, speed 95 km.p.h. *Avro 504N* serial 110, c/n 49 of 1927, built

Avro 504N (Copenhagen)

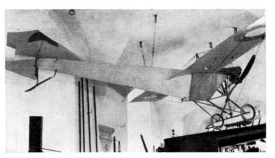

Berg and Storm Monoplane (Copenhagen)

Royal Dockyard, Copenhagen. Used by Navy until 1935 when 997 hours had been flown. *Hawker Dancock* Fighter serial 158, built 1927 at Royal Dockyard. Armstrong-Siddeley Jaguar 4 engine, speed 235 km.p.h. *Fieseler FZG-76 V1. Spitfire HFIXe* RDAF 41-401, ex NH417 of 127, 313 (Czech) 118, 441 (Can) and 329 (Free French) Sqdns is stored. *Gloster Meteor F.8* RDAF 461 also stored; in Ryvangen Barracks? *Republic F-84G Thunderjet* marked K-50 "SI-G 'Ludwig'" near main railway line—at Svanemollen Barracks?

At Copenhagen's Kastrup Airport is *Hunting Percival President* OY-AVA c/n 79 (for museum). Formerly prototype G-AOJG, to RDAF as 697. Flying from here are many vintage types:—*DH. Tiger Moth* OY-DET c/n 84589 ex T6122, G-ANTV, D-EKUR owned and flown by Kr. Loth Hougard & Ptnrs. *Douglas DC-3C* OY-DMN c/n 13637 ex 42-93697, SE-BBO. *Lockheed 12A* OY-AOT c/n 1285 ex Y-0233 G-AGDT, HM573, SE-BTO, LN-BDF. Both of Faroe Airways. *DC-3C* OY-DNP c/n 11638, ex 42-68711, LN-IAI, LN-IKI, SE-BSN; Danish Aero Lease. *Douglas C-54E* OY-DKG c/n 27336 ex 44-9110, NC90903, SX-DAC; Gronlandsfly A/S.

Ellehammer 1911 (Elsinore)

ELSINORE. Technical Museum. *Ellehammer 1906 biplane.* The first and oldest Danish aeroplane, flown by inventor-pilot J. C. H. Ellehammer 12 September 1906. *Ellehammer Standard Monoplane of 1909*, built of balloon linen and iron pipes, with folding wings. *Ellehammer 1911 helicopter* with 1904 engine. First flown 5 Sept. 1911. *Robert Svendsen "Glenten"* (The Kite) a Danish-built Henri Farman training aeroplane. Built

"Glenten" (Elsinore)

Hawker Dancock (Copenhagen)

1910/11 by Svendsen, first pilot to cross The Sound, used 1912 by Danish Naval Air Force as first machine, 80 km p.h. *Donnét Lévèque "Maagen 2"* (The Gull) flying boat biplane bought from France 1913 for Danish Naval Air Force with another of same type, "Ternen" (The Tern). In 1914 "Ternen" rebuilt and renamed "Maagen 2". Speed 135 km p.h. Reported "Maagen 2" is at present fitted with a replica of the hull of "Maagen 3" to make it look like the Danish-designed F.B.II of the Naval Dockyard. It is planned later to build wings for the replica hull so that the museum will then have both "Maagen 2" and a *replica* "Maagen 3." (Thanks to Hans Kofoed for this data.) *Polyt II glider* OY-65 and *Lars Larsen 1925 glider* also here.

"Maagen 2" (Elsinore)

FREDENSBORG. Airfield. *Piper L-4H Cub* OY-AFG c/n 10858 ex 43-29567, LN-MAP, SE-CEW; F-Bohnstedt-Petersen Ptnr.

FREDERICIA, Airfield. *Piper L-4H* OY-TRP c/n 11964 ex 44-79668, OO-MCG; H. Jensen.

FUENEN. Kvaerndrup. Egeskov Veteranmuseum. Verify times with Hans Kofoed, P.O. Box 20, DK-2740 Skovlunde, sending International Reply-Paid Coupon— or check in Denmark with Tourist Office, Copenhagen or main cities. On display, 1973:—*GAL Monospar ST.25* OY-DAZ c/n 95 ex G-AEYF, used as air ambulance from 1939. *Fairchild PT-26 Cornell* serial 253 ex R Nor AF. *DH. Tiger Moth* OY-BAK c/n 86356 ex NL913, G-AOFR, SE-COX but painted S-11 of Danish Air Force. *Lockheed 12A* ex R. Neth A.F. serial L2-38, was OY-AOV c/n

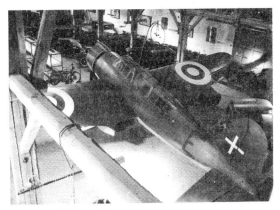

SAAB B17A (Fuenen)

1306, SE-BXR. OH-ETA, LN-BFS. *N.A. Harvard IIB* serial 324, RDAF. *Hollaender A.H.I.* OY-ADO; home built single-seater of 1957. *KZ II Sport* OY-DOU c/n 13. *SAAB J29F* serial 29487 ex F.3 Wing RSwedAF code 07. *SAAB 17* (B17A) serial 17320, painted as aircraft of Danish Brigade in Sweden 1945, codeletter E. Nose-section of Douglas DC-7 OY-KND also displayed. Presently in storage awaiting exhibition-space:— *DH89 Dragon Rapide* OY-AAO c/n 6775 ex NR676, G-AIWY. *Fairchild Argus II* OY-EAZ c/n 962 ex 43-14998, HB724, SE-CPA. *Klemm Kl 35* SE-AKN; c/n 1873 *KZ III* SE-ANY c/n 45, second prototype; and *KZ VII* OY-SAI c/n 135 (for restoration) *Percival Proctor III* OY-ACP c/n H274 ex HM364, RDAF 605;. *Hans Lund HL-1* home built. *Miles Gemini 1A* G-AJWA c/n 6290. *Moelhede Pedersen XMP-2* home-built autogyro. *Republic F-84G Thunderjet* 51-9792 RDAF KP-K (tail of 51-1094.) Many gliders including:—*DFS Weihe* OY-VOX. former holder of World Altitude Sailplane record. *SG 38* OY-86. *Grunau Baby IIB* OY-AHX. *Hogslund-Olsen 2G* OY-ATX. *Polyt II* OY-98. *Hutter 17* OY-AXH. *Focke Achegelis Fa 330. Ellehammer 1906 biplane* (replica). A fascinating collection which all visitors to Denmark should see.

GREVE STRAND. Airfield. *Tiger Moth* OY-DNR c/n 82104 ex N6849, G-AHRV; Tiger Group.

HADERSLEV. Playground. *Republic F-84G-16-RE* 51-10598 A-598 of 725 Sqdn, RDAF.

HELLEBAEK. In Forest. *NA Harvard IIB* RDAF 31-306 formerly RAF FH114.

HERNING. In Park. *Republic F-84G-16-RE*, with nose of 51-9844 and fuselage of 51-10660. *J. C. H. Ellehammer*

Standard monoplane of 1909 (replica) is owned here by M. Dyhr-Thomsen.

Ellehammer 1909—replica (Herning)

KARUP. RDAF base. *Gloster Meteor F.8* RDAF 44-491. *Republic F-84G-16-RE* RDAF A-477 "SI-L" ex 51-10477.

MOGELGAARD. Jutland. Chr Nielsen has, as coffee-bar *Douglas DC-6A* OY-BAS c/n 43837 ex N568, XA-KIR, formerly of Sterling Airways A/S.

RIBE. Playground. *Republic F-84G-11-RE* 51-10124 from 725 Sqdn. RDAF.

SKRYDSRTUP. RDAF base. *Gloster Meteor F.4* RDAF 469, c/n G/5/302. *Republic F-84G-16-RE RDAF* A-603 "SY-C" ex 51-10603

SONDERBORG. Airfield. *Bf 108* OY-AIH c/n 1561 ex F-BBRH; H. Poulsen.

SUNDBY. Airfield. *Tiger Moth* OY-DYJ c/n 85223 ex DE153, D-EDOM; C. R. Kristensen & Ptnr.

TIM. Airstrip. *Tiger Moth* OY-DGJ c/n 82981 ex R5086 G-APIH, D-EMEX; Tim Flyvreklub.

VAERLOSE. RDAF. *Republic F-84G* 51-10731 of RDAF. *Armstrong Whitworth Meteor TT20* (ex NF11) RDAF H-517, ex WM400, SE-DCG and *RDAF H-519* ex WM 402, SE-DCI.

VOJENS. Playground. *Republic F-84G-16-RE* RDAF A598 of 725 Sqdn, formerly 51-10525

FINLAND

HALLI (Kuorevesi) Air Force Base. *DH. Vampire FB.52* VA-2, believed VO692, delivered 1955/6, one of first 9 jets in Finland, retired 16 July 1965. Displayed outdoors.

Vampire FB.52 (Halli)

SM-1Z (Mi-1) serial HK-1, outside museum building. *Vihuri 2* VH-18. *IVL. C.24* coded 8F.4. *IVL. D.27 Haukka 2* HA-41 of 1928. *Bristol Bulldog IVA* BU-59 c/n 7810—Winter War survivor *VL Sääki II* LK1, 2-seat trainer biplane of 1929 in Finnish Customs colours. *Caudron G.III* 1E.18, forward fuselage, *plus one other* "Bathtub" unmarked. These seven a/c stored in hangar pending restoration. *Focke-Wulf Fw.44J* SZ-4 in flying condition. *Douglas C-47* DO-5 fuselage.

Bristol Bulldog IVA (Halli)

HAMEENLINNA. Lakeside Square. Used as Coffee Bar. *Douglas DC-2* DO-1 "Hanssin Jukka" c/n 1354 ex KLM's "Haan" PH-AKH; SE-AKE; then Finnish Air

Douglas DC-2 (Hameenlinna)

Douglas DC-2 (Hameenlinna)

Force DC-1 used as bomber in Winter War. Then Marshal Mannerheim's aircraft. Post-War mapping-ambulance. Last flight 29.5.55. Now raising funds for juvenile delinquency work.

HELSINKI. Seutula Airport. *Folland Gnat F.1* GN-106 ex HävLv 21 (displayed.) *Junkers A.50 Junior* OH-ABB "Junnu" world's first all-metal aircraft 1931, flown by Major Bremer on expeditions, including round-world Owned by Finnish Aeronautical Assn but reported for sale, 1972. Formerly D-1915, c/n 3530. *Lockheed Lodestar* OH-VKU c/n 2006 ex F-ARTF, of KAR-AIR Oy. *Piper L-4H* OH-CHP c/n 12043 ex 44-79747 SE-ATG; O. Riekka Ptnr. *DH. Vampire T.55* VT-9. *Pyry II* PY-27 (fuselage for rebuild) *Sääski II* SA-131 (fuselage for restoration). *Thulin Parasol F.4* in store (fuselage). *Airspeed Oxford*—confirmation? *Hansa-Brandenburg* 11-120/A.22 said being rebuilt by Finnair? *Douglas DC-2* DO-3 c/n 1562 ex OK-AIC, D-AAIC, OH-DLB, OH-LDB, said to be near city—confirmation, photos and details of future, please. *DH.60X* OH-ILD *Moth* c/n 8 built by Veljekset Karhumaki, ex K-SILD being restored—details/photo wanted. *LaGG-3* rear fuselage & wings stored—for restoration?

IITTI. Store. *DH.60X Moth* OH-EJA ex OH-MAH, c/n quoted as 1029.

ILMAJOKI. Airstrip. *Fw. 44J* OH-SZI c/n 2773 ex SZ-20; A. Manninen.

Gourdou-Leseurre B.3 (Jyvaskyla)

Lockheed Lodestar (Helsinki)

Dakota (Jyvaskyla)

Gourdou-Leseurre B.3 (Jyvaskyla)

JYVÄSKYLÄ (Luonetjärvi) Air Base. *Bristol Blenheim IV* BL-200 c/n 7810 with "Bull" emblem of Lt-Gen. R. Artola first of 17 delivered Jan. 1935, preserved opposite the Finnish Air Force Memorial. *Gnat F.1* GN-107 on pole. *Martinsyde F.4 Buzzard* MA-24 ex D4326. *Vampire T.55* VT-8. *Gourdou-Leseurre B.3* GL-12 ex 8F.12 now restored. *Dakota* DO 12 airworthy.

KAJAANI. Airfield. *DFS Kranich* glider OH-KAA.

KARHULA. Airfield. *Taylorcraft Plus D.* OH-AUH c/n 184 ex LB325, G-AHXF; K. S. I. Kannatusyhsistys.

KARSTULA. Airfield. *Fairchild F.24R4-6A* OH-FCF c/n 959 ex 43-14995, HB721, LN-HAM; Tauno Huhtanen.

KAUHAVA. Air Force Base. *Rumpler 6B* 5A1—for rebuild.

KOKKOLA. Airfield. *Auster 6A* OH-AUK c/n 3731 ex TW577: Kokkolan Ilmailukerho.

KUUSA. Airfield. *Viima II* OH-VII ex VI-16: H. Korhonen.

KYMI. Airfield. *Harakka* glider H-12 stored.

LAPPEENRANTA. Airfield. *Auster IV* OH-AUF c/n 856 ex MT100, G-AKRC; Lappeenrannan Ismailuyhdistys.

MANUKONE. Airfield. *Klemm L 25D* OH-ILI c/n 1129; P. Terho.

MIKKELI. Airfield. *Klemm L 25A* OH-KLA c/n 137 ex OH-ABA, K-SABA; Korsimann & Kumpp.

DH.60X Moth (Tampere)

NAARAJARVI. Airfield. Gliding Club has *DFS. Weihe* OH-WAB; *PIK-5A* OH-PAK; *Sisilisko* OH-SAB c/n 1.

NUMMELA. Airfield, *Salamandra* glider OH-SAA.

OTANIEMI (near Helsinki) Technical High School Museum. *Folland Gnat. F.1* GN-105. *PIK-11* "Tumppa" OH-YMA c/n 1.

OULU. Airfield. *Fairchild F24R* OH-FCH c/n 869 ex 43-14905, HB632, G-AJBF; Oulun Laskuvarjokerho ry.

PIEKSAMAKI. Airfield. *Piper L-4H* OH-CPC c/n 12109 ex 44-79813, G-AJBE, NC6400N, G-AKNC; Moottorimatkailu ry.

Bristol Blenheim IV (Jyvaskyla)

PORI. Air Base. *DH. Vampire FB.52* VA-6 (V0696) flown Finland 15 September 1953 by Pat Fillingham it was FAF's last serviceable single-seater. Flown 965 hrs, 1,614 landings. Powered by Goblin 35 serial 8994. *Viima II* OH-VIH ex VI-12; J. Forsman Ptnr (flying).

RAYSKALA. Airfield. *Fieseler Storch* OH-FSA c/n 2430 ex ST-112, OH-VSF.

RISSALA. Air Force Base. *Avro 504K* AV-57 ex E448, G-EBNU, restored.

SALO. Airfield. *Fw.44J* OH-SZE c/n 2891 ex SZ-2; E Lehtiniitty.

TAMPERE. Technical Museum. *SM-1Z (M1-1)* HK-2. *IVL.A.22 Hansa* IL-2 c/n 2 ex 4D.2. *Valmet Pyorremyrrky Pyry I* PY-1. *Saaski II. DH.60X Moth* OH-ILA c/n 447 ex K-SILA—the machine which made the Finnish people air-minded when flown to Helsinki by Captain Hubert S. Broad in October 1927. It was bought by the Air Defense League of Finland and used for 10 years for intense propaganda work all over the country. *Taivaan Kirppu* (Flying Flea) OH-KAA c/n 1/35. *Fokker D.10* FO-42 (fuselage frame only). For rebuild? At TAMPERE Airport, stored, are the following:—*Bell P-39Q-15-BE Airacobra* 44-2664; Soviet Air Force Nr 26. *DH. Vampire T.55* VT-6 (forward fuselage only). *Focke-Wulf Fw.44J* SZ-25. *VL. HM-671 Humu I* c/n 632567 (Russian M-63 engine) *Pyorremyrsky I* PM-1. *Pyry II* PY-35. *VL.Tuisku* TU-178. *VL Viima I* VI-1. first prototype, open cockpit.

TURKU. Airfield. *Klemm L 25D* OH-ILL c/n 1230 (rebuild?).

UTTI. Air Force Base. *Messerschmitt Bf 109 G-6* MT-452 (from Santa Hamina) *Bf 109 G-6* MT-507 Werk-Nr 165227, restored to flying condition at Rissala.

Bf 109 G-6 MT-507 (Utti)

Bf 109 G-6 (Utti)

VAASA. Airfield. *Fairchild F.24W-41A* OH-FCK c/n 287 ex 41-38843, EV779, G-AKIZ; Vaasan Laskuvarjokerho ry.

VANTAA. Airfield. *Focke-Wulf Fw.44J* OH-SZF c/n 2782 ex SZ-15: T. Heininen.

VARKHAUS. Airfield. *Fairchild F.24R-Argus 3* OH-FCT c/n 977 ex 43-15013, HB739, SE-BCH, OH-FCD, SE-EGG; Timi Varkauden Lento.

VESIVEHMAA. Air Force Base. Museum store hangar. *Adaridi* monoplane of 1924. *Breguet 14A-2* 3C30. *Aero A.11* AE-47, Hispano engine. *Aero A.32* AEj-59 with Jupiter 420 hp. *Caudron C.59* CA-50. *Caudron C.60* unserialled. *Caudron C.714* CA-556 c/n 8538 coded "6". *Blackburn Ripon II* RI-140 (with engine). *Fokker C.V* FO-75 (fuselage). *Fw.44J* SZ-23 fuselage. *Gloster Gamecock* (fuselage frame). *Hawker Hurricane IIC* HC-452. *I-16UTI* UT-1. *IVL D.26 Haukka I* HA-39. *IVL Kurki*, 4-seat transport mono. *IVL Kotaka II* Sea-Recce and Day Bomber, KA-147. *Morane-Saulnier MS.50C* MS-52. *Karhu 48B* OH-KUA c/n 6 ex OH-VKL. *Harakka* glider H-5. *Kassel 12A* glider "13". All aircraft except Ripon are engineless—engines sold for scrap.

VILPPULA. Army Depot. *Polikarpov PO-2*, captured Suulajärvi, 1943.

VIMPELI. Airfield. *Piper L-4J* OH-CPA c/n 12471 ex 44-80175, SE-ATF; E. Vesala.

FRANCE

ABBEVILLE. Airfield. *Dassault Ouragan* No 215 on gate. *Potez 60/48* F-PFOD c/n 01 and dismantled *Caudron* (details please).

Ouragan (Abbeville)

AIRAINNES. Garage. *Boisavia Mercurey* F-BHTL c/n 21. *Miles Hawk Tr 3* F-BDPD c/n 1778 ex P6423 has now been completely destroyed.

Hurricane IIC (Vesivehama)

Blackburn Ripon II (Vesivehama)

AIX-LES-MILLIES. Airfield. *Dassault MD 312 Flamant* No 281 coded "316-KK" on pole outside clubhouse.

AMBOISE-DIERRE. Airfield. *Dassault Ouragan* No 308. *Dassault 311 Flamant* No 271.

ANGOULEME. Airfield. *Percival Proctor IV* F-BBTL c/n H.738 ex NP367 at gate.

ARRAS. On N39 (near city) *Nord Norecrin* F-BEUE, c/n 166.

AUCH. Airfield. *Potez 600* F-PNUX, c/n 3873 ex F-ANUX

AUXERRE-MONTENAU. Airfield. S.N.C.A.S.E. *SE 535 Mistral* (French built DH. Vampire) No 50 at gate. *DH. Hornet Moth* F-AQBY c/n 8038 ex HB-OBE.

AVIGNON. Caumont Airfield. *Abraham 2* F-PBFV c/n 01.

BERCK. Playground. *Lockheed L1049G Constellation* F-BGNF c/n 4515 ex Air France.

Constellation (Berck)

BESANCON. Airfield. *Caudron 510 Pelican* F-BDXK c/n P2.

BEYNES. Airfield. *Govier* glider F-CRAY.

BLOIS-LE-BREUIL. Airfield. *Dassault Ouragan* serial 165. *Douglas RB-26 Invader* 44-39162 in markings of C.E.A.M. (Centre d'Essai Aérien Militaire). The equivalent of A.&.A.E.E., Boscombe Down, England.

BORDEAUX. Merignan Base. S.N.C.A.S.E. *SE.2010 Armagnac* F-BAVI c/n 8, for inspection. A large four-engined airliner seating up to 160 passengers, type first flown April 1949. Nine built (F-BAVA-BAVI) and although built for Air France were used by S.A.G.E.T.A. on runs from France to Indo-China during Viet-Minh war. At Yvrac Airport. *Dassault MD 450 Ouragan* No 153. *Caudron C.601 Aiglon* F-BFLB c/n 18 ex F-ANXX.

CAEN. Carpiquet Airport. *Dassault MD 312 Flamant* No 161. *SFCA Taupin* F-PMEM c/n 10, also known as Lignel 44. *Dassault 452 Mystère IIC* No 52 coded "10-LF".

CAMPO D'EL ORO. Airfield. *Morane-Saulnier MS. 500* No 820.

CANNES. Airport. *Auster V* 3A-MAC c/n 1551 ex F-BGXQ of Monaco Aero Club.

CASTELNAUDRY. Airfield. *Bücker 133C Jungmeister* F-BBRI c/n 1. *Caudron C.272 Luciole* in nearby amusement park and *Lockheed 1049G Super Constellation*

F-BHBA c/n 4620 ex Air France in Parque de Madame du Bois.

CHAMBERY. Airfield. *Dassault Mystère IIC* No 147 coded "5-OR" *Dassault Ouragan* No 120 coded "2".

CHARTRES. Airfield. *Morane-Saulnier MS. 502 Criquet* F-BDQS c/n 695 used for glider-towing.

CHATEAUDUN. Air Base *F-84F* 29061.

CHAVENEY. Villepreux CIC de Lognes. *Morane-Saulnier MS. 315* F-BGFR c/n 301.

Morane-Saulnier MS.315 (Chaveney)

CHENNEYIERS. Scrapyard. *Morane-Saulnier MS.* 571 F-BEJT c/n 676. *Nord 1203 Norécrin* F-BBKN c/n 74 and F-BEMQ c/n 98—were displayed. Confirmation and photos please to enable preservation action.

CLERMONT-AULNAT. Airfield. *Dassault Mystère IVN* prototype 2-seat all-weather fighter, first flown 19 July 1954, equipped with radar nose and 128 rocket capacity. Details of status and photo please.

COGNAC. Air Base. *NA T-6G Texan* 114522 "31" displayed.

COLMAR. Meyenheim. *NA F-86K Sabre* 54641 exhibited.

COMPIEGNE. Margny Airport. *Bücker Jungmeister* F-BLGM c/n 39 ex U-92, HB-MIB. *Schulgleiter SG.38* No 159.

COUCHEY. Nr Dijon. *Lockheed Constellation* F-BAZP c/n 2550 ex S.A.R. L-23 "Chateau le Francozae" as Bar.

COULOMMIERS. Airfield. *Zlin 12* F-AQDS c/n 164.

CREIL. Airfield. *Boeing B-17G* aircraft of Institut Geographique Nationale—airworthy:—F-BDRS c/n 32376 ex 44-83735; *F-BEEC* c/n 8627 ex 44-85718; *F-BEEA* c/n 8552 ex 44-85643; *F-BGSP* c/n 8246 ex 44-8846; *F-BGSO* c/n 8289 ex 44-8889A; *F-BGSQ* c/n 8503 ex 44-85594A. Also *F-BGOE* c/n 32369 ex 44-83728, static. *F-BGSH* c/n 7190 ex 42-32076, SE-BAP, OY-DFA, RDAF 672; now fuselage only. *Hurel Dubois HD-34* F-BHOO c/n 01; *F-BHOP* c/n 02; *F-BICQ* c/n 3; *F-BICR* c/n 4, *F-BICT* c/n 6; *F-BICU* c/n 7; *F-BICV* c/n 8. *Percival Proctor V* F-BESV c/n Ae 65 ex SU-ACH, G-AKPB, SU-AFG. Let us hope some of these a/c will be preserved, in France or elsewhere!!

Boeing B-17G (Creil)

CUERS-PIRREFEU. Airfield. *Vought F4U Corsair* serials 363, 376, 378, 393, 417, 670, 690, 696, were here—up-dated information wanted. Surely some can be preserved in Europe?

DIEPPE. Airport. *Bristol 170 Mk 32 Superfreighter* F-BLHH c/n 13132 ex G-ANWH of Silver City, ex C.A.T. as Bar-Clubhouse.

DINARD. Airport. *Avro Triplane IV* (replica) from "Magnificent Men" film. *Douglas Dakota 3* F-BNPT c/n 25459 ex 43-48208 KG792, G-ALBG, Marshal of the RAF Sir Arthur "Bomber" Harris's wartime machine—this ought to be preserved—preferably in England.

DIORS. Musée des Trois Guerres. Nr Chateauroux. *Heinkel He 46*, captured by Marquis at La Martinerie, 20 August 1944 after demolition charge failed to explode. Complete even to rear flexible gun—would value report on condition, with photo.

DONCOURT. Airfield. *Potez 600* F-PIHA c/n 3945, ex F-AOBD.

DREUX. Vernouillet Airfield. *Percival Proctor IV* F-BDJN c/n H781 ex RM178 was static here—report and photo wanted.

ETAMPES-MONDÉSIR. Airfield. *Dewoitine 520 DC* (two-seat conversion) details and pic please. In a hangar on Etampes Air Force Base Jean Salis and others have in store:—*DH.89A Dragon Rapide* F-BGON c/n 6541 ex X7381, G-ALZF; F-BHGR c/n 6844 ex NR756, G-AOAO. *Sipa 121* F-BLKH. *NA.T-6* F-BMJP. *DH. Tiger Moth* F-BGEE, c/n 86618 ex PG732. *S.V.4*—two examples—details please. *Morane-Saulnier MS. 341* F-ANVS c/n 4234/3—all above airworthy.

EVREUX. Airfield. *Breguet 765 Sahara* No 4.

FAYENCE. Gliding Centre. *Morane-Saulnier MS. 502* F-BAOU, c/n 149 and F-BAYN, c/n 2005. *Nord 1002* F-BAUZ, c/n 246. *Sipa 1000 Coccinelle* F-BHHL, c/n 01 ex F-WHHL.

FLERS. Airfield. *Dassault MD315R Flamant* No 51.

FONTENAY-TRESIGNY. Airfield Restaurant. *Breguet 763 Deux-Ponts* F-BASV ex Air France, c/n 9.

GRANVILLE. Airfield. *SFCA Taupin* coded 82-PP.

GUISCRIFF. Airfield. *Dassault MD315 Flamant* No 43.

GUYANCOURT. Airfield. *Nord 1203* F-BEBI c/n 39; *Starck AS70* F-PBGS c/n 12. *Ambrosini F4 Rondone* F-BGTU c/n 019.

HESDIN ST. POL. Roadside. *Percival Proctor V* F-BFVP c/n Ae 138 ex G-AMKM on display—report on condition wanted.

HOURTIN. Naval Air Base. *Sud Aquilon* 59-S-8 French-built version of DH. Sea Venom F.20.

ISSOURIS. *Morane-Saulnier MS. 502* F-BAYE c/n 752 displayed.

ISTRES. Scrapyard. *Nord NC 856 Norvigie* Nos 50, 92 "YI" and 106, available for preservationists.

LA BAULE. *Short Sunderland III* ML796 (50-S-3) ex Flotille 27F Dakar 1951; Escadrille Lanveoc Pulmic 1960. Over 2,400 hrs flown. Moved from Moisdon-le-Riviere Hydrobase. Static as attraction.

LA FERTÉ ALAIS. Jean Salis and others have here:—*Avion Bugatti* (from museum at Croisie). *Breguet 763 Deux-Ponts* F-BASO. c/n 4. *Brochet MB 80* F-BGLD, c/n 4, F-BGLJ c/n 10. *Bücker Bü 131 Jungmann* F-BOMF. *Bu 133C* F-BOHK. *Caudron 69* F-AFHH. *Caudron C.275 Luciole* F-ALLL c/n 1, F-PJKE c/n 7153/16 ex F-AOBS *Caudron C.282/9 Phalene* F-AMGJ c/n 6720/5. *Caudron 710 Rafale Caudron C.800 glider* F-CAZX. *de Havilland DH.94 Moth Minor* F-BAOG c/n 94038 ex G-AFNJ. *DH. Tiger Moth* F-BGFA c/n 86347 ex NL904; F-BFVU c/n 86603 ex PG706; F-BGDH c/n 86556 ex PG647; F-BGDM c/n 86565 ex PG 656. *Dewoitine 514*—serial? *Fairchild Argus* F-BEXY c/n 1070 ex 44-83109, KK452; F-BEXC c/n 998 ex 44-83087, KK380; F-BEXX c/n 926 ex 43-14962, HB688. *Fouga CM 8/15* F-CABN. *Mignet HM.8*—no identity known. *Miles M.14 Hawk Trainer* HB-EEB c/n 431 ex L5999. *Morane-Saulnier "A"* remains. MS27 or MS29. *Morane-Saulnier MS.181* F-AJRQ c/n 01; F-PALY c/n SM.I ex F-BALY, plus one other. *Morane-Saulnier MS.315* F-BCNT c/n 350. *MS.?* F-AQDN. *MS.130 Morane-Saulnier MS.502 Criquet* F-BAYN c/n 2005, F-BBUS c/n 320, F-BBUG c/n 226. *Morane-Saulnier MS.500* F-BJQA c/n 41. *Mauboussin M127* F-PBTB c/n 92. *NA.T-6* F-BMJO. *Nord 1002* F-BAUF c/n 173. *Potez 600* F-AOSE c/n 4184. *Sipa-Arado*

Caudron G.3—replica (La Ferte Alais)

Bleriot XI F-PERV (La Ferte Alais)

121 No 57, F-BLKH. *Salmson D.7* F-BFNG c/n 9 *Stampe SV4c* F-BDEO c/n 594; F-BCFM c/n 254; F-BAGZ c/n 1117; F-BCLD c/n 304; F-BCLB; c/n 302; F-BASM c/n 1100; F-BCLN c/n 314. *SFAN.2* F-WBTE (license-built BAC Drone). Flying replicas *Bleriot XI* F-PERV; *Caudron G.3* F-PSYL, ex F-WSYL. Non-fliers include *Wright Baby, Demoiselle, Avro Triplane, Antoinette*. The Caudron F-PSYL is often flown by stunt-pilot for films Gerard Streiff, and may be seen at various airfields. The Bleriot XI F-PERV "Jean Baptiste Salis", flown by Nicole Perceval is said to have original parts and was previously F-WERV which the late Jean Salis, father of the present owner, flew to Lydd to mark the 50th anniversary of the Bleriot Channel crossing of 1909. There are many rotary engines, propellers etc, and many of the a/c may be dismantled and under restoration so please do not visit without first making an appointment with Jean Salis.

LA PAGNE. Airfield. *Nord 1002* F-BFUY.

LA ROCHE-BERNARD. *Super Constellation* F-BHBG c/n 4626 as Bar.

LE CASTELLET. Airfield. *Fouga Magister* No 491 "Patrouille de France" markings.

LES MUREAUX. Air Base. *Dassault Ouragan* No 294 displayed. Many *NC-701 Martinet* aircraft in store here, (licence-built Siebel Si204D).

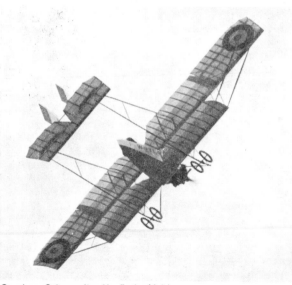

Caudron G.3—replica (La Ferte Alais)

LEZIGNAN. Airfield. *Salmson CFA Phrygane* F-PJXQ.

LIMOGES. Castle battlement in town centre. *Reggiane Re 2000 "Ariete"* fighter. One of 60 delivered to Luftwaffe 1944; 25 actually flown, the others destroyed by

Reggiane Re 2000 (Limoges)

Nazis at Caproni works, Taliedo, April 1945. Several used against French partisans in Limoges area and this example was shot down by partisans and erected as monument. It was the last remaining machine of the 60. Development of the Re 2000 with more-powerful Piaggio P.XIX RC.45 engine.

LISSEN. On N.6 highway. *Stampe SV.4*c F-BCOK c/n 374 in yard—available for preservation?

LONS-LE-SAULNIER. Caserne Bouffez. *Sikorsky H-19.*

LORIENT. Airfield. *Sud Aquilon* No 203, coded "160F-16" and "53"; Aeronavale. *NA SNJ-5* No 981; Aeronavale.

LUXEIL-LES-BAINS. On N.64 in "Mougens" furniture showroom. *T-6 Texan* 51-15012.

MILLAU LARZAC. Airfield. At the hotel. *Nord 1002* No 44 is displayed.

MIRANDE. Airfield. *Nord 1002* F-BBBZ c/n 127.

Consolidated Catalina (Nice)

MITRY-MORY. Airfield. *Bücker Bestmann* F-BCSB c/n 127 and F-BGMX c/n 107, ex F-BCRG.

MONTARGIS-VIMORY. Airfield. *Morane-Saulnier MS.181* F-AJQK c/n 3. *Caudron C.277 Luciole* F-ALUR c/n 6.

MONTBAZIN. Sorigny. *Ouragan* No 214.

MONTPELIER L'OR. Airfield. *Caudron C.272 Luciole* c/n 6730, static—no regn.

MONT-DE-MAISON. Air Base. *Republic F-84F* 28882 "14".

MONTIGNY-LE-BRETONEUX. Airfield. *Nord 1101* F-BAUC c/n 158 by roadside.

MORMANT. Near Rly Station. *SO-95 Corse*; *SO-7010 Pegase* F-WEAG.

MURET. Airfield. *Mauboussin 202* F-BAOI c/n 01; record-breaker.

NANCY-ESSAY. *Dassault 311 Flamant* No 261.

NANTES. Airfield. *Potez 585* F-PNDG c/n 3608 ex F-ANDG.

NICE. Airfield. *Lockheed 12A* F-BFUD c/n 1277 ex 42-38349, LA621, G-AGVZ, N79820; *F-BHVT* c/n 1211 ex NC17311, 42-38352, LA620, G-AGWM, OO-AFA; *F-BJJY* c/n 1287 ex NC33615, BuAer 02947, G-AGTL (formerly F. S. Cotton's "Caprice". Mr. Cotton made history just before World War II when he took photos of the German Fleet from a similar aircraft; this led to his forming the Photographic Recce Units of the RAF). *Vickers Viking* F-BJRS c/n 264 ex G-AKBH (still here?) *Consolidated PBY-5A Catalina* F-ZBAQ of Protection Civile—(details of earlier history please).

NIMES. Courbessac Airport. *Dassault Mystere IIC* No 143 "5-DP" *Dassault Ouragan* No 232 "TP". *Republic F-84E* 9600. *Morane-Saulnier MS. 502* F-BJHV c/n 617. *Dassault Ouragan* No 231 here as instructional airframe. At Nimes Garon is believed to be *DH. Rapide* F-BGDB (?)—details please.

NOGARO. Airfield. *Caudron C.600 Aiglon* F-PNZE c/n 64/7119 ex F-ANZE.

ORLEANS. Saran. *Dassault MD312 Flamant* No 269 "316-KD" ex Navigation Training Display.

Lockheed 12A (Nice)

THE Bleriot (Paris)

PARIS. Conservatoire National de Arts et Metiers, 292 Rue St. Martin, Paris 3. THE *Bleriot*—flown from Barraques to Dover on 25th July, 1909, to make aviation history in Europe (see the Bleriot in stone-outline in the grounds of Dover Castle). *Ader Avion III* (and the 30 hp steam engine from the Avion II). *REP of 1906* (Robert Esnault-Pelterie). *Breguet Type R.U1* No 40 of 1911. Also scale-models of the Deperdussin on which Vedrines broke the world-speed record in 1911, and of a Vuitton helicopter, plus four others. Also a non-man-carrying 1905 Dufaux replica of 5-foot length.

PARIS. Les Invalides. (See SALON for SPAD VII). It may be that the *Nieuport XVII* (is this Nungesser's No 880) is stored somewhere here but, alas, we now know that the missing Lysander "Lise" presented by the RAF to honour SOE (Special Operations Executive) *WAS* scrapped by the French.

PARIS. Musée de l'Air, (in park of the O.N.E.R.A.) 8 Rue des Vertugadins, in CHALAIS MEUDON (Hauts-de-Seine). Open weekdays 0800-1700; Saturdays, Sundays, Public Holidays 1000-noon and 1400-1800 (1700 winter). Entrance free. Access by bus 136 from Porte St. Cloud to Vertugadins. By rail (line Invalides-Versailles) to Meudon Val-Fluery. Private car parking indicated by arrows from Meudon. Guided visits for groups ring 227-07-35. For the benefit of intending visitors aircraft are listed in the order of the official catalogue except that those in reserve (stored) will be shown at the end with details of impending arrivals. In sequence:—1879 *Biot* glider. 1895 *Lilienthal* (said to be 1928 replica). 1896 *Chanute* glider. 1906 *Vuia* Franco-

Rumanian "Bat monoplane". 1907 *Voisin biplane* No 1 bis—replica with original parts. 1908 *Santos-Dumont Demoiselle*. 1909 *Levavasseur Antoinette*. 1910 *Henri Fabre Hydravion*—first successful seaplane. 1910 *Nieuport 2 N-28CV* racing monoplane. 1910 *Wright Baby racing seaplane*, built by Soc. Ariel. 1911 *Maurice Farman Longhorn* No 446 coded "15" used by King Albert and Belgian Army. 1912 *Donnet-Leveque Type A*, flying-boat biplane. 1912 *Henri Farman F.20 Shorthorn*. 1913 *Bleriot XI-2* 2-seat military version, No 686. Wings marked "Pegoud". 1913 *Morane-Saulnier type G*—first a/c to cross Mediterranean. 1913 *Caudron G.III Type XII C.324*. 1913 *Deperdussin Monocoque* No 334—attained 127.7 mph. In Gordon Bennet Race, flown by Maurice Prevost. 1913 *R.E.P. Type K*—first Turkish military aircraft. 1914 *Voisin LA 5 B 2* bomber-ground attack. Marked Voi 5B[2]. 1915 *Nieuport XI* N976. 1915 *Caudron G.4* C.1720. 1917 *SPAD S.XIII C.1* serial S.15295. 1917 *Fokker D.VII (Alb)* 6796/18 licence-built by Albatros. 1917 *Breguet XIV A 2* No 2016, photo-recce a/c. 1918 *Pfalz D XII*. 1918 *Packard Lepere C II*, SC.42133, USA Signal Corps. 1918 *de Havilland DH.9* F1258 marked "A Battery 2nd Siege Artillery Reserve Brigade". 1918 *Nieuport-Delage 29 C.1* No 010; world altitude record 1919. Tail marked PV761/PU167/PC178/PT1150. 1919 *Farman F.60 Goliath* No 2 F-HMFU "Ile de France" of Air Union,—fuselage only displayed. 1921 *Morane-Saulnier A 1 (MS. 30)* F-ABAO c/n 2283, flown by Alfred Fronval. 1926 *Schreck FBA 17HT.4 Hydravion* F-AJOR c/n 195—flew until 1964. 1926 *Breguet 19 Grand Raid* No 1685 of the Nungesser & Coli 1926/7/8 record flights. 1929 *Bernard 191 Grand Raid* "Oiseau Canari" F-AJGP; first French West-East Atlantic crossing 13/14 June

Hydravion and Demoiselle (Paris)

Breguet "Super-Bidon" (Paris)

Polikarpov "Chicka" (Paris)

Morane-Saulnier MS.230 (Paris)

1929, with Asolant, Lefevre, Lotti. 1929 *Breguet "Super-Bidon" 19GR*. "Point d'Interrogation" set up world distance record with first East-West transatlantic flight 1/2 September 1930 when Costes and Bellonte flew Paris-New York in 37 hrs 17 mins. 1929 *Morane-Saulnier MS. 230 Et2* No 1048. Repainted ex F-BGMR. 1933 *Potez 53* No 3402 "10" Racer. Winner of "Coupe-Deutsch", 1933. 1935 *Polikarpov 1-153 "Chicka"* serial 9. Russian markings. 1937 *Habicht No II glider,* built by *DFS* for Hanna Reitch and sold to Marcel Doret to become F-CAEX. 1937 *Dewoitine D.530* F-AJTE c/n 06, flown by Marcel Doret. 1938 *Morane-Saulnier MS.406C1* ex Swiss Air Force, now in French marks. 1939 *Caudron C.714 R* built for air-speed record 1939 but never flown. 1939 *Dewoitine D.520 C.1* No 408. 1942 *Supermarine Spitfire IX* BS464 "GW-S" No 340 "Ile de France" Squadron markings. 1942 *Focke Wulf Fw 190 A-8* built as SNCAC NC.900 A-8 serial No 62, in Luftwaffe markings. 1942 *Focke-Achgelis Fa 330* rotakite, in Luftwaffe markings. 1943 *Yakovlev Yak 3* "18" of Escadrille Normandie Niemen. Russian marks. 1944 *Heinkel He 162A Volksjager* No 3, also reported as 02. History not known, possibly French evaluation aircraft. 1944 *Mignet HM 280,* built for use by Resistance. 1946 *Leduc 010 experimental* No 03 "Rene Lorin" ramjet research. 1949 *S.O. 1110 Ariel II* helicopter F-WFRQ c/n 1—prop-jet. 1948 *Hurel-Dubois H.D.10* F-BFAN c/n 01. 1953 *S.O.1220 Djinn* F-WGVD c/n 02. 1953 *S.O. 9000*

Trident "O1-Y" experimental. 1957 *SNECMA C.400 P2 "Atar Volant"* VTOL. Plus magnificent models, engines etc. Held in store (1973) for restoration and/or future display:—1910 *R.E.P. Type D.* 1914 *Deperdussin Type B* 1915 *RA. Factory BE.2C* No 9969 built by Blackburn. 1918 *Sopwith Type 1 A 2* (from La Ferte Alais?) 1918 *Junkers D 1* (J9) 1918 *Junkers F.13* (JL.6) c/n thought 600, Junkers-Larsen assembled USA 1919. *Hanriot HD.14* of 1921. 1921 *Spad Herbemont 52*, developed from SPAD 29; aerobatic demonstrator. 1921 *Caudron C.60* F-AINX c/n 49/6184. 1922 *Spad Herbemont 54*—two-seat version of SPAD XIII. 1923 *Dewoitine D.7.* 1924 *Perrin (STAé/helicopter.* 1923 *Pescara F.3 helicopter. Caudron C.109* of 1925. 1938 *S.G.38* glider c/n 173. 1928 *Cierva C.8LL* G-EBYY which made first cross-Channel rotary flight. 1929

Cierva C.8LL (Paris)

Morane-Saulnier MS.149, two-seat trainer "OO". 1929 *Farman 192* believed F-BAOP c/n 4 1929 *Potez 36* two-seat monoplane probably F-ALAB. 1932 *Caudron C.277 Luciole* F-AOFX c/n 14. 1932 *Avia 40p glider*. 1933 *Caudron 366 racer*; Regnier engine. 1931 *Caudron C.282/8 Phalene*. 1934 *DH. Rapide* F-BHCD c/n 6706 ex HG721, G-ALGB. 1935 *Oehmichen No 6 helicopter*. 1935 *DH. Puss Moth* F-ANRZ c/n 2151 ex CH-271. 1936 *Potez 58*. 1935 *Farman F.455 Moustique*. 1937 *Gourdou-Leseurre Type B.7* F-APOZ c/n 3—Fernard Malinvaud's a/c. 1936 *Liore & Olivier C 30 2*, licence-built Cierva. 1937 *Junkers Ju 52/3m* Aeronavale licence-built AAC.1 No 216. 1942 *Martin B.26 Marauder*—serial wanted. 1943 *NA P-51 Mustang* 44-63871 which was R.Swed.AF 26039 and ex-Israel, then N9772F at Nice and Cannes. 1943 *Republic P-47 Thunderbolt* 44-20371. 1943 *Douglas C-47 Dakota*—serial please. 1944 *Douglas A-26 Invader*—serial please. 1946 *Caudron C.800*—registration wanted. 1945 *SNCAN Stampe SV4C* —No 38. 1945 *Morane-Saulnier MS.500 Criquet*. Details wanted. 1946 *SNCASO 6000 Triton* first French jet F-WFKY c/n 03. 1947 *Jodel D.9 Bebe* F-PEPF c/n 01 (prototype) .1948 *S.N.C.A.S.E. 3101* single-seat helicopter "01" 1949 *Castel-Mauboussin C.M. 8-13 glider* "Emouchet". 1948 *Armstrong Whitworth Meteor NF.11* believed ex-WM301 and probably serial 24 in France.

Jodel D.9 (Paris)

1951 *S.E.535 Mistral* (license-built Vampire) probably "004". 1951 *SAAB 29 (J29F)* donated R.Swed.AF—serial wanted. 1953 *Hispano HA-1112-MIL* (Spanish 109) serial please. 1955 *Republic F-84F Thunderstreak* 52-8875. 1953 *Piper Super Cub L-18C*—details please. 1954 *Payen P.A. 49b* F-WGVA delta experimental "Katy". 1957 *Nord 1500 "Griffon"* 02. André Turcat's 1959 record a/c. 1958 *Nord 3400* serial 131, high-wing observation monoplane. 1965 *Dassault Mirage III-V* serial 01; Mach 2 fighter. It is reported that many other machines are awaiting delivery to the museum or store including:— *Boeing B-17G* F-BGOE c/n 32369 ex 44-83728. *Caravelle* F-BHHI c/n 02. *Brochet 850. Sikorsky H-19. Vertol H-21. Sipa Minijet. Sud Ludion 001. Hirsh HR 100. Potez 58*. It is also thought that the following are in long-term storage:—*Massa-Biot 1880 Ornithopter; Grassi Ornithopter* of 1938; *DFS Kranich II* of 1939; *Breguet G.III* F-WFKC; *Morane-Saulnier Parasol L.A.* of 1914; *Paul-Schmitt 1914 variable-wing photo-recce a/c; Nord 1203 Norécrin No 373;* F-BICY c/n 128; *Avia XVa glider; Granau Baby glider. Bruel, Duhammel, Molinari BDM-01 helicopter* F-WEPH of 1958. Application must be made in writing, well in advance, to 91 Boulevard Pereire, 75017, Paris, to visit, with no guarantee. In the Jardin d'Acclimatation there is said to be *Dassault MD 312 Flamant*—serial and photo please.

PAU-USSEIN. *Nord Noralpha* F-WJDQ c/n 150, the Astazou test-bed.

PERSAN BEAUMONT. Airfield. *Boisavia B606 Mercury* F-BHCH c/n 3; *Brochet MB80* F-BGLG c/n 7 (stored). *Kranich glider* F-CBBA; *Rhonsperper glider* F-CABK.

PONT-SUR-YON. Airfield. *Morane-Saulnier MS.181* F-AJQK c/n 3 airworthy.

REIMS. Airfield. *Morane-Saulnier MS.505* F-BEJE; *Tiger Moth* F-BGCS, c/n 85946 ex DF210.

ROCHEFORT. French Air Force. Instructional a/c (viewable with prior permission from C.O.):—*Dassault 315* Nos 17, 65, 135. *Mirage IIIC* No 46. *Mystère IVB* No 08. *Mystère IVA* Nos 04, 38, 52, 109. *Super-Mystère* No 17. *Fouga Magister* No 21. *Nord 2506* No 01. *Nord 2501 Noratlas* No 4; No 34. *SO4050 Vatour IIN* No 04. *LTV F-8 Crusader*. serial wanted. *SO 90 Corse* No 41. *Fouga 170M* No 02 and one other. *Sikorsky HSS-1* No 512. *Beech SNJ-6* 3820. *SO-30 Bretagne. Morane-Saulnier 733 Alcyon. Dassault Etendard IV* Nos 01; 04. *Breguet 1050 Alize* No 02. *Lockheed P2V-6 Neptune* 126622. *Lockheed P2V-7 Neptune* serial 685. Do NOT visit without written authority.

ROMANIN-LES-ALPILLES. Airfield. *MD315 Flamant* No 92 and *Harvard* 53-4611.

ROMANS. Airfield. *Avia XVa glider* No 35. In local Motor Museum; *Leopoldoff L.55* F-APZP c/n 8.

ROMORANTIN. Airfield. *Dassault Ouragan* No 297 displayed. *Morane-Saulnier MS.341* F-ANVS c/n 4234/3—only one flying.

ROUEN. Boos Airport. *Potez 439* F-AMPF c/n 3445. *SG.38 glider* No 137. On route N14. near Shell Garage, south of city, *Nord NC856* No 76. Nearer Le Havre *NC856* No 32.

ROYAN. *Proctor 5* F-BCJC c/n Ae 111 by road.

ST. AUBAN. Gliding Centre. *Morane-Saulnier MS.502* F-BCME c/n 600; F-BEJG c/n 653. *MS.500* F-BAUV c/n 73.

ST. CYR Airfield. Stored (for Musée de l'Air?) *Auster J/1 Autocrat* F-BEPC c/n 2034 ex OO-ABH, LX-ACD, LX-ABH *Morane-Saulnier MS.563* F-BBGC c/n 01 ex F-WBGC. *Nord 1002* F-BDYT c/n 258, F-BEOY c/n 146, F-BFOJ c/n 269, Dismantled; F-BNDS c/n 229 ex F-OTAN-4. *Nord 1101* F-BLQC c/n 43 (for restoration?) *Nord 1203* F-BEOB c/n 117. Dismantled. *Nord NC854S* F-BDYP c/n 5 F-BFSI c/n 65. *Nord NC858S* F-BBRP c/n 142, F-BEZX c/n 116.

ST. DIZIER. Air Base *Republic F-84F* "1ET" in I/I Corse markings. Serial wanted.

ST. JEAN BARREME. South of Digne. At Petrol Station. *Nord 1002* marked F148N but possibly No 241.

ST. JUNIEN. Airfield. *Proctor IV* F-BFXV c/n H769, ex RM166 as gate guardian.

ST. VINCENT-DE-TYROSSE. *Super Constellation* F-BGNB c/n 4511 as Bar.

SALON-DE-PROVENCE. French Air Force Academy. In entrance hall *SPAD VII* "Le Vieux Charles" of Guynemer—from Les Invalides, Paris. In front of college *Dewoitine 520* (possibly amalgam of two—serials please). *Nord Norvigie* also staked out here. *Breguet Taon* is in store here.

SANTENY. Airfield. *Sikorsky H-19*—serial please.

STRASBOURG-ENTZHEIM. Air Force Base. On display *Republic RF-84F* 37577 "33-CK", inside gates. At Neuhof Airfield there is said to be *Messerschmitt Bf 108 Taifun*—details please. Near Pont-du-Rhin is *Super Constellation* F-BHMJ c/n 4669 as Bar.

TOUL. Casern Courtyard. *Republic F-84F* 28879 "4-VU".

Spitfire LFXVIe (Tours)

TOURS. Air Base. *Spitfire LF XVIe* RR263 ex 66,416 (Can), 5 Sqdns, 3 CAACU and RAF Kenley gate-guardian, painted as TB597 of 340 (Ile de France). Used in "Reach for the Sky" film and donated to French Air Force 1967. *Vertol H-21* and *Dassault Ouragan* 154/UU, 187/UI, 227/UN, 320UQ displayed.

TOUSSUS-LE-NOBLE. Airport. *Lockheed 12A* EI-ALVc/n 1226 ex NC18130, G-AHLH, of the Earl of Granard. *Stinson Reliant* F-BBCS c/n 3/5846; *Nord 1101* F-BBJG c/n 115, F-BBJR, c/n 44, F-BLRZ c/n 69, F-BLTM c/n 160, F-BLTU c/n 107. *Breguet 763 Universal* F-BASX c/n 10 ex Air France "Deux Ponts"; for possible clubhouse. *Potez 437* F-APXO c/n 3588. *Nord NC858* F-BDZN c/n 4. *DH.89A Rapide* F-BHGR c/n 6844 ex NR756, G-AOAO.

TROYES. Motel near airfield. *AT-6D Harvard* F-BJBM c/n 88-14510.

TRUSLY-BREUIL. On Soissons-Compiegne Rd. *Nord 1101* No 108 near flats.

VANNES-MEUCON. Jean Frelant of Morbihan has Westland-built *Supermarine Seafire III* PP972 ex Aeronvale Store, Hyeres; under active restoration.

VERDUN. City Museum. *Nieuport XI (replica)* constructed by late Jean Salis.

VILLENEUVE-SUR-LOT. Airfield. *Caudron C.275 Luciole* F-PPHO c/n 7496/20 ex F-APHO.

GERMANY (EAST)

DRESDEN. Saxony Army Museum. *Fokker E.III* said displayed here—details please.

MAGDEBURG. Kulturhistorischen Museum. *Hans Grade* type machine of 1909 (original or replica not known) displayed here. This is the type Hans Grade flew in October, 1909 to win a 40,000-Mark prize for the first flight in Germany by a machine of German construction.

GERMANY (WEST)

AACHEN-BRAND. Lützow Kaserne. *Lockheed F-104 Starfighter* unserialled, of WsLw 10, WGAF. *Lockheed T-33A*, unserialled, WGAF.

AACHEN-BURTSCHEID. Ingenieurschule. *Bristol Sycamore* serial unknown, of HTG 64, WGAF. Details of above, please.

AACHEN-MERZBRÜCK. Airfield. *Auster V* D-EKBO c/n 1012 ex NJ618 HB-EOI; H. Steffens. *Tiger Moth* D-EGIT c/n 83580 ex T7129 G-ANTW; Luftsportverein Aachen. *Piper L-4J Cub* D-EJIB c/n 12522 ex 44-80226, LN-SAG, K. Daum & Ptnrs (Lingen).

AACHEN. Technical University. *Hispano HA-1112-MIL* c/n 213 now painted as Messerschmitt Bf 109 G-6 of 6.JG 26 coded 4+ and with authentic DB engine. Also *1927 Schulgleiter* glider to be restored. *Republic F-84F* may also be restored here.

AALHORN. WGAF base. *Republic RF-84F* EA+101 of AG 51. *Nord Noratlas* 53+56 of LTG 62, WGAF and *Sabre 6* JA+110 ex JB+370 in markings of JG 71, C.O. Erich Hartmann, *Bristol Sycamore* 78+37 acts as Bar for HTG 64.

AHRENSBURG. Airfield. *Tiger Moth* D-EKAL c/n 83683 ex T7213, G-ANGD; M. Schmitz.

ALTENMARKT. Airstrip. *Piper L-4J Cub* D-EJAX c/n 12089, ex 44-79793; D. Reif.

ANGERSTEIN. Airfield. *L-4A Cub* D-ECIZ c/n 8391 ex 42-15272; H. Apetz.

ARNZBERG. Airfield. *Piper L-4J Cub* D-EFIL c/n 12320 ex 44-80024, HB-OBT; W. Molz.

ASCHAFFENBURG. Airfield. *L-4J Cub* D-EFPE c/n 12882 ex 44-80586, OE-AAR; Flugsportclub Aschaffenburg.

AUGSBURG. Airfield. *Piper L-4J Cub* D-EMAT c/n 12484 ex 44-80188, HB-OIL; S. Kautzmann. At the Aeroclub is said to be *Fieseler Storch* D-EBOY c/n 4389 for sale after taking part in American TV film about the attempt on Hitler's life (20 July 1944). The a/c has logged 1,142 hrs with 2,640 take-offs/landings. At the nearby Messerschmitt-Bölkow-Blohm GmbH factory *Messerschmitt Me 17 "Ello"* of 1925, D-779, with Bristol Cherub engine, thought to be hangared. *Bf 108 Taifun* A-208 of Swiss AF c/n 2064, all-blue, without registration, is at the plant. Also *HA 1112-MIL* is here, minus R-R engine.

Messerschmitt Me 17 (Augsburg)

BAD DURKHEIM. Airfield. *Piper L-4J Cub* D-EOMA c/n 12622 ex 44-80326, F-BFBI; A. Zemke.

BAD REICHENALL. Airfield. *L-4A Cub* D-EJAF c/n 8437 ex 43-5045, HB-OAD; Reichenhall Alpenflug.

BADEN BADEN. Oos Airport. *Percival Prince* D-CAKE (preserved?)

BAMBERG. Airfield. *Comte AC.IV* D-ELIS c/n 34 ex CH-262, HB-IKO "Spirit of Bamberg" now flown by F. Dioszegny. *Piper L-4H* D-EMUX c/n 11496 ex 43-30205; Aeroclub.

Comte AC.IV (Bamberg)

BERLIN. Templehof Airport. *Douglas C-54 Skymaster* 0-50557 c/n 36010 as USAF Airlift Memorial (Luftbrucken Denkmal).

BERLIN. Berliner Verkehrsmuseum (Transport Museum) *Klemm L 25* of 1929 Werk-Nr 138 F-PCDA, restored 1971/72 by RAF Gatow personnel, now with Hirth and not Mercedes engine. Any further details greatly appreciated for next edition. *Junkers Ju 52/3m* Werk-Nr 35,210 D-2201, bought back from Spain 1965 for symbolic payment of One Mark, to represent Lufthansa's first Ju 52. Actually a CASA 352. *Santos Dumont Demoiselle* (replica) PPS/DEM/1 from "Magnifi-

cent Men" film. *Eardley Billing 1910* (replica) from same film. *Kondor Sailplane*, original. *SG.38 trainer glider*, original. *Focke-Achgelis Fa 330* rotary kite, original. *Lilienthal glider* (replica).
Deutsche Luftfahtsammlung e.V. Berlin-Lichterfelde, Schütte-Lanzstrasse. *Rumpler C-IV fuselage* without covering, upper wing covered, faint lozenge camouflage. Mercedes 160 hp engine on loan from Daimler-Benz, Stuttgart, for Rumpler. *Schulgleiter S.G.38* dismantled but complete, on loan from Polizei-Sportgruppe. *Holzwarth Schwingenflugzeug 1938/45.* Complete but not entirely finished owing to early death of constructor—loaned by his family. *Lilienthal Eindecker* (replica).

Junkers Ju 52/3m (Berlin)

Demoiselle—replica (Berlin)

Eardley Billing—replica (Berlin)

Klemm L 25 (Berlin)

BIELEFELD. Airfield. *Piper L-4H Cub* D-EDOT c/n 11671 ex 43-30380; Dr. M. Koppler.

BINGEN. Airfield. *Piper L-4H Cub* D-EHAL c/n 10993 ex 43-29702, G-AIYX; Aeroclub Bingen.

BONN. Hangelar Airport. Federal Republic of Germany own:— *HawkerSea Fury FB.11* D-CACY c/n 3617 ex WG599, G-9-66. *Sea Fury T.20* D-CEDO c/n 9506 ex VZ351, G-9-53. *Sea Fury T.20S* D-CADA c/n ES3612 ex VZ365, G-9-61. D-CACE c/n ES3613 ex VX302, G-9-62. D-CACO c/n ES3615 ex VX281, G-9-64. D-CACU c/n ES3616 ex WG655, G-9-65. D-CAFO c/n ES8509 ex WG652, G-9-57. D-CAMI c/n ES8502 ex VX300, G-9-24, D-FAMI. D-CATA c/n ES8503 ex VZ345, G-9-30, D-FATA. D-CIBO c/n ES8501 ex VX309, G-9-27, D-FIBO. D-COCO c/n ES9505 ex VZ350, G-9-59. D-COTE c/n ES8504 ex WE820, G-9-49, D-FOTE. Also *Harvard IV* D-FABA ex 53-4631, *IVM* D-FABE ex 52-8578. *Harvard IV* D-FABO ex 52-8593, under same ownership. *Klemm L 25 DVIIR* D-EJOL c/n 798; H. Frintup & Ptnrs.

BRAUNSCHWEIG. Airfield. *Zaunkönig* D-ECER c/n V.4 owned by Professor Dr. Ing H. Winter. *Piper L-4J* D-EGAR c/n 12591 ex 44-80295, HB-OBR; A. P. Koch.

BREMEN. Airport. *Fairey Gannet*—German National flag on tail—serial and history, please; with photo. Flying here:—*DH. Dragon Rapide* D-IGEL c/n 6347 ex OH-BLA, OH-VKH, OH-DHA, OY-DAS; G. Seuffert. *Piper L-4H Cub* D-EKWU c/n 11210, ex 43-29919, HB-ONN, OE-ABE; Mehrwald & Co. At VFW-Fokker Werk 1, *VFW-614* full-scale wooden mock-up, *H2*, single-seat helicopter. *VAK-191* (VTOL test-rig).

BREMERHAVEN. Airfield. *Piper J-3C-65 Cub* D-ELWY c/n 13058 ex 44-80762, F-BEGB; Aeroclub Bremerhaven.

BREMGARTEN. WGAF base. *Republic RF-84F* EA+101 of AG 51.

BUECHEL. WGAF barracks. *Republic F-84F* DC+319 ex 53-7045 displayed. *F-86 Sabre* JA+332 said at Fire Section—report on condition, please.

Republic F-84F (Buechel)

BUCHLO. Airfield. *Bücker Bü 181 Bestmann* D-EKOR c/n 25091 ex Fv 25091 SE-CBB; A. Lederle.

BUCHOLTWELMEN. Airfield. *Bücker Bü 131 Jung-mann* D-EDEF c/n 63, ex HB-ESA; G. Stalter.

Focke F.61—replica (Buckeburg)

BUCKEBURG. Hubschraubermuseum (Helicopter Museum). Open weekdays 0900-1700; Saturdays, Sundays, Public Holidays 1000-1700. Entrance adults 1.00 DM, children 0.50 DM. As at 1st March, 1973, the following are exhibited:— *Havertz HZ-5* prototype, D-HAJU. *Focke F.61* of 1936 D-EKRA (replica). *Siemetzki ASRO—4* prototype, no registration/serial. First flight 22 Jan. 1965. *Wagner Rotocar—III* prototype, unregistered. A roadable built and tested 1964/65. *Merckle SM-67*, prototype serial V-3, registered D-9506, c/n 1. Turbine-driven helicopter, flew 7 July 1959. *VFW H-2* serial V-1 D-HIBY, c/n 152. Experimental single-seat helicopter, first flew 30 April 1965. 72 hp McCullogh engine. *Bolkow BO-102 "Helitrainer"* serial 4502. *Bolkow BO-103* prototype D-7505. *Bolkow BO-46*, serial V-1, D9514. *Bolkow Sky Jeep* prototype. *BO-105* D-HAJY, c/n V-3. *Saro Skeeter AOP.12* XN348; ex British Army Air Corps. *Bristol 171 Sycamore* 78+20 c/n 13478, of HTG 64, WGAF. *Bristol 171 Sycamore* 78+33 c/n 13493, of HTG 64, WGAF. *Vertol H-21 Workhorse* 83+07, c/n WG.7. *Bell 47 G-2* 0-85348 U.S. Army. *Sud Aviation SO. 1221/S Djinn* 7—FR 8, c/n 250; ex French. *Gosslich "Pedalcopter"* prototype, built 1928; from Deutsches Museum. *Borgward-Focke BFK-1 "Kolibri"* main gearbox, rotor-head, rotor-blades, tail-rotor section. The only parts remaining of the two helicopters built by Borgward in 1958, the rest destroyed when the company closed-down. There are also other fascinating exhibits, and this museum is well-worth a visit if you are in Germany. Werner Noltemeyer is curator and postal address is Postfach 1310.

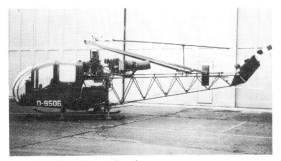

Merckle SM-67 (Buckeburg)

BUDINGEN. Airfield. *Luscombe 8F* D-EBVY c/n 6211 ex N1584B; E. Thielmann.

BURG FEUERSTEIN. Airfield. *DFS-Jakobs Kranich* D-1768 reported still active with pupil-students in 1973.

DARMSTADT. In town shopping centre *DC-4* D-ADAB, c/n 27353 ex 44-9127, N90901, SA-R4, HZ-AAW, G-ASRS, OO-FAI.

DETMOLD. Army barracks. *Saro Skeeter AOP.12* XL739 displayed.

DORTMUND. Airfield. *L-4H* D-EHIT c/n 10675 ex 43-29384, I-GINU. Dortmunde Luftfahrt.

DURBACH. *Tiger Moth* D-EGJH c/n 85851 ex DE991, F-BGJH; O. Leible.

DUSSELDORF. Airport. *Auster IV* D-ELIT c/n 906 ex MT170 G-ANHP; J. Langenohe. *Blume BL.503* D-EKUB c/n BL.02 the only one flying, owned by Min. fur Wirtsch.

EGELSBACH. Airfield. *Beech D.18S* D-INOL c/n A.471 ex N9472, PH-UDS; Aero Photo GmbH. *Fw. 44J Stieglitz* D-EMIL reported static here. *Miles M.28 Mercury* D-EHAB c/n 6268, ex G-AHAA: H. Kirchner. *Taylorcraft Plus D.* D-ELUV c/n 173 ex LB314, G-AHHX, D-ELUS; W. Luttner. *Piper L-4H Cub* D-EGOV c/n 11417 ex 43-30126: P. Steinbach.

EINOD. Airfield. *Piper L-4J Cub* D-EGAF c/n 12943, ex 44-80647, HB-ONI; W. Zimmermann.

ENSHEIM. Airfield. *Piper L-4J Cub* D-EDUH c/n 12640 ex 44-80344, F-BDTL, SL-AAC, SL-ABC; Aeroclub Saar.

ESCHERSHAUSEN. near Hannover. *Vickers Viscount V814* D-ANAC c/n 370 reported as a restaurant. Photos please.

ESSEN. Airport. *Piper L-4J Cub* D-ELYN c/n 12451 ex 44-80155, HB-OCV; Kundenkreditbank; who also own *L-4H* D-ENAK c/n 11275 ex 43-29984.

FRANKFURT. Rhein Main. *Tiger Moth* N82TM c/n 3815 ex N6478 G-AOGS; Capt. Schweaker, USAF.

FREIBURG. Airfield *Fiesler Storch* D-ELYN c/n 119253 ex Fv 3918, OE-ADO; K. Eckert (damaged).

FRIEDRICHSHAFEN. WGAF. *F-84F* BF+101 ex 53-7146 at gate.

FRIESENER WARTE. (near Bamberg) Airstrip. *Jakobs Weihe* D-9062 *Hirth Goppingen Go-4* (Goevier) D-1084. Both gliders still very actively flying here.

FUERSTENFELDBRUCK. WGAF. *F-84F* and *RF-84F* at gates—details wanted.

FULORN. Airfield. *Piper L-4H Cub* D-EBIS c/n 12341 ex 44-80045; Fa. H. Walter.

GELNHAUSEN. Airfield. *Piper L-4H* D-EGIS c/n 11030 ex 43-29739. *L-4J* D-EBIW c/n 12500 ex 44-80204, HB-OCF. *Tiger Moth* D-EDEM c/n 86403 ex NL971. *Tiger* D-EDIS c/n 85506 ex DE526; all Aeroclub Gelnhausen.

GEY. Airfield. *Piper L-4J Cub* D-EBYR c/n 12741 ex 44-80443; R. Werts Ptnrs.

GIENGEN/BRENZ. Airfield. *Piper L-4J Cub* D-ECAS c/n 12809 ex 44-80513; Fliegergruppe Giengen/Brenz.

GÖPPINGEN-BETZGENRIED. Fritz Ulmer Collection. Near Geislingen, east of Stuttgart. Here are several rare aircraft and gliders including:—*Junkers A.50 Junior* HB-UXI of 1930 ex CH-358, with Siemens SH.13 engine. *Klemm L 25* D-ENAF c/n 277 ex CH.272, HB-EFU. Ernst Udet flew this for films and it is fitted with many refinements. *Klemm KL35D* D-EMHN c/n 1842 ex Fv 5065, SE-BPL; Hans Meeder of Firma Hirtha, Nabern-Teck, Built 1940, rebuilt 1960-66 after 1,250 hrs had been recorded. Engine Firth HM 504 A.2; closed canopy, one-leg undercarriage. *Bucker Jungmann* HB-USR c/n 25 ex A-16 of 1938. *Bucker Jungmeister* D-ENOW c/n 6 ex U-59 Swiss Air Force, HB-MII. *Arado 79* D-ECUV c/n 0047 ex SL-AAP, of 1940, once owned by Luftwaffe, then French Hochkomissar, later A. Philippi, Saarland. Last survivor of type. Hirth 4-cylinder HM.504 A.2 of 105 hp. Wings rebuilt. *Grunau Hirth Baby IIb; Schulgleiter SG-38. Hutter H-17 B. Schleiches Rhonbussard. Rhonsperber* (last in world). *Hirth Minimoa* (last?) *Olympia Meise,* Germany 1932. *Goppingen Go 4* (Goevier) side-by-side two-seater glider. *Piper L-4H* D-ECAV c/n 12077 ex 44-79781, SL-AAA flies locally: R. Nussle.

Piper L-4H (Goppingen)

GOSLAR. WGAF. *Canadair Sabre 6* GS+338.

GRENZLAND. Airfield. *Piper L-4J Cub* D-EGUM c/n 12859 ex 44-80563, HB-OAF; Motorfluggruppe.

GROTZINGEN. Airfield. *Auster V.* D-EMXA c/n 803 ex MS938, HB-EOK; F. W. Peppler.

GUNDELFINGEN. Airfield. *Auster 5.* D-EHYS c/n 3408; Luftsportverein Bez.

HAGEN. Airfield. *L-4J* D-EDUS c/n 12851 ex 44-80555, OO-AVM, F-BBIJ, E. Rafflenbau.

HAMBURG. Hartenholm. *Lockheed L1649A Starliner* D-ALUB c/n 1034 as nearby café. At the airport several vintage types flying, including:—*Piper L-4H Cub* D-ECIV c/n 11364 ex 43-30073, SL-AAK; Karlsberg Brauerei. *Piper L-4H* D-EHID c/n 11874 ex 44-79578, HB-OSH; HBF Motorfluggruppe. *Klemm Kl 35D* D-EHKO c/n 1854, ex Fv5020, SE-BHR, D-EBIB; H. Rohl.

HAMBURG. Fuhlsbuttel military base. Two *Grumman Albatross* said to be here, ex West German Marineflieger—preserved? *L1049G Super Constellation* D-ALIN c/n 4604 on public display (small charge for interior viewing).

HAMMERAU. Airfield. *Piper L-4B Cub* D-ELSU c/n 9059 ex HB-OWX, OE-ABF; Reichenhaller Alpenflug.

HEIDELBERG. Airfield. *Piper L-4J Cub* D-EBAS c/n 12998 ex 44-80702; W.Houfek.

HELSEN. Airfield. *Piper L-4H Cub* D-EBIR c/n 11578 ex 43-30287, HB-OAM; C. Ritter.

HERZOGENAURACH. Airfield. *Piper L-4H Cub* D-EHYM c/n 10776 ex 43-29485, PH-NAE, PH-NFI, D-EDIF; Air Service Memmert Co. *Auster 5* D-ENIS c/n 1812 ex TW473.

HILGERTSHAUSEN. Airfield. *Fairchild Argus 1* D-EKAS c/n 322 ex 42-32117, FK313, G-AJGW, OO-ACF; H. Breindl Ptnrs.

HOHN. WGAF base. *Nord Noratlas* 53+55 in markings of LTG 63 WGAF, ex LTG 62 machine.

HUSUM. LeKG 41 barracks. *Republic F-84F* of JaboG 35. *Fiat G.91R.1* 35+41 in markings of LeKG 41, ex Italian AF.

IDAR OBERSTEIN. Airfield. *L-4A* D-EHXA c/n 8910, ex 43-36786. F. Stein.

INGOLSTADT. WGAF. *RF-84F* EA+326 ex 52-7375 at gate.

ITZEHOE. Airfield. *Tiger Moth* D-EKIF c/n 83891 ex R5216, G-AOED; also D-EMWT c/n 82003 ex N6730, D-EMWE; both H. Huss.

JAGEL. WGAF base. *Hawker Sea Hawk* VA+007 ex Kriegsmarine.

JEVER. WGAF. *Canadair Sabre 6* BB+103 at gate.

KARLSRUHE. Airport. *DH.Rapide* D-IGUN c/n 6437 ex HB-AME, HB-APE; G. Nitzsche. *Piper L-4H Cub* D-ECSA c/n 12138 ex 44-79842, F-BBII; H. Trappenberg.

KARLSRUHE-RINDHEIM. WGAF. NA F-86K on pylon uncoded—details please.

KAUFBEUREN. WGAF. *RF-84F*—details wanted.

KEIL. Airfield. *Piper L-4J Cub* D-EBEN c/n 12566 ex 44-80270, HB-OFZ; H. Gellner.

KIEL. Marineflieger. Reported another ex-Pollensa *Dornier Do 24* may come here. Details and photos if confirmed, please.

KLINGENBERG. Airfield. *Piper L-4H Cub* D-EJIX c/n 11540 ex 43-30249; B. T. Pfister.

KOBLENZ. Airfield. *Tiger Moth* D-EFPH c/n 83786 ex T7410; R. Fehlhaber.

KOLN. (Cologne). Wahn airfield. Barracks area. *NA F-86 Sabre* BB+237 ex 51-111 displayed. *F-86* JC+361 in Fire Section; ex 51-605. Confirmation and photos please. *F-104F Starfighter* details please.

KONSTANZ. Airfield. *Piper L-4J Cub* D-ECID c/n 12953 ex 44-80657; Dreilander Flugdienst.

KREFELD. Airfield. *Auster V* D-EMAG c/n 992 ex MT356, HB-EOE; H. Dillmann.

LAARBRUCH. RAF base. *Auster III* G-ATAX c/n 546 ex NJ916, R-13 R.Neth.AF, PH-UFP; with Flying Club.

LANDSBERG. WGAF. *NA Sabre*, *Fouga CM-70 Magister*, *Bristol Sycamore* (ex HTG64) and *Nord 2501 Noratlas* (ex LTG-61); *NA Harvard* AA+666. displayed here. Confirmation/photos please.

LECHFELD. WGAF. *F-84F* DD+367 ex 51-1645 at gate.

LECK. Luftwaffe Base. *Republic RF-84F* EB+250 displayed, ex 52-7355.

LEUTKIRCH. Airfield. *Piper L-4J Cub* D-EGYS c/n 12769 ex 44-80473, HB-OAA; Fliegergruppe Leutkirch.

LINDAU. Airfield. *Piper L-4J Cub* D-EFRI c/n 12771 ex 44-80475, HB-OSO; E. Zankert.

LINGEN. Airfield. *L-4J* D-EJIB c/n 12522 ex 44-80226, LN-SAG; K. Daum Ptnrs.

LUBECK. Airport. *Piper L-4J* D-EGPL c/n 13367 ex 45-4627, PH-UCO, D-EGPI; Kommanditgeselleschaft. Some of the Hawker Sea Furies (see BONN) operate out of Lubeck-Blankensee airfield, along with ten ex-Luftwaffe Noratlas in markings of "Eleeflug".

MAINZ. Airfield. *L-4H.* D-EGZG c/n 11295 ex 43-30004, G-AIYV, N9829F; Luftfahrtverein.

MANNHEIM. Airfield. *L-4J* D-EKEG c/n 12512 ex 44-80216; Dr. G. Rotta.

MARKTINDERSDORF. Airfield. *Klemm Kl* 35D D-ECIC c/n 2013 ex Fv5064, SE-BHU; P. Stein.

MEERSBURG. Lake Constance. Dornier Museum. Closed during Winter. Open from Spring-Autumn daily 0930-1200 and 1330-1800. DM 1.00. *Dornier Do 24T-3* Werk-Nr 5345 ex HD5-4 of Spanish Air Force marked "SAR", the last airworthy example of twelve supplied by Luftwaffe during WW II (with allied approval) to form "Life Saving Group No 804" for rescue of airmen of all nationalities in Mediterranean and Spanish

Dornier Do 24T-3 arrives (Meersburg)

coastal waters. A ceremonial last flight was made on 28 August 1971 from Pollensa, Balearic Isles, to Friedrichshafen, Lake Constance, for the museum. Of the two then remaining one—believed HD5-1 Werk-Nr thought 5342—is thought earmarked for Spanish Air Force Museum, Madrid. The third may go to KIEL although there are interested parties in U.K. Dimensions of the Do 24—72 ft 2 ins long, 88 ft 6 ins span, 18 ft 10 ins high; weight empty 20,600 lbs. loaded 30,200 lbs. Top speed 205 mph, cruising 179 mph, normal range 1,800 miles, max range 2,920 miles.

MEINERSHAGEN. Airfield. *Klemm Kl 35D* D-ELOX c/n 1959, Fv5040, LN-TAI; E. Schwartz.

MEMMINGEN. WGAF base. *F-84F Thunderstreak* in JG 34's marks on plinth. Details of serial and photo wanted please.

MITTELBIBERACH. Airfield. *Focke-Wulf Fw44J* D-EHEQ c/n 664, ex Fv664 SE-BZI; E. Ackermann.

MONCHEN-GLADBACH. Airfield. *Rhein RF 1* D-IGIR (only example) stored. *Harvard IV* AA+633 coded "A" (all-yellow) of Flugzeugfuhrersschule WGAF here, together with some former target-towers including *D-FABI* and *D-FABU* (out of service since 1972. See BONN also). Some may be available for preservation together with *Hunting C.Mk 54 Pembroke* aircraft of WGAF and Navy, including 54+15, 54+22, 54+23 and 54+25. Bids to Federal Government, Bonn.

MOSBACH. Airfield. *Bucker Bu 131 Jungmann* D-ECNF c/n 74, ex A-61, HB-USB; Sigmund-Flugtechnik.

MUNICH. Deutsches Museum. *Lilienthal Biplane* of 1896. *Lilienthal Monoplane* 1900. *Wright Biplane* of 1908. *Hans Grade Erster Monoplane* 1909 "Libelle" (Dragonfly) Lanzpreis-Gewinner. *Bleriot XI Kanalflugtype* of 1909. *Etrich-Rumpler-Taube* 1910 Werk-Nr 19, Kathreinerpreis-Gewinner. *Fokker DVII* 4404/18 of 1918. *Klemm Kl-25e-VII* SE-ANF of 1935 c/n 980. *Fieseler Fi 156 C-3 Storch* c/n 4299 ex HB-ARU, A-96 of Swiss Air Force. *Junkers Ju 52/3m* serial 363, French built AAC-1, hung & sectioned to show construction. *Messerschmitt Bf 109 E-1* Quoted as Werk-Nr 790 and allegedly flew in Spanish Civil War, code "AJ+YH". Brought back

from Spain in 1959. Manufacturer's plate gives date of 18.7.39. *Messerschmitt Me 163* Werk-Nr 120370 ex RAF Biggin Hill, *Messerschmitt Me 262 A-1b* Werk-Nr 500071 of 3/JG7 which landed at Dubendorf aerodrome 25 April 1945 and was interned by Swiss authorities until 1957. *Dornier Do 27B-1* D-EHAV c/n 27-1104-360, formerly 56+66. Non-authentic civil registration *Dornier Do 32* D-HOPA. *Junkers F 13* Werk-Nr 1035 from Afghanistan (outside awaiting restoration.) *Canadair Sabre 6* JD+105 of JG 74 but markings are incorrect. Is believed to be formerly KE+105 c/n 1659. *Sikorsky H-19B Chickasaw* USAF 0-34458 of 526th TFS, 17th AF. *Lockheed F-104F Starfighter* 29+03, WGAF of JG 74. *Junkers W34* ("W" for Werkflugzeug or general-purpose) said to be marked "J+KL"—further details please. *EWR-Sud VJ-101C X2* D-9518. Many interesting old gliders either exhibited or stored:—*Milan Segelflugzeug* D-1001 Werk-Nr 5 of 1934. *Hutter 17A Segelflugzeug* D-8129 of 1938. *DFS Kranich II* D-6171. *SG.36 Primary. Wolfmuller* glider, 1907. *Pohemuller* of 1870.

Deutsches Museum aircraft (Munich)

Bf 109 E-1 (Munich)

Messerschmitt Me 262 A-1b (Munich)

Dornier Do 32 (Munich)

EWR-Sud VJ-101C (Munich)

Spatz glider. *Wings of Horten IV* Nr 7856. *Olympia* glider D-6336. *Vampyr Segelflugzeug* of 1921. *Opel-Sander* rocket aircraft. *Focke-Achgelis Fa 330. V2* rocket. *Martin Matador* rocket (outside with some of aircraft, 1973.) *Bachem Ba 349* (stored). *Nike Apache* of DFVLR on launching platform. At Munich-Auding. Technical School *RF-84F* EB+331 ex 52-7379. At Munich Reim Airport. *Taylorcraft Plus D* D-ECOD c/n 228 ex LB381 G-AHKO; R. Ettengruber. *Auster V* D-ECIL c/n 1575 ex TJ527, G-ANIL; D. Bohner Ptnrs. *Piper L-4J* D-EJGI c/n 13204 ex 45-4464, HB-OVO, OE-ABD; of Dr. Studemann may be stored here. At the Messerschmitt factory is said to be a *Bf 108* and *Hispano HA 1112 MIL*—details and pics please. At Munich's Technische Universität is *Fieseler Fi 156 Storch* D-EKLU c/n 110061 ex Fv3809.

MUNSTER. *Hirth Minimoa.* D-1163 restored to fly by Max Muller.

NECKARELZ. Airfield. *NA AT-16 Harvard IIB* D-FHGK c/n 14-324 ex FE590 U-322, G-AXCR; G. Roth.

NEHEIM-HUSTEN. Airfield. *Fieseler Fi 156 Storch* D-EGON c/n 8156, ex PH-NEL, LN-BDE; K. H. Bigge.

NEUBIBERG. At the Fachhochschule der Luftwaffe (FHSLw) *Bell 47G-2* AS+092 FFS "S" and *Sud Alouette II.* Also *Fouga CM-170* AA+291 and *F.84F* DD+302 ex 52-6601 of JaboG 34.

NEUBURG-DONAU. WGAF base. *NA F-86K Sabre* on pylon marked "JG-74". Previously JD+172.

NEULAND. Airfield. *Tiger Moth* D-EBUN c/n 83223 ex T5490, G-ANVE; H. Bohn.

NEUMARKT. Airfield. *Fieseler Fi 156 Storch* D-EKLA c/n 5837 ex Fv3824 DI+PC; Flugsport Neumarkt.

NEUMUNSTER. Airfield. *Fairchild 24H* D-ECAF c/n 3222 ex HB-EIL; P. Skogstad. This aircraft was caught up in WWII and was used by HQ ATA at White Waltham for a few months from November 1939.

NEUWULMSTORF. (near Hamburg). *Lockheed L1049G* D-ALOP c/n 4605 used as coffee-bar.

NORDHOLZ. Naval Air Base. *Fairey Gannet AS.4* UA+113 ex MFG 3, WGAF.

NUREMBURG. Airport. *Piper L-4H Cub* D-EMYM c/n 11124 ex 43-29833; H. Worl Ptnrs. *Stinson L-5 Sentinel* D-ELKO c/n "VW2493" (damaged.).

OBERHAUSEN. Airfield. *Klemm Kl 35D* D-ECCI c/n 1904 ex Fv5069, SE-BHX; W. Fenten.

OBERNAU. Airfield. *Auster V* D-EERK c/n 1603 ex TJ587, G-AMNU, D-EFIR, D-ELIR; Flugsportclub Move EV.

OBERSCHLEISSHEIM. Airfield. *Piper L-4H Cub* D-EFUL c/n 11313 ex 43-30022, HB-OAI; J. Koller.

OBERWURZBACH. Airfield. *Stinson HW.75* D-EMUB c/n 7249 ex 41-5143; F-BESY, SL-AAN; R. Vester.

OLDENBURG. WGAF. *Canadair Sabre 6* ex LeKG 43.

OTTOBRUN. Airfield. *Piper L-4J Cub* D-EHTU c/n 12602 ex 44-80306, OE-ADV; Sportfluggruppe Neubiburg.

PFARRKIRCHEN. Airfield. *Auster V* D-ELYD c/n 1790 ex TW446, G-ANKI; Segelfluggruppe Pfarrkirchen.

PFATTER. Airfield. *Piper L-4J Cub* D-EBAF c/n 13197 ex 45-4457, F-BDTF, SL-AAR; P. Wimmer.

PFERDSFELD. (SORBERNHEIM) WGAF barracks. *NA Sabre* coded JC+102 with Jabo 42 badge (G-4) on tail, though code is Jabo 73. It is reported there are still several *Thunderstreaks* here—DB+308; DD+306 (53-6639); DD+343; DD+346; DD+352. Confirmation of status please if existing 1973.

PFULLENDORF. Airfield. *Auster V* D-EGAT c/n 1159 ex RT497, G-AKSI, HB-EON, I-METE; Flugsportverein.

PINNEBURG. WGAF. *Canadair Sabre 6* BB+239.

PREUSSISCH-OLDENDORF. (Wittage). *Douglas DC-6* D-ABAH c/n 42855 ex Germanair as restaurant "Zum Flugzeug". Second production DC-6 built 1946 for American Airlines as N90702, "Flagship California".

PRIEN. Airfield. *Klemm Kl 35D* D-EBBW c/n 3171 ex OE-ABW; J. Koch.

RAMLINGEN. Airfield. *Piper L-4H Cub* D-EJYD c/n 11658 ex 43-30367, G-AJDS; Dr. G. Meyer.

REGENSBURG. Airfield. *Focke-Wulf Fw44J Steiglitz* D-EFUR c/n 1899 ex Fv617; H. Hanni.

RETHEM. Airfield. *Piper L-4J Cub* D-EBUK c/n 12593 ex 44-80297, OO-AHP; M. Liebisch.

RHEINBOLLEN. Airfield. *Piper L-4J Cub* D-EBYS c/n 12520 ex 44-80224; E. Lulzer.

ROSDORF. Airfield. *Fairchild Argus 2* D-EHIB c/n 834 ex 43-14870, HB597, HB-EAK; P. Hulshoff.

RUHPOLDING. Airfield. *Klemm Kl 35D* D-EFES c/n 1853 ex Fv 5019, SE-BGI; W. Frome.

SAARBRUCKEN. Airport. *Piper L-4J* D-ENAC c/n 12802 ex 44-80506, F-BFQB, SL-AAX, University Flugsport. *Fairchild Argus 3* D-EMYB c/n 1132 ex 44-83171, KK514, F-BDAQ, SL-AAW; A. Paul.

SCHAMEDER. Airfield. *Auster V* D-ENIS c/n 1812 ex TW473; Flugsportverein.

SCHLESWIG. Kriegsmarine base. *Hawker Sea Hawk* reported—serial?

SCHLOTTENSTEIN. Airfield. *Piper L-4J Cub* D-ELUM c/n 13249 ex 45-4509, HB-OFG; A. Mahnicke.

SCHMALLENBERG. Airfield. *Auster V* D-ELUT c/n 1236 ex RT607, HB-EOC; Flug Rennefeld.

SCHWARZENFELD. Airfield. *Piper L-4J* D-EMUR c/n 12914 ex 44-80618, HB-OCE; Aeroclub.

SCHWELM. Autobahnkreuz. Mr. Waldefried Eilhoff plans to convert ex-Luftwaffe *Noratlas*, code 52+37, into a "Flugzeug-Restaurant" (aircraft restaurant).

SEESTER. Airfield. *Focke-Wulf Fw44J* D-EFUD c/n 83 ex Fv631, SE-AWT; P. Hell.

SIEBERG. Airfield. *Messerschmitt Bf 108* D-EHAF Werk-Nr 730253; F. Wirth. Formerly PH-PBC, used by Prince Bernhard of Netherlands.

SIEGERLAND. Airfield (Verkehrsflughafen, near Burbach) *CASA 2111* (Construcciones Aeronauticas SA, Tablada, Spain) Spanish built Heinkel He 111H-16. D-CAGI coded 6J+PR owned by Gp Cpt T. G. Mahaddie, flown to Germany to publicise "Battle of Britain" film. Not now airworthy and may return to England for Battle of Britain Museum, Chilham Castle, Kent. Probably G-AWHA c/n 025. *Focke-Wulf Fw44J Stieglitz* D-EMOF c/n ASJA-82, ex Fv630 SE-CBE; Luftsportverein Siegerland, also *D-EDYV* c/n 2549, ex Fv 935. *Auster 5* D-ECUZ c/n 3414 ex G-APUL; E. J. Clade Ptnrs.

CASA 2111 (Siegerland)

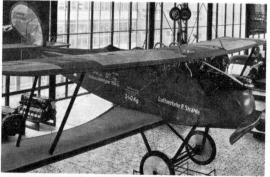

Halberstadt CL.IV (Stuttgart)

Luftwaffenmuseum (Uetersen)

SIERSBERG. Airfield. *Messerschmitt Bf 108* D-EDIH c/n 1660 ex D-IDBT, G-AFZO, ES955, G-AFRN, HB-ESL, SL-AAV; B. Klein.

SONTHOFEN. WGAF base. *NA F-86 Sabre* and *Lockheed TF.104F Starfighter* outside Bundeswehrkaserne. Serials & pics please.

SPEYER. Airfield. *Tiger Moth* D-EGXY c/n 84641 ex T6193, G-AMCK, HB-UAC; W. Scherpf.

SPRENDLINGEN. Airfield. *Piper L-4H Cub* D-EDOH c/n 10612 ex 43-29321, F-BGQV, SL-AAZ; Sport-Rhode.

STRASKIRCHEN. Airfield. *NA AT-6F Texan* D-FDEM c/n 121-42500 ex 44-81778, D-IDEM. *Klemm Kl 35D-160* D-EDUX c/n 3001; both owned and flown by J. Hossl.

STUTTGART. Daimler-Benz Museum. *Halberstadt CL.IV* original 2-seat ground-attack aircraft re-worked with 160 hp Daimler 3A to carry pilot and two passengers. Used from January 1921 as D-71, owned by Paul Strähle former CO Jadgstaffeln 57 and 18 (14 victories Ace.) Operated early German civilian scheduled air service. Max speed 103 mph, 3-hr endurance. *Fieseler Fi 156 Storch* OE-ADS Werk-Nr 3819 was reported based at Stuttgart Echterdingen—confirmation?

TARP. West German Navy. Barracks of MFG 2—*Sea Hawk* serial?

HA-1109-MIL (Uetersen)

TOGING. Airfield. *Piper L-4H Cub* D-EAXY c/n 11905 ex 44-79703, F-BFQX; F. Berger.

UELZEN. Airfield. *Piper L-4H Cub* D-EMYL c/n 11740 ex 43-30449, HB-OSR; R. Detel Ptnr.

UETERSEN. Luftwaffenmuseum. Contact Oberstabsarzt Dr. Boecker 2082 Uetersen, Appener Hauptstrasse. Aircraft reported at 1st March, 1973:—*Bucker Bu 181 Bestmann* NE+IR; Probably ex Swedish. *CASA 2111B* restored as Heinkel He 111 G1+AD. *Dornier Do 27A-4* 57+38 of LekG 43, WGAF. *Fairey Gannet AS.4* UA+106 of MFG 3, WG Navy. Possibly UA+110. *Fiat G-91R-4* BR+239 of WGAF, of FFS "A". c/n 0113. *Bristol 171 Sycamore 52* 78+04 c/n 13442 of HTG 64, WGAF. *Hispano HA-1109-MIL*, Spanish-built Bf 109. *North American Harvard IV* AA+622 ex Flugzeugfuhrerschule "A" WGAF. Previously 52-8570. *Lockheed T-33A* EB+399 of AG 52, WGAF. *Lockheed TF-104F Starfighter* 26+06 ex 59-5002, from WsLw 10. *Canadair Sabre 6* JB+110 of LeKG 43, WGAF, c/n 1643. *Republic F-84F Thunderstreak* BF+106 of TsLw 1. *Republic RF-84F* EB+344 of AG 52, WGAF. *Sikorsky H-34G* 80+34, ex CA+351; VIP transport of F1BerBMVtg. c/n 58-1099. *Fouga CM-170 Magister* AA+014 c/n 229. *DS 10 Fledermaus 2* D-9534. *Martin Matador* rocket on trailer. *Nike Ajax* and *V2*. Other exhibits are being sought to make this one of Europe's most interesting collections of military a/c.

ULM. Boelke-barracks. *F-84F-30RE* no markings but delivered ex DE+368, and mounted on pylon; ex 51-1816.

UNTERBOHRINGEN. Airfield. *Klemm Kl 35D* D-EFUB c/n 1810 ex Fv5011, SE-BGH, HB-UXC; H. Reichart.

UNTERGLAUHEIM. Airfield. *Auster IV* D-EGUK c/n 900 ex MT163, G-ANHN; J. Gotteschall Ptnr.

UNTERWOSSEN. Alpine Gliding School. Reported there are two *1939 Mu 17s* and one *1938 Mu 13a* gliders. Photos with confirmation, appreciated.

WAHN. (Cologne) WGAF HQ. *Lockheed F.104F.* Serial wanted.

WARSTEIN. Airfield. *Piper L-4J Cub* D-EFQK c/n 12308 ex 44-80012, OO-ZOU, F-BFQK; K. Bock.

WASSERKUPPE. (on top of) Rhön-Museum. *Grunau (Hirth) Baby IIb* D-4303 "Landkreis Fulda" *Schulgleiter SG-38* "Bockenheimer Brot". *Lilienthal monoplane glider* (replica) Plus another glider, similar to the Lilienthal and many models and other items. Photos please.

WEIL-AM-RHEIN. Airfield. *Piper L-4J* D-ELRO c/n 12144, ex 44-79848, F-OBAX, F-BFNM; K. Koppenhofer.

WERNSTEIN. Airfield. *Fairchild Argus 3* D-EFML c/n 947 ex 43-14983, HB709, HB-EIR; K. L. F. von Kuenssberg

WERSAU. Airfield. *Piper L-4J* D-EMYR c/n 12967 ex 44-80671; H. Loffler.

WIESBADEN. Airport. *Fairchild Argus 2.* D-EHUL c/n 857 ex 43-14893 HB620, HB-EAB; H. Fisch.

WILDENRATH. RAF base. With Flt Lt Jeremy Collins No 60 Sqdn. *Gloster Gladiator II* N5589 remains; for possible restoration after expedition on behalf of RAF Museum—other remains at Henlow, Beds.

WITTAGE. (see Preussisch-Oldendorf.)

WITTMUNDHAFEN. WGAF. *Canadair Sabre 6* JA+000 of JG71.

WOLFERSHEIM. Airfield. *Auster V* D-ENIR c/n 1815 ex TW477, G-AOSL; W. Schmitt.

WUNSTORF. Airfield. *Fieseler Fi 156 Storch* D-EKUS c/n 741 ex HB-LKA; R. Klimmik. At WGAF gate *F.84F* DE+101 ex 52-6687 ex Jabo G35.

WURZBURG. Airport. *Focke-Wulf Fw44J Stieglitz* D-ECUX c/n 91 ex Fv 639, SE-BXN; Flugsportsclub Wurzburg. *Piper L-4A Cub* D-EMOG c/n 9296 ex 42-36642, OO-AAH; A. Seufert.

GREECE

ATHENS. Airport. *Douglas C-47B* SX-BBE c/n 26459 ex 43-49198, KG782 (RAF) reported to be preserved. Other *Dakotas* operating from here include SX-BAG c/n 26880 ex 43-49619; SX-BAH c/n 26565 ex 43-49304; SX-BAK c/n 26095 ex 43-48834; SX-BAL c/n 25923 ex 43-48662; and SX-BBF c/n 4860 ex 41-20090, PH-NDV; All with Olympic Airways. Reported now based at Athens Airport, from Bahrein, the fleet of oil magnate John W. Mecom, including:—*Douglas B-23 Dragon* N86E c/n 2745; *Lockheed Lodestar* N5231N c/n 2512; *Curtiss C-46D-10 Commando* N9588Z ex 44-77572; *Fairchild C-82A Packet* N127E c/n 10150, from 45-57190/57780.

ATHENS. War Museum. *Farman Biplane Replica* of Greek Army aeroplane flown by Lt Camberos in 1912. Built at the State Aircraft Factory under the supervision of Mr. Alex Ardis, 1968. *Curtiss SB2C Helldiver. Piper Cub* serial 241 of Army Air Service. *North American F86D Sabre* 518404.

LARISSA. Air Base. *Republic F84G* serial 23110 mounted on concrete blocks.

Douglas B-23 Dragon (Athens)

Farman Biplane—replica (Athens)

Boeing-Stearman E.75 (Tatoi)

Spitfire IX (Tatoi)

MEGARA. *Boeing-Stearman E.75*'s of Social Welfare Ministry SX-EAG c/n 75-8514 ex Bu-43420; SX-EAZ c/n 75-8499 ex Bu-43405; SX-EBB c/n 75-8537 ex Bu-43443; and SX-EBF c/n 75-8191 ex Bu-38570.

TATOI. Air base. *Republic F84G* serial 26901. *Supermarine Spitfire IX* serial MJ755, despatched by 33 MU, Lyneham via 222 MU to Casablanca in February, 1944, but no details of operations recorded. Transferred to Royal Hellenic Air Force in 1947 and based at Elevsis, Sedes, and Tatoi. To State Aircraft Factory in 1950 for overhaul, later stored at Hellenikon Airport. Now at *Air College Museum, Tatoi*. *Boeing-Stearman E.75* SX-EAV c/n 75-8399 ex Bu-43305; and SX-EBC c/n 75-8073 ex Bu-38452; both Royal Aeroclub of Greece.

HUNGARY

BUDAPEST. Kozlekedesi Museum, in centre of city. Curator of aviation, Mr. Pol Rev. Displayed outside *Benez-Mraz Sokol* HA-REA, dark-green, immaculate condition. Inside: *Junkers F 13* restored by Mr. Erno

Magyar Lloyd Biplane (Budapest)

Benez-Mraz Sokol (Budapest)

Rubik, designer of the Kanya. Registered CH-59 in livery of Ad Astra, the forerunners of Swissair, lettered "OO" under wings. Originally a floatplane it was confiscated after landing in Hungary 1921. After conversion to landplane was used by Regent of Hungary. In excellent condition. *Magyar Lloyd* biplane—first Hungarian fighter. *Aladar Zselyi* monoplane (replica) the first Hungarian aircraft to fly. There are also many engines and include the one from the original Zselyi, the Ardorjan and Dedica of 1909, Hungary's first aero-engines. *Gyongyos 33*, first Hungarian glider now displayed here. In store at the old gliding airfield, half-an-hour from Budapest by car, seen only by prior appointment and in company of museum representative:— *Fabian Levante* HA-LEB parasol primary trainer with 105 hp Hirth HM-504A engine. *Rubik R-18 Kanya II* HA-RUF and *HA-RUG* high-wing STOL glider tugs with 160 hp M-11-FR engine. *Brandenburg D.1* of 1927. *Samu-Geonczy S.G.2 Kek-Madar* HA-BKF, with 105 hp Hirth HM-504A. A low-wing cabin monoplane which won post-war design competition organized by National Hungarian Aviation Association. Prototype completed 50 hrs flying but did not go into production. *Koma* glider HA-5070. *Lepke* glider HA-1039. *Pilis* glider.

Fabian Levante (Budapest)

ICELAND

AKUREYRI. Airfield. *Auster 5A* TF-LBP c/n 1577 ex TJ592; J. Fossdal & Ptnr. *Piper J-3C Cub* TF-JMF c/n 10606 ex 43-29315; Nordurflug.

MULAKOT. Airfield. *Fleet Finch II* TF-KAL c/n 293 ex RCAF 4491. and *Finch II* TF-KAN c/n 651 ex RCAF 4772; A. Gudmundsson & Ptnrs.

REYKJAVIK. Airport. *DH82C Tiger Moth* TF-KBD c/n 1407 ex RCAF 1204; T. Einarsson. Awaiting rebuild to flying condition. *Stearman PT-17* TF-KAU c/n 75-1556 ex 41-7997; M. Matthiasson. Awaiting rebuild to flying condition. *Auster J/1 Autocrat* TF-ACC c/n 2207 ex G-AIGV; H. Arnorss. *Piper J-3C-65 Cub* TF-KAP c/n 12156 ex 44-79860, G-ALGH; K. B. Gudmundsson. *Republic RC-3 Seabee* TF-RKH c/n 171 ex N6002K; G. Sirgurbergsson. *Klemm L 25 E7r* TF-SUX c/n 847 ex D-ESUX, presented by German Government in 1936, being restored. Owned by A. K. Hansen. *Douglas C-47A* TF-ISB c/n 9860, ex 42-23998, FD939, G-AIBA (ntu) G-AKSM and *C-47A* TF-ISH c/n 25306 ex 43-48045, KG762, are operated from here by Icelandair. One may be preserved. Also at the airfield is a *1940 home built* with unofficial registration TF-OGN. Construction commenced by two mechanics in 1932; a one bay, two-seat biplane with 90 hp Gipsy engine. First flew 23-11-40 but further flying after the fourth flight banned by RAF because of war.

Piper J-3C Cub (Reykjavik)

ITALY

BARI. Museo de Bari. *Idrovolante* 1917, ex Austrian A.F.

BERGAMO. Museo del Risorgimento. *Ansaldo A-1 Balilla* serial 16553, flown by Italian Ten. Dil. Antonio Locatelli *Nieuport Bebé,* also reported here, flown by Locatelli; but in absence of picture would like confirmation. *Stinson L-5* I-AEGD ex MM52847 flying locally, may be preserved. *Piper J-3C-55 Cub* I-BOBO c/n 12128 ex 44-79832, I-PIST; and *I-SARI* c/n 12612 ex 44-80326, SE-BFE, D-ELIC here with A. C. Bergamo.

Ansaldo A-1 (Bergamo)

BOLOGNA. Airport. *Tiger Moth* I-BANG c/n 85482 ex DE486, G-APRY. *Piper J-3C-65 Cub* I-CAID c/n 13203 ex 45-4463 and *I-VOLE* c/n 11412 ex 43-30121; all A. C. Bologna.

NA-Cavalier Mustang (Florence)

BRESCIA. Airfield. *Fairchild F-24R.46A Argus III* I-FRIF c/n 1036, ex 44-83097, KK418; *Piper J-3C-65 Cub* I-AGAA c/n 12079 ex 44-79783 and *I-PIPA* c/n 13142 ex 45-4402; all three owned and operated by A. C. Brescia.

BRESSO. Airport (Milan). *Fairchild F-24R.46A Argus III* I-AIAT c/n 1041 ex 44-83080, KK423, I-FULN and *I-SIEN* c/n 955, ex 43-14991, HB717, OO-FAB; Accademia Paracadustica Italiana. *Tiger Moth* I-APLI c/n 86562, PG653, G-APLV, I-RIBU; D. Pertile. *Bucker Bu 131 Jungmann* I-CERM c/n 57, ex A-45, HB-UTW; A. C. Milano. *Piper J-3-65 Cub* I-MALU c/n 11950 ex 44-79654; A. Rastelli. *Caproni Ca.100* I-ABMT of 1934 ex MM55914; I. Ballerio (restoring?)

CASALE MONFERRATO. Airfield. *Bucker Bu 131 Jungmann* I-GEVA c/n 7 ex HB-UTY; M. Lucchini. *Ansaldo SVA.* A-O Balilla owned nearby by Fam. Palli.

COMO. Aeroclub. *Caproni Ca.100 Seaplane* I-ABOU, c/n 3992; Also *I-COMA, Piaggio P-136.*

Caproni Ca. 100 (Como)

CREMONA. Airfield. *Auster IV* I-ALLO c/n 945 ex MT295; A. C. Cremona. *Viberti Musca* I-DIAN (rarity).

CUNEO. Airfield. *Piper J-3-65 Cub* I-BISI c/n 13121 ex 44-80825, F-BCPG; A. C. Cuneo.

FANO. Airport. *Stinson L-5B* I-AEEJ ex MM52897 with stretcher-case hatch along fuselage. At the nearby Vitali Garage may still be displayed *Percival Proctor V* I-ADOH (publicised in Italy as I-ADOM) c/n Ae 80, ex G-AHWX, MM56707.

FLORENCE. Airport. *NA-Cavalier F-51D Mustang* I-BILL ex 44-74694 N6851D; Ditta Billi & Co. *Fairchild Argus III* I-FULC c/n 1032 ex 44-83071, KK414. *Bucker Bu 131 Jungmann* I-CABI c/n 21 ex A-12, HB-UTZ; both owned by A. C. Firenze. *Piper J-3-65 Cub* I-FIVI c/n 11255 ex 43-29964. *I-NUBI,* c/n 12125 ex 44-79829, both owned and flown by P. Guerrini.

GARDOLO. Shell Garage F.lli De Gasperi. *Nardi F.N.305*

GARDONE. Vittoriale Museum. *Ansaldo SVA 5 "V-2"* flown by Gabriele d'Annunzio, 1918.

GORIZIA. Aeroclub Campoformido. *Fairchild UC-61*—details wanted. *Ali Viberti Musca* I-CAIA, c/n 11 said to bè preserved here. *Fiat G.46-1B* I-AEHN c/n 14 ex MM52781 and *G.46-4B* I-AEKA c/n 180 ex MM53304 are now flying here.

LATINA. School of Artiglieria Foce Verde. *Spitfire IX*—serial/pic.

LINATE. Airfield. *Cessna UC-78 Bobcat* I-JLEP c/n 4907 ex 43-7387; Soc. I.R.T.A.

LUGO-di-ROMAGNA. Castle. Museo Baracca. *SPAD VII* flown by Francessco Baracca, hangs from ceiling above his personal gear and some engines from the aircraft he shot down.

Caproni Ca.3 (Milan)

MILAN. Museo Nazionale Della Scienza E Della Tecnica. Full details required. *Henri Farman* of 1909, constructed by Savoia. *Bleriot XI* of 1910, *Nieuport* of 1910, constructed by Macchi. *Ricci* triplane. *Breda 15* of 1929. *de Havilland DH.80A Puss Moth* I-FOGL c/n 2114 *Cierva C-30A Autogiro* MM30030 c/n 753 ex G-ACXA, I-CIER. Avro built of 1934. *Arado Macchi MC 205*. *DH.100 Vampire* MM6112 *Savoia Marchetti S.M.102 Nardi F.N.333* Anfibio. *Magni Vale* of 1937. *Caproni-Campini* experimental. *Caproni T.M.2* of 1943, military transport glider. *Zoegling* glider. And very many fascinating engines and other exhibits from the Anzani of 1907 (dirigible) Anzani 1909, to the de Havilland Goblin of 1948 and Pratt & Whitney 91 of 1950. *Caproni Ca.3* moving here; with many other exhibits from Turin.

NAPLES. Airport. *Beech UC-45J* 03558, US Navy, based here, confirmation wanted. At 1st. Fermi Is *Fiat G.59* MM52774.

PALERMO. Airfield. *Fairchild Argus III* I-FRIB c/n 1024 ex 44-83063, KK406; with A. C. Palermo.

PAVIA. Airstrip. *Piper J-3C-65 Cub* I-MICI c/n 10900 ex 43-29609; P. Pietra.

PERUGIA. Children's Play Park. *Aeromacchi M.416* ex I.A.F., also *Fiat G.59* MM53526 and *Piaggio P.136L* MM80077.

PISA. Technical School *Canadair Sabre 6* serial 19782.

RAVENNA. Airfield. *Piper J-3C-65 Cub* I-NITA c/n 10905 ex 43-29614; A. C. Ravenna.

REGGIO EMILIA. Airfield. *Piper J-3C-65 Cub* I-SASC c/n 9916 ex 43-1055; A. C. Reggio Emilia.

RIMINI. IAF base. *Canadair Sabre 6*—serial & pic please. *Republic F-84 Thunderstreak* 26375 minus starboard wing (which stands mounted on ground with squadron history inscribed thereon. In the local Children's Park (Disneyland) *Fiat G.46* unserialled.

ROME. Urbe Airport. *Fairchild Argus III* I-BIOR c/n 1049 ex 44-83088, KK431, MM56699; now U. Piazzesi. *Auster 5D* I-FOTO c/n 1814, ex TW472, F-OAJP, TS-BJP; G. Castaldi. *DH. Tiger Moth* I-JENA c/n 84682 ex

T6256, G-APLR; Balbo Ptnrs, also *Tiger Moth* I-RIBI ex NL765, G-APJK. *Stinson L-5* I-AEKW ex MM52864; *Fiat G-46-6* I-AEKT c/n 216 ex MM53491 also fly here. *Fiat G.12* and *Fiat G212* reported static. At Rome's Museo del Genio is *Bleriot XI* c/n 412 of 1911; from Lybic War 1911-13. At the Institute Galilei is the *Sikorsky S.51*

At the Francesco de Pinedo Institute is *Fiat G.46B* I-AEHP c/n 11 ex MM52778 and *V.785 Viscount* I-LIRG c/n 284 ex N6594C of Alitalia.

See under *VENEGONO* and *VIZZOLA TICINO* for Caproni Museums.

ROVERETO. Museo St. It. Guerra. *Nieuport XVIII* of 1916 described as Ni 10, constructed under license by Macchi, with Gnome Rhone 90 hp engine. A serial 13469 has been quoted but whether for airframe or engine not known.

SARZANA. Airfield. *DH. Tiger Moth* I-GIVI c/n 84559 ex T6068, G-AISR; V. Grimaldi.

TURIN. Museo Del Volo (Aeronautica Militare Italiana) *Bleriot XI* of 1913 constructed under license by S.I.T. *Blume B.L.160*. *Hanriot H.D. 1*, constructed under license by Macchi. *Caproni Ca.33* trimotor (450 hp) of 1917. *Macchi M 39* for Schneider Trophy 1926. *Macchi MC 72* built for 1931 Schneider Trophy race; unable to compete but established seaplane record 440.68 mph. *Fiat CR 32*, camouflaged. *Macchi MC 205* MM9546. *Fokker* of 1930. *Fiat G.5 bis* I-BFFI. c/n 5 ex MM290. *Fiat G.82* MM53886 "19" c/n 3. *Fiat G.46*—serial wanted. *Fiat G.49* MM556. *Macchi MB.323* MM554, was coded RS.10 (only one built). *Caproni Trento F.5* MM553 (only one built). *Caproni-Campini CC.2*, first prototype (known also as N-1) first flew 27 August 1940 applying jet principle of propulsion by using 900 hp Isotta-Fraschini piston engine in a duct (the fuselage) driving 3-stage compressor, with a ring of fuel injectors to heat compressed air. After 1941 Milan-Pisa-Rome flight the project, beset by troubles, was dropped. *DH.113 Vampire Mk 54 (NF.10)* MM6152, built by Macchi. *NA P-51D Mustang* serial 4323 "RR"—further details wanted. *Aerfer Sagittario II* MM561 (one built) *Aerfer Ariete* MM569. *Ambrosini Supersette S.7* MM558. *Piaggio*

Macchi MC 72 (Turin)

Caproni-Campini CC.2 (Turin)

DH.Vampire Mk 54 (Turin)

Savoia-Marchetti Sm.79 (Turin)

Macchi MC.202 (Vigna-di-Valle)

Ansaldo SVA (Vigna-di-Valle)

P.150 MM555 (only one built). *Savoia-Marchetti SM.79* L-112 ex Lebanese Air Force, Beirut—one of several "successes" of early V. and V. editions in that a reader-report was transmitted to the RAF Air Attache in Rome who alerted the Italian authorities who quickly obtained this rare machine as a gift from the Lebanese. At last check there were still two SM-79 aircraft in the open near Beirut. There is also a *Wright* biplane (replica) displayed in Turin. Now please see VIGNA DI VALLE, for the museum's other exhibits.

Flying from Turin (Orbassano) are several vintage types:—
Fairchild Argus III I-AIAO c/n 1028 ex 44-83067, KK410, I-FULI, Soc. Aeroscuola Cerrina. *Piper J-3C-65* I-ALDO c/n 13071 ex 44-80775, HB-OES; M. Dogliani & M. Carossia also *I-TESC* c/n 12296 ex 44-80000: A. C. Apuano. From Turin Aeritalia N. flies *Argus III* I-FULF c/n 1033 ex 44-83072, KK415 of Soc. Aeral.

UDINE. Technical School. *Macchi MC 205V* MM91818; *F86E Sabre* "2-37" of 2nd Aerobrigatte, believed MM-16680; *Fiat G.46* unmarked.

VARESE. Airfield. *Auster 5* I-DOGE c/n 1253 ex RT-624; A. C. Vergiate. *Tiger Moth* I-MOMI c/n 83790, T7276, G-APTV; C. Guidi. *Piper J-3C-65 Cub* I-REDO c/n 11438 ex 43-30147 and *I-SISI* c/n 12474 ex 44-80178; both A. C. Vergiate.

VENEGONO SUPERIORE. Museo Aeronautica Caproni di Taliedo, near Milan. Permission must be obtained before visiting. *Caproni Ca.1* of 1910 with 25 hp Miller engine. *Caproni Ca.22* of 1913, Parasol—Gnome Rhone 80 hp. *Caproni-Bristol* of 1913, Gnome Rhone 80 hp. *Gabardini 2* of 1913 with Le Rhone 80 hp. *Caproni Ca.20* of 1914 with Gnome Rhone 110 hp. *Caproni Ca.36* of 1917, 3-motor IF 150 hp, 2378. *Ansaldo SVA 5* of 1918—a serial 11777 is quoted. *Gabardini* biplane of 1918 with Gnome 110 hp. *Fokker D.VIII* of 1920, serial MM2916 with Oberurstel VR 12 of 120 hp—the world's only example of a D.VIII. Other exhibits may come from Vizzola Ticino on rotation.

VENICE. San Nicolo Airport. *Fairchild F-24W.41A Argus II* I-MARC c/n 416 ex 43-14452, FS535, MM4314452; A. C. Venezia.

VERGIATE. Società Italiana Aeroplani Idrovolanti. *SIAI SM.50.*

VIGNA-di-VALLE, Near Rome. Aircraft of the Museo del Volo, Turin. Official restoration centre, visit by appointment only. *Republic P-47D Thunderbolt* MM4653 ex 51 Sqdn IAF. *Macchi MC.202 Folgore* MM-9667 ex 63 Sqdn IAF. *DH. Vampire F52* MM6085. *SPAD VII* with Hispano Suiza 150 hp engine. *SPAD VII* (già di Cabruna). *Ansaldo SVA* of 1918 with Spa 6 engine. Serial 11721 of 87a squadriglia. *Ansaldo AC-2* fighter 1208. *Wright* (replica). *Fiat C.29. Fokker* of 1930. *Fiat G.80. Fiat G.82. Macchi MC 200 Saetta* (Lightning) serial MM8307 of IAF, single-seat fighter. *Macchi M.39 Speedplane* of 1926. *Macchi MB.326*, under restoration. *Macchi 416. Cant Z.506 B Airone* (Heron) MM45425 mid-wing mono floatplane torpedo-bomber, some converted to air/sea rescue. *Savoia Marchetti SM.55* from lake for rebuild. *Piaggio P.136.* MM80078 and MM-80083. *Republic F-84G Thunderjet. F-84F Thunderstreak*

MM111049, plus another, 51st Aerobrigade. *RF.84F Thunderflash. N. A. Harvard. Lockheed T-33. Canadair F-86 Sabre* MM19724; 4th Aerobrigade. *M.D.B. 01 aeroscooter. Fiat G.59.* MM53772. *SAAB J.29F* Fv29543, donated by R. Swed.A.F. *Fiat G.91R.* The compiler would be grateful for serials and further details (with photos if possible).

Republic P-47D Thunderbolt (Vigna-di-Valle)

VINCENZA. Airfield. *Saiman 202* I-BIOM of 1937 ex MM52193; A. C. d'Italia.

VIZZOLA TICINO. Malpensa Museo Aeronautico di Taliedo. Available for visits 1973. *Caproni Ca.6* of 1910 with Rebus 50 hp engine. *Caproni Ca.18* of 1915 with Le Rhone 100 hp. Serial 231. *Caproni Ca.53* of 1917, triplane with Tosi V.12 300 hp. *Macchi 20* of 1923 I-AABO c/n 3588, 2-seat with 50 hp Salmson, *Breda Ba 19* of 1932 serial MM70019. *Caproni Ca.100* with Fiat A/50 90 hp engine ex MM56271, I-BIZZ. *Caproni Ca.100 float-plane* version I-DISC with Colombo S.63. *Caproni Ca. 113* of 1938 I-MARY c/n 3473 with Piaggio P.VII 370 hp. *Fairchild 24 C/8* I-GENI c/n 2622, imported 1935. *Caproni Ca.163* I-WEST of 1937, with Walter Minor 130 hp. *Ambrosini SAI.2S* of 1936 I-LANC. *Savoia Marchetti SM.80* of 1934 ex I-IATI then I-ELIO c/n 30-003 with Pobjoy Niagara 86 hp. *Saiman 202M* of 1938 I-BIOL c/n 5 ex MM52163 with Alfa 110/bis 120 hp. *Caproni Ca.193* prototype (only one) twin-engined 4-seat tourer I-POLO c/n 5736 last a/c built after the war by the Caproni Taliedo works. Walter Minor 180 hp engine. *M.D.B. 02 aeroscooter* of 1961 with Praga D. 75 hp. I-SELI, c/n 002. *Avia F.L.3* of 1947 I-AIAE c/n A-16 with CNA D/4 engine. *Republic Seabee* I-SIBI c/n 331 with Franklin 6A8 of 215 hp. *Badini* 1943 prototype with Alfa 110 engine. *Savoia Marchetti 102* of 1947. Under restoration here and destined for Museo del Volo, Turin:— *Caproni Ca.9* of 1911 with Anzani 35 hp. *Caproni Ca.100* of 1934 I-GTAB c/n 1 with Colombo S.63. *Caproni-Reggiane Re.2000 Falco* (Falcon) fighter with Piaggio P.XI. *Caproni-Reggiane Re.2002 Ariete* (Ram) fighter-bomber. *Caproni-Reggiane Re.2005 Sagittario* (Archer) single-seat fighter, serial MM92351—48 delivered to Regia Aeronautica. There are also many fascinating dirigible exhibits and engines from Anzani of 1910 to the Isotta Fraschini V. 4.

LAPPLAND

There are known to be several wrecked aircraft here including *Junkers Ju 52/3m* Werk-Nr 5596 code G6+OM. *Junkers Ju 88 A-5* and a *Bf 109 E* coded DB+3F. It is thought attempts will be made to obtain these probably for the Finnish Air Force Collection.

LUXEMBOURG

FINDAL. Airport. *Piper L-4J Cub* LX-ABO c/n 12847 ex 44-80551, HB-OAB, OE-ABO; Aero-Sport. *Focke-Wulf Fw44J Stieglitz* LX-OOI ex Fv648, SE-AYY, D-EBOB, HB-EBO; owned & flown by N. Theisen. *Klemm L 25 R15* LX-MAF c/n 772 ex LX-SAF; H. Kraemer.

MALTA

VALLETTA. The Palace Armoury. *Gloster Sea Gladiator* N5519 sole survivor of the legendary trio "Faith, Hope and Charity" which defended the George Cross Island until the first Hurricanes arrived. Post-war research has tended to play down the legend, put about for propaganda purposes. The aircraft is now more symbolic of the overall Maltese defence.

Gloster Sea Gladiator (Malta)

Macchi 20 (Vizzola Ticino)

NETHERLANDS

AALBURG. Nr Veen. *Harvard* OO-JBP c/n 121-42480 ex 44-81758, F-BJBP; at tyre dealers.

ACHTERVELD. "Jeugddorp De Rudolfstitching" (playground). *NA Harvard* B-30 c/n 14A-1440 ex 43-13141, FT400, including parts of c/ns 14-894, 14-1536, 14-1721. In poor shape!

ADUARD. Firm. Knoop (car-breakers) On their roof: —*Harvard* PH-UBO c/n 78-6384—is it there now?

ALPHEN a/d **RIJN.** "Avifauna playground" *Harvard* B-133 c/n 14a- ex 43-13052, FT311, with parts of B-8 and B-143; once displayed in Breda.

Aviodome, Schiphol (Amsterdam)

Cierva C.30A (Amsterdam)

AMSTERDAM. Schiphol Airport. Aviodome. Open daily except 5th, 25th, 26th and 31st December. On right of Amsterdam-Hague motorway. Free buses from airport car-parks. From Amsterdam railway station No 55 bus stops at Aviodome. Entrance 2.75 guilders. Times 16 March to end September 1000-1700 Mondays-Saturdays. 1 October 15 March 1030-1600. Sundays all year 1200-1700. Displayed 1973:—Fokker F.VIIA painted H-NACT (destroyed by bombing at Schiphol 10/5/1940.) This machine is actually c/n 5054 ex CH-158 of Balair, 1928 OY-DED of D.L.S., then SE-ASE, OY-ASE; in 1955 to Schiphol as H-NACT of the National Luchvaart Museum (Dutch National Air Museum). Fokker C.V.D. 618 believed assembled from parts of

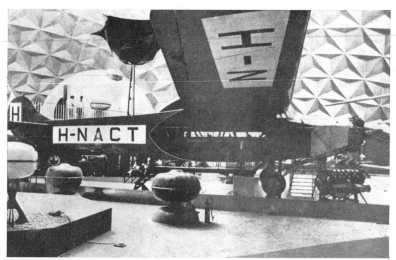

Fokker F.VIIA (Amsterdam)

Tiger Moth (Amsterdam)

Zogling glider (Amsterdam)

Fokker S.14 (Amstèrdam)

Hawker Hunter T.7 (Amsterdam)

Mercury capsule—replica (Amsterdam)

Hawker Sea Fury (Amsterdam)

several a/c. Once at Delft and at Soesterberg 1968/70. *Cierva C.30A* SE-AFI c/n 735 ex LN-BAD found in Swedish hanger and donated by K. Oberman in 1962. In WW II many aircrew were rescued from the Ostsee by Swedish pilot Rolf van Bahr in this a/c. *DH.82a Tiger Moth II* A-38 of R. Neth AF c/n 83101 ex RAF R5242. Finally used for glider-towing. Donated R. Neth AF. *Fokker S.14* prototype PH-XIV jet trainer ex R. Neth. AF K-1 c/n 6289. 1st flight 19.5.51. *Nederlandse Helicopter Industrie H-3 Kolibrie* PH-NHI, originally PH-NGV; c/n 3007 (real PH-NHI had c/n 3001). *Gloster (Fokker-built) Meteor F.8* I-189 but painted 7E-5 of Major Wansink "Ruiten Vier" (Diamond Four) team—loaned from Soesterberg but ex Leeuwarden AFB gate where it was Y9-15 ex 322/326 Squadrons. *Hawker Sea Fury FB.11* 6-43 ex WJ290, ex Delft Technical School. *Douglas C-47A-75-DL Dakota* of Rijks Luchvaart Dienst (Dutch Dept of Civil Aviation) PH-PBA c/n 19434 ex 42-100971, is destined for the museum as this is typed. Previously used as Prince Bernhardt's personal aircraft. *Grunau Baby 2A* glider PH-170 c/n 6052 built by Fokker after WW II formerly owned by K.N.V.v.L. *Zogling* glider PH-1—first glider registered. *Fokker 1911 Spin "Spider"* (replica). *Wright Flyer of 1903* (replica). *Lilienthal 1894* glider (replica). And many engines and other splendid exhibits. A *Mercury capsule* (replica) is on loan from NASM, Washington, and there are replicas of a Lunar module and a Sputnik. Negotiations are in hand for a Fokker D.VII and it is expected that K.L.M. will offer

machines as they become available. This Aviodome, costing 4 million Dutch guilders was built with joint contributions of the State of the Netherlands, Fokker, K.L.M., the Schiphol Airport Authority and members of the public. We hope the Aviodome will get the support it so richly deserves.
Flying from Schiphol with the Dutch National Aerospace Research Institute is *Hawker Hunter T.7* PH-NLH formerly XM126, then N-320 of R. Neth AF, c/n 41H-695342. This may go to the Aviodome when its useful work has ended. *Douglas DC-3 Dakota* PH-MAG c/n 12472 ex 42-92648, KG437, G-AGYX flying here with Moormans V.NV.

BEEK. Zuid Limburg Airport; next to Autoroute E9. *Gloster Meteor T.7* I-320 R. Neth AF ex VW417 (or 412) once with steps into cockpit for children to view; now may go to Soesterberg. *Stampe SV.4C* F-BCVC c/n 423, allotted PH-AFA but R.L.D. did not give permission—was standing in AFCENT hangar.

BOXMEER. Static is *Harvard* OO-JBW c/n 14a-190.

DEELEN. LETS (Air Force Technical & Electronics School) near Arnhem. The Netherlands AF Fire School. As this is compiled three unburned machines are here:—*Hawker Hunter 4* N-150 (former Deelen gate guardian). *Hawker Hunter 4* N-180 ex Nijmegen gate guardian. *CS-2A Tracker* 185-H (Canadian Navy 1507) ex R.N.N. Let us hope they can be offered for preservation. *Republic F-84F Thunderstreak* P-115 ex 52-7158 is reported as Deelen's new gate a/c in silver colourscheme. *Nike Hercules* serial 10383, booster 1450 also on base.

DE KOOY. Airbase. R. Neth Navy Air Station. *Grumman TBM-3 Avenger* coded 037 and possibly one ex Amsterdam Navy Yard coded 050. Earlier serials please. *Beech C-45G* serialled G-7 R. Neth AF ex 43-33336 was at the MLD Technical School here in good condition—photo please. *Sikorsky S-55* (HO4S-3) "Salomé" c/n 13777 ex MLD 8-2 then 076 is at the school with probably two *Harvards* 043/K c/n 14a-1216 ex 43-12917, FT176, R. Neth AF B-56, and *098/K* c/n 14a-1494 ex 43-13195, FT454, R. Neth AF B-84.

DELFT. Kluyverweg 1. Technical University. Visits by prior approval only. Aircraft change, but 1973:—*Republic F-84E-31-RE Thunderjet* R. Neth AF TP-2 of 306 Sqdn, ex 51-9583 USAF. Now numbered K-8. Also *Thunderjet K-6* R. Neth AF TP-25 of 306 Sqdn ex 51-9591 c/n 1358. *Hawker Sea Fury FB.11* 6-14 with Spitfire XIV propeller. (Confirmation of this a/c wanted.) *NHI Kolibrie H-2* PH-NFT c/n 2001 prototype. *Republic F-84F-61-RE Thunderstreak* 8T-7 ex 314 Sqdn R. Neth AF ex 53-6550; tail of Thunderstreak c/n 1638. *NA AT-16 Harvard IIB* RAF's FT228, ex 43-12969, c/n 14a-1268—R. Neth AF serial wanted. *Fokker S-13* PH-NEI c/n 6288, the prototype and only one. First flew as PH-NDW, then R. Neth AF as D-101, then PH-NEI. *Dornier Do.27A* OC+054 ex Luftwaffe, c/n 231 or 239. *Dornier Do.28A-1* 5N-ACQ c/n 3006 ex D-IHYL, PH-ACU, from Schreiner Aero Contractors, Nigeria. *Fokker F.27-100 Friendship* PH-NIV, first prototype c/n 10101; first flew 24 November 1955. *SAAB 91A Safir* PH-UEA c/n 91.125 from R.L.S. *Hawker Hunter F.4* N-102 R. Neth AF, Fokker-built c/n 8614. *Martin TM-61-C Matador.* In another building is *DHC Beaver 1* N7904C c/n 1288 (fuselage) and Link Trainer PH-TEE, and there are many parts of aircraft of all nationalities, some from WW II and some post-war. Reports of a piloted VI flying bomb and a V2 in an Army Museum are difficult to confirm and up-dated report and photos required.

DELFZIJL. The War Museum. On the roof of the building:—*Spitfire IX* MJ271, painted TA-26 of 313 Sqdn R. Neth AF and earlier claimed to be PT989 then PT873/3W-8/H-26. Believed ex-Volkel.

DEN HAAG (The Hague) Netherlands Luchtvaart Museum. Daily. *Free Balloons* PH-BOX and *PH-BVH* c/n 8619 "Marco Polo" and "Nibbo". Anthony Fokker School (for Aviation, Electronics, etc) Brinckhorstlaan 251. By appointment. *Grumman TBM-3W2 Avenger* 045 ex M.L.D. *NA AT-16 Harvard IIB* B-103 R. Neth AF. c/n 14a-1459 ex 43-13160, FT419. Also *B-199* c/n 14-610 ex 42-12363 FE876. And *B-179* c/n 14a-807, ex 43-12508, FS667, PH-NID. *Fokker S-14* L-11, R. Neth AF c/n 7356. *Hawker Hunter T.7* N-305 R. Neth AF, c/n 41H/693457. Expected at the school are a *Grumman Tracker* of MLD and *Thunderstreak*. Confirmation and photos/serials please.

DEN HELDER. Deibel Camp, R. Neth AF. *Hawker Hunter F.6* N-226.

EINDHOVEN. R. Neth AF base. *Republic F-84G Thunderjet* TB-1 of 315 Sqdn (formerly painted TC-1, 316 Sqdn.) *Spitfire IX* MK959 painted H-15 (formerly thought to be MJ289 and was painted VL-V of 167 Sqdn. re-numbered 322 (Dutch) Sqdn, RAF.) Originally with 302 Sqdn. 329 Sqdn, 165 Sqdn RAF. In the city at "Philipswonderland" is *F-84G* P-192 ex 53-6921 and there may also be a *Hunter*—details?

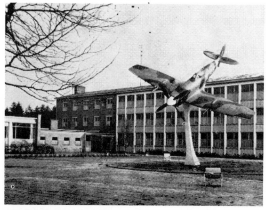

Spitfire IX (Eindhoven)

GELDROP. "The Puttershoek" Puttensedreef. *Hawker Hunter T.7* N-310—ex Eindhoven.

GILZE-RIJEN. R. Neth AF base. *Hunter F.6* N-258 ex 322 Sqdn and Leeuwarden gate. *N.A. Harvards* here:— B-175 c/n 14-765 ex 42-12518 FH131, and B-178 c/n 14-739 ex-FH105, 42-12492—possibly for exchange to get aircraft for R. Neth AF Museum. Stored here for this museum is *Harvard* B-182 c/n 14a-808 ex 43-12509 FS668. Reported also stored here *Fieseler Fi 156 Storch* D-EDEC all-silver and thought to be the machine used by Otto Skorzeny when he liberated Mussolini on the

Gran Sasso, Italy, 12/9/43. This machine became I-FACC before going back to Germany—confirmation would be appreciated, also future of aircraft. Flying here *N.A. Harvard* PH-BKT c/n 14a-1020 ex 43-12721 PS880, B-135, R. Neth AF; now J. A. H. M. Thurling.

HAARLEM. Technical School, Veldzichtlaan 1. *Fokker S-14* and *Grumman Tracker*—details please.

HAASTRECHT. Provinciale Weg Oost playing-garden. *Mraz M.1D Sokol* PH-NFK c/n 359.

HARDERWIJK. Firm. Block & Maneschijn. Static. *N.A. Harvard* B-136 c/n 14a-1053 ex 43-12754, FS913.

HILVARENBEEK. "Beekse Bergen" holiday-camp. *N.A. Harvard* B-14 c/n 14a-971 ex 43-12672, FS831—nose of *B-9* c/n 14-622 ex 42-12375 FE888. In pop-art name "Pekanus".

HILVERSUM. Airfield. *NA AT-6 Harvard* PH-NKD c/n 78-6922 ex 41-16544, Fv. 16291, OY-DYE, D-IGAL, D-FGAL, used for sky-writing in Holland. Also *AT-16 Harvard IIB* PH-SKL c/n 14a-868 ex 43-12569, FS728, B-104. Both owned by J. Daams.

HOEVEN. Nrd. Brabant. Swimming Pool/Playing Garden. *Consolidated PB2B-1 Catalina IVB* (built by Boeing) 16-212 of MLD. Believed formerly JX365 "P" of 205 Sqdn, RAF in Far East.

Catalina IVB (Hoeven)

HOOFDDORP. Airstrip. *Auster III* PH-NGK c/n 344 ex MZ231, R-18; Tugair NV.

LEEUWARDEN. R. Neth AF base. In use by "Impesa" Scouts. *N.A. Harvard* B-82 c/n 14a-1188, ex 43-12889, FT148; from LETS and the Deelen dump.

LEUSDERHEID. R. Neth. Army Camouflage School. *Gloster Meteor F.8* 9Y-25 from 323 Sqdn.

NIEUW LOOSDRECHT. Rading 74. Home of J. Daams. *Auster iii* PH-NGI c/n 295 ex MZ170, R-12; in garden.

NIJMEGEN. R.Neth.AF Barracks LIMOS (counterpart of our RAF Regt.) *F-84F Thunderstreak* P-183 ex 53-6626 ex 8T-4 of 314 Sqdn. At an Army Barracks here is *AT-16 Harvard* B-176 c/n 14-719, ex 42-12472, FE985. At the Blind Institut St. Henricus, Panovlaan:—*Beech D-18S* PH-UBX c/n A-105 ex NL-505, RIS, from Eelde.

OUD GASTEL. Moerdijk-Roosendaal Rd, Breakers Yard. *Bucker Bu 181 Bestmann* PH-KPK c/n 25112 ex D-EMEG. Reported still here—confirmation please.

NA Mitchell (Overloon)

Meteor F.8 (Soesterberg)

NA Mustang (Soesterberg)

Fokker S.14.1 (Soesterberg)

Piper L-18C Super Cub (Soesterberg)

OVERLOON. War Museum—Open-Air Display. *NA B-25D-20-NA Mitchell* coded 2-6 c/n NA 87-8957, ex 42-30792, FR193 "L" of 320 (Dutch) Sqdn, RAF, then B-6, M-6, A-17 of MLD. At Dunsfold, Surrey 1944. *Spitfire PR.XI* PL965 one of four used by Neth. AF Tech. School at Langham, Norfolk, then at LETS, Deelen. Painted 3-W but, like the Mitchell paintwork, is incorrect. *Fieseler Fi 103 V1* hangs over vehicle in which Dutch Royal Family left to join Royal Navy destroyer in 1940 when escaping from Occupied Holland.

ROTTERDAM. Zestienhoven Airport. Many vintage:— *Fairchild 24R-46A Argus* PH-NDH c/n 923 ex-43-14959, HB685; C. C. A. Kries. *Argus* PH-NDL c/n 961 ex 43-14997 HB723; National Vliegclub Beheer. *Piper L-4J Cub* PH-NLA c/n 12732 ex 44-80436, OO-GEI, OO-AVL; NV Nationale Luchtvaartschool. *Auster III* PH-POL c/n 274 ex MZ138; T. H. de Waal. *Piper L-4J Cub* PH-UCG c/n 13347 ex 45-4607; Cortinair. *PH-UCH* c/n 13348 ex 45-4608; W. Daams. *PH-UCI* c/n 13351 ex 45-4611; NV Nationale Luchtvaartschool. *PH-UCS* c/n 13228 ex 45-4488; C. J. Bleeker Ptnr. *PH-UCZ* c/n 13236, ex 45-4496; N.V.N.L.

SOESTERBERG. R.Neth. A.F. Base. *Hunter F.4* N-129 ex 325 Sqdn. *Gloster Meteor F.8* I-187—both on display. In hangar 3 is the R. Netherlands Air Force Museum, opened mid-1968 and opened to the public every Saturday from 1000-1600. Free. Curator, G. W. Glerum. Many aircraft are stored and changes are made as restorations are completed, or machines donated. Displayed:—*Avro Anson C.19* VM352 formerly 58 Sqdn, Coastal Com Sqdn, 232 OCU, RAF; ex RAE Llanbedr; flown from there 18 May 1971 by Neville Duke and Major Lauffenberg, R. Neth. A.F., now painted as R. Neth. A.F. machine D-26. *NA B-25* Mitchell painted as M-464 but ex Neth. East Indies AF and AURI, was 44-31258, N5-264, donated by Indonesian Govt and presented by HRH Prince Bernhard 23 October 1971. *Gloster Meteor F.4* I-69 ex VZ409 RAF, with 322 Sqdn, from Gilze Rijen May, 1968. *NA AT-16 Harvard IIB* B-184 c/n 14a-1100 ex 43-12801, FH124. *DH.82A Tiger Moth* A-10 c/n 86587 ex PG690, PH-UFC, built Morris Motors. *Hiller H-23C Raven* 0-36 c/n 937 ex 57-6521 (OH-12A). *DH.89A Dominie* V-3 "Gelderland" ex NF869 c/n 6740 ex PH-VNC (United Nations in Israel) V-3, PH-RAE, PH-TGC, PH-OTA (KLM Aerocarto and Aero Camera, Ritterdam). Was in Avifauna playground at Alphen, then 1968 to Soesterberg. *Supermarine Spitfire IX* MJ143 painted 3W-1,was in Schiphol Museum until 1968. Flew with No 1 CAACU as H-1, then 322 Sqdn R.Neth.AF. Originally 485 Sqdn, 66 Sqdn in RAF. *NA P-51K Mustang* H-307 c/n 111-30358 ex 44-12125, once at Delft Technical School, then Gilze Rijen. *Piper L-21A Super Cub* R-213 c/n 18-847 ex 51-15682. Was a glider-tug at MVK Valkenburg. *Hawker Hunter F.4* N-122 with 325 Sqdn badge—from Gilze Rijen, formerly "Paraat-exposition-aircraft". *Fokker S-14.1* L-17 c/n 7362 in service R.Neth.AF 1956/1967. Plus many exciting relics of early Dutch aviation with engines, propellers, guns etc. In store (see also Woensdrecht) *Republic F-84E Thunderjet* K-18 ex TP-9 of 306 Sqdn. *Auster V* PH-NET c/n 1416 ex TJ347,G-AIPE. *Piper L-18C Super Cub* R-87 c/n 18-3185 ex 53-4785 ex L-111 Belgian Army. May go to Gilze Rijen for storage. *DH. Mosquito FB.VI* TA122 ex 605 (County of Warwick) Sqdn.—fuselage etc, for restoration. Standing along the Utrecht-Amersfoort Rd at Soesterberg:— "Avio-Resto" Café-Restaurant are

Vickers Viking (Soesterberg)

coffee-bars comprising:—*Vickers Viking* G-AGRU c/n 112 (donated by Channel Airways) by air to Soesterberg January 1964 ex VP-TAX, one-time BEA's "Vagrant". *Vickers Viking* G-AGRW c/n 115, one-time BEA's "Vagabond" then to Hunting-Clan and Autair. *Vickers Viking* G-AHPB c/n 132, ex BEA's "Variety" then Hunting-Clan and Autair. All three now named after famous Dutch pilots "Henri Wijnmalen" "Flores Albert van Heijst" and "Marinus van Meel".

TWENTE. R. Neth. A.F. base. On pole at south side *NA F-86K-18-NA Sabre* Q-283 ex 54-1283, of 700 Sqdn, then 702 as ZX-6. First Dutch F-86K with 1,000 flying hours.

NA Sabre (Twente)

VALKENBURG. Air Base. Here are (or were) four cocooned *Lockheed SP-2H Neptunes* of MLD, serials 202, 203, 207, 214. Let us hope one is preserved in the Netherlands Museum and that the others are made available to other collections.

VEEN. Airfield. *AT-16 Harvard* PH-KMA c/n 14a-1216 is thought still airworthy with C. Honcoop who has bought many Harvards in recent years, some now re-sold to UK. It would be helpful to know if others are still here.

VOLKEL. R.Neth.A.F. It is believed that *"Starhunter"* A *Hunter* with Starfighter nose, tiptanks and tailplane, may be here—details and serial(s) please.

WESTERSCHOUWEN. "Duinrand" Camping-Café. *NA Harvard* (B-72 or B-193) but claimed c/n 14a-822 ex 43-12523 ex FS682—check on serial please.

WOENSDRECHT. R.Neth.AF. *Hunter F.4* N-173 is by the NCOs mess. The store for the Soesterberg Museum is here and has:—*Beech D-18S* PH-UDT c/n A-472 ex RIS from Eelde Airport. *NA F-86K Sabre* Q-296 ex 54-1296 "Cheesehunter" from Playing Garden at Koudekerk. *Republic F-84G Thunderjet* DU-24 (from Gilze Rijen)—(previous serial and history wanted.) *Republic F-84F Thunderstreak* P-134—thought to be ex-56-6726 of 314 Sqdn—confirmation please. *Gloster Gloster Meteor T.7* I-19 (ex WH233) once displayed here. *Hunter F.6* N-281, once with Air Scouts. Check please? *Hunter F.4* (two examples—serials please). *NA Harvards* B-64 and B-165 may be here—they are on museum list as stored. Details awaited—with photos. *Lockheed T-33* thought to be earmarked—serial?

YPENBURG. R.Neth.AF near Den Haag-Rotterdam road. *Fokker S-14* serial L-18 on pole near Avio-Diepen factory. *S-14* (with false serial L-26) also reported preserved here.

ZUIDHORN. Near Groningen. On roof of merchant's. *NA Harvard*—serial and history wanted please.

NORWAY

ALESUND. Airfield. *Grumman Widgeon* LN-HAL c/n 1332; SE-ARZ; Morefly A/S. *Norseman* LN-HAO c/n 810, ex 44-70545, SE-AYF; Nor-Wings A/S.

ASKER. Airfield. *DH.Rapide* LN-BEZ c/n 6838 ex NR750, G-AKIF, donated to Norwegian Paralift by Rothman's, for eventual preservation by N.A.H.S.

BARDUFOSS. 9353 Salangsverkert. Erling Njelstad. *R.A/c Factory BE.2e* serial 133 ex A1325. Let us hope this is restored for display somewhere.

BEKKELAGET. Airfield. *Luscombe 8F* LN-BWK c/n S-75 ex N3543G; A/S Orbis.

BODO. R.No.A.F. *Spitfire LFIXe* MH350 "M-FN" ex 349 (Belg) 331 and 332 (Norge) once "AH-V". Flown from Dyce (Aberdeen) to Sola 19 May 1945. *F-86K Sabre* 41245 "RI-Z" of 334 Sqdn. *Tiger Moth* LN-VYG c/n 85328 ex DE282,G-ANSB, LN-BDN flies here, owned by T. Naess.

Spitfire LFIXe (Bodo)

BREKSTAD. Airfield. *Piper L-4H Cub* LN-PAO c/n 12103 ex 44-79807 is with Orland Flyklubb.

DOVRE. Lake Lasjavann (Lesjaskog.) Not exhibited. *Gloster Gladiator II* N5579 (previously reported N5641) This is now known to be the machine in which P/O Mc Namara of 263 Sqdn shot down a Heinkel 111 over Lesjaskog on 25 May 1940 (the Heinkel still exists where

Gloster Gladiator II (Dovre)

it crash-landed on the mountain behind the lake). This Gladiator was recovered and a special shed was built to house it. Other than missing fabric and the boxed-in-with plywood rear fuselage, it is more or less complete and one hopes that in time it may be moved to a museum for public display. (See HENDON, England and WILDENRATH, Germany, for details of other Lesjaskog a/c).

ELVEBAKKEN. Airfield. *L-4H Cub* LN-SAE c/n 12852; 44-80556; Alta Flyklubb.

FAGERNES. Airfield. *Piper L-4J Cub* LN-RAK c/n 12889 ex 44-80593; Valdres Flyklubb.

FETSUND. Farm. *Schweitzer SGU 1* LN-GBR "Lille-balja" and *SGU.2* LN-GBT "Store-balja" gliders.

FORNEBU. Airport. *Piper J/4A Cub Coupe* LN-HAD c/n 4-568 of 1939 bought by Norwegians to train Finns for Winter War 39/40. Is it still here?

GARDERMOEN. R.No.A.F. *Taylor Cub* LN-FAB "Fabian" c/n 980 built 1937 was here, owned by Corporal Wadal—confirmation? Aircraft are, apparently, being stored here, for a possible R.No.A.F. Museum, and reports indicate the following:— *DH. Vampire 28C* c/n or serial 28456/93, built in Sweden under license, motor RM 1A/4122. This 2-seater donated by R.Swed. A.F. *NA F-86F Sabre* serialled J47-27 and an *F-86E* without engine—Previous serials and histories please. Also a *Bell H-13* stored.

HAMAR. Airfield. *L-4J Cub* LN-IKH c/n 12608, ex 44-80312, SE-BNI; A. S. Flytransport. *L-4J* LN-PAM c/n 12807, ex 44-80511 LN-RTM, SE-CGY; P. A. Munch.

HONEFOSS. Airport. *Beech D.18S* LN-BWG c/n A.954 ex N270M, SE-CHA; Nor-Fly A/S.

KIRKNESS. Airport. *UC-64 Norseman* LN-BIU c/n 59 ex RCAF 2486, R-AN; A/S. Varangfly.

KJEVIK. R.No.A.F. School of Technical Training. *Fairchild PT-26B* 43-36487 ex FZ708 RCAF "L-DM". Used at "Little Norway" Canada during WW II for training Norwegians for the RAF.

Fairchild PT-26B (Kjevik)

KONGSBERG. Airfield. *Piper L-4J Cub* LN-AEU c/n 12783 ex 44-80487; B. Svinningen.

LAKSELV. Airfield. *Piper L-4J Cub* LN-RAL c/n 12904, ex 44-80608; L. J. Sivertsen.

LISTA. R.No.A.F. *F-84G Thunderjet* "MU-S"; *F-86F Sabre* "AH-L" 31220.*V1*.

NAUSTE. Airstrip. *Auster 6A* LN-KCN c/n 3743, ex* VF514, SE-ELM; M. Reitan Ptnrs.

NESODDEN. Airfield. *Luscombe 8A* LN-VYF c/n 4891 ex LN-MAH (and parts from LN-MAK):— K. H. Johensen.

OERLAND. R.No.A.F. On display at the entrance. *Republic F-84G-31-RE Thunderjet* 52-2912 "MU-J" ex 338 Sqdn.

Loening Amphibian (Oslo)

Bleriot (Oslo)

OSLO. Norsk Teknisk Museum. Still awaiting additional space and many splendid exhibits remain stored. Following displayed:—*Rumpler Taube* "Start" of 1912, the first Norwegian aeroplane, in which Lt. H. F. Dons crossed Oslo Fjord 1 June 1912. *Bleriot II* "Nordsjoen" of 1914, c/n 794 (or M.57) the plane in which Lt Tryggve Gran made first North Sea crossing 30 July 1914 from Cruden Bay, Scotland to Revtangen, south of Stavanger. *Maurice Farman Longhorn* of 1913, the first military type used initially by the Norwegian Army and later by their Navy. The other, sometimes unrestored, machines include:—*Maurice Farman Shorthorn* of 1918, used by Norwegian Army. *Avro 504K*—serial wanted—of 1918, ex Norwegian Army. *Loening Amphibian* LN-BAH of 1935 —the plane in which Thor Solberg flew from New York over Greenland, Iceland, Faeroes, to Bergen and Oslo, July 1935. *R.A/c Factory B.E.2e*. serial wanted. *Deperdussin*, used by Norwegian flying enthusiast, Jul Hansen, 1912. At Akershus Castle, in store for Norwegian Aviation Historical Society c/o The Army Museum:—*Farman F.40*, parts of XL.11; PU.227K, PC 148K and "79" ex Army Air Force, from which it is hoped to make one machine. *Henschel HS.293* gliderbomb Werk-Nr 21816. Gerat Nr 109-507. B.1. On fin 0-20455. *DH.Tiger Moth* SE-ANL Norwegian built c/n 161, flown into Gardermoen in C.130 5 May 1971 and *Fairchild Cornell* LN-BFI c/n T-40-266, ex R.No.A.F. 115; L-AG; said to be held by Norsk Flyhistorisk in or near Oslo whether for NAHS or R.No.A.F. Museum not known—details? *Kjölsern X-1* helicopter stored. At Air Mechanic School R.No.A.F. *F-86K Sabre* "RI-G". Flying from Oslo's Flying Club and with others—*Auster J/I* LN-BFV c/n 2005 ex G-AGYN; L. E. Johensen: *Auster 6A Tugmaster* LN-AEV c/n 3744; Olso Flyklubb. *Noorduyn Norseman* LN-BFE c/n 60 ex RCAF 2487, R-AU Hardangerfly A/S. *Piper L-4J Cub* LN-MAV c/n 13157, ex 45-4417; H. Brun. *Luscombe 8E Silvaire* LN-PAU c/n 5281 ex N2554K; W. & E. Jansen. *LN-PAV* c/n 5208 ex N2481K; Aero-Colour A/S. *Luscombe 8F* LN-BWL c/n S.76 ex N3544G; T. Tunheim Ptnrs.

Longhorn (Oslo)

OSTERAS. Airfield. *Piper L-4J Cub* LN-RAH c/n 12764 ex 44-80468; E. Vestby Ptnr.

RAKKESTAD. M. Korsvold's Aviation Museum. *Wideroe C-5 Polar* LN-DBW c/n 1 ex LN-11—a one-off. (photo please) *NA Harvard IIB* LN-BNN c/n 14a-1057, ex FS917 RDAF 310; ex Fjellfly. *Republic F-84G*—details wanted please. *Tiger Moth* LN-BDM c/n 85294 ex DE248, G-ANSC. *Sailplanes* also reported—details please.

RYGGE. R.No.A.F. *Spitfire PR-XI* PL979 c/n 6S. 583719 "AZ-B".

SAEBOVAGEN. Airfield. *Piper L-4J Cub* LN-MAU c/n 13163 ex 45-4423; L. Lunde Ptnr.

SANDVIKA. Airfield. *Auster V* LN-IKB c/n 1550 ex TJ541, G-AJLE, SE-BZC; W.Wien Ptnr.

SKIEN. Geiteryggen Airport. Fjellfly A/S. *Noorduyn Norseman* LN-BDP c/n 64 RCAF 2491, R-AV and LN-BDR c/n 92, RCAF 2492, R-AK.

STAVANGER. Airport. *Douglas DC-3* LN-TVA, ex 502 of Muscat & Oman Air Force—full history please.

STAVANGER/SOLA. R.No.A.F. *Republic F-84G* 110161 "L-MU" ex 338 Sqdn.

STORHAMAR. Airfield. *Piper L-4H Cub* LN-IKJ c/n 12081 ex 44-79785, SE-ASO; P. A. Munch.

VADSO. Airfield. *Beech AT-11 Kansan* LN-BWN c/n 3696 ex 42-58205, TF-BVB; Air Cargo Transport.

VAERNES. R.No.A.F. The following are stored for the planned Royal Norwegian Air Force Museum:—*Fokker C.V.D* observation type of 1927 serial 349; used by Norwegian Army Air Service 1930 until 1940. Jupiter series VIFH engine serial J6835 of 1930. *DH.Tiger Moth* with Gipsy "3" 175HK—serial wanted. *Fairchild PT-19 Cornell* T40-208 "L-AB" ex 42-76477 with Ranger C-3 engine modified to C-4. *DH.Vampire 3* VO184 "ZK-U" with Goblin engine. *Vampire 3* serial P42408 "SI-D" of 337 Sqdn, 1949-55. *Republic RF-84F-26-RE Thunderflash* 51-17053 "AZ-G" with 3127 hours recorded. Engine J65-B7C No B-644014. *Republic F-84G-26-E Thunderjet* 51-11209 "MU-5" engine J65-3A No 506319, ex 338 Sqdn, Oerland 1954/60. Reported that a SAAB J-29 due from R.Swed.A.F.—confirmation and photo appreciated when firm.

Fokker C.V.D. (Vaernes)

POLAND

CHORZOW. Near Katowice. In park. *Yak 23*, Polish AF *Lisunov Li 2* (Russian-built version of DC-3).

DAJTKI. Airport. *Polikarpov Po 2* SP-BXU, as air ambulance.

GDYNIA. (Danzig). On waste land near the British Embassy. *Yakovlev Yak 11*, serialled C-11, ex Polish Air Force. *Yak 9P*, unmarked, is in War Museum.

KRAKOW. Old military airfield. Polish National Air Museum. Here, in one hangar, under the control of Mr. Marian Markowski, with his assistant director Zhigniew Baranowski, will be found the 23 machines which—in varying stages of damage—survived the destruction of the famous Berlin Air Museum in 1943. Restoration proceeds and the museum is not open to the public, although written application may procure admittance for readers. Here, first, the former Berlin aircraft:—*Albatros B IIA* (Mercedes DIII) "MG+UA" late example of 1917/18 German standard trainer. *Albatros C I* (Benz BzIII) No 197/15; reconnaissance

aircraft of 1915. *Albatros H I* (Siemens Halske Sh III) Called H 1 this is actually a *Siemens Schukert D IV* fighter of 1918 modified 1920s by Albatros for altitude research; very long-span wings fitted. *Albatros L 101* (Argus As8A Series III). Parasol wing two-seater monoplane 1929/30 vintage, D-EKYQ c/n 245. *Antoinette.* Genuine example of 1910 model in good condition. *AEG "Euler".* First AEG aircraft, built 1911, uses steel-tube fuselage construction of typical AEG design serial 1911/12. *Aviatik C III* (Mercedes D III). Reconnaissance aircraft of 1917. C.1225/17 c/n 1996. *Curtiss Hawk II* (Wright Cyclone) D316. One of pair purchased 1933, flown by Ernst Udet. "Iris" crashed 1934 so this must be "Irtis". Fuselage covering almost entirely missing but 1936 Olympic badge clearly visible. *de Havilland DH9A* (Liberty) F.1010, Westland-built, was operated by 110 Sqdn, Independent Air Force and on sixth raid (on Kaiserslautern) was forced down October 5th, 1918, *DFW C.V.* (Benz Bz IV) C.17077/17 c/n 473, Aviatik-built example of one of the later German reconnaissance aircraft. *Fokker Spin.* Spidery example of 1914 Fokker design, in good condition. *Geeste Mowe* (Mercedes D1). A vintage Taube type of 1913. *Grigorovitch M.15* (Hispano). In very good state, this Russian flying boat was built 1917. Dark grey upper surfaces, light grey below with Czarist markings visible. *Halberstadt CL II* (Mercedes D III) serial 1545 9/17. Ground attack aircraft 1917/18, this example was personal machine of Kommd General der Luftstreitflotte, Grosses Hauptquartier. *Heinkel He 5e* "D-1". Three-seat seaplane of mid-1920s. *Jeannin Taube* (Argus As II). Another Taube of circa 1914. *LVG B II.* Two-seater trainer built late 1918. *Messerschmitt Me 209* V-1 D-INJR. Fuselage of the former holder of Air Speed Record for piston-engined aircraft. Wings and engine reported destroyed during raid on Augsburg Messerschmitt factory, so aircraft may not be ex-Berlin Museum. *PZL P.11C* (Bristol Mercury) c/n 562. Painted as aircraft No 122 Sqdn, 2nd Air Regiment but may not have served with squadron. Original olive colour detectable beneath layers of green.

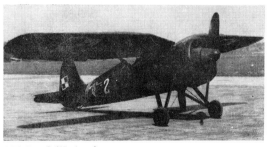

PZL.P.11C (Krakow)

CSS.13—civil (Krakow)

CSS.13—military (Krakow)

Ilyushin Il-10 (Krakow)

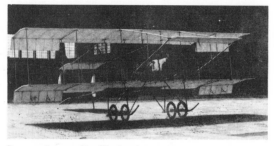

Farman F.4—replica (Krakow)

MD-12F (Krakow)

Roland D VIb (Mercedes D III). No 2225/18, tail-less; but otherwise fair condition. *Rumpler Taube* (Mercedes D1) 1914 Taube in what appears to be Austrian markings. *Sopwith Camel F.1*, B7280, No 210 Sqdn, RAF, missing September 15th, 1918, with 155 airframe and 15 hours engine, but believed flown by Germans, as German wicker seat fitted. *Stinson L-5* USAAC serial 42-98643—a mystery, as one wonders if this was in Berlin. The other aircraft in the hangar represent Polish-built and flown machines since WW II. *Bucker Jungmann* SP-AFO (Hirth HM 504A). German built but completely rebuilt by Z. S. L. S. Poznan. *BZ-1 GIL* (Hirth HM 504A2) SP-GIL-prototype presently stored. *BZ-4 ZUK* (WN-4) Prototype two-seat helicopter, presently stored. *CSS 13* (M.11 of various models). There are five examples of this license-built version of the *Polikarpov Po 2*, in the collection. On show are SP-API, modified for crop-dusting, with hopper in rear cockpit *SP-AXT*, ambulance version with stretcher under raised decking behind pilot. *"5"* An armed version in Polish Air Force markings. *SP-ADE* is in store; along with a *Russian-built Po 2* with original wooden struts. *Farman F.4* replica with unidentified

modern French radial. Flying replica built at Lublin by Pawel Zolotow and flown extensively by him before presentation to museum. Mr. Zolotow is said to be the only private pilot permitted to own his own aircraft, a *Piper Cub*. In his seventies he has been flying since before WW I and, an enthusiast for early aircraft, has recently completed a *replica Bleriot XI*, using small modern radial and Piper Cub propeller. *Ilyushin Il-10* (AM-42) coded "4" in Polish Air Force colours. *LIM-2* (RD-45F) Polish-built *MiG-15* coded "712". *LWD Junak 1* (M.11D) SP-GLA (the prototype—presently stored). *LWD Junak-3* SP-BBU, *LWD Szpak-2* (Siemens Halske Bramo SH.14A4) SP-AAA (prototype-stored). *LWD Szpak-3* (Siemens Halske Bramo SH.14A4 (SP-AAB (prototype-stored). *LWD Szpak-4T* (Siemens Halske Bramo SH.14A4) SP-AAG, production model c/n 48-004. *LWD Zak-3* (Cirrus Minor 4-111) SP-AAX, initially Walter Mikron III *LWD Zuch-1* SP-BAD (Cirrus Minor 6-III). Prototype-stored. *LWD Zuch-2* SP-BAM (Siemens Halske Bramo SH.14) production version. *LWD Zuraw* SP-GLB (M.11FR) Prototype stored. *PZL MD 12F* (4 × WN-3C) SP-PBL. *Pegaz* (XL-GAD) SP-590, prototype powered-glider. *Piper Cub* (Continental A-65) SP-AFP, a standard version. *PWS 26* (Wright Whirlwind) SP-AJB, but in spurious Air Force camouflage of green "coded S". *RWD 13* (Walter Major) SP-ARL one of two examples of pre-war RWD light aircraft brought back from Romania. In excellent condition. Ex SP-MSZ *RWD 23* (Walter Major) SP-AKG, needs restoring. Under civil paint, Romanian Air Force markings (stored). *TS-8 Bies* (WN-3) serial 0309, a standard production aircraft. *The prototype TS-8* SP-GLF, which broke distance records in 1956 is currently stored. *Tupolev Tu 2* (2 × ASh-82 FNV) used by Polish Air Force for ejector-seat trials. An open cockpit with metal wind deflector is fitted aft of wing. *WSK SM-1W* (AI-26B) a production example displayed. *Yakovlev Yak-11* "36" (ASh-21) standard production model. *Yakovlev Yak-17UTI* (RD-10A) "02" jet trainer based on Yak-9. *Yakovlev Yak 23* (RD-500) a standard production model—no canopy.

GLIDER SECTION.

ABC/A unregistered. *CZAJKA*, SP-1640. *Jastrab IS-4* SP-1391; *IS-1SEP* SP-552, *IS-3* SP-1697. *Komar SP-*

PWS.26 (Krakow)

985. *Kranich* SP-1213, plus one other. *Lunak* SP-1146.
Minimoa SP-148. *Motobaby* SP-213. *Olympia* SP-380.
Rhonlander—unregistered. *Rhonsperber* unregistered.
Staaken (Rhineflungzg) unregistered. *Swallow* SP-1535.
SZD-6X Nietoperz. *Weihe* SP-1029. *WWS.1 Salamandra*
SP-322 c/n 003. *WWS.2 Wrona Bis*. *ZABA* SP-167.

KRAKOW. Pobiedmik Aero Club. *Po 2* SP-AMC;
Zlin-26 SP-ARM; *Jastrab glider* SP1383.

LISIE KATIE. Airfield. *Polish Lunak* (Cadet) SP-ABI
2-seater, 125 hp M-11D, 5-cylinder radial, for towing at
gliding club.

RADOM. Airfield. *Polikarpov Po 2s* SP-ABF and SP-
ANK. (Still flying?)

Yak 23 (Warsaw, Goclaw)

WARSAW. Goclaw Airfield. *Yak 23* unserialled mounted for exhibition.

Pe 2 (Warsaw, Army Museum)

WARSAW. Peoples Army Museum grounds (Closed
Tuesday). Group of incorrectly-painted Russian
aircraft in dark-green and bright sky-blue instead of
olive-green and very light sky-blue. *Ilyushin Il-2* Polish
markings, standard version. *Ilyushin Il-10* Standard
version Polish markings. *LIM-2*. A licence-built MiG

Tiger Moth (Alverca)

Yak 23 (Warsaw, Army Museum)

15bis serial "1964" on nose sprayed over, landing light
in intake division. *Petlyakov Pe 2*. Standard version.
Polish markings. *Polikarpov Po 2*. Russian markings,
small Polish markings cockpit area. Rocket rails.
Tupolev Tu 6 Identifiable by 4-bladed propellers as
development of Tu 2. Polish markings. *Yakovlev Yak
9U* Polish markings. Standard version. *Yakovlev Yak 23*
"17" in red on nose, sprayed over. Pilot's seat in tan
pigskin; matt pale-green interior.
Tu 2 in Polish markings, green/grey; 4-blade propeller.
Ilyushin Il 28 coded "22" natural metal, Polish markings.

WARSAW. Aeroclub. *Po 2s* SP-APM and SP-KPE
Jastrab glider SP-1376.

WARSAW. Technical Museum. *Lilienthal* glider
original.

PORTUGAL AND CAPE VERDE ISLANDS

ALVERCA. The Air Museum. *Avro 631 Cadet* no
serial, licence-built with Armstrong Siddeley Coventry
engine AS9861. Possibly an Avro 626 in reality. *DH.
Tiger Moth* c/n 3650, delivered to Portuguese Air Force
pre-war, later civilianised as CS-AAA. Now restored
with Air Force serial 111. *Grumman Widgeon* serial 129.
Junkers Ju 52/3m 6315. *NA T-6 Texan* 1635. *DH. Rapide*
1307. *Sikorsky H-19* serial 9101. *Lockheed T-33* 1951.
Bristol Beaufighter TT10 BF-10 (believed in RD239-285
batch) this machine not on display and future unknown.
Caudron G.III (replica) honouring PAF's first type.
DH. Vampire FB.5 5801, donated by South African Air
Force. *Maurice Farman* (replica). *Savoia-Marchetti*
(further details wanted). *DFS Grunau Baby IIb* CS-
PAE c/n 3567. Details requested, please, and photos,
of above and any other types earmarked for preservation.
Flying from Alverca airfield (civil side):— *Piper J-3C-65
Cub* CS-AAP c/n 21984 ex G-AKBT and CS-ABF c/n
17389. *PA-11 Cub Special* CS-AAJ c/n 11-233; owners,
Nacional Macidade Portuguesa and D.G.A.C. PAF
side has *Junkers Ju52/3m* 6301 and 6306.

Beaufighter TT10 (Alverca)

BOA VISTA. Airfield. *Douglas C-47A* CS-TAI c/n 12060 ex 42-92277 FL633, TC-YOL; Universal Air Leasing.

CASCAIS. Tires Airport. *Culver 5* CS-ACY c/n 348, dismantled. *Paulistinha 56-C* CS-ALC c/n 1214 ex PP-HPR, also dismantled. *AT-6 Texan* 51-14770 c/n 182-457; *51-14991* c/n 182-679; *51-14794* c/n 182-481 and *51-14800* (were destined for Biafra—future unknown). Infantil Park. *NA F-86 Sabre* donated by USAF—serial and photo please.

NA F-86 Sabre (Cascais)

COIMBRA. Airfield. *DH. Tiger Moth* CS-AEL c/n P-65; CAAAC. *J-3C-65 Cub* CS-ABT c/n 2954 of 1939; DGAC. In Children's Town: *Junkers Ju 52/3m* 6304.

COVILHA. Airfield. *Fleet 80 Canuck* CS-ACQ c/n 068 ex CF-ACQ, CF-DQP; A.C.A. de Carvalho, who also own *Caudron 635 Simoun* CS-ADG ex French A.F., preserved static. *Tiger Moth* CS-AFZ c/n DHTM.16a; CAAAC.

ESPINHO. Airfield. Aero Clube da Costa Verde. *Tiger Moth* CS-AEO c/n P-37; *CS-AFF* c/n DHTM.18A; *Piper J-3C-65 Cub* CS-ABK c/n 17674.

EVORA. Playground. *Junkers Ju 52/3m* 6303.

GRANJA DE ALPRIATE. Gliding Club D.G.A.C. *DFS Kranich* CS-PAD c/n 983 of 1947. *DFS Weihe A.3* CS-PAF c/n 244 of 1947.

LISBON. Naval Museum. Praca do Commercio. *Fairey IIID* F402 "Santa Cruz". On 30 March 1922 Captain Cago Coutinho (navigator) and Commander Sacadura Cabral (pilot) attempted ocean crossing 4,367 nautical miles to Rio de Janeiro. Portuguese Admiralty allowed initial £5,000 to include cost of aircraft. On 5th leg (18 April) F400 lost due to leaking floats. F401 arrived Fernando Norohna 6 May, returned to last point flown, took off 11 May but was lost—crew saved. Portugal and Brazil opened subscription list and F402 took off 5 June, arriving Rio de Janeiro 17 June, 60 hrs 14 mins flying time but $2\frac{1}{2}$ months elapsed time. Average speed $72\frac{1}{2}$ knots. Commander Cabral disappeared over North Sea flying Fokker seaplane Holland-Portugal $2\frac{1}{2}$ years later but navigator lived to become Admiral and died 1960. *Schreck FBA* flying boat c/n 203 "2" also displayed.

Fairey IIID (Lisbon)

Short Solent (Lisbon)

Ju 52/3m (Ota)

DH. 89 Rapide (Cuatro Vientos)

Breguet 19 (Cuatro Vientos)

Cierva Autogyro (Cuatro Vientos)

Flying from Lisbon Airport is *Grumman G.44 Widgeon* CS-AHG c/n 1242 of D.G.A.C. and in Monsanto Park is *Widgeon* serialled 2401, c/n 1248 of 1942, formerly used for photo-reconnaissance work. It is believed that one of the three *Short Solents* G-AHIN, G-ANYI and G-AOBL may still be on the River Tagus, the others have been scrapped. A plan was in hand to try and get at least one back for display at Rochester—details appreciated by compiler.

MIRANDELA. Airfield. *Piper J-4 Cub Coupe* of 1939 CS-ABQ, c/n 4-486; D.G.A.C.

MONTIJO. Air Force base. *Republic F-84*—details wanted.

PEDROUCOS. Institute of Higher Military Studies. *Lockheed T-33* serial 1953.

OTA. Air Force base. On plinth *Republic F-84* (believed G) painted 5201. Full serial wanted and photo. *Junkers Ju 52/3m* 6320 also here.

SANTA CRUZ. Airport. Aero Clube de Torres Vedras. *Piper J-3C-65 Cub* CS-ABY c/n 17243 of 1946.

SANTANA. Airfield. *Tiger Moth* CS-AFC c/n P-12 ex Portuguese Air Force, now Aero Clube da Ilha Verde.

VISEU. Aero Clube. *Junkers Ju 52/3m* 6311.

ROMANIA

BUCHAREST. Central Military Museum. *Mig-15; Il-10; La-9; Yak-23; S-102; Nardi FN-305; Fleet F-10G; Vuia No 1; Vlaicu II; I.A.R.-811; I.A.R.-813;* Technical Museum has *I.A.R.-813* and unidentified *Bücker*.

SPAIN

BARCELONA. Sabadell Airport. Many vintage types:— *DH. Rapide* EC-AKO c/n 6345 ex G-AERN; Metamar S.A. *Percival Proctor III* EC-AHB c/n H.463 ex LZ681, G-AMCO; L. de P. Batile. *Fairchild F.24R Argus III* EC-AEN c/n 946 ex 43-14982, HB708, OO-PET. *Piper J-3C-65 Cub* EC-AKP c/n 11114 ex 43-29823, HB-OFC, EC-AKP, HB-OUC; J. L. Sallares. Also *EC-ALG* c/n 12240 ex 44-79944, HB-OIZ; *EC-AKQ* c/n 11190 ex 43-29899, HB-ONR; R.A.C. de Barcelona.

CUATRO VIENTOS. Airport (Madrid). *Auster IV* EC-AXR c/n 799 ex MT255, G-ANHU; Aeropost *DH.89 Rapide* EC-AGP c/n 6879 ex NR803, G-AMAI; C.E.A.P.S.A. *DH.60G-III Moth* EC-AIT c/n wanted, ex MM30-82; Subsec de Av. Civil, also *DH.60G-III* EC-AFQ ex MM30-89 and *DH. Tiger Moth* EC-AFM ex MM30-162, EE1-162. *Auster V* EC-AJJ c/n 1798 ex TW457, G-ANIG. *G-44A Widgeon* EC-AJU c/n 1402 ex N41971; R. C. Flandes. *Auster V* EC-AKX c/n 1052 ex NJ668, G-AJTN, HB-EUA; J. A. C. Blanco. *DH.60G-III* EC-AEL c/n 465, ex M-CEAA, EC-EAA, EC-BAJ, MM30-75, once rebuilt using parts and c/n of Avian IV is believed again under restoration here. At the Spanish Air Force side *CASA C2111* BR.21-14 "403-3" and BR.21-129 "403-4" at the AISA factory *AT-6/C6* serials 126, 163, 178 and *AT-16* 61,109, 114. It is reported that several machines are stored with the Spanish Air Force here for the projected Spanish Aviation Museum to

Ju 52/3m (Cuatro Vientos)

be established in Madrid:—*Breguet 19* "72". *Fiat CR.32* biplane fighter (may be a license-built Hispano Suiza HA-132-L "Chirri".) *Cierva Autogyro No 1* (reported this may, in fact, be Avro-built C.30A G-ACWM ex AP506 c/n 715 ex Staverton 1965). *DH. Rapide* G-ACYR, c/n 6261 the machine chartered from Olley Air Services to fly Franco from Morocco to Spain pre-war. It was dismantled at Desford post-war and thought sold to General Franco 1954 for the museum. *Dornier Do 24T-3* HD5-1, thought Werk-Nr 5342, is said to be earmarked for this museum; also examples of the Spanish-built Me 109, He 111 and Ju 52—details requested, please.

GETAFE. Spanish Air Force. *CASA C352L* (*Ju 52/3m*) T-2B-189 and T-2B-260 "911-1"

GRANADA. Airport. Not vintage but a rarity:— *Hispano Suiza HS-34* EC-AFJ c/n 1; R.A.C. de Granada.

LERIDA. Airfield. *Piper J-3C-65 Cub* EC-AQZ c/n 12494 ex 44-80198, HB-OSG; R.A.C. de Lerida.

LUGO. Airfield. *Auster V* EC-AKE c/n 1526 ex TJ479, HB-EOB; R.A.C. de Lugo.

MADRID. Barajas Airport. *Lockheed P-38L Lightning* EC-ANU or EC-WNU c/n 8204 was reported—confirmation? *Hispano HA-1109-MIL* G-AWHL c/n 186 ex C4K-122 and G-AWHS c/n 228 ex C4K-170 were here for the Patton film. Details of present location please. *Airspeed AS.65 Consul* EC-AGI c/n 3096 ex LX265, G-AHRK, VP-RBM, EC-WGI; Iberia, *DH.87B Hornet Moth* EC-ACA c/n 8039 ex, EC-W51, EC-EBE, EC-CAI, and *Miles M.3 Falcon* EC-ACB c/n 197 ex EC-BDD, EC-CAO, said to be static here—let us hope they are preserved! *Boeing B-75NI Stearman* EC-AMD c/n 75-4721 ex 42-16558, N55050; EC-AID c/n 75-6508, Bu05334, ex N67955 and *EC-AIF* c/n 75-5513 ex 42-17350, N4657V here with Servicios Agricolas Aereos S.A., also *EC-ATY* c/n 75-6714 ex Bu07110. *Douglas R5D-3* EC-BQH c/n 10738 ex 42-72633, Bu56516, T4-14; *EC-BQI* c/n 22200 ex 43-17250, Bu56546; and *EC-BQJ* c/n 10589 ex 42-72484, KL978, Bu92003 are here with Subsec. de Av. Civil.

MALAGA. Spanish Air Force. *CASA C2111* (Heinkel He 111) 272nd Squadron thought to exist with a number of machines—compiler would value details of serials and whether airworthy. *Fairchild F.24W Argus II* EC-AJZ c/n 663 ex 43-14699 FZ723, HB-EAP flies here from civil airfield with R.A.C. de Malaga.

MURCIA. Airfield. *Miles M.38 Messenger 2A* EC-ACU c/n 6360 ex G-AJEZ, EC-EAL; L. R. Liano.

SAN SEBASTIAN. Airport. *DH.60G Gipsy Moth* EC-ACN c/n 1916 ex EC-TTA, MM30-54, EC-BAV; R.A.C. de San Sebastian.

SEVILLE. Airport. *DH.60G* EC-ACO c/n 1918, ex EC-UAH MM30-88; *DC-4* G-APID as restaurant attraction.

SILS. Near Gerona. Hostal de Rolls. Motor Museum. *Fairchild Argus* EC-AJB and unmarked *DH. Hornet Moth*. Registration of DH. 87B wanted, please. Is it EC-ACA?

TORREJON. Air Force base. *CASA C352L* (Ju 52/3m) T2B-244 "901-20" dismantled—available for a museum?

VALENCIA. *Piper J-2 Cub* EC-ALA c/n 1166 ex G-AFFH and *Taylor J-2 Cub* EC-ALB c/n 971 ex G-AEXY are stored here—details please of restorations.

VILAVERDE. Route N.IV south of Madrid. Scrapyard. *Airspeed Consuls* EC-ANL c/n 5167 ex HN719, G-AJXH and *EC-ARU* c/n 5151 ex HN980, EI-ADC, AP-AGK, HB-LAU. Efforts ought to be made to preserve at least one from the two. *Sikorsky H-19-ZD*, 1B-21 "803-3" also reported here.

VITORIA. Airfield. *Auster V* EC-AJR c/n 1505 ex TJ517, EC-WJR; R.A.C. de Vitoria.

ZARAGOZA. Airfield. *Auster V* EC-ANI c/n 1262 ex RT635, HB-EOG; R.A.C. de Zaragoza.

MAJORCA

PUERTO DE POLLENSA. Spanish Air Force *Dornier Do 24 T-3* thought still available here for preservation —non-airworthy. Serial wanted, please, and news of re-location if sold.

CANARY ISLANDS

LAS PALMAS. Airport. *Airspeed AS.65 Consul* EC-AHU c/n 5102 ex BG152, G-AIVA. *Piper J-3C-65 Cub* EC-AJI c/n 21962 ex G-AKBV; both R.A.C. de Gran Canaria.

SANTA CRUZ DE TENERIFE. Airport. *Auster V* EC-AJT c/n 1665 ex TJ645; *Piper J-3C-65 Cub* EC-AKD c/n 11691 ex 43-30400, G-AISP; both R.A.C. de Tenerife.

SWEDEN

ALVADALEN. Airfield. *Piper L-4H Cub* SE-ATH c/n 12844 ex 44-80148; Alvadalens Flygklubb.

ALVSBYN. Airfield. *Auster V* SE-CMB c/n 1791 ex TW455, G-AOJL; Alsvby Flygklubb.

ARJEPLOG. Airfield. *Noorduyn UC-64A/S Norseman* SE-CLZ c/n 492 ex 45-35418, SE-ASC, Fv78001; Turistflyg.

ARVIDSJAUR. Airfield. *Piper L-4J Cub* SE-AUF c/n 12387 ex 44-80091; Arvidsjaur Flygklubb.

ASARUM. *Tiger Moth* SE-CWG c/n 3364 ex G-ADLV BB750, G-AORA; E. Svenson.

BANDAGEN. Airstrip. *Piper L-4H Cub* SE-ATP c/n 12057 ex 44-79761; S. A. Andersson.

BOLLNAS. Airfield. *Piper L-4J Cub* SE-AWK c/n 12418 ex 44-80122; Bollnas Flygklubb.

BOLLSTA. Airfield. *Auster 5* SE-CGK c/n 3411 ex G-APRE; Bollsta Flygklubb.

BORAS. Airfield. *Piper L-4J Cub* SE-AUH c/n 12685 ex 44-80389; Aerobolaget i Boras.

ENSKEDE. Airfield *Beagle Auster 6A* SE-ELP c/n 3738 ex TW 537; Borje Centergren.

ESKILSTUNA. Airfield. *Auster 6A* SE-ELI c/n 3727 ex TW529, G-ARLN; Eskilstuna Flygklubb; *SE-ELK* c/n 3739 ex VX935; Tuppz Flygklubb. *Tiger Moth* SE-COO c/n 86372 ex NL929, G-ANKJ; Eskilstuna Flygklubb.

GALLIVARE. Airfield. *UC-64 A/S Norseman* SE-CGM c/n 780, ex 44-70515, RA-F, LN-TSN; *SE-CPB* c/n 89, ex RCAF 3538, R-AY RNoAF; AB Norrlandsflyg.

GOTHENBURG. Industrial Museum. *Albatros B.II* SE-ACR ex SE-94 (minus engine) *Weihe* glider. *SG.38* (Gothenburg built) plus others under restoration. Photos wanted. At the nearby R. Swedish Air Force F9 Wing are:- *Flyforvaltningens Verkstad (F.F.V.S.) J22. SAAB J-21* serial A-3; *Seversky Republic EP-106* J-9. Flying from the Goteborg Airport; *Piper Cubs:- L-4H* SE-AST c/n 12007 ex 44-79711: Mjorns Sjoflygskola. *L-4H* SE-AUW c/n 11686 ex 43-30395; K. E. Gustafsson Ptnrs. *L-4B* SE-CAL c/n 9994 ex 43-1133, LN-SAT; F. Bergman.

HAJUM. Airstrip. *Piper L-4H Cub* SE-ASU c/n 11708 ex 43-30417; A. Nilsson.

HALMSTAD. Airfield. *Tiger Moth* SE-CPW c/n 83689 ex T7219, G-ANND; K. Nilsson Ptnrs.

HAMMERSTRAND. Airfield. *Auster 5* SE-CME c/n 3410, ex G-APNN; A. Y. Sandstrom.

HELSINBORG. Airstrip. *Piper L-4H Cub* SE-CET c/n 11304, ex 43-30013, LN-MAE; Firma Flygreklam.

HEMAVAN. Airfield. *Auster 6A* SE-ELH c/n 3737; K. Berglund.

HUDIKSVALL. Airstrip. *Luscombe 8A* SE-AZS c/n 4111; A. Kring.

HURVA. Airstrip. *Piper L-4H* SE-ATE c/n 11965, ex 44-79669; Per Envald Espgard.

JAKOBSBERG. Airfield. *Focke Wulf Fw. 44J Stieglitz*

SE-EGT c/n 81, ex Fv. 629; Per Tomas Stovling.

JOSSEFORS. Airfield. *L-4J* SE-BCX c/n 12672 ex 44-80376; E. Nilsson.

KAGEROD. Airfield. *Piper L-4H Cub* SE-BFK c/n 11821 ex 43-30530; *Miles Gemini* SE-AYM c/n 6296 ex G-AKDA; both G. Esbjornsson.

KALMAR. R.Swed.A.F. F12 Wing. *SAAB-32B (J32B)* 32544; said to be first of a possible collection here. Flying locally is *Piper L-4H Cub* SE-AUM c/n 10875 ex 43-29584, D-ELOL; B. A. Ebesson Lundgren.

KIRUNA. Airfield. *Noorduyn UC-64 Norseman* SE-EGF c/n 44 RCAF 2471, R-AL RNoAF, LN-BIT; F:a Fjallflyg. *Stinson SR-10J Reliant* SE-CLN c/n 5-5820; T-Aero.

KLOVSJO. Airstrip. *Piper L-4H Cub* SE-ASR c/n 10486, ex 43-29195, SE-ASR, D-EDOZ; A. H. Morlind Ptnr.

KRISTIANSTAD. Airfield. *Miles M38 Messenger 2A* SE-BYY c/n 6703 ex G-AKAO; A. Johnson.

KUNGSANGEN. Airfield. *Piper L-4J* SE-CAN c/n 12475 ex 44-80349; C. Magnus of Ugglas.

LANDSKRONA. Museum. *Thulin NA* displayed plus engines of some of Dr. Enoch Thulin's 14 types (he built 100 a/c).

LAXA. Airfield. *Auster 5D* SE-CMF c/n 1376 ex TJ295, VR-RCC, OY-ADY; Laxa Flygklubb.

LJUNGBY. Airfield. *Piper L-4J Cub* SE-CDH c/n 12583 ex 44-80287, LN-RAP; Feringe Flygklubb.

LJUNGBYHED. R.Swed.A.F. *SAAB-29(J29F)* 29666 "64" from F4. Many a/c reported undamaged in fire section.

LJUSDAL. Airstrip. *Piper L-4J* SE-BYX c/n 12650 ex 44-80354, LN-SAH, LN-NAO; Ljnsdals Fly.

LOS. Airship. *Piper J-4A Cub Coupe* SE-CTE c/n 4-612 ex G-AFWS, ES923, OH-CPB; S. Johansson.

LUND. Airfield. *Fairchild UC-61A Argus 2* SE-AYI c/n 572, ex 43-14608; B. G. Kjellstrom.

LYCKSELE. Piper L-4J SE-CGU c/n 13202 ex 45-4462, LN-RAI; S. A. Nasstrom.

MALMBERGET. Airstrip. *Piper J-2 Cub* SE-AGO c/n 993; K. O. V. Tallberg.

MALMEN. R. Swedish A. F. Wing F3 The Royal Swedish Air Force Museum:— *ASJA/RK26 (Sk10)* serial 536 c/n 20 *ASJA/DH82A (Sk11A)* serial 515, c/n 47 ex SE-BYM airworthy. *ASJA/Hawker Hart (B4A),* serial 714, c/n 52 with Mercury 309, operated with Finnish Air Force during Winter War 1940. Major Hugo Beckhammer (Later F3 C.O.) survived with this machine. *Bucker Bu 181B (SK25)* serial 25000. *Can-Vickers PBY-5A (Tp47)* ex 2 Wing serial 47001, flew until August 1966. coded "79". *CFM Albatros (SK1).* serial 04 of 1925. *CFM Tummelisa*

0-1 serial 3656—c/n 147 of 1928 airworthy. *CFM Phonix 122 (J1)* serial 947 of 1919. *Fokker CVE(S6b)* serial 386—still flying. *CVV/Fw 44J (SK12)* serial 670, restored to 1940 colour scheme. *DH100(J28A) Vampire FB1* serial 28001. *DH100 (J28B) Vampire Mk 50* serial 28311—engine RM1A No 4101. *DH 115 (J28C) Vampire T55* serial 28451—engine RM1A No 3268. *DH112(J33) Venom Mk51* 33025 ex SE-DCD c/n 12374 *Fiat CR42(J11)* serial 2543. *FFVS 22 (J22B)* serial 22280 "panic fighter" in F3 markings—the interim type before F3 converted to the *DH Vampire*. *Gloster Gladiator(J8A)* serial 278, Bristol Mercury M42047 Mk 8, used by Finnish Air Force in Winter War—8 Russian aircraft destroyed for loss of 3 Gladiators. *Grunau Baby IIb* SE-SAP. *Holmberg*—ultralight built by officers, 1930's. *Hawker Hunter Mk 4 (J34)* serial 34016, engine RM5B No 3417; ex F9 "06". *Junkers Ju*

86-K4 (B3C-2) serial 155 c/n 0412. *Klemm Kl 35B (Sk15)* serial 5081 c/n 1596 ex SE-AIG "81" "5". *Macchi M-7* serial 945 of 1919. *Nieuport IV-G* serial M-1 of 1912, still airworthy. *North American P-51D-20-NA Mustang (J26)* serial 26020 ex 44-63992 USAF. With F16 Wing Uppsala 1945-52; sold to Israel 1953 and operational in Sinai campaign. Recovered by "Action Group". *N.A. (Sk16) Harvard* 16109. *Pou Du Ciel* unmarked. *Reggiane Re-2000 (J20)* serial 2340 ex F3 but presented by Wing F70. *SAAB 17 (B17B)* serial 17005. *SAAB B17A* 17239 ex SE-BYH. *SAAB 21A-3 (J21A-3)* serial 21364. *SAAB 210 "Lill-draken"*—the SAAB 35/Draken's research aircraft *Seversky Republic EP-106 (J/S9)* serial 2134. *Sparman S1 A (P1)* c/n 8 serial 814 "61". *Vertol 44* ex Swedish Navy. It is thought that *NA Harvard* ex RSwed.AF "75" c/n 16047 ex LN-MAA may be based locally; owner Jan Murer. *SAAB J-29F* code "F".

Tummelisa (Malmen)

RK26 (Malmen)

Phonix 122 (Malmen)

Hawker Hart (Malmen)

FFVS 22 (Malmen)

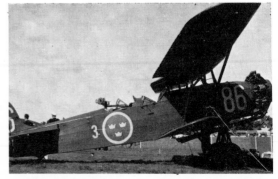

Fokker CVE (Malmen)

Albatros (Malmen)

Phonix 122 (Malmen)

Fokker CVE (Malmen)

DH.Venom Mk 51 (Malmen)

Fw 44J (Malmen)

Junkers Ju 86-K4 (Malmen)

Gloster Gladiator (Malmen)

Junkers Ju 86-K4 (Malmen)

Macchi M-7 (Malmen)

Nieuport IV-G (Malmen)

NA Mustang (Malmen)

SAAB 21A-3 (Malmen)

SAAB 210 (Malmen)

SAAB J-29F (Malmen)

Sparman S1A (Malmen)

MALMO. Technical Museum. *Fairey Firefly TT.1* SE-CAW c/n F6121 ex PP392 from Svensk Flygtjanst. *Klemm Kl 35 (Sk15a)* ex RSwed.AF. *Douglas DC-7B* SE-ERB c/n 45087 ex N818D. *Rearwin 9000 Sportster* SE-AGB c/n 567D minus engine. Flying from Malmo Airport is *Piper J-3C-65 Cub* SE-AYZ c/n 13264, ex 45-4524; J. Lilja.

MOLLTORP. Airfield. *Stinson V-77 Reliant* SE-BZP c/n 6375 ex FB536,OO-NUT; Captain T. Davidsson, Soderhamn Paratroop School.

MOTALA. Airfield. *Piper L-4H Cub* SE-ATT c/n 11979 ex 44-79683; Motala Flygklubb.

NORRKOPING. R.Swed.AF base. There is a *Junkers Ju 86-K4* (B3-C2) here with nose and engines burned. It would, surely, be possible to return this to Germany

for restoration and display? Flying here is *Auster V* SE-CBT c/n 841, ex MS977, G-ANIU, LN-BDU; M. Walk.

NORRTALJE. Airfield. *Tiger Moth* SE-COY c/n 85882 ex DF133, G-ANDN; Roslagens Flygklubb. *Piper L-4H Cub* SE-AUU c/n 11661, ex 43-30370; Bo. Stensson Cederblom. In a local park a *Douglas DC-3* is reported in use as restaurant—registration and history appreciated.

OSTERFARNEBO. Airfield. *Piper L-4H Cub* SE-ATZ c/n 12319 ex 44-80023; Foreningen Farnebo Flyg.

OSTERSUND. R.Swed.AF. F4 Wing. *SAAB J29F* on post, coded F4-29—serial wanted.

ROSSAN. Airstrip. *Piper L-4J Cub* SE-ATO c/n 12517 ex 44-80221; G. Andersson.

SIGTUNA. Airfield. *Auster V* SE-BZR c/n 1552 ex TJ511; F: a Aeroproject.

SJOBO. Airfield. *Piper L-4H Cub* SE-AUL c/n 12066 ex 44-79770; Ystada Flygklubb.

SKELLEFTEA. Airfield. *Piper L-4H Cub* SE-ASP c/n 11928 ex 44-79632; J. T. Lundberg.

SKOVDE. Airstrip. *DH. Tiger Moth* SE-CHG c/n 85867 ex DF118, G-APOU; A. G. Backman & Ptnr.

Stinson Reliant (Molltorp)

SLOINGE. Ugglarps Museum. Lennart "Svedino" Svedvelt. On display or under restoration for display:— *de Havilland DH.60G* SE-ABS. *Focke Wulf Fw 44J. Gotaverken GV38* SE-AHY c/n 15. *Auster J/1 Autocrat* SE-CGR c/n 2230 ex G-AIZW. *Heinkel He 35* SE-SAM (Sk5 of Flgvapnet) *SAAB J29F* 29203 ex F16 Uppsala. *J28C Vampire T.55* serial 28444 "74" from F5. *J34 Hunter F4*—serial wanted. *SK16A Harvard* serial 16033 ex "72" F17—photo please.

SODERHAMN. Airfield. *Piper L-4H Cub* SE-ATU c/n 12146 ex 44-79850; S. Siggstedt Ptnr.

SPANGA. Airfield. *DH.85 Leopard Moth* SE-BZM c/n 7061 ex G-ACRW, AX733, LN-TVT; G. Back (red and white livery).

16433, R.No.AF 2593, G-AGIJ, OH-VKP. *Fairchild F-24W Argus 1* SE-BXE. c/n 862 ex 43-14898, HB625, LN-MAD. *Pou Du Ciel. Gotaverken GV38. DFS Kranich glider* SE-SCC of 1943. *Grunau Baby glider* SE-SAZ of 1941 *Riesler/Bendel* S-AAR c/n RIII. *DFS Weihe glider* SE-SNK. Cabin of *Junkers Ju 52/3m* SE-ADR c/n 4017 ex Fv907. Currently flying from Arlanda are thought:— *Gloster Meteor Mk 7* SE-DCC c/n G5-1525 ex G-ANSO, G-7-1 also *SE-CAS* c/n G5/1496 ex WF833, both of Svensk Flytjanst AB. SE-DCC was built by Glosters as the private-venture prototype G.44 Reaper, ground-attack version of the Meteor with strengthened F.4 wing and F.8 rear fuselage. First flown 1951 it was de-militarised 1954 when the single-seat front fuselage was exchanged for a two-seat T.7 type, tip-tanks with stabilizing fins fitted and, painted larkspur blue, it

DH.Leopard Moth (Spanga)

STOCKHOLM. Technical Museum. Many aircraft stored or undergoing restoration; displayed:—*Junkers F.13* SE-AAC c/n 715 ex D-343, S-AAAC first a/c of A. B. Aerotransport. *Cierva C.30A* SE-AEA c/n 740. *Donnet-Leveque L-11* serial 10. of Swedish Navy, 1912. *Thulin "A"*. Bleriot XI copy of 1915. *SAAB J21-A3* serial 21286. *Lilienthal glider* (replica) *Fieseler VI.* Stored—: *Bleriot Nyrop* No 1. Swedish-built. *Thulin "N". Thulin "B"* with floats; *Thulin "G"* serial 15.

At Stockholm's Arlanda Airport a Museum of Civil Aviation is being established and before making a special journey Mr. Enger should be contacted for permission to view machines, some in the open under tarpaulin wraps. Including:—*Bucker Jungmann* SE-AGU of 1937 c/n 846. *Bell 47G* not yet identified. *DH. Moth Major* SE-AGF c/n 5132 of 1935. *Fairey Firefly I* SE-BRG c/n F6071 ex DT989. *Focke Wulf Fw 44J Stieglitz* SE-BWX ex Fv 2816. *Junkers W.34* SE-BYA ex R.Swed.AF 1935, c/n 2835. *Lockheed Lodestar* SE-BZE c/n 2593 ex 43-

Junkers F 13 (Stockholm)

was used by Hawker Siddeley as a demonstrator until modified to T.7 standard it was sold to Sweden 1959. Although Swedish records state G-5-15125/1525 as c/n, British documents state that c/n is G5/1525 although manufacturer's plate reads 05-15125. Both aircraft are painted yellow. Also registered to Svensk Flygtjanst AB

Gloster Meteor Mk 7 (Stockholm)

are:—*Douglas AD-4W Skyraider* SE-EBA, Bu 127950, ex WT952, G-31-4; *SE-EBB*, Bu 127947, WT949, G-31-5; *SE-EBC*, Bu 127960, WT962, G-31-6; *SE-EBD*, Bu 127948, WT950, G-31-7; *SE-EBF*, Bu 127955, WT 957, G-31-9; *SE-EBG*, Bu 127942, WT 944, G-31-10; *SE-EBI* Bu 124777, WV185, G-31-12; *SE-EBK*, Bu 126867, WT984, G-31-13; *SE-EBL*, Bu 127922, WT924, G-31-14; *SE-EBM*, Bu 127949, WT951, G-31-15; *SE-EBN* Bu 126849 (other details wanted, plus photos and news of these machines, some of which, surely, should be preserved for display in Sweden and elsewhere in Europe.) *Cierva C.30A* SE-AZB c/n 954 is owned by R. von Bahr. *Tiger Moth* SE-ALM c/n 172 ex R.No.AF. 173 and *SE-ATI* c/n 3113, ex Fv568, SE-ADF are with Kungl Svenska Aeroklubben. *Luscombe 8A* SE-AZU c/n 4865 flies with A. Martin & Ptnr. *Auster 6A* SE-ELA c/n 3724 ex VX110, G-ASHY is owned and flown by B. Svensson & Ptnr and *SE-ELD* c/n 3733 ex WE553 by Kungl Svenska Aeroklubben. Photos appreciated. Flying from Stockholm's Bromma Airport:—*Lockheed 18-56 Lodestar* SE-BUU c/n 2076 ex G-AGBT, VP-KFA of Load-Air AB. *NA.AT-6A Harvard* SE-CHP c/n 77-4524 ex 41-16443, Fv16269; B. O. Lowgren. It is thought that *Messerschmitt Bf108 Taifun* SE-BZN c/n 5138, ex LN-DAT, may be hangared here—the last on the Swedish register. Also *Siebel 204* SE-KAM c/n 172 (French built as NC701) —confirmation please.

STROMSNASBRUK. Airstrip. *Piper L-4H* SE-AWL c/n 11871 ex 44-79575; G. Bertil & Ptnr.

SUNDBYBERG. Airfield. *Auster 6A* SE-ELG c/n 3736, ex VF600; L. E. Andersson.

TIERP. Airstrip. *Piper L-4H* SE-AUK c/n 11697, ex 43-30406; Norra Uppslands Flygklubb.

TULLINGE. R.Swed.AF. F18 Wing. *Hawker Hunter F.4* (J34) serial 34006 on display.

UPPSALA. Airfield. *L-4J* SE-BFD c/n 12535 ex 44-80239; S. A. J. Hjortshagen. *Auster 6A* SE-ELB c/n 3732, ex TW538; C. E. B. Aberg.

VASTERAS. Airfield. *Auster 6A* SE-ELE c/n 3734 ex WJ373; Vasteras Flygklubb.

VAXJO. Airstrip. *L-4H* SE-ATL c/n 11243 ex 43-29952· S. Karlsson.

VILHELMINA. Airstrip. *Piper L-4H* SE-AUT c/n 11615 ex 43-30324; A. Backman.

VINDELN. Airfield. *Auster 6A* SE-ELF c/n 3735 ex TW571; Vindelns Flygklubb.

VINNINGA. Airstrip. *Piper L-4H Cub* SE-ASX c/n 11711 ex 43-30420; Vinninga Bil-och Lant.

VISBY. Airport. *Percival Vega Gull* SE-ALA. Believed impressed as X1085 ex D-IXWD but details obscure. Believed still owned by N. J. Bjorkman, though not currently airworthy. Let us hope this historic machine will be preserved and displayed.

Douglas Skyraider (Stockholm)

SWITZERLAND

AGNO. Nr. Lugano. *Potez 600* HB-SPM at home of J. Berger, with collection of engines.

ASCONA. Airfield. *Messerschmitt Bf 109 B-1* HB-ESM; c/n 370114 ex D-IJHW of German Embassy London, captured at Croydon 3 September 1939 impressed as AW167, restored erroneously as G-AFZO. *DH.85 Leopard Moth* HB-ABA c/n 7097 of 1935; ex CH-416.

BELLECHASE. Airfield. *Comte AC-4A* HB-USI c/n 33 of 1930, oldest on Swiss register, ex CH-249.

BEROMUNSTER. Airfield. Glider HB-309 identification wanted, please. Also *DFS Meise* HB-384.

COLOMBIER. Airfield. *Grunau Baby* glider HB-234.

DUBENDORF. Swiss Air Force. Nr Zurich. Museum in two hangars, seen only by C.O.'s authority and prior appointment:—*Bucker Bu 133 Jungmeister* U-61. *Dewoitine D26* serial U-288 c/n 320 ex HB-RAE. *Rech Monoplane. Soldenhoff Delta. Fokker C.V-E.* serial C-331. *Nieuport 28* serial 607. *E.F.W. C-3603* serial C-549 (flying still?) *Messerschmitt Bf 108 Taifun* A-209. *NA.AT-16 Harvard* U-328 ex FE824 (other serial etc wanted.) Plus many engines and other interesting items. Currently flying here for para-drops and communications and used in films "Where Eagles Dare" and "The Counterfeit Traitor" are *Junkers Ju 52/3m* which from outbreak of WW II became Ju 52/3m.G4E:—A-701 Werk-Nr 6580—HB-HOS from 1948/59. A-702 Werk-Nr 6596—HB-HOT from 1951/59. A-703 Werk-Nr 6610—HB-HOP from 1947/59 One of these machines will, it is thought, enter the museum here when its flying days are over. Let us hope the other two are also preserved in Europe.

E.F.W. C-3603 (Dubendorf)

Junkers Ju 52/3m (Dubendorf)

Bf 108 Taifun (Dubendorf)

ECUVILLENS. Airfield. *Miles Whitney Straight* HB-EPI c/n 349 of 1937.

EIKEN. Airfield. *Comte AC-4* HB-ETI, c/n 15 ex CH-180; Franz Berger. *Erla 5* HB-SEX c/n 14 ex D-ENAL.

GENEVA. Airport. *Percival Gull 6* HB-OFU c/n D65 owner Alfredo Habib. *Luscombe 8A* HB-DUS c/n 923 of 1939 (often at Basle). *Beech D.17S* HB-UIH, c/n 4920 ex 43-10872, OO-VIT, SE-BRY; *Antoinette No 2* (replica) ex "Magnificent Men" being rebuilt here for Mr. Simsa and on the main road out of Geneva at a garage there are said to be two *Avro 504* (replicas) for taxying, made for a film project.

LA COTE. Airfield. *Dewoitine D26* HB-RAI c/n 276 ex S.A.F. 284, being restored for flight.

LAUSANNE. Airport. *DH.60 Moth Major* HB-UPE c/n 5078 of 1934, ex CH-348.

LES AVANTS. Chatelard School. *DH.83 Fox Moth* said owned here by member of staff—details please.

LOMMIS. Airstrip. *Moswey IIA glider* HB-257.

LUCERNE. Swiss Transport Museum. Air and Space Exhibition Hall, opened 1 July 1972. Planned when the main museum opened in 1959, building work started 1967; total cost of £1¾ million being shared by many contributors including Swissair and Longines. The main hall is 200 ft long, 110 ft wide and 42 ft high, housing 23 of the 25 a/c, with elevated galleries for viewing. Outside are:—*Douglas DC-3C* HB-IRN, c/n 33393, ex 44-77061, KN683; Swissair since 1945. *EKW (Federal A/c Factory) N-20* prototype of the first Aiguillon (Sting) STOL jet fighter-bomber, with four early SM-1 engines. Taxied and "hopped" from 8 April 1952 but never flew as no funds for production were made available. Indoors (some hanging) all easily photographed:—*Dufaux No 4* of 1910; biplane built by brothers Armand and Henry Dufaux of Geneva and used by Armand for first flight over Lake Geneva 28 April 1910, the longest flight made over water at that time—66 km in 56 minutes. The 25 hp Anzani 3-cylinder engine produced maximum speed 75 km per hr and this signalled the real beginning of Swiss Aviation. *Bleriot XI No 23* of 1913 constructed by Bleriot Works the type used by Swiss pioneer Oskar Bider who flew over Pyrenees for first time 23 January 1913, 512 kms (with 70 hp Gnome engine). He later made four epic flights including Berne-Domodossola-Milan (first flight over Jung-

N-20 (Lucerne)

Bf 109 E-3 (Lucerne)

fraujoch—3,600 m.) Some of Bider's equipment is in
the Bleriot displayed. *Messerschmitt Bf 109 E-3 J-355*
Werk-Nr. 2422 one of batch J-311/390 ex Germany
1939/40 for Swiss home defence. *Hanriot HD-1* No 653
of 1922. *Nieuport 28.C.1 Bebe* No 607 which landed
Samaden 1 June 1918 and was interned. *Fokker FVIIA*
HB-LBO c/n 5005 of 1927, Balair's original CH-157,
renovated by Swissair apprentices at Kloten. *Comte
AC-4* HB-KIL c/n 35 ex CH-264, of 1930. *Pou-du-Ciel*
HB-MH8 ski-equipped, VW-powered, built by Roland
Py-Guignard at Vallee de Joux. *Dewoitine D27* serial
J-257 of 1934, Swiss-built. *E.K.W.* (Eidgenössische
Konstruktions Werkstätte) *C-35* serial C-180, biplane of
1937, replacing Fokker C.V-E. *Dornier D-3801*, license-
built Morane M-S 406, serial J-276, built by Swiss
Dornier-Werke AG at Altenrhein. *Bucker Bu 133 Jungmeister* serial U-60. *Fieseler Fi 156 C Storch* A-97 which
landed in Switzerland 1943 and was interned. *NA
P-51D Mustang* J-2113; served 1948-58. *E.F.W.* (Eidgenössische Flug-zeug-Werke) *C-3603* ground-attack two-
seat fighter-bomber, 295 mph, first-flown 1941 with
Oerlikon cannon and four 7.5 mm guns, plus four
110/220 lb bombs. Serial C-537. *DH. Vampire Mk 6*,
Swiss-built—J-1068. *E.K.W. Arbalete* (Crossbow) the
3/5ths-scale N-20 powered by four Turbomeca Pimene
1 engines, flown successfully 91 times before the
Aiguillon was dropped. *Bell 47G-1* HB-XAE from Heli-
swiss Co. Several fascinating gliders are here:—
Chanute-type Hang glider built 1933 by Donat Guignard
of Ste. Criox and flown by him wearing skis. to give the
necessary speed for take-off in downhill run! *WF-7
biplane glider* "32" built by Willi Farner, 1934. *Zogling
training sailplane.* A *Mercury capsule* loaned by USA is
in the Space Section. Presently outdoors is a *Con-
traves Zenit sounding rocket* an example of which was
launched successfully from Sardinia in 1967. Design
ceiling 136-217 miles, depending upon payload. Many
other machines are still flying, eg *Pilatus P2* serial U-138
or are in store and will be rotated or added when
possible. The director, Mr. Alfred Waldis and his
associates have done a fine job for preservation.

Dewoitine D 27 (Lucerne)

NA Mustang (Lucerne)

Pilatus P2 (Lucerne)

Miles Gemini (Schanis)

SCHANIS. Airfield. *Spyr IIIb* glider HB-112; *S-15K*
glider, HB-327, and unknown *glider* HB-362 reported
here—details? *Miles Gemini* HB-EEA.

SCHUPFART. Airfield. *Bucker Bu 180 Student* HB-
EFO c/n 2106 of 1938. *Grunau Baby II* HB-87, oldest
glider flying in Switzerland also *Rhonadler* HB-312.

SILTERDORF. Playground. *Beech C-18S* HB-GAI.
ex 44-87150, S.A.F. B-6.

SPECK. Airstrip. *Gliders* HB-230 and *Moswey III* HB-
374—details wanted.

STANS. Airfield. *Dornier D-3801* (license-built Morane
Saulnier MS406) two examples here dismantled—
request serials and prospects of preservation—price
required etc?

ST. MORITZ. Hotel grounds. *Boeing B-17G Flying
Fortress* 42-38160 "Lonesome Polecat" recovered from

Swiss lake where landed during WW II and then displayed at St. Gallen. It is believed available for disposal—details appreciated, also photo.

THUN. Airfield. *Auster V* HB-EOW c/n 1004 ex N3611, flying.

TURKEY

CUMAOVASIR. Disused airfield 10 miles south of Izmir. Turkish Air Museum being established here with:— *Curtiss CW-25 Falcon*—no registration—details please. *de Havilland DH.89 Rapide*, until recently used for advertising, one of ten in use pre-war/post-war. Would value details of regn. and history. *MKEK 4 Ugur* TC-KUJ—believed airworthy. *Miles M.14A Magister* TC-KAH, marked "THK 1925". *NA T-6 Texan* serial 06, airworthy. *NA. F-86D Sabre* serialled 19207. *Republic P-47 Thunderbolt* marked "TC-21". *Republic RF-84F Thunderflash* 11901. *Republic F-84G Thunderjet*—2 examples; serialled 19953 and U-572. Histories please. *Turkish-built P.Z.L.24* unmarked. *Turkish-built glider* TC-PBP. *Douglas C-47, Beech AT-11 Kansan* and *Lockheed T-33* due as this is written—details please and photos; also of opening days and times, admission price etc.

Curtiss CW-25 Falcon (Cumaovasir)

P-47D Thunderbolt (Cumaovasir)

ESENBOGA. Ucakla Zirai Koruma A.S. *Auster V* TC-AYL c/n 1375 ex TJ299, ex G-AKWK, TC-AYLA. *Beech C-45* TC-KUM c/n 1009; Tapu Ve Kadastro. *Beech C-45* TC-KOM and TC-KON; Devlet Havadan Meydanlari. Fuller details would be valued.

ESKISEHIR. Turkish Air Force. Said to be a *Russian-built WW.I a/c* here, captured near Trabzon. USSR help has been sought to identify and facilitate restoration. Now believed 1914 *Grigorovitch M.5* flying-boat with Gnome Mono. To go to Cumaovasir.

ESTIMESGUT. Airfield. *P.Z.L.24* OK-L was displayed here, Polish-built.

ISTANBUL. Yesilkoy Airport. *Beech AT-11 Kansan* "30" of Turkish Air Force based here. *Miles M.14 Magister* TC-KAI (coupe) c/n 35; TC-KAR, c/n 78; and TC-KAY c/n 60 of Havacilik Kuluba Istanbul (Istanbul Flying Club). It is thought there are also some MKEK 4 Ugur a/c stored.

U.S.S.R.

CHKALOVSK. Museum. *ANT-25* stated to be displayed here, flown by Chkalov; but not known if this is the machine which made the non-stop 7,711 miles flight Schelkovo-Moscow-Tula-Ryazan in 1934. Chkalov later flew non-stop to USA in 1937 in the all-metal cantilever low-wing monoplane produced by P.O. Sukhoi and team, with A.N. Tupolev supervising. The military version was the Tupolev RD-DB-1 and compiler would be grateful for a photograph and confirmation of which a/c is here.

LENINGRAD. Arctic Museum. The *amphibian* flown by Babushkin. Can a reader please give complete details of type and provide photo? It is also reported that there is a Naval Museum containing a *Polikarpov 1-16 Rata*. Again, details and photo would be appreciated.

GAGARIN. On the main Moscow-Smolensk road, about 5 miles east of the re-named birthplace of the astronaut, as a war memorial, is a *Yak-3* monoplane fighter, mounted with undercarriage retracted in banking position on concrete plinth. It is painted a drab greyish-green overall; no markings.

MONINO. Air Forces' Red Banner Academy, 30 miles from Moscow, a museum dating from 1960, in which are about 30 machines, mainly in the open:— *Sopwith Triplane* (under cover) details wanted. *Voisin Pusher* of WW.1—(under cover). *Antonev An-2*, 12-seater feeder-line a/c of 1947; 1,000 hp USN-62IR engine. *Ilyushin Il-10*, two-seat ground-attack, first operated February 1945 over Germany. *Ilyushin Il-28* "04" NATO code-name "Beagle" first flown 1947, two VK-1 turbojets. Over 10,000 built. *Lavochkin La-7* "27", said to be Ivan Kojedub's a/c—with 63 "kills". Top speed 422.5 mph. Three 20 mm ShVAK cannon in front upper fuselage decking, two offset to port, one starboard. *Lavochkin La-11* "20" last piston-engined fighter designed by Sergei Lavochkin and last to attain production in USSR. Too late for WW II but used by Communist Northern Air Force in Korea. *Lavochkin La-15* the first of Semyon A. Lavochkin's jet fighters in production. Power plant RD-500 turbojet, USSR version of Rolls-Royce Derwent. NATO code-name "Fantail". *Mikoyan-Gurevich MiG-9* "01" first known as the I-300, test-flown 24 April 1946, max. speed 566 mph. NATO code-name "Fargo". One 37 mm, two 23 mm cannon. *Mikoyan-Gurevich MiG-15* "27" famous for its part in the Korean War this A. I. Mikoyan and M. I.

Gurevich a/c with NATO code-name "Fagot" served with at least 12 air forces and was license-built in Poland and Czechoslovakia. Prototype first flew 30 December 1947 powered by Rolls-Royce Nene engine, later models having the RD-45 (later called VK-1) engine, virtually copied from the Nene. In Poland a/c was known as the LIM-2 and in Czechoslovakia S-102. *MiG-15* unserialled, also shown in "cutaway". *Mikoyan-Gurevich MiG-17* (serial wanted) built for 21 air forces and under license in China, Czechoslovakia, Poland, NATO code-name "Fresco" with mixed bag of armament including air-surface weapons. *Petlyakov Pe-2* twin-engined fighter-bomber tested 1939, production from mid-1940. Code-named "Buck"; maximum bombload 6,615 lbs. *Polikarpov Po-2*, designed by Nikolai N. Polikarpov as the U-2 trainer, the U-2VS became a night-bomber and, after Polikarpov's death in 1944 was re-named the Po-2 in honour of the designer. Maximum speed only 90 mph and range only 267 miles but gave very good performance against the Nazis. *Tupolev Tu-2* first flown October 1940, production early 1942, two 1,850 hp ASh-82FN engines, top speed 342 mph. In production until 1948, in action in Korea and NATO code-name "Bat". Soviet, Chinese and Polish AF. *Yakovlev Yak-12*—light communications aircraft. *Yakovlev Yak-17* fighter of 1947, improved Yak-15 jet fighter, NATO code-name "Feather"; two 23 mm cannons. *Yakovlev Yak-23*, all-metal development of Yak-17, with copy of R-R Derwent. NATO code-name "Flora". *Yakovlev Yak-24*—tandem-rotor helicopter. It is believed other types are to be added—details and photos gratefully received by compiler.

MOSCOW. Central House of Aviation and Cosmonauts. *MiG-15* fighter—serial wanted. *Mil Mi-1* helicopter. *Kamov Ka-18* helicopter CCCP 31300. And many models etc. At the Central Museum of the Armed Forces:—*MiG-15*. *MiG-17* and *MiG-21F* "01" NATO code-name "Fishbed-C" short-range clear-weather fighter, two 30 mm cannon, max-speed 1,320 mph. Also here the wreckage of a Heinkel He 111 and of the Lockheed U-2 flown by Gary Powers. The Zhukowski Aircraft Museum is worth a visit although it is not known if full-scale a/c there. Space Pavilion in the Mir Prospect has a *Vostock rocket* outside and full-size mockups of a Yak-40 and Tu-134, with some replicas of USSR space vehicles. Moscow Park of Industries displayed *Tupolev Tu-124* CCCP-45052.

SARATOV. District Study Museum. *Yakovlev Yak-18* in which the late Major Yuri Gagarin (first man in space) flew his initial solo in 1955.

TUSHINO. Airport. Two of Yakovlev's designs are exhibited—*Yakovlev UT-1* of 1936, with 160 hp radial engine. *Yak-30* two-seat jet trainer, 1959 prototype—it was not produced.

YUGOSLAVIA

BELGRADE. Surcin Airport. *Boeing PT-17 Stearman* YU-AER c/n 75-437 ex 40-1790; *YU-AET* c/n 75-2706 ex 41-8517; *YU-AEV* and *YU-AEW* (histories wanted). *Boeing N2S Stearman* YU-BAB c/n 75-7118 ex Bu07514; *YU-BAD* c/n 75-7614 ex Bu37993; *YU-BAE* c/n 75-7527 ex Bu07923; *YU-BAH* c/n 75-4930 ex Bu55693; and *YU-BAI* c/n 75-4931 ex Bu55694. In a compound

Lavochkin La-11 (Monino)

Lavochkin La-15 (Monino)

MiG-17 (Moscow)

MiG-21F (Moscow)

Hurricane IV (Belgrade)

Bf 109 G-2 (Belgrade)

Ilyushin Il-2 (Belgrade)

Junkers Ju 52/3m (Belgrade)

P-47D Thunderbolt (Belgrade)

Short Sealand 1 (Belgrade)

near the JAT maintenance base are stored the machines formerly at Zemun, for the proposed Muzej Jugoslovenskog Vazduhoplovsta. A site on the approach road to the airport has been earmarked but for the time being anyone wishing to view the stored aircraft must apply to the aiport's Air Traffic Control officers or to JAT who may open the hangar if their personnel are available. As at 1st April, 1973, the following are preserved in varying conditions, some almost beyond restoration, alas:—*Saric 2*—kept in JAT maintenance hangar. Oldest a/c in Yugoslavia. Built and flown by Ivan Saric in 1911 at Subotica. Powered by Saric-built and designed 50 hp engine. *Fizir FN 9009* c/n 9. Two-seat biplane of 1930s. Dismantled in the hangar. Was allocated YU-CHY, carries pre-war national insignia. Flew with A. K. Novisad 120 hp Walter engine. *DH.Tiger Moth* YU-CHX/0802. In hangar. Was light-blue, is now dark-blue. Operated by Belgrade and Novisad flying clubs and probably ex-RAF, donated 1945. *Bucker Bu 133 Jungmeister* 9102 c/n 1069. Silver overall, flown post-war, by Sava Poljenec, famous Yugoslav pilot. *Fieseler Fi 156 Storch* YU-COE/9393. Fuselage dilapidated outside; wings stored, need recovering. *Hurricane IV* 9539 "T", traces of serial 319 on wings, was with 351 (Yugo-Slav) Sqdn of RAF in WW II, Middle East/Italy. *Spitfire VC* 9486 ex 352 (Yugo-Slav) Sqdn, RAF. Code "H" was added when displayed at Kelemagden Park, Belgrade 1950s. *Fiat G.50bis* 3505 Croatian markings on fin. Used for home defence, one of ten supplied 1941. *Focke-Wulf Fw 190 F-8* Werk-Nr 930838 coded "43'. C/n plate lettered "hmw" but manufacturer not identified. Captured Zagreb-Pleso 1944. *Messerschmitt Bf 109 G-2* 9663 (JRV serial) From Bulgaria post-war. Flown for a time by training unit. *Yakovlev Yak-3* 2252. Dismantled in hangar. Olive drab. *Yak-9P* 2826. In poor state. May not be restored. *Petlyakov Pe-2* serial unknown, ex JRV. May be scrapped. *Ilyushin Il-2 M3* unserialled, ex JRV. From USSR 1945. *Junkers Ju 52/3m* (AAC-1; from France post-war). Serialled 7208, was used by JAT 1946-50. Regn. unknown. Was earlier reported as 7203/203—confirmation wanted. *Republic P-47D-30-RE Thunderbolt* 13024 supplied under Military Aid Programme 1951. Another (13021) is also stored. *Short Sealand 1* 0662 ex-JAT, purchased 1952 and formerly YU-CFJ or YU-CFK, ex G-AKLR or G-AKLS, c/ns SH1566 or 1567. *Folland Gnat F.1* 11601 c/n FL.14 ex G-39-8. One of two evaluated 1958. Accepted by JRV 21.6.58, after first flight Chilbolton 7.6.58. *Douglas C-47A-25-DK Dakota* YU-ABB c/n 13713 ex 42-93765; *C-47A-30-DK Dakota* YU-ABG c/n 14035/25480 ex 43-48219, KG803, G-AHLX. Both formerly with JAT. *Lisunov Li-3* 7011 (Jugoslav designation for Li-2 re-engined with Wright Cyclones). Alias licence-built Dakota. *Cvjetkovic CA-51*. Two examples, YU-CMH, ex-A. K. Osijek and *YU-CMK* ex Zagreb A. K. With 25 hp Volkswagen engines. *Konstrukcijska Letalske Zveze Slovedije KB-6 Matajur* YU-CFD c/n 177 ex A. K. Celje. Built at Ljubljana. *Aero 2*, two examples. YU-CVB/0875, dismantled in hangar. Unmarked prototype of 1946 with Aero 3 canopy now fitted. *Student* YU-CKK c/n 01. Designed and built by Jovan Cubrilo and Mirko Josipovic and Belgrade students. Volkswagen engine. *Yugoslav Govt S.49A* 2319 dismantled. Initial wooden-fuselage version of fighter based on Yak-9, produced 1950 at former Ikarus plant, Zemun. With 1,222 hp Klimov engine VK-105PF-12. *S-49C*, with Hispano-Suiza 12Z-Ily engine. Dilapidated. Unserialled. *Vajic V.55* YU-CMR, from Zagreb A.K. with 105 hp Walter Minor

4/111. *S-451M Zolja* Prototype, dismantled. Built 1953 with two Palas 056A jets. Registered YU-COH, established international record 19.5.60 in FAI sub-class C.1c at 310 mph. *S-451MM Matica* 2001, experimental indigenous 2-seat jet. With Marbore II. On 19.5.60 established international FAI record in sub-class C.1d at 466 mph. *J-451MM Strsljen* 21001. Single-seat S-451 MM. *B-5 Pionir*, unserialled. Prone-pilot research a/c. With two 55hp Walter Mikron. Completed 1939 and stored during WW II. Re-assembled 1949 but now dismantled. *Type 451*. Unserialled. Prone-pilot research a/c with two 160 hp Walter Minor B-111. Built 1951. Dismantled. *Type 214*, two examples. Serial 61004, slightly-damaged. Airworthy YU-ABP/61019 (both built 1958). *Jadran glider*. Unmarked. *Kosava glider* YU-5022. *CAVKA glider* YU-2179, basic trainer of 1952. Also parts of other a/c and promises of F-84, F-86, Po-2 etc.

S-451 Matica (Belgrade)

LJUBLJANA. Airport. *NA F-86K* 14307 and 14325.

POSTOJNA CAVES. Northern Yugoslavia. *Primary Glider* YU-5040 in children's playground.

J-451 Strsljen (Belgrade)

ZAGREB. Pleso Airport. Across road from airport buildings. *NA F-86D-45NA Sabre*—serial wanted please. The Zagreb Technicki Muzej, Savska 18, in city centre displays, as at April, 1973:—*Aero 3* serial 40001, prototype of 1956, all-yellow. *S-49C* serial 2400. Yugoslavia's first post-war indigenous fighter, powered by 1500 hp Hispano-Suiza 12Z-Ily, built Zemun 1963. *DAR-9*, unmarked but thought to be YU-CGJ/9786. Copy of Fw 44J Stieglitz, built by Darjavna Aeroplane Rabotilnitza at Sofia, during WW II. *Cijan C-3 Trojka* YU-CGT, but originally with JRV as serial 0777. Production a/c built Pancevo near Belgrade by UTV in early fifities. *Jastreb glider* YU-3015. *Fizir biplane* (thought stored). Weekdays the museum opens from 0700 to 1800 and Sundays 0800 to 1200. Easily reached by tram or bus from central bus terminus. Although signs forbid use of cameras, ask the staff at entrance, indicating that you are a "foreign visitor". Ask for permission to go up to the gallery for best views of the collection which is in the centre of the museum building.

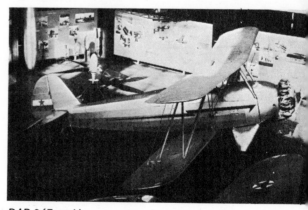

DAR-9 (Zagreb)

NA F-86D Sabre (Zagreb)

S-49C (Zagreb)

Cijan C-3 (Zagreb)

NEAR EAST, MIDDLE EAST AND AFRICA

ALGERIA

DAR-EL-BEIDA. Airport. *Fairchild F.24R.46A Argus III* 7T-VBX c/n 1019 ex 44-83058, KK401, F-OABG, of Protection Civile.

SKIKDA. Airfield. A.C. de Skikda. *Fairchild F.24R.46A Argus III* 7T-VOS c/n 1072, ex 44-83111, KK454, F-OACS.

TIARET. A.C. de Tiaret. *Argus III* 7T-VMT c/n 1006 ex 44-83045, KK388, F-OAFT.

TOUGGOURT. *Beech C-45H* 7T-VBW c/n AF-170 ex 51-11613; Nouvelle Hydraulique Algerianne.

CYPRUS

AKROTIRI. No. 1 Overseas Sqdn., ATC. *Percival Pembroke C.Mk 1* WV706.

EGYPT

All attempts via military and civil sources have failed to confirm existence of Spitfire at Almaza or other vintage types — can anyone help?

ETHIOPIA

ASMARA. Airfield. Imperial Ethiopian Air Force. *Fairey Firefly I*, ex Royal Canadian Navy serial 613 (2-seater). *Fairey Firefly II*, ex Royal Canadian Navy serials 610, 612, 616 and 617. Single-seaters. These aircraft are believed to be for sale — details of location requested when moved.

IRAN

SHIRAZ. In the Park Farah ex-Imperial Iranian AF *N.A. Harvard.*

NA Harvard (Shiraz, Iran)

TEHRAN. Merebad. *Republic F-84G* on plinth in I.A. AF. colours. *Douglas C-47* 44-17203 ex R4D-5, Bu 17203 flies here with U.S. Military Assistance programme.

IRAQ

HABBANIYAH. Airfield. Several (perhaps 20) *Hawker Sea Fury FB.11*; believed for sale.

Avia S.199—Bf 109 G (Israel)

Spitfire IX (Israel)

ISRAEL

Not surprisingly, information is difficult to obtain but (1973) the authorities confirm the existence of:— *Avia S.199* (Jumo-Bf 109G built Prague) known as the Mezec (Mule), bought from Czechs 1948 and ferried out in DC-4 Skymasters of IDF/AF. Whether there is one example (formerly marked "4" and on a pylon at 101 (F) Sqdn base) or this and another, cannot be established. *Supermarine Spitfire IX* Israel Defence Forces/Air Force serial "57" and with "registration" 17-1351 (Merlin 66 195417) sometimes flown by Brigadier Ezer Weizzman. Bought in 1949 from Czech Air Force and presumably one of the former 310/312/313 Sqdn aircraft flown to Prague in 1945. Any details of original serial appreciated. Another *Spitfire IX* painted "105" with six Arab "kill" marks and camouflaged blue-brown may be at the Haaretz Museum Complex where there is a *Harvard* "65".There is also (here or at a military base) *NA P-51 Mustang*, "148" ex R. Swedish AF, survivor ot fhe 1957 Sinai Campaign. Also a *MiG 15* mounted in nose-down position at another base; captured in 1956. It is reported that the sole surviving *Douglas DC5* VH-ARD of Haifa Technical College has been scrapped—confirmation?

TEL AVIV. Lod Airport. *Gloster Meteor T.7*, camouflaged. *Armstrong Whitworth Meteor NF.13* 4X-BET c/n 5582 is with Israel A/c Industries. *Noorduyn UC-64A Norseman* 4X-ARS c/n 769 ex 44-70504 and *Harvard* 4X-ARC c/n 88-17025, thought ex 42-85244, with Marom Ltd. *Boeing PT-17 Stearman* 4X-AII c/n "2929-335". *Harvard* 4X-ARA c/n 14-186 ex 42-629, FE 452. *4X-ARB* c/n 88-17716 ex 42-85935; both with Avitor Ltd.

LEBANON

BEIRUT. Near the Rayak Road. *Proctor IV* L-02. *Savoia-Marchetti SM.79* L-111 ex LR-AMA, L-113 ex LR-AMC. Up-dated report welcomed on condition.

LIBYA

BENINA. Airport. *Auster AOP.6* "194" c/n Tay. 460H. *Gomhouria* (Egyptian-built Bu 181 Bestman) c/ns 091 and 092.

MALI

MOLODO. Airfield. Mali Sport Flying Club. *Gomhouria* (*Bucker*) *181* TZ-ABQ c/n 166. *TZ-ABZ* c/n 167 (also flies from Bamako airfield).

MOROCCO

CASABLANCA. Anfa Airport. Cie Agricolair Maghreb. *Noorduyn UC-64A Norseman* CN-TEE c/n 774 ex 44-70509, I-AIAK, YE-AAD, EC-ANO. *Beech E18S* CN-TTD c/n BA-310 owned by Omnium Nord Africain.

FEZ. Sefrou Airport. A.C. Royal de Fez. *Piper J-3C-65 Cub* CN-TUB c/n 11165 ex 42-29874, F-DAFG. *CN-TVI* c/n 11211 ex 43-29920, F-OAIK. *Auster V* CN-TUD c/n 2061 ex TW518, F-DAAN; A.C. Royal de Casablanca. *CN-TZD* c/n 1079 ex NJ691, G-ALJD, F-DAAG; N.T. Tom. *Fairchild Argus III* CN-TZV c/n 1120 ex 44-83159, KK502, F-OAFY; M. Bennis. *Aeronca II Chief* CN-TYZ c/n 264 ex F-OAEE; F. Petolet.

KENITRA. Airfield. A.C. Royal de Casablanca. *Piper J-3C-65 Cub* CN-TVO c/n 12417 ex 44-80121 F-BDTK, CN-TUK, F-DACK. *Jodel D.92* F-PFEB c/n 6 (oldest flying).

MARRAKESH. Menara Airport. A.C. Royal de Maroc. *Miles Hawk Tr. III*. CN-TZE. c/n 843 ex N3795, G-AIUC, F-OAGQ; no longer airworthy. *NA Harvard* 07, 24, 33, 70 and 97, of Ecole de Pilotage. R. Maroc A.F. (ex French A.F.).

MEKNES. Airport. A.C. Royal de Meknes. *Fairchild Argus III* CN-TUF c/n 1090 ex 44-83129, KK472, F-OACF. *Piper J-3-65 Cub* CN-TUC c/n 12205 ex 44-79909, F-DAEC; *CN-TUE* c/n 9856 ex 43-995, F-DAAM.

RABAT. Ville Airport. D.G.Securite Nationale. *Beech D.18S* CN-MAL c/n A-932.

TANGIER. Tanger Airport. A.C. Royal de Tanger. *Piper J-3C-65 Cub* CN-TYA c/n 12356 ex 44-80060, F-BCPL. *Auster V* CN-TZC c/n 1440 ex TJ371 F-OAOD, HB-EOL; M. Cohen.

TIT MELLIL. Airfield (near Casablanca.) A.C. Royal de Rabat. *J-3C-65 Cub* CN-TTK c/n 11882, ex F-DAFA. *Argus III* CN-TTN c/n 1082, ex 44-83121, KK464, F-OAAV; M. Mulero. *DH. Dragon Rapide* CN-TTO c/n 6940 ex RL958, G-AKRP, F-DAFS is with the Parachute Club de Maroc.

PORTUGUESE GUINEA

BISSAN. *A-W Meteor NF.14* G-AXNE ex WS 804, captured en route to Biafra September 1969. News of future wanted.

SAUDI ARABIA

RIYADH. Airport. *Douglas Dakota* HZ-AAX, presented to King Abd-al-Aziz 1945; now Saudi Arabian Airlines.

SOMALI REPUBLIC

BERBERA. Airfield. *NA P-51* ex Israeli AF reported—details wanted.

SYRIA

DAMASCUS. War Museum Courtyard. *Harvard* and *Piper Cub* reported—Details and photos wanted also news of the *Spitfires* (fifteen Mk F.21) believed stored somewhere in or near Damascus.

Dakota (Riyadh, Saudi Arabia)

EAST AFRICA. RHODESIA. SOUTH AFRICA. CENTRAL WEST AFRICA.

ANGOLA

ILHA DO LUANDA. *F-84G Thunderjet* 6158 of F.A.P. *Fairchild PT-26 Cornell* CR-LBI (confirmation wanted). *Miles Gemini* CR-LCX. c/n 6510 ex G-AKHS. *DH. Rapide* reported airworthy—reg'n please.

KENYA

NAIROBI. Embakasi Airport. Near the Nairobi Road. *DH. Venom FB.4* WR493 near Fire Training School. Can this be saved? Up-dated report and photo please. *Luscombe 8A* 5Y-KDD, c/n 946.

MALAWI

BLANTYRE. Airport. *Vickers Viking* G-AHPG c/n 139 ex VP-YHJ and one time BEA "Velocity" as Hot Dog Stall — details and photo please.

MOZAMBIQUE

BEIRA. Manga Airport. *Lockheed PV-2 Harpoon* 4610 of Portuguese A.F. mounted on poles. *DH Hornet Moth* 5201 and *Tiger Moth* 1184 of P.A.F. *DH. Hornet Moth* CR-AAC c/n 8104; Aero Club de Mocambique.

LOURENCO MARQUES. Airport. On the dump said to be *PV-2 Harpoon* 4604 and *Junkers Ju 52/3m* CR-AAK c/n 5967 "Quelimane" and *CR-AAL* c/n 5973 "Nampula". Restorable? *Lockheed 14H2* CR-AAZ c/n 1511. *Lockheed 18 Lodestar* CR-ACT, c/n 2261 ex 42-55871 *DH Rapide* CR-AAU c/n 6440. *Beech D.17S* CR-AEU, c/n 4925 ex 43-10877, G-AJJE; *DH. Tiger Moth* CR-AFP c/n P.55. All owned by DETA who may donate some to local museum which now houses *DH. Hornet Moth* CR-AAA "Vila Cabral" c/n 8099 their first a/c.

DH.Hornet Moth (Lourenco Marques)

RHODESIA

BULAWAYO. Airfield. *DH. Tiger Moth* VP-YOI c/n 84245 ex T7873, ZS-DEK; J. R. Onions.

SALISBURY. In playground. *Fairchild F.24R Argus* VP-YNF (?) ex ZS-BES c/n 1095 ex 44-83134, KK477. In same playground or another is *Beech AT-11 Kansan*

Spitfire F.22 (Salisbury, Rhodesia)

ZS-CFN c/n 3239. At Air Force Headquarters, New Sarum, near Salisbury *Spitfire F.22* S64 (formerly RRAF 64) shown in recent photo as "R64" — clarification wanted please. *Harvard IIB* SR-50, *Tiger Moth* SR-26 "9" c/n 746 ex DX 658; and *Vampire T.55* R-100 and reported stored here for possible exhibition — histories of all appreciated. It is thought the Spitfire (as also below) comes from the PK350/55 batch. Original serials wanted. *Douglas C47* R7307 "Chaminuka" (African for "rain maker") is flying on cloud-seeding operations; the pilot Flt. Lt. I. A. Holshausen who flew Mustangs/Sabres in Korea. Flying from a local airfield are *DH. Tiger Moth* VP-YDC c/n 732 ex DX644, 7Q-YDC; YDC Syndicate. Also *VP-YNV* ex DX609; V.G.A. Braughton.

THORNHILL. Rhodesian Air Force base. *Spitfire F.22* S65 (formerly RRAF-65) once in Bulwayo Museum. All other RRAF Spitfires were sold to Syria and could still be there?

SOUTH AFRICA

BARAGWANATH. Airfield. *Dragon Rapide* ZS-DLS c/n 6773 ex NR674, G-AGZU dismantled, owner D. Steyn. *DH.90A Dragonfly* ZS-CTR c/n 7526 ex CR-AAB (believed going to USA — details of location please.) *Fairchild F24R Argus 3* ZS-BAY c/n 1145 ex 44-83184, KK527, (static); *Beech D17S Traveller* ZS-BBZ c/n 6768 ex 44-67760, CR-LBF (flying). Also here are a number of *DH. Tiger Moths* including ZS-BGL c/n 84221 ex T7852, 571; S. Levin. ZS-CDJ c/n 84811 ex T6457; N. J. Otten. ZS-CNR c/n 82619; B. T. Zeederberg. ZS-CTN c/n DH4033; D. Jones. ZS-CTS c/n 84077 ex T7683; P. F. Nicholas. ZS-DKY ex 2465; S. M. Shnier. ZS-DNP ex SAAF 4695; Johannesburg Light Plane Club. ZS-FEY c/n "1999 SA/BS"; V. G. Dobson. ZS-FZF c/n 728 ex DX640; R. L. Hay. ZS-CKX ex SAAF 2193; G. van den Bosch. ZS-DEC ex T5478; S. Liederman. ZS-DHE c/n 84435 ex T8123; J. A. Duplessis.

BENONI. Brakpan Airport. Nr Johannesburg. *Hornet Moth* ZS-AOA c/n 8161; J. D. Haupt. *Fairchild 24W-41A Argus* ZS-DCX c/n 285 ex 41-38841, EV777, G-AKJB; M. S. Bosman. *Tiger Moths* ZS-CGR c/n "T3621"; A. D. Howett. ZS-CKZ c/n "LA703"; A Harvard and Ptnr. ZS-DMC c/n 85351 ex DE317; S. L. Hill and Ptnr. *Taylorcraft BL-65* ZS-ARZ c/n 1356; E. C. Jane. On farm nearby reported to be ex-*RAF Oxford* and *Anson*(s). Details of serials and conditions valued.

BLOEMFONTEIN. Airfield. *DH. Tiger Moth* ZS-DFU c/n 84440 ex T8128; C de Villiess.

BULFONTEIN. Airfield. *Taylorcraft BL-65* ZS-APO c/n 1167; T. C. H. Pieterse.

CAPE PROVINCE. CAPETOWN. Jan Smuts Airport. South African Airways use ex-SAAF *Lockheed PV-1 Venturas* for apprentice training, in natural metal finish with SAAF Technical School serials:— TS302; *TS303* ex USN 34965; *TS304* c/n 6059 USN 48823; *TS305* ex USN 34959; *TS306* c/n 2690 ex USN 49474; *TS307*—no details. Atlas A/c Corpn also believed using Venturas here. Flying from here *DH. Tiger Moth* ZS-BCU c/n 85028 ex T6741; W. A. Gerdes, *ZS-BXB* ex SAAF 4636; G. P. de Wet. At Paarden Eileen, Capetown, S. A. Metal & Machinery scrapyard *Sikorsky S-51* ZS-HBT c/n 51-102 ex SAAF A-1 is mounted at entrance and here there are complete (and parts of) Ansons, Harvards, Venturas, Vampires and it is said, Spitfires. On farms around Mamré, 36 miles from Capetown are the following:— *B-34 Ventura* 6120 c/n 4646 ex AJ508 "Irene". *B-34 Ventura* 6066 coded "Y" and "W". *B-34 Ventura* 6075 c/n 4633 ex AJ495 "S". *B-34 Ventura* 6112 code "GZ-OU". *B-34 Ventura* 6130 coded "LB-G" of 21 Sqdn, 2 Group, RAF. Let us hope one can be saved for preservation — perhaps in England.

DUNNOTAR. Transvaal. SAAF base. *Fieseler Fi 156 Storch* VD-TD ex Air Min 99, Farnborough, medium-brown mottle top surfaces, pale-blue under surfaces, azure serial no, yellow u/s of nose.

Fieseler Storch (Dunnotar, R.S.A.)

DURBAN. Virginia Airfield. *Lockheed Lodestar* ZS-ASN c/n 2026 of Aircraft Operating Co. Known as "Grand Old Lady", assembled S.A. 1940 by S. A. Airways but commandeered during WW II by SAAF as 1372, flying to Cairo, then Italy. Used on Royal Tour 1956, carrying Queen's staff.

Vampire FB.5 (Fort Klapperkop)

FORT KLAPPERKOP. Old Boer War Fort. Now Military Museum. *N.A. Harvard IIA* painted spuriously as SAAF 7729 but with Belgian Congo serial H-15 visible.

One of four "refugees" flown to South Africa during Congo-Katanga crisis. Thought ex EZ310. *DH. Vampire FB.5* 208 displayed, standard current finish.

GRAFF REINETT. Airfield. *Fairchild 24R Argus 3* ZS-BLG c/n 1099 ex 44-83138, KK431, being restored.

DH.9 (Johannesburg)

Hawker Hartebeeste (Johannesburg)

JOHANNESBURG. South Africa's National War Museum, Saxonwold. *de Havilland DH.9* believed c/n 2005 an Imperial Gift a/c. Once coded "IS-8" of 70 Air School, then ZS-AOE. *R.A/c Factory S.E.5* — no serial, Imperial Gift, once at Natal University for technical training. *Hawker Hartebeeste* quoted earlier as 850 now thought 851, only survivor of 65 built A/c & Artillery Depot, Roberts Heights, Pretoria as SAAF version of Hart with R-R Kestrel V. Used East African campaign 1940 coded "B". *Hurricane IIC* 5285 ex LD619 delivered 1943, was "AX-E" 11 OTU. *Spitfire FVIII* believed JF294 serialled 5501 SAAF, from Cairo 1947; first Spitfire to fly in South Africa. *Spitfire IX* W5630 said here for restoration. *Messerschmitt Bf 109 F (Trop*) captured No 7 Sqdn, SAAF and given serial "777", painted as JG27, N.Africa. *Messerschmitt Bf 109 E* built by Arado, shot down Devonshire 1940; code "2+FA". Displayed outdoors unrestored. *DH. Mosquito PRIX* LR480 ex 60 Sqdn. SAAF, originally "Anne" now quoted as Cairo-Pretoria record-breaker "Lovely Lady". *Focke-Wulf Fw 190* thought ex-AM77 of Fw 190/Ju 88 "Mistel", Farnborough. Also quoted as possible ex-AM 10 with Werk-Nr 55012? *Messerschmitt Me 262 B-Ia/U1* "EL-K" one of two sent from Farnborough, not authentic markings and once believed marked "8" or "305" possibly ex AM 50 or Luftwaffe 500443. Moved, with Fw 190, from

Messerschmitt Bf 109 F (Johannesburg)

Bf 109 E (Johannesburg)

Hurricane IIC (Johannesburg)

Vickers Viking ZS-DKH (Near Johannesburg)

DH.Mosquito PRIX (Johannesburg)

Fort Klapperkop. Thought to be at Johannesburg, Malan Airport:— *Lockheed Lodestar VP-WCN* dismantled. *Lockheed 18-08* ZS-ATL c/n 2058, is with Commercial Air Services. *Douglas DC-3* (ex Cyclone-powered) ZS-DPO c/n 1994 ex N18118, N402D is a clubhouse. *DH Hornet Moth* ZS-ALA c/n 8121; M. W. Spencer. *Aeronca 65C* ZS-APY c/n 2879; B. D. Jones. *Spitfire IX* MA793 is being restored to fly by Larry L. Barnett, with the remains of 5631 and four other Spitfires from Capetown dump and elsewhere: 5631 was last Spitfire to fly in S.A., used to train pilots for Korea. In a local scrapyard are said to be some Kittyhawks with "sharkmouth" markings — surely worth investigating? *Fairchild 24R Argus* ZS-BLP c/n 1118 ex 44-83157, KK500, has been converted, in North Johannesburg to ZS-UFW—a homebuilt biplane. *Vickers Viking* ZS-DKH c/n 121 ex G-AHOT of BEA "Valkyrie" mounted on roof of Vic's Viking Garage on the Salisbury-Vanderbijl Rd, 8 miles from Johannesburg. Formerly Protea and Trek Airways.

Messerschmit Me 262 (Johannesburg)

Focke-Wulf Fw 190 (Johannesburg)

KRUGERSDORP. Airfield *DH. Tiger Moth* ZS-CMD ex SAAF 4963; C. J. Hattingh.

LANGEBAANWEG. SAAF base. *Vampire FB.9* "235" mounted on concrete pylon as tribute to the type's long service. Ex 2 Sqdn and Air Ops School. A coastal wreck in area said to contain brand-new WW II aircraft — let us hope a "rescue" takes place.

LYTTLETON. SAAF Technical Training School. *DH. Vampire FB.5* "207". *Harvard II* "7681" (history please).

Beechcraft D17S (Roodebank)

PORT ELIZABETH. P.E. Museum. *Miles Gemini 1A* ZS-BRV c/n 6444 for new Transport Wing of Museum. The museum may also acquire a Ju 52 from Mozambique and a/c from SAAF. From the airport fly *Tiger Moth* ZS-BCN c/n "372" and *Fairchild 24R Argus 3* ZS-DDP c/n 1129 ex 44-83168, KK511; and also ZS-DGG c/n 1165, ex 44-83204, KK547, ZS-AXE, VP-YGW; being rebuilt.

PRETORIA. Airport. *DH. Heron C(VVIP)3* XM296 c/n 14130 ex Queen's Flt reported here for British Defence Liaison Staff—let us hope this now-rare type will be preserved in England.

ROODEBANK. Airfield. *Hornet Moth* ZS-DIH c/n 8117 ex ZS-AKG, VP-YIW; P. J. Viljoen. *Beechcraft D17S* ZS-PWD c/n 295 ex 39-139, DR628, NC91397, G-AMBY, VP-YIV, thought hereabouts: from Rhodesia. This aircraft was used in WW II frequently by Prince Benhard of the Netherlands, and previously the American Embassy, London.

Vampire FB.9 (Langebaanweg)

Constellation (Warmbaths)

SNAKE VALLEY. 15 Air Depot, S.A.A.F. Restoration/ Storage. *Lockheed PV-1 Ventura* 6534 Bu 48775, ex 17 and 22 Sqdns "MT-Z" almost restored—for museum display? *Lockheed PV-1 Venturas* stored here include:— 6521; 6472 "D"; 6473 "P"; 6504 "MS-W"; 6428 "MS-X"; 6525 "MS-T"; 6478 "MS-K"; 6483 "MT-F"; 6534. 6494 "MT-S"; 6509; 6513 "MT-Q". 6430. Above are either bomber version, d/earth top/surfaces, sky under/ surfaces or coastal patrol version extra dark sea-grey top/surfaces and sky or PRU-blue under/surfaces. Following are ex-VIP Transports natural metal finish, white top; blue cheat line. 6487; 6481. Following was target tug, all-over yellow with black diagonal bands:— 6499. Let us hope some are obtained for the world's aviation collections. Several Harvards are stored including *Harvard III* 7570 ex 41-34016, EZ143, Also *Canadair Sabre 6* and *Vampire FB.5* Details of serials would be of value. *Hurricane II* 5124 marked "214" is now here for—we hope—restoration. History would be appreciated.

STILFONTEIN MINE. West Transvaal. Garden of Remembrance. *NA Harvard IIA* 7506 in 40 Sqdn markings.

VALHALLA. S.A.A.F. Gymnasium. *Vampire FB.5* 205; *Harvard III* 7731 thought ex H-210 of Belgian AF, Congo. Inside the camp it is thought there are display a/c including *Vampire FB.5* 209 and *Harvards* 7732 (ex H-9 or H-223) and 7681. Clarification would be welcomed.

VOORTREKKERHOOGTE. S.A.A.F. *Harvard IIA* 7647 (replaces 7654). *Vampire FB.5* 210 ex 1 Sqdn "AX-V". Standard finish with matt red bands instead of dayglo. At the Medical Institute is *Lockheed PV-1* 6487—ex personal transport of General J. C. Smuts; used for training medical attendants.

WARMBATHS. Transvaal. On main road Pretoria-Rhodesia. *Lockheed L-1649A Starliner* of Trek Airways ZS-DVJ "Super Star" c/n 1042, ex D-ALOL, N45520, LX-LGX. Flown from Jan Smuts airport to specially-prepared runway at "Little Kariba" holiday resort where owner, Mr. Pelser, plans to convert it into a restaurant.

WATERKLOOF. S.A.A.F. base. *Spitfire IXe* 5518 ex RAF TE213, formerly inaccurately painted W5581.

WONDERBOOM. Airport. *Percival Prentice* ZS-EUS ex VS609 G-AOPL; static.
Before leaving the Republic of South Africa it may be worthwhile to mention several reports from reasonably-reliable sources stating that at Alexandersfontein, Kimberley, many SAAF a/c were gathered at end of WW II and some may still be restorable—one contact mentions a Vickers Valentia, a Fairey Battle, etc. In the Orange Free State, at Tempe Bloemfontein, No 1 Parachute Battalion are said to have a Spitfire! An Airspeed Oxford is reported at Pietermaritzburg, Natal, a Catalina in the Thousand Hills near St. Lucia, a Warwick in Eastern Transvaal (Belfast) and a Sunderland sunk in shallowish waters in Richards Bay, a freshwater lake. The compiler would like to have up-dated information with any photos for the next edition, provided of course, that the machines ARE restorable and transportable.

ZAMBIA

NDOLA. Airport. *Gloster Javelin* XH890 of 29 Sqdn, left, unflyable, when detachment returned UK, for children's playground use. *Lockheed Lodestar* 9J-RBM c/n 2066 ex VP-YWY, ZS-ATM of Hunting Surveys; also in playground.

Spitfire IXe (Waterkloof)

THE FAR EAST

AFGHANISTAN

KABUL. Airport. Reports abound that there are still Hawker Hind parts sufficient to make more exhibits—details would be appreciated. Meantime *Douglas DC-3* YA-AAD c/n 18910 ex 42-100447, VT-DGV flies with Ariana Afghan.

BURMA

RANGOON. Aung Sang Park, Royal Lakes. *Spitfire LFIXe* UB431 (or 441) is here, but details and a photo seem impossible, despite years of correspondence (one-sided) with British and Burmese authorities. It is stated that the aircraft logbook is held by the Mayor of Rangoon and that after flying with the RAF the Spitfire went to Prague with Czech Wing, was later sold to Israel and flew against Egypt. In 1954 it was flown from Lydda via Turkey, Iran, Bahrein, Sharjah, Jamawi, Karachi and Calcutta, flying with Burmese Air Force as UB431 (triangle markings and tailflashes) against Ku Ming Tung troops on borders of Burma/China. Surviving to become a National Monument it was presented to the nation 24th April, 1956 by Air Commodore T. Clift, CAS, Burmese A.F. General Aung Sang organized an underground army which he led against the Japs in 1945. Assassinated 1947 he is regarded as a symbol of Burma's independence just as Spitfire is a symbol in Britain. Can a reader PLEASE confirm present serial and original serial, with photo.

CEYLON (SRI LANKA)

COLOMBO. Defence HQs. *Boulton Paul Balliol T2* CA310 c/n BPA/10C ex WG224, G-APCN. The Walrus, alas, was sold for scrap and is now in many kitchens as part of a pot or pan.

CHINA

PEKING. Thought to be kept in store (and exhibited in the city on occasions). *Boeing PT-17* in Nationalist China markings. *North American B-25H Mitchells* with codes 120 and 329. *North American P-51D Mustang* displayed in Chicom markings. *North American F-86F-30NA* CNAF F-0672 ex USAF 52-4441 in Nationalist markings. *Ryan Firebee drones*—wreckage exhibited from time to time *Sikorsky R-6, Tachikawa Ki-36 "Ida"* in Chicom markings. *Tupolev Tu 2* serialled 2130 and in Chicom markings.

FORMOSA

PINGTUNG. Nationalist Chinese Airfield, south of village. *MiG-15* serialled 1765 on display.

TAINAN. Air Base. *Republic F-84G* (serial wanted). *Martin Matador Missile*. Both at main gate on display.

HONG KONG

HONG KONG, Kai Tak. Airport. Former 80 Sqdn RAF and Hong Kong AAF *Spitfire F.24 VN485.* Also reported, ex RAF Sek Kong. *DH Venom FB4* WR539 ex 28 Sqdn.

MiG-15 (Pingtung, Formosa)

Spitfire F.24 (Hong Kong)

162

INDIA

AGRA. Indian Air Force. *Douglas DC-3* HJ905.

AMBALA. Indian AF. *Spitfire FR.XIV* HS365 "N-M".

BANGALORE. Indian AF. *Douglas DC-3* BJ496, BJ764, IJ242, for internal service flights.

COCHIN. Airport. Can anyone up-date, please, the reports of a *Short Sealand* and *Fairey Firefly* said to be static here.

DEHRA DUN. Doon School. *NA Harvard II* FT105 in SEAC marks. *Spitfire XIV* SM832 has been re-located to the grounds of the Indian Military Academy here, but is deteriorating fast.

DELHI. Cantonment, Western Air Command. *Spitfire XIV* HS877. *Folland Gnat* IE1061.

JALAHALLI. IAF Technical College. In use:— *Consolidated B-24J Liberator* painted T-18. *Spitfire XIV* painted T-20. *Vampire FB.52* T-27. Also several *C-47* a/c., a *Percival Prentice, HT-2,* and *Ilyushin Il-14.*

JORHAT. IAF. *DC-3* HJ230 and J247.

KARNAL. Sainik (Cadet) School. *Harvard IIB.*

NA BHA. Sainik School. *NA Harvard III.*

NEW DELHI. Asian Trade building. *Folland Gnat* IE1053. At Safdarjang airfield, New Delhi, is *Beech E17B* VT-AKK c/n 233 ex Indian Airlines static.

PALAM (New Delhi) The Indian Air Force Museum. *Auster V* IN959, silver, black wingtips. *Consolidated B-24J-90-CF Liberator* HE924 "L" 6 Sqdn, IAF, ex 44-44213. *Dassault Ouragan "Toofani"* IC-554 camouflaged. *DH. Vampire NF.10* ID606 of 10 Sqdn IAF. *Folland Gnat Mk 1* IE1059, 23 Sqdn IAF. *DH. Tiger Moth* HU512. *Hurricane IIB* AP832 (RAF) 6 Sqdn IAF. *Hawker Tempest II* HA623 ex MW848—natural aluminium. *NA F-86-F40 Sabre* 25248—remains of a/c shot down by 7 Sqdn IAF over Halwara Air Base 6 Sept 1965. *NA AT-16 Harvard IIB* HT291 "S" may be FS787, 43-12626, though c/n 14A-927 on plate. *Percival Prentice* IV336—from IAF Academy, Jodhpur. *Sikorsky S-55* IZ1590 ex 104 Helicopter Unit. *Sukhoi Su-7* tail displayed—remainder stored for future; flown back by Wg Cdr H. S. Mangat after flak damage. *Spitfire VIII* NH631 (RAF) named "Plumber", flown by AV-M. Harjinder Singh. Blue overall. *Spitfire XVIII* HS986, ex 14 Sqdn IAF, natural aluminium. *Westland Lysander IIIT* 1589, shipped UK-Canada 1941, flown only 61 hours, 400 Sqdn, RCAF; donated Canadian Armed Forces in return for IAF Liberator October 1967 (see Rockcliffe, Ontario).

Spitfire XIV (Delhi)

Hurricane IIB (Palam)

Hawker Tempest II (Palam)

Spitfire VIII (Palam)

Westland Wapiti (Palam)

Lysander IIIT (Palam)

Liberator HE846 (Poona)

Westland Wapiti, thought IIA, painted K183 but possibly from K1254-1309 batch. ex "A" Flt 1 Sqdn, then Kanpur No 1 Base Repair Depot for 20 years. *Jap Naval Arsenal Ohka II*—recovered by No 4 Sqdn IAF during service in Japan with British Commonwealth Forces. Flt Lt I. P. Alexander, IAF, is the helpful curator and hopes to add to the museum as types become surplus to requirements.

PATALIA. Airfield. *DH82A Tiger Moth* VT-DBX c/n 83044 ex R5182, VH-BMJ; owned by Capt Daljit Singh who hopes to fly round the world in this aircraft as soon as he has found financial backing.

PATNA. IAF. *Hurricane I* V6846, thought ex-312 (Czech) Sqdn also 3, 17, 87, 242 Sqdns, RAF.

POONA. IAF base. The following machines were up for disposal, though, alas, most may now be scrapped as costs of making airworthy are prohibitive:—*B-24J-CF Liberator* HE841 ex 42-99787 "H"; *HE839* ex 44-10526; *HE843* ex 44-39248; *HE712* ex 44-39261 "Z"; *HE923* ex 44-44181; *HE848* ex 44-44262 "D"; *HE846* ex 44-44263, "T"; *HE845* ex 44-44280. *B-24L-FO HE833* ex 44-49052 c/n 5786L; *HE807* ex 44-50206 c/n 6707L. Also *HE926*, details unknown. Report from visitor says 10-12 engineless *Tempests* also here—some, surely, worth acquiring for displays?

PUNJAB. Chandigarh Engineering College. *DH. Tiger Moth* T-13. *Spitfire XIV* HS674. *Kanpur II* BR570 indigenously designed and built AOP/Light Utility aircraft.

SANGANEN. National Cadet Corps HQs. *Spitfire XIV* T-17.

SAROJNI NAGAR. Lucknow. Sainik School. *Dassault Ouragan* IC867.
It would be greatly appreciated if a reader could fill in some of the gaps insofar as previous serials and histories are concerned and let the compiler know of any other vintage types, flying or static, in India. For example a civil register dated June 1968 lists Auster 3(1), Auster 5(5), Avro Anson (12), Beech 17(1), Beech 18(15), Cessna 140(1), Curtiss C46 (18), DH. Tiger Moth (45), DH. Fox Moth (2), DH. Leopard Moth (1), DH. Rapide (5), Dakota (53), Fairchild Argus (5), Noorduyn Norseman (6), NA AT-6F (3), Piper Cub (17), Stinson Sentinel (55) and Vultee BT-13 (1).

INDONESIA (JAVA)

DJAKARTA. Airport. *C-47* O-48316 with US Embassy, ex Mildenhall.

JOGJAKARTA. On roadside between airport-town *Vultee Valiant,* said to be first Indonesian AF aircraft—serial and photo, please, also of *Valiant* B605 at Jogja Zoo.

Fairey Gannet (Surabaja, Java)

SURABAJA. Djuanda Naval Air Base. *Fairey Gannet* A500 marked "Angk Laut" at gate. Another *Gannet* and *Sikorsky S-55* instructional airframes.

JAPAN

AICHI PREFECTURE—
KOMAKI. Nagoya Airport. Terminal building. *NA F-86D* 84-8105, JASDF. *Handley Page HPR1 Marathon* JA6009 c/n 136 ex XA277, G-AMHY. Municipal Science Museum. *NA T-6G.* 52-0036

AOMORI PREFECTURE—
OMINATO. Air Station. JMSDF. *Westland WS-51 Dragonfly* 8831.

CHIBA PREFECTURE—
NARASHINA CITY. Nihon University. *Okamura-Shiki N-52* JA3024 c/n 1.

SHIMOFUSA. Air Station. *Grumman (Gen. Motors) TBM-3S2 Avenger* s/n 2347, JMSDF.

TATEYAMA. Air Station. *Beech JRB-4* 6409 USN Bu 44665. *Grumman TBM-3R* Bu 91195—both with JMSDF.

URAYASU. Okayama Airport. *Aero Commander 520* JA 5001 c/n 1 ex N4100B, the first!

FUKUI PREFECTURE—
FUKUI. Airport. *Hiller UH-12B* JA7002 c/n 341.

FUKUOAKA PREFECTURE—
ASHIYA. Air Base. *Fuji T1A* 85-5801. *Lockheed T-33A* 51-5610 and 51-5642. *NA F-86F* 85-5801. All with JASDF.

KURUME. Ishibashi Cultural Centre. *NA-T6G.* 52-0098.
GIFU PREFECTURE—

KAGAMIHARA CITY. Gifu Air Base Displayed—*DH. Vampire TII* 63-5571, *Kawasaki KAL-2* 40-1555 c/n 30001, with JASDF

HIROSHIMA PREFECTURE—
HIROSHIMA. Airport. *NA T-6G* 52-005.

KURE. Local Station *Grumman TBM-3S2* 2344, JMSDF.

HOKKAIDO PREFECTURE—
HOKKAIDO. Chitosi City. *Piper L-21B* JG 12047, JGSDF 7th Group.

HYOGO PREFECTURE—
TOKARAZUKA Park. *Douglas DC-4* JA6003 c/n 3115 ex 42-32940, N 86556.

IBARAGI PREFECTURE—
TSUCHIURA CITY. Kasumigaura School. *Kawasaki KAL-1* JG20001 c/n 1001 JGSDF.

ISHIKAWA PREFECTURE—
KOMATSU. Airport. *Lockheed T-33A* 51-5649. *North American T-6F* 52-0017.

KANAGAWA PREFECTURE—
ATSUGI US. *NAS. Vertol UH-25B* Bu 128527.

MIE PREFECTURE—
YOKKAICHI. Health Centre. *DH 114 Heron 1B* PK-GHH c/n 14023.

MIYAGI PREFECTURE—
SENDAI CITY. Miyagi Senior High School. *NA T-6G* 52-0089.

SENDAI. JGSDF Station. *NA T-6G* 72-0146 and *Piper L-21B* JG12038.

YAMOTO-CHO. Matsushima Air Base. *Lockheed T-33A* 51-5626. *North American T-6G* 52-0080, with JASDF.

NARA PREFECTURE—
NARA CITY. JASDF Officers' School. *NA F-86D* 84-8100.

OSAKA PREFECTURE—
OSAKA. Traffic Museum. *Kawasaki KAL-1* JA 3074 c/n 1002. *Ansaldo SVA9* (replica) sponsored by Alitalia.

SAITAMA PREFECTURE—
IRUMA (Johnson). Air Base. *Jap Naval Arsenal Ohka 11. Kawasaki Ki-61-II Hien (Tony). Lockheed T-33A* 51-5625 and 51-5638 *Lockheed TF-104J* 36-5011. *North American F-86D* 84-8103, *F-86F* 62-7461. *Douglas XSAM-A-7* Nike-Ajax. *Vertol H-21* (serial wanted).

KUMAGAYA. JASDF 4th Technical School. *NA F-86F* 82-7849. *NA T-6G* 52-0079. *NA T-28B* 63-0581 c/n *NA-218-1.*

SHIZUOKA PREFECTURE—
HAMAMATSU CITY. JASDF Hamamatsu South. *Maurice Farman* (stored). *Mitsubishi A6M5a* 43-188 c/n 4685, ex Guam, formerly 1st Air Fleet, 343 Fighter Group,

Kure, pilot Major Ozaki. *North American F-86F Sabre* 82-7808. *Texans* 6172, 6177, 6187, 6194, 6198, 6209 reported here—histories?

KOYAMA-CHO. JGSDF Officers' School. *Piper L-21B* JG12009.

TOKYO AND DISTRICT—
CHOFU-CITY. *North American T-6D* 52-0004. At Chofu Airport, Nihom University. *Nichidai NM63 Linnet* is stored.

Kawasaki "Tony" (Kanda)

KANDA. Kotsu Transportation Museum, 21-1 Sudo-Cho. *Farman Shorthorn* No 266. *Hatachi Tachikawa R-HM* JA-3094 c/n 3. Japanese built Pou-du-Ciel. *Kawasaki Ki-61-II "Tony". Nakajima Ki-115. NA T-6G* 52-0062.

KOGANEI-CITY. Koganei Industrial High School. *Toyo TT-10* JA-3026 c/n 531. Tokyo Technical Research Institute, Ministry of Transport *Nakajima Ki-115* stored.

Ohka 11 (Iruma, Japan)

Mitsubishi A6M5a (Hamamatsu City)

MATSUCHIEGEVIL. Tokushima Air Station. *Kawasaki KAL-2* 9001 c/n 3002, JMSDF.

TAMA-TEC. Minamitama-gun. *Handley Page HPR1 Marathon* JA6010 c/n 137 ex G-AMHZ, XA278.

TOKYO. International Airport. *Nikon YS-11* JA8611 c/n 1. Prototype. Technical High School (Aeronautical Dept.) 10-140. Senju-cho, Arakawa-ku, in store:—*Auster J5G Autocar* JA3029 c/n 3054, *Chrislea Super Ace* JA3062 c/n 112 ex G-AKVD, *Fletcher FD-25A* JA3062 c/n 531, *FD-25B* JA3092 c/n 2. *Nakajima Ki-115. North American T-6G* 52-0099. *Piper PA-22-135* JA3036 c/n 22-776 *Sikorsky R-6A* 43-4590 (USAF). *Yomiuri Y-1* JA 7009 c/n 1. Technical Museum (Science) Kasumigaseki, Chiyoda-ku. *Mitsubishi Mu-2 prototype* JA8620 c/n 001 *NA F-86* (serial wanted).

TOKYO STATION. JGSDF. Nerima-ku. *NA T-6G* 52-0078. Tachikawa Aircraft Co (New) *Tachihi R-53* JA3070 c/n 2.

TOKUSHIMA PREFECTURE—
TOKUSHIMA-CITY. Naruto Technical High School. *NA T-6G* 52-0096.

WATE PREFECTURE—
MORIOTA CITY. JGSDF Iwati Station. *NA T-6G* 72-0147.

YAMAGUCHI PREFECTURE—
BOFU SOUTH. Air Base. *North American F-86F* 52-7403. *North American T-6D* 62-0008 and *T-6G* 72-0134. Will readers kindly-up-date information and provide photos for next edition.

KOREA (SOUTH)

SEOUL. UN Korean War Allies Association. *Boeing B-29-BW Superfortress* 45-21739 c/n 13633 coded "48".

TEAGUE. K-2 Air Force Base. Republic of Korea AF. *NA TF51D-NA* "201" Temco conversion. *NA. T-6G-NA* —serial wanted and pics.

YONGDUNPO. Republic of Korea AF base. *NA-TF51 Mustang* "205" ex 44-73494.

F-86 Sabre (Sargodha, Pakistan)

PAKISTAN

PESHAWAR. Pakistan Air Force Museum. Although (April 1973) Gp Cpt Akber Khan says no complete a/c yet displayed, it is thought that *Vickers V.649 Viking 1B*

J750 c/n 261 is earmarked and that a *Sea Fury, DH. Dove,* and other aircraft will eventually join the exhibits. Rumours abound of *Tempests* and *Spitfires*—details appreciated.

SARGODHA. Airfield. On display on plinth *NA F-86 Sabre* 51-13447.

THE PHILIPPINES

BASA. Air Base. Front of officers' club. *NA.F-51D Mustang* 44-74627 "001" (*F-86* mainwheels).

Phillipine Air Force Museum (Lipa City)

LIPA CITY. Fernando Air Base. Philippine Air Force Museum displays (1968). *Beech T-34* serial 59-06101. *Bell H-13, Boeing PT-13* marked "500". *Hiller UH-12. North American F-86F Sabre* 52-4468. *North American F-86D Sabre* 52-10015. *North American T-6* serial 20162. *North American T-28* serial 17500. *Taylorcraft L-5.*

NICHOLS AIR BASE. *North American F-51D.*

SINGAPORE

CHANGI. Airfield. *Gloster Meteor T7* VW487 with 1574 Flt, ex No 1 Sqdn 1949. Claimed to be longest serving RAF operational a/c. *Scottish Aviation Twin Pioneer* XP293 ex 209 Sqdn, RAF, with Air Scouts

SELETAR. Airfield. *Auster AOP.9* WZ729 (ex Army) restored by 390 MU, RAF, for Air Cadets. *DH. Vampire T.11* XH358/7763M "Z" and *Gloster Meteor T.7* WH226/ 7818M were displayed.

Auster AOP.9 (Seletar, Singapore)

THAILAND

BANGKOK. Don Muang. Royal Thai Air Force Museum. Viewing by arrangement with curator at airport. *Beech AT.18(C-45F)* HS-TBE ex 44-87152. *Boeing P-12-100E* Fighter Trainer. Silver overall, Thai cockade, c/n 1487 or 1488. *Cessna L-19 Bird Dog* 26231.

Curtiss Helldiver (Bangkok)

Grumman Widgeon (Bangkok)

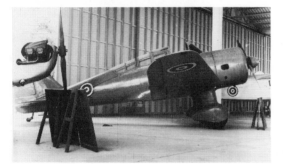

Tachikawa "Ida" (Bangkok)

Vought V-93S Corsair (Bangkok)

Curtiss Hawk 3, Cyclone engined, natural metal with cockade. Engine No 23399 *Curtiss Hawk 75*, natural metal with cockade; Engine No 27307. *Curtiss SB2C Helldiver* 3-4/97 "4" c/n 366, midnight-blue, engine No 124457—history please. *DH. Tiger Moth* coded "21" all-yellow, cockade; c/n quoted as 2494—details wanted, but possibly ex R4877, G-AMGB c/n 82794? *DH. Chipmunk* 9-5/93 ex Thai Flying Club. White & Maroon c/n 133 coded "5". *Fairchild F-24J Argus*; two examples, SS793E and 7201AM. *Fairey Firefly Mk I* SFII ex MB410 c/n F.7402—midnight and pale blue, red spinner. *Grumman F8F Bearcat* 15-178/98, metallic finish with cockade, white rear fuselage band. *Grumman G-44-A Widgeon* 2494 c/n 1449, silver, black & yellow; coded "4" and "Rescue". *Hiller UH-12B* 4 c/n 597, silver & yellow, black markings. *NA. T-6 Texan* serialled "122" —stored. *Percival Prince* Thai serial 2-4/96. *Piper L4J Grasshopper* Thai serial "301". *Republic F-84G Thunderjet* "4314" on nose. *Sikorsky YR.5A* 43-46607, silver, black, yellow. *W/Sikorsky S51A Dragonfly* ex G-AMJW c/n WA/H/120 "Rescue". *Tachikawa Ki36 "Ida"* thought sub-contracted Mitsubishi Type 98 Karigane III (Ida.) Listed in museum as Tachikawa. *Vought V-93S Corsair* sold to Thailand 1934, O3U design of which 195 built for US Navy in various versions. It is thought this is the oldest Vought a/c existing. P & W Hornet 14682. *V/Supermarine Spitfire FRXIVe* 2493 coded "1" under paint, silver with red wingtips and spinner. *Sikorsky H-19 Chickasaw* 3-3/97 painted "6313" said c/n 55757 of 1954, silver and black with yellow badge "Valour without Arms". *Vultee-Stinson L-5B Sentinel* 44-16985, silver, black anti-dazzle panel. Outside museum:— *NA F-86 Sabre* "4322" on fuselage, 5060 on tail. *F-86L* "1215" on fuselage, 30681 on tail. Royal Thai Air Force School (opposite museum) *Two Sabres*—serials unknown. It is thought there are vintage gliders (or replicas)

and information would be valued, including any original serials which for most machines have been painted out. Outside Government Buildings, Bangkok stand *Grumman F8F Bearcat* 15-43/93 (with bombs/rockets) *Grumman F8F Bearcat* unserialled. Details wanted. At the Armed Forces Academy School stands *Grumman G-44A Widgeon* NC41972.
At Civil Aviation Training Centre are *Beech C-45* HS-SFB and *T-6 Texan* HS-TCA.

BANGKOK-AYNDYA (on road between) One mile apart Two *F-84 Thunderjets*—serials wanted.

NAKORN-SAWAN. Wing 4 on main gate. *Grumman F8F Bearcat* "342".

Grumman Bearcat (Nakorn-Sawan)

TAKHLI. R.Thai AF. *F8F-1* "4000". *Republic F-84G* "4311" with T-33 tiptanks.
It is still thought that at least one *Spitfire XIV* exists of the four sent to an airfield "up country" and reports with photos are sought.

Grumman Bearcat (Bien Hoa, Vietnam)

VIETNAM (SOUTH)

BIEN HOA *Grumman F8F-1B* 121510 "G 1510" on tail.

NHA TRANG. Long-Van Air base. *F8F-1* 93569 "35-69" on tail.

TAN SON NHUT Air Base. *Grumman F8F-1* 95255 and 95338.
In view of changes in Vietnam as this is typed, up-dated information would be appreciated for 5th edition.

PACIFIC ISLANDS

NOTE:— There is considerable activity in this area and some aircraft may well be on the way to Australia, Canada or USA when this edition reaches you. Details are as at 1st April 1973 according to the compiler's information.

FIJI

SUVA. Nausori Airport. *Tiger Moth* DL-FAG c/n 83502 ex T5773, NZ678, ZK-AIE (engine from DHA. Drover); Nausori Flying Group. At the Derrick Technical Institute, for eventual display at Nausori, is *Dornier 12 Libelle* "Dragonfly" flying-boat VQ-FAB c/n 117 of 1927 powered by a Cirrus III 508/3, manufactured Croydon 1929. Stored for many years after hurricane damage, this, the first machine to pioneer air services in Fiji, is one of the oldest Dornier a/c in existence and needs only a few parts for restoration.

NETHERLANDS NEW GUINEA

BIAK. A *Fairey Firefly* is reported mounted at entrance to the Naval HQs—details and photo wanted.

NEW BRITAIN

MALMALUEN. Coastwatchers' Memorial Lookout. *Mitsubishi A6M Zero*, on pylon, rescued from Kokopo and restored by Rabaul Lions Club. Photo appreciated.

RABAUL. Airport. *Curtiss Robin* VH-CSB said to be stored here, ex Crowley Airways—details please.

NEW CALEDONIA

NOUMEA. Airport. Confirmation wanted of 1935 *Stinson* and *Caudron Aiglon* flown by Henri Martinet.

NEW GUINEA/PAPUA

ALEXISHAFEN. Airport. Will a reader kindly confirm *Junkers W.34* VH-UKW still there and suitable for rebuild.

GOROKA. Branch of New Guinea Museum. *Bell P-39 Airacobra* 41-6670 (believed) from Tadji airstrip.

LAE. Airport. *Douglas DC-3 Dakota* VH-PNA c/n 16355 ex 42-76771, A65-99 ex Ansett, for use of local technical college students.

MYOLA. *Ford 5-AT-C Tri-motor* A45-1 c/n 5AT-60 ex NC401H, G-ABHO, VH-UBI, was reported here, overturned here but possibly restorable—up-dated report please.

PORT MORESBY. Kodoka Track War Memorial Museum. Said to have *Bell P-39D Airacobra* 41-6802. At a spot 2 miles from Ward Strip, fenced-off, are many aircraft owned by the War Historical Society, including, it is said:— *Republic P-47 Thunderbolt* 42-8068. *P-38 Lightning*, serial wanted. *Curtiss P-40 Warhawk*, being restored in colours of Sqdn Ldr Jackson (after whom Jackson Field so-named.) also a *Thunderbolt*, minus one wing. In store is *CAC Wirraway CA-1* A20-685 painted A20-13, to represent one based at Rabaul in WW II. This is from Tom King of Melbourne.

TALDORA. Dept of Civil Aviation Training College. *Mitsubishi A6M Zero* and other wrecks for possible rebuild.

NEW IRELAND

KAVIENG. In clearing; *Mitsubishi "Betty"* owned by Tom King and said to be bound for Melbourne.

AUSTRALIA AND NEW ZEALAND

AUSTRALIA

AUSTRALIAN CAPITAL TERRITORY

CANBERRA. Australian War Memorial. Displayed, 1973:— *Albatros D.Va* D5390/17; shot down 7 December 1917 by 3 Sqdn, Australian Flying Corps, Ploegsteert, Wood, when Lt Sandy and Sgt Hughes engaged six German a/c. Both Sandy & Hughes were killed by single bullets and their machine flew 50 miles before it, too crashed. *R.A/c Factory SE.5a* C9539 "V" and boomerang marking. A type flown by No 2 Sqdn, AFC, but actually a gift from UK in 1920 and re-serialled A2-4, RAAF. *Avro Lancaster 1* W4783 coded "AR-G" of 460 (RAAF) Sqdn, flown by 29 different crews on 90 "Ops" and shot-up at least 30 times. Its first regular captain was the late Flt Lt J. Saint-Smith DFM, hence "Saint" insignia. Flown to Australia 1944 by Flt Lt E. A. Hudson DFC & Bar for war-savings campaign. Donors or buyers of £100 bonds got a flight, those who gave £10 a ground inspection tour. Re-serialled A66-2 RAAF post-war. *Spitfire IIA* P7973 ex 452 (RAAF) Sqdn was flown by the late Sqdn Ldr K. W. Truscott DFC & Bar,

Wg Cdr R. Bungey DFC and the late Sqdn Ldr R. Thorold Smith DFC. Coded "R-H". *Commonwealth A/c Corporation CA.5 Wirraway* II A20-103. Flown by Flt Lt Archer when he shot down a Zero near Gona, New Guinea, 26 December, 1942. *Deperdussin Type A* bought by Australian Flying Corps 1912 for the first military flying course at Point Cook, Victoria. Flown by Lt Eric Harrison and many others who achieved fame. The Deperdussin is recorded as C.F.S.5 and is ex-Point Cook, Victoria. *Fieseler V 1* flying bomb.

Also displayed are panels from Sunderlands P9605 and W3983, tail rotor from Bell Sioux A1-637 shot down in Vietnam and many other magnificent exhibits well worth a visit when in Australia. In store as this is compiled:— *Gloster Meteor F.8* A77-368, formerly WA952, with No 77 Sqdn, Korea as "Rosemary", then with City of Sydney Sqdn. Citizen Air Force. To Canberra September 1960. *Pfalz D.XII* 2600/18, forced-down by pilots of No 2 Sqdn, AFC near Dieppe 9 October 1918. Two Camels escorted a/c to allied aerodrome after enemy had used up his ammunition. (Under restoration as this is compiled). *V2 rocket*—used in tests at Woomera.

Albatross D.Va (Canberra)

Meteor F.8 (Canberra)

R.A/c Factory SE.5a (Canberra)

Wirraway, V1, Lancaster, Spitfire (Canberra)

Deperdussin (Canberra)

Pfalz D.XII (Canberra)

FAIRBAIRN. RAAF Airfield for Canberra. *DH. Vampire T.35A* A79-830 at the entrance. *DH. 82a Tiger Moth* VH-ULR, c/n 1019 built 1942 as A17-584, was sold post-war to the Royal NSW Aero Club as VH-RSG, later to Airland when it became VH-WOG. Now owned and flown by Major Charles Miller who also owns *DH. 83 Fox Moth* VH-UUS c/n 4044 which left England as G-ACCS in 1933 as part of the Houston Expedition. Blown over at Allahabad it was shipped back to UK, was later sold to J. A. Mairs of Portrush, 1935, but left for Australia and became later the RAAF's A41-3. It is said that this a/c actually carried *twelve* souls from Wau to Lae in New Guinea during the Jap invasion, the pilot still alive in Brisbane today. It is the only Fox Moth on the Australian register and is being restored to fly again after being stored at Archerfield. After war was registered VH-CCH. Major Miller plans to restore a DH. 60 when the Fox Moth is flying and has in mind either the *DH. 60M* VH-UMO c/n 1379 or *DH. 60G* VH-UFV c/n 1, ex A7-112 both currently stored fuselages, for which Major Miller has a set of mainplanes from his VH-ULM days. Hats off to this pilot who formerly flew the Monospar now at Newark, England. *CA. 18 Mustang Mk 22* A68-187 formerly on pylon at Bankstown is here, fitted with Rolls-Royce Dart and nicknamed "Dartang".

NEW SOUTH WALES

ALBURY. Airport. *Tiger Moth* VH-ART c/n 592/T.185 exA17-417; E. B. Fraser; *VH-BCN* c/n 876/T.267 ex A17-459; K. L. McLean. *Ryan STM*, unregistered at present, under restoration.

BALMAIN. Airfield. *Auster V* VH-SED c/n 1668, ex TJ631, VH-PIC; B. Baudin.

BALRANALD. Airfield. *Auster 3F* VH-CYH c/n 413 ex NK126, A11-41; J. J. Coates.

BANKSTOWN. Airport. Marshall Airways Collection: *Avro Cadet II* VH-AGH c/n 1058, ex A6-23, VH-AHH. *Douglas DC-2* A30-9 c/n 1292 ex NC13782, VH-CRK; *A30-11* c/n 1286 ex NC13736, VH-CRE. *Messerschmitt Bf 109 G-6* Werk-Nr quoted as 16382 which is thought to be a G-14. *Morris Penguin*, pre-war Australian-built ground trainer. *Comper Swift* VH-UVC c/n S32/10 ex G-ACAG (being restored) *Nakajima Ki-43 Hayabusa* (Peregrine Falcon) known by allies as "Oscar". *Short Scion Mk I* VH-UUP c/n S.776 ex G-ACUX; once fitted with floats. *Spitfire HF.VIII* MV154 ex A53-671 and *MV239 (incomplete) Westland Widgeon III* VH-UGI—first a/c to fly Coral Sea. Flying from Bankstown or undergoing restoration:— *Douglas DC-2* VH-CDZ c/n 1376 ex PK-AFL of KNILM, VH-CXG, 44-83227; (bound for USA—new registration and location please). *DH. Dragon* VH-AQU c/n 2048 ex A34-59; Marshall Airways. *DH. Puss Moth* VH-UQB c/n 2051 ex G-ABDW. *DH. Tiger Moth* VH-AJA c/n 629/T.192 ex A17-437; J. W. Cameron. *Bristol Sycamore 4* VH-BAW

Nakajima "Oscar" (Bankstown)

Bf 109 G-6 (Bankstown)

Short Scion (Bankstown)

Spitfire HF.VIII (Bankstown)

Douglas DC-2 (Bankstown)

Hawker Sea Fury 11 (Bankstown)

Lockheed 12A (Bankstown)

c/n 13070 ex G-AMWI and *VH-SYC* c/n 13504 ex XN448; Associated Helicopter Services. *BA Swallow 2* VH-AAB c/n 461 ex G-AFBB, VT-AIG (restoration). *Commonwealth CA. 18-20 Mustang* VH-BOY c/n 1364 ex A68-39 and *VH-BOZ* (CA18-22) c/n 1524 ex A68-199; Air Training Pty Ltd. *Hawker Sea Fury Mk 11* VH-BOU ex WH588; A. Glass. *CA.18 Mustang* VH-IVI c/n 1444 ex A68-119; Ray Whitbread. *Beech D.17S* VH-MJE c/n 4922 ex 43-10874, G-AJJJ; J. R. Palmer. *Cierva C.30A* VH-USR c/n 792 is in Royal Aero Club of NSW hangar. *DH. Sea Venom FAW.53* WZ946 is mounted as in flight at Chieftain Flying Club. *Fairchild Argus* VH-BVF c/n 416, ex 43-14416, A36-1, VH-ACV; J. Stewart. *Lockheed 12A* VH-ASV c/n 1236 ex VH-TLZ, VH-DMC, VH-ABH is reported here with A. Fisher. *DH. Vampire T.33* A79-649 and A79-673 also here. *Spitfire XVI* TE384/7207M ex 603 (City of Edinburgh) and RAF Syerston, Notts, is said here with Mr. Treloar, as part of the deal which took Seagull VH-ALB to RAF Museum. It is, however (April, 1973) suggested that this Spitfire (or MV154) may go to Mildura, Victoria. Will a reader please give fate of *CA. Mustang* VH-WAS c/n 1443.

DH.9 (Bathurst)

B.A. Eagle 2 (Bathurst)

BLACKTOWN. Australian Air League. *Fairey Firefly AS.6* WD827.

BATHURST. St. Stanislaus Vincentian College. *de Havilland DH.9* G-EAQM ex F1278 in which Ray Parer and John McIntosh became the second team to fly from England to Australia, taking 6 months and 25 days in 1920. (See Adelaide for first flight). On loan from Canberra and in a specially-built hangar at Parer's old school. Parer (who died July, 1967) also flew a Fairey Fox in the 1934 England-Australia Race and took 116 days to reach Melbourne (Geoff Hemsworth, who flew with him, lost his life discovering the Jap task force prior to the Coral Sea Battle). Flying from the local airfield *DH. Tiger Moth* VH-BGJ c/n 83185 ex T5460; J. Honeyman. *BA Eagle 2* VH-UUY c/n 128 not currently registered.

BROKEN HILL. Airfield. *DH. Tiger Moth* VH-ASD c/n LES.6 ex VH-BOC, VH-RVB; K. R. Smith.

CAMDEN. Airport. Museum of Aviation. Mr. G. H. Thomas and his son. Open 1030-1750 Sundays & public holidays (except Good Friday/Christmas Day. Admission 30 cents, 5 cents for children; or 60 cents a family. By prior appointment at other times: Displayed, 1973:— *Avro Anson Mk I* R9883 ex VH-AVT, VH-AGA. Painted as N5151. *Bristol Sycamore HR.51* XR592, c/n 13505. *CAC CA-16 Wirraway III* A20-685. *DAP Beaufighter 21* A8-186 ex 22 Sqdn, RAAF, then Instructional Airframe No 8 at RAAF, Wagga. *DH. 60G Moth* A7-75 c/n 1060 ex VH-ULT (fuselage) *DH. Tiger Moth* A17-680 c/n 82348 ex VH-ADH. *DH.94 Moth Minor* VH-AGT, c/n 94075. *DH. Mosquito FB.VI* HR621, being restored. ex 805 Sqdn, and *DH Sea Venom FAW. 53* WZ907, *WZ945. DH. Sea Vampire T.22* XA101. *DH. Vampire F.30* A79-14. *Fairey Firefly AS.6* WH632 from Marrickville Air League. *Fairey Gannet AS.1* XA334, ex Bankstown (with Vampires). *Gere Biplane*, unregistered. *Gloster Meteor F.8* A77-868 ex WK674—from Ultimo. *Gray Monoplane*, homebuilt of 1929. *Hawker Sea Fury FB.11* VW647 from Dept of Works, Ryde. *Percival Proctor III* VH-BXU. c/n K.401, ex Z7212, G-ANWY. *Percival Proctor IV* NP336 c/n H.707. *Spitfire HF VIII* MV239, from Bankstown. *Victa R.101 Gyrocopter* VH-MVB. *Vultee Vengeance 1A* EZ999 ex A27-99 "NH-V". Cockpits of Beaufighter A8-386 and Beaufort A9-703. The cockpit of Avro/GAF Lincoln B.30 A73-27 is also displayed and this growing collection deserves the support of all enthusiasts in or visiting Australia.

Anson Mk I (Camden)

Beaufighter 21 (Camden)

Firefly AS.6 (Camden)

DH.84 Dragon (Camden)

Vultee Vengence (Camden)

B.A.Eagle 2 (Camden)

Flying from Camden or undergoing restoration:—
B.A. Eagle 2 VH-ACN c/n 138 ex G-AFAX; C.Monk.
DH. 84 Dragon VH-SNB c/n 6088 ex VH-URU, A34-2;
Rev. Les Nixon. *Fairchild 24R Argus* VH-ABZ c/n 3314
ex A36-2; and *Norduyn UC-64A Norseman* VH-GSF
c/n 274 ex 43-5289, VH-BNL; both with Skyservice Avn
Pty. *Republic Seabee* VH-ECZ ex VH-BBJ (damaged)
and VH-MJC c/n 416; K. Olsen, thought still hangared
here.

COONAMBLE. Airfield. *DH. Tiger Moth* VH-BAR c/n
816 ex A17-666; P. M. Lefebre.

COOTAMUNDRA. Airfield. *DH. Tiger Moth* VH-ALU
c/n 1035 ex A17-600; D. McKenzie.

COWRA. Auto Museum. *Tiger Moth*—serial please.

FORBES. On pylon. *DH. Vampire F30* A79-109.

GAREMA. Airfield. *DH.60G* VH-UAE c/n 192 ex
A7-88; A. A. Wright.

GILGONDRA. Airfield. *DH. Tiger Moth* VH-CYA c/n
986 ex A17-551; K. Anderson.

GOULBURN. Airfield. *Fairchild Argus II* VH-BLB c/n
856 ex 43-14892; HB619, G-AIXM; B. Gash.

GRIFFITH. Returned Servicemen's League. *Fairey
Firefly TT.6* WB518, as memorial.

GUNDAGAI. Airfield. *DH. Tiger Moth* VH-DAD c/n
1076 ex A17-745; A. McGillivray.

HAY. Airfield. *DH. Tiger Moth* VH-SEC c/n 189/T.245
ex A17-188, VH-AXH, VH-BXH, VH-RVH; Air Group.

HOLSWORTHY. Australian Army HQs. *V2 rocket*
displayed.

INVERELL. Airfield. *DH. Tiger Moth* VH-APN c/n 331
ex A17-312; P. A. Finlen.

JERILDERIE. Airfield. *Ryan STM 2* VH-AHC c/n 492
ex S-56, A50-29 and *VH-AHD* c/n 469 ex S-33, A50-34;
V. T. Chapman.

Ryan STM 2 (Jerilderie)

KATOOMBA. Airfield. *DH. 60M Moth* VH-UQV c/n 783, ex CF-ADC; M. J. A. Honeysett.

KOORINGAL. Airfield. *DH. Tiger Moth* VH-RIN c/n 1023, entered RAAF 25 July 1942 as A17-588 "Kuringai Municipality" bought by local citizens. Sold as war disposal 4 October 1957, now owned by Terry Mahoney for joy-riding and crop-dusting.

LITHGOW. Airfield. *Fairchild Argus I* VH-ALF c/n 339 ex 42-32134, FK330, G-AKJL; Lithgow Air Park Pty Ltd.

LONGOEVILLE. Airfield. *Taylor J.2 Cub* VH-UYM c/n 959; L. G. Carey.

MAITLAND. Airfield. *DH. Tiger Moth* VH-RNI c/n 108/T.35 ex A17-111, VH-ALH; Royal Newcastle Aero Club.

MOSS VALE. Airfield. *Auster V* VH-ABA c/n 1050 ex NJ667, G-AJJR; G. S. Anderson. *Auster 3F* VH-FBA c/n 483 ex MT393, A11-45, VH-WAI; L. F. Cooper.

MURWILLUMBA. Airfield. *Fairchild Argus II* VH-AZL c/n 308 ex 41-38862, EV798, G-AKCJ; J. K. Bryant.

NARRABRI. Airfield. *DH. Tiger Moth* VH-BUG c/n LES.9 ex VH-WET; A. H. Baker (also flies at Wee Waa).

NARROMINE. Airfield. *Tiger Moth* VH-PCL c/n 3786 ex N6456, VH-BPW; C. Pay.

NOWRA. HMAS Albatross, Royal Australian Naval Air Station. Displayed at entrance gates:— *Fairey Firefly AS.6* WJ109. *Hawker Sea Fury FB. 11* VW623 (ex 1946 for HMAS Sydney, Korea). Just inside the gates *Sycamore HR.51* XD653: *Grumman S-2E Tracker* 151646. In store or for instruction:— *Westland Wessex Mk 31* (WA217 quoted but believed incorrect—confirmation please). *DH. Sea Venom FAW.53* WX895 and WZ931 (931 to go on pole). *Fairey Gannet AS.1* XA435 (to go on display). Reported (1973) for possible disposal:— *DH. Sea Vampire T.22* XA167 and N6-766, N6-770 (original serials wanted if a/c not scrapped.) *DH. Vampire T.35* A79-840 and A79-842. *DH. Sea Venom F.53* WZ944, WZ897, WZ943, WZ903, N4-901, N4-904, N4-930, N4-935.

ORANGE. Airfield. *Proctor III* VH-SCC c/n H.44 ex BV544, G-AKWO; Dick Bland. *Chrislea Ace* VH-BAE c/n 129 ex ZK-ASJ; F. Graf. *Auster IV* VH-BHA c/n 881 ex MT108, G-ANGX, VH-AZJ, VH-TLS, VH-DDW; L. H. Kerr.

OSBORNE PARK. Airfield. *Lockheed Hudson 3* VH-AGS c/n 6041 ex 41-23182, A16-112, VH-BNJ, VH-EWA, VH-AIU, also *VH-AGX* c/n 6051, ex 41-23192, A16-122; Adastra Aerial Surveys.

Lockheed Hudson 3 (Osborne Park)

PANANIA. Airfield. *Ryan STM.* VH-AGR c/n 466 ex S-30, A50-18; L. R. Barnes.

PARKES. Airfield. *BA. Eagle* VH-UTI c/n 109, was stored here by Jack Hodder—news please.

PELICAN BAY. Airfield. *Stinson V.76* VH-ACZ reported stored in hangar; J. Hilder.

PORT MACQUARIE. Airfield. *Klemm L 25 D.11* VH-UUR c/n 796 ex HB-XAL; A. Oliver.

Klemm L 25 D.11 (Port Macquarie)

REGENTS PARK. No 2 Stores Depot, RAAF. *Gloster Meteor F.8* A77-858. *DAP Jindivik* A92-20. These are RAAF recruiting display a/c stored here. *DH. Vampire T.35* A79-561 will be mounted at this base.

RICHMOND. RAAF. *Junkers A50* VH-UCC c/n 3517 once at Wiseman's Ferry, said to be under restoration here by RAAF airman—up-dated report please. *Auster 3F* VH-ALS c/n 293 ex MZ168, A11-55, RAAF Gliding Club.

Firefly AS.6 (Nowra)

Junkers A 50 (Richmond)

Sandringham VH-BRF (Rose Bay)

ROSE BAY. Sydney Harbour. Flying Boat Terminal. *Short S25 Sandringham* VH-BRC c/n SH.55c, ex Sunderland III JM715 (RAF), ZK-AMH and *VH-BRF* ex Sunderland III ML814 of 422 (Canadian) Sqdn and NZ4108 of RNZAF. Both now still with Ansett Flying Boat Services. Let Australia ensure that one or both are preserved when flying ends, to honour No 10 (RAAF) Sqdn!

RYDE. Commonwealth Dept of Works. *Hawker Sea Fury FB.11* WG630 for wind & rain tests on building materials.

SCHOFIELDS. HMAS Nirimba. Navy Apprentice Centre. *DH. Sea Venom FAW.53* WZ898 and WZ937. *Firefly TT.6* WD826. *Fairey Gannet AS.1* XA329. *Grumman S-2A Tracker* 133160. For instruction—one may be displayed at entrance.

SCONE. Airfield. *Noorduyn UC-64A Norseman* VH-GSG c/n 269 ex VH-GSB; Pay & Williamson Pty. Ltd.

SYDNEY. Mascot Airport. With Qantas Airways. *Avro 504K* A3-4 on permanent loan from Australian War Memorial, Canberra, converted to take in-line Sunbeam Dyak to represent first Qantas a/c of 1921. Believed ex H2173, (if serial A3-4 is genuine) it now has a bottle-green fuselage with silver surfaces, polished brass radiator and varnished struts with tyres from an M.G. car. A lovely sight. Also here the engine from BE.2e C6985, G-AUBF, flown by (Sir) Hudson Fysh in 1921. Flying from Mascot several vintage types:—

Demoiselle—replica (Sydney, Mascot)

Lockheed Hudson 4 VH-AGJ c/n 6464 ex VH-SMM; *VH-AGP* c/n 6034 ex VH-SMO; Adastra Aerial Surveys Pty. *Demoiselle No 2 (replica)* from "Magnificent Men" thought to be here with Ansett/ANA pilot.

SYDNEY Technical College, Ultimo. *Bristol Sycamore HR.50* XA220 c/n 13064; *DH. Sea Venom FAW.53* WZ910; *Forney F.1A. Aircoupe* N3017G. *Hunting Jet Provost T.2* G-AOHD c/n P84/12. Sole Mk T.2 built Luton 1956 and used for trials in Australia as A99-001 from May 1959. Here for instruction.

The Sydney (Ultimo) Museum of Applied Arts & Sciences:— In storage/awaiting display space— *Bleriot XI* believed flown by Maurice Guillaux July 16-18 1914 on first Melbourne-Sydney airmail—longest in world at time. Did first loop in Australia and later owned by R. F. Carey. Flew first airmail South Australia Adelaide-Gawler. Carey was first civilian to obtain license—at Point Cook, at age of 42! Also stored:

Avro 504K (Sydney, Mascot)

Catalina VI VH-ASA (Sydney, Ultimo)

Consolidated PB2B-2R Catalina VI VH-ASA ex RAF JX630, RAAF's A24-385 of Nos 11 and 43 Sqdns, 112 ASR Flight. Flown by the late (and great) Captain Sir Gordon Taylor GC, MC, (see Brisbane) on pioneering survey of 8,500 miles in 1951 to Chile via, Suva, Samoa, Tahiti, Easter Island, as "Frigate Bird II". The Catalina was towed by barge from Rathmines for storage pending eventual display—but when? *DH. 60 Cirrus Moth* VH-UAH c/n 245 built UK 1925; stored. *Hawker Sea Fury FB.11* VX730—stored.

TAMWORTH. Airfield. East West Airlines Ltd. *Avro Anson I* VH-ASM ex W2086, from Bankstown, the first aircraft used by East West and under restoration for display purposes.
Flying from here their three veteran Dakotas:—
Douglas C-47 Dakota VH-EWE c/n 6007 ex 41-18646, VH-AER VH-EWF; *C-47A-20-DL* VH-PWM c/n 11869 ex 42-92105, A65-21, VH-EWB; *C-47A-20-DL* VH-PWN c/n 9286 ex 42-23424, A65-9, VH-EAM, VH-EWK.

Meteor F.8 (Wagga Wagga)

WAGGA WAGGA. RAAF. Forest Hill. At the main gates *Gloster Meteor F.8* A77-871 ex WK791 and A77-874 ex WK909, both from No 77 Sqdn, RAAF, Korea, painted in colours of "Meteorites" aerobatic team. As instructional and only seen by appointment:— *WS.51 Dragonfly* A80-75 and A80-374 (ex A80-1). *CAC CA-26 Sabre 30*

A94-101 (prototype). *CAC CA-22 Winjeel* A85-364. A85-618. *DH. Vampire FB.31* A79-390 will be displayed on pylon here. *Cessna C-34 Airmaster* VH-KWM c/n 339, the only one on Australian register is currently hangared in Wagga, fitted with Warner Super Scarab 165D with Hamilton constant-speed metal prop, owner W. D. Hietbrink & Ptnr. *C-34* VH-KGM (G.Bathen) thought stored here.

WALCHA District Historical Society displays the *Tiger Moth* VH-PCB c/n 41 ex A17-44, VH-ASQ—the first Tiger to spread superphosphate in NSW. *Auster 3F* VH-MHT c/n 635 ex NJ797, A11-49 flies here; G. J. Ireland.

CAC Boomerang (Williamtown)

WILLIAMTOWN. RAAF. Near Newcastle. The collection initiated by Wg Cdr (now Gp Cpt) Keith Isaacs AFC:— *CAC CA-12 Boomerang* A46-30; *Bristol Bloodhound* 8513. *CAC CA-27 Sabre Mk 32* A94-951. *Meteor F.8* A77-875. *DH. Vampire FB.30* A79-1; *DH. Vampire T35A* A79-822.
It is of interest that the Boomerang, ex 83 and 85 Sqdns, played the part of the Lockheed Altair VH-USB "Lady Southern Cross" in the Kingsford Smith film. The Meteor flew in Korea with 77 Sqdn, then with the

Cessna Airmaster (Wagga Wagga)

"Meteorites" and finally became Instr. A/c No 7 at
Wagga. It is hoped that the collection will increase in
scope.

YAMALA. Airfield. *Comper CLA-7 Swift* VH-UVC c/n
GS 32/10 ex G-ACAG; W. J. Kelman.

YOUNG. Airfield. *DH. Tiger Moth* VH-CXL c/n LES. 8;
operated here by F. W. King & Sons.

NORTHERN TERRITORY

ALICE SPRINGS. Airport. Miss Christine Davey flies
DH. Tiger Moth VH-CCD c/n 823 ex DX 780, A17-673,
VH-RNP. *Auster III* VH-PRW c/n 660 ex NJ838, A11-51,
not currently flying—is it stored?

DARWIN. East Point Military Museum, Aviation
Section, Curator John M. W. Haslett is currently
restoring *Spitfire VC* A58-232 from components of this
and other Spitfires lost in defence of the area during
Japanese attacks in 1943. This will serve as a memorial
to the pilots who flew in RAF and RAAF squadrons
here. Original serial of A58-232 appreciated. Also here
Curtiss P-40 parts, CAC CA-27 Sabre cockpit, Mitsubishi G4M-1 "Betty" wingtip. Let us hope some of the
wrecks in the Territory and elsewhere will make exhibits
here in time. Flying from Darwin Airport *Waco EGC/8*
VH-AAF c/n 5051; L. A. Clarke (said for disposal 1973).
DH.90 Dragonfly VH-UXS c/n 7546, ex A43-1, was
reported stored here—up-dated news please of condition. *Douglas Invader* also reported—serial wanted and
photo. *Taylor J.2 Cub* VH-BPK c/n 958 ex VH-UYT,
VH-PCM flown here by C. E. Henderson. *DH. Rapide*
VH-ECW c/n 6530 ex X7370, G-AJXB, SE-CBU was
here—condition please. Aircraft one-time BEA "William Gilbert Grace".
The compiler would very much appreciate details
of any other vintage types, flying or static in Northern
Territory.

QUEENSLAND

AMBERLEY. RAAF. *DH. Vampire FB.31* A79-440
displayed.

ANNERLEY. Private Strip. *Percival Proctor I* VH-BCX
c/n K.305 ex P6271, G-AHTV; K. T. E. Shersby.

BRISBANE. Museum. *Avro 581E Avian* G-EBOV c/n
5116 prototype with Cirrus Mk 1 in which the late Sqdn
Ldr H. J. "Bert" Hinkler AFC, flew the first solo from
England to Australia 7-22 February, 1928 after flying
London-Riga non-stop and Riga-Berlin-London as a

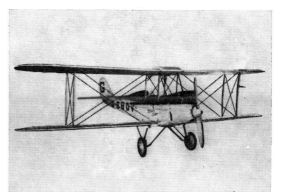
Avro Avian (Brisbane)

Avro Baby (Brisbane)

"warm-up". He lost his life in Italian Alps 8 January
1933 during further attempt on London-Australia
record, flying Puss Moth CF-APK. *Avro 534 Baby*
VH-UCQ c/n 534/1 ex K-131, G-EACQ, G-AUCQ, first
flown 16 May 1919. As K-131 it won Victory Trophy Race,
Hendon, July 1919; was then flown by Hinkler as G-EACQ
non-stop Croydon-Turin 31 May 1920, As G-AUCQ
Hinkler made historic 800 mile flight Sydney-Bundaberg
11 April 1921, and taxied to his mother's home in
Bundaberg. Re-registered VH-UCQ 1928 it flew until
1937 and in recent years it was found under a house in
Melbourne! A second cockpit was seen to have been
constructed but whether by Hinkler or Jim Smith of
Melbourne is not reported. Stored at Brisbane's
Archerfield Airport:— *Cessna C-37* VH-UZU c/n 357
(J. F. Webster), also *DH. Tiger Moth* VH-RKW c/n
LES 1, first Lawrence Engineering-assembled aircraft,
believed no longer airworthy. For preservation? At
Eagle Farm Airport is housed the magnificent *Fokker
FVII/3m* "Southern Cross" US serial 1985, originally
"Detroiter" of the Wilkins Alaska expedition, 1926.
Construction number 4954 allotted and after the large
wing of the "Detroiter" had been unsuccessfully tried
on the broken-winged "Alaskan" F.VII, the original
fuselage/wing of "Detroiter" was married together in
Seattle by the Boeing A/c Co and sold to Kingsford
Smith, a new rudder fixed in Los Angeles and the
famous trans-Pacific flight followed, Oakland-Brisbane
1928. The Tasman Sea, from Richmond, NSW-to
Christchurch, NZ, in 1928, then the Atlantic from Ireland-
Newfoundland, 1930. The first non-stop crossing of
Australia from Point Cook-Perth and the flight to
England were other historic flights. In 1935 the late

Last flight of "Southern Cross" (Brisbane)

"Southern Cross" at Eagle Farm (Brisbane)

Captain Sir Gordon Taylor gained the Empire Gallantry Medal (converted to the George Cross in 1940) in this aircraft during the ill-fated Jubilee Airmail flight to New Zealand when—in flight—Taylor transferred oil from a dead engine to a dying engine, as he clung to the struts over the Tasman Sea, the aircraft being forced to turn back, with the mail etc. jettisoned. The aircraft later became G-AUSU and then VH-USU. "Alaskan" with which it is sometimes confused, is in Bismarck, North Dakota, USA, in the local musuem there.

Aeronca K. (Clifton)

BRODIES PLAINS. Airstrip. *DH. Leopard Moth* VH-BAH c/n 7016 ex G-ACKY, VH-ADV, VH-RSL; D. W. Ruming.

CAIRNS. Airport. *Stinson L5* VH-BEN c/n 17025 ex 44-17025, VR-HEO; D. E. Faithful (the Sentinel formerly flying Mt. Hagen, New Guinea, now dismantled.)

CLIFTON. Airfield. *Porterfield 35/70* VH-UVH, c/n 242 and *Ryan STM.* VH-RAE c/n 467 ex VH-ARS. Also *Tiger Moth* VH-AZR c/n 1041/T.321 ex A17-606, all owned by John Bange Flying Group. *Aeronca K.* VH-ACK c/n KS162 ex N18888; W. T. Appleton. The *BA. Swallow 2* VH-AAB c/n 461 ex G-AFBB, VT-AIG is believed stored here.

COOLANGATTA. Airfield. *Avro 643 Cadet* VH-AFX c/n 861 ex A6-12, now airworthy, owner Cliff Douglas. At Gilltraps Auto Museum *DH.94 Moth Minor* VH-ACR c/n 94067, ex G-AFNN, VH-ACR, A21-42 is hanging.

CUNNAMULLA. Airfield. *Short S.16 Scion II* VH-UTV c/n S793 ex G-ADDW, ex Connellan Airways, Alice Springs. Up-to-date news please of condition and future.

DALBY. Airfield. *Fairchild Argus* VH-ACW c/n 415, ex 43-14451, FS534; K. Torr & Ptnrs.

GYMPIE. Airfield. *DH. Tiger Moth* VH-BGE c/n 308 T.124 ex A17-289; G. C. Sutherland.

HERVEY BAY. Airfield. *DH. 60 G. Gipsy Moth* VH-AFN ex A7-44 being restored by Don Adams, owner of local Aerial Spraying firm.

INGHAM. Airfield. *DH. Tiger Moth* VH-SNR c/n T.314 ex VH-AZC, VH-BOO; S. Sheahan. Also *VH-BGT* c/n 8221/T.004 ex A17-672; S. T. Hobbs.

JAMBIN. Airfield. *Aeronca 65C* VH-ACH c/n C1618; K. R. Wilson.

LONGREACH. Airfield. *Fairchild Argus* VH-ADF c/n 407 ex 43-14443, FS526, A36-4; F. L. Bird.

MUNDINGBURRA. Airfield. *DH. Leopard Moth* VH-UUE c/n 7109: W. H. Taylor Ptnr.

PIALBA. Airfield. *Piper J.3 Cub* VH-APO c/n 2381 ex VH-CGG; Peaker Bros.

STANTHORPE. Airfield. *Tiger Moth* VH-DBE c/n 11; E. T. Clarke.

STONE'S CORNER. Airfield. *DH. Hornet Moth* VH-AMJ c/n 8066 ex G-ADMJ; T. Drury.

TOOWOOMBA. Aero Museum, displaying:— *CAC CA.12 Boomerang* A46-25, A46-54, A46-142 (CA-13.) *CAC CA-9 Wirraway* A20-606. *CA-27 Sabre Mk 31* A94-923 (incomplete). Fuselage of *Viscount* VH-TVL c/n 197, cockpit of VH-TVJ.
At 7 Stores Depot, RAAF, Drayton, Toowoomba:— *DH. Vampire T.35* A79-656 displayed. *DH. Tiger Moth* VH-BXF c/n 152/T.186 ex A17-151, VH-AXF, VH-BWF and *VH-RJA* c/n AW/A/16 ex VH-MBC, fly locally.

Vickers Vimy (Adelaide)

SOUTH AUSTRALIA

ADELAIDE. West Beach Airport. *Vickers Vimy* G-EAOU, the first aircraft to fly from England to Australia. With the brothers Ross and Keith Smith, and Sergeants Bennett and Shiers it did the Hounslow-Darwin trip in 135 flying hours spread over the 28 days 12th November-10th December, 1919. Winning the prize offered by the Australian Government, the brothers were knighted and the NCOs were awarded the Air Force Medal and then commissioned. Part of this magnificent glass-fronted memorial housing the *Vimy* is a lifelike sculpture of the crew. Ex RAF's F8630 (Vimy IV) allotted A5-1 by RAAF.

Waco YKS-6 VH-UYD (Adelaide)

Bristol M.1C Monoplane (Minlaton)

Flying from Adelaide's Parafield airfield, the light aviation centre, are many vintage types including:— *DH. Tiger Moth* VH-ART c/n 592/T. 185 ex A17-417; Ron Smith and John Freeman; *VH-CDM* c/n 589 ex A17-414, VH-AOM; Bob Burnett-Read, vintage enthusiast, who also has *Proctor III* VH-SCC c/n H.44 ex BV544, G-AKWO. *Tiger Moth* VH-BNI c/n 1048 ex A17-613; R. A. Smith. *Clyde Cessna C.C.I* (replica) is owned by Ross Aviation. *Waco YKS-6* VH-UYD c/n 4534, is not in my current register but one hopes it is still here and for preservation if J. H. Treloar is not flying it again.

ADELAIDE. RAAF HQs, North Adelaide. *de Havilland (Aust) Vampire FB30* A79-202.

BIRDWOOD, Near Adelaide. Private Museum, mainly of cars but with:— *de Havilland DH. 60G Gipsy Moth* VH-ULJ, c/n 1074, minus engine, and *de Havilland DH 60M Moth* VH-ULO c/n 1405 (needing restoration).

EDINBURGH FIELD. RAAF. *Mraz Sokol M.1C* VH-BXY (first in Australia, sold by Bob Burnett-Read to RAAF officer, is believed undergoing restoration here.) Details please.

GAWLER. Chain of Ponds. *Douglas C-47A-25-DK* VH-ANW c/n 13624, ex 42-93685, VH-GAK of Ansett/ A.N.A. Donated to playground for local children.

GOOLWA. *Westland Widgeon* VH-UKS is dismantled on Don Dennis's Farm—for preservation, we trust.

MINLATON. The Butler Memorial. *Bristol M.1C Monoplane* C5001. With the 110 hp Le Rhone engine, this type of machine in 1916 attained the then-incredible speed of 132 mph, but landing-speed of 49 mph was declared too high for the Western Front and only 125 were ordered—mainly for Middle East. Captain Harry Butler, AFC, bought this from War Disposals at Waddon, Surrey, and flew it after 1919 as G-AUCH, later VH-UQI "Puck", but always known in Australia as "The Red Devil". Butler, with Lt H. S. Kauper, RFC, also brought to Australia an *Avro-504* and the pair did much to make South Australia and Victoria air-minded.

In September, 1920, Butler won Australia's first Aerial Derby, with Captain Frank McNamara, Australia's first Air VC, and Lt. F. S. Briggs, RAAF, also competing. After the contest Butler and McNamara gave a thrilling aerobatic display which "stunned the crowds" to quote a newspaper of the time. When the Vickers Vimy reached Adelaide after the first UK-Australia flight it was Butler in "The Red Devil" who flew out to escort them into Butler's own landing field, which he made available to the record-makers. On 11th January, 1922, alas, Butler suffered engine failure in the *Avro 504* and although his passenger miraculously escaped injury, Butler was very badly hurt, and although plastic surgery partially restored his face, his flying was curtailed and on 30th July, 1923 he died from cerebral troubles, the result of that crash 18 months earlier. His funeral was attended by a huge crowd and was a moving ceremony for Harry Butler had brought a new and exciting experience into the lives of many Australians. His Memorial is a MUST for all who can get to Minlaton.

PENOLA. Airfield. *Avro 594 Avian IV* VH-UQE c/n 531; A. G. Murrell.

PORT MACDONNELL. Airfield. *DH. Tiger Moth* VH-BPU c/n 85639, ex DE709; D. A. McBain.

RENMARK. Airfield. *Tiger Moth* VH-FSS c/n 1072 ex A17-741; Renmark Tiger Group.

SALISBURY. Airfield. *Percival Gull 6* VH-CCM c/n D.46 ex G-ACUP, VH-ACM; A. Nixon.

Percival Gull 6 (Salisbury, S.A.)

WAIKERIE. Airfield. *Miles M3A Falcon Major* VH-AAT c/n 193, ex G-ADHG, A37-3; John Smothers (USA teacher).

WOOMERA. Department of Supply. *DH. Sea Hornet F.20* TT213 has been reported and it is hoped to recover it for Salisbury Hall, Herts—news please.

TASMANIA

HOBART. The Air Museum. Operated privately by Mr. R. K. Morgan with:— *DH82A Tiger Moth* and *CAC 6 Wackett Trainer*, registrations not known, more details please.

LAUNCESTON. Airport Terminal. *Desoutter Mk II* VH-UEE c/n D30 "Miss Flinders", In a basement room of this modern new terminal is housed one of Australia's most historic machines. The *Desoutter Mk II* was a development of the Dutch Koolhoven FK23 and, with various aerodynamic refinements it was built by M. Marcel Desoutter in the U.K. in the late

Desoutter Mk II (Launceston, Tas.)

1920s. One of 41 built, powered with a de Havilland Gypsy Mk III engine, beginning life as EI-AAD of Iona National Air Taxis, 1931. Early 1932 it was acquired by two Melbourne men, 'Messrs. Jeffereys and Jenkins who flew it, now registered G-ABOM, via India, to Australia. Here it was purchased by Mr. L. McK Johnston, registered VH-UEE, initiating Launceston-Flinders Island schedules. In 1933 Tasmanian Aerial Services purchased the a/c, retaining Mr. Johnston as chief pilot. In turn this became Holyman Airways, the forerunner of Australian National Airways. In 1935 the a/c was sold for £A350 and later became VH-BQE, flying until 1961. The Launceston Air Force Assn acquired and renovated it for display.

MOONA. D. Holten has *Stinson L-5 Sentinel* VH-BFR under restoration—details and pic please.

VICTORIA

ABBOTSFORD. Airfield. Gliding Club of Victoria. *Auster 3F* VH-GCV c/n 258 ex MZ123 A11-56; *VH-MBA* c/n 436 ex NX500, A11-53.

AVOCA. Airfield. *Rearwin 9000L* VH-UYS c/n 535D; R. J. Nuttall.

BENDIGO. Private Strip. *DH. Tiger Moth* VH-PME c/n L.V.1 believed restored by Les Penna—confirmation and history please.

BERWICK. Casey Airfield. Victorian Chapter of Vintage A/c Club of Australia. Transport Museum, ground leased by Ian McArthur, enthusiast & pioneer of Moorabbin Museum, some aircraft transferred from there for display of transport from bullock drays to aeroplanes, which includes:— *DH. 60G Gypsy Moth* VH-UKV c/n 1066 ex A7-79, first machine of the Australian Aircraft Restoration Group (AARG). *CA-6 Wackett Trainer* VH-ALV c/n 256 ex A43-22. *Desoutter II* VH-UPR

Leopard Moth VH-UUL (Berwick)

Westland Widgeon III (Boort)

c/n D35. *Fairey Firefly AS.6* WD833 (Lt-Col Keith Hatfield) *Primary Glider* (minus wings). The above are static. *DH.85 Leopard Moth* VH-UUL c/n 7111, restored and flown by enthusiast Lt-Col Keith Hatfield, Neil Follett, Ross Williamson; pale-green fuselage and silver wings. *Percival Proctor I* VH-DUL c/n K.246 ex P6187, G-AHFU; owned & flown by E. Lippman. *DH. Tiger Moth* VH-TIG ex PK-VVT, A17-624, VH-AMH; P. A. Williams & Ptnr—airworthy.
There are usually other vintage aircraft as visitors to make Berwick a "MUST" for preservationists.

BOORT. Airfield. *Westland Widgeon III* VH-UHU c/n WA. 1695 ex G-EBUB; A. L. Whittaker. also here, *DHC. Chipmunk T.10* VH-BAC c/n CI/0041 ex WB600; P. H. Weaver. From the first production batch and one of the oldest flying; border-line vintage but surely worthy of note.

COLDSTREAM. Airfield. *DH. Moth Minor* VH-KHJ ex A21-10; Nelson Wilson.

EAST BENTLEIGH. Airfield. *DH. Tiger Moth* VH-GMC c/n 798 ex A17-648; P. Andreason & Ptnr.

EAST IVANHOE. Airfield. *Auster 3F* VH-BYJ c/n 333 ex MZ220, A11-27, VH-BCK; R. A. Arnold.

EMERALD. Airfield. *Tiger Moth* VH-AYW c/n 400 ex A17-365; Emerald Flying Group.

FRANKSTON. Airfield. *Ryan STM* VH-AGW c/n 465 ex S-29, A50-22; W. F. Suhr.

KERANG. Airfield. *Tiger Moth* VH-AAR c/n T.038, Kerang Tiger Group.

LAVERTON. Service Station. *DH. Vampire FB31* A79-165 but painted A79-1 (which exists as an FB.30 see Williamtown, NSW.) It is said that at the nearby RAAF base there is a *Lockheed P2V-5 Neptune* marked A891-A-TA which is said for preservation—confirmation wanted and photo, please.

MELBOURNE AREA

Royal Melbourne Institute of Technology has *NA.P-51D Mustang* A68-648 with wings removed outboard of undercarriage and thought to be stored here. History please. At Melbourne's Essendon Airport are based some vintage types including:— *DH. Tiger Moth* VH-ATJ c/n 873/T.253 ex A17-456; A. G. Mulhauser, also the aptly-registered Mineral Resources Bureau *Douglas C-47A* VH-MIN c/n 13459 ex 42-93536, KG647, G-AIAZ, VH-SMI.
At the Institute of Applied Science of Victoria, 304-328 Swanston St, C.1, *Duigan Biplane.* The first Australian-built aeroplane to fly was constructed by John Robertson Duigan in 1910 at Mia Mia, near Heathcote, Victoria. Country-born, but educated at Brighton Grammar School and later at a London technical college, Duigan returned to Australia as an electrical engineer but eventually went back to his father's farm "Spring Plains" Mia Mia. He first attempted a pair of wings with a hole for his body then—in 1909—he tried a glider based on the Wright Brothers, finally he planned and built his own aeroplane which he flew 24 feet on 16th July, 1910, later achieving 200 yards at a height of 20 ft in October. Duigan served with No 3 Sqdn, AFC, gaining the

Duigan Biplane (Melbourne)

Military Cross—he died on 11th July, 1951, aged 69. The Duigan Biplane is of ash and red pine tensioned with piano wire, length 28 ft, wingspan 25 ft, all covering material specially-made light rubber-coated fabric. Two wheels under wings and an ash skid at rear. A bicycle wheel at front prevented forward tilting. Weight on wheels (about 620 lbs) was cushioned by home-made pneumatic shock absorbers. The 20 hp engine made by J. E. Tilley, Melbourne, was of the 4-cylinder vertical type with water-cooled heads. Power was transmitted by chain and sprocket to a propeller of $8\frac{1}{2}$-ft diameter. *CAC CA-16 Wirraway* A20-651, former Point Cook RAAF training aid, restored by CAC.

Currently awaiting allocation to a Museum or Collection is the fabulous 2-seat *Mitsubishi A6M2 Model 21 Zero*, retrieved from a lagoon off Rabaul and bought by Geoff Pentland (of Kookaburra Technical Publications) and Barry Coran, and since restored in Melbourne. Japanese bank manager, 64-year-old Tomoyoshi Hori, who commanded 151st Naval Air Wing ,Rabaul, states this a/c was one of two specially converted 2-seaters modified to carry out a sneak bombing raid on Admiralty Islands early 1945. Little damage was inflicted but this raid greatly boosted 100,000 Japanese army and navy personnel pinned down at Rabaul. Mr. Hori speculates that the pilot, after failing to rendezvous with the other Zero, probably lost his bearings in the dark. Both a/c had been rebuilt from Zeros damaged after US and RAAF attacks, the second seats being provided for either navigator or radio operator. The Zero which did

Mitsubishi Zero (Melbourne)

return was subsequently destroyed at Rabaul. Mr. Hori wished to thank the Australians for restoring this Zero fighter, now in original colours.

At the Pascoe Vale Garage, Preston (a suburb) *CAC. CA-16 Wirraway* A20-652 is mounted for display. In Williamstown, Melbourne, *Avro 707A* WD280, the true forerunner of the Vulcan bomber, having wingroot intakes, is in Mr. G. Mallet's garden, bought from the Australian Govt. *Fairchild F24W Argus 2* VH-EMP c/n 837 ex 43-14873, HB600, G-AJSG, VH-DDG, VH-EMF; is said to be undergoing restoration in or near Alphington. News please.

MELTON. Fogarty's Field. *Douglas C-54B* VH-INX c/n 18327 ex 43-17127, NC 74628, ZS-BYO, G-ALEP; donated from Ansett/A.N.A.

MENTONE. Airfield. *DH. Tiger Moth* VH-SGC c/n 82503 ex N9449, G-ANUL, VH-RSF; W. S. English.

MILDURA. Airport. "Warbirds" Aviation Museum. The driving-force at this former RAAF base is Pearce Dunn who has led a team of enthusiasts in recovery and restoration. Almost 2 acres is now wired-in and with workshops erected we look forward to hearing of opening-date and hours for a splendid collection. Currently there complete or in varying stages of restoration:— *CAC. CA-3 Wirraway II* A20-99; *CA-7 Wirraway II* A20-233. *CA-8 Wirraway II* A20-395; *CA-9 Wirraway II* A20-502. *CA-16 Wirraway III* A20-656, A20-687, A20-719. *CA-12 Boomerang* I A46-55; *CA-19 Boomerang II* A46-249. *CA-18 Mustang 21* A68-105 (from Moorabbin Air Museum). *CA-27 Sabre Mk 31* A94-901 and *A94-906. DH. (Aust) Mosquito PR.XVI* A52-600. *Percival Proctor I* VH-AVG c/n H224 ex BV658, G-AHVG, to be restored as Fleet Air Arm communicator. *Consolidated Catalina* A24-46 (parts only so far) *DH. Dove* VH-CTS. *DH. Vampire FB.31* A79-202. *DH. Sea Venom FAW.53* WZ903; *TT.53* WZ944.

NA.P-51D Mustang A68-674, A68-679 and a third unidentified, from which it is planned to complete one to represent Col. Howard's "Ding Hao" 38374. There are parts of *DAP Beaufort* A9-143 (fuselage and wing centre section) *DAP Beaufighter 21* A8-366 (cockpit) *Curtiss P-40E Kittyhawk* Ia (cockpit & engine of A29-28) *Mitsubishi A6M Zero* (rear fuselage and tail section) *Vought Sikorsky Kingfisher* A48-2 ex 107 Sqdn RAAF, "JE-B", Bu. 2475; (fuselage only but complete restoration hoped-for.) Pearce Dunn writes that he hopes to get a Spitfire—possibly TE384 or MV154 (see Bankstown NSW)—also a Meteor F.8, C-47, Jindivik, Pika, Blue Steel missile etc, so a magnificent collection is envisaged and deserving of support. We look forward to photos of completed a/c.

MOORABBIN. Airport. Off Nepean Highway or Cheltenham-Mentone railway stations. Dating back to 1962 when the AARG drew up aims of a non-profit organization dedicated to preservation. The Department of Civil Aviation allocated a 300 ft × 100 ft area (now 600 ft × 140 ft) and in May, 1965 an 8-ft man-proof fence enabled the first a/c to arrive. As at 1973 the following are reported:— *CAC. CA-1 Wirraway* A20-10, the 8th production and oldest; painted in colours of No 2 SFTS of 1941. *DH. Vampire FB.31* A79-422, recovered from Lord Mayor's Holiday Camp and being repainted. *DH. Sea Venom FAW.53* N4-901 of R.A.N (history please). *Fairey Firefly TT6* WD828, flown in 1967 and run-up weekends; Formerly at Nowra with Nos 723 and 851 Sqdns, RAN as operational trainer and target tug. Later at Avalon, Victoria for target-towing and radar tracking. Bought from Dept of Supply and flown in by Terry Brain. *Fairey Gannet AS.4* XG789—from Dept of Supply. *Gloster Meteor T.7* A77-707, originally from CFS, Little Rissington (original serial wanted.) In Australia from 1955 with No 22 (City of Sydney) then No 23 (City of Brisbane) from Dept of Supply. *Southern Cross Aviation* (Queensland) SC.1 prototype, VH-SCA, proposed 4-seat tourer—only one built.

Stored at Moorabbin for restoration and/or display: *Avro Anson Mk I* VH-FIA ex AW965, formerly of Flinders Island Airways. *BA. Swallow* VH-UUM c/n 409—donated by Bob Burnett-Read. *Bristol Sycamore 3* VH-GVR c/n 12894 ex G-ALSZ, WV695, A91-1. *CAC. CA-16 Wirraway* A20-649, purchased for refit to fly. *DAP Beaufighter 21* A8-328 with 30 Sqdn, RAAF (post-war)—from Lord Mayor's Camp. *DAP Beaufighter Mk I* A19-43—in poor condition. *Percival Proctor I* VH-UAC donated by B. Treloar. *DH. Hornet Moth* VH-RKM c/n 8036 ex VH-UUD VH-PMG, VH-BMG; for rebuild. *McKenna-Heath Parasol*, homebuilt, fuselage only. *DH. 82A (Aust) Tiger Moth* A17-377 c/n 418 ex VH-AQM and *Tiger Moth* VH-AYY—for restoration. *Vickers Viscount V816* VH-TVR c/n 318 donated by Trans-Australia Airlines with Darts donated by Ansett. *Douglas DC-3* VH-ANH "Tullana" c/n 4120 ex NC33657, 41-7698, VH-CDJ is reputedly coming here (or to Berwick?) from Ansett—A.N.A. *Miles Messenger 2A* VH-AVQ c/n 6373 ex G-AJKG, once Lord Casey's aircraft and *Percival Proctor V* VH-BJY c/n Ae91, donated by Lindsay Ball, plus *Wackett Trainer* VH-AGP ex A3-167, of member Andrew Lucas, are not included in latest lists from Moorabbin Museum's President, Joseph A. Vella, nor on the Berwick listing—are some at Melton (Fogarty's Field)? A visitor might be advised to visit all three locations. We congratulate the A.A.R.G. on behalf of all preservationists and look forward to further details and illustrations for the next V. and V. Flying from Moorabbin (Cheltenham) *Avro Anson Mk I* VH-BAF ex MH120 rebuild c/n BB1 a rebuild of VH-BAB, VH-BAF and VH-BIX by Brain & Brown Pty Ltd.

CA-18 Mustang (Mildura)

B.A. Swallow (Moorabbin)

CAC. Wirraway (Moorabbin)

MORWELL. Airfield. Latrobe Valley Aero Club. *Millicer Airtourer* VH-FMM the wooden prototype of the Victa Airtourer is preserved here. *DH. 84 Dragon* VH-AGC c/n 2045 ex A34-56, VH-ASO, VH-FDA; is being restored by W. Miller.

NEWTOWN-GEELONG. Airfield. *Percival Proctor III* VH-BXQ c/n H.565 ex LZ804, G-ANGC; C. J. Hunt.

POINT COOK. Near Melbourne. The "Cranwell" of RAAF. The RAAF Museum has at last begun to collect more a/c and presently displays:— *CAC.CA-18 Mustang Mk 23* A68-170 sole surviving Mk 23, from RAAF, Drayton, Queensland (to be made airworthy.) *DH.(A) Vampire FB.31* A79-175. *T.35* A79-636. *GAF Pika* A93-2 (from Edinburgh Field, S.A.) *Messerschmitt Me 163 B-1* Werk-Nr 191907. *Messerschmitt Me 262 A-2* Werk-Nr 500210 ex AM81. The last two on loan from Australian War Memorial. *Glóster Meteor T.7* A77-702 ex A77-305, once 77 Sqdn then RAAF Laverton gate.

It is understood the museum is open to the public from Mondays to Fridays (except holidays) but intending visitors should contact the RAAF PRO or Guardroom before travelling.

Meteor T.7 (Point Cook)

PORTSEA. Lord Mayor of Melbourne's Holiday Camp. *GAF Canberra T.4* A84-502 for children.

TOTTENHAM. RAAF Stores. *DH. Vampire T.35* A79-816.

TULLARMARINE. Airport. *Douglas C-47* VH-SBA c/n 6021 ex 41-18660, VH-AES of Trans-Australia Airlines, the first Dakota on the Melbourne-Sydney run, Sept, 1946. Originally named "Shanghai Lil", flown for 49,571 hrs, over 7 million miles (14 return trips to the moon.) Retired 1971.

WANDIN NORTH. Airfield. *Curtiss P-40E Kittyhawk* A29-133 being restored by Nelson Wilson who flies *DH.94 Moth Minor* VH-AIB c/n DHP.17.

Me 262 A-2 (Point Cook)

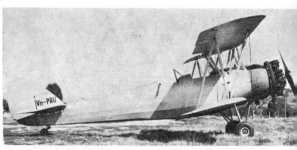

Avro Cadet (Wodonga)

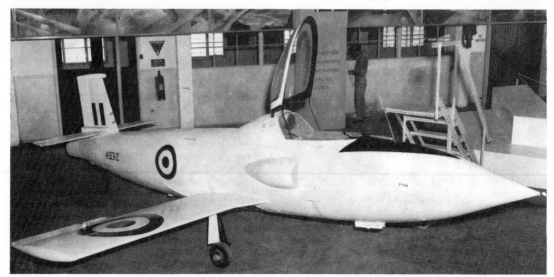

GAF Pika (Point Cook)

WODONGA. Parkers Road, two miles south of Wodonga off the Hume Highway, Drage's Historical Aircraft Museum. The largest collection of biplanes in Australia under one roof: Open all day weekends and holidays from 1000 hrs. *Avro 643 Cadet* VH-PRT c/n 1059 ex VH-BPS, VH-AGC, A6-32; *VH-PRU* c/n 1060 ex VH-AEI, A6-25 is believed stored. *Beech F.17D Staggerwing* VH-ACU c/n 248 ex A39-1. *DH.60M. Moth* VH-ULM c/n 1403—from Bendigo. *DH.82A Tiger Moth* VH-WEM c/n 1005 ex A17-570, VH-AQH, VH-RVJ. *DH. 84 Dragon* VH-AON c/n 2019 ex A34-30. *DH.94 Moth Minor* VH-ACS c/n 94047 ex G-AFOW. *Genairco* VH-UOG, c/n 16. Some of the a/c are thought to be airworthy.

DH.60M Moth (Wodonga)

WESTERN AUSTRALIA

BEVERLEY. Aeronautical Museum of Shire Council. *Ford "Silver Centenary"* VH-U (applied in anticipation but never granted.) Built 1929 by the late Selby Ford and a Mr. Shackles, successfully flown but never granted C. of A., though claimed superior to best light a/c of its day. Built from chalked plans on a powerhouse floor it flew from Beverley to Perth and return (162 miles) on 1st July 1930, later repeating the trip and carrying out many others. It cost £600 to construct and is worth a visit as *DH Vampire T.35* A79-638 and many other aviation relics are also housed here.

BROOME. Airport. *CAC CA-6 Wackett Trainer* VH-AIY c/n 265, ex A3-31, owned by Harry Miller, founder of Robertson Miller Airline. C. of A. lapsed 1964 but a/c preserved.

BUNBURY. Airport. *DH. Tiger Moth* VH-AMW c/n 209 ex A17-208; Lance Lime Co.

DH.84A Dragon (Capel)

CAPEL. Airfield. *DH. 84A Dragon* VH-AML c/n 2081 ex A34-92, VH-BDS. Now owned and flown by H. Hockin, this aircraft was allotted British registration G-AJKF in March 1947 but failed to arrive in U.K.

GNOWANGERUP. Private Strip. *DH 60G* VH-UAO c/n 613, ex A7-92. Acquired for £A50 in Adelaide in 1945, it was rebuilt at Royal Aero Club of W.A. and then re-sold several times lastly to present owner's father who hoped to learn to fly, although over 60—his son, George Aylmore keeps it beautifully—and airworthy.

KELLERBERIN. Airfield. *DH. Tiger Moth* VH-AMU c/n 397 ex A17-362, VH-BKC, VH-WFY; M. S. Forster.

PERTH DISTRICT

BELMONT. No 15 Flight, ATC (near airport) *DH. Vampire T.35* A79-606, coded "TA-34".

CLAREMONT. ATC HQs, Stirling Highway, *DH. Vampire T.35* A79-620. "TA-35".

FREMANTLE. ATC. *Vampire T.35* A79-664 "TA-36".

GERALDTON. Chamber of Commerce. *DH. Vampire T.35* A79-651.

Avro Lancaster VII (Jandakot Perth)

JANDAKOT. Airport and Air Force Assn, BATEMAN:—*Avro Anson I* VH-BEL ex RAAF Disposals 1946 for £A250.00 used for air ambulance, charters etc, then sold to No 9 Flt, ATC for *two shillings* as instructional aid—from Kalgoorlie; for display. *Avro Lancaster VII* NX622, later WU-16 of French Navy, presented by them in 1963 and repainted by No 25 (City of Perth) Citizen Air Force members as "C-AF" (Citizen Air Force) and "A-FC" Australian Flying Corps" on either side, above authentic Bomber Command camouflage. *Supermarine Spitfire F.22* PK481, once at RAFA HQs in Sussex, England, and for years on pylon at Memorial House, Perth. Marking "AF-A" is for Air Force Assn, this Spitfire having no wartime history. *CAC. CA-16 Wirraway III* A20-606 and *A20-688* (ex Midland Tech.) *CAC. CA-17 Mustang 20* A68-71 ex Technical College. *DH. Tiger Moth* VH-BKS (fuselage only, to be rebuilt.) *DH.94 Moth Minor* VH-THT (history please). *DH. (Aust) Vampire FB.31* A79-36. (possibly Perth ATC Sqdn a/c.) Inst. 20, *DH. (Aust) Vampire T.35A* A79-821. *Heath Parasol* (unregistered.) *Man-powered aircraft* (details wanted.) *Miles Gemini 1A* (fuselage, being restored fully) VH-GBB c/n 6486 ex G-AKEN, VH-BTP. *Percival Proctor II* VH-BQR ex Bunbury. c/n K392 ex Z7203, G-ALIS. *Vultee Vengeance IV* A27-247 (ex Kalgoorlie scrapyard) Previous history, serials, etc. wanted. *Stinson Reliant* is being restored at Jandakot—details? (Is this *VH-CWM* c/n 9766 ex VH-KAF of G.B. Yool?)

CAC. CA-6 Wackett Trainer VH-AJH c/n 283 ex A3-49, VH-AGN; modified as KSAS Cropmaster—now with AF Assn. Flying here: *Comper CLA 7 Gipsy Swift* VH-ACG c/n GS32/2 owner Doug Muir, ex Kalgoorlie, ex G-ABWH, NC27K. Long may it fly.

MT. YOKINE. TV Station TVW7 now has a museum; with:— *CAC. CA-28 Ceres* VH-DAT c/n 14 ex VH-CEP, damaged by fire 16.2.68 at Kojonup, WA, painted as Wirraway A20-47 with modified canopy. *DH. (Aust) Tiger Moth* A17-161, ex VH-AHP, c/n 162 built Mascot NSW 1940. 1946 allotted VH-AXM but not taken up in WA 1946-66 with various owner-pilots. Sold to Channel 7 1968. *DH. Vampire T.35* A79-660 and A79-665. *Slingsby Gull I glider.*

PEARCE. RAAF Base. *Vampire T.35* A79-603 "TA-38". We wish the Air Force Association and all working for preservation in the Perth Area, great success.

No recent reports have been received of the aircraft at **KALUMBURU MISSION STATION** (Drysdale Strip WW II) but *Beaufighter IX* A19-144—ex 31 Sqdn RAAF ex JM135 and *Mk XI* A19-144—ex JL946, 31 Sqdn may still be worth saving. *Lockheed Hudson* A16-244 and *NA Mitchell* N5-161 "Mississippi Dream" were also reported hereabouts and further details would be appreciated, especially accompanied by recent photos.
Up-dated information concerning the Spitfires at Truscott strip up coast from Derby would also assist, together with news of the often-reported but never confirmed Spitfire (or Mustang) allegedly unregistered but flying in WA and NT.

NEW ZEALAND (SOUTH ISLAND)

BALCLUTHA. Airfield. *Auster VC* ZK-AZF c/n 1272 ex TJ187, G-ALKI; AZF Flying Club. *Tiger Moth* ZK-BLI c/n DHNZ. 128 ex NZ 1448; A. J. Pugdett.

BLENHEIM. Airfield. Golden Age Flying Group have on loan *Proctor V* ZK-AQZ c/n AE.143; from Peter Dyer, Christchurch. (Aero Club, NZA). *Simmonds Spartan* ZK-ABZ c/n 43 imported from UK 1930 for Air Travel, Marlborough owned by Sid Lister, Temuka, is with Golden Age for rebuild to airworthiness, it flew until 1945 then static for displays. *DH. Tiger Moth* ZK-BSN c/n 501 ex NZ1415 with 27 Sqdn, ATC believed airworthy. It is reported that Mustang NZ2427 ex 45-11518 has been scrapped, the wings to John Smith, Maheno. In Redwood town Park is *DH. Vampire T.55* NZ5701 c/n 15009, to NZ, 1952 with No 14 Sqdn etc;

Comper CLA.7 Gipsy Swift (Jandakot, Perth)

finally stored Woodbourne. Sold as scrap 1963. *Hudson III* NZ2035 c/n 3858 ex RAF AE503, RNZAF "SJ-A" No 1 Sqdn, with Mr. L. Holdaway—owned by MOTAT.

CHRISTCHURCH. Harewood Airport, 8 miles from city. *Auster V* ZK-AUH c/n 1834 ex TW502, G-AJVU; A. M. Richards; *Auster VD* ZK-BMD c/n 1035 ex NJ635, G-ALZM; P. C. Shand; *NA.P-51D Mustang* ZK-CCG c/n 124/48260 ex 45-11507, NZ2417 of No 3 Sqdn, owned by J. S. MacDonald & R. Fechney, sold as scrap but restored to airworthiness. May now be stored. At the Canterbury Brevet Club, on pole, is *Spitfire XVI* TE288, donated to NZ 1963 by RAF after flying with 61 OTU, 501 (County of Glos) RAuxAF, 102 FRS, North Luffenham, then 33 MU Lyneham as instructional airframe. Later displayed Kenley, Rufforth, Church Fenton, Dishforth. Honours all Kiwis of the South Island who flew the type. Stored at Harewood for the newly-formed Ferrymead Aeronautical Society is *Douglas LC-47M* Bu 17221 "Yankee Tiki A Te Hau" used by the USN in Antarctica. *DH. Mosquito FBVI* TE758, NZ2328 of 75 Sqdn "YC-C" is being restored here with wings & undercarriage from

P-51D Mustang (Christchurch)

Simmonds Spartan (Blenheim)

HR339 (no RNZAF serial allocated.) Mt. Cook Airlines have promised a DH. Rapide and parts of Oxfords (inc NZ2144) are in store for a future project. An RNZAF Vampire may also come. *Proctor V* ZK-APH c/n Ae.126 also near here on display.

Spitfire XVI (Canterbury Brevet Club)

CROMWELL. Airfield. *Tiger Moth* ZK-ATI c/n 82901 ex R5006, NZ891; owned & flown by B. L. Drake & Ptnrs.

DUNEDIN. Airport. *Tiger Moth* ZK-AKH c/n DHNZ. 57 ex NZ807; J. R. Hanlon; *ZK-BGP* c/n DHNZ. 174 ex NZ1494; Y. P. Neill.

FAIRLIE. Airfield. *Auster V* ZK-AVH c/n 1412 ex TJ342, G-AKOU; A. A. Innes.

GORE. ATC Sqdn. *Tiger Moth* INST-103 ex N9172, NZ865; c/n 82283.

GREYMOUTH. Airfield. *Auster VD* ZK-BGU c/n 1757 ex TW387, G-ANHY; J. K. Crook & Ptnr.

HOKITIKA. Airfield. *DH. Dragon Rapide* ZK-AHS c/n 6423 ex NZ559, ZK-AGT; West Coast Airways.

HORORATA. Airfield. *Auster V* ZK-AXP c/n 1586 ex TJ567, G-AKPJ; D. W. Stone & Ptnrs.

MAHENO. Oamaru. Gardiners Valley. J. R. Smith:—*DH. Mosquito* FBVI NZ2336 ex TE910 ex 75 Sqdn "YC-B" being restored to taxiing state. *NA.P-51D-25-NT* NZ2423 c/n 124-48266 ex 45-11513 ex No 1 (Auckland) Sqdn, flown only 261 hrs. *Curtiss P-40N-20-CU* NZ3220 c/n 30901 ex 43-22962 "Gloria Lyons", served with several operational units in SW Pacific, claiming 2½ victories, finally "FE-T", No 2 OTU, Ohakea. Also *P-40E-1-CU* NZ3043 ex 41-36410, RAF EV156; for rebuild. *Lockheed Hudson GR.III* NZ2013 c/n 3826 ex RAF V9241, post-war at School of Navigation, Wigram, now with J. W. Clarke, Maheno; only a possibility for rebuild. *Hudson GRIII* NZ2049 c/n 6465 ex USAAF RA-29A-LO 41-36976, lease-lend to RAF FH175, to RNZAF 1942 Nos 3 and 4 Sqdns; now John R. Smith for possible restoration. *DH. Tiger Moth* ZK-ASA c/n 3630 ex ZK-AFO, NZ720; John R. Smith (airworthy).

NELSON. Airport. *Proctor V* ZK-AVW c/n Ae.78 ex G-AHWW; A. J. Bradshaw.

OMAKAU. A *Bleriot* (replica) has been constructed here but believed from photos only—fuller details and photo please.

PORT CHALMERS. Airfield. *Miles Messenger 4* ZK-ATT c/n 6343 ex G-AIRY; A. J. Wilson.

QUEENSTOWN. Airfield. *Dragon Rapide* ZK-BCP c/n 6648 ex HG649, NZ-524; Now Southern Scenic Air Services. In the Queenstown Motor Museum is *Tiger Moth* ZK-CCH c/n DHNZ110 built Rongotai as NZ1430, sold 1955 as ZK-BLN, later re-registered.

TEMUKA. Airfield. *Tiger Moth* ZK-AVK c/n 425 ex A17-384, VH-AXZ; S. R. Brodie.

TIMARU. Airport. *Porterfield 35W* ZK-APJ c/n 316 ex ZK-AFT, NZ581, ZK-AHJ, NZ598; W. R. Willmott. *Dragon Rapide* ZK-AKY c/n 6653 ex HG654, NZ525; Mt Cook Airlines (who may have *Rapide* ZK-ALB c/n 6655 ex HG656, NZ527 stored for preservation.)

WIGRAM. RNZAF. CFS. *NA Harvard II* NZ909 c/n 66-2702 ex 2 SFTS, Woodbourne from 1941. Now INST-909.
At Wigram it was thought that *Harvards* NZ1017, 1058, 1060, NZ1061, 1065, 1066, 1075, 1076, 1078, 1079, 1080, 1083, 1085, NZ 1087, 1092, 1096, 1098 and 1099, may still be airworthy and that NZ1005, 1009, 1012, 1024, 1025, 1033, 1034, 1037, 1038, NZ 1040, 1050, 1051, 1052, 1053, 1057 and 1091, are in store. It would be appreciated if up-dated information, with earlier serials etc, could be provided, also news of any being added to the civil register or preserved for display. Australia would surely be interested in some?

NORTH ISLAND

AUCKLAND. The Domain War Memorial Museum. *Spitfire XVI* TE456 "43" of Nos 3/4 CAACU, Exeter, then RAF Dishforth. Donated 1957 at request of ACM Sir Keith Park GCB, KBE, MC, DFC, DL, who commanded No 11 (F) Group in 1940 and is now (1973) retired to his native Auckland, and still active on the City Council and with ex-Servicemen, though 82 years of age. What we owe to his brilliant command in the Battle of Britain and later at Malta and in Middle East and Far East, has never properly been told. Let us hope the powers-that-be will soften their hearts and donate a Hurricane—the type he flew throughout WW II—to Auckland. Also here *Mitsubishi A6M3 Zero 22* serial 3844, Unit code

Mitsubishi Zero (Auckland)

2-182, captured at Kara, South Bougainville, flown to Kieta by Wg Cdr Kofoed, RNZAF. Restored for Ohakea Air Display 1958 but incorrectly repainted. Given serial NZ6000. Now known to have been a land-based a/c assigned to Japan's 8th Fleet, 2nd Air Group. Retains arrester-hook and folding wingtips. *Fieseler FZG76 flying bomb*, grey-green splinter camouflage, brought back from Europe by NZ forces and was displayed at Ohakea. Stored here is *Gloster Meteor F.3* NZ6001, later INST147 and previously EE395 sent from England November 1945 for jet familiarization. Flew from Ohakea until grounded by over-stressing during aerobatics. Can someone provide photograph, please. It has been reported that these aircraft will one day go to Western Springs Auckland, for exhibition.

MOTAT (Museum of Transport & Technology) Western Springs, Auckland 2. Telephone 869 030 to check opening times etc. As advised in 1973, the following are displayed:— *Avro Lancaster MR VII* WU13 completed as NX665, to French Navy 1951 after storage. Served with 24F, 10F, 10S.9S; presented to New Zealand 1964 and flown from Tomtouta, New Caledonia, to honour Kiwis of Bomber Command. Now includes major components of NX666 (WU05 of Aeronavale.) Painted 1944 camouflage but starboard as ND752 "AA-O" 75 (NZ) Sqdn, port PB457 "SR-V" 101 Sqdn, RAF. Both were lost over Germany and markings chosen as two typical—not famous—bombers. *Commonwealth CA 28C Ceres* ZK-BZO c/n CA 28-9 ex VH-CEL presented by James Aviation Ltd. *Curtiss P-40E-1-CU Kittyhawk* NZ3009 ex 41-25158 RAF's ET482, on RNZAF charge Hobsonville 1942, to 14 Sqdn Hood Field, Masterton. Subsequent history unknown except 17 Sqdn Seagrove, Sept 1943, finally 2 OTU Ohakea "FE-F". Sold for scrap 1948, wheels, internal fittings and everything forward of firewall removed. Wings replaced 1965 from NZ3202 ex 42-106403—permanent loan from d'E.C. Darby & R. H. Mc Garry. *DH.82A Tiger Moth* ZK-BJH c/n 84664 ex RAF T6238. Reconstruction includes cut-down forward fuselage. Presented by Manawatu Aerial Top-dressing Co; displayed as crop-duster. *DH.84 Dragon* ZK-AXI c/n 2057, Australian-built ex RAAF A34-68, to Qantas as VH-AEF before sale to Rolvin Airways NZ. Donated by N.Z. Insurance Co. *DH.Vampire FB.9* WR 202. To 60 Sqdn, RAF, Selatar, Singapore, 1952. To 14 Sqdn RNZAF 1965, to New Zealand as Inst 171 Hobsonville, but painted Inst NZ1717. Donated by RNZAF. *Lockheed 10A Electra* ZK-BUT c/n 1138 built for Standard Oil Co as N21735, later N10Y. Imported into NZ 1957 for Trans Island Airways, withdrawn after ground-loop at Harewood and became fire-fighting hulk. Presented by Dept of Civil Aviation and restored in Union Airways colours as ZK-AFD. *Lockheed Lodestar* ZK-BVE c/n 2020. Built for United Airlines as NC25630, transferred to RAF as AX756, BOAC as G-AGCN. Back to RAF as AX756 then Spanish Air Force, and Minnesota Airmotive as N9933F. Converted for aerial top dressing and imported by Fieldair August 1958. Flown to MOTAT 1970 as gift from Airland Ltd. *Miles Magister II* L8353 c/n 779 of 1938, ex No 8 Elementary & Reserve FTS, Woodley coded "O". Post-war renamed 8 Reserve Flying School and coded "FDT-E". Total hrs flown 3,587 and stored 5 MU, Kemble. Sold to Rollasons, Croydon and civilianised as G-AMMC in October 1953. Shipped to Waitomo Aero Club to become ZK-AYW on 3 Dec 1953. Last flight 2 Sept 1962 when total hrs 4,302. Presented by L. R. Nicolson of Waharoa. *Miles Gemini IA*

P-40 Kittyhawk (Auckland, MOTAT)

DH.84 Dragon (MOTAT)

Lockheed 10A (MOTAT)

.NA Harvard (MOTAT)

Pearse Monoplane and Lancaster (MOTAT)

Sunderland MR.V (MOTAT)

Short Solent 4 (MOTAT)

Auster 7c (MOTAT)

ZK-ANT c/n 6322, imported for Wellington Aero Club and donated 1964 by A. B. Baker of Cambridge, NZ. *N.A. Harvard II* NZ944 c/n 66-2757. Shipped to NZ 1941, with 2 SFTS, Woodbourne coded "44", then INST 153 at 1 TTS Hobsonville. Presented by RNZAF. *Pearse Monoplane* unregistered; constructed by Richard Pearse of Temuka probably 1930s but never flown. Tubular steel, fabric covering, variable pitch prop, engine which could be run either as 2-stroke or 4-stroke and could be tilted to provide downward thrust for short take-off or hovering. Tail rotor to counter torque, leading edge slats and conventional elevator-aileron control surfaces. Salvaged from river-bed and donated by late George Bolt. *Short Sunderland MR.V* NZ4115 c/n SH1552 ex RAF SZ584 and G-AHJR, BOAC. Not flown by RAF and used as trainer BOAC 1946/8. To RNZAF 1953/1966 as "KN-B" 5 Sqdn, Luathala Bay, then "Q" 5 Sqdn. Finally Maritime Search & Reconnaissance Unit, Hobsonville. Presented by RNZAF; 6,270 hrs flown. *Short Solent 4* ZK-AMO c/n SH1559 with TEAL 1950/1960 on trans-Tasman Auckland/

Wellington to Sydney and from 1954 the only machine flying the Coral route Auckland-Fiji (Lauthala Bay), Cook Islands (Aitutaki), Western Samoa (Satapuala) and Tahiti (Papeete.) Total hrs approx 14,500. Presented by TEAL/Air NZ Ltd. The following are currently stored or under restoration:— *Auster 7c Antarctic* NZ1707 ex RAF WE563, reserve a/c for British Antarctic expeditions early 1950s. Purchased RNZAF 1956, subsequently operated on wheels or floats, first with Antarctic Flight, Scott Base, Antarctica, later 3 Sqdn, for Army Co-op. Crashed into Kaipara Harbour 22 August 1966 and airlifted next day to Hobsonville by UH-1D NZ3802—presented by RNZAF. (stored) *Avro Anson Mk I* NZ412 ex RAF DG701. On charge 1942 and navigation trainer School of GR, New Plymouth. Presented by C. H. Dodge, Christchurch. (stored) *Vought FG-1 Corsair* NZ5612 Bu 88090 to MOTAT 1971 from Asplins Supplies. *DH. Mosquito T.43* NZ2305, laid down as FB.40 at Bankstown, NSW; then A52-19, but converted before completion to A52-1053 (T.43). With 75 Sqdn, Ohakea; donated by L. R. Coleman of Marton. *Gere Sport Biplane*. Ultra-light of early 1930s with 40 h.p. Szekely engine; donated by G. Cohen & B. S. Smith. (stored) *Lockheed Hudson GR III* NZ2031 ex RAF AE499 with Nos 2 and 4 Sqdns. Presented by Messrs. W. and T. Garr of Dunedin (stored). *Lockheed RB-34 Lexington* (US Army version of Ventura) NZ4600 c/n 4773, ex 41-38117, RAF FD665. To RNZAF for coastal patrols and crew training at Whenuapai: from J. D. Russ, Nelson. *Hawker Hind* NZ1518 ex K6717 of 88 Sqdn, RAF, Boscombe Down ex 3 SFTS Ohaka is a long-term restoration task. *Mignet Pou-de-Ciel "Flying Flea"* ZM-AAA (not ZK) presented by D. B. Monteagle of Havelock North. Registration ZK-AAB also quoted but believed inaccurate. *Ryan STM-2* ZK-BEM c/n 489. Netherlands East Indies Air Force S.53; escaped to Australia 1942 and flew with RAAF as A50-13, post-war to VH-AGS. To New Zealand 1954. Presented by Miss K. Quinn. *Vickers Vildebeest III* under restoration from various parts found in New Zealand and will probably become NZ102 or NZ105. Vickers Vincent parts (from NZ313/K6355 and NZ353/K6345) currently being used for Vildebeest—a Vincent project may be possible later. *DH.83C Fox Moth* ZK-APT c/n FM48. Post-war Canadian built; donated by B. S. Smith. *Lincoln Sport*, homebuilt, being restored, possibly to airworthiness and donated by B. S. Smith. *Glider (homebuilt)* of 1936—not flown—donated by D. B. Monteagle. *DH. Tiger Moth* ZK-AIN c/n 83202/DHNZ.25 ex RNZAF NZ775, reconstructed from fuselage of AIN and other parts—not listed but believed stored. Also here or in Auckland store, a *DFS Weihe 1942 glider* built in Reich Protectorate of Bohemia & Moravia, Czecho-Slovakia (Avia bolts).

Ornithopter built by R. Adams during 1960s, weight 60 lbs, donated. *Bennett Aviation Airtruck* ZK-BPV/ ZK-CKE of 1960/63, being restored as one a/c by D. Subritsky, using Harvard parts. First commercially-developed a/c in N.Z. *Fletcher FU.24* will be assembled from damaged parts; agricultural a/c. There is also a flight deck, engines & Components display of Hastings C.3 NZ5801 ex 41 Sqdn, RNZAF. A Link Trainer has also been donated from RNZAF and other exhibits will be displayed when additional space becomes available. Do make a point of going to MOTAT if you are within striking distance of New Zealand.

At Auckland's Central Institute of Technology is *DH. Vampire FB.5* NZ5717 and *Harvard II* NZ1069 may come here or to another educational establishment. In the Howick area of Auckland, John Chambers has:— *Curtiss P-4OE-1-CU* NZ3094 ex RAF ET433 impressed into USAAF for 68th Pursuit Group, Tonga. Transferred to 15 Sqdn, RNZAF October 1942, later "HQ-C" of 14 Sqdn, "FE-LI" of 2 OTU. Sold as scrap 1948. Also *Curtiss P-40M-10-CU* NZ3119 c/n 27501 ex 43-5813, to 16 Sqdn, RNZAF 1943 as "XO-T" and 2 OTU as "FE-P". Sold for scrap 1948. John would be happy to exchange one Kittyhawk for another WW II fighter. *DH. Vampire FB.52* NZ5732 with 14 and 75 Sqdns, RNZ AF. Sold from Woodbourne as scrap 1963.

Flying in the Auckland area many vintage types:— *Tiger Moth* ZK-AIA c/n 3697 ex ZK-AGI, NZ 721, Auckland Gliding Club. *DH. Moth Minor* ZK-AKM c/n 94012 ex G-AFON, ZK-AHK, NZ597; D. Lilico. *DH. Tiger Moth* ZK-AQA c/n 82355 ex N9254, NZ863; A.G.C. *DH.83 Fox Moth* ZK-ASP c/n 4097 ex ZK-ADI, NZ566; R. M. Robertson. *DH. Tiger Moth* ZK-ATC c/n DHNZ. 88 ex NZ838; D. L. Sterling. *Grumman G.44A Widgeon* ZK-AVM c/n 1466 ex VH-AZO; *ZK-CFA* c/n 1439 ex N9096R; *ZK-CHG* c/n 1356 ex USCG. 37726, N91702; all with New Zealand Tourist Air Travel. *Tiger Moth* ZK-BFX c/n

Grumman Widgeon (Auckland)

83145 ex T5378, G-ANPZ; Weedair Ltd. *Tiger Moth* ZK-BVN c/n 85768 ex DE883 G-ANSU, ZK-BGY; with BVN Flying Group. *Tiger Moth* ZK-CDU c/n 84711 ex ?T6296, G-ALAD, ZK-BAW; L. F. Karl & Ptnrs. *DH.89A Rapide* ZK-AKU c/n 6662 ex HG663, NZ528 may be stored at Ardmore.

DEVONPORT. Airfield. *Miles M.11A Whitney Straight* ZK-AXD c/n 506 ex U-0227 NF747, G-AFZY; R. S. Lockley.

FEATHERSTON. Airfield. *Tiger Moth* ZK-APM c/n 3226 ex G-ACWB, NZ737; I. C. Dittmer.

GISBORNE. Airport. *Tiger Moth* ZK-BAL c/n 82793 ex R4876, G-AMMG; P. O. Nicholls. *Lockheed 18/56 Lodestar* ZK-BUV c/n 2152 ex 41-29631, RAF's EW984, EC-22, N9930F; Fieldair. (may also be seen at Oringi, Dannevirke and was said to be available for donation to RAF Museum if a Hurricane donated to MOTAT.)

HAMILTON. Airport. *Tiger Moth* ZK-AJO c/n 489, built Australia and assembled Rongotai as NZ1403, at 2 EFTS, Ashburton 1941/2, post-war Canterbury Aero Club. To James Aviation 1949 as first topdressing a/c flying 6,914 hrs on agricultural work until 1966. Now displayed. Flying here *Tiger Moth* ZK-CCQ c/n DHNZ. 132 ex NZ1452; T. J. Bindon & Ptnrs. *Hudson* fuselages —NZ2059 and others, reported in scrapyard here.

HASTINGS. Airfield. *GAL Monospar ST.25* ZK-AFF c/n 84 imported 1937 as G-AEJW; New Zealand Aerial Mapping Co. Also *Beech AT-11 Kansan* ZK-AHO ex 42-37208. *Tiger Moth* ZK-BBG c/n 85829 ex DE969, G-AMPN flies for Marshall & Neville Ltd. and *Piper J-3C-50 Cub* ZK-AHD c/n 2707 is thought under restoration here.

HAVELOCK NORTH. Playground. *Grumman TBF-1C Avenger* NZ2539 c/n 5782 USN Bu 48016, from 30/31 Sqdns, RNZAF. Post-war as target tug Ohakea, sold as scrap 1959. *Avro 626 Prefect* ZK-APC c/n 811, ex NZ203 of A Flt, CFS, Wigram "A-3" INST 90; under restoration by J. Frogley nearby.

HOBSONVILLE. Yacht Club. *Sunderland MR.V* NZ4112 ex VB881 of 201 Sqdn, re-serialled RN272/ 6534 M. Re-activated for Berlin Airlift. Engines sold to Australian Co who presented a/c to club.

GAL Monospar (Hastings)

LOWER HUTT. Len Southward's Car Museum. *Tiger Moth* ZK-AOX c/n 503 built Australia and assembled Rongotai as NZ1417. To Southland Aero Club December 1947 as ZK-AOX. Also owned by Len is the *Vickers V.22 Bleriot* (*replica*) from "Magnificent Men" which is exhibited at air displays in the season.

MANUREWA. Airfield. *DH. Moth Minor* ZK-AKL c/n 94061 ex ZK-AHJ NZ591; D. F. C. Muir & Ptnr—may be stored.

MASTERTON. *DH. 94 Moth Minor* ZK-ALN c/n 9400 ex G-AFRD, VH-AAO, ZK-AHI, NZ596 (may go to Ardmore, Auckland.) *DH. Tiger Moth* ZK-BAT c/n 82139 ex G-AFSH, X5106, G-AFSH; T. C. Williams.

METHVEN Playground. *NA Harvard II* NZ946.

MT. MAUNGANUI. Airfield. *Tiger Moth* ZK-BCB c/n 83707, ex T7386, G-AMMN; Tauranga Aero Club.

NAPIER. Airfield. *Rearwin 9000KR* ZK-ALF, c/n 613D imported as ZK-AGQ, impressed as NZ599. Post-war to New Plymouth Aero Club. Believed under rebuild. Flying here *Tiger Moth* ZK-BLV c/n 85071 ex T6802, G-ANSJ; L. E. Harris Sons.

ROTORUA. Airfield. *EoN Baby glider* ZK-GAF c/n EoN/B 002 ex G-ALRS, BGA626 is owned by J. D. Lane. With 29 Sqdn ATC is *Tiger Moth* ZK-DAM c/n NZ165 ex NZ1485, INST. 151. *Grumman TBF-1C Avenger* NZ2527 c/n 5625, USN Bu 47859, with 30/31 Sqdns RNZAF and post-war Ohakea as target-tug. Registered ZK-CBO 1962 for aerial topdressing but project dropped and aircraft now in Kuiau Park on display.

STRATFORD. Airfield. *Tiger Moth* ZK-AZH c/n 84736 ex T6362, G-AHRL; D. E. Farquhar.

TAKAPAU. In playground *AT-16-ND Harvard IIB* NZ 1100, RAF KF403 c/n 14A-2103, later INST. 149.

TAURANGA. Airfield. *DH.83C Fox Moth* ZK-AQB c/n FM.49, imported from Canada for Auckland Aero Club; now W. Patterson. In playground *NA Harvard II* NZ980 ex RAF AJ867, ex 2 SFTS, Woodbourne, then INST.136 at Taieri.

TE AWAMUTA. Airfield. *Tiger Moth* ZK-BAB c/n 83350 ex T5672, G-ALRI; C. H. R. Liddell.

TE PUKE. Airfield. *Tiger Moth* ZK-BFG c/n 82039 ex N6754, G-ANFB; J. P. Galpin.

Grumman Avenger (Te Rapa)

NEW PLYMOUTH. Airfield. *Tiger Moth* ZK-BUO c/n 83393 ex NZ795, ZK-APS; New Plymouth Aero Club. *DFS Weihe glider* ZK-GAE c/n 535 ex G-ALKG, BGA433, is also flying here.

PAHIATUA. Playground *NA Harvard II* NZ918 c/n 66-2784 ex 2 EFTS, Woodbourne, then INST 135 and INST A.100 Taieri.

PALMERSTON NORTH. Airport. Many vintage types flying:—*Proctor V* ZK-ARP, c/n Ae 97 ex G-AIEO; F. A. Brittain. *Tiger Moth* ZK-BAA ex 84893 ex T6564, G-AMKN; S. J. Skilton. *DH.94 Moth Minor* ZK-BFP c/n 9403 ex. G-AFRR, HM579; Earlybird Flying Ltd. *Rearwin 9000KR* ZK-AKF c/n 654D ex VH-ADM, ZK-AHM, NZ568; *Lockheed 18/50 Lodestar* ZK-CGV c/n 2051 ex ZS-ATE, SAAF 244, VP-KIB, N94546; N777Z; Airland (NZ) Ltd.

PETONE. Central Institute of Technology. *Vampire FB.5* NZ5757 allocated here for instruction.

TE RAPA. RNZAF. Main Auckland-Wellington Highway. *Grumman TBF-1 Avenger* NZ2504, was INST. 182. With 30 Sqdn, Gisborne, 1943, than 31 Sqdn; post-war with 42 Sqdn as target-tug. Will go to MOTAT when base closes.

WAIPUKURAU. Airfield. *Tiger Moth* ZK-BLQ c/n 84120 ex T7738, G-ANSL; J. I. Mackie.

WAIROA. Airfield. *DH. 60G Moth* ZK-ADT c/n 1101 ex G-AAJO, owned Hon. Loel Guiness and others. In 1934 F/O S. G. White, New Zealander in the RAF, bought it and flew it solo to Sydney, shipping it from there to Auckland and flying it on to Hastings. In 1937 Union Airways Social Club acquired and named it "Huia", Currently owned by D. Matches & Ptnrs and thought to be stored (1973).

WELLINGTON. Flying from Northland, *Tiger Moth* ZK-ATC c/n DHNZ.88 ex NZ838; D. L. Sterling. *Tiger Moth* ZK-BEF c/n 83323 ex T5625, G-AIDR; L. Darcy. Thought flying at Paraparaumu Airport are *Avro Avian IVM* ZK-ACM c/n 499 of K. C. Trillo who restored it in 1964. It was originally imported in 1931 by Goodwin-Chichester Aviation. *Auster B.8* ZK-BMJ c/n B.102 is with Associated Farmers (Aerial Work), also Auster B.8 *ZK-BXO* a rebuild with c/n AIRP. 860, and *ZK-CCU* c/n B.105 a rebuild of ZK-BMM. Further details appreciated, with photos. A new group of local preservationists led by Ross Macpherson and John Regan have acquired *Grumman TBF-1 Avenger* NZ2505 c/n 5220, USN Bu. 24337, ex 30/31 Sqdns and moved from Opunake Beach. They (or other preservationists) also have *Aeronca 100* ZK-AKA c/n AB 105 ex VH-UXV, VQ-FAJ, thought likely to become airworthy again.

WHAKATANA. Airfield. *Tiger Moth* ZK-AUZ c/n 85349 ex DE315, G-AJHR; D. J. Billinghurst.

WHANGEREI. Airfield. *Piper J-3C-65 Cub Special* ZK-ATU c/n 9538 ex USAAF 43-677, VQ-FAG; L. W.

Tarr & Ptnr. The *Short Sunderland MR.V* NZ4114, ex RAF SZ561, of Northland Coastguard HQs, has been up for disposal and it is thought it may go to an Australian Preservation Group in NSW.

Before ending the New Zealand section could a reader kindly advise what has happened to some of the "veterans" listed in the 3rd edition of V. and V. and not shown here. We know that Widgeon ZK-BAY crashed and was totally destroyed 24.12.1971 and that Rapide ZK-AKT crashed and was written-off, also that the Catalina NZ4055 was broken up for scrap 1971 as not restorable. Perhaps some of the "oldies" like Whitney Straight ZK-AUK (c/n 507 ex G-AFJX) are in store— Details appreciated, also locations of the Percival Prentice G-AOMF ex VS316 flown from Australia May, 1969? These types are fast disappearing and ought to preserved when no longer airworthy. *Harvard II* NZ1041 c/n 88-13190 ex 41-37717, RAF EX744 is with Air NZ and *Harvard II* NZ1044 c/n 88-13193 ex 41-33720, EX747 is with NAC, both for use of airframe apprentices and both from CFS, Wigram store. Details of *where located* wanted, please.

CANADA

ALBERTA

ACADIA VALLEY. Airfield. *DH.82C Tiger Moth* CF-DFG c/n 1516 ex RCAF 3855; Hall & Rtal.

BURNS LAKE. Airfield. *Harvard IV* CF-UFZ c/n CCF4-112; A. Beach.

CALGARY. Centennial Planetarium—Director Mr. S. Wiesser; P. O. Box 2100 Calgary 2 for details of viewing:—*Avro Lancaster B.X* FM136 in No 50 (RAF) Sqdn colours—mounted on pylon at McCall Field.

Lancaster B.X FM136 (Calgary)

Vampire Mk 3 CF-RLK (Calgary)

Sikorsky H-5 (Calgary)

At Planetarium—*Avro CF-100 Mk3 "Canuck"* 18126, example of Canada's first jet fighter, the world's first straight-winged combat aircraft to exceed Mach 1 (Dec 18 1952, in a dive.) *DH. Vampire Mk 3* CF-RLK ex 17069, N6877D, ex Calgary contingent of Confederate Air Force. *Beechcraft D18S Expeditor* CF-GXC c/n A.547. In storage are:—*DH.82C Tiger Moth* CF-DAL c/n DHC644 ex RCAF4314. *NA Harvard IV*—serial/registration unknown. Under restoration:—*DH. Mosquito B.35* CF-HMS ex RS700 from Spartan Air Services. *Hawker Hurricane IIB* 42024 (*44019* is at present in Saskatchewan on lease.) *Sikorsky H-5* 9607 coded "OU-607" RCAF (also known as S51.) *Sopwith Triplane* with 130hp Clerget; under construction, believed replica for flying. Details awaited. *McDonnell Banshee* reported coming here. Readers note that many of the original Air Museum aircraft have been dispersed or scrapped and some are currently being traced. We wish this project well under the new management. *Westland Lysanders* 1205, 1206 and 1209 are thought to be with Martin Riehl somewhere in Calgary. Flying from Calgary are many vintage types including:—*DH.60G Gipsy Moth* CF-APA c/n 1322, restored from scrap by Jack Landage. *Harvard IV* CF-UAB c/n CCF4-189; CF-UAD c/n CCF4-212; CF-UAE c/n CCF4-254; CF-UNL c/n CCF4-175; Rainer Developments Corpn. *Harvard IV* CF-UZW c/n CCF4-222; Chas. Money. CF-WWI c/n CCF4-127; Robt. C. Wilkinson. CF-MWN c/n CCF4-267; Douglas M. Nelson. CF-RQC c/n CCF4-109; Edwin Goertz; CF-SWW c/n CCF4-53; F. G. Wetherall. *Auster VI* CF-OMW c/n 2862 ex RCAF 16684; Cu-Nim Gliding Club. CF-LOE c/n 2600 ex RCAF 16672; Frank Shaban. *Auster VII* CF-KYB c/n 145ES ex RCAF 16692; Fred Halkow. *Consolidated PBY-5A Catalina* CF-HHR c/n 300 ex N18446; Field Aviation. *Beech D17S* CF-DTF c/n 403; George Money & Son. *Grumman G-44A Widgeon* CF-GWL c/n 4870; Geo. L. May; CF-IJO c/n 1458; Pastew Ltd. At the Calgary Memorial, *Lockheed T-33 "Tee-Bird"* 21231 built by Canadair.

CARDSTON. Airfield. *Grunau GB.II glider* CF-ZBH c/n 1533; J. B. Woslyng.

CASTLEGAR. Airfield. *Beech AT-11 Kansan* CF-IBT c/n 1195; Waneta Airways. *Cessna T-50 Crane* CF-STT c/n 5013; N. Kostiuk. *WACO YKS6* CF-LWP c/n 4513 is owned and flown by Dr. J. V. Hall. First-flown Sept 1, 1936 by John Livingstone of WACO & Monocoupe fame at Troy, Ohio it became NC16522, executive a/c for Socony Vacuum Oil Co. but was stored during WW II and until 1954 when restored and sold to Lee Nemeti, New York. In 1960 it moved to Canada, was flown by Sqdn Ldr Morris RCAF 1961-65 and J. V. Hall M.D. bought her in June 1968.

Seafire F.XV PR410 (HMCS Tecumseh)

HMCS Tecumseh. *Supermarine Seafire F.XV* PR410 (painted in error as PR451) *Hawker Sea Fury FB.11* WG565 from Institute of Technology.

Sea Fury FB.11 (Cold Lake)

COLD LAKE. Canadian Armed Forces. *Avro Canada CF-100* displayed, serial wanted. *Hawker Sea Fury FB.11* WH589 ex Royal Australian Navy and Bankstown, NSW, owned and flown by Ormond Haydon-Baillie of 448 Experimental Sqdn, Englishman in CAF. It is understood this will come to Southend, Essex, with other aircraft when Ormond's tour of duty ends. It has flown with successes in many USA Races and has created enthusiasm wherever seen. (See page IX)

DRAYTON VALE. *Harvard IV* CF-RUQ c/n CCF4-85; M. McCullagh.

EDMONTON. Airport. *Canadair F-86 Sabre* 19101 (the first) mounted here by RCAF Assn. *Bleriot XI* replica, ex Air Museum of Canada bought by Edmonton City Council but is it displayed? Flying:—*Fairchild M62A3 Cornell* CF-FKB ex FX192; S. Snider; *CF-FDU* ex FV703; J. Harrold. *Fairchild 24W46 Argus* CF-FZQ c/n W46-322; J. Franklin. *NA B-25 Mitchell* CF-OND ex 44-28866; NW Air Leasing Ltd, *Rearwin 185* CF-OML c/n 1869; N. Halomen. *Cessna T-50 Crane* CF-MFA c/n 7562; R. V. Coambs. *Douglas A-26B Invader* CF-PGF ex 44-35875 and *B-26C* CF-PGP ex 44-35898; Airspray Ltd. *A-26B* CF-BVH ex 44-34724; Dontuss Industries. *Harvard IV* CF-UZH c/n CCF4-217; Adrian Hobart; *Harvard II* CF-MMT c/n 07-184; V. Clothier; *CF-MWP* c/n 07-166; Gail Schmidt. *Lockheed 18 Lodestar* CF-PPL c/n 2345; Sterling A/S. *Consolidated PBY-5A Catalina* CF-SAT c/n 9757; W. P. Bernard. *DH.82C Tiger Moth* CF-CLW c/n 1373 ex RCAF 1170; Maclan Construction; *CF-CSZ* c/n 1430 ex RCAF 1227; George Chivers. *Howard DGA-15P* CF-OJE c/n 1730; T. H. Sydia. *Grumman G-44A* CF-SPA c/n 26; Wright Equip Ltd. *AX-SM Balloon* CF-POP; Sandy McTaggart (fun entry).

GRANDE PRAIRIE. Airstrip. *Tiger Moth* CF-CIH c/n 636 ex RCAF 4306; Edward Kinipe. *Fairchild M62A3 Cornell* CF-CVP ex FV730; J. H. Dalen.

LADNER. Airfield. *Harvard IV* CF-WLO c/n CCF4-55; Victor McMann; *CF-VFK* c/n CCF4-42; R. W. Haslam; *CF-WWO* c/n CCF4-52; R. R. Weaver.

LETHBRIDGE. Airfield. *Fairchild M62A3 Cornell* CF-CVO ex FV729; D. McLean.

NAMAO. Canadian Forces Base. *Mosquito FB.VI* VA114 coded TH-F, on gate.

NANTON. By roadside. *Avro Lancaster B.X* FM159, built by Victory Aircraft of Canada, arrived UK May, 1945, no operations and flew back September for modification. Served with 407 Sqdn coded RX159 which is painted on one side with 407 badge, starboard carries code "B" and name "Bull Moose".

PURPLE SPRINGS. Strip. *Harvard II* CF-MWJ c/n 3188; Kinniburgh SS.

RED DEER. Canadian Forces Base. *Harvard IV* 20370, built Canadian Car & Foundry Co., displayed here.

SPRUCE GROVE. Airfield. *DH.82C Tiger Moth* CF-CIX c/n 1417 ex RCAF 1214; Les Shep.

Lancaster B.X (St. Albert)

ST. ALBERT. Airport. *Avro Lancaster B.X* CF-TQC (also reported as TQR) the former MR.X KB976 ex 405/408 Sqdns, flown into McCall Field, Calgary for the proposed Air Museum, and then acquired, allegedly to become CF-AMD of "The Lancaster Club"; now airworthy for water-bombing. *Fleet Finch Mk I* CF-AAE c/n 243, ex RCAF 1001 here with Stanley Hodgson.

VAUXHALL. Airstrip. *Harvard IV* CF-SRJ c/n CCF4-191; James Swartz.

Avro Avian IV (Wetaskiwin)

WETASKIWIN. Reynolds Pioneer Museum, Box 728. *Avro 594 Avian IV* CF-CDV c/n 316 with Genet 5-cyl radial. Originally built by Ottawa Car Manufacturing Co Ltd for RCAF. *Curtiss JN-4D "Jenny"*

G-CATE c/n 77832 ex G-CABX, originally at Camp Borden for pilot-training and after WW I flown as "City of Edmonton" until purchased and flown by RFC Lt. Edward A. Reynolds, 1920s. *DH.60GM Gipsy Moth* CF-AGX c/n DHC127, with Gipsy 4-cyl upright engine; on Short Bros floats. *DH.60 Cirrus Moth* G-CYYG with Cirrus 4-cyl upright engine. *Fairchild Cornell* trainer with Ranger 6-cyl inverted—serial please. *Hurricane IIB* serial 44057 with Merlin 29.

BRITISH COLUMBIA

ABBOTSFORD. Airport. Conair Aviation Water-Bombers *Grumman TBM-3 Avenger* CF-KCF c/n 53554; *CF-KCN* c/n 53732; *CF-KCM* c/n 53420; *CF-KCH* c/n 53072; *CF-KCL* c/n 53638; *CF-KCG* c/n 69327; *CF-IMI* c/n 53337; *CF-IMM* c/n 53241; *CF-IMN* c/n 53139; *CF-IMK* c/n 85597; *CF-MUD* c/n 86180; *CF-MUE* c/n 91426; *CF-MXN* c/n 53632. *Douglas A-26C* CF-BMS ex 43-22357; *CF-DFC* ex 41-39398; *CF-BMR* ex 41-39359; *A-26B* CF-MSB c/n 28719; *A-26B* CF-FBV ex 44-34607. *NA.AT-6 Harvard* CF-MFK c/n 2957; E. Fossen and *Harvard IV* CF-NSN c/n CCF4-164 fly here. Preservationists ought to watch for disposal of time-expired Conair machines.

ALERT BAY. Airstrip. *WACO AQC6* CF-CCW c/n 4646; H. J. Pickup.

BELLA COOLA. Airfield. Wilderness Airlines. *Stinson SR10 Reliant* CF-KLH c/n 5953.

CAMPBELL RIVER. Island Airlines. *Fairchild F11 Husky* CF-EIR c/n 12.

CHASE. *Consolidated Liberator VI* KK237 and *VIII* RCAF 11120 reported dismantled here. Fuller details valued if, in fact, these two machines are restorable?

P-51 Mustang (Nanaimo)

CHILLIWACK. Brett's Garage. *Fairchild Cornell* on roof, details please.

COWICHAN. Airstrip. *Fairchild F24R46A Argus* CF-GZV c/n R46-341; J. A. Hunt.

DAWSON CREEK. *Auster VI* CF-KGZ c/n 2589 ex RCAF 16665; Sandy Duane.

DELTA. Airfield. *Stinson V77* CF-XND c/n 77-156; D. Diston. *Fairchild M62A3 Cornell* CF-FLY c/n M-288; W. Lannon.

KAMLOOPS. Airport. Farnsworth A/c Ltd. *Cessna T-50 Crane* CF-NPT c/n 7387. Four *B-25J Mitchells* reported static here; CF-NTU ex 5203 RCAF; *CF-NTV* ex 5234, SV-234; *CF-NTW* ex 5247, SV-247 and *CF NTX* ex 5249, SV-249. Is one worth saving?

KIMBERLEY. *Harvard IV* CF-VTT c/n CCF4-231; Flying Club.

LANGLEY. Airfield. Skyway Air Services. *AT-6 Harvard* CF-MSZ c/n 3070. *Tiger Moth* CF-CIE c/n 986.

LETHBRIDGE. Airfield. *Harvard IV* CF-RUL c/n CCF4-167; B. Durfee.

MILE HOUSE. Airstrip. Cariboo Canim Ranch. *Howard DGA-15P* CF-LRM c/n 503.

MISSION. North-West Aero Ltd. *Howard DGA-15P* CF-NTY c/n 869—was in 1971 London-Victoria Air Race as "40".

NANAIMO. Airport. *NA P-51 Mustang* CF-RUT ex RCAF 9221, owned & flown by D. McGillivray—one of two airworthy examples in Canada.

NEW WESTMINSTER. Airport. *Stinson HW-75* CF-BZL c/n 7175, B. Johnson. Is *Beech AT-11 Kansan* still at Woodlands School?

NORTH BURNABY. Airfield. *Stinson SR5E Reliant* CF-MXH c/n 9256A; J. Taylor.

OKANAGAN FALLS. *Stinson 10 Voyager* CF-HIK c/n 7584; Margaret Hester.

PENTICON. Airfield. Rapid Air Services Ltd. *Cessna T-50 Crane* CF-NIU c/n 3037.

Howard DGA-15P (Mission)

PRINCE GEORGE. Airfield. Imperial Airways operate *Grumman G-44A Widgeon* CF-IIQ c/n 1265. *Fairchild F24R46A Argus* CF-MXW c/n R46-313 is flown by G. Jack. *Auster VI* CF-LIC c/n 2591 ex RCAF 16667; by M. H. Pearson.

PRINCE RUPERT. Airfield. North Coast Air Services *Grumman G-44A* CF-HEN c/n 1311; *Fairchild F11 Husky* CF-EIM, c/n 3.

QUESNEL. Airstrip. *Tiger Moth* CF-CIK c/n 851 ex RCAF 5052; R. F. McLeod/D. K. Styan.

RED DEER. Canadian Forces Base. *Harvard IV* 20370, built by Canadian Car & Foundry Co, on display. *Beech D17S* CF-GLL c/n 6914 ex Bu. 23724; flies here; Harry Leader.

RICHMOND. Airfield. Western Aviation *Tiger Moth* CF-CLH c/n 1238 ex RCAF 5935. *NA.AT-6* CF-MTA c/n 2591 flown by W. Bagosi/P. Kalnin. *Culver LFA* CF-HQQ c/n 383 (believed only one in Canada); L. Purnell. *DH.82C* CF-OQT c/n 1060 ex RCAF 4869; R. W. Coulter. *R.A/c Factory S.E.5a (replica)* CF-QGM c/n G70-003; C. R. Goguillot.

SAANICHTON. Airport. *Mono Monocoach Model 201* CF-AAT ex NC114K (the only one) C. M. Price.

SANDSPIT. Airstrip. *Auster IVA* CF-XNF c/n TAY-207V; H. H. Bronch.

SECHELT. Airfield. Sechelt Air Services. *Fairchild F71C* CF-BXF c/n 523 of 1943.

SIDNEY. Airport. Flying Fireman Ltd, Water-Bombers. *Harvard IV* CF-SNJ, CCF4-74; *Consolidated PBY-5A* CF-FFW c/n 46596; *CF-FFZ* c/n 46602; *CF-NTL* c/n CV383; *PBY-28/5AC* CF-IHN c/n 441; *Stinson L-5E/1 Sentinel* CF-IIM ex 44-18071, H. D. Thomas. *Ryan ST-3-KR* CF-XNO c/n 1691; Precision Engineering. On Salt Springs Island (approached by Ferry) Mr. G. A. Maude has *Curtiss P-40 Kittyhawk* 1034, restored here. He donated his Bolingbroke to CNAC, Ottawa.

SOUTH BURNABY. Airfield. *Harvard IV* CF-WLA c/n CCF4-66; F. A. Durant.

ST. JOHN. Airfield. North Caribou Flying Services. *Stinson SR-9/FM* CF-OAY c/n 5732.

STRATHMORE. Airfield. *Harvard IV* CF-RUU c/n CCF4-148; Rainier Developments.

SURREY. Airfield. *DH.82C Tiger Moth* CF-BEK c/n 1498, RCAF 1295; A. P. Kusch. *WACO YKC-5* CF-QGG c/n 4231; R. A. George. *NA. AT-6* CF-NIA c/n 3832; L. C. Abbey.

VANCOUVER. Sproat Lake, Vancouver Islands. *Martin JRM-3 Mars* CF-LYK "Hawaii Mars" ex Bu. 76820 and *CF-LYL* "Phillipine Mars" Bu.76823, carrying

P-40 Kittyhawk (Sidney)

Martin JRM-3 Mars (Vancouver)

Martin JRM-3 Mars (Vancouver)

Harvard IV (Victoria)

12,000 imperial gallons as forest-fire tankers; F. I. Flying Tankers. Flying from Vancouver Airport many vintage, including:—*Grumman G-21A Goose* CF-HUZ c/n B83; *CF-IOL* c/n B107; CF-ETJ c/n B70 ex RCAF 390; all Canadian Forest Products Ltd. *Goose* CF-VFU c/n B101; Forest Industries Flying Tankers. *Goose* CF-RQI c/n 1145; Airwest Airlines. *Goose* CF-NIF c/n B129; *CF-VAK* c/n B142; *CF-UVJ* c/n B6; *CF-UMG* c/n B145; *CF-UAZ* c/n 1077; Trans-Provincial Airlines (sometimes based at TERRACE, BC.) *Grumman G-44 Widgeon* CF-JXX c/n 1235; *G-44A* CF-NNH c/n 1431; Harrison Airways; *G-44* CF-PNT c/n 1334; Canada Kelp Co. *Harvard IV* CF-RZP c/n CCF4-123; Sandford Pearce. *Fairchild F11 Husky* CF-SAQ c/n 8; West Coast A/s. *CF-BQC* c/n 1; Industrial Wings. *CF-MAN* c/n 9; Harrison Airways. *Porterfield CP-65* CF-RKU c/n 1029; Ian Neville. *SE-5A (replica)* CF-QGL c/n 002; D. W. Mc-Gowan. *Cessna C-50* CF-CSH c/n 2243; Bryan Mahon.

VICTORIA. Colwood. Royal Roads Military College. *Canadair Sabre 5* serial 23060 ex No 442 Air Defence Sqdn, Sea Island, Vancouver, than Chatham NB. Over 2,000 hrs logged, 1956/58. At Victoria's British Columbia Provincial Museum *Fleet 2* CF-AOD c/n 6, a 1930 import. Flying from Victoria Airport:—*Fairchild M62A3 Cornell* CF-CVD ex FV733; R. J. Grant. *Howard DGA-15P* CF-JSO c/n 796; Sooke Lake Lumber. *Harvard IV* CF-UZG c/n CCF4-192; A. R. Cockburn (was in 1971 London-Victoria Air Race.) *Harvard IV* CF-UVQ, CCF4-128; D. A. Butler. *Grumman G-21C* CF-BCI c/n 1203; Dept of Highways.

WELLINGTON. Airport. *Harvard IV* CF-UAT c/n CCF4-89; A. Garside.

MANITOBA

BROOKHAVEN BAY (near Winnipeg) Airfield. *Heath Parasol* CF-PYC c/n 14794; Gerald Sage. *Grunau IIB glider* CF-ZEE c/n 468950 owned by "The soarers of 951 Hector Avenue."

BROOKLANDS. Airfield. J. W. W. Borys. *Stinson HW-75* CF-BSU c/n 7044.

CARMAN. Airfield. Bob Diermert, Canada's great preservationist has a remarkable collection including: — *Aichi Navy 99 Val 2* (Aichi D3A1 "Val") CF-TZT serial 3179, fitted with Pratt & Whitney R-2600 from Mitchell and test-flown by Bob to Portage La Prairie. Also from the Solomon Islands and currently being restored *three Nakajima Navy-O Zeke* aircraft, one of which it is said may go to CNAC, Ottawa. *CAC Mustang 23* A68-175 from Australia. *Fairey Firefly V* CF-CBH ex

Aichi "Val" (Carman)

WD840 from Bankstown, NSW to be restored as a Mk 1. *Avro Anson V,* believed one to be restored from 12116/12125, to be painted as last Mk V flying at Portage La Prairie. *NA.AT-6C* CF-MGZ c/n 2557. *DH. Moth Minor CF-AOO* c/n 94095, ex G-AFUV, VH-AFQ, A21-30—imported from Australia. *NA B-25J Mitchell* N3152G ex 44-30456. A growing collection, applauded by all enthusiasts.

ERIKSDALE. Airfield. *Stinson HW-75* CF-CHI c/n 7025 owned & flown by L. A. Heroux & C. Leonard.

GROSSE ISLE. Airfield. *Stinson HW-75* CF-MJK c/n 7219; W. J. Ridgeway.

LAUDER. Airfield. *Funk B85C CF-IEM* c/n 345; E. L. Hicks.

LYNN LAKE. Airfield. Chiupka Airways Ltd. *Anson V* CF-PAC c/n BRC1357.

MANITOU. Airfield. *Stinson 10A Voyager* CF-BPJ c/n 7596; G. Carswell.

PETERSFIELD. Airfield. *Stinson HW-75 CF-CH1* c/n 7025; Arthur Franks.

Prototype CT-41 Tutor (Portage la Prairie)

PORTAGE LA PRAIRIE. Canadian Forces Base entrance *Canadair CT-41 Tutor* in colours of Golden Centennaires and serialled "000". In the local Island Park a *Lockheed T-33* is mounted on pylon—authentic serials please.

STEINBECK. Airstrip. *Harvard IV* CF-RZW c/n CCF4-213; T. Lodobruk.

ST. JAMES. Central Northern Airways. *Anson V* CF-GJV c/n MDF932.

SWAN RIVER. Airfield. *Stinson HW-75* CF-BSI c/n 7190; G. E. Windsor.

THOMPSON. Airfield. *Howard DGA-15P* CF-OGL c/n 561; E. J. Kiss. *Stinson HW-75* CF-BSV c/n 7250; J. A. Macdonald.

WINNIPEG. Portage Avenue West. *Lockheed T-33* mounted in park—serial wanted please. Flying from Winnipeg's International Airport:—*Anson V* CF-GRO c/n BRU122C; Percy Horsley. *DH.82C Tiger Moth* CF-COU c/n 1325 ex RCAF 1122; 1942-built and trainer at Medicine Hat, Battle Creek, Maple Creek & Calgary; now Dr. Stewart & Red River Tigers. *DH.83C Fox Moth* CF-DIX c/n FM24; Henry Boulanger. *Consolidated PBY-5A Catalina* CF-DIL c/n 427; *CF-GLX* c/n 560; *CF-NJE* c/n CV437; *PBY-28/5AC* CF-CRR ex RCAF 9767; *CF-PIU* c/n 64092; all with Ilford Riverton Airways. *Grumman G-21A Goose* CF-GFC c/n B98 ex N94750; *CF-PVE* c/n 1200, Midwest Airlines. *CF-WCP* c/n B139; Ilford Riverton. *CF-HBC* c/n B128; Hudsons Bay Co. *Grumman G-44 Widgeon* CF-NHG c/n 1298; Don Paterson. *Lockheed 18 Lodestar* CF-TCY c/n 2064; W. Hanaway. *CF-TDB* c/n 2220; Northland Airlines. *Meyers MAC-45* CF-VIP c/n 220; I. Sapper. *Stinson L-5 Sentinel* CF-STC c/n 76-050; Winnipeg Gliding Club. *Stinson 10 Voyager* CF-NPP c/n 7553; L. Hall. *WACO YKC-6* CF-AYS c/n 4267; Transair Ltd. *WACO ZKS-6* CF-BBQ c/n 4524; George Gregory.

NEW BRUNSWICK

CHATHAM. Canadian Forces Base. On Display *Canadair Sabre 5* 23355 (also reported as 19355 "Golden Hawks").

EDMUNSTON. St. Jacques Airport. On display *Avro Lancaster AR.X* KB882 ex 428 Sqdn, a B.X. in England then modified for 408 Sqdn to Mk X AR, coded MN882.

FREDERICTON. Airport. *DH.82C Tiger Moth* CF-FYW c/n 1673 ex RCAF 8871 owned by Dr. R. H. Bradley. *Fleet 80 Canuck* CF-DPC c/n 029 owned by M. Archer-Shee of Senneville.

GAGETOWN. Airfield. *Stinson HW-75* CF-BJN c/n 7259, owned by Robert Lees

MONCTON. Centennial Park. *Avro CF-100* 18488 on pylon. Flying at the local airport with Maritime A/S *Grumman TBM-3E* CF-XON c/n 85829; *CF-XOM* c/n 69324.

ST. JOHN. Airport. Forest Patrol Ltd. *Grumman TBM-3* CF-IMO c/n 85833. *Douglas B-26C* CF-ZTC ex 44-35857.

NEWFOUNDLAND

CORNER BROOK. Airfield. Newfoundland Air Trans. *Grumman G-44A Widgeon* CF-KPT c/n 1415.

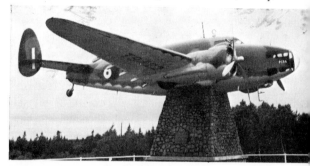

Lockheed Hudson IIIA (Gander)

GANDER. International Airport. On plinth *Lockheed Hudson IIIA* painted as T9422 but actually BW769 c/n 6448 ex 45 Group, Ferry Command and post-war, to Canadian Pacific as CF-CRJ, then to Kenting Photographic Surveys. Retired 1960s and stored Oshawa. Donated to Gander Aviation Museum Committee, ferried and restored by Eastern Provincial as first Hudson ferried to Aldergrove 25th Oct 1940, when AV-M Don Bennett led six across.

ST. JOHN'S. Airport. *Consolidated PBY-5A Catalina* CF-OFI c/n CV343; *CF-IGJ* ex Bu.48429; *CF-IZU* ex Bu.46655; *CF-NCJ* c/n CV420; *PBY-28/5AC* CF-CRP ex RCAF 9837. All operated by Government of Newfoundland & Labrador.

Lancaster AR.X (Edmunston)

NORTH WEST TERRITORIES

MAY RIVER. Airport. Carter Air Services. *Lockheed 10A Electra* CF-HTV c/n 1005, ex NC14258, NM-16, N1836M.

RAE. Airfield. *Howard DGA-15P* CF-OJN c/n 1004 and *Stinson SR-10/J3* CF-KVY c/n G3-5939.

RANKIN INLET. Airfield. *Cessna T-50 Crane* CF-HZO c/n 5083; K. M. Ross.

SNOWDRIFT. Airfield. *Stinson SR-8/CM Reliant* CF-AZV c/n 9733.

YELLOWKNIFE. Air Terminal. *Bristol 170 Freighter Mk 31* CF-TFX c/n 13137 ex G-AMRV, purchased from Transair 1957, retired 1969 and erected on pedestal. It is said that *Fairchild 82-D* CF-MAK c/n 64 ex McAvoy Air Service is also preserved—news please and photos of both required. *Fairchild F-24W46* CF-EKK c/n W46-324; W. England. *Stinson SR-9/FM* CF-BIM c/n 5729; M. A. Thomas; *CF-OAW* c/n 5704; Ptarmigan Airways.

NOVA SCOTIA

GREENWOOD. Canadian Forces Base. *Avro Lancaster B(MR)X* KB839 but now painted KB976; post-war in maritime usage.

MCKAY. Airfield. *Fleet 80 Canuck* CF-DPI c/n 035; Picton Co.

McDonnell Banshee (Shearwater)

SHEARWATER. Canadian Forces Base. Near Dartmouth. *McDonnell Banshee* 126402 ex VR870 Sqdn, RCN, displayed. *DH.82C Tiger Moth* CF-IVO c/n 1667 ex RCAF 8865. *DH.80A Puss Moth* CF-PEI c/n 2187 ex G-AHLO, RAF's HM534, USN8877—a rarity in Canada. Built 1931, used by US Naval Air Attache, London. Acquired by Rev. John MacGillivray who has obtained the registration PEI (Prince Edward Island) to honour the first CF-PEI which was earlier CF-AGV and flown by Mrs. Louise M. Jenkins of Charlottetown. Father MacGillivray also has his famed *Miles M.2W Hawk Major* CF-NXT c/n 215 ex G-ADWT, acquired during one of his RCAF tours of duty in Europe in 1964. Also at Shearwater for restoration is *Grumman Avenger* 85861, ditched 6 August 1953 and recently recovered from the sea. It is also reported that the Dartmouth Chapter, 305 of the Experimental Aircraft Association, have a *Seafire XV* undergoing rebuild—serial and pics please. Also of the Avenger when restored and exhibited.

ONTARIO

ATHENS. Airfield. *WACO YKS-7* CF-BDY c/n 4621; W. N. Barraclough.

Miles M.2W Hawk (Shearwater)

Canadair Sabre 5 (Belleville)

AURORA. Airfield. *Fairchild M62A3 Cornell* CF-CVE ex RCAF FV724; E. Stewart.

BARRIE. *Stinson SR-10J Reliant* CF-HAW c/n 8717; L. Martin.

BELLEVILLE. Centennial Park, off Highway 2, near Glenora Causeway. *Canadair Sabre 5* 23053 in "Golden Hawks" markings.

BOLTON. *Fleet 7B Fawn* CF-CEQ being restored here.

BRACEBRIDGE. Airfield. *Harvard IV* CF-GUY c/n CCF4-27; P. R. Watt.

BRAMPTON. *Stinson SR-8B* CF-RXE, c/n 9701; Harry Bray.
The EAA Hangar houses NA.64 Yale, RCAF 3396 ex Simmons. *Auster VI* CF-KJP c/n 16663 of Ronald Travell; *Auster VII* CF-KPL c/n 146ES, Dr. J. D. McClure.

BRANTFORD. Airfield. Southern Soaring Association. *WACO UPF7* CF-JAU c/n 5516.

BROCKVILLE. Services Club. *Canadair Sabre 5* 23649.

BURLINGTON. Airfield. *Fairchild M62A3* CF-FXX ex RCAF FV705; P. Nelson.

CARP. Airfield. Bradley Air Services *Beech AT-11* CF-KJI ex 42-37099. *Grumman G-44A* CF-HPD c/n 1315.

CLINTON. Canadian Forces Base. Displayed:— *Canadair Sabre 2* 23245; *Avro CF-100 Canuck* 18241; *Lockheed T-33 (Canadair) Tee-Bird* 21129. It is said base may be closing—details of new locations wanted.

COPPER CLIFF. Canadian Nickel Air Services. *Anson V* CF-HOT c/n BRC1567, ex RCAF 12103, PT-AVD.

CORNWALL. Airfield. *WACO VKS7* CF-LWL c/n 6117; R. Silmser. *Stinson 10A Voyager* CF-DZN c/n 8149; L. Marren.

DOWNSVIEW. Airport. Toronto. *Stinson 10A Voyager* CF-LUY c/n 7957; K. H. Smith. At de Havilland Aircraft of Canada. *DH.60G Moth* CF-AAA c/n 1840 ex G-ABJJ, BK842, bought by test-pilot George Neal on a visit to England. He also flies *Sopwith Pup (replica)* CF-RFC c/n C552 which he built in seven years from authentic plans and using 80 hp Le Rhone. Awarded trophy as Canada's best "amateur" aircraft of 1968. Also *DHC.4 Caribou* CF-LAN c/n 2 and *DHC.6 Twin Otter* CF-DHC c/n 1 fly here and are said earmarked for preservation later. *Nieuport 17* part-size (replica) flying. *DH.89A Dragon Rapide* CF-PTK c/n 6254 ex G-ACPP and *DH.87B Hornet Moth* CF-EEJ c/n 8092 ex G-AEET, X9319 also flying here. The Rapide is the fifth built and oldest survivor. Originally registered as Dragon Six to Railway Air Services in 1934; it flew throughout the war on internal services. Shipped to Canada in 1961 it was not uncrated for some four years and has had a remarkable survival.

DUNVILLE. War Memorial. *Harvard II* serial 2766 as tribute to airmen of No 6 SFTS RCAF, and BCATP.

FENWICK. Airfield. *Auster VI* CF-LWK c/n 2598 ex RCAF 16670; Elliot Traver.

FORT ERIE. *Fleet 21M* CF-DLC c/n FAL 11, owned and flown for many years by Canada's "senior" pilot, Thomas Williams, who only stopped aviating in his eighties. He has refused good offers to date as he wants it to stay where it was built.

FORT WILLIAM. Airport. *Stinson SR-10F* CF-FUE c/n 7-5815 and *Vultee TB-13A Valiant* CF-HJB c/n 5886; Superior Airways.

FRANCES. Rainy Lake Airways operate *Grumman G-21A Goose* CF-SBS c/n 1153.

GANANOQUE. Near town, at small airport. *Can-Vickers Catalina* CF-NJL built Montreal 1944, RCAF 11093, now for sale in excellent state for 50,000 Canadian dollars; David T. Dorosh of Edmonton.

GODERICH. SKYHARBOUR. *Lancaster X.SR* FM213 ex 107 (Rescue) Unit Torbay, Newfoundland. Mounted as tribute to BCATP's 12 EFTS. *Cessna C-37 Airmaster* CF-NEV c/n 355; George Morley. *Fairchild 24W/41A* CF-FUH c/n 649; Lloyd Attfield. *Porterfield 35-70* CF-AYK c/n 163 with Le Blond 5 DE engine, owned by John Hopkinson, dismantled for rebuild.

GORMLEY. Airstrip. Cam-Roy Ltd. *Harvard IV* CF-SPC c/n CCF4-145.

GRAVENHURST. Airfield. *Fairchild 24H* CF-BKB c/n 3218; L. Street.

GUELPH. Airfield. *Grumman G-44A* Widgeon CF-LGZ c/n 1473; Thos. Smith.

HAMILTON. Airport. *WACO ZQC6* CF-BDW c/n 4643, said to be for sale by J. C. Tait.

ISLINGTON. Airfield. *Fairchild. 24W/46* CF-EKC c/n W46-193, D. N. Platts.

KAPUSKASING. 647 Sqdn, Canadian Air Cadets. *Spitfire VC* AR614/5378M ex 312 (Czech) 610 (County of Chester) 130 and 222 Sqdns, 53 OTU then instructional airframe St. Athan 1945, is here from Calgary where it was listed as 7555M and confirmation of serial appreciated. *DH. Mosquito B.35* VR796 ex CF-HML of Spartan Air Services is being restored to airworthy state by Don Campbell and his cadets who have erected their own hangar. *DH. Vampire III* 17057 also here from Calgary and a *DHC Tiger Moth* from the estate of the late Herbert Foxcroft—serial/regn wanted.

KENORA. Airfield. *DH.83C Fox Moth* CF-DJB c/n FM28; J. H. Edwards. *Consolidated 28-5AC Catalina* CF-OWE c/n 11074 also reported. At Gratton's Weldwood Farm, a Pioneer museum south of city, Highway 4, is *NA Yale* 3355 and a *Swordfish III*-serial wanted but thought NS122-156 batch. From Simmons, Tillsonburg sale.

KINGSTON. Royal Military College. *Canadair Sabre 5* 23221 displayed. *Tiger Moth* CF-BHK c/n 1819 ex RCAF 9662 ex Mount Hope, 1942, Toronto Gliding Club and other owners, now owned by Officer Cadet James Thomson for restoration. May be based St. Catherine's Flying Club, Niagara District Airport later.

LAMBETH. Royal Canadian Legion. *CF-100 Mk 2* 18106 instructional 615B on fuselage. VC under port and FBK under starboard (18102 which crashed was coded FB-K also.)

LANCASTER. Airfield. *Stampe SV4C* CF-AYF c/n 548 ex F-BDCS, G-AVYY; owned by R. A. Munro, thought the only one in Canada.

LISTOWEL. Airfield. *Avian 2/180 Gyroplane* CF-JTO-X c/n 65/6, only one on register. Built Georgetown, Ont. the company is now out of business. This, the 4th metal prototype, is owned by Harvey Krotz.

LONDON. Airport. *Harvard IV* CF-WWQ c/n CCF4-144 S. J. Roberts. *Auster VI* CF-LGM c/n 2580 ex RCAF 16656; J. C. Knowles.

MALTON. Airport. Toronto. *Fairey Firefly V* CF-BDH ex WD901, N7649, owned by Canadian Warplane Heritage, a band of enthusiasts determined to save—and fly—WW II machines. Being restored in colours of HMS Magnificent ex 816, 723, 724, Sqdns RAN. *Lockheed 18 Lodestar* CF-CEC c/n 2132 is with Aries Service Co and *Consolidated PBY-5A* CF-IZZ c/n 64064; *CF-UKR* c/n CV281, *CF-HTN* ex Bu.48275; with Field Aviation. *Douglas A-26 Invader* CF-CCR was flying here with Canadian Comstock. It is static; likewise *B-25 Mitchell* CF-NWJ? *Consolidated PBY-5A* CF-UAW c/n CV201; *CF-NJB* c/n CV249; *CF-NJF* c/n CV283, Kenting Aviation A/c Ltd. *PBY-5A* CF-JCV c/n CV357 and *CF-IEE* c/n 1566; Austin Airways. *Lockheed 18 Lodestar* CF-OZO c/n 2209; Kenting Aviation. *Lockheed 18* CF-BAL c/n 2283; Murray Watts Exploration. *Harvard II* CF-MTX c/n 3191; S. Castle; *CF-TSV* c/n 3771; C. Clark. *CF-OHG* c/n 3276; Robt C. Smith; *CF-PST* c/n 3776; H. J. Vear. *Harvard IV* CF-UUU c/n CCF4-4; Sam Mazary; *CF-RZQ*, CCF4-132; H. Krautzum; *CF-WGA* CCF4-168; Currie Donald. *NA.P51 Mustang* CF-LOR ex 44-74446A; G. Oates, H. Malagie. *Fairchild M62A3* CF-CVF ex RCAF FV702; Bernice Ruther. *Douglas DC-3* CF-TRY c/n 4585 "Arctic 7" in this Pop Group's psychedelic colours of cream, yellow, brown and green; D. G. Harris Promotions.

MAPLE. Airport. *Nieuport Scout 24 Bis (replica)* CF-ZOT c/n 1917; owned and flown by D. P. Bromley. Said for sale; 3,000 dollars. *Miles M2H* Hawk *Major* CF-AUV c/n 123 ex G-ACYZ, VH-ACC, A37-4 (RAAF) now Cliff Glenister.

MARKHAM. Airfield. *Rearwin Sportster* CF-BEX. *Avro Lancaster* X KB889 ex Age of Flight, Niagara Falls, being restored to fly; Ken Shortt.

MERLIN. Airfield. *Stinson HW-75* CF-BBV c/n 7117; M. Broadbent.

MIMICO. Airfield. *Fairchild M62A3* CF-HXH c/n FC-140; B. Provoden.

MISSISSAUGA. Airfield. *Thruxton Jackaroo* CF-QOT c/n 82168 ex N6924, G-APHZ; Miss Patricia Witty.

MOONBEAM. Airfield. Mattagmi Skyways Co *Bellanca 31-55A* CF-DCH c/n 4.

MOUNTAIN VIEW. Canadian Forces Base. It is said *Avro CF-100* serial 18434 stored here for CNAC.

MUIRKIRK. Messrs. R. Spence & E. Sharpe, RR.2 *Swordfish II* HS554 being restored.

NIAGARA FALLS. Airfield. *Beech E.18S* CF-ANA c/n BA333; *CF-ANT*, c/n BA386; Air Niagara. *Harvard II* CF-NWH c/n 203; L. F. Ross. Mounted behind a garage is *NA Yale*—serial please.

NIXON. Airfield. Norfolk Aerial Spraying. *Grumman TBM-3E Avenger* CF-AYL c/n 86091.

Douglas DC-3 (Malton)

Thruxton Jackaroo (Mississauga)

NORTH BAY. Lee Park *Avro CF-100* 18626 donated to city by RCAF.

NORWICH. Airfield. *Fairchild 24R/46* CF-PHO c/n R46-139; R. Gee.

OAKVILLE. Airfield. *Stinson HW-75* CF-BUP c/n 7026; A. K. Thomson. *Harvard IV* CF-VMG c/n CCF4-203 Sidney H. Bonser.

ORILLA. Airfield. Orthia Air Services. *Stinson SR-10F* CF-HVP c/n 5951. *Consolidated 28-5AC* CF-VIG c/n 46662; Great Lakes Paper Co.

ORLEANS. Airfield. *Cessna T-50 Crane* CF-FGF c/n 1355; D. Wardle.

OSHAWA. Airport. *Rearwin 9000L* CF-BEX c/n 565D; D. C. Oldfield. *Grumman G-21A* CF-CNR c/n 1136; Robson Leather. *Boeing B-17G* CF-HBP c/n 32455 ex N66571 believed static here (or Malton) To be preserved?

OSTRANDER. Airfield. *Harvard II* CF-RWN c/n 3830; Hicks & Lawrence.

OTTAWA/ROCKCLIFFE/UPLANDS.

The National Aeronautical Collection of Canada began as an experiment in 1964 by displaying the combined aircraft etc of the R.C.A.F., Canadian War Museum and the National Aviation Museum in three World War II hangars at the historic Rockcliffe site. The arrangement was so well received by the public that it has continued as a permanent collection under a co-operative arrangement among the three founding agencies. In the Spring of 1967 it became part of the newly-formed National Museum of Science and Technology, Ottawa. Some machines and other exhibits are rotated between the four locations and are here; marked (r) for Rockcliffe Air Station, North Ottawa (u) Uplands Airport; (w) War Museum, Sussex Drive,

Avro CF-100 (North Bay)

Ottawa; (st) National Museum of Science & Technology, 1867 St. Laurent Boulevard, Ottawa. On display (or in store) as at 1st June, 1973:— *A.E.A. Silver Dart No 2 (replica)* constructed in 1958 and flown Baddeck, Nova Scotia 23 Feb 1959 by W/Cdr Paul Hartman on 50th anniversary of J. A. D. McCurdy's first sustained controlled flight by a British subject at any place in the British Empire. He flew the 35 hp biplane half-a-mile over frozen Bras d'Or Lake, Baddeck Bay. The replica has a Continental engine. (r). *A.E.A. Silver Dart No 3 (replica)* a non-flying reproduction, also constructed by RCAF, Trenton, 1958, with reproduction of Curtiss

A.E.A. Silver Dart—replica (Rockcliffe)

Avro 504K G-CYFG and Museum (Rockcliffe)

A.E.A. Silver Dart—replica (Ottawa)

A.E.G. GIV (Rockcliffe)

V-8 (st). *Allgemaine Elektricitäts Gesellschaft A.E.G. GIV* 574/18 with two 180 hp Mercedes. Shipped to Canada in SS Venusia 28 May 1919, restored CFB Trenton 1968/9; 180 Mercedes to be replaced by 260 hp when possible (r). *Aeronca C-2* CF-AOR c/n 9 ex N525V. Purchased 1967 and flown Rockcliffe June 1967 with fin & rudder of C-3. *Airspeed Consul* G-AIKR c/n 4338, with two Armstrong Siddeley Cheetah 10; 1946 Conversion of RAF Oxford PK286. Purchased 1965 for restoration as Oxford, now stored Rockcliffe. *Auster VI* ex CF-KBV c/n 2576 ex RCAF 16652; purchased 1965, repainted VF582 (RAF) in markings of Capt. P. J. A. Tees when winning DFC in Korea (w). Note the *real* VF582 became instructional airframe 7595M. *Avro Avian IVM* CF-CDQ c/n R3/CN/314, originally RCAF 134; RCAF Stores Depot 1930, re-allotted Camp Borden 23 April 1930, Moose Jaw Flying Club 1932, Winnipeg Flying Club 1935. Donated 1968 from estate of Charles Graffo. Fuselage built Manchester, all other components by Ottawa Car Mfg Co Ltd. Stored, Rockcliffe. *Avro 504K* G-CYFG purchased from J. H. C. Palen, Rheinbeck, 1966. Restored as CAF/RCAF a/c at Trenton, previously N8736R/A1958 but markings in wings indicate A1995 and A1996. Reg'n given by museum. Clerget 9B,130 hp serial 15281. (r). *Avro 504K* G-CYCK believed manufactured Grahame White Aviation Co. Le Rhone 110 hp 8954. Purchased by Major Appleby from Mrs. Jared H. Gallup, Connecticut about 1961,

fuselage rebuilt with new wood by him and sold to RCAF May 1966. Completed at Trenton and flown 1966/67. Restored as G-CYCK of CAF/RCAF but previously flown with serial D8971. Stored Rockcliffe but used in museum's flying displays. *Avro 504K (replica)* G-CYEI reproduction by Trenton, 6RD, based on G-CYFG/G-CYCK and flown 1967 with Le Rhone 110 hp 100779. Stored Rockcliffe. *Avro Anson V* 12518 "CK-D" built McDonald Brothers A/c, Winnipeg, two Pratt & Whitney Wasp Jr. stored 1945/48 then ATC, CEPE, Arnprior, CEPE Uplands, 1948/54. (r). *Avro CF-100 Mk V*—awaiting assignment of machine. *Avro Lancaster X* KB944 built by Victory A/c Ltd Malton, Ontario. To 6 Group, England, no history known, returned Canada June 1945 for storage. To Greenwood, N.S. Jan 1955/1957 then stored. Refurbished as "P" 428 Sqdn. (r). *Bell HTL-6(47G)* 1387 RCN, originally USN 142386. From CFB Shearwater N.S. (st). *Bellanca Pacemaker* CF-ATN c/n 181 ex US NC196N, originally El Paso Air Services, Texas, then Alaska Coastal Ellis Airlines. To be restored with Wright J6-9. (r). *Bleriot XI* built 1911 from Bleriot plans and parts by Jack Hamilton of Pala Alto, Calif. Has Gibson propeller and Elbridge 4 cyl, 2-cyle 60 hp serial 301. Partially restored and in storage Rockcliffe. *Boeing 247D* CF-JRQ c/n 1699 ex NC13318 National Air Transport 1933/4; United Airlines 1934/37; Western Air Express and Pennsylvania Central Airlines 1937. CF-BQS Canadian Govt

A.E.G. GIV (Rockcliffe)

Dept of Munitions 1940; 7638 RCAF 1940/42; CF-BVX Quebec Airways 1942/43; Canadian Pacific 1943-45; NC41809 Macquire Industries 1945, "Zigzag" Airways 1948; Central Aircraft, Yakima, Washington about 1956; CF-JRQ California Standard Oil of Calgary 1959/64 (rebuilt); W. B. Patrick (sec. Chevron Standard) about 1961, presented to CNAC 1967 by Standard Oil. Two Pratt & Whitney R-1340 (r). *Bristol Beaufighter TT. 10*, RD867 last of T.F.X batch RD130-867; converted post-war and donated by RAF Museum minus engines, propellers and cowlings, in exchange for Bolingbroke. Outside storage Rockcliffe—to be restored. *Bristol Bolingbroke IVT* 9892 built Fairchild A/c Longueil, Quebec. To ITC, JATP 1942, 4TC 1942, stored from 1944. Donated by Mr. G. Maude. Total hours flown 178.55; two Bristol Mercury XX. (r). *Canadair C-54GM* (CL-2 Mk I) 17515 c/n 122 four R-R Merlin 622s; 426 Sqdn RCAF from 1948, to museum December 1965 (r). *Canadair CL13B Sabre Mk 6* 23651 c/n 1441 ex "Golden Hawks", fuselage partly cut away for display. Orenda 14 engine serial 2066 (st). *Canadair CL 13B Sabre Mk 6* 23455 c/n

Cessna Crane (Rockcliffe)

Canadair CL-2 Mk I (Rocklciffe)

Bellanca Pacemaker (Rockcliffe)

Beaufighter TT.10 (Rockcliffe)

Bolingbroke IVT (Rockcliffe)

Canadair Sabre 6 (Rockcliffe)

Canadair Silver Star 3 (Rockcliffe)

Consolidated Canso II (Rockcliffe)

1245, Orenda 14 2185, in NATO markings of 444 Sqdn (r). *Canadair Silver Star 3* 21574 c/n T-33-574, R-R Nene 10 1427 ex McDonald, 1 AFS, Saskatoon, AFT, Portage, in "Red Knight" markings (r). *Cessna T-50 Crane I* 8676 c/n 2226, ex 4TC, 15 SFTS 1942, No 2TC, Prairie Airways 1943. Stored from 1946 (r). *Consolidated Canso II SR* 11087 c/n CV423, built by Canadian Vickers Ltd, Montreal. Two Pratt & Whitney Wasp. Ex EAC, NWAC, 10RD, ADC Sea Island, 102 CR Trenton, 103 CR, Greenwood. Restored in markings of Flt Lt Hornell VC 162 Sqdn. Stored Rockcliffe. *Consolidated Vultee B-24L Liberator* RCAF serial 11130 allotted,as for 44-50186 AAF, but authentically 44-50154, HE773 from Indian Air Force. Built Ford Motor Co, Michigan. Exchanged for Lysander III (r). *Curtiss JN-4* C227, built Canadian Aeroplanes Ltd Curtiss OX-5 serial M3491. Ex US Army 39158, U.S. civil 111. Purchased 1962 and restored as a/c of 85th Sqdn. (st). *Curtiss HS-2L* G-CAAC c/n A1876, gift to Canadian Govt 1919 from U.S. Navy. Loaned to St. Maurice Forest Protective Assn (a/c named "La Vigilance") then Laurentide Air Services 1920. Crashed on take off Foss Lake 1922, wreck located and salvaged 1968/9. Hull, instruments and tools on display, Rockcliffe, remainder in storage. Wings and tail surfaces of NC652 (formerly AL135 Pacific Marine Airways) to be used. *Curtiss P-40 Kittyhawk* 1076, with Allison F3R 6330/206634; loaned from RAF 1942; to 132 (F) Sqdn, 3TC, 2TC, SR Vulcan. Stored 1945-1964 (r). *Curtiss Seagull* with Curtiss C-6 engine 451. Used by 1924/5 Dr. Hamilton Rice Expedition, Parima River, Brazil. Acquired on loan 1968 from Science Museum, Kensington, for restoration, Rockcliffe. *DH.60 Cirrus Moth* G-CAUA c/n 630 with ADC Cirrus 408; Built de Havilland, England, to International Airways of Canada 1928 (Canadian Airways later). Various owners 1933-42. Donated by C. F. Burke, and rebuilt by de Havilland of Canada employees. Displayed in Uplands Airport Terminal Annexe. *DH.82C Tiger Moth* CF-FGL c/n 724 ex RCAF 4394, purchased from Mr. Bertrand, Montreal In storage Rockcliffe. *DH.82C Tiger Moth II* 4861 c/n 1052; version with Menasco D4 engine 4039/18130; 2 TC Winnipeg 1941, converted to elementary trainer. (r). *DH. Mosquito XXB* KB336 (RAF) two R-R Merlin 33. Built de Havilland A/c of Canada; from RAF 12 June 1944 to WAC, SR Moncton 1945, SR Calgary 1951. (r). *DH. Vampire I* TG372 (RAF) brought to Canada for winterization trials 1946. Wings have been cut. Stored Rockcliffe. *DH. Vampire 3* 17074 (RCAF) ex 1 (F) OTU, 438 Sqdn. DH. Goblin 2 (r). *DHC-1B2 Chipmunk 2* 12070 (18070) c/n 208-246, given CF-CIA for Ferry Flight. Ex Centralia, Dunnville, Mt. View, Portage, Saskatoon 402 CFTSD. Flown Mount View to Rockcliffe 25 April 1972. Stored Rockcliffe. *Douglas C-47 Dakota IV* KN451 (RAF) ex USAF 44-76590; to Canada from overseas 1946 transferred Camp Borden as trainer 1951. To museum 1964. Stored Rockcliffe. *Fairchild PT-26A Cornell II* 10738 c/n FC239 with Fairchild Ranger 6-440-Ct. Built Fleet A/c. With 4TC 1943, then stored Portage (r). *Fairchild FC-2W2* G-CART c/n 128, Pratt & Whitney Wasp "C". Originally US NC6621, Aerial Survey Corpn, Philadelphia. Presented by V. Kauffman. Restored as G-CART (c/n 126) of Canadian Transcontinental Airways (r). *Fairchild 82A* CF-AXL c/n 61, built Fairchild A/c, Longueuil, Quebec. With Starratt Airways and Transportation 1937-41, Canadian Pacific Airlines 1941-47, Ontario Central Airlines 1947-51, then various owners Alberta and Saskatchewan to 1967. Donated by Canadian Pacific Airlines. Displayed Uplands Annexe.

Fairey Battle I(T) R7384 (RAF), with R-R Merlin III 18179/ 14402. Taken on RCAF strength 18 Jan 1941, converted to Gun Battle by fitting turret 20 Dec 1942, to 2 TC (3BGS) St. Res. Preserved in markings of BCATP Gunnery Trainer "35" (r). *Fairey Swordfish*, authentic serial unknown, built Fairey Aviation, Hayes, Middlesex. Bristol Pegasus XXX P36872FA. Purchased from E. Simmons of Tillsonburg, Ont, 1965. Restored in markings of RCN a/c "TH-M" NS122 Mk III. (r). *Fleet Model 2*, built Fleet A/c Ltd, Fort Erie, Ontario, less upper wing and engine, purchased in Ottawa, for restoration—serial to be allotted. Stored Rockcliffe. *Fleet Model 16B Finch* 4510 c/n 408, with Kinner B-5, serial 1777. Built 1940; Central A/c, London, Ont, 1942. Sold in USA and registered NC1327V, purchased by Flt Lt Dr. A. D. McLean and donated to museum, refurbished by 12 Wing (Aux.) (r). *Fleet Model 50K Freighter* CF-BXP c/n 202, minus engine. Salvaged Labrador 1964 ex CF-BJU and RCAF 799, formerly of Labrador Mining and Exploration Ltd, donors of a/c. Wing panel and smaller components from CF-BJW recovered from O'Sullivan Lake by M. L. McIntyre. To be restored—at Rockcliffe. *Fokker DVII* 2071/18 with Hall-Scott L-6 HS94672 (to be replaced by 180 hp Mercedes.) Wings built by Fokker, fuselage original but maker unknown. US regn N1178, lower wing "No 3659 FL No". Purchased

B-24L Liberator (Rockcliffe)

Curtiss JN-4 (Ottawa)

Curtiss JN-4 (Ottawa)

Curtiss Seagull (Rockcliffe)

Fairchild Cornell II (Rockcliffe)

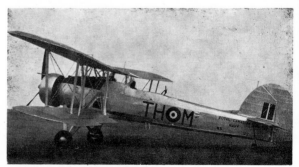

Fairey Swordfish (Rockcliffe)

DH.Mosquito XXB (Rockcliffe)

Fairchild 82A (Ottawa)

Fairchild FC-2W2 (Rockcliffe)

Fairey Battle I(T) (Rockcliffe)

Gibson Twinplane—replica (Rockcliffe)

Hurricane Mk XII (Rockcliffe)

Hawker Sea Fury FB11 (Rockcliffe)

Junkers J1 (Rockcliffe)

Heinkel He 162 A-1 120076 (Rockcliffe)

Junkers J1 (Rockcliffe)

Junkers W 34f/fi (Rockcliffe)

from J. Nissen and Mrs. Mathiesen San José, Cal—used in film "Hell's Angels". Under restoration by J. De Fiore; at Rockcliffe. *Gibson Twinplane (replica)* manufactured by Walker Displays of Vancouver for Department of Transport and used 1969 at Rockcliffe to display museum's original Gibson engine. Now on loan and stored Rockcliffe. *Hawker Hurricane Mk XII* 5584 with Packard Merlin 29 serial 552/19308, built Canadian Car and Foundry Co, Fort William, Ont. 2 TC Nov 1942, WAC, SR Portage, SR 6 RD 1958. (r). *Hawker Sea Fury FB 11* TG119 (RCN) with Bristol Centaurus

XVIIIC serial C87487, of 30th Air Group, RCN Sqdn VF871. Donated by Bancroft Industries (r). *Heinkel He 162 A-1* 109509 with BMW 003. A war prize, to be restored—in store at Rockcliffe. *Heinkel He 162 A-1* 120076 with BMW 003, refurbished in markings of 3JG 77. War prize (r). *Junkers J1* serial 586 Werk-Nr 252 with Benz BZ52974. War prize shipped to Canada in SS Venusia May 1919. Not restored but on display (r). *Junkers W 34f/fi* CF-ATF c/n 2718, with Pratt & Whitney R1340 42-12956. With Canadian Airways from 23 Dec 1932, re-engined with P & W Wasp, 1939 to Central B. C.

Lockheed CF-104 Starfighter (Rockcliffe)

Lockheed 10A (Ottawa)

McDonnell Banshee (Rockcliffe)

Nieuport 12 (Rockcliffe)

Nieuport 17—replica (Rockcliffe)

Messerschmitt Me 163 B (Ottawa)

Airways 1946, Pacific Western Airlines 1957; Pacific Wings, Vancouver 1960. Donated by Mrs. J. A. Richardson, Winnipeg, 1962 (r). *Lockheed CF-104 Starfighter* serial 700 (RCAF) the a/c used to set new Canadian altitude record of 100,110 ft Dec. 1967, pilot Wg Cdr R. A. White. Displayed in that configuration (r). *Lockheed 10A Electra* CF-TCA c/n 1112, two Pratt & Whitney R985 AN-14B. Trans-Canada Airlines 1937, CF-TCA; to Dept Nat'l Defence as RCAF 1526 1939. War Assets to Thunder Bay Flying Club 1946 registered CF-BRD, to Illinois N79237, re-registered N1285 "Lady Alice" 1951 to various owners and back to N79237 1962. Round-world flight to commemorate Amelia Earhart flight of 1937, 7 June-10 July 1967 with pilots Mrs. Ann Pellegreno and Col. W. Payne, navigator W. Polhemus and owner L. Koepke. To Air Canada and back to CF-TCA 1968. Donated to museum 1968 and on display at Annexe of Uplands Airport. *Lockheed 12A* CF-CCT c/n 1219, two Pratt & Whitney Wasp. Flown on first dawn-dùsk flight Montreal-Vancouver 30 July 1937 with pilot J. H. Tudhope, co-pilot J. D. Hunter, engineer Lew Parmenter; passengers Hon C. D. Howe and other Government officials. Donated by Dept of Transport (r). *McDonnell Banshee F2H-3* serial 126464, ex RCN Sqdn VF870—outside storage Rockcliffe. *McDowall Monoplane* with Anzani 25 hp (fan type). In 1910 Robert McDowall, Town Engineer of Owen Sound, Ont. purchased Anzani engine from bankrupt flying school, Long Island, NY, after being inspired by seeing Louis Bleriot's cross-channel Bleriot XI in Europe. Construction began in Ferguson's carriage shop, Owen Sound during 1912 but flight attempts were not made until 1914, at Jack Riddell's farm, north of Annan, Ont. After several unsuccessful attempts to rise more than a few inches McDowall stored the machine. In 1916 he sold to Edward Pratt of Durham, Ont, who used engine, propeller and fuselage, fitted with skis, as ice-scooter to pull skiers and sleds on McLean's Lake, near Durham. A/c then sold to K. G. Hopkinson of Sky Harbour Air Services, Goderich, 1964 and purchased from widow 1967. Stored Rockcliffe for restoring. *Messerschmitt Me 163 B* 191095 with Walter 109.509C. A war prize in storage Rockcliffe. *Messerschmitt Me 163 B* 191916. War prize refinished in markings of 1 JG 400 by Canadian War Museum (w). *Hispano HA-1112-MIL* 471-39 (Spanish AF.) c/n 164 (C4K-114) with R-R Merlin, in storage Rockcliffe for restoration as Bf 109. *Nieuport 12* A4737 (RFC) with Clerget 110 hp 3855. A gift from French Government, in storage Rockcliffe for restoration. *Nieuport 17* (replica) B1566 (RFC) markings of Lt Col W. A. Bishop VC. Aircraft built by C. R. Swanson, Illinois and flown 1967 by Wg Cdr P. A. Hartman. Damaged and restored Trenton. Le Rhone JB 110 hp engine 6202 (r). *Noorduyn Norseman Mk VI* 787 (RCAF) c/n 136 with Pratt & Whitney Wasp R1340-AN 1. Ex

Nieuport 17—replica (Rockcliffe)

Noorduyn Norseman (Rockcliffe)

Harvard II (Rockcliffe)

NA Mitchell (Rockcliffe)

R.A/c Factory B.E.2c (Ottawa)

Sikorsky S51 (Rockcliffe)

Goose Bay, 412,408 Sqdns, 121 C. and R. 1945-1954 (r). *North American Harvard II* 2532 (RCAF) c/n 66-2265; with 3 TC SFTS, 2TC, SR Weyburn, FTS Claresholm, SR Dunnsville, 1940-1962 (r). *NA Harvard II* 3840 (RCAF) c/n 81-4107 with Pratt & Whitney R1340,2096B (instructional). No history recorded. Donated by RCAF 1961— displayed outside Canadian War Museum. *NA Harvard IV* built Canadian Car & Foundry, Fort William. 20387 (RCAF) c/n CCF4-178, with Pratt & Whitney Wasp. Ex Centralia, Lincoln Park, Moose Jaw, Calgary. Stored Rockcliffe. *North American B-25 Mitchell 3 PT* 5244 (RCAF) with two Pratt & Whitney R2600-29A. Turret from NASM, Washington on loan. Nose from Fairey Aviation. Ex TC Trenton, 1952, 2 AOS Winnipeg, CEPE, 6RD 1962. Restored as "D" 98 Sqdn. (r). *North American P-51 Mustang Mk IV* 9298 (RCAF) c/n 122-39806 USAF 44-73347, formerly with Vancouver Auxiliary Sqdn now in markings of 442 Sqdn of 1944 (r). *Northrop Delta* 673 (RCAF) c/n 183 built Can-Vickers Ltd. No engine. Recovered 1969. Ex 8 (BR) Sqdn 1937 —lost flying Ottawa-Sydney Sept 1939. First RCAF war casualties. Found 40 miles N. of Fredericton N.B. Crew never found, stored Rockcliffe for rebuild. *Piasecki HUP 3* 116623 (RCN) with Continental R-975-46. Ex Royal Canadian Navy. Stored Rockcliffe. *Pitcairn PCA-2* NC2624 c/n 8 with Wright R-975E-2 originally loaned from CAHA, Hebron, Conn, but now bought from them. To be restored as CF-ARO at Rockcliffe. *Royal A/c Factory B.E.2c* 4112 (RFC) built British & Colonial Aeroplanes Co, with RAF 1a engine. The a/c in which 2nd Lt F. Sowrey shot down Zeppelin L.32 at Billericay, Essex 24 Sept 1916. His son, AV-M F. B. Sowrey CB, CBE, AFC, is serving still; donating the original propeller (w). *Sikorsky S51/H5* 9601 (RCAF) c/n 5118 with Pratt & Whitney R985-AN-5 serial 21954. Ex CAC Trenton, 9(T) Rockcliffe, K Flt Edmonton, 6 RD,CJAC Rivers, Cold Lake, Chatham. 1947-59. Stored Rockcliffe. *Sikorsky HO4S-3* 55877 (RCN) with Wright R-1300 Canadian Armed Forces Navy Rescue Helicopter "Shearwater Angel". Donated to museum 1970 (r). *Sopwith Camel 2F.1* N8156 (RNAS) with Clerget 130 hp 9E,3941. Built Hooper & Co. At Camp Borden 1928, restored by C. R. Swanson, Sycamore Ill 1966/67 and flown 1967 by Wg Cdr P. A. Hartman. (w). *Sopwith Snipe 7F.1* E6938 (RAF). Built Ruston Proctor & Co with B.R.2A serial 50131, tested 22 Sept 1918. Imported USA 1926 by Reginald Denny for movies. To Los Angeles Museum to 1950. Restored and flown by Jack Canary 1953/61 and loaned USAF Museum. Purchased by Canadian War Museum 1963. First flight Canada 21 May 1964 by Wg Cdr P. A. Hartman at Rockcliffe. Flown

Camel (above) and Snipe (over Rockcliffe)

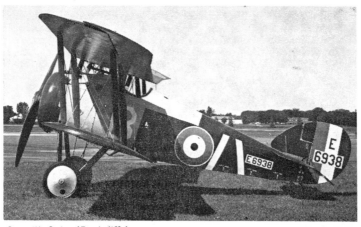

Sopwith Snipe (Rockcliffe)

Sopwith Camel (Ottawa)

Snipe E8107 fuselage (Ottawa)

again 1967. Visited RAF College, Cranwell and Science Museum, 1970. (r). *Sopwith Snipe 7F.1* E8102 (RAF) (fuselage only) built Sopwith Aviation Co Ltd; the machine in which Major W. G. Barker won his V.C. (w). *Sopwith Triplane* N5492 (*replica*) from original drawings; by C. R. Swanson—with Clerget 130 hp 9E,21327. First

Sopwith Triplane—replica (Rockcliffe)

flown 1967 by Wg Cdr P. A. Hartman, Rockcliffe and again 1971 at Rockcliffe & Abbotsford; (r). *SPAD SVII* B9913 RFC c/n 103 built Mann, Egerton & Co, with Hispano-Suiza E 180 hp 5337. To USA after WW I and in Col Jarrett's Museum, Atlantic City during 1930s then sold to Frank Tallman who gave it to J. Rust in return for Pfalz restoration. Sold to J B Petty who restored in markings of SPA.3. Loaned to USAF Museum and sold to CNAC 1965, (r). *Stearman 4EM* CF-AMB c/n 4021 with Pratt & Whitney Wasp SC 2255. Originally a 4E purchased by John Paterson of Thunder Bay, Ont, from Dean Wilson of Idaho. Restored by Nat'l Av'n Museum as CF-AMB (c/n 4016) and test-flown by John Paterson Dec 1969, before presentation by him (r). *Supermarine Spitfire IIB* P8332 with Packard R-R Merlin 29 A3545. A 1941 presentation a/c paid for by State of Soebang, Netherlands East Indies and named "SOEBANG (N.E.I.)" With 222 Sqdn 1941/2. To TC Mountain View 7 May 1942 then 2 TTS Camp Borden 1947, used as instructional A166 and 166B. Was painted "SO-P" 145 Sqdn "Boron" but will be returned to "SOEBANG (N.E.I.)", (st). *Spitfire LF IX* NH188 "AU-H" with R-R Merlin 76 serial 189703. With

Sopwith Triplane—replica (Rockcliffe)

SPAD SVII (Rockcliffe)

Spitfire LFIX (Rockcliffe)

Stearman 4EM (Rockcliffe)

Spitfire LFIX (Rockcliffe)

Spitfire IIB (Ottawa)

Westland Lysander III (Rockcliffe)

308 (Polish) and 416 (RCAF) Sqdns 1944. To Netherlands Army Air Force 1947 as H-64, to Belgian Air Force 1952 as SM39, sold to COGEA, registered OO-ARC, 1956, bought by John Patterson, restored as CF-NUS and flown in 421 (Red Indian) Sqdn colours. Donated by him to museum and last flown 6 June, 1964. (r). *Spitfire XVI* TE214 with R-R Merlin 266 serial 563413. Central Gunnery School, Leconfield, Yorks, 1945, displayed Ternhill 1956 as TE353 "DN-T". Loaned to RCAF for B. of B. Display, Ottawa, 1960 and donated by RAF to museum. (w). *Taylor Cub E2* N14735 c/n 142 with Continental A40-4 serial 1256. Registered N14735 October 1934 and to various owners until November 1966. Bought by museum 1971. Stored Rockcliffe. *Travel Air 2000* CF-AFG c/n 720 with Curtiss OXX-6, serial unknown. U.S. Regn C6291 to Canada 1929 and rebuilt Ontario 1930, flown until 1941 when retired due to wartime restrictions. Bought by museum 1968 from Mrs Hopkinson of Goderich. Stored Rockcliffe. *Vickers V.757 Viscount* CF-THI c/n 270, four R-R Dart. Air Canada Fleet No 627, donated by Air Canada November 1969 and displayed outside at Rockcliffe in Trans-Canada Airlines markings. *Fieseler Fi 103 (VI)* with

Argus pulse-jet engine. Acquired 1963 from Montreal Historical Museum. Restored by Canadian War Museum 1966. (w). *Westland Lysander III* (given R9003 (RAF))—wings built by N.C.C. Malton, Ontario. Bristol Mercury XX 24098 engine. Restored with components from three British and Canadian aircraft as Centennial project, CAF Winnipeg under Captain Bernard Lapointe who performed first test-flight 29 Dec 1967, demonstrating a/c at many places. Machine refinished as R9003 which served overseas with 110 Sqdn RCAF in 1939. Presented to CNAC (r). *Boeing M1M-10B Super Bomarc* 60446 c/n 656, with 2 Marquardt RJ43-MA-7 Ramjet, 1 Thiokol XM-51 Rocket Booster (inert). Manufactured 1960—to museum 1972; stored St. Laurent Boulevard. There are also magnificent engines, propellers, aircraft noses etc etc, making this one of the world's top collections—do not miss seeing it. Flying from Ottawa's Uplands Airport:—*Consolidated PBY-5A* CF-JJG c/n 48423 of Spartan A.S. *28-5ACF* CF-MIR c/n 46633 of Geoterrex Ltd. *Harvard IV* CF-PTP c/n CCF4-1 of Nat'l Research Council. *Ercoupe 415C* CF-JZH c/n 72 of 1942 is flown by Wg Cdr Phil Markham once of 604 (County of Middlesex) Sqdn, and friends.

Beech D17S CF-CCA c/n 203 is flown by C. V. Hyderman Ptnrs. *Grumman G-21A Goose* CF-BXR c/n 1059 ex NC2788 by Laurentian Air Services and *CF-MPG* c/n B77 by Royal Canadian Mounted Police Air Division.

OWEN SOUND. Airfield. *Proctor VI* CF-EHF c/n Ae 140, ex X-1 of Percivals; dismantled. *Auster VI* CF-LXT c/n 2590 ex RCAF 16666; Kenneth W. Rowe.

PETERBOROUGH. Displayed on pedestal *Canadair Sabre* erected 1971 by 428 Wing, RCAFA with Trenton's help. Flying here is *Harvard IV* CF-NUQ c/n CCF4-172; P. McIlwain. *Grunau IIB* CF-ZCP c/n 004497; Central Ontario Soaring Assn. *Grunau Baby 28M* with Volkswagen engine CF-PNR c/n 1; M. Offierski.

PICKERING. Airfield. *DH.80A Puss Moth* CF-AVC c/n DHC 225; Bruce N. Smith.

PICKLE LAKE. Airfield. Hooker Air Services:— *Anson V* CF-GIU c/n MDF367; *Bellanca 66-75* (only one flying) CF-BTW c/n 721, with P. & W. Hornet. Total flying time since 1936 over 12,000 hrs and formerly Trans-Air Ltd, Northern Manitoba, Mackenzie Air Services, Canadian Pacific and Central Northern.

PORT ARTHUR. Airstrip. *Harvard AT-6C* CF-MEQ c/n 3167; J. Springer.

PORT CREDIT. Airfield. *Auster VI* CF-LWA c/n 2599 ex RCAF 16671; C. C. Armstrong.

PORT PERRY. Airfield. *Aeronca Super Chief* CF-EXJ c/n 11CC-273; Scugog Aviation.

REDDITT. *Grumman G-21A Goose* CF-IWW c/n 120 Ontario Central Airlines.

RED LAKE. Airfield. Green Airways. *Stinson SR-9FM Reliant* CF-BGN c/n 5702.

REECES CORNER. Highway 7, Pioneer Museum. *Harvard II* serial 2684 in RCAF all-yellow scheme.

REXDALE. Airfield. *Stinson HW-75* CF-BST c/n 7055; R. L. Shore. *PBY-5A* CF-JMS c/n 48287; Questor Surveys.

ROCKWOOD. W. A. Gregg of RR.2 has *NA.64 Yale* serials 3350 and *3390* from estate of Ernie Simmons, for rebuild. Construction nos believed 2206 and 3303.

SCARBOROUGH. Airfield. *Lockheed 12A* CF-EPF c/n 1269 ex NC17397, WPB-1, NC2; F. Oystrick.

SIOUX LOOKOUT. Airport. *Fairchild 24R/46* CF-GZL c/n R46-250; A. Maxwell. *F24K Argus* CF-BRG c/n 3320; A. Guest.

SIOUX NARROWS. Airfield. *Grumman G-21A Goose* CF-HUY c/n B55 ex RCAF 386; Sioux Narrows Airways.

SMITH FALLS. On static display *NA Harvard* RCAF "443". Memorial to 443 Sqdn.

SPRINGFORD. Near Tillsonburg. *Harvard II* RCAF 3140 near "Sunoco" garage.

ST. CATHERINE'S. Airfield. *Ryan ST3-KR* CF-KTD c/n 1676; F. Liddycoat. *Alexander Eaglerock* CF-AAR, to be restored with the regn of an Eaglerock at Barker Field, Toronto pre-war. The owner, Keith Mitchell, has imported this a/c from USA.

ST. MARY'S. Airfield. *DH.82A Tiger Moth* CF-BNF c/n 327 said to be the oldest Canadian built version still flying in Canada; Frank Ball. Nearby at RR.1 with R. Ratcliffe is *NA.64 Yale* serial 3445, for rebuild.

ST. THOMAS. Municipal Airport. *Harvard II* CF-RWN c/n 3830; Hicks & Lawrence Air Services.

STRATFORD. Airfield. *Harvard II* CF-MGI c/n 3275; A. McCann.

STURGEON FALLS. Airfield. *Grumman G-21A* CF-JRV c/n 1389; Field Lumber Co.

TEMAGAMI. Airfield. Lakeland Airways. *Stinson SR-9FM Reliant* CF-BGM c/n 5701.

TILLSONBURG. Airfield. *Howard DGA-15* CF-NWK c/n 896, *CF-OGI* c/n 981; Hicks and Lawrence.

Millardair DC-3s (Toronto)

TORONTO. Island Airport. Austin Airways Ltd said to operate:—*Anson V* CF-HQZ ex RCAF 12477, *CF-IVK* ex RCAF 12082; *CF-JAW* c/n 4274. *Consolidated 28-5AC*

CF-AAD c/n 1658. Also flying here *Harvard II* CF-TSV c/n 3771; Colin Clark and *CF-MTX* c/n 3191 of Stanley Castle. From Malden Airport, Carl Millard of Millardair operates a *Douglas DC-3* fleet of seven, including CF-WIC c/n 11625 ex 42-68698; *CF-WCN* c/n 43082; *CF WCO* c/n 19737; *CF-WGN* ex 44-77036 plus three others; *Beechcraft 18s* including CF-WGP c/n A38; and more modern types. A former senior captain with Trans-Canada, who learned to fly 1935 in an Eaglerock, he is noted for his charter work with Dakotas. In Toronto's Canadian National Exhibition Grounds, Ontario Park, *Avro Lancaster* B.X FM104 built Victory Aircraft, Canada, flown to England for No 6 (Canadian) Group early 1945 and no operations recorded. Flown back June 1945 and refurbished at Trenton for display. Nearby in the new Exposition Area *Spitfire PR.XIX* PM627, which was HS964 at Palam, India ex 101 (PR) Sqdn, IAF. Now owned by Toronto City authorities. In the city's Centennial Centre of Science is *Avro CF-100* serial 11525. Ontario Place, along the waterfront may be exhibiting Bob Diermert's *Val* (see Carman, Manitoba) although it is said it could go to CNAC, Ottawa, in time. What can now be added is that it came from the Island of Ballale, British Solomons and was flown from the carrier "Zuikaku" 4th-7th May 1942 in the first major Coral Sea engagement, fought entirely by carrier aircraft. At Buttonville, Toronto, is *Seafire XV* PR503, owned by Canadian Warplanes Heritage, possibly for display in Toronto. It has been reported that a *Fairchild KR-34* biplane belonging to Ontario Department of Lands may be going on show at Toronto City Museum —details please.

TRENTON. Trenton Community Gardens off Highway 2 *Canadair Sabre* 23641 ex "Golden Hawks", presented to Mayor, September 1967.

WATERLOO. Four *NA.64 Yale* a/c ex Tillsonburg being rebuilt.

WESTON. Airfield. *Fleet 16B* CF-GDM c/n 550 of Cliff Glenister and *DHC.1 Chipmunk* CF-DJS c/n 6 (thought the oldest flying) owned by D. M. Shaw. J. De Pippo has *Yale* for rebuild.

WHITBY. Airfield. *Stinson V-77* CF-XND c/n 77-434; M. D. Norwick.

WILLOWDALE. *Stinson 108* CF-DAF from Indiana—now D. MacRitchie.

WINDSOR. Jackson Park Sunken Gardens. *Avro Lancaster B.X* FM212 of 408 (RCAF) Sqdn, flown back from England June, 1945. Coded "CF-S" which is not squadron's wartime code. At Windsor Airport. Don Plumb, enthusiastic preservationist has *Spitfire T.9* TE308 c/n CBAF 4494 ex Irish Air Corps 163 and G-AWGB. Now registered CF-RAF, Don has painted codes "RA-F" and it looks magnificent. He also has *N.A. P-51 Mustang* 44-74850, later N2116 which he plans to register as CF-USA in wartime USAAF colours. We wish him well with his enterprising aviating. *Tiger Moth* CF-CLE c/n 1133 ex RCAF 4942; originally Menasco powered, is also said to be part of this "stable".

WOODSTOCK. Airfield. *Harvard II* CF-MKA c/n 3222; N. Beckham & R. Hewitt.

PRINCE EDWARD ISLAND

SUMMERSIDE. Airport. *Fairchild M62A3* CF-FES ex FV679; J. E. Armstrong. *NA AT-6 Harvard* CF-MGO c/n 0762; N. Clement.

QUEBEC PROVINCE

ASBESTOS. Airfield. *DH.83C Fox Moth* CF-DIW c/n FM22; Eugene Jolin.

BELOEIL. Marcel Dorion has acquired the *Barkley Grow T8P-1* c/n 8 CF-BQM of 1940 ex Midwest Airlines, Winnipeg, apparently to be used for charters in James Bay region. Photo and details wanted.

DRUMONDVILLE. Airfield. *Rearwin 185* CF-PBB c/n 1617; G. Gagne.

JETTE. Airfield. Aerial Photography Cooperate *Beech AT-11 Kansan* CF-JNW c/n 4616 and *CF-LFW* ex 42-37627. *Auster VI* CF-KBW c/n 2579 ex RCAF 16655; and *CF-LPA* c/n 2853 ex RCAF 16675 also reported here with Quebec Soaring Club.

KIPAWA. Kipawa Air Services. *Stinson SR-10F* CF-FBB c/n 5905.

KNOWLTON. Brome County Historical Society. *Fokker DVII.A1b* 6810/18, considered one of the finest examples in the world.

Spitfire T.9 (Windsor)

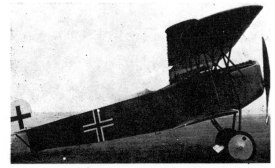

Fokker DVII (Knowlton)

LACHINE. Airfield. *Fleet 16B* CF-FUL c/n 4738; R. Allen & F. Deveaux.

LAVAL. Airfield. *Stinson HW-75* CF-BPI c/n 7246; G. Doucet.

MONTREAL. Dorval Airport. At the College of Aviation *Avro CF-100 Mk 3* serial 18172 said in use for instruction. Flying from here:—*Lockheed 18 Lodestar* CF-TDG c/n 2465; *CF-EAE* c/n 2291 ex 42-32201; both with Execaire Aviation. *Lockheed PV-1 Ventura* CF-MFL c/n 4676; Canadian Inspecting & Testing Ltd. *Curtiss C-46* CF-CZM c/n 22453 ex 44-78630 N48794V; Nordair Ltd—understood for preservation. With No 737 Sqdn, Air Cadets is said to be a *Vickers Vedette* undergoing restoration—more details please. Also with F. D. Emmorey 1060 University St, *Westland Lysander III* 2346 but confirmation unobtainable. Inrormation wanted.

POINT DU MOULIN. Airfield. *Stinson HW-75* CF-CHH c/n 7261.

QUEBEC. Airport. *Travel Air E-4000* CF-JLW ex N9953 c/n 1151 of 1929 is now fully restored by Captain J. Wendel Reid, a senior airline pilot. Well done!! *DH. 82C* CF-FDZ c/n DHC.1179 ex RCAF 5876 is with Quebec Soaring Club. *Lockheed 18* CF-SYV c/n 2273 and *CF-XHA* c/n 2238, both with Lacie de Photog. Aer Ltee. *Consolidated PBY-5A* CF-PQF c/n CV333; *CF-PQK* c/n 9830; *CF-PQL* c/n CV417; *CF-PQM* c/n CV245; *CF-PQO* c/n CV427; *CF-PQP* c/n 11079—all with Dept of Transport and Communications. *NA.Harvard II* CF-HWX formerly AJ583, RAF; J. Cowan. *Falrchild FM62A3* CF-ILA c/n FC110; Bedard & Hayeur; *CF-KAL* c/n 10512; Houghton & Langford.

ROXBORO. Evergreen Air Service. *Grumman TBM-3* CF-IMX c/n 86098; *CF-IMR* c/n 53610; *CF-IMW* c/n 85928; *CF-IMV* c/n 85665; let us hope some are preserved when flying ends. Messrs. Kelly & Cousinau have *Culver V* CF-EHG c/n V.74.

ST. GEORGES de BEAUCE. Airfield. *Rearwin 185* CF-XHZ c/n 1876; B. Poulin.

ST. JEAN. College Militaire Royale. *Avro CF-100* 19746 mounted. At Canadian Forces Recruit Depot on display:—*Avro CF-100-2T* 18104 "PX104" training serial 611B. *Canadair Sabre* 19118 training serial 593B. *Canadair Silver Star* (T-33) 14678, training 599B "678" *Canadair Sabre* coded "131" serial wanted.

ST. JOSEPH de BEAUCE. Airfield. *Cessna C-50 Crane* CF-DMD c/n 5285; F. Cloutier.

ST. JOVITE STATION. Wheeler Airlines. *Consolidated 28-5AC* CF-ILK c/n 464. *PBY-5A* CF-DFB c/n 605, ex TF-RVG.

ST. LAURENT. *Beechcraft D17S* CF-BJD c/n 201; *CF-EKA* c/n 4813; both with Ronald Uloth. *Stinson 10 Voyager* CF-LUY c/n 7957; P. Mandryk.

TROIS RIVERS. Airfield. St. Maurice Air Transport. *Cessna C-50 Crane* CF-HAD c/n 3838 ex 44-70363.

TWEEN RIVERS. Airfield. *Fairchild M62A3* CF-ECH c/n A131; E. Brazil and V. Bolger.

VALD'OR. Airfield. *Monocoupe 90-AF* CF-JGA c/n 861, believed undergoing rebuild. Details please.

Canadair Silver Star (St. Jean)

SASKATCHEWAN

ASSINIBOIA. Airfield. *Harvard IV* CF-VIR c/n CCF4-125; H. Whereatt.

DINSMORE. Airfield. *Harvard IV* CF-WXY c/n CCF4-255; G. Nelson.

DRINKWATER. Airfield. *Harvard IV* CF-WWM c/n CCF4-110; B. Cornea.

ELBOW. Airstrip. *Harvard IV* CF-VYF c/n CCF4-; Arthur Knutson.

KINDERLEY. Airfield. *Harvard IV* CF-VIJ c/n CCF4-173; D. M. McTaggart.

LA LOCHE. Airfield. *Bellanca 35-55A* CF-DCE c/n 32; C. & M. Airways. *Harvard IV* CF-VCM c/n CCF4-8; R. M. Ruelling.

LEADER. *Funk B85C* CF-HAR c/n 311; L. P. Nagel.

MAIDSTONE. Airfield. *Stinson HW-75* CF-DLM c/n 7087; E. Lundell.

DH.Humming Bird—replica (Moose Jaw)

MEADOW LAKE. *Harvard IV* CF-UJI c/n CCF4-88; L. M. Ruelling.

MOOSE JAW. Canadian Forces Base. *Harvard IV* 20456 mounted on plinth and coded "456". It is scrubbed by students whenever their misdeeds are frowned upon by authority. Stretches of good-conduct, however, have allowed other fliers to nest and raise young behind the airscrew. Now flying here at the local airport is *DH.53 Humming Bird (replica)* CF-OVE c/n DH.6063. built by Stan Green of Calgary. Now owned by Ronald G. Davidson. *Harvard IV* CF-XJC c/n CCF4-58 owned and flown by R. Elliott.

NORTH BATTLEFORD. Airfield. *Harvard IV* CF-RUJ c/n CCF4-64; H. Jaeger.

PRINCE ALBERT. Airfield. *Consolidated PBY-5A* CF-IDS ex Bu11629, N74680; *CF-IZO* ex Bu46645; North Canada Air Ltd. Pine Trees Soaring Club *Grunau II glider* 3 CF-ZBT c/n 468950.

REGINA. Airport. *WACO YKS-7* CF-KYI c/n 4615; L. J. McKenna.

SASKATOON. Western Development Museum. *Pheasant H-10* G-CASR c/n 121, ex NC5411, built Memphis, Missouri 1927; purchased 1928 by Norman Cherry, Cherry Airways, flown to Saskatoon. Force-landed 1931, dismantled and stored. Rebuilt by 406 (City of Saskatoon) Auxiliary Sqdn, RCAF. From the airport *Fairchild F24/W46* CF-SFU c/n W46-299; G. T. Thompson & N. Menzies. *Harvard IV* CF-RFS c/n CCF4-116 of Ray's Flying Service.

ST. LOUIS DE TERREBONNE. Airfield. *Harvard IV* CF-WPS, c/n CCF4-46; J. M. Brandin.

YUKON TERRITORY

WHITEHORSE. Airport. *Fairchild F24R/46A* CF-FVR c/n W46-291; M. Grant and W. Whittaker.

UNITED STATES OF AMERICA

ALABAMA

ATMORE. Displayed. *Lockheed T-33A* 51-8604

BAYOU LA BATRE. Displayed. *Lockheed T-33A* 51-6794

BIRMINGHAM. National Guard Station. Displayed. *Republic F-84F-15-RE Thunderstreak* 51-1487; *NA F-86D/L Sabre* 51-2993 and *52-4243.*

BROOKLEY. Air Force Base. *Republic F-105B-1-RE Thunderchief* 54-0102.

CLANTON. Airfield. *DH. Tiger Moth* N5300 c/n 83424 ex T5703, G-AMES; M. V. Love.

DOTHAN. Airport. *Boeing B-17* N3701G ex 44-8543; and *N5017N* ex 44-85740; Dothan Aviation Corp.

FLORALA. Displayed. *Lockheed T-33A* 53-4938.

Bell XH-40 (Fort Rucker)

FORT RUCKER. Near Ozark. U.S. Army Aviation Museum. Visiting hours 0900-1600 Monday-Friday: 1300-1700 Saturday, Sunday and Holidays (closed Christmas). Exhibits Curator, Jim Craig. Founder Brigadier General Carl I. Hutton—to tell the story of Army Aviation. Admission free, photography encouraged, parking free. In addition to aircraft (only half of which can be currently displayed at one time) there are in-sequence galleries of mangificent exhibits. The aircraft:—*Aeronca L-16A* 47-924 c/n 001 ex N6408C of the Utah Wing, Civil Air Patrol. *American Helicopter (Fairchild) XH-26 Jet Jeep* serial 50-1840, prototype. *Beech L23A Seminole* painted 21700 but thought 52-1800. *Bell H-13B Sioux* 48-827 with 4-wheel landing gear. *Bell H-13B Sioux* 48-845 (may be out on loan.) *Bell H-13D Sioux* 51-2468. *Bell OH-4A* 62-4201 c/n 001. *Bell XHU-1 Iroquois* 55-4459 c/n 001. *Brantley B-2 (YHO-3-BR)* 58-1496 c/n 9. *Cessna L-19A Bird Dog* 50-1327; first L-19 for US Army, used Korea by General Eisen-

Helio-Courier (Fort Rucker)

McCullough YH-30 (Fort Rucker)

hower. *Cessna U-20A (195)* 51-6998. *Cessna YH-41 Seneca* 56-4244, the only Cessna helicopter. *Curtiss-Wright VZ-7AP* 58-5508—only one built. *DHC L-20A Beaver* 52-6135. *Del Mar DH-1A* c/n 002, no serial, with hoverplatform. *Helio YL-24HE Courier* 52-2540—the only L-24 accepted by US Army. *Hiller H-23A Raven* 51-3975; tricycle gear, with litters. *Hiller YH-32 Hornet* 55-4965 c/n 8. *Hiller (FH1100) OH-5A* 62-4206. *Hiller XROE-1* 54-004 c/n 3. (serial believed incorrect.) *McCullogh (MC-4C) YH-30* 52-5837 c/n 003. *McDonnell XV-1 Convertiplane* 53-4016, one of two built. *Piper L-4B(r) Grasshopper* 42-15174. *Piper L-18C Super Cub* 52-2536 ex N555X. *Piper TL-21A-PI Super Cub* 51-15782. *Piasecki H-25A Army Mule* 51-16616, *Ryan L-17A Navion* 47-1344. *Ryan VZ-3RY Vertiplane* 56-6941; only one built. *Sikorsky YH-18A (S-52)* 49-2888. *Sikorsky UH-19D Chickasaw* 55-5239. *Sikorsky XH-39 (S-59)* 49-2890 one of two built—world's first turbine-powered helicopter. *Vertol CH-21C Shawnee* 56-2040. *Vultee-Stinson L-5G* 45-34985. *Vultee-Stinson L-5 Sentinel* 42-99103 (formerly painted 44-17582 in error). *Hughes OH-6A Cayuse* 62-4813, 13th production and holder of 23 world records. *Sikorsky CH-34A Choctaw* 53-4526. *Lockheed VC-121B Constellation* NASA-422; was 48-613, General McArthur's a/c "Bataan" Korea. Then NASA in Pacific until 1966. Flown from Baltimore. *Sikorsky R-4B* 43-46521 (not believed authentic) loaned by USAF Museum

Sikorsky XH-39 (Fort Rucker)

MIL-4 Hound (Russian helicopter). Now that the Vietnam contribution has been withdrawn a permanent Army Aviation Memorial will be erected here and one hopes that all interested in what Army fliers have done will make a visit.

Hiller YH-32 Hornet (Fort Rucker)

GULF SHORES. *Northrop F-89D Scorpion* 51-443 displayed.

HUNTSVILLE. Alabama Space & Rocket Centre; open seven days a week. Many audience-participation exhibits and free wide-screen cinema. Largest collection of rockets in the world:—*A-4 rocket (V2); N. American A-1 Hermes; Chrysler Juno II; Jupiter Booster; Chrysler Jupiter C; Saturn 1; Chrysler Mercury-Redstone; Chrysler Saturn V* (Apollo moon rocket) *Chrysler SM-78; Jupiter IRBM; Chrysler XSM-A-14 Redstone; Ford JB-2,* unknown serial (found in Mount Vernon, Indiana) *North American AGM-28A Hound Dog* 60-2110 (loan from USAFM) Borman & Lovell's *Gemini VII; Bell X-1B* 48-1385 (loan from USAFM) high-speed research, carried to launching altitude under "mother" plane, first powered flight 8 Oct 1954, Flying from Huntsville:—M. D. Edwards *DH. Tiger Moth* N8879 c/n 83098 ex R5239, G-ANVV, OO-ACI, PH-NLC; *WACO QDC* NC11470 c/n 3513 of R. F. Johnson, AAA. At Redstone, Huntsville, *Douglas C-47A* 43-15688.

MAXWELL. Air Force Base, Darque Hall. *Northrop T-38A-15-NO Talon* 59-1601 c/n N3114 (USAFM loan).

Bell X-1B (Huntsville)

Convair F-102A and Bomarc (Anchorage)

MOBILE. USS Alabama, Battleship Commission Park. *Chance-Vought OS2U Kingfisher* "60" Bu 0951 ex Mexican Air Force, rebuilt Brookley AFB as memorial to all who flew the type or who served in this battleship; a wheeled version with Grumman floats. Parked nearby:—*Douglas C-47B-DK Skytrain* 44-76326 ex Blytheville, Arkansas. *Vertol CH-21B-PH Workhorse* 51-15859 from USAF, Homestead, Florida. *Vought F4U-7 Corsair* Bu 133704, from NAS, Pensacola, in USMC colours. *NA P-51D-NA Mustang* 44-74216, painted in General Chenault's "Flying Tigers" marks and (like the CH-21B and C-47D) loaned from USAFM. It is hoped to acquire an Avenger, Hellcat, "Rex" and, with luck, a Seafire for this excellent display owned and operated by the State. *Lockheed T-33A* 53-6123 reported at Mobile—location wanted. At a "Duster Strip" 91st Ave/Indian School Rd, Bob Bean said to have 8 *Corsairs* and a *Lockheed 10*.

MONTGOMERY. Airport. *Republic RF-84F-20-RE Thunderstreak* 52-7249; *NA F-86 Sabre* 53-566 and *53-806*. On Highway 80 *Sabre F-86K* 53-847 is exhibited. *F-86L* 53-973 also reported.

ROBERTSDALE. *T-33A* 51-9104 on show.

RUSSELLVILLE. *Lockheed T-33A* 51-6554 displayed.

SELMA. *T-33A* 51-6707 on display.

TUSCALOOSA. *T-33A* 53-5109 displayed. Exact locations of all these individual aircraft—with photos—appreciated.

ALASKA

ANCHORAGE. Transport Museum. So far believed on show:—*WACO Model UIC* of 1933 N13409 c/n 3756—on floats. *Fairchild 24G* N19121 c/n 2981—on wheels. *Stinson SR-JR* of 1933 —reg'n wanted. *Fairchild 71* NC119H c/n 657 of 1929—a legendary aeroplane in Alaska, used by Bob Reeve to pioneer many present routes. Fitted with special wide wooden skis for snow, mud and ice. *Stinson SR-6 Reliant* N15135 c/n 9637 of 1935.Nose section of a JN-4 recovered from Nome. Rest-

oration continuing on 1939 Aeronca and other airframes. At the adjacent International Airport, Anchorage, reported:—*C-47A* 43-15200 and *Convair F-102A Delta Dagger* 56-1282 (ex 317 FIS Alaskan Air Command) are preserved. Also *Boeing CQM-1Q Bomarc* missile 59-2028. US Coast Guard *Grumman J2F-6 Duck* 794 reported—confirmation wanted. Flying from the civil airport here said to be:—*Curtiss C-46* N10012 c/n 33271 and *Lockheed 10A Electra* N1986R c/n 2007, ex ZK-CLX of Air New Zealand, both with Reeve Aleutian. Photos and confirmation please. *Boeing YL-15 Scout* N4770C c/n 20012 ex 47-432 static & privately-owned.

ELMENDORF. Air Force Base. *Fieseler Fi 103 (V1)* in original markings was said to be here—news please.

HOMER. Airfield. *Travel Air S6000B* N9084R, believed here with Bill de Creeft.

ARIZONA

APACHE JUNCTION. Legion Post, on pole, *T-33A* 56-6008.

BUCKEYE. Municipal Airport. *Stearman PT-17* Cropdusters N1263N c/n 75-5316, *N49666* c/n 75-2023, *N56058* c/n 75-901,and *N9484*.

CASA GRANDE. Airport. *Northrop JF-89C Scorpion* 51-5776 at entrance, said to be dilapidated. *Stearman C-3* N787H c/n 6002 cropdusting.

CHANDLER. City Park. *NA F-86D Sabre* 51-6261 (tail 52-10115). Flying from airport. *Navy N3N* cropdusters N4515, *N44814* c/n 4447, *N9831Z* c/n 2960, *N45255* c/n 2864. *Stearmans PT-17s* N9147Z c/n 75-3109, N9146Z c/n 75-3117, N48765 c/n 75-2931, N68164 c/n 75-7281, N9834H, c/n 75 -7192.

DOUGLAS. *Lockheed T-33A* 52-9608 displayed.

GLENDALE. Airport. *NA B-25J Mitchell* N9877C ex 44-29145 owned and flown by C. R. Crowe. *Stearman 4D* N11724 c/n 4026 of Rex Williams.

GLOBE. *NA F-86D/L Sabre* 51-5915 displayed.

MARANA. Air Park. On Phoenix-Tucson Road, US Forestry Service. *Lockheed P-2H* tanker N126Z ex Bu 124904 (only one) *NA T-28 Trojan* N132Z ex Bu 137645, *T-34* N144Z c/n BG-160, *N183Z*, c/n BG-168. *Boeing B-17* N809Z ex 44-83785 marked "C 71" Up-dated news of condition, please.

MESA. Pioneers Park, *Grumman F9F-5 Panther* 125316. At Falcon Field. near Phoenix. Cropdusting—Aero Specialities (Borate bombing) operate the following—*Boeing B-17* N17W ex 42-29782, *N620L* ex 44-85840, *N621L* ex 44-85774, *N9139G*, *N9563Z* c/n 83563—with another (perhaps N93012 ex 44-82575 unregistered, for spares. Histories wanted. *NA B-25* N9117Z ex 44-29199, N6123C ex44-86893. *Douglas A-26* N9163Z ex 44-34659, N3328G *Lockheed Lodestar* N34E c/n 2082. *Lockheed PV-2 Harpoon* N6718C ex 151415, *N6852C* ex 151456, *N7270C*. *Grumman TBM-3* N9590Z ex Bu 91733, N9926Z, N9927Z ex Bu 85869, N7219C, ex Bu 86280. Also here flying/static:—*NA AT-6* N8218E, N1467 c/n CCF4-270, N17400 c/n CCF4-252. *L1049H Super Constellation* N173W. c/n 4674 ex YV-C-AMI, N9746Z. *Sabre*—unreg (52-3504 perhaps). *Beech 17* N1083B. *Douglas A-26C Invader* N52NM c/n 1302. *Canadair Sabre 6.* 23504. *Stearman PT-17* N51440 c/n 75-7163. N55987, c/n 75-247, N56940, c/n 75-725, N1311N, c/n 75-5779, N70074 c/n 75-3404 (cropduster).

MOHAVE. County Airport. At entrance *Lockheed Super Constellation* N45515 c/n 4843 ex PH-LKN.

MOSELEY. Airfield. West of Phoenix. *Vought F4U-4 Corsair* 97142, *97264, 97330, 97349, 97359, 97389, 97390*, reported here ex Olathe or Seattle NAS—details of disposal welcomed.

PEDRIA. Airfield. *WACO VKS7* N2309 c/n 5239 flying.

PHOENIX. Flying from International Airport:—*Meyers OTW* N26483 c/n 36, a former WW II trainer—serial and history please. *St. Louis YPT-15* N67328 ex *AAF* 40-6 c/n 106 with Pratt & Witney 450 hp reported.

BISBEE-DOUGLAS. Airport. *PV-2 Harpoon* N7080C c/n 15-1465, *N685C* c/n 15-1156, *N7261C* c/n 1173 ex Bu 37107, *N7263C* c/n 1247, ex Bu 37281 (chance for museums?)

PHOENIX-LITCHFIELD. Municipal Airport offers:—*Douglas B-18 Bolo* N66267 ex Roberts A/c, Boise, Idaho—airworthy? If not, should be saved. Also *Nor can FJ-3 (F-1C) Fury* 135883; *Grumman F9F* 141675; *NA B-25 Mitchell* N87Z; *Bell H-13 Siou F-86D Sabre* 51-6071; *Douglas B-26* N4819E ex 44- and *N4827E*, with *Beech JRB-6* N9256 ex 39957, are to be assembled for the *Global Air Museum*, forming . 1973—further details of serials, histories, and photos please, with exact final location. Also here *Consolidated PBY-5A Super Catalina* N2763A, c/n 21232, ex Alaska Airlines. Sanders Airport, Phoenix has a *Stinson V-77 Reliant* N69395, c/n 77-477. *Navy N3N* cropdusters N45283 c/n 2623, *N45306* c/n 1998, *N45117* c/n 1780, *N45184* c/n 2837, *N45043* c/n 2716, *N45299* c/n 4445, *N45106* c/n 1801. Near the Goodyear airfield, was *NA F-86D/L Sabre* 53-763.

RYAN FIELD. West of Tucson 15 miles. *Columbia XJL-1* and *Standard J-1* being rebuilt—details please.

SCOTTSDALE. *Perth-Amboy Bird A* N88K c/n 1050, restoration. *Lockheed T-33A* 53-5915 displayed.

TUCSON. International Airport. *Lockheed F-94C Starfire* 51-5623; *Republic F-84F* 51-1637 (dismantled) *Lockheed T-33A* 51-8676 and *53-5917. Douglas A-26 Invader* 44-35858, 44-45808, 44-35994, 44-34642, 44-35901, 44-35267, 44-35372, 44-355411, 44-35867, 44-34153, 43-22877, 44-22559, 44-35880, 44-35357, 44-35365, 43-22730, 44-211, 44-34736, 44-35671, 44-34581, 44-35385, 44-34612, 44-35637, 44-35609, 44-35860 and N91317 ex 41-39398. It would be nice if one, at least could be displayed in Europe! Also here. *Fairchild C-82 Packet* 44-23009, 44-23005, 44-23033. *Boeing KC-97G* 53-0307, 53-3816, 53-0208, 53-0224, 53-0218, 53-0240, 53-0282, 53-0285, 53-0289. David Kubista has *DH.98 Mosquito PR-41* VH-WAD ex A52-210 then A52-319 "The Quokka" ex Perth, W. Australia. At the Davis-Monthan Air Force Base, the Military Aircraft Storage and Disposition Center had 6,000 aircraft in March, 1973, with many more expected as the Vietnam fighting ended. In 3/5,000 acres of open storage (only 11 inches of rain a year) there should always be around 50 different types. Mr. L. Railing, Office of Information will provide-up-dated details to clarify the position insofar as USAF Museum aircraft, Pima County Air Museum Aircraft, and straightforward stored aircraft are concerned. Space does not permit complete listing but the following are held on behalf of USAF Museum: —*NA F-100C Super-Sabre* "Discovery" 54-1823. *Boeing*

Boeing 707 prototype (Tucson)

WB-50D Superfortress 49-351. *Convair B-58A Hustler* 61-2080. *Douglas RB-66B Destroyer* 53-466. *Douglas C-133B Cargomaster* 59-527. *Sikorsky R-6A* serial unknown. *Lockheed X-7 Ramjet* missile—serial unknown. *Lockheed X-17* nose-cone re-entry research vehicle (26 built). *Boeing 707* prototype N70700 "Dash Eighty" is held here for the National Air & Space Museum, Washington, DC. One of the 12 most significant a/c of all time (quote). Model 367-80, first flown 15 July 1954. At the adjoining site, the *Pima County Air Museum* —organized in 1966 by a group of local businessmen (most of them ex-Air Force) purchased a parcel of 320 acres of land, with County backing, from funds provided by the Tucson Air Museum Foundation, a non-profit activity organized to operate this museum for the County. The land adjoins Davis-Monthan on the south and is readily accessible from a recently-completed freeway. As funds become available aircraft will be moved across the base and on to this land, to provide the best and largest museum west of Wright Field. The following is the 1973 listing and of these aircraft some will, obviously, remain at Davis-Monthan for a little time but, eventually, will be the focal point of a 275-acre regional park with large machines in the open and smaller types, with interesting displays, within a modern museum building. First let us list loaned USAF Museum Aircraft:—*Douglas RB-23* (UC-67) *Dragon* 39-51 c/n 2737 ex N534J. *NA TB-25N Mitchell* 43-27712, of 10th A.F., c/n 108-34725. *DB-26C Invader* 43-22494, ex Holloman ADC. *Boeing TB-29 Superfortress* 44-70016 c/n 10848, ex 4715th REVRON (ECM) *NA.AT-28E Trojan* 0-13788, Survivor of two COIN turboprop conversions. *Republic F-84F* 51-1725. *Boeing EB-47E Stratojet* 53-2135 c/n 44481 from 380th S.W. *Boeing KB-50J Superfortress* 49-0372 from T.A.C., c/n 16148. *Martin EB-57D Canberra* 53-3782. *Douglas WB-66D Destroyer* 55-395, c/n 45027. *Lockheed UC-36A* 42-56638 c/n 1011 ex N4963C, NC14260, NW Airlines. *Curtiss C-46D Commando* 44-77635. *Douglas C-47A Dakota* 41-7723, the 2nd C-47 procured for USAF. *Douglas C-54D Skymaster* 42-72488. *Lockheed C-69 Constellation* 42-94549. c/n 1970 ex N90831 "Star of Switzerland" TWA. *Boeing KC-97G Stratofreighter* 53-151. *Fairchild C-119C Boxcar* 49-0157. *Lockheed VC-121B Constellation*, 48-614, c/n 2606. *Douglas C-124A Globemaster* 49-0236. *Lockheed F-80C Shooting Star* 45-8612 ex Kansas ANG. *Republic F-84F Thunderstreak* 52-6563. *NA F-86H Sabre* 53-1525 ex New Jersey ANG. *NA F-86L* 53-0965. *Northrop F-89J Scorpion* 53-2674. *Lockheed F-94C Starfire* 50-980. *Douglas A-26A* (ex B-26K) 64-17651. *Convair F-102A Delta Dagger* 56-1393. *Sikorsky UH-19D Chickasaw* 56-1559. *Vertol CH-21C Shawnee* 56-2159. *Lockheed P-38L Lightning* 44-53247. *Bell P-63E King Cobra* 43-11727; was N9003R at Phoenix. *Culver* (TD2C-1) *PQ-14B* 44-21819. *Ryan PT-22 Recruit* 41-15736 c/n 1765, was NC54003, N1180C. *NA T-6G Texan* 49-2908 c/n 168-12 (was AT-6B 41-17246 c/n 84-7624). *Grumman HU-16A Albatross* 51-0022 c/n 96. *North American AGM-28A Hound Dog* 59-2866 and 60-2092. United States Naval aircraft on loan:—(Air Force Museum Programme) *Beech UC-45J Expeditor* 39213 "7L" was SNB-2/SNB-5. *Bell* (47K) *TH-13N* 145842. *Kaman OH-43D* 139974 "WB-7" USMC. *NA AF-1E Fury* 139531. *Douglas F3B Demon* 145221 "AK-104" USS "Shangri-La" *Douglas F-6A Skyray* 134748 c/n 10342 *Grumman RF9-J Cougar* 144426 c/n 110 "7X-45"/VMJ-4 Sqdn, USMC. *Grumman F-11A Tiger* 141796 c/n 113 "3L"/VT-26 Sqdn. *Douglas TF-10B Skyknight* 124629

AT-28E Trojan (Tucson)

Grumman Tiger (Tucson)

Douglas Skyraider (Tucson)

c/n 7499 "NJ-196"/VF-121 Sqdn. *Douglas EA-1F Skyraider* 135018 c/n 10095 "GD-703"/VAQ-33 Sqdn. On loan from National Air & Space Museum:—*Boeing FB-5* A-7114 c/n 820 Biplane Marine Corps 1927 fighter. *Martin PBM-5A Mariner* N3190G ex 122071, amphibian, only one known. *Boeing S-307B Stratoliner* N19903 c/n 2003, from Mesa. with Pan American February 1940 "Clipper Flying Cloud", later allocated ZS-BWV. to Haitian A.F. "2003", 1954/57 and restored N9307R '57. *Lockheed R50-5 Lodestar* N15A c/n 2411 ex Bu. 12481 On loan from individuals:—*Douglas B-18A Bolo* N18AC c/n 2505 ex 37-505, XB-LAJ. *Taylorcraft L-2M Grasshopper* N59068 c/n 5714 ex 43-26402. *Fairchild PT-19A Cornell* N53963 c/n T41-613 ex 41-14675. *Piper L-3B Cub* N46067 c/n 13434 ex 43-28413. *Vought FG-1D Corsair* 92085, from Marine Corps Training Ctr. Lincoln, Neb. Donated by US Navy:—*Douglas A3D-1 Skywarrior* (YEA-3A) 130361. *Douglas A4D-2* (TA-4B) *Skyhawk* 142928. *Grumman F9F-8* (TAF-9J) *Panther* 141121. *Grumman F8U-1* (DF-8A) *Bearcat* 144427. *Grumman F11F-1* (F-11A) *Tiger* 141821. Donated by US Army:—*Sikorsky CH-37B* 58-1005. The following are owned by Pima

Liberator (Tucson)

County Museum:—*Consolidated B-24J-90-CF Liberator* 44-44175 formerly HE877 Indian Air Force, KH304 (RAF) flown in as N7866 "Pima Paisano" in stages from Palam. *Vultee L-5B* 44-16907, was N4981V of Arizona Wing Civil Air Patrol. Being rebuilt at Cochise College. *Vultee BT-13A-VU Valiant* 42-42353 c/n 9103 from Tucson High School. *Fairchild Cornell* N1270N ex FC34, RCAF 10530. *Northrop YC-125A Raider* XB-GEY c/n 2521 ex 48-636, from Bisbee-Douglas, Arizona. *WACO ZKS-6* N16523 c/n 4512, being rebuilt by James Davis of EAA. The following are in process of acquisition or loan:—*Cessna AT-17A Crane* N68779 c/n 2472 ex 42-13788, FJ271 of RCAF, CF-GET. *Budd Conestoga RB-1* XB-DUZ, stainless-steel transport; from Bisbee-Douglas airport. *Columbia XJL-1* N54205 ex Bu. 31400. *Howard GH-3 Nightingale* N63592 ex 45022. *Boeing KC-97G Stratofreighter* HB-ILY, flown as C-97G by Balair in Biafran Airlift; formerly 52-2626 c/n 16657. *Lockheed F-94A-1-10 Starfire* 49-2517 c/n 7039 is at present disassembled. A *Douglas A4D-2 Skyhawk* (TA-4B), *Grumman F9F-8 Cougar* (AF-9J) and *Grumman F8U-1* (DF-8A) *Bearcat* will be joining the museum, also *EC-121H Constellation* 53-535 c/n 4350, and *Douglas C-133B Cargomaster* 59-527 c/n 45578. We wish this project the success it so richly deserves and look forward to news of further additions, with photos for the next V. and V.

WILLIAMS. Air Force Base. *F-86E-6 Sabre* 52-2844.

ARKANSAS

BATESVILLE. Airfield. *Stearman PT-17* N75696 c/n 75-8804 of 1943, owned and flown here by Russ Amos and Jack Hopwood.

BLYTHEVILLE. *T-33A 51-8965* displayed.

FAYETTEVILLE. Razorback Field. *Travel Air A6000A* N377M c/n A6A-2003 of 1929 with Bob Younkin, believed

Tiger Moth (Heber Springs)

only one airworthy. Also *Grumman F4F-3* N12371, ex 86750. *Curtiss CW-1 Junior* of 1931.

FORT SMITH. Air National Guard. *F-86D/L* 52-36

GRAVETTE. *T-33A* 53-6073 displayed.

HEBER SPRINGS. *DH. Tiger Moth* N1300D c/n 86582 ex PG685, A-4 (Dutch AF)'from California with B. L. Davidson.

HELENA. *T-33A* 51-8965 displayed.

JONESBORO. *T-33A* 53-5933 displayed.

LITTLE ROCK. Airfield. *Boeing B-47E* 52-595 and *F-86D/L* 52-3653 displayed. Histories wanted.

MAGNOLIA. *T-33A* 51-6678 displayed.

NORTH LITTLE ROCK. *T-33A* 53-5342 displayed.

WILSON. *North American F-86D/L Sabre* 53-1047 on display.

CALIFORNIA

ALHAMBRA. *NA F-86D/L Sabre* 53-563 displayed. Location wanted.

ANAHEIM. *NA P-51D* N6519D of Leroy Penhall believed located here—ex Mojave racer. On Placentia Avenue is *Grumman F9F-6P Cougar* Bu 127484 formerly in colours of Air FMF, PAC and now reported in protective skin in green concrete!

APPLE VALLEY. At old airport (now closed) *F-86F* "Beauteous Butch" mounted on plinth on Highway 18—serial and pic please; Capt. Joseph Cornell Memorial.

ATHERTON. Airfield. *Navy N3N-3* of 1941 N45102 c/n 4499; Jack Gougler.

AUBURN. *F-86D/L* 51-13012—location please.

XF-84H (Bakersfield)

BAKERSFIELD. Kern County Airport. *Republic XF-84H-RE* 51-17059 with turboprop in nose, splendidly displayed on plinth. *NA P-51 Mustang* N8673E ex 44-74430; R. A. Hevie. *CAC Mustang* A68-198, RAAF colours was here—up-dated details please. *Stearman PT-17* N51440 c/n 75-679.

BANNING. Municipal Airport. *F-86E* 51-13067 on plinth—was formerly in small park.

BEALE. AFB. *F-86D/L* 51-6056 displayed.

BEVERLEY HILLS. Bob Guilford has *Vought F4U-7 Corsair* N693M ex Bu 133693 ex "93-WR" of VMF-312— may be flying locally.

BIG BEAR LAKE. *T-33A* 52-9172 displayed.

BLYTHE. Airfield. *Lockheed P-38* c/n 8502 under rebuild—serial, history and pic wanted. Bob Bean reported to have two *F4U-4 Corsairs* here—details appreciated. *F-86D/L* 51-2998 reported on show

BORON. *YF-102A* 53-1785 exhibited—where?

Wichita Fokker D.VII (Buena Park)

BUENA PARK. Planes of Fame Museum, 6900 Orangethorpe Blvd. Alongside Movieland Museum's Cars of the Stars. The aircraft are on show seven days a week from 1000-2200 and the project is under control of Jimmy Brucker and Ed Maloney, exhibiting (1973) the following: In front of the museum *Lockheed F-80C Shooting Star* 47-33866 (first jet to shoot down a jet fighter). Also *NA F-86 Sabre* 49-1318. *Bell Rascal* air-ground missile. Inside:—*Octave Chanute hang glider* of 1898. *Curtiss Pusher 1910 (replica)*. *Hanriot HD-1 Scout* 5934 of 1916-18, brought to USA by Captain Nungesser (45 victories Ace) for first WW I aviation film of 1923. *Wichita Fokker D VII (replica)* from "Hell's Angels" and "Men with Wings" films. *Flugesel secondary glider* of 1920s, built by Mr. Gettings. *Boeing P-12E/F4B-3* biplane fighter serial 32-17, N33606, airworthy, in General "Hap" Arnold's markings. *Boeing P-26A "Peashooter"* 33-123, N3378G, in markings 34th Pursuit Sqdn. First all-metal and last flyable of type. *Curtiss P-4CN Warhawk* 42-8954. *Seversky P-35A(2PA)* 38-483, restored as "Buzz" Wagner's a/c. *NA P-51D Mustang* N5441V ex 45-11582 "Spam Can" "D" Day paint. *Fieseler FZG 76 (VI)*. *Heinkel He 162A* 120077. *Messerschmitt Bf 109 G-10/U4* Werk-Nr 611943. *Spitfire PR XIX* PS890—gift from King of Thailand. *Messerschmitt Me 262 A-Ia/U3* ex T2-4012—this saw combat. *Mitsubishi A6M5 "Zero"* "HK-102" c/n 5347 s/n 61-120. *Mitsubishi J2M3 Raiden "Jack"* c/n 3014. *Mitsubishi J8M1 Shushui* c/n 403. *Yokosuka MXY7 Model 11 Ohka "Baka"* c/n 1049 "Cherry Blossom" captured Okinawa 1945. *Grumman FM-2 Wildcat* (minus starboard wing) unserialled. *Grumman F6F-5 Hellcat* N4994V ex Bu 93879. *NA B-25J Mitchell* believed

Boeing P-12E (Buena Park)

Seversky P-35A (Buena Park)

Boeing P-12E (Buena Park)

Boeing P-26A (Buena Park)

Raiden "Jack" (Buena Park)

Mitsubishi Shushui "Sword" (Buena Park)

Bf 109 G-10/U4 (Buena Park)

Me 262 A-1a/U3 (Buena Park)

44-30761 c/n 130257—broken partly, for use in TV film "Sole Survivor". *Consolidated B-24J-20 Liberator 44-49001*—part only. *Boeing B-50A* "Lucky Lady II" 46-010 c/n 15730, fuselage only—of round-world flight (first a/c to fly non-stop.) *Grumman F-11F Tiger* 14168 ex "Blue Angels". *Bell P-63A King Cobra* 42-69080, said used by USSR in WW II. *Lockheed T-33A T-Bird* 53-5541. *Stits SA-1 Junior* N1293 c/n 68-9—claimed worlds' smallest a/c, wingspan 8 ft 3 inches. *Douglas SBD-5 Dauntless* NZ5062, NZ marks; no wings yet. Not here when visited November, 1972, but may come, are some aircraft also owned by Ed Maloney:—*Lockheed P-38J* N74883 ex 42-2691 (stored Buena). *Curtiss SB2C-3 Helldiver* Bu 19075. *Republic P-47G Thunderbolt* 42-25234, in marks of Bud Mahurin, 56th Fighter Group. Damaged and presently stored Buena. *Bell YP-59A Airacomet* 42-108777—first US jet. *Northrop N9M-B Flying Wing* c/n 0039—the last one. *Douglas D-558-II Skyrocket* 37973 (one of three). *US Navy Bat* guided bomb, first US guided missile WW II. *Radioplane RP-5* world's first target-drone, developed by Reginald Denny in 1930s. Also many engines and other fascinating exhibits. Make Riverside Route 91 (near Disneyland) a MUST. Also reported in or near Buena Park *Northrop F89C* 51-5757 but not, apparently, museum property.

BURBANK.

BURBANK. Airfield. *Lockheed 1649A Constellation* N1102 c/n 1001 (prototype) ex N1649 preserved and *Douglas DC-7* N6323C c/n 44287 in use as Married Couples Club. *Douglas DC-3* N16096 c/n 2136 of Mercer Airlines (ex American Airlines May 1939) and *Lockheed 12A* N908MA c/n 1271, flying from here.

CAMARILLO. *NA F-86H Sabre* 53-1230 displayed.

CAMPBELL. *Lockheed T-33A* 51-6825 displayed. Location?

CARPENTARIA. *Vought FG-1 Corsair* N91522 ex USN 87853; G. Miller.

CHICO. Airfield. *NA F-86D/L Sabre* 53-903, ex CAL ANG. This aircraft may be moving—new location please.

CHINA LAKE. US Naval Weapons Centre. On display *Philco AAM-N-7 Sidewinder*; *NOTS Rat*; *Holy Moses*; *Mighty Mouse*; *Tiny Tim*; *Weapon A*. Stored nearby:—*Boeing B-29* 44-69983; 45-21739; for USAFM disposition. *Douglas A4D-1 Skyhawk* 137814 is mounted on plinth here. *Douglas XF4D-1 Skyray* 124587 and *Grumman F11F-1 Tiger* 138647 are reported preserved, to be mounted later.

Douglas Skyray (China Lake)

King Cobra (Buena Park)

Curtiss Helldiver (Buena Park)

CHINO. Airport. *Curtiss P-40N* 44-7203 "Pilot Lt Gardwell" displayed here. At the Headquarters of "Yesterday's Air Force" on the old Air Corps Field, enthusiast David Tallachet is gathering a fantastic collection, some airworthy, some for long-term restoration, as follows:—*Consolidated B-24J-CF Liberator* 44-44272 ex HE 771 of Indian Air Force and donated by Indian Government. *B-24D Liberator* 42-40461 ex BZ734 (RAF) 599 RCAF, *B-24D* 42-40557 ex BZ755 (RAF) 600 RCAF, dismantled. *NA B-25J-30-NC* 44-31032/N3174G—airworthy. *NA B-25J-30-NC* 44-86701/N7681C; *NA B-25J-20-NC* 44-29366/N9115Z; These Mitchells were converted to TB25N for the film "Catch 22". *Martin B-26 Marauder* 40-1416, to be made airworthy and *B-26 Marauder* 40-1459, static. Both recovered from Arctic. *Curtiss P-40N* 44-7983, ex Tallman, to be licensed. *Curtiss P-40N-1-CU* A29-405 ex 42-104818; *A29-528* and *A29-1134*, both ex 42-106101, from Papua-New Guinea for restoration, plus a *P-40E*, serial wanted, from elsewhere. *NA P-51D-20-NA* 44-63893 ex 9560 RCAF, CF-PIO now N3333E. *Bell P-39M-BE* 42-4949, from Canada, damaged. *Bell P-63 King Cobra* 42-69097, to be static. *Convair F-102A Delta Dagger* 56-1413, ex Calif. ANG, static (USAF on loan). *Lockheed P-38 (F5-G) Lightning* N9957F ex Tallmantz 44-53015; to fly. *Lockheed T-33A T-Bird* 53-5156—static (USAFM a/c loan) *Vought FG-1D Corsair* 92132 ex N3466G from Ontario Air Museum, to be re-licensed. Was in "Pappy" Boyington's marks. *DAP Beaufort* A9-577, *A9-679* and *A9-?*, to be restored on arrival from Papua-New Guinea, probably to make one machine. *Stearman PT-17* N56732 c/n 71585 of 1941—airworthy. *Stearman C-3R*—ex cropduster—to be re-stored. *NA AT-6F* N81854 ex 44-81857—flying. *Bristol (Fairchild) Bolingbroke IV* 9048 "B-T", *10073, 10076*, from Canada, to be restored as one or more aircraft. *Grumman TBM-3 Avenger* N9710Z ex USN 53804 and N7239C ex 91450 ex RCAF; one more to follow. *Naval A/c Factory N3N-3* N2896 c/n 2896, being restored in Navy marks. *NA F-86A Sabre* 49-1195 ex Calif ANG, being restored (at Long Beach.) *Stearman 4E "Bull"* N485W c/n 4033—unlicensed. *Westland Lysander* (built National Steelcar) 1176, to be licensed. *Stinson L-5 Sentinel*

N3N-3 (Chino)

N29846 ex 42-98468—flying. *Boeing B-17* 44-83663 (USAFM loan) and *B-29* 44-61669 (USAFM loan) *Grumman TBF-1* and *Lockheed P-38* from MGM Studios —serials and condition unknown. This is obviously to become one of the largest collections in the USA and we wish Dave Tallachet, Monty Armstrong and all concerned every success when they open to the public (in 1974 it is hoped). Also at Chino Airport (Aerosport Hangar) are many vintage flying types:—*NA P-51D* N210D, ex 44-84952, Joseph Hartney; *N6340T*, ex 44-73149, Ernest Beehler; *N5436V* ex 44-84753, M. L. Grant; *N117E* ex 44-73832, David Webster; *N51JK*, Kister; *N5411V*, Whiteman; *N11T*, Beal; *N44727*, Ward; *N74978* ex 44-74978, Richard Vartanian; *N9146R* ex 44-73027, MPC Inc; *N5465V* ex 44-73423, Edward Bliss; *NA AT-6* N8203H ex 49-3241, Bill Miller; *N7767C*, Mehterian; *N7491C*, Heogh. *P-51* N6519D, several Canadair Sabres and Lockheed T-33s are for sale at Fighter Imports. *Catalina* N5583V and *B-17G Flying Fortress* 44-83684 (N5441V) of "Twelve O'clock High" film, are reported here, together with *B-25J Mitchell* N3675G ex 44-30423, *P-51A* 43-6251, *Grumman F6F-5K Hellcat* 94473, *Vought FG-1D Corsair* N3470G ex 92436, colours of Ira Kepford's No 29, *NA SNJ-5* 90790 said to be here, owned still by Edward Maloney but future uncertain. Details please. Is the (replica) Fokker DR 1 based here from the former Ontario Air Museum? Up-dated listing of aircraft NOT at Buena Park appreciated. Not vintage really, but *DH Vampire* 2-seater N11921 and Pete Regina's *Vampire* fly from here.

Sopwith Pup—replica (Columbia)

COLUMBIA. Airfield. *Nieuport XI* (*replica*) N1485 c/n 101 and *Sopwith Pup* (*replica*) N54T c/n 101, airworthy and owned by constructor Joe Pfieffer. *Davis D-1W* N854N c/n 127 reported, also *Vought F4-U4 Corsair* N6667, Bu 97259 of Eugene Akers.

COMPTON. Airfield. *Grumman F8F-2 Bearcat* 122629 "Phoenix I" with Wright R3350 engine. Holds world's piston-engine climb record; Lyle Shelton.

CONCORD. Airfield. *Ryan PT-22* N48748 c/n 1683, N 54876 c/n 2097; Elton J. Eddy.

CORONA. Airpark. *DHC. Chipmunk* N2533 c/n CI/0685 ex WP793, G-APOE of London School of Flying said here with Hellen Harwood.

CULVER CITY. Hughes Airport. *Douglas A-20G* said owned by Howard Hughes—reg'n please.

DIXON. *NA F-86D/L Sabre* 51-2950 exhibited.

EDWARDS. AFB. In front of Base HQs Bldgs. *Bell P-59B* (painted as YP-59A) *Airacomet* 44-22633, the last on USAF register. *Bell X-IE* 46-63 c/n 6053, at NASA offices.

EL MIRAGE. Airfield. *Avro Anson C.19* N7522 ex VM 351, G-AWSB.

EL MONTE. It is reported that a Mr Hardwick has three *Hispano HA-1109-MIL* (Spanish-built Me 109) direct from Spain, plus a *P-47N, P-40N, P-51B* and *P-59*. Confirmation with serials/pics please.

EL SEGUNDO. Aerospace Corporation Complex. *Douglas SM-75 Thor-Agena* 58-2268 c/n 157.

FOWLER-SELMA on old 99 (some distance from Dinuba) roof of Bruce's Lodge, nose-down *Vultee BT-15 Valiant* 41-10067 "0-308".

FREMONT. Airfield. *Ryan ST-3KR* N48701, Kinner R-56; H. R. "Dick" Bungers.

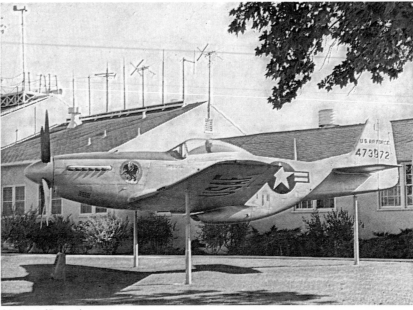

Mustang (Fresno)

FRESNO. Air National Guard Base. *NA F-86D/L Sabre* 53-642; Air Terminal has *NA P-51D* 44-73972; *F-86A* 49-1272; *Convair F-102A* 53-1804 and *Lockheed T-33A* 52-9640, all mounted on poles near Headquarters buildings, as 194th FIS Museum. *Northrop F-15 Reporter* N9768Z of AEI/Aero Enterprises said to be here.

GAVIOTA. Vista del Mar School. *F-86F* 51-13082.

GRIFFITH PARK. Travel Town Museum *Chance Vought F7U-3M Cutlass* 129655; *Grumman F9F-2 Panther* 123420; *Lockheed P2V-3W Neptune* 124359. *Ford JB-2 (US-built V1.)*

GUADALUPE. *Lockheed T-33A* 51-6923—location please.

HALF MOON. Airport. 25 miles south of San Francisco. Pacific Warbirds Museum forming here with:— *NA P-51D* N5460V ex 44-72192; *NA AT-6D* N6979C ex 42-85408; *NA B-25* (owned by four members—reg'n wanted). *Grumman F8F Bearcat*—reg'n wanted. *Vought F4U-4 Corsair* N5218V ex Bu 97264, restored to fly.

HANFORD. Airfield. *Timm Collegiate* of 1928 NR337E c/n 101; Frank Reed.

HAWTHORNE. Airfield. *T-33A* 51-4424. Flying here is *DH.60G* NC916M c/n 117 of 1928; Ed Clark.

HEMET. Airfield. *T-33A* 51-8827. *Grumman TBM-3E Avenger* N7833C ex 91289 and *N9082Z* reported as water-bombers. *Product Design Inc.* N9799C with Franklin 2A 4 engine reported here.

HERMOSA BEACH. *Standard J-1* being restored by Ray Folsom.

INDIO. Airport. *NA P-51B Mustang* NX28388, Jacqueline Cochrane's Bendix Racer reported stored. *DH.Tiger Moth* N5444 c/n "3312", possibly ex Dutch East Indies; G. F. Adams.

INGLEWOOD. Airfield. *WACO 10* NC7968 of 1928, with Curtiss OX-5 being restored by Wm R. Lewis.

Douglas Skyrocket (Lancaster)

Sea Fury (Lancaster)

Sea Fury (Lancaster)

LAKEWOOD. In Park Korean Memorial. *Douglas F3D-2Q (F-10B)* 125870 "7L-17" beautifully mounted.

LANCASTER. Antelope Valley College. *Douglas D-558-II Skyrocket* 37975. At Fox Field nearby, the Western Aerospace Museum has *Bell P-63A* (ex Fresno) unserialled—details wanted (loan USAFM); *Boeing C-97G* 53-272 (loan from USAFM); *Convair TF-102A* 54-1353 (see page XI.) Stored hereabouts *Travel Air "Mystery Racer"* NR613K of 1928 bought by Wm and Florence Barnes from Tallmantz. *Tiger Moth* N5445 c/n 85652 ex DE722, G-AIXH, VR-HEL, VR-HFH, owned and flown by W. E. Barnes. *Taylorcraft L-2M* N99211 and *Harlow PJC-2* N65296 c/n 7 fly here. *Grumman F9F-5 Panther* due; presumably for museum—serial appreciated when known. Howie Keefe's *P-51D-30-NA* N991RC ex 44-74536 and *P-51D-15-NA* N79111 ex 44-1561 of Frank Sanders may be here. Frank also thought to own *Hawker Sea Fury FB 11* N232, ex TG114. *Sea Fury* N260X c/n 41H-636334 may be here or nearby.

LAVERNE. American Aerospace and Military Museum. *C.V.F4U-7 Corsair* N693M ex 133693.

LEMOORE. NAS. *Douglas A-1H (AD-6) Skyraider* 137062; *Douglas A-4D Skyhawk* 142094.

LIVERMORE. Municipal Airport. *Curtiss P-40E* N94466 ex AK899, RCAF, owned by John Paul, who also has *PT-26 Cornell* being painted RCAF-yellow—reg'n and history wanted. *P-40E Kittyhawk* N1207V c/n 18796, flown by Dick Woodson. *P-40N Warhawk* N151U c/n 18723 by Tom Camp (from EAA, Wisconsin). *Fairchild PT-19* N56216 ex 42-3067 now owned by Jack

Kittyhawk (Livermore)

Warhawk, Mustang, Kittyhawk (Livermore)

F4U-7 (and A-7A) Corsair (Laverne)

Perrars (ex J. Paul). *Thomas Morse S-4C* was reported under restoration here also a *Nieuport XI (replica)* built by Pfieffer—details wanted.

Travel Air 4000 (Lodi)

LODI. Airfield. *Stearman PT-17* N62906 c/n 75-021 and *Navy N3N* N44937 c/n 3067, cropdusters. Is *Travel Air 4000* N3977 c/n 326 of 1928 still flown here (with others) by Precissi Brothers?

LOMPOC. *Martin Titan 1* missile displayed—donated from Vandenberg AFB. *F-86D/L Sabre* 53-703 at Arroyo Grande.

LONG BEACH. Municipal Airport and main Douglas Aircraft plant. It is estimated there are often 500 a/c here and so only a fraction can be included:—*Douglas DC-3A* N25668 c/n 2241 of 1940; *N137D* c/n 2249 American Airlines N25629 of March 1940) *N74B* c/n 3299 (NC-

1949 of TWA March 1941). *Hawker Sea Fury FB 11* N878M ex WG567 RN/RCN; (may move to Merced, Calif.) *DH.Vampire F.3* N41J; *Douglas A-26* N240P c/n 7140; *NA B-25 Mitchell* N9958F and N9167Z ex 44-86777; *Grumman J2F-6 Duck* N1214N; *NA F-86 Sabre* 53-1238; *Beech AT-11 Kansan* N6960C ex 42-36926, N7179C c/n 3811. Catalina Airlines operate *Grumman G-21A Goose* N11CS c/n 1166, *N12CS* c/n 1085, *N324* c/n B.66. *Cessna UC-78 Crane* N61808 c/n 5826. *Consolidated (Canadian-Vickers) Cansos* N6108 c/n 22022, *N5583V*. *Aeronca 65CA Scout* N36810 c/n c17661. At Flight Test Research Centre *Canadair Mk 6 Sabre* N166X formerly RCAF 23454 —sold for static display to Air Museum of Calgary and illegally re-sold as airworthy. *N186F*, c/n 1244 ex CF-AMH of Milt Harradence, also said here. *T-33s* (ex RCAF) N156X c/n 192, *N157X* ex 21024, *N109X*, ex 21298. *NA Super-Sabre F-100* N100X c/n 23-035, formerly on pole in Arizona, reported no longer flying. Still preserved at Long Beach is the *Hughes H-4* transport flying-boat, the 8-engined prototype NX37602, built Culver City and assembled Long Beach which Howard Hughes flew for a short distance 2 November 1947. Power plant eight 3,000 hp P & W R-4360-4. Span 320 ft, length 219 ft, gross weight 400,000 lb. Cruising 175 mph at 2,500 ft, for 3,000 miles, with 150,000 lb load. Almost entirely of wood, designed by Henry Kaiser 1942 to carry urgent wartime materials. Let us hope it is not scrapped. Also reported—confirmation please—*Consolidated PB2Y Coronado*, also owned by Howard Hughes. It has been stated (mid-1973) that he is prepared to donate one or both but costs of removal would obviously be enormous. Photos appreciated for 5th V. and V. Is the *Howard Hughes H-1* world-speed-record aircraft also here?

LOS ALTOS. *Boeing FB-5 "6F2"* serial 7104 of 1927 for sale. Details wanted.

LOS ANGELES. International Airport. *Lockheed Lodestar* N22G c/n 2430 of Garret Air. Other vintage types seem to be visitors, not locally-based.

LOS GATOS. Airfield. *Ryan PT-22* N53189 c/n 1265 and *Ryan STM-S2* PI-C324 c/n 494 of 1940, ex S-58 (Dutch) A50-3 (RAAF) VH-AHG, VR-HDK—both owned by Bob DeVries.

McCLELLAN. AFB. Nr Sacremento. *Republic F-105B Thunderchief* displayed.

MADERA. *T-33A* 52-9769 displayed.

MADEVIA. Airfield. *Vultee BT-15 Valiant* N66982 c/n 1304 one of nine still airworthy, with AT-6 engine.

MEDFORD. Airport. H-V. Flying Services *PBY "Super Catalina"* N6453C ex 64041. *Douglas B-26B* N7719C; *Boeing B-17G* N3702G c/n 9613—waterbomber.

MERCED. Airport. *Lockheed F-80 (TV-1)* 456, in colours of 450 FIS.

MILL VALLEY/SANTA CRUZ. *F-86D/L* 53-3682 displayed.

MILPITAS. Airfield. *Fairchild 24-R* N81234 c/n R46-135; Vern and Cora Posateri.

Bearcat "Conquest I" (Mojave)

MOJAVE. Airport. Boeing 377 Stratocruisers were in open storage by Aero Spacelines—news please. *Grumman F8F-2 Bearcat* (modified) N1111L "Conquest I" ex Bu 121646, with P & W R-2800, of Darryl Greenamyer, which set new world piston-engined record of 483.041 mph is reported here from Van Nuys. Also his *P-51D Mustang* N5480V ex 44-73129. *Grumman F9F Panther* of Wally McDonald also thought here—registration and history wanted. *P-51D* N332 ex 45-11471 of David Maytag listed here.

MONTCLAIR. *NA F-86D/L Sabre* 52-10170 displayed—where?

MONTEREY. Airfield. *Tiger Moth* N14659 c/n 809 ex A17-659, DX752, VH-RVN, VH-BEQ; A. Cissen. *Grumman F8F-2 Bearcat* N198F ex Bu 122637, painted mid-Blue; *F4U-5 Corsair;* and *PBY-6* N15KL ex Denmark with John Church. *Bearcat* N184F ex Bu 121787 of Darold Joliff may also fly here.

MORGAN HILL. South of Jan Jose. Jan and Irving Perlitch Transportation Museum. *DH.84 Dragon* N34DH ex G-ADDI c/n 6096, originally first a/c of Railway Air Services "City of Cardiff" 1935; then owned by the late James Hay Stevens, brilliant aviation writer. *Stearman-Hammond 4E* N663K c/n 4005 ex Gillespie Field, San Diego. *Ford 5AT-B Tri-Motor* N9651 c/n 34. *Curtiss Robin* N348K c/n 475. Pictures wanted, also viewing details.

MORRO BAY. *NA F-86D/L* 52-4159 exhibited—location?

NEWHALL. *Tiger Moth* N5446 c/n 434 ex A17-392, VH-ATL, VH-BKB; R. M. Wefel, chairman EAA Moth Club.

NORTHRIDGE. Airstrip. *American Eagle 101* NC3738 c/n 82 of Claude Grey. *Tiger Moth* N524R c/n 85332 ex DE298; C. P. Robertson.

NORTH SACRAMENTO. *Lockheed F-80A* 47-537 displayed.

NOVATO. *NA F-86H* 52-2102 displayed.

Mitchell landing (Oakland)

OAKLAND. North Field, International Airport. The American Air Museum, a non-profit organization of William Penn Patrick, Ralph Johnson, and William Bottoms, is forming here with, to date:—*Boeing B-29A-95BW* N91329 "137" on fin, c/n 13681, ex 45-21787, ex USN P2B-1S Bu 84029. This aircraft, named "Fertile Myrtle" was NACA "mother-ship" for the Bell X-1A, X-1B, X-2, series and for the X-1, the first a/c to exceed speed of sound 14 Oct. 1947 (Chas Yeager). NACA serial 137. Panel on port nose records the many launchings. *B-25 Mitchell* N86427. *Bushmaster 2000* N7501V c/n 1. *Lockheed T-33* N123MJ ex 51-9127. *P-51 Mustang*. *AT-6 Harvard*. *Stearman PT-17* N707R c/n 75-544. *Meyers OTW* N34342 c/n 87. *Piper J-3 Cub*. The owners of the museum (where all aircraft are kept flying) are negotiating for a P-40, and F-86 Sabre. If in time, details will be added, with registrations etc of above machines. *Douglas DC-3* N423MB c/n 27079 (C-47B-20-DK 43-49818) which was KN213, RAF, is owned by William F. Bottoms. *Lockheed 18 Lodestar* N611N c/n 2555 reported here, airworthy, also *PT-17* N49793, c/n 75-2312, *WACO UPF-7* N30149 c/n 5546; *Ryan ST-2* N74801 and N57085, *P-51 Mustang* N5460V ex 44-72192, *Douglas B-26* N9536E and *Cessna 195 Airmaster* N9883A c/n 7585 are reported here (1973) but owners unknown. Details wanted. *P-51D* N7715C ex 44-84961 of Chas Hall may be based.

Spitfire IX (Oxnard)

OXNARD. Airport. *Spitfire IX* N93081 ex MK923, SM37, OO-ARF; Cliff Robertson. Colona Park. *Douglas F-6A (F4D-1) Skyray* 134875.

PACIFICA. *DH.82C Tiger Moth* CF-COV c/n 870— Billy Orbeck; flying?

PALMDALE. Airport at Plant 42. *NA Sabre* 52-2054.

PALM SPRINGS. Airport. *Bird Innovator* N5907 (Catalina with Lycomings outboard of P. & Ws.).

PASO ROBLES/SHANDON. *F-86D/L* 51-8415 displayed.

PLACENTIA. *Mosquito FB.VI* PZ474 with James Merizan for rebuild.

POINT MUGU. HQs Pacific Missile Range, Missile Park. *Chance Vought SSM-N-8A Regulus I; Chance Vought SSM-N-9A Regulus II Lockheed Polaris; Ling-Temco-Vought MGM-52A Lark; Oerlikon (Swiss) Oriole; Martin ASM-N-7 Bullpup; ASM-N-7 Bullpup B; Northrop/Raytheon XM-3 Hawk; Philco AAM-N-7 Sidewinder; Raytheon AAM-N-6 Sparrow I* and *Sparrow III*.

PORT HUENEME: *T.33A* 51-6781 displayed.

REDDING. *F-86F* 52-5459 on display.

REDONDO BEACH. *Tiger Moth* N10RM c/n 85830 ex DE970, G-AOBJ, D-EBIG; R. McElhose.

RIALTO. *F-86H* 53-914 and *53-1380* displayed; where?

Short Solent (Richmond)

RICHMOND. Foot of South 10th Street. Owned, it is said, by Howard Hughes and possibly now available:— *Short Solent 2* N9945F c/n S1303, ex BOAC's G-AHIO "Somerset" VH-TOD; *Solent 3* N9946F c/n S1295 was Seaford NJ203, G-AKNP "City of Cardiff" BOAC, VH-TOB. *Solent 3* N9947F c/n S1298 ex Seaford NJ206 G-AKNT "Singapore" BOAC.

RIO LINDA. *NA F-86D/L* 53-1160 displayed. Location wanted.

RIVERSIDE. Fla-Bob Airport. *WACO 10* N7258 c/n 3065; *Arrow Sport* N220K c/n 419; *Rearwin Cloudster* N25403 c/n 803. *NA F-86H* 52-2074 reported displayed but confirmation and location wanted. *P-51D* N79111 c/n 109-35934, "Galloping Ghost" No 77 of 1946/9 Cleveland Races believed damaged here, owned by Dr. Clifford Cummins. *Sopwith Triplane (replica)* built by Earl Tavan said for sale, with 165 hp Warner.
At March AFB, Riverside. *Boeing Minuteman II* displayed. There is also *KC-97E* 51-209 parked, but for preservation, unknown.

Bird Innovator (Palm Springs)

ROSEVILLE. *Lockheed F-80A* 44-85374 displayed— where?

SACRAMENTO. California Exposition Grounds. *Lockheed F-104A Starfighter* 56-801, presented to City by General William A. Veal on behalf of Air Force Air

Material Area. The plaque states that the type has been produced for 14 friendly nations. *Beech T-34A-BH Mentor* 52-7662; *NA F-86F Sabre* 52-5241.

SAN BERNARDINO. Norton AFB. *Boeing Minuteman II.* Other vintage a/c only come for Armed Forces Day. Nearby *T-33A* 53-5286; *F-86A* 49-1248, *F-86D/L* 51-13037 and *53-1515*, confirmation wanted.

SAN CARLOS. *SPAD VII* B9913 c/n 103 built Mann Egerton, ex J. B. Petty, Gastonia NC, used for films, now with James F. Ricklefs, due to fly 1973. This machine was also owned by the Army Air Force, Enrigo Balboni, Col. G. B. "Reid" Jarrett, Frank Tallman and Robert E. Rust. It is surely one of the world's great veterans. Long may it fly. *Curtiss JN-4D Jenny* of 1917 serial 123 Dept of Commerce No' 3868. Manufactured by Howell-Lesser Airplanes of San Francisco, with Curtiss OX-5 V-8 water-cooled engine. Owners include "Tony" Dekleva, who got it from Mather Field, Sacramento. Then owned by Jim Brown and obtained by Rick Helicopters 1971 for restoration. *Sopwith Pup (replica)* (when flying is based at Meadowlark Field, Livermore with SPAD and where Jenny will fly). Serial A635 is shown on machine, FAA reg'n N6018 (not on a/c). Built by Carl R. Swanson 1966-71, test-flown by Walter J. Addems April 1971 and then by James S. Ricklefs July 1971. The original A635, built by Standard Motors saw service with 46 Sqdn and 66 Sqdn, RFC, and was captured by the Germans intact. Rick Helicopters are building up an impressive antique "chopper" collection, currently including:—*1943 Sikorsky R-6A* two-place WW II observation, serials 43-45451 and *43-45473* (one registered as N5282N). 1944 *Sikorsky R-4B* N68351 c/n 136—US Army serial wanted. 1958 *Hiller YH-32A Ram Jet* 55-4974 FAA N575H, two-place experimental helicopter with vane yaw control. Three built. 1960 *Hiller YROE-1 Rotorcycle* serials 5 and 6. Twelve built, 40 hp Nelson 4-cyl, 2-cycle engine. Airframe designed Hiller, built Saunders Roe, England.

SAN CLEMENTE. Airfield. *Grumman TBM-3 Avenger* N7961C "92"; Daro Inc.

Sea Dart (San Diego)

SAN DIEGO. North Island NAS. *Grumman F6F Hellcat* 66237 recently recovered from the sea and is being restored for Aerospace Museum *Martin P5M Marlin* 5534 "QE-8" of VP-40 is here, also *Douglas F4 Skyray* 151452 "DC" of VMF-A-122 is stored, with other types —further details wanted. The San Diego Aerospace Museum is in Balboa Park (1649 El Prado)—a non-profit corporation, admission free to General Aviation, Armed Forces, and Spacecraft Sections, plus historical

Ryan M-I (San Diego)

Ryan PT-22 (San Diego)

library and archives, Hall of Fame of International Aerospace etc, drawing 40,000 visitors each month to see:—*Aeronca C-2 Collegian* N6626N of 1928—accessible for research (ar). *Aeronca C-3 Master* N14564 of 1935 c/n 515—on public view (pv). *Aeronca K Scout* NC19755 of 1937—at entrance (pv). *Bowlus Experimental Glider* "Baby-Albatross" N28804, (pv). *Chanute 1909 Hang Glider (replica)* built Waldo Waterman 1963 (pv). *Consolidated PT-3 Husky* 28-311 of 1928 (pv). *Convair YF-102 Delta Dagger* 53-1787 in store (s). *Convair XF2Y-1 Sea Dart* 135763 of 1953, one of four completed examples which exist (the 5th, the second example actually, 135762, disintegrated in flight November 1954 during a press tour at San Diego). (s) *Bee Aviation Queen Bee* N8474H c/n 1 of 1957 (pv). *Coward, Chana, Montijo 1948 Wee Bee* NX90840, one of world's smallest a/c (pv). *Curtiss A I Triad (replica)* copy of the first USN 1911 hydroplane (pv). *Curtiss JN-4D*, serial unknown, on loan from USAFM; being restored. *Curtiss-Fife Pusher* "Little Looper" (replica) R4161K (pv). *Essery Glider* "Baby Bomber" of 1939 (pv). *Grumman J2F-6 Duck* N1273N c/n A-633504 of 1944 (s). *Grumman F9F-5P Panther* 126274 (pv). *T.P. Hall Flying Car* NX79711 of 1938 (pv). *Lockheed T-33A Shooting Star* 53-5963N (pv). *Luscombe I Phantom* NC1010 c/n 111 (pv). *Mitsubishi A6M5 "Zeke"* 4323, on loan from USAFM (s). *Montgomery Gull 1883 Glider* (replica), built 1962 (pv). *NA F-86F/L Sabre* 52-10032 (s). *Piper J-3 Cub* N88185 c/n 15802 of 1946, being rebuilt. *Ryan M-I* 2532, silver overall, "Spirit of North Dakota" "Hisso" powered (pv). *Ryan NYP "Spirit of St. Louis" (replica)* N-1967T (pv). *Ryan S-T Sport Trainer* prototype 17351 c/n 193 (pv). *Ryan SCW-145* N18910 c/n 204, under restoration. *Ryan PT-22 Recruit* 41-15390 c/n 1419 (pv). *Ryan FR-I Fireball* 39707—loan from NASM, Washington. *Ryan XFV-5A mock-up (replica)* of 62-4505 V/STOL (pv).

Saalfield Skyskooter N345L c/n 1 (pv). *Sikorsky (HH-19G) HO4S-3U Chickasaw* 1309 Coastguard version (pv). *Urshan UR-1 Air Chair* N20K c/n 1 (pv). *Vultee BT-15* N67627 c/n 11513, as Aichi "Val" for film(s). *Waterman Early Bird* N94299 (pv). *Waterman Chevy Bird* N262Y(pv). *Wright 1903 Kittyhawk* (replica) (pv). *Ford JB-2 (VI).* *Curtiss P-40N-30-CU* N4161K ex 41-4192 and *Fleet 7* N8620 are said to be joining this fine collection—glad of confirmation. Flying from Lindbergh Field (where some museum a/c stored) *Howard DGA-15P* N67425 c/n 1744, Joe Hecker and *N68259* c/n 548 Bob Myers. *Vultee BT-13* N87866. *WACO EQC-6* of 1936 reported, owner Lee de Line—reg'n please. *Cessna C-38 Airmaster* N18037, Jack Polk. *Catalina* N5583V. *Avenger* N9650C.

Douglas Dauntless (San Fernando)

SAN FERNANDO. Airport. *Douglas A-24B Dauntless* N74133 ex 42-54682; John McGregor. *Fleetwing F-401/F-5 Seabird* NC16793 c/n 1 of 1936, rebuild to airworthiness at Glendale College, by Channing Clark and students. Stainless steel single-engined amphibian with Jacobs 755A-2 radial of 300 hp. *Stinson V-77* N67070 c/n 77-13—in US Army AT-19 colours.

SAN FRANCISCO. Palace of Fine Arts Exploratorium *John L. Montgomery's 1911 Glider* (replica), rebuilt by Lockheed A/c using original parts. On loan. In Carl Larsen Park on Route 1 is *NA FJ-2 Fury* 132115.

SAN JOSE. State College. *Republic F-84E* 49-2348. *Hiller YH-32* 55-4974; *Sud-Ouest YHO-3 Djinn : NA F-100 Super Sabre* (serials please). Flying from the Municipal Airport *P-51D Mustang* N5444V ex 44-73751; *Stearman PT-17A* N104H c/n 75-2820; *Beechcraft 17S* N44561 c/n 6922. From Reid-Hillview Airport here fly *Stearman YPT-9B* N795H; Frank Luft. *Cessna T-50 Bobcat* N1202N; *Fairchild 24-C8F* N77665, c/n R46-365. *DH.89A Rapide* N683DH c/n 6782 ex NR683, G-AHXW, one-time BEA islander class "John Nicholson" claimed to have been the last Rapide used for aerial survey work—by Pre-

cise Surveys, Worcester until 1971. Now owned by J. R. O'Brien and R. M. Puryean. *DH.Tiger Moth* N7966 c/n 83462 ex T5753, ZK-AIW; W. A. MacDonald *DHA. Vampire T.35* N11921 ex A79-613, RAAF—details of ownership and state please. Ernest E. Fillmore said to own the unique *Stinson SM-7 Junior* NC 933W "Western Air Express", built 1930.

SANTA ANA. Orange County Airport. The Movieland of the Air Collection—with Frank Tallman in charge:— (some aircraft are reported for sale and changes may have taken place by the time you read this). *Boeing B-17G* (for sale). *Boeing 100 (F4B-1)* N873H c/n 1144; *Boeing-Stearman PT-17A* N63588 c/n 75-8024; *Curtiss CW-1 Junior* of 1930; *Curtiss 1910 Pusher (replica)* N8234E c/n 1; *Curtiss TP-40N* N923 ex 33915—two seater Warhawk; *Douglas B-26 Invader* N4815E ex 44-35505 with Cinerama nose. *Morane-Borel* monoplane of 1911. *NA AT-6* N7446C c/n 121-42541 painted as "Zero" for filming. *NA B-25J Mitchell* N1042B ex 44-30823 with Cinerama nose. *NA P-51B* NX1204 c/n 103-26385—the Paul Mantz all-scarlet racer. *Mantz Standard J-1 (replica)* —was airworthy, reg'n wanted. *Fokker DR-1 (replica)* —and two *SE.5 (replica)* 2/3rds-scale, from the film "Darling Lili"—reg'ns please. *Fokker D.VII (replica)* —in fact a former Hall biplane, 3-seater, with in-line Ranger engine, faked to look like a Mercedes. *Sopwith Triplane (replica)* N5492 c/n ET-1 built Lou Stomp—for sale. *Orenco* observation aircraft of 1918 with 180 hp Hispano, painted A-197, believed used in film "Wings of Eagles". *Wright Flyer (mock-up). Nieuport 28 (replica)* built 1935, N12237 c/n 3; *Roadaire 1,* experimental roadable aircraft. *Stampe SV4C* N1606 c/n 190 ex F-BCFI, *Stinson L-5* (from "Catch 22") reg'n please. *WACO UPF-7* N30141 c/n 5538; *Thomas Morse S4-C Scout*

Fokker DR-1—replica (Santa Ana)

DH.89A Rapide (San Jose)

Boeing B-17G (Santa Ana)

Mitchell (Santa Ana)

Grumman Duck (Santa Ana)

38898; *Grumman J2F-6 Duck* Bu 7790 from film "Murphy's War". *Stinson L-1 (0-49)* N63230 ex 40-3102; *Hughes 500 helicopter* prototype (mock-up). *"Kate", "Val"* and *"Zero" mock-ups* constructed for "Tora, Tora, Tora"—details of former serials/registration please. Also reported that at least two other Mitchell a/c used in "Catch 22" may still be here and possibly *Tiger Moth* N6970 c/n 1608, RCAF 3947, CF-CIT. As there would seem to be some dealing with Buena Park (or Edward Maloney) an up-dated check would be valuable. It is not known exactly what remains at the adjacent Inter-national Flight and Space Museum, but possibly:— *McDonnell XF-85 Goblin* 46-524; *F-84 Thunderstreak* (serial please) *Hiller Ramjet;* Reports (November, 1972) say that a *Lockheed Orion* is here or nearby undergoing restoration—all-metal monocoque fuselage—confirmation and registration please. USAF Museum listing includes *NA YF-107A* 55-5118 stored Orange County Airport, also *Lockheed F-80C* 49-1872; *49-1810* and *49-0851; Vultee XP-81* 44-91000 and *44-91001* shown as "stored in California"—Are these also at Orange County Airport—if not, where?

Bleriot —replica (Santa Barbara)

SANTA BARBARA. Airport. *Bleriot (replica)* N3433 built and flown by 67-yr old Bert Lane with Continental C-85 "bad for authenticity, good for flying!" It took two years and 3,000 working-hours to build. The *Focke Wulf Fw 190 D-9* FE-118 received at Wright Field for evaluation August 1945 is now reported in Germany for rebuild for David Kyte—will it return to USA? Information and photos please. *Lockheed P-38 Lightning* N517PA c/n 8187, *N53753* reported; *P-51D Mustang* N5436V ex 44-84753.

SANTA CLARA. Airfield. *Ryan NR-1* (modified) N66622 c/n 1129 of 1941; Bob Yates.

SANTA MARIA. *Convair F-102A Delta Dagger* 56-995 and *Lockheed T-33A* 52-9221 displayed.

SANTA MONICA. Airport. *Douglas M-2* NC1475 c/n M-338, the 1927 machine of Western Air Express reported stored here. *Ford 5-AT Trimotor* N414H c/n 74 also here. *Fairchild 71* N2K c/n 675 flying here.

Bleriot —replica (Santa Barbara)

Hanriot HD-1 (Santa Rosa)

Tiger Moth (Santa Rosa)

SANTA PAULA. Airfield. *Bücker 133* N44DD c/n 27 of Mira Slovak; *Travel Air 2000* N241 c/n 1; *Funk B* of 1937 N9000 c/n B-2 Ted Ball; *Piper J-3C* N42330 c/n 14580 "Little White Bear" TWA Captains Perry Schrettler and Robt Van Ansdell; *Bleriot XI* of 1909 N9781 c/n 9, oldest airworthy in world, restored 1970 after last previous flight 1917, owner-pilot Mrs. Shirley B. Wardle. *Piper J3C-A65-8* N6513H c/n 19698 of Nick G. Stasinos.

SANTA ROSA. Napa County Airport. *McDonnell F2H-2 Banshee* 125052 "7F". *Bücker Jungmeister* N133BJ c/n 3 ex U-56, HB-MIN; *DH.60GM Moth* N151OV, although quoted as c/n 506, ex G-CAPA of 1927, it is in fact c/n 1322 of 1929 and formerly CF-APA. *Lincoln Page LP3* of 1928 N3830 c/n 156; *Buhl LA-1* N320Y c/n 180; *WACO UPF-7* N32114 c/n 5736. At Sonoma County Airport, Santa Rosa, the fabulous *Hanriot HD-1* N75 formerly Belgian AF. No 75 later H-1 and civilianised as OO-APJ, G-AFDX, now N-75 again, owned and flown by Marvin K. Hand. This is the historic plane of Willy Coppens, flown at the Nice 1922 Air Show, later to Shuttleworth and sold to Marvin in 1963 who restored it to airworthiness. Marvin visits Willy Coppens in Belgium regularly and, as this is written, plans to bring the Hanriot back to Europe to fly at Old Warden etc. Also flown here by Marvin and friends:—*Ryan PT-22* N57081 c/n 1505; *Ryan ST-3KR* N51707 c/n 1778; *Meyers OTW* N34355 c/n 99; *Ryan STA* N17346 c/n 149; *Fleet 7* N795V c/n 346; *Tiger Moth* N9714 c/n 83896 ex T7467 of 29 EFTS, 10 RFS, then G-ANIZ of Skegness Air Taxis, now Capt. Roger Sherron, Pan Am. *Tiger Moth* N1350 c/n 1039 ex A17-604, VH-AIN, VH-SNZ; H. E. Williams. Borate Bombers of SIS-Q Flying Service Inc fly from here or Napa County Airport, including:—*Grumman F7F Tigercat* N7626C "E42" ex Bu80404, *N7195C* ex Bu 80532, *N7178C*, *N7238C* ex 80525, *N6179C* ex 80494, *N7195C* ex 80532, *N7629C* ex 80374; There are also *Grumman Avengers*—N13692, *N68663* ex 53334, *N7961C*, N90782 ex 44917, N9711Z ex 53697 (they are dispersed during fire-hazard months.) *Vultee BT-13 Valiant* N128M c/n 6475 also here.

SARATOGA. Henry Hoelling restoring rare 1939 *Security S-1B*—reg'n please.

SIERRA MADRE. *NA F-86D/L* 51-13064 displayed.

SOUTH PASADENA. Airfield. *WACO 10* N7258 c/n 3065 of 1928; Al Kiefer.

STOCKTON. Wayne Kerr, 1511 North Carlton Ave said to have:—1929 *Fleet 2* N617F c/n 193 with original K-5 100 hp Kinner, airworthy; 1928 *Curtiss Robin* N78900 with original OX-5, being restored; 1936 *Aeronca LC* N17425 c/n 2054, original Warner 90, being recovered; 1946 *Fairchild 24W* modified with R680, 225 hp Lycoming, reg'n wanted; 1946 *Taylorcraft BC12D* for rebuild; *WACO VKS-7*—for rebuild; *DH.90 Dragonfly* ZS-CTR c/n 9526 ex CR-AAB said to be coming—see South Africa. *Fokker DR-1* (replica) also reported.

SUN VALLEY. John W. Caler. *Messerschmitt Bf 109 K* FE-124 (T2-124) from Atlanta, Georgia for re-build. *Mosquito* remains from Whitman Air Park, Pacoima, also said to be with John—let us hope restoration possible.

TORRANCE. Airfield. *Harlow PJC* N18978 c/n 1 of 1938; Mel Heflinger; *Stearman 4C* of 1930 N788H c/n 6003; Ray H. Stevens. *Thomas Morse S-4B Scout* N38923 c/n 1; Replica built by Ernest Freeman. *P-51D Mustang* N5416V ex 44-84896.

TULARE. *Boeing DB-17G-105-VE* 44-85738 displayed as American Veteran's Memorial now near Freeway, Route 99. Flown in by General Maurice A. Preston ex 379th Bomb Group, later 41st Combat Wing; Tulare his hometown.

VAN NUYS. Airport. Impossible, for restrictions on space to cover more than a fraction of the vintage types based:—*Spartan 7W Executive* N4444; *Vampire F.3* N6878D ex RCAF 17072, Pete Regina; *F-80C-10-LO* N10DM ex 47-2518, from Fuerza Aerea Colombiana, now with Dick Martin; *NA B-25* N3699G ex 44-30801 "Executive Suite" of Challenge Publns; *Bell P-63* NX90805 ex 42-69021; *Beech 18* N7825 ex RCAF 2282; *Culver LCA* N32464; *Vought FG-1D Corsair* N92059 ex N9150Z Bu 92059; John Van Andel; *P-40N-30-CU* 44-7369 ex Ed Maloney, for restoration; Field Av'n; *NA P-51D N64CL* ex N182X, 44-74423; Clay Lacey; *P-51F-6C* N5528N "90" winner of 1949 of Bendix Races, said owned by Jimmy Stewart; stored. *Grumman F8F Bearcat* N618F awaits restoration here; *Temco Buckaroo* N1135T; *DH.2 (replica)* N32DH flying. And countless others—please send details of the best.

VICTORVILLE. Victor Valley Community College. *Douglas F5D-1 Skylancer* NASA 708; *NA F-86D/L* 53-804.

WATSONVILLE. Airfield. *Douglas B-18A Bolo* N18AC ex XB-LAJ one of 217 built 1937/8 (plus 20 in Canada). Over a hundred converted to B-18B for submarine-tracking and the first B-18 was the DB-1 prototype. *Stearman PT-17* Cropdusters N686W c/n 75-3772, *N3961B* c/n 75-5511, *N68324* c/n 75-7797, based.

WEST COVINA. *NA F-86D/L* 52-3784 displayed.

WOODLAND. *Lockheed T-33A* 51-9025 displayed.

YUBA COUNTY. Airport (near Marysville). *NA P-51D Mustang* N5450V ex 44-63542; *Stearman PT-17* N50210.

YUCAIPA. *F-86E* 51-12985 displayed. Mr. R. Ward said to have *Vought FG-1D Corsair* N9150Z ex USN92509.

COLORADO

BOULDER. *Lockheed T-33A* 53-6028 displayed. *Tiger Moth* N126B c/n 85642 ex DE712, G-APJL; Pete Bartoe.

BRIGHTON. *NA F-86D/L* 53-1067 on display.

BROOMFIELD. Airport. *Vought FG-1D Corsair* N6604C ex 92050; Robert Mitchum.

COLORADO SPRINGS. Norad HQs. *Douglas XSAM A-25 Nike-Hercules.* USAF Academy:—*Republic F-105D Thunderchief* 60-482 (from 10 a/c damaged S.E. Asia) *Lockheed F-104* (serial please) *McDonnell RF-4C Phantom* 64-0799, damaged over S.E. Asia, repaired for display at Hill AFB. *Northrop X-4* 46-676 (one of three built) research plane in X-1/X-15 series.

Northrop X-4 (Colorado Springs)

DENVER. Buckley ANG Base. *Lockheed P-2H (P2V-7)* 128402 "6F"; *Vought F8U Crusader* 145349 "7K". DHA. *Vampire T.35* N11929 ex A79-644 flying. At Denver Metropolitan College *Douglas F4D-1 (F-6A) Skyray* 134936. At the Emily Griffith Opportunity School is another *Skyray*—serial wanted, donated by the Naval Air Reserve Training Detachment, ex NAS Olathe, Kansas. Stapleton International displays *Curtiss JN-4D* SC1918 "65". Flying:—*Piper J-5A* N38715 c/n 5-1072 of Morris McEntyre; *Lockheed Lodestar* N68643.

ENGLEWOOD. *NA F-86D/L* 50-731 displayed.

FORT COLLINS. Colonel Max Hoffman of Confederate Air Force *Spitfire XIV* TZ138 now N5505A, being restored to fly, once CF-GMZ and N20E at Perry Airport Minneapolis. *Spitfire IXTr* HS543 ex Indian Air Force, being restored here for Kansas Senator to fly. Two *P-51D Mustangs* reported also.

GRAND JUNCTION. Airport. *Fairchild 24W* N77648 c/n W46-398; Joe Kendrick.

PETERSON FIELD. HQs ADC, USAF. *Republic P-47N Thunderbolt* 44-89425 on loan and *Curtiss P-40 Tomahawk* said to be airworthy in 14th AF marks—serial please.

PUEBLO. Airfield. *Consolidated Vultee V-1A* NC16099 c/n 25 of Harold Johnson, now restored and flying again.

YUMA. *T-33A* 51-8667 on display.

CONNECTICUT

BRIDGEPORT. Airport. *Vought (Goodyear) FG-1D Corsair* 92460 mounted in USM markings "217". It was built at Stratford, Conn. flight-tested at Bridgeport and sold to El Salvador Air Force—donated by them to be memorial. *T-33A* 52-9338 displayed. *Goodyear FG-1D* N7225C ex 92508 flies here, also *Vultee SNV-1 Valiant* N64930. A *Sikorsky R-4B* is with Museum of Art Science and Industries—details please. *Boeing M1M-10 Bomarc* AF57256 exhibited here.

CANAAN. Airfield. *Tiger Moth* N24SS c/n 1660 ex RCAF 3939, CF-CLB, N7990 of Stanley Segalla.

DANBURY. Ron Reynolds of Norwalk said to have *Grumman 8F Bearcat,* restoring after accident when landing-gear collapsed. Reg'n please.

MERIDEN. *NA F-86D/L Sabre* 53-1367 displayed.

SIMSBURY. Airport. *Grumman TBM-3E Avenger* N4039A, *N6580D, N53489, N5681D, N6583D* ex 53503, These are reported as static—a chance for preservationists.

STAMFORD. Airport. *Nord 1002* N108U c/n 188 painted as Bf 108 and flown by John H. Van Andel. *Douglas B-26* N86481 for disposal (may be Bridgeport).

WILLIMANTIC. Airfield. *P-51D Mustang* N8676E; ex 44-74008 Richard Foote.

Boeing Stratojet (Windsor Locks)

WINDSOR LOCKS. Bradley International Airport. Bradley Air Museum of Connecticut Aeronautical Historical Association. Modern metal machines displayed at airport with rarer specimens in CAHA Airdome, 7,200-square feet clear span floor area in air-supported structure:—*Silas M. Brooks 1886 Balloon* "Jupiter"; oldest surviving aircraft in USA; *General Development Gas Navy Training Balloon* of 1956 with WW II basket; *Raven S-40 Hot Air Balloon* "Vulcoon" serial 108, N12000 of 1963, flown by Barbara Keith as "Barkris" (nickname). *Boeing B-17 (299Z) Flying Fortress* N5111N ex 44-85734, the 1945 P. & W. engine flight test aircraft with T-34 in nose. *Boeing WB-47E-12-BW Stratojet* 51-2360, modified weather-recce. *Chance Vought XF4U-4 Corsair* 80759 ex armament tests. *Bunce*

Grumman Panther (Windsor Locks)

Curtiss Pusher serial 1 of 1912, oldest Connecticut a/c. *Consolidated PBY-5A Catalina* N3936A was 33966 US Coastguard WW II. *Convair F-102A Delta Dagger* 55-3450 ex Wisconsin ANG and *56-1221* ex "Connect", loaned by USAFM. *Douglas AD-4N Skyraider* 125739—flew in Korea. *Douglas C-133B Cargomaster* 59-529 ex 60th MAW, Travis AFB, Calif, used for transporting Atlas, Thor and Jupiter; USAFM loan. *Douglas A-26C Invader* N86481 ex 43-33499, modified solid nose. *Douglas C-54E Skymaster* 44-9040, former a/c of Chief of Staff USAF, Germany; USAFM loan. *Douglas C-124C Globemaster II* 51-0119 ex 905th MAG. *Dyndiuk Parasol Sport* a/c No 1 of 1934, Conn. homebuilt. *Fairchild C-119C Flying Boxcar* 51-2616. *Fokker Universal* NC7029 c/n 434 of 1928, the sole remaining US-built example. *Gee Bee Sportster A* N901K c/n 8, believed only one in USA. *General Motors FM-2 Wildcat* 74120 of 1943. *Grumman F9F-2 Panther* 125155—first to use P. & WA jet. *Grumman HU-16B Albatross* 51-25—USAFM loan. *Kaman K-16B VTOL* tilt-wing of 1960. *Laird LCDW-300 Solution* NC10538 c/n 192—Thompson Trophy winner. *Lockheed 14 Super Electra* CF-TCO c/n 351 of 1939, ex Trans-Canada Airlines and loaned from USAFM. *Lockheed SP-2E (P2V-5FS) Neptune* 131427 of 1952. *Lockheed T-33A-5-LO T-Bird* 53-6146 ex Conn. A.N.G. *Lockheed F-94C-1-LO Starfire* 51-13575 ex Penn. A.N.G., Tower City. *Lockheed L-749A Constellation* N6695C c/n 2167, ex N6025C, G-ANNT of BOAC and N4901C of Capital Airways; flown in by Captains Derrick Wilson and Robt E. Franks (who flew a/c 1958 with BOAC). *Macchi Castoldi MC 200 Saetta,* Italian WW II fighter of 1942. *Nixon Special* No 1 of 1920; Conn. home built sportsplane. *NA B-25H Mitchell* N3970C ex 43-4999—75mm cannon version. *NA FJ-1 Fury* 120349, established speed record Seattle-Los Angeles in 1948. *NA F-86H-10-NH Sabre* 53-1264 from Puerto Rico ANG. *NA F-100-1-NA Super Sabre* 52-5761, Conn. ANG's oldest F-100. *Northrop F-89J-85-NO Scorpion* 52-1896, from Maine ANG. *Republic RF-84F Thunderflash* 52-7374 from Michigan ANG. *Sikorsky S-39B Amphibian* c/n 904, historic CAP rescue plane. *Stinson SR-5A Reliant* NC13838 c/n 9203 of 1934. *Vultee BT-13 Valiant* of 1941—reg'n wanted. *Gyrodyne XRON-1 Rotorcycle* 4005 of 1955. *Kaman K-225* N401A c/n 5, oldest surviving Kaman a/c. *Kaman HTK-1K* 128654—drone modification, 1953. *Kaman HOK-1* 129801 of 1954. *Piasecki HRP-1 Rescuer* 111809—first production example, also *HRP-1* 111813 "Flying Banana" from Philadelphia (stored). *Sikorsky VS-300* Lift & Torque device of 1938. *Sikorsky UH-19D Chickasaw* 56-4257, US Army's S-55. *Sikorsky CH-37B Mojave* 57-1643, US Army's S-56. *Sikorsky S-59* N74150 c/n 52004—first Sikorsky turbine type. *Sikorsky S-60*

Mojave, S-59 and Chickasaw (Windsor Locks)

Skycrane N807 c/n 60001; prototype. *Boeing IM-99A Bomarc* 57-2756 rocket & ramjet, anti-aircraft. *Chance Vought RGM-3 (SSM-N-8) Regulus I,* turbojet, 1955. *Douglas MIM-3 (SAM-A-7) Nike-Ajax* anti-aircraft rocket, 1953. *Fairchild SM-73 Goose* turbojet decoy missile 1958. *Radioplane OQ-2* 1943 target drone. *YOQ-19* 1956 target drone. Incomplete (less than 50 per cent) aircraft for potential restoration:—*Bourdon Kittyhawk* of 1928; *Sikorsky S-39B Amphibion* NC58V c/n 920. *Standard J-1* c/n 129 of 1917. WW II unidentified fighter. *Platt La Page XR-1A* helicopter of 1945. We wish all concerned with this magnificent project every success in the future. We would like to know days and times of opening and if a charge is made.

DELAWARE

DELAWARE CITY. *Lockheed T-33A* 56-1650 displayed.

DOVER. *Lockheed T-33A* 51-17431 displayed.

NEWCASTLE. Greater Wilmington Airport, *NA F-86H-10-NH Sabre* 53-1286 is displayed.

SUMMIT. Airport (is this Delaware City?) *Commonwealth Aircraft Mustang* A68-1, the prototype Australian built, once at the Emu, South Australia, atom bomb test site, later flown to Adelaide, arrived in USA but suffered, it is said, irreparable dockside damage during unloading. Is this true and if so, surely this historic machine can be preserved as a static exhibit? News please.

WILMINGTON. Aidair Museum Inc. *Tiger Moth* N4808 c/n 82700 ex R4759, G-ANKN, CF-JJI; *Ryan PT-22A* N262SR c/n 1799 is flying with Gus Musante.

DISTRICT OF COLUMBIA

The National Air and Space Museum, near 10th and Independence Avenue, SW Washington, D.C. Open seven days a week (except Christmas Day) from 1000-1730. With the ending of the Vietnam conflict, it is hoped to open a new structure in 1976, designed by Gyo Obata, to stand opposite the National Gallery, with about the same dimensions. The new director, former Apollo astronaut Michael Collins, says the new building will give the public chance to assess past, present and future air and space programmes all under one roof. It will offer ample space for exhibits that will educate and inspire the estimated annual six to eight *million* visitors. As long ago as 1969, S. Paul Johnston, then the museum director spoke in terms of 50 million dollars being needed but rising costs will obviously increase the final figure. Let us hope that this much-needed new building WILL come about so that the many stored items can at last be viewed. Paul Johnston made it clear, before handing over, that of the 200-odd airframes and 300/400 engines in store, only a relatively small fraction are of sufficient historical value to be considered for public display and it does not follow, alas, that all entries here will eventually come to the new building. This listing is based on a personal friend's summer, 1972, visit but, as is well known, exhibits are changed and generously loaned, so that not all may be where stated. At the Smithsonian Institution, Arts & Industries Building:—Outside are *Jupiter, Vanguard, Atlas* and *Polaris* missiles; Inside, main entrance hall:— *North American X-15A-1* 56-6670, research aircraft. Elsewhere:—*Wright 1903 Flyer*, 16 hp engine, span 40 ft 4 inches, the biplane which changed the world's history at Kitty Hawk, North Carolina, 17 December 1903. *Langley A Aerodrome* of 1903. *Wright Ex "Vin Fiz"*—first to fly coast to coast, 1911—Sheepshead Bay NY to Long Beach Cal. in 84 days, with 70 landings; actual flying

Missiles, NASM (Washington, D.C.)

X-15A-1 (Washington D.C.)

time 82 hrs for 4,321 miles. *Wright 1909 Military*—world's first heavier-than-air military machine, purchased by Signal Corps 2 August 1909 for 30,000 dollars, designated S. C. Aeroplane No 1. Used October 1909 for flight instruction to Lts. Latham and Humphreys and in 1910 to Lt. Foulors. March 1911 retired as "no longer fit for use". *Caudron G4* serial C4263 (may now be in store) *Curtiss Headless Pusher* of 1912 (may be under rebuild) *Fokker D VII* OAW/4635 18F, captured by First Pursuit Group at Battle of Verdun. Now restored as "U.10". *SPAD VII* "3" S248 of 1916, later NX18968 then N4727V at Tallmantz, sold to Wings & Wheels, Santee SC, and on loan to NASM. *SPAD XVI*—Billy Mitchell's machine serial AS9392 c/n 959. *Curtiss JN-4D Jenny* 4983 ex US Army, Hempstead Field. *Ryan NYP* NX-211 "Spirit of St. Louis" in which Lindberg made first solo Atlantic crossing Long Island-Paris 20/21 May 1927. *Curtiss Robin* NR526N c/n 723 "Ole Miss" in which Al Gene and Fred Key set world endurance record of 653½ hours in 1935. *Bell X-1* 46-062A "Glamorous Glenniss" first manned Mach. 1 (Mach 1.47 Oct 14 1947).

Bensen Gyrocopter N2588B c/n 194 of 1957. *Bowlus-Dupont Falcon* G-13763 of 1934, gained *glider* altitude record 9,094 ft (Warren Eaton). *Douglas DC-7* nose section only N334 c/n 45106. *Hawker Hurricane IIC* LF686 ex 7270M, Bridgnorth and Colerne, donated by RAF in return for Typhoon. *Lockheed 5-C Vega* "Winnie Mae" NR105W, in which Wiley Post and Harold Gatty flew round-world NY-Sealand (Chester)-Berlin-Irkutsk (USSR)-Alaska-NY 15,474 miles in 8 days 15 hrs 51 mins 23 June 1 July 1931. *Lockheed 8 Sirius* NR-211 c/n 140 "Tingmissartoq" Lindbergh's aircraft, 1929. *Northrop Gamma* "Polar Star" NR12269 c/n 2, 1933 of Ellsworth Trans-Antarctic Flight. *Piper PA-12* NX2365M "City of Washington" c/n 12-1618. *Popular Mechanics Hang Glider (replica)* of 1909. *Wittman Buster* monoplane N-14855 of 1930 "20". The following are reported "Research Accessible" for serious researchers, not to general public, these will almost certainly be at Silver Hill, a city suburb actually in the State of Maryland but included here for ease of reference:—*Aeronca C-2 Collegian* N6626N c/n 3774. *Akerman Tailess* (U. Minn)

Wright 1903 Flyer (Washington D.C.)

Fokker D VII (Washington D.C.)

SPAD VII—loan (Washington D.C.)

SPAD XVI (Washington D.C.)

JN-4D and other exhibits (Washington D.C.)

Close-up of JN-4D (Washington D.C.)

Lindbergh's Ryan NYP (Washington D.C.)

Wright "Vin Fiz" (Washington D.C.)

Hurricane IIC (Washington D.C.)

X-14880. *Albatros D.Va* D7161. *Arado Ar 196* A-3 623183 "GA-DX" from "Prinz Eugen". *Arlington 1A Sisu* Sailplane N1100Z c/n 102, first to exceed 1,000 kms. *Beech D18S* "Red Devil" N1313G of 1946. *Bell XP-59A Airacomet* 42-108784. *Bell Model 30* NX41867 c/n 1a, first flown 1942. *Bell VTOL* N1105V of 1954. *Bell VH-13J* 57-2728, President Eisenhower's a/c. *Bellanca CF* (tail missing) of 1924. *Benoist-Korn* of 1913, flown by Korn Bros, incomplete. *Bensen Gyroglider* of 1954. *Berliner Helicopter* of 1924. *Bleriot XI* "Demonjoz" 1910; flown Roosevelt Field as Serial 340. *Boeing 247D* NR-257Y "Adaptable Annie" of England-Australia Air Race of 1934, Mildenhall-Melbourne. *Boeing (Stearman) N2S-5*

Kaydet 61064, 1944. *Boeing B-17D* 40-3097 "Swoose", built from remains of oldest Flying Fortress, the only one to see duty throughout 1941-5 with 19th Bomb Group, 3 years of which was as Lt-Gen. George Betts' a/c. *Boeing B-29 Superfortress* 44-86292 "Enola Gay" which dropped atomic bomb on Hiroshima 6 August 1945 (Col. Paul W. Tibbets, pilot). *Bowlus Baby Albatross* Sailplane X18979 of 1932. *Bucker Bu 181 Bestmann* K-2227, FE-4611, of 1931. *Burgess-Curtiss* of 1909. *Crowley Hydro-Air Vehicle. Culver TD2C-1 Turkey* 120035 of 1944. *Curtiss NC-4* A-2294 "4" first aircraft to cross the Atlantic, in stages 16-31 May 1919 from Trepassey Bay, Newfoundland to Plymouth via Azores and Lisbon. The flying

Lindbergh's Ryan NYP (Washington D.C.)

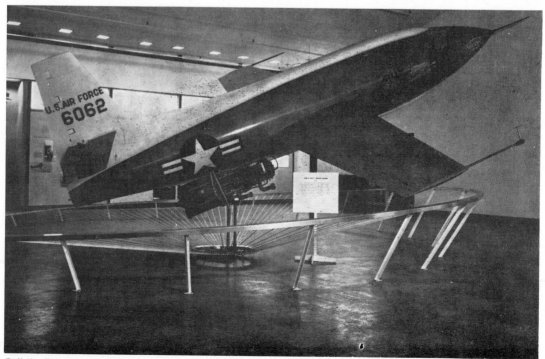

Bell X-1 (Washington D.C.)

Lockheed Vega (Washington D.C.)

Lockheed Vega (Washington D.C.)

Northrop Gamma (Washington D.C.)

Wittman Buster (Washington D.C.)

Bleriot XI (Washington D.C.)

Curtiss NC-4 (Washington D.C.)

Dornier Do 335 A-1 (Washington D.C.)

Curtiss Sparrowhawk (Washington D.C.)

World Cruiser "Chicago" (Washington D. C.)

Douglas Skystreak (Washington D.C.)

boat was commanded by Lt. Cdr. A. C. Read, USN. The NC-4 returned to USA aboard USS Aroostock and was displayed in Central Park, NY. It later flew exhibition flights and then was again dismantled and put on outdoor display at foot of the Washington Monument, before going to the Smithsonian. It was displayed outdoors on the 50th anniversary. *Curtiss TS-1* of 1923 used as TR-1 trainer in 1925. *Curtiss F9C-2 Sparrowhawk* painted as 9056 but actually 9264 XF9C-2, with carrierhook, trapeze-hook and belly tank fitted, made from original drawings but not vintage. Designed as lightweight carrier fighter was chosen to equip airships ZRS.4, USS Acron and ZRS.5 USS Macron. Six production a/c built (9056-9061) joining XF9C-1 prototype and Consolidated N2Y-1 trainers to form Heavier Than Air Unit, Navy Airships. Acron crashed at sea without loss of a/c. Macron was lost with 4 a/c. One final Sparrowhawk was built by Curtiss at their own expense, the XF9C-2, allocated NX-986M and, purchased by the Navy, given serial 9264 and is now returned to F9C-2 configuration. *Curtiss P-40E Kittyhawk* N1048N c/n 1047 (any military serial?) *Curtiss SB2C-5 Helldiver* 83479. *Custer CCW-1 Channel Wing. de Havilland DH.4 (replica)* N249B "Old 249" c/n 249, with some original parts and 400 hp Liberty engine. Built 1961/68 by Bill Hackbath after original crashed Utah 1922. Bill flew it San Francisco-Washington 1968 to mark 50th anniversary of US Airmail. Flight took 13 days and Bill was 67 at the time. *DH.98 Mosquito B/TT35* TH998 ex 3 CAACU, donated by RAF. *Dornier Do 335 A-1 Pfeil (Arrow)* 102 "VG+PH" given FE1012. *Douglas DWC-2 World Cruiser* "Chicago"—see Dayton, Ohio. *Douglas XB-43* 44-61509 "Versatile II". *Douglas DC-3* N18124 c/n 2000 ex Eastern Airlines, delivered 7.12.37, to Smithsonian May 1953. *Douglas C-54C* 42-107451 c/n 7470 "Sacred Cow" President Roosevelt's Skymaster. *Douglas D-558-II Skystreak* 37974, Mach 2 a/c, NACA 144. *Douglas R4D-5* Bu 12418 ex C-47A-20-DL 42-23496 c/n 9358, "Que Sera Sera" first a/c to land South Pole October 1956. *Fairchild FC-2* NC6853. *Fieseler Fi 156 Storch* of 1944. *Fokker F IV(T-2)* AS64233 of 1921, first non-stop flight across USA (Kelly & Mcready). *Franklin PS-2 Eaglet Glider* 502M c/n 202, the machine in which Frank Hawes was towed across USA. *Fulton FAM4 Airphibian* N74154. *Grumman FM-1 Wildcat* (built by General Motors) Bu 15392 of 1942. *Grumman F6F-3K Hellcat* Bu 41834—used as drone. *Grumman F8F-1 Bearcat* Bu 90446. *Grumman F9F-6 Cougar* Bu 126670. *Grumman TBF-1 Avenger* Bu 24085. *Hiller YHO-1E Flying Platform. Hiller YROE Rotocycle* 4022 c/n 596022. *Huff-Daland Duster*, 1925 biplane, a tribute to C. E. Wooman who became Delta Airlines first pilot. *Kellett XO-60 Autogiro* 42-13610. *Kugisho Okha 11 (22)* of 1944. *Laird LCDW-500 Super Solution* NR12048. *Lockheed 5B Vega* NR7952 c/n 22, of 1928, Flown by Amelia Earhart, first solo Trans-Atlantic flight by a woman, Harbour Grace, Newfoundland-Londonderry, N. Ireland, 2,062 miles in 14 hrs 54 mins 20/21 May 1932. A/c was formerly at Franklin Institute, Philadelphia. *Lockheed XC-35 Electra* 36-353, used for pressurized cabin tests. *Loening OA-1A* "San Francisco" amphibian AC26-431. *Macchi C. 202 Folgore* (Thunderbolt), given FE300, received Wright Field, May, 1945. *J.V. Martin K-111 Kitten* of 1920. *McDonnell FH-1 Phantom* 111759 of 1946. *F-4A Phantom* 145307 of Project "Sageburner", set low-altitude world speed record 902.769 mph 28 August 1961 when Lt Hunt Hardisty USN flew a/c at 125 ft over White Sands Missile Range, New Mexico. *Messerschmitt Bf 109 G-6 Gustav*, given FE-496. *Messer-*

schmitt Me 163 B-la Komet 191190, FE-500. *Messerschmitt Me 262 A-1a* 500491 ex JV-7 a/c, given FE-111, known as Schwalbe (Swallow) arrived Wright Field 1 August 1945. *Mignet (Crossley) Pou du Ciel* "Sky Louse". *Mitsubishi A6M5 Zero-Sen "Zeke"*. *Nakajima Kikka* (sometimes quoted NXM1 Kikka) jet. *Nieuport XII* (83E) of 1915. *North American AT-6 (SNJ-4) Texan* 51398. *North American P-51D Mustang* 44-74939. *North American F-86A Sabre* 48-0260. *Northrop P-61C Black Widow* 43-8330, high-altitude version. *Pitcairn PA-15 Mailwing* N2895. *Princeton University Air Rho Car. Republic P-47D 30-RE Thunderbolt* 44-32691. *SAAB (J 29)* from Swedish Air Force, serial? *Sikorsky (JRS-1) S-43* Bu 1063 *Sikorsky (XR-4) VS-316* 41-18874. *SPAD S.XIII* c/n 7689—downed 7 e/a (with 220 Hispano engine). *Stout Skycar. Spitfire VII* EN474—given FE-400, 161522 on fin—from RAF for evaluation 10 June 1943, Wright Field. World's only Mk HFVII. *Vought F4U-1D Corsair* Bu 50375. *Chance-Vought XF8U-1 Crusader* Bu 138899. *Waterman Aerobile* N-54P. *Waterman Whatsit* X12272. The following machines are stored, some crated, not normally accessible even to researchers:—*A-4* (V2 rocket). V4 Werk-Nr 342, given FE-4615. *Abrams Explorer* X19897 *Aichi B7A1 Ryusei "Grace"*, 1944. *Aichi M6A1 Serian II* of 1943 *Arado Ar 234 B-2 Blitz* Werk-Nr 623167, FE-1010 (Luftwaffe 140312). *Avro (Canada) VZ-9V Avrocar. Bachem Ba 349-B1 Natter (BP-20.) Baldwin Red Devil* of 1911. *Beech A-35 Bonanaz "Waikik"* N80040 of William Odoms' Honolulu record (still airworthy, not arrived). *Bell RP-63A King Cobra* 42-70255. *Blohm and Voss BV 155B* given FE-505 (sometimes described 155 V3). *Consolidated PT-1* of 1926. *Convair 240* N240K "Caroline", c/n 89. *Curtiss E Boat* —hull only, of 1914. *Curtiss CW-1 Junior* N10965 c/n 1143. *Curtiss XP-55 Ascender* 42-78846. *de Havilland DH.4* A15101, "Alaskan Flier" of 1920. *Douglas XB-42 A Mixmaster* (Fuse) 43-25253. *Ecker Flying Boat. Fairchild 71* NX8006 c/n 140 "Stars & Stripes" incomplete. *Fairchild PT-19A Cornell* 43-33842. *Felixstowe (Naval A/c Factory) F5L* (hull only) serial 3022. *Fisher XP-75C Eagle* 44-44533. *Focke Wulf Fw 190 F-8/R1* Werk-Nr 640069, was T2-117. *Focke Wulf Ta 152 A* Werk-Nr 0003, was FE-112. *Fowler-Gage Tractor* of 1912 (parts only). *Gallaudet Hydro Kite* of 1921. *Grumman G-44 (J4F-2) Widgeon* (XP5M-1) 32976. *Grunau Sailplane* given T2-2600 (incomplete). *Heinkel He 162 A Salamander* (called "Volksjäger" by German publicists) originally Werk-Nr 120230, with new tail fitted Werk-Nr 120222 allocated. Was "White 23". FE-504. *Heinkel He 219 A* T2-614 of 1944. *Helioplane No 1* N939OH. *Herrick HV2A Vertoplane* N13515. *Herring-Curtiss 1910* a/c incomplete. *Hiller XH-44 Hiller-Copter* NX30033. *Hiller HOE-1* 138652. *Horten Brothers Primary Glider* of 1943. *Horten Brothers Ho 111 Glider* FE-7 (incomplete). *Horten Brothers Ho 229* FE-490 (listed by some as Go 229 V3). *Hughes XV-9A Hot Cycle Heli. Interstate TDR-1* 33529. *Jet Supported Platform Rotorcraft*, NACA. *Junkers Ju 3 88 K Störtebecker* Werk-Nr 880430650, FE-1400. *Kaman K-225 (XHOK-1)* 125477, world's first turbine-driven helicopter, 10 December 1951. *Kawanishi P1Y2-5 Kyokko "Frances"*—quoted by some as Yokusuka P1Y1 Ginga "Frances. *Kawasaki Ki-45 Tory "Nick" II* serial 701. *Kellett XR-8* 43-44714. *Kyushu J7W1 Shinden* T2-326. *Lilienthal Glider* of 1894. *Lippisch DM-1 Delta Wing* of 1945. *Lockheed P-38J Lightning* 42-67762. *Lockheed XP-80 Shooting Star* 44-83020. *Martin B-26B-25-MA Marauder* 41-31773 "Flak Bait". *Martin PBM* quarter-scale test vehicle, 1940. *Martin Wm. H. Glider* (incomplete) of 1908. *Maupin-Lanteri Black Diamond* of 1910. *McDonnell XHV-*

Douglas R4D-5 (Washington D.C.)

C-V Crusader (Washington D.C.)

Amelia Earhart's Vega (Washington D.C.)

Spitfire VII (Washington D.C.)

Loening OA-1A (Washington D.C.)

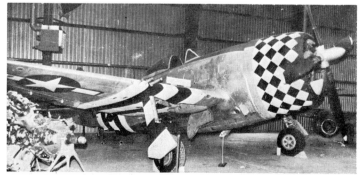

Thunderbolt (Washington D.C.)

Focke-Wulf TA 152 (Washington D.C.)

Junkers Ju 388 K (Washington D.C.)

McDonnell XHV-1 (Washington D.C.)

Ryan Vertijet (Washington D.C.)

1 *Convertiplane* 53-4017 (to come). *McDonnell XV-1 Helicopter. Messerschmitt Me 410 A-3 Hornisse (Hornet)* FE-499. *Mitsubishi G4M2 "Betty" 24* T2-2205—nose only. *Montgomery Santa Clara Glider* of 1905, incomplete. *Montgomery Evergreen Glider* 1911, incomplete. *Nagler Rolz 54V2* of 1943. *Nakajima Ki-115 Tsurugi. Nakajima C6N1 Saiun "Myrt 2"* serial 1702. *Nakajima J1N1S Gekko "Irving 2"* serial 700. *Naval A/c Factory N3N* 3022 "Yellow Peril". *Noorduyn YC-64 Norseman IV* 42-5046 c/n 78. *North American RO-47A* 37-279 (sometimes CS-47A). *North American XP-51 Mustang* 41-038. *North American P-51C Mustang* 44-10947 c/n 111-29080, now N1202 "Excalibur III". Charles Blair flew first ever solo across Arctic and North Pole, May 29 1951 in this aircraft. *Northrop XP-56 Black Bullet* 42-38353. *Northrop N-1M Flying Wing* NX28311. *Northrop M2-F1 Lifting Body* (coming from Edwards AFB). *Olmstead Pusher Amphibian* of 1912 (incomplete). *Pentecost E III Hoppicopter* NX31222 of 1945. *Piper L-4B Grasshopper* 43-1074. *Cierva C.8L Mk IV* NC418 of 1928. Built by A. V. Roe for Harold F. Pitcairn and made first autogiro flight in USA, January 1929. Presented to Smithsonian 1931. *Pitcairn Cierva PCA* X95N of 1930. *Pitcairn AC35 Roadable* NX70 c/n J-91 of 1940. *Platt-Le Page XR-1* 42-6581. Early twin rotor helicopter. *Ryan X-13 Vertijet* 54-1619. *Shoemaker Biplane* of 1910 (incomplete). *Standard J1 Lincoln* N1375 of 1917. *Stearman-Hammond* NC15533 of 1935. *Stinson SR-10F Reliant* NC2311. *Stinson L-5 Sentinel* 42-14798. *Vertol (Piasecki) PV 2* NX37061. *Vertol XHRP-X Dog Ship* 01045 of 1947. *Vertol VZ-2 VTOL. Verville Sport Trainer* N457M. *Voisin MOD.8 Bomber* of 1916. *Vought V-173 Flying Flapjack* 02978, 1942. *Vultee BT-13A Valiant* 41-22124. *WACO 1922 Glider* (incomplete). *Weissman-Cooke* 1911 aircraft. *Yakovlev Yak-18 Bedck "Charlie"* captured Korea. It is believed that in 1973 additions will be:—*Roscoe Turner RT-14* Racer "Miss Champion", the 1938 Thompson Trophy Race winner. *WACO 9* of 1926 with 90 hp OX-5, from Clay Brutner of Troy, Ohio. *Goodyear F2G-1D Corsair* 88454, from Norfolk, Va, and *Douglas DC-3* N67000 (c/n 1498 the oldest and fifth production) due from California; ex NC16004 American Airlines "California", 42-56096, NC16004. In the new Space Building a growing collection of the world's spacecraft and ancilliary exhibits:—*Lockheed Agena; Mercury Spacecraft* "Friendship 7" of Colonel John H. Glenn 20 February 1962; *Gemini IV; Titan* missile (in which public are allowed). *Moon Vehicle* of type first to land men, with "Old Glory" in showcase, plus many ever-changing items as men return from space. Details appreciated with dates, serials etc. Let us hope that this fantastic collection will soon be properly housed. Aircraft at present out on loan are shown at their current locations to avoid duplication. *Bucker Jungmeister* N15196 which reached U.S.A. in the "Hindenburg" (destroyed by fire at Lakehurst N.J. 6th May 1937) being restored as memorial to Bevo Howard.

In John F. Kennedy Playground, 7th and O. Streets are:—*Lockheed T-33A* 51-9294 and 53-5208. *NA F-86H* 53-1348 also reported—but where exactly? The National Naval Memorial Museum, Old Washington Navy Yard offers, outside:— *Chance Vought RGM-6 Regulus II; General Dynamics Advanced Terrier* (two examples) *Bendix RIM-8 Talos AA Target Mk 52 Mod2* serial E-429. Inside museum:— *General Dynamics SAM N-7 Terrier; Raytheon AIM-7D/E Sparrow; ASM-N-2 Bat; Gyrodyne YRON-1* single-seat helicopter; *Yokosuka MXY7-K2* two-seat glider trainer—for Ohka suicide bomb pilots—in original paint. There are also many

"Friendship 7" (Washington D.C.)

Bucker Jungmeister N15196 (Washington D.C.)

guns, tanks, submarines etc, *Focke Achgelis Fa 330 A-1* FE-4618 (from NASM) may be here.

FLORIDA

ARCADIA. *Lockheed T-33A* 52-9696.

BAY COUNTY. Municipal Airport. *Douglas M1M-14A Nike-Hercules; Ryan AQM-34 Firebee 2382.* Displayed.

BEAUFORT. MCAS. At gate, *North American FJ-2 Fury* 135841 "9".

BELLE GLADE. Airfield. *WACO QDC* N11489—one of two in USA; *WACO QSO* N837V c/n 3133; *WACO ASO* N7091; *WACO ASO* N752K c/n A153—all sprayers.

BOCA RATON. Airfield. *NA Harvard* N8201E (ex SNJ-5 90995).

BRADENTOWN. South Florida Museum (see Miami for store). *Martin HGM-25A Titan 1* 4508. *Globe GC-1B Swift* N80684 c/n 1089 flies here with B. F. Staub.

CAPE KENNEDY. Patrick AFB. Air Force Space Museum. Many items stored; intending visitors should write to Arthur B. Hicks, Museum Officer, Florida 32925 to verify viewing facilities to see:—*Bell GAM-63 Rascal; Boeing IM-99 Bomarc; Boeing Minuteman; Convair SM-65 Atlas D; Convair SM-65 Atlas E; Chrysler SM-78 Jupiter; Chrysler XSM-A-14 Redstone; Douglas MB-1 Genie; Douglas SM-75 Thor; Douglas Skybolt; Douglas XSAM-A-7 Nike-Ajax; Fieseler FZG-76 (V1); Firestone XM4E1 Corporal; Hughes GAR-1D Falcon; Hughes AIM-26A Falcon; Lockheed Polaris 1; Lockheed Agena; Martin ASM-N-7 Bullpup A; Martin ASM-N-7 Bullpup B; Martin SM-78 Titan 1; Martin SSM-A-12 La Crosse; Martin TM-61 Matador; Martin TM-76 Mace; Martin Pershing; McDonnell Asset; McDonnell GAM-72 Quail; North American Navaho; Northrop SM-62 Snark; Philco AAM-N-7 Sidewinder; Ryan Q-2 Firebee.*

CECIL FIELD. NAS. *Douglas A-4A Skyhawk* 142167 mounted.

CROSS CITY. *T-33A* 51-4200 displayed.

DADE. *NA F-86D/L Sabre* 53-728.

DAYTONA BEACH. Museum of Speed. *XM-11878 Missile; Martin TM-61C Matador; Convair F-102 Delta Dagger* 0-60986. Details of opening and admission welcomed. At Dayton Beach Airport, Embry Riddle Aeronautics said to have *Beech C-18* and *D-18,* also veteran *DC-3,* details appreciated. Also flying *Fleetwing F-5 Seabird* N19191 c/n F.502; *A-26 Invader* N42ER; *Stinson V-77* N69386, c/n 77-332.

DE FUNIAK SPRINGS. *T-33A* 51-8959 displayed.

DE LAND. Airstrip. *Mooney M-18 Mite No 1;* Ray Campbell.

DELRAY BEACH. Airfield. *DH.89A Rapide* G-AJGS c/n W1001 ex rebuild of pre-war G-ACZE by DH. at Witney 1947; Fred Ludington.

EAU GALLE. Chamber of Commerce Park. *NA F-100-45-NH Super Sabre* 55-2882 "FW882". *Boeing LGM-30A Minuteman I* of 655th ATW.

EGLIN. AFB. Museum. *T-33A* 53-4987.

FLORIDA CITY. Highway 27 *F-86L* 53-0998.

FORT LAUDERDALE. Hollywood International Airport. *Lockheed T-33A* 53-5936 displayed. Flying from here *NA P-51D Mus'ang* N6165U ex 44-85634 coded "K-GI"; Aviation Business Enterprises; *PBY-5A Catalina* N8875G; *N48129* ex 64071, *N68766. B-25 Mitchell* N3512G ex 44-30456; *McDonnell F2H Banshee* N4282A; *Stearman PT-17* N5598L; *Douglas A-26 Invader* N52NM c/n 1302, *N30355; Lockheed 10* N3749 and N5705. *Fairchild C-82* N8009E. ex 44-23027. In playground said to be *Chance-Vought F7U Cutlass* serial?

FORT WALTON BEACH. *Convair F-102A* 53-1799 on small grass strip along main street; *TF-102A* 56-2333 "333" in park.

GLYNCO. *Grumman F11F Tiger* 141790 displayed, on Route 17.

HOMESTEAD. Executive Airport. *Junkers Ju 52/3m* ex Mexico reported owned here by George Hamilton— reg'n? *Northrop SM-62 Snark* on traffic island. *NA P-51H* N313H ex 44-64415 of Bill Hogan (and may fly from Hamilton Airport).

HURLBURT. AFB. (part of the Eglin Complex). At main entrance *Douglas A-26K Invader* 64-17666 (was 44-35483 c/n 28762) ex 1st Special Operations Wing; *Cessna O-1E Bird Dog* 56-4208; *Douglas A-1E Skyraider* 51-598; *Helio U-10A Courier* 62-3606.

INDIAN ROCKS BEACH. *NA F-86D/L* 51-6059.

JACKSONVILLE. NAS. *Grumman F-11F Tiger* in "Blue Angels" colours—serial wanted.

KISSIMMEE. Mark Morrison reputedly paid 40,000 dollars-plus, for the *Boeing SST prototype mock-up* (cost to USA more than 12 million dollars). Shipped by rail from Seattle at enormous cost (12,000,000 dollars— £400,000.00 quoted) including erection by 30 men, to be the centrepiece of a display they say, eventually, to be 600 aircraft!!! Details please.

LAKELAND. Luther A. Young, 2 *Fairey Swordfish III* ex Brantford, Ontario.

MAITLAND. *Northrop F-89H Scorpion* 54-396 exhibited.

MIAMI. International Airport. *NA P-51D* N103TL; Wallace Garrick; *DH. Comet 1XB* CF-SVR c/n 06017 ex RCAF 5301 delivered 29th May 1953; reported still static here. *Boeing SA-307B Stratoliner* NX19904 c/n 1997, sold to Howard Hughes for round-world flight "Flying Penthouse" also said hangared—confirmation please. *WACO UPF-7* N17470; and *Demoiselle (replica)* with Joe Mangeri. *Boeing 100 (PT-12)* reported with Ted Voorhees for rebuild. *Lockheed P2V-7* in children's playground—serial wanted. *Tiger Moth* N100MH c/n 119 ex A17-122, VH-BKB, VH-BTS, VH-WFV with L. M. Hill. Aviation Trades Training School:—*Curtiss C-46* 44-77838. *Douglas C-47* 45-916 (ex USA-Brazil Mission); *45-1119. Fairchild C-82A* 45-57762. W. G. Dickinson, Bi-Planes Inc, said to have *WACO UIC* N13577 c/n 3829 of 1933 (ex Texaco 18) and *Boeing Stearman* N163ER c/n 75-2173, N55735 c/n 75-2616. *Stinson V-77 Reliant* NC69377, c/n 3060. *JN-4D* (rep.). In the Pan Am hangar a 1927 *Laird Swallow;* 1932 *Aeronca C-2,* and 1934 *Taylor Cub* owned by John H. McGeary for a possible museum. Reg'ns please.

OPA-LOCKA. Airport. *Lockheed C-89 Constitution* N7673C c/n 85165 reported not to become restaurant— let us hope to be preserved, though. Flying:—*Ryan PT-22 Recruit* N53826 c/n 1522; *FM-2 Wildcat* N2876D Bu 41760; *Stearman PT-17* N9998 ex 41-1059; *P-51D Mustang* N12067 ex 45-11371. Reported static (on display, perhaps) *Douglas A-4A Skyhawk* 142166 "10/6F" and *NA F-1E Fury* 143591, also *Lockheed P-2E Neptune* 124871.

ORANGE PARK. *NA F-86L* 53-4063.

ORLANDO. Naval Reserve Training Centre, displayed *McDonnell F2H-2 Banshee* 126680. Lock Haven Park has *Martin TM-61C Matador; Northrop SM-62 Snark.* At Sentinel Star Building, *Martin GM-12D Bullpup.* At the Municipal Airport, *Martin ASM-N-7 Bullpup A.*

PANAMA CITY. *NA-F-860D/L* 52-10133.

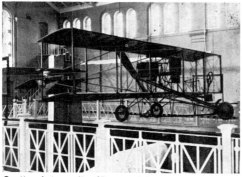

Curtiss A-1—replica (Pensacola)

N3N-3 and Boeing F4B-4 (Pensacola)

Douglas A-1H (AD-6) Skyraider 135300, which made the last Navy prop-driven combat strike over Vietnam 20 February 1968. *Douglas A4D-1 (A-4A) Skyhawk* 137830. *Douglas F4D-1 (F-6A) Skyray* 123806 from NAS Patuxent River, Md. *Grumman F8F-2 Bearcat* 121710 from NTS Bainbridge. *Grumman F9F-2 Panther* 123050, from NAS Pensacola. *Grumman TF11F-1 Tiger* 141828, Cdr Wheat's "Blue Angels" a/c. *Grumman J2F-6 Duck* (manufactured by Columbia) 33581, from NAS Norfolk. *Grumman TBM-3E Avenger* 53403 from NAS Jacksonville. *Kaman OH-43D (HOK-1) Huskie* (K-225) 138101 from Davis-Monthan AFB. *McDonnell F2H-4 Banshee* 127693. *North American FJ-4 (F-1E) Fury* 139486 from NAS Glynco. *Sikorsky S-55 (CH-19E) Chickasaw* 142432. *Vertol HUP-3 (UH-25C) Retriever* 147600, from Litchfield Park, Ariz. *Vought F4U-5N Corsair* 122189 from NTS Bainbridge. *Chance-Vought F8U-1 (F-8A) Crusader* 145347. The following are stored and not accessible:— *Bell TH-13M (HTL-6) Sioux* 142377 from NAS Ellyson Field. *Curtiss MF Seagull* 5483. *Grumman F6F-5 Hellcat* 94203 and *F6F-5K* 79863, the latter donated by Grumman. *Gyrodyne YRON-1 Rotocycle* 4013, from Bethpage, NY. *Naval A/c Factory N3N-3 "Yellow Peril"* 1359, from NAEC, Philadelphia. *North American AT-6 (SNJ-5B) Texan* 51968, donated by Paul Pribble of Downey, California. *Sikorsky S-51 (HO3S) Dragonfly* 124352. *Vought F4U-7 Corsair* 133704, recovered from French via MAAG. There is also a *Naval Aircraft Factory MF-Boat* Bu 5483, purchased from Mr. George S. Waltman of NY and completely restored. It is thought that just inside the main gates there is *Grumman F11F-1 Tiger*, probably 141884, from MCAS, Cherry Point, "Blue Angels" aircraft. See Quantico, Va for loaned-out aircraft. Pensacola Municipal Airport also has *Grumman F11F-1*, in "Blue Angels" markings, mounted on plinth; serial wanted.

POMPANO BEACH. *Northrop F-89H Scorpion* 54-318

SARASOTA. Airport. Cavalier Aircraft—several *P-51 Mustangs* including N6167U ex 44-63775—with Rolls-Royce turboprop. N7724C of Trans-Florida Aviation, and *NA P-51* N851D ex 44-84658, the only dual-control Mustang.

VALPARAISO. Doolittle Memorial *NA JB-25J Mitchell* 44-30854 c/n 108-34129 as Tokyo Raider.

WEST HOLLYWOOD. North Perry Airport. *PBY-6A* N6454C ex 64106; *Stinson SM-8A* N941W c/n 4099. *Aeronca Chief* N46425 of 1939; Melville E. Dillon.

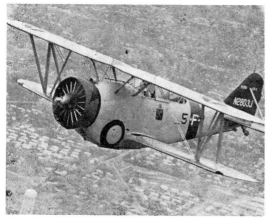

Grumman FF-1 (Pensacola)

PENSACOLA. Naval Aviation Museum, USN Air Station. A new building is planned and officer-in-charge should be contacted—postal address Florida 32508, for visiting. On public view (1973)—*Burgess N-9H* sometimes referred to as Burgess-Curtiss, now completely restored here, on loan from NASM. No serial. *Douglas D-558-1 Skystreak* 37970, recovered from Calif State Polytechnic College. Set world-speed record 1947 of 964.105 mph. *Boeing F4B-4* 9241, completely restored, loaned by NASM, NR9329. *Curtiss A-1 (replica)* reproduction of Navy's first a/c, from NASM. *Grumman FF-1* (Bu 9351 assigned arbitrarily by Grumman) discovered in a Nicaraguan Air Force salvage yard 1962 by J. R. Sirmons; after 3 years restoring he flew it to USA as N2803J in 1966. Assumed to be one of the G-23 models assembled by Canadian Car & Foundry in 1937 and exported to Nicaragua 1938. Grumman returned it to FF-1 configuration before donating to museum, in "Fighting Five" colours. *Mercury Space Capsule "Aurora 7"* of Scott-Carpenter's earth orbit 24 May 1962 is on loan here. The following exhibits are available only to serious researchers:—

WEST PALM BEACH. Airport. *Douglas B-23 Dragon* N4000B c/n 2743. *DH. Vampire* N350S.

WINTER HAVEN. *Northrop F-89H Scorpion* 54-337.

GEORGIA

ADEL. *Lockheed T-33A* 52-9633 displayed.

ATLANTA. Peachtree-de-Kalb Airport. *Douglas AD-4 Skyraider* 123827 ex NAS. At the Atlantic Museum (in the backyard, 1972 report) *Mitsubishi A6M5 Zero*—said to be first captured. At 3689 Shadow Lane John C. Youngblood is said to have *Thomas Morse S.4C* original, under rebuild. Technical & Vocational School here has the *Lockheed L-329 Jetstar* N329K, second prototype c/n 1002, presented by Lockheed A/c. Powered by Bristol Orpheus turbojets.

AUGUSTA. *Lockheed T-33A* 51-6746 displayed.

BRUNSWICK. Airport. *NA B-25 Mitchell* N37L ex 43-4899 and *Ryan PT-22* N59200. *Tiger Moth* N9146 c/n 82710 ex R4769 PH-UFK, D-EKIL owned and flown by M. M. Leveilland. *Tiger Moth* N8878 c/n 86536 ex PG627, PH-UAM; *N4970* c/n 86294 ex NL838, F-BGEP, and *N4797* c/n 85962 ex EM731, F-BGED; all H. L. Routh.

CARTERSVILLE. *Republic F-84* reported on display-serial?

COLUMBUS. *NA P-51D Mustang* N6303T, ex 44-63481 of R. Kestle flies locally.

CORDELE. On display *F-84F* 52-6438 and *T-33A* 51-6699.

DOBBINS AFB. *F-86K* 51-5896 at gate ex Georgia ANG.

DOUGLAS. *T-33A* 53-6132 displayed.

ELLENWOOD. *Tiger Moth* N3862 c/n 926/T.256 ex A17-503, VH-BMY, VH-RNM; K. R. Martin.

FAYETTEVILLE. *Tiger Moth* N8232 c/n 85886 ex DF137 PH-UAG; R. E. Rust.

GRIFFIN. Municipal Airport. *T-33A* 53-6096.

HAHIRA. *T-33A* 51-6727 displayed.

HUNTER-STEWARD AFB. *Bell H-13G* 48-845, on loan from Fort Rucker, Alabama.

LAKELAND. *T-33A* 51-8555 displayed.

MACEN. *T-33A* 52-9574 displayed.

MARIETTA. Cobb County Youth Museum *Republic F-84F Thunderstreak* 51-9382—on loan from USAFM.

RICHLAND. *Northrop F-89H Scorpion* 49-2449 displayed.

SAVANNAH. P. Richart flies *Tiger Moth N657DH* c/n 86566 ex PG657, F-BGDN. At ANG Bldg. Trafis Field *F-84D* 48-741 and *F-86D* 51-5891 displayed.

STONE MOUNTAIN. Airport (near Atlanta) *WACO UPF-7* N39377. *Stinson SM-2* NC6871 c/n 1007, with Warner engine, owned by Carl Francis and R. G. Jenkins.

THOMASVILLE. *T-33A* 52-9191.

VALDOSTA. *NA F-86D/L Sabre* 52-10057 displayed.

WADLEY. *NA P-51D Mustang* N10607 ex 44-74466, Mojave Racer, owned and flown by John Sliker.

WARNER ROBINS. *T-33A* 52-9225 displayed.

WAYNESBORO. *T-33A* 51-6635 displayed.

WILLACOOCHEE. *Lockheed T-33A* 51-6612 displayed.

HAWAII

HONOLULU. Hickham AFB. *NA F-86F-5-NA* 51-2841—formerly used for rescue training and *NA F-86L* 52-4191, displayed at ANG HQs. *NA B-25J* being rebuilt for Aviation Branch of Bishop Museum—serial? *Mock-up of Curtiss P-40* used in "Tora, Tora, Tora" in ANG lot, for possible rebuild for display, with *F-102*; to be rebuilt after explosion. *NA P-51D Mustang* N5413D is said based here; serial? At International Airport *NA T-6* N3163G ex 85039 and *Beech AT-11 Kansan* N3954C—the latter static, believed for restoration. University of Hawaii, Honolulu Commercial Technical College has *Douglas A-26C Invader* N5636V; *NA B-25J* N9763Z (hardnose); *Stinson L-5*, *Lockheed T-33*, *Beech 18*, *Beech C-45J* and *NA T-6*—serials and histories appreciated.

WHEELER AFB. *Mock-up of P-40* from "Tora, Tora, Tora" exhibited. Remains of *Republic P-47* which ditched off Bellows Field, Oahu, 1943, are being recovered for possible restoration and display. Serial and further details, with pic, wanted. Lt-Col S. C. Burgess flies *Bucker Jungmeister* N859K ex PI-X-388 of Alfredo Carmelo, Manila.

IDAHO

BLACKFEET. *NA F-86D/L* 51-6074 displayed.

BOISE. Airport. *Convair F-102A* 0-31816 ex 124th F. G. Idaho ANG displayed. *Douglas A-26C* 43-22606 also reported displayed. Flying from here *P-51D* N5482V ex 44-73343 of Mike Loening, Mojave Racer; *Boeing B-17G* N9823Z, N9324Z ex 44-83542, N9193G; *Grumman TBM-3 Avenger* N9590C ex 53784; N7026C; At Glider Air Park, J. L. Terteling has the fabulous *Sopwith 1F.1 Camel* B7270, built by Clayton & Shuttleworth and restored in markings of Capt. Roy Brown of the "Red Baron" combat, 209 Sqdn, RAF. Rebuilt by Richard Day of State College Pennsylvania. Airworthy and registered N86678. Also *Avro 504J/K* B3182 built A. V. Roe 1916 as J and converted to K. War history wanted. To USA after 1918 and purchased early 1920s by rancher and used in Mexican Central Highlands. It is said that the first woman to solo in Mexico used this machine. Refabriced 1925 and loaned to a Trades School until 1931, then stored in shed until 1968. Now authentically restored to 1916 configuration and flown again 3 August 1972—what a magnificent project.

Camel (right) and Avro 504 (Boise)

BURLEY. *Lockheed T-33A* 52-9594 displayed.

IDAHO FALLS. Airport. *NA F-86D/L* 53-1022 displayed, Idaho ANG colours.

KELLOGG. Airport. *DH. Tiger Moth* N5050 c/n 635 T. 208 ex A17-440, VH-AYG, ZK-AWB; *N5050C* c/n 86321 ex NL875,, F-BGEU, G-AYHU; both owned/ flown by C. E. Henley.

LEWISTON. Nez Perce County Airport. *T-33A T-Bird* 0-16717 of 124th F. G. ADC, Idaho ANG, mounted.

NAPA. City Park. *Northrop F-89B Scorpion* 49-2457 displayed, ex Idaho ANG.

POCATELLO. *F-86D/L* 52-10079 displayed; *Ryan PT-22* N48552 c/n 1039, owned/flown by Ron Bowie. *Franklin Sport (replica)* owned by Dick Gregerson; *Fairchild 24G, Vultee BT-13* and *Interstate Cadet* of 1942 being restored—details wanted.

TWIN FALLS. Airport. *Lockheed T-33A* 56-1660 displayed; *Grumman TBM-3 Avengers* N7157C, N7015C ex 85854, flying here.

ILLINOIS

ALTAMONT. *NA F-86D/L* 51-6211 displayed.

AURORA. In Park. *Lockheed F-80C-11-LO Shooting Star* 45-8357 ex 169th FS, Illinois ANG, Oklahoma ANG.

BIGGSVILLE. *Piper PA-12 Super Cruiser* N3469M c/n 12-2347; Robert Seymour.

BROOKFIELD. Park *NA-F-86L-55-NA Sabre* 53-700.

BURLINGTON. Airport. *Spartan Executive Model 7W* stored by J. Jennings—reg'n please.

CAHOKIA. Bistate Parks Metropolitan Airport. *Douglas C-47-80-DL Skytrain* 43-15331, in USAF marks, said to be earmarked for National Museum of Transport, St. Louis, Missouri—up-dated information please.

CENTRALIA. *Lockheed T-33A* 52-9651 displayed.

CHAMPAIGN. University of Illinois Airport *Grumman FM-2 Wildcat* N6290C c/n 5804 of Rudy Frasca; *NA F-51D* N2870D ex 44-63350 of Dr. Mark R. Foutch; Training airframes:—*Lockheed T-33A* 51-4039 and 53-5979; *C-47A* 42-23727/N2217S; *Douglas VC-47A* 42-93066/N2216S; *Hiller H-23A* 51-16110 (in pieces). *Beech C-45F* 44-47691; *C-45G* 51-11585; *51-11878.*

CHICAGO. Midway Airport. *Curtiss Condor* N12303 c/n 23, of American Airlines, reported here for restoration. Can a reader please confirm and send photo. At The Museum of Sciences and Industry, East 57th Street and South Lakeshore Drive, open Monday-Saturday 0930-1600, Sundays and Holidays 1000-1800, During daylight saving (from end April) weekdays to 1730. *Wright Brothers 1911-12 Biplane,* a composite model with ailerons instead of warping wings. Rausenberg 8 cyl, 75hp engine. Span 40ft, length 28ft, height 10ft, wing area 538 sq ft. Weight empty 800 lbs, loaded 1,132 lbs. Max speed 48 mph, landing 30 mph. Flown Dayton International Air Races 1924 by Lt John A. McCready. Natural wood and varnished. Loaned by Charles F. Kettering, Dayton Ohio. Recent report says not displayed—is it stored or under restoration? *Morane Saulnier Type 1916,* thought to be 80 per cent reproduction from original Morane "G" which Walter Brock took back to USA 1914 after winning London-Manchester Aerial Derby and London-Paris-London Races. He purchased Auban Flying Field, Chicago. A Lady Peel is said to have bought Brock's original fuselage and other parts to help the RFC in 1914. Donald J. Lockwood who inherited much of Brock's Collection is now trying to reconstruct the Morane

"G" from engine and parts—up-to-date progress news wanted. *Curtiss Pusher Biplane* 1910, SC.8384, NR10362. *Curtiss JN-4D Jenny* 2421 c/n 553, donated by John L. Brown. Blue fuselage, yellow wings, number on tail and wing in black. *Boeing 40-B NC288*, donated by United Airlines Transport Co. This machine pioneered first privately-operated Great Lakes to Pacific Coast services. Span 44 ft, length 33ft, height 12ft, weight loaded 6,079 lbs. Max speed 132 mph, landing 57mph. Light green fuselage sides, pine green top and bottom, with light green on bottom of wings inner area, red trim, black numbers. *Travel Air Texaco No 13*, NR1313, flown by Lt Cdr Frank Hawks to establish many speed records including Los Angeles-NY 13 hrs 26 mins 15 secs. Max speed 235mph, cruising 150 mph, landing 70 mph. Red wings and wheel pants, stripe on fuselage and numbers trimmed in black. Rest white, white numbers on wings trimmed black. Donated Texas Co. *Supermarine Spitfire IA* P9306 ex 74 (Tiger) Sqdn, RAF Hornchurch, flown by Pilot Officers Cobden and St. John. Five enemy aircraft officially credited from 6 July 1940 to October 1941 when relegated to training. Colour —blue—loaned by RAF. The official museum listing supplied to V. and V. includes *Pitcairn PCA-2* "Miss Champion" NC-11609, with Wright Whirlwind E, 300 hp.S an 30ft, length 23ft, height 13ft. Rotor sweep 45ft, Empty weight 2,025 lbs, loaded 3,000 lbs. Flown by Capt. Lewis A. Yancy. Is this in store now? List also quotes "Missile and Drone exhibits" but visitors have not seen any. It is known the Ju 87B. dropped twice in lowering for cleaning, is now with EAA Museum, Wisc—have other exhibits gone there? News wanted. At Chicago's Vocational Technical School (Mr. Woodbill in charge) *Cessna UC-78* N50137—photo a/c; *Lockheed T-33A* 51-4309; *51-4271A*. *Stearman PT-17 Kaydet* "201" in AAF training colours—serial wanted.

Morane Saulnier 1916 (Chicago)

JN-4D (Chicago)

Boeing 40-B (Chicago)

Spitfire IA (Chicago)

Travel Air Texaco (Chicago)

DIXON. Walgreen Field. Junkers Ju 52/3m N130LW bought by barber Lester Weaver (ex Flying Fortress pilot) from Quito, Ecuador. Flown in by George Hamilton via Mexico and Miami. Said to have been flown in Spain during Civil War and later in Sweden until moved to Ecuador by a Luftwaffe veteran, earlier serials/reg'ns please. Also flying locally *Stinson SR-7B* N16130 c/n 9693; Gordon Rutt; *Rearwin 6000M Speedster* N19415 c/n 307; Leon Self.

DUNDEE. Airfield. *Ryan PT-22* N48773; Buck Hilbert.

ELMWOOD PARK. Airfield. *Naval A/c Factory N3N-3* N933R; Bob Halmchen & Joe Ciapattoni. *N3N-3* N6399T c/n 3046 "Ed" Prose. *N3N-3* N12063; D. A. Powers.

HARVARD. Airfield. *Harvard IV* (Canadian Car & Foundry) N7552U and N7553U, believed ex RCAF 20427/8.

HIGHLAND. *Lockheed T-33A* 53-4914 displayed.

HILLSBORO. *NA F-86D/L* 51-6126 displayed.

HINSDALE. Airfield. *NA T-6G* N1190 c/n 182-648 "RB 007" and *Grumman G-44* N4018, both of Dick Burns. *Interstate S-1A* N37217 c/n 60 of 1941, Mary Burns.

LAKE BLUFF. Airstrip. *Ryan STM-E2* N8146 c/n 457 of 1940, in Dutch colours; Dorr Carpenter.

LOCKPORT. Lockport Aero College. Viewing by appointment only:—*Douglas C-47* N12046 ex 0-16392; plus one other, serial wanted. *Beech UC-45J* 51227; *Lockheed T-33A* N11986 ex 51-8915; *N11987* ex 51-9106; *N11988* ex 51-9128; *N11989* ex 53-6091.

MATTOON. City Park. *Republic F-84F* 51-9339.

MOLINE. Airfield. *Ryan ST-3KR* N48307 c/n 1269; *Fleet 2* N431K c/n 154; John & Joan Richardson.

Lockheed 18 (Mundelein)

MUNDELEIN (Ivanhoe) Polidori Airstrip. The Victory Air Museum, Paul Polidori, director; Earl Reinert curator. Telephone LO 6-6469. Many fascinating restorations under way, including:—*Beech AT-11 Kansan* N81Y ex 42-37240; *Consolidated SNV-1* Bu 34491. *Brewster F2A-3 Buffalo* N9622C dismantled and minus tail, ex Naval Technical School. *Consolidated PBY-6A Catalina* N33RS Bu 64002—sank Lake Michigan —to museum 1966 for restoration. *Chance Vought F8U Cutlass*, incomplete, Bu wanted. *Douglas RB-26C-40-DT Invader* 44-35590 "Nightmare", markings of 3rd Bombardment Group. *Grumman FM-2 Wildcat* Bu 46867 serial 121214, dedicated to "Butch" O'Hare and Joss Foss one wing for USN, one for USMC. Formerly at Wheeling. *Grumman F6F-3 Hellcat* Bu 40467, ex VF-16 of Carrier Lexington, 1944 and then Navy Technical School, Chicago. *Henschel Hs 129*, incomplete but world's only example and obviously subject for restoration, was FE-4600. *Lockheed 18* CF-TCY c/n 2064, painted to represent Hudson of RAF Coastal Command, with unorthodox marks ER-V (for Queen Elizabeth II and Churchill). Gesture of goodwill from former merchant seaman Earl Reinert who remembers hospitality in Liverpool, Southampton—and Hong Kong and Sydney. *Lockheed T-33A-5-LO* 51-4298—fuselage only. *NA P-51K/F6 Mustang* 44-12840 photo-reece version, fuselage. *NA.T-28A Trojan* 49-1738 N7692C. *SNJ-6* N9826C. *NA B-25J* 44-323043 ex Indiana in 5th AAF South Pacific markings of 8th and 90th BW, Bismarck Sea Battle. *Republic P-47M Thunderbolt* NX4477N c/n 227385, the former W. P. Odom, Bendix Racer, owned by Earl

Reinert since 1948. *Jap Naval Air Technical Arsenal Ohka 11*, 1-13, or 1-20; one of six captured in cave at Okinawa in 1945, believed the finest existing and only intact wooden-wing operational example (wing weighs 400 lbs against 75 lbs for metal wing). There are also fuselages or remains of NA Sabre, Me 262, Me 163, engine of a Fieseler VI and other engines. A collection worthy of your support. Also at Mundelein *Spitfire XIV* RM694 ex Hornchurch, and *RM927* (ex 91 Sqdn and SG25 of Belgium) owned by John Lowe and Larry Matt for rebuilding. Six of the *Hispano HA-1109-MIL* (Spanish Bf 109) are here, serials/reg'ns appreciated, also future locations and registrations.

NAPERVILLE. Airfield. *Curtiss JN-4C Canuck*, formerly with Paul Franklin, Salem, Oregon, now being rebuilt by R. A. McDaniel. He (and all of us) would value history and serial. *Great Lakes 2T-1E* N108CH c/n 235, reported with John C. Leubke—confirmation please, with pic.

OAK LAWN. Airport. *NA AT-6B* N5849N and *N7231G*; J. Brabant. *Boeing P-12E* 31-559, owned by B. & F. Supply Co, said to be here dismantled, minus wings— a case for rebuild?

ODIN. *Republic F-84F* 51-9343 displayed..

PEORIA. *Republic F-84F-1-GK Thunderstreak* 51-9313 ex Illinois ANG.

PEWAUKEE. Airfield. *P-51D Mustang* N5471V ex 45-11381 of Jack Hursmann.

QUINCY. Park. *Lockheed T-33A* 52-9770, from Springfield.

Convair RB-36H (Rantoul)

RANTOUL. Chanute AFB. Some aircraft on display and others, used as training airframes, only when moved from hangar to hangar or annually during May. Best to write to Officer Commanding before making a long trip to see:—*Douglas A-26C Invader* 44-35204, now painted as 434314 B model of 8 BS, 3 BW, Captain Walmsley's MH a/c 44-34314. *NA TB-25N Mitchell* 44-30635 painted as 02344 B model, Doolittle's Tokyo Raider 40-2344. *Boeing B-29 30-MO Superfortress* 45-21749 to be painted "Enola Gay". *Convair RB-36H* 51-13730 to be painted as 44-92065 of 92 BW. *Boeing XB-47 Stratojet* 46-066—the second prototype. *Convair YRB-58A Hustler* 55-666 painted as "Greased Lightning" 12059, Tokyo-London speed record, 1963 (61-2059). *Lockheed F-80B Shooting Star* 45-8501, painted as B model, 80 FBS, 8 FBW, Major Loring's MH a/c 91830 (49-1830). *Republic YF-84A Thunderjet* 45-59494 painted as G model of 1953 Thunderbirds Aerobatic Team with T-33 tip tanks, 116719 (51-16719). *North American F-86A Sabre* 47-614 painted as F model of 39 FIS, 51 FIW of Capt. McConnell, sixteen MiG Ace of Korea, 12910 (51-2910). *North American P-51H Mustang* 44-64265 painted as "7" a D model of 99 FS, 332 FG, 15 AF, Italy. The above machines are all on loan from USAFM. *Republic F-84F Thunderstreak* 51-9531—from 101 Fighter Sqdn, Mass ANG. *Grumman HU-16B Albatross* 51-7200, prototype B model, from Luke AFB, Ariz. *Douglas VC-47D Dakota* 43-49336 from England AFB, Louisiana, 4403 TFW. Boeing *C-97G Stratofreighter* 52-898 from Delaware ANG. *Douglas C-133A Cargomaster* 56-2009 from Dover AFB, Delaware. *Boeing B-52E Stratofortress* 56-708. In addition to the above six base-allocated a/c the following machines, used as training airframes, join the main display every May on public viewing days: *Boeing B-52B* 52-8714; *Martin RB-57B Canberra* 52-1584 (ex W-P AFB Trials A/c). *Douglas RB-66B Destroyer* 53-412. *Lockheed T-33A T-Bird* 51-9282; 51-9797. *Cessna T-37B* 54-2739; 55-2972. *North American F-100A Super Sabre* 53-1663, *F-100C* 54-1784, *54-1785.*

McDonnell F-101B Voodoo 56-273. *Convair F-102A Delta Dagger* 56-1264; *TF-102A* 54-1351. *Lockheed F-104A Starfighter* 56-732. *Republic F-105B Thunderchief* 54-104; 54-112. *General Dynamics F-111A* 63-9767. We hope to hear that this great assembly of aircraft can be maintained and extended for public viewing.

RIVERDALE. Airfield. *Piper J-3C* of 1946 N3655K c/n 22345; Dan McGarry.

ROCKFORD. Airport. *Travel Air D4D* NC606K c/n 1282; Nick Rezich. *Piper J-5A Cub Cruiser* N35829; J. A. Braemel. *Ryan STA* N17368; John Lamb. *NA SNJ-5* N666MC ex 85066; Mark Clark. *Stinson Monoplane* 5488, being restored here following crash—updated details and photo please.

ST. CHARLES. Du Page County Airport. Many changes in the William D. Ross Collection with return of Spitfire to U.K., and crash of *Grumman G-32A* N7F c/n 447 (which we hope to hear will be restored by new owner if only for static show). This was once personal a/c of Leroy Grumman, seeing service with AAC as the UC-103 and was registered as N46110, with tail marking F3F-20447 (not completely authentic). *Curtiss P-40E* ex CF-OGZ, AK905 RAF, 15286 RCAF and *Grumman F6F-3 Hellcat* N1103V, bought by Bill Ross from Pete Brucia. *Lockheed P-38 Lightning* N9005R ex 45-3095 "Der Gabelschwanz Teufel". Also flying here *Douglas A-26* N600D c/n 28017 of Norm Kleman & John Glatz. *Spartan 7W* N836 c/n 15, also Norm Kleman.

YRB-58A Hustler (Rantoul)

Boeing Stratofortress (Rantoul)

P-40E (St. Charles)

Stinson Monoplane (Rockford)

SOUTHERN. Illinois Airport. *Lockheed T-33A* 51-4374 on display with nose-fitted guns.

SPRINGFIELD. Airfield. *Porterfield LP-65* of 1941 N34706 c/n 872 with Lycoming 65; Bill Gore.

TUSCOLA. Flying Services of Earl M. Adkisson *Demoiselle (replica)* N6162, c/n 1.

VILLA PARK. Airstrip. *NA SNJ-4* N173V c/n 88-13779 of Carl Vik.

WEST ALEXANDRIA. Airfield. *Vultee BT-13A* of 1941 N63838 c/n 2276 and *N67789* c/n 1715 of Louise & Paul Pfoutze.

WEST UNION. *Lockheed T-33A* 52-9604 displayed.

WHEATON. Airfield. *Luscombe 1 Phantom* N1286 c/n 106 of Gene Ruder.

WHEELING. Chicagoland Airport. *Taylor E-2 Cub* of 1928 c/n 60, owned by Art Mueller, the lowest surviving serial. Details of registration, with photo wanted. *Grumman F6F-5K Hellcat* N7896C ex 79863—ex 2PL photoship. *Ryan STA* N17361, c/n 166. *Ryan ST-3KR* N48587 c/n 2073; *Ryan STM* N11D c/n 181; *AT-6* N7056C ex 27512. *Beech AT-11 Kansan* N7340C ex 43-10404— photo aircraft. Details of owners, with photos appreciated. From Wheeling's Paulwaukee Airport fly:— *Cessna C-165 Airmaster* N19464 c/n 450; *Lincoln Page* of 1929 N5735; C. D. Balling. *WACO UPF7* N32084 c/n 5716, and N39756 c/n 5889.

INDIANA

ANDERSON. Park. *NA F-86H-1-NA Sabre* 52-2004.

BRAZIL. Outside County Legislature Building *NA-F86F-25-NH Sabre* 52-5434 "FU-434".

BROWNSBURG. *Lockheed F-94C Starfire* 50-975 displayed.

CHURUBUSCO. City Park. *NA F-86H-10-NH* 53-1298 ex 137th F.I.S., NY Air Guard and Maryland ANG.

COLUMBUS. *Beech XT-34A Mentor* 53-3342 displayed.

COVINGTON. *Lockheed T-33A* 52-9326.

ELKHART. *Republic F-84F-10-GK* 51-9350 displayed.

GARY. *Lockheed T-33A-1-10* 51-9079.

GRENCASTLE. Jesse Lee Post VFW. *Fieseler Fi 103/RE* 11378-2, a V1 flying bomb with provision for pilot, cockpit faired over. Captured by USN. Further details and a photo would be very helpful.

GRISSOM AFB (formerly Bunker Hill AFB). Near Peru; growing Collection loaned by USAFM—contact Officer in Charge for viewing:—*Boeing B-17G-95-DL Flying Fortress* 44-83690. "Tarnished Angel" "D" Day markings 305th BG. *Boeing B-47E Stratojet* 52-271 ex 30th BG. *Convair B-58A-CF Hustler* 55-663. *Lockheed T-33A* 52-9563. *NA B-25J* 44-86843.

HUNTINGTON. *Lockheed T-33A-1-10* 51-6745.

INDIANAPOLIS. World War Memorial Plaza. *NA F-86E Sabre* 50-632. At Weir-Cook Airport Museum, *Laird-Turner Meteor*, winner 1938/9 Thompson Races.

LAFAYETTE. Purdue Airport. *NA F-86 Sabre* N651P flying.

MONTPELIER. Kiwanis Park. *Republic F-84F* ex 122nd TAC Fighter Wing, Baer Field, Ind. Serial wanted.

MOORESVILLE. *Lockheed T-33A-1-10* 51-6782.

MUNCIE. *T-33A-1-10* 51-8609.

PORTLAND. *Lockheed F-94C-1-10 Starfire* 51-5621.

PERU. Ma-Con-A-Quah Park. *McDonnell F-101A-5-MC Voodoo* 53-2423—mounted.

ROANOKE. *Lockheed T-33A-1-10* 53-5392.

SOUTH BEND. Airfield. *Fairchild 22* N9481 c/n 911; Jack Faney. *Rearwin 7000 Sportster* N14485 c/n 403; Wm. B. Hasleton. *WACO I-BA* of 1932 N12453 c/n 3603; Ed Packard. *Beech D-18S* N500 c/n A-223 ex N80242; Tony Hulman, Indianapolis Motor Speedway.

TERRA HAUTE. Court House Lawn. *Republic F-84 Thunderjet*. Confirmation and serial please.

IOWA

BLAKESBURG. Antique Airfield, 1½ miles NE of town. The Airpower Museum (P.O. Box H. Ottumwa). Of the following aircraft listed as on display, only two, the OQ-19D and LH-2 are not kept in flying state, the museum motto being "Keep the Antiques flying":— *Arrow A2-60* N9325 c/n 341 of 1929, loaned by John Talmadge; *Arrow F* N18000 c/n 18 of 1937; *Beech AT-11* N311Y, ex 42-37432; *de Havilland DH.60GM* N1586 c/n 160 loaned by Dudley Kelly; *Fairchild 71* NC9727 c/n 603 of 1927 ex P.A.A.; *Fairchild 24W* N20638 c/n W102 loaned by Paul Lahman; *Fairchild PT-26* N73520 c/n T43-4536 ex 44-19424 of 1943, loaned Ed Nedderman; *Lark-Termite H-1* N1036 c/n 10 of 1967 loaned by Robert L. Taylor; also the *Lockheed DL-1B Sp.Vega* NC12288 c/n 161 of 1933, and the *Pietenpol B4 Aircamper* c/n AAA1 NX4716 of 1929; *Monocoupe 90* NC170K c/n 504 of 1930; *Stinson JR-S* NC12165 c/n 8074 of 1931; *Radioplane OQ-19D*; *Van Dellen LH-2* N4826E, 1958, loaned by Clarence H. and Ethel M. Van Dellen of Pella, Iowa. *Aeronca K* NC18883 c/n K147 of 1937 is being rebuilt to fly; *Anderson Z* ex 12041 of 1925 also being rebuilt; *Fairchild KR-21B* NC854V c/n 1502 of 1931, being rebuilt; *Stearman 4E Junior Speedmail* NC791H of 1930 c/n 4023 also being rebuilt. The 1929 unregistered *Kari-Keen Coupe* and 1942 *Rearwin 8135T* NC37885 c/n 910; 1917 *Standard J-1*; 1931 *WACO Primary Glider* are all stored. There are many other splendid exhibits including basket from an early Free Balloon, a 1917 American LaFrance Firetruck, and a marvellous assembly of aero-engines, veteran, vintage and modern. We applaud what is happening here and hope to hear of many more aircraft being loaned or donated, especially for the Fly-In occasions. It is understood that a *Rearwin Cloudster* is due from Ken Rearwin; *Aeronca LC* of 1936 from D. Czerwinski; *Eaglet I* biplane; *Eaglet II* parasol monoplane, both designed and built by Dr. Martin Williams. More details of these and photos of all of value for next V. and V.

BURLINGTON. *T-33A-1-10* 52-9697 in Darkwardt Park. Flying locally *Curtiss-Wright CW-1 Junior* N696V c/n 1078; Donald Guegler; *Curtiss JN-4D* "Memory Jenny" reportedly rebuilt and then flight-tested by Art J. Hartman on his 71st birthday in 1959, said to be here. Can someone confirm and give serial, also up-dated information on Art J. Hartman?

CEDAR RAPIDS. *T-33A-1-10* 53-5916 and *F-84F* 51-9444 on display; *Piper L-4 Cub* N5869V c/n 9384 of 1943, flying with C.A.P.

DES MOINES. Historical Memoral & Art Buildings. *Bleriot XI (replica)* N4W, with Continental engine; *Benoist* of 1915—further details and photos please. Flying locally:—*Lincoln Beachey Pusher (replica)* of E. D. Weeks; *Meyers OTW* N26466 c/n 19 Geo. Clark; *N31413* c/n 57, Harold Lasoner; *N34318* c/n 62, Bob Carney: *N34344* c/n 89 Max Anderson. *WACO YKS-7* N17701 c/n 4617; Donald Grimm; *Piper J-3F* N41112 Ken Smith.

Lincoln Beachey Pusher—replica (Des Moines)

FORT DODGE. Airfield. *Spartan C3-225* of 1930 N720N c/n A14, Earl Kopp.

EMMETSBURG. *T-33A* 52-9626 displayed.

GREENFIELD. Airfield. *Fokker E.III (replica)* N3363G c/n 401 of John Schildberg who also owns *DH.Tiger Moth* N8966, c/n 1767 ex RCAF 8965, CF-FEN.

Fokker E III—replica (Greenfield)

GREENVILLE. Route 1, Mid-Continent Air Museum. Contact Shelby B. Hagberg for viewing times:—*Alexander Eaglerock A-3* 8240 c/n 714; *American Eagle 101* 536N c/n 700; *Bird CK* 726N c/n 4037; *Commandaire 3C3* 7885 c/n 530; *Curtiss Robin* 263E c/n 116; *9206* c/n 276; *397K* c/n 489. *Travel Air 2000* N6217 c/n 669. *Detroit-Parks P-2A* N499H c/n 101 of 1930.

IOWA CITY. Airport. *NA F-86L-55-NA Sabre* 53-0750N.

MARENGO. Airfield. *NA P-51 Mustang* N169MD ex 44-73140 and N6337T of Dr. Burns M. Byram.

MAQUOKETA. Airstrip. *Tiger Moth* N82TM c/n 3815 ex N6478, G-AOGS; R. Schwenker.

NEWTON. *F-86D-40-NA Sabre* 52-3640.

OETWIN. *Lockheed T-33A-1-LO* 51-4406.

OSCEOLA. Airport. *Meyers OTW* N15784 c/n 1, Dale Derby; *N26489* c/n 42 John Schildberg.

OSKALOOSA. Airfield. *Culver PQ-14B* (piloted Turkey Drone) N5526A c/n N-917, Bob Campbell.

OTTUMWA. Airport. *Stinson S* N13141 of Richard Bach.

ROCK VALLEY. *T-33A-1-LO* 52-9612 displayed.

SERGEANT BLUFFS. *Republic RF-84E Thunderjet* 52-7267.

SHELDON. *T-33A-1-LO* 52-9614 displayed.

SIOUX CITY. Airport. *Republic RF-84F-56-RE* 52-7226, ex Iowa ANG. At Iowa Technical College. *Beech RC-45J* 29645 from Alameda. *Piper J-3C* N5956V c/n 9369; *NA SNJ-5* N3670F ex 43855. *Taylor E-2 Cub* NC14330 c/n 97 of 1934 flown locally by Chet Peek.

SLOAN. Airfield. *Piper PA-12* of 1946 N7781H c/n 12-679 of Glenn Mittenberger.

SPIRIT LAKE. Airfield. *Ercoupe 415C* N93841 c/n 1164 of Jim Jackson.

URBANDALE. *NA F-86 D/L* 53-924.

WAVERLEY. *Lockheed T-33A-1-LO* 53-4951.

KANSAS

AUGUSTA. *Lockheed T-33A-1-LO* 52-9488 displayed.

BALDWIN. Airfield. *Stearman A-75* of 1941 N50058 c/n 75-1135 owned by Del Chaney

COLBY. *T-33A-1-LO* 51-6617 displayed.

DODGE CITY. Airport. *Douglas B-26* 0-35627 "Dodge City".

FORT MITCHELL. Airstrip. *Harvard IV* CF-RZO c/n CCF4-201 of RCAF, owned and flown by J. Strang.

GARDNER. On Interstate 35, SW of Kansas City. *Aeronca Champion 7AC* N84177 c/n 7AC-2865; Bill Nevius of Springfield. *Stinson Model 108-3* N6153M c/n 108-4153; Frank Burton. *Stinson Model 108-1* N97831 c/n 108-831; Harlan McKain. *Taylorcraft BC12-D* N40099 c/n 7799, all-yellow; Calvin Mummery. *Luscombe 8F* N26324 c/n 6782; Utility Sales Inc. *Globe GC-1B Swift* N3260K c/n 1253; Chas Van Trease.

GRAIN VALLEY. East Kansas City Airport, Interstate 70. *Porterfield CP-35* N32339 of 1940 c/n 797, owned by Lee and Allen Evinger. *NA SNJ-5* N7997C ex 85005; Billy W. Merriner; *SNJ-5* N21JD ex 90996, damaged after belly-flop. *Luscombe 8E Silvaire* N1956K c/n 4683, owned by William Numbers—static for last seven years. *Mooney M18C Mite* N486M c/n 240; Allen Teters & Anthony Peltier.

HIAWATHA. *NA F-86D/L Sabre* 53-718 displayed.

INDEPENDENCE. *T-33A-1-LO* 52-9258.

KANSAS CITY. Fairfax Municipal Airport. Flying:— *NA P-51D* N6321T ex N37492, 44-74502; Edward Fisher. *NA P-51D* N5461V ex 44-73210 *Monocoupe 90A* N38904 c/n A-827; *Lockheed P-38J* N1107V, c/n 8342

LAWRENCE. Municipal Airport. *Grumman F-11A Tiger* ex "Blue Angels"—serial please. *Aeronca C-3* N13010, c/n A-225. *Ford 4-AT-E Trimotor* N8407 c/n 69; Dale Glenn. In Centennial Park *Grumman RF-9J Cougar* "7" ex NAS, Norfolk Va.

LEAWOOD. Airfield. *Great Lakes* N863K c/n 124 of 1932 *Stearman PT-17* N29654 both Si Royce.

LEMASTER FIELD. Just South of Ottawa. *Boeing 247D* N18E c/n 1722 of 1933—still flies, owned by Charles Lemaster (Cropduster) seating for 18 passengers.

MANHATTAN. Municipal Airport. *Lockheed F-94C-1-LO Starfire* 51-5676.

OLATHE Beside Route 10. *Douglas F-6A Skyray* 134816 "7K/116" ex NAS, Olathe and *Chance Vought F7U-3 Cutlass* 129565 displayed on poles. At Johnson County Airport. *Meyers OTW-160* N26466 c/n 19; Chas Van Trease.

OVERLAND. City Park. *Chance Vought F4U Corsair*—serial wanted.

RANTOUL. Dempsey Field. SE of Ottawa. Run by Bill Dempsey of Confederate Air Force who flies water bombers. Owns *North American 0-47B Owl* N73716 c/n 51 1011 now under restoration. *Grumman TBF-3* N9593C ex Bu 69472, converted to spray plane, owner Clayton Curtis of Boise, Idaho, but flown by Bill Dempsey. *Fairchild 24G* N23E c/n 2926, of Grant Nichols, Olathe. *Beech AT-11 Kansan* N6669C ex 41-27391, owner Lee Chemicals. *Kansan* XA-SED, with flag of Mexico on vertical stabilizers. *Beech C-18S* N8040H c/n "AF8455" De D Acro Spraying Co. *Lockheed PV-2 Harpoon* N6657D c/n 151606 of 1940 fibreglass belly; Wenair Co. also *PV-2* N6853C c/n 151125; *PV-2* N7086C c/n 151410 of Central A/c Maintenance Co. *Douglas B-26B* N9682C ex 41-39230, was to have become

water bomber but being converted to sprayer. *Stinson L-5E* N2745C ex 44-18025, owned by Ed Wilt. *NA SNJ-4 Texan* N9522C ex 26912, of De D. Aero Spraying, also *SNJ-4* N7008C ex 88-13784—both front cockpits used for spray storage. *Lockheed Lodestar* c/n 2013 of 1940, owned by Bill Dempsey. *Meyers OTW* N26485 c/n 38 of 1941 is owned and flown by Charles Botts of Olathe—may be at Ottawa Municipal, Kansas.

SALINA. Municipal Airport. *Boeing RB-47H Stratojet* 53-4299. *Interstate S-1A* N37394 c/n 237 of 1942 flying with Toby Tobiason.

SPRINGHILL. Airfield. *Stearman N2S-3* of 1943 N12M; Curtiss Murdock.

STANLEY. Airfield. *Piper J-5A* N35385 of 1941; Harry Krummel.

STATE LINE AIRPORT. South of Kansas City. *Stinson 108 Universal* c/n 108-2008; Lawrence Strickland. *Fairchild 24-G* N16900 c/n of 1937; Lee Brown.

STILWELL. Airfield. *Ercoupe 415C* N2969H c/n 3594; Kelly Viets.

A. K. Longren Pusher Biplane (Topeka)

TOPEKA. Kansas Historical Museum. Gifted by Robert Billard. *A. K. Longren Pusher Biplane* of 1912, the second Longren built, with Hall-Scott 8-cyl. Aeronautic motor. Right foot pedal fed gas, left foot was brake. It was owned by Captain Phil Billard, killed testing aircraft in France during WW 1. Max speed 60 mph. Scales hanging on pilot's seat were attached to axle and tied to tree by rope or chain. When scales showed 300 lbs of pull as pilot raced motor there was sufficient take-off power and rope was cut or chain unfastened. *Lockheed T-33A* 50-383 is displayed in Gage Park, ex Lincoln AFB.

WICHITA. Municipal Airport. *Boeing B-47H* 0-34218 on pylon. Flying here *Curtiss Robin* N8337 c/n 210 of 1928; David Blanton. *Travel Air 2000* N6282 c/n 721; Max Walton, 1927 machine. *Stearman B* of 1942 N32459 c/n 1; Glenn Stearman. At the Beech Factory it is said the first *Beechcraft 18* built 1936 is preserved, brought back from California. At the Cessna Plant's Commercial Aircraft Division the *Cessna 180* of Jerrie Moch is reported as exhibited. May we have these two registrations and photos please. The Wichita Area Vocational Technical School stated to have *NA F-86 Sabre* ex 175th TAC FG from Baltimore, Maryland. Serial please. Reported on Hury 54 West of Wichita *Boeing B-47H* 0-34213—is this additional to the one at Municipal Airport? Reported that there is now (or is to be) a National Antique Air Museum and Hall of Fame in Wichita, with Mr. Louis Anderson as curator. The

Solbrig-Benoist Biplane of 1914, used until 1917 by Solbrig was stored and then hung from ceiling of the Davenport Museum, Iowa. Powered by 4-cyl. Roberts 2 Cycle engine. It is said to be on loan to City of Wichita from Mrs. Ruth Adams, Solbrig's daughter. May we have photo of this and any other aircraft in this new museum.

KENTUCKY

FORT KNOX. General George H. Patton Museum. Dedicated 11 November 1972 it is primarily tanks, halftracks and other armoured vehicles—Fort Knox being regarded in USA as "the home of armor". *Bell AH-1G Huey Cobra* gunship N209J c/n 20001, the prototype, donated by Bell Helicopter has been restored to original configuration with TAT-102A 7.62 mm minigun turret system and retractable landing gear (all production Huey Cobras fixed gear). *Bell OH-13E (H-13E-BF) Sioux* 51-13746 is on display in front of the Aviation Squadron barracks.

Bell Huey Cobra (Fort Knox)

FULTON. *Lockheed T-33A-1-10* 51-8614 displayed.

LOUISVILLE. Aircraft Industries Museum. *NA B-25J Mitchell* 44-30378. *Boeing B-29-55-MO Superfortress* 44-86402. *Douglas A-26C-50-DT Invader* 44-35923. *Boeing B-47B-30-BW Stratojet* 51-2095. *NA F-86D/L-40-NA Sabre* 52-3628. *Northrop F-89D-20-NO Scorpion* 51-11341. It is said that a *Douglas AD-5 Skyraider* may be coming—details of serial please, also viewing. From the Louisville Airport *Monocoupe 90A De Luxe* N15427 c/n A-727 is flown by Shelly L. Abramson. *Republic F-84F* ex TAC HQs, said with private citizen; serial and address appreciated.

STURGIS. *NA F-86D/L Sabre* 52-3694 displayed.

LOUISIANA

ABBEVILLE. Airfield. *Lockheed P-38L Lightning* N38LL ex 43-50281, N138X; of Revis Sirmon—from Van Nuys, Calif.

ALEXANDRIA. Thunderstreak Park. *F-84F Thunderstreak* confirmation and serial wanted.

BARKSDALE. AFB. *Boeing B-47E* 53-2276 exhibited.

BATON ROUGE. Airfield. *Beech G17S Staggerwing* N911 c/n B-12 of N. H. Holloway.

GRETNA. *NA F-86D/L Sabre* 53-822 displayed.

HOUMA. Airport. *Grumman F8F Bearcat* N700A c/n 1262 ex Cornell Aero Labs, with J. W. Fornoff Jnr. *Beechcraft 17S* N192H, c/n 6723. *Lockheed T-33A* 51-9091 is on a plinth.

KAPIAN. *T-33A* 52-9492 displayed.

MANSFIELD. *T-33A* 51-6601 displayed.

MINDEN. *Northrop F-89C-1-NO Scorpion* 50-743 displayed.

NEW ORLEANS. Lake Shore Airport. *B-25* N3453G. *Consolidated PBY-5A Catalina* N5585V, ex 46522. *Douglas B-23 Dragon* N5345, c/n 625. *Stinson V-77 Reliant* N79556, c/n 77-380.

RUSTON. *F-86D/L* 53-1029 and *T-33A* 52-9349 displayed.

Grumman F6F Hellcat (Andrews AFB, Maryland)

SHREVEPORT. Airport. *Cessna 199* N2103C c/n 16088—only example—a modified Cessna 195 with 450 hp P. & W. R-195 and 5½-ft 3-blade Hartzell propeller, owned by R. F. Marston.

THIBODAUX. Airfield. *Aeronca 65-TAC Defender* N36816 c/n C1661TA, of Bill Taylor. Details of other V. and V. fliers here welcomed.

WHITE CASTLE. *NA F-86D/L Sabre* 53-1032 displayed.

MAINE

BATH. David G. Perkins restoring *Grumman F6F-5 Hellcat*—serial please.

BRUNSWICK. NAS gate. *Lockheed SP2-E Neptune* Bu 128392 at Brunswick 1952-70 with Navy patrol squadrons 7, 10, 11, 21, 23 and 26. Now painted as "1" of VP-21 "LH", with pilot's name, Lt. Irving Click, under cockpit.

WATERVILLE. *Northrop F-89J* 52-1856 displayed.

MARYLAND

ABERDEEN. US Army Ordnance Centre and School Museum, Mr. R. Kempf in charge—Maryland 21005 for details—do not travel until viewing times confirmed:— *Aerophysics XSSM-A-23 Dart*. *Douglas XSAM-A-7 Nike-Ajax*. *D.XSAM-A-25 Nike-Hercules*. *Firestone XM-4E1 Corporal*. *BV-143 Missile*. *Douglas XM-47 Little John*.

Douglas M-30 Honest John. Martin SSM-A-12 La Crosse. Northrop XM-3 Hawk. Chrysler XSSM-A-14 Redstone. Entac Missile. Explorer 1. Henschel 117 Schmetterling. Henschel Hs 293 and Hs 298. Fieseler Fi 103 V1. A-4 (V2). Nord SS 10. Rheintochter. Ruhstahl X 4. C 3 Wasserfall Up-dated listing appreciated and full details of opening times.

ANDREWS. AFB (Washington DC borders). At ANG buildings *NA F-86H* 53-1387 and *F-100* 53-1574. Naval side *Grumman F6F Hellcat* 77722, mounted.

ANNAPOLIS. US Naval Academy. *Douglas A4D-1 Skyhawk* 139968; *McDonnell F-4A Phantom* Bu 148275.

BAINBRIDGE. Naval Training Centre. *Grumman F9F-8 Cougar* 131230; *Douglas F-6A Skyray* "106"—serial please.

BALTIMORE. Friendship Airport. Flying: *T-33A* N144M ex RCAF 21342; *NA B-25 Mitchell* N75755, and N69345, c/n 108-47686. *Martin TM-61 Matador* at Maryland Wing HQs. At Martin Airport, ANG entrance, *NA F-86H Sabre* 53-1339 in colours of 104 TFS, Maryland.

BETHESDA. John Recreational Park. *NA F-1E Fury* 139536.

CLINTON. Hyde Field Airport. *NA F-86H* 53-1348—reported neglected.

CRISFIELD. *NA F-86H* 52-2023 displayed.

CUMBERLAND. *Lockheed T-33A* 51-4157 displayed.

ELLICOTT CITY. *NA F-86H* 52-2048 displayed.

ESSEX SKYPARK. *Columbia XJL-1* N54207 ex Bu 31399, the first of three purchased by Navy, being restored by Bernie Ulbrich.

FERNDALE. HQs Maryland Wing CAP. *Martin MGB-13 Mace.*

GAITHERSBURG. Montgomery County Air Park. *Lockheed T-33A* 51-16988.

HIGH POINT. Naval Reserve HQs. *Vought SSM-8-A Regulus 1.*

HYATTSVILLE. Perry Boswell had *Miles M.5A Sparrowhawk* NC191M c/n 264 ex G-ADWW in 1950s—can a reader say if still in existence? A report states it crashed at Palm Beach in 1959 but it may still be extant.

LANHAM. *NA F-86H* 52-3864 displayed.

PATUXENT RIVER. NAS. At main gate, Naval Air Test Centre *NA A-5A Vigilante* 146697—tested here 1960-69. *Martin SP-5B (P5M-2) Marlin* 155355 marked "QE" ex VP-40 flown from San Diego, as last airworthy Marlin, to be held here for NASM. Confirmation of serial please. *Douglas F4D-1 Skyray* 144764 is here in Test Pilot School marks. *Douglas C-54D* 56501 c/n 10636, the NATC "hack" may be preserved.

PRINCESS ANNE. *NA F-86H* 52-2066 displayed.

ROSEMONT. Airfield. *Pietenpol B-4 Air Camper* N34278 c/n 1; Willard Steichen; *B-4* N12937 c/n 1 of 1933; Wallace Hanson.

SILVER HILL. NASM Store (see Washington D.C. for list).

WHEATON. Regional Recreational Park. *Chance Vought YF7U-3M Cutlass* 129722.

WORCESTER. On Route 13, American Legion Post 93, ex Bangor Air Defence Sector. *Lockheed T-33A* 52-9650.

MASSACHUSETTS

BEDFORD. Airfield. *Harlow PJC-2* (for Pasadena Junior College where Max Harlow taught) N64760 c/n 3 is owned and flown by Capt. Kesting, American Airlines.

BROOKLINE. Airstrip. *NA T-6G* N9890C ex 49-3048; Henry Faulkner.

FALL RIVER. USS Massachusetts. *Vought OS2U-3 Kingfisher* 5909 "BB 59" on loan from NASM, with incorrect centre float; *F-94C* 51-5520.

FALMOUTH. *Lockheed F-94C Starfire* 51-5692 displayed.

FRAMINGTON. Airfield. *Tiger Moth* N8223 c/n 86443, ex NM123, PH-UAI; P. McHugh.

MARLBOROUGH. Airport. The Marlborough Antiquers—vintage aircraft owners, flying:—*WACO QCF.2* N11468 c/n 266, white with red sunbursts; *Curtiss Robin C-2* N348K c/n 475 of 1929, rebuilt by Perrotti brothers after flight from Alaska. Red and Diana cream, sold to Don LaCouture 1964 after being Grand Champion, AAA National Fly-In, 1962. *Travel Air D-4000* (converted 2000) N674H c/n 1219 of 1929, cream & orange, black striping, owners Carman D. Perrotti Jnr & Theodore Perrotti (who also own the WACO). *Travel Air D-4000* (converted from 2000) N9803 c/n 958 of 1929, all-red black trim; same owners. *Fleet 16B* N1238V c/n 512 of 1941, blue & yellow military trainer (USA) colours. Rebuilt by Dale E. Means Snr from basket case, to tiptop condition. *Great Lakes 2T1* N308Y c/n 195 of 1931, was being restored by Hugh Wamboldt for aerobatics—up-dated report please. *Taylor J-2 Cub* NC19502 c/n 1618 of 1937. Restored by August McCarthy and others—is it flying now? *Ryan ST3-KR (PT-22)* N59411 c/n 1366 of 1941. Red and cream, black trim, checkerboard underside wings; Wm J. Purcell. *Fairchild 24R46* N77695 c/n R46-336. Bronze and beige; James Colbaugh. The best wishes to Don LaCouture and all concerned.

MONUMENT BEACH. *Lockheed F-94C* 50-1054 displayed.

OTIS. AFB. *NA F-86H* 53-1377, *T-33A* 51-4335 and *Bomarc IM-99B* 59-3731 displayed.

PILGRIM AIRPORT. Near Hatfield. *Spartan C-35* NC285M c/n 120 believed here for rebuild.

PROVINCETOWN. Airport. Provincetown Boston Airlines. *Stinson SM8A Detroiter Jr* N205W c/n 4029 gives joyrides. Two *Lockheed 10* aircraft fly schedules to Boston—registrations wanted.

SPRINGFIELD. Airfield. *Miller A/c Corpn Zeta*, designed by the late Mark Granville, built 1937, a low-wing 2-seat sportster with Menasco C-4, cruising to max 125 mph. Did not go into production and proto-type preserved here for museum.

TURNERS FALLS. Airport. Reported that "Damn Yankee Air Force" disbanded. Details of re-location of aircraft valued.

WEYMOUTH. Airfield. *Piper J-3C* N7499H c/n 20768, and *J-3L* N30926 c/n 5205 of 1940 owned here by Paul G. Babcock.

MICHIGAN

ADRIAN. *T-33A* 51-4322 on display.

ALMA. Airfield. *Pasped Skylark* N14919 of 1935; Bob Greenhoe.

AUBURN. Oak Park. *Republic RF-84F/K* 52-7262.

BAD AXE. *T-33A* 51-8786 on display.

BATTLE CREEK. Kellog Airport. *NA F-86 Sabre* 53-789 (also reported as 53-1096) confirmation of correct serial please.

BELLEVILLE. *RF-84F/K* 52-7259 on display.

BIRMINGHAM. *NA F-86D/L* 53-4028 displayed.

BREKENRIDGE. *T-33A* 51-4067 displayed.

CARO. *T-33A* 53-6099 displayed.

CENTER LINE. *T-33A* 51-4159 displayed.

DEARBORN. Greenfield Village. Here is the Henry Ford Museum including truly historic aircraft, to which additions are being made as suitable exhibits become available. Here, as at 1st July, 1973.—*Bleriot XI of 1909*, apparently Channel-type with 7-cyl. rotary engine. *Laird 1916 biplane*, no registration; used by E. M. Laird

on loop-the-loop flights. *Standard J-1* 823H, from Hall Flying School, Warren, Ohio, with Hisso engine. *Curtiss JN-4* serial 8428. *Curtiss MF Seagull* No 257, Hisso engine, plywood hull. *Fokker FVIIa/3M Trimotor* "Josephine Ford" of Byrd Arctic Expedition—first aeroplane over North Pole 9th May, 1926, flown by Floyd Bennett and Richard E. Byrd. Two Curtiss-Reed twisted metal and one Hamilton-Standard forged propellers. Wright Whirlwind engines, floats and skis. This aircraft, the second F.VIIa built, c/n 4900, first flew 4th September 1925 and took part in the Ford Reliability Tour. Later allotted registration C267 but carried marking BA-1 for Expedition. *Junkers W-33b* "Bremen" serial D-1167, c/n 2504, in which Baron von Huenefeld, Captain Koehl and Major James Fitzmaurice made first successful westward Atlantic cross ng April 12/13, 1928. *Ford 4-AT Trimotor* of Stout Metal Airplane Co, NX4542 "Floyd Bennett" used as Admiral Byrd 28/29, November 1929, for first aeroplane flight over South Pole; floats and skis. *Stinson Detroiter* NC857, "Pride of Detroit" used by William S. Brock & Edward F. Schlee for world flight which ended in Tokio (round-world except Pacific) in 18 days (28th Aug-14th Sept, 1927). Condition marred by people writing on fuselage. *Stinson Detroiter* X-7654—first Diesel-powered flight 19th Sept., 1928: Capt. L. M. Woolson and Walter Lees, Packard CR-980 engine. *Pitcairn Autogiro PCA-2* NC799W, built 1931 with Wright Whirlwind R-975—in mint condition. *Boeing 40 B-2* NC285 ex United Airlines. *Piper J-3* N6003 J-3 Cub *N6003 Zoegling Glider*. *American Biplane Glider* No 10211. *Ford Ultra-light Monoplane*, No 268 "Flivver". *Vought-Sikorsky VS-300* NX28996, de-signed by Igor Sikorsky 1938, first flew 14th Sept, 1939, the first practical helicopter built in USA. On 6th May, 1941, Sikorsky established International Helicopter Endurance Record (1 hr, 32 mins 26.1 secs.) Power plant was 75 hp Lycoming. *Rhinehart-Baumann-Dayton-Wright Racer* RB-1 of 1920 Gordon Bennett Race. First retractable landing gear and variable camber wing. *Lockheed Vega 1* N965Y, bought from Tallmantz Collection for 18,000 dollars. Used by Con-tinental Airlines for promotional tours, painted in the colours of Varney Speed Lines Inc. Airworthy. *Ryan Monoplane* marked NX211 NYP "Spirit of St. Louis" but actually a/c B30066 of Ryan Airlines, San Diego, 1927 and rebuilt in 1957 to duplicate Lindbergh's Ryan. Used by James Stewart in movie "The Spirit of St. Louis" and donated by him to the museum. The 2-seat front compartment closed to represent the extra fuel tank. *Lockheed 10A* N79237 c/n 1112, Ann Pellagreno's 30th anniversary commemoration aircraft (of the Amelia Earhart round-world flight) said on loan to Ford Museum.

Vought-Sikorsky VS-300 (Dearborn)

Ryan Monoplane (Dearborn)

DETROIT. Airport. *Lockheed Lodestar* N789F ex ZK-AOP was with Mason Inc. A *Northrop F-89D Scorpion* 51-435 is on display hereabouts and it is said *Douglas C-47* has arrived from Wurtsmuth AFB for a new aircraft museum—details awaited please.

FREELAND. Airfield. *NA P-51 Mustang* N6327T ex 44-74417 of Garland R. Brown.

GRAND BLANC. Airfield. *NA P-51 Mustang* N6518D ex 44-63872 of Gerald Walbrun.

GRAYLING. *T-33A* 51-8673 displayed.

GROSSE POINT WOODS. *RF-84F/K* 52-7275 on show.

HAZEL PARK. *RF-84F/K Thunderflash* 52-7254 on show.

HOLLAND. *Lockheed F-94C Starfire* 51-5611 displayed.

IRON MOUNTAIN. *T-33A* 53-5610 on show.

ISHPEMMING. *T-33A* 50-453 displayed.

KALAMAZOO. Airport. *Grumman FM-2 Wildcat* N86581 ex 86581 and *Grumman F8F-1* N9G c/n 18 of Gunther Balz; *FM-2 N1FE* of Ted Edison. *F8F-1 Bearcat* N3351 of M. Balch. *NA T-6G* N3749G ex 49-3141; T. Wood. *Curtiss Robin* N9283 c/n 337 of 1928; *Tiger Moth* N4446 c/n "29552" both owned by John Bright. *Stinson L-5 Sentinel* N60190 c/n 76-91. Bruce A. Dillon said to have a *Mitsubishi A6M5 Zero* with Pratt & Whitney 1130 hp engine, capable of giving him 350 mph at 20,000 ft. Details wanted.

LIVONIA. *RF-84F/K* 52-7260 displayed.

MENOMINEE. Airfield. *Mercury BT-120* reported—details please.

MIDLAND. *T-33A* 53-6081 displayed.

MOUNT CLEMENS. *NA F-86D/L* 53-663 displayed.

MOUNT PLEASANT. Airfield. *Ryan PT-22* N47554 c/n 1811 flying in military pain scheme with John Bergeson.

MUSKEGON. Airfield. *Piper J-3C* N32509 c/n 5406 of 1940 and *J-3C-85* N7174H c/n 20435 of 1946 with Robt. F. Weigand.

OAK PARK. *F-84F Thunderstreak* 51-9359 on show.

OTSEGO. *T-33A* 51-9078 displayed.

RIVERDALE. Airfield. *Fokker D.VII* (replica) N5125R c/n 1 of Orville Lippert.

SAGINAW. Michigan Military Museum—details of exact location and opening hours appreciated. Following aircraft all loaned from USAFM Program:—*Martin RB-54A Canberra* 52-1463. *Douglas C-47D* 43-48459. *Boeing KC-97G* 52-2646. *Fairchild C-119G Flying Boxcar* 52-5846. *Douglas C-124C Globemaster II* 51-126. *Hughes YOH-6A* 62-4211. *Republic RF-84F* 51-1896. *Grumman HU-16B (SA-16B-GR) Albatross* 51-7169. *Sikorsky UH-19D-SI Chickasaw* 55-3186 is also reported as in Saginaw—is it at museum? (See page XI).

SEBEWAING. *T-33A* 53-5073 displayed.

SOUTHFIELD. Swann D. Allen is restoring to fly. *American Eagle 101* NC7157, of 1929, with OX-5.

TECUMSEH. Airfield. *Meyers OTW* N34307 c/n 51 of Ed Johnson and *N34357* c/n 102 of Al Meyers.

WARREN. Airport. *DH.82C Tiger Moth* CF-CLE c/n 1133 ex RCAF 5830, of V. W. Martin.

MINNESOTA

ALBERT LEA. *Lockheed T-33A* 53-5158 on display.

BRAINARD. Paul Bunyan Amusement Park, Highway 371, West of town. *NA TB-25N Mitchell* 44-29812 displayed.

CHISHOLM. *Lockheed F-94C* 51-13560 on show.

FAIRMONT. Airport. *NA F-86H Sabre* 53-1302 on plinth, in colours of 11th FIS. *Sabre* 52-5757 displayed elsewhere, probably Route 16 to Jackson.

LUVERNE. City Park. *NA F-86D-30-N Sabre* 51-6038.

MINNEAPOLIS. At the International Airport many vintage types fly or are in store, including: *Douglas DC-3* N21728 c/n 2144 ex Eastern Airlines which flew 83,032 hrs on scheduled flights, wearing out 550 main tyres, 25,000 spark plugs, 136 engines, burning 8 million gallons of fuel. It then flew as an airborne laboratory for a paint firm—is it still clocking up the hours? *Douglas B-23 Dragon* N774Q was with McDonald Lumber Co; *Lincoln PTK* N275N c/n 602 of 1930 and *Curtiss Robin* N50H c/n 403 of 1929, with Norman Sten. *Curtiss JN-4D* 2404 with Dan Neuman Snr. *Anderson-Greenwood AG-14* N3904K with Wm McPhail. *Ryan SC-145W* (mod) NC18912 c/n 206, with B. J. Larsen. *Howard DGA-11* N14887 c/n 79 with John Witt. *Lockheed B-37 Ventura II* ex AJ311 of USAAF is stored in Minneapolis for USAF Museum. *Chance Vought F7U-3 Cutlass* is at the local NAS. *NA P-51D Mustang* N711UP ex 44-73856G, is with Gale Aero Corpn. A Reno Racer. The Minnesota Aircraft Museum is at 714 West 77-1/2 Street, Minneapolis, offering:—*Bell P-63C King Cobra* N52113 c/n 33-37 of 1944, in store. *Bleriot XI* (replica) N605WB, still airworthy. *Curtiss MR-1 Pusher* (replica) serial N91258 c/n 1, is this N8234E, built by Pruett then sold to Tallmantz, used in the "Great Race" film, with 65 hp Continental, then sold to Novak Autos? It is now in store here. *Curtiss JN-4D Jenny* N5391 c/n 396, in store. *Curtiss CW-1 Junior* N10943 c/n 1121, still airworthy. *de Havilland DH.60* GIII *Moth Major* N2726A, in store. This aircraft is a bit of an enigma since the quoted c/n "V4760" would appear to be the RAF serial applicable to a Queen Bee—a radio-controlled target version of the Tiger Moth. Queen Bees initially were produced on the Moth Major production lines and were very similar to them—but the circumstances of a Queen Bee turning up in the US are unknown. Most of the early productions were destroyed in the war. *Fleet N2648M*—on display. *Morane-Saulnier MS.230* N7461 c/n 1079 ex F-BGJX, a 1936-built machine still flying. Used in film "Blue Max" and previously at Weston, Eire. *Nelson BB-1 glider* N33687, in store. *North American 0-47B Owl* N73722 c/n 51-1025 ex XB-XUW, airworthy. *NA AT-6D Texan* N7095C ex 42-84678, airworthy. *AT-6 (SNJ-5)* N7130C, ex 90712, flown as "Kate" in "Tora, Tora, Tora", still so painted. *North American B-25J Mitchell* N3156G ex 45-8884. *Northrop F-89J Scorpion* 52-1851—on public view. *Pietenpol B4A1 Scout* N12941, still flying. *Pitcairn PA-7 Mailwing* N95-W c/n 147 of 1936. *Standard J-1* N2826D c/n 1598 of 1918. *Stinson V-77 Reliant* N5443N c/n 297, 1943 serial. also *N91091* ex FK883—both stored. *Taylor J-2 Cub* NC19565 c/n 1765 of 1937, airworthy. *Vought F4U (FG-1D) Corsair* N9154Z ex 88297, airworthy. *Vultee BT-13A Valiant* N52411 c/n

2548—on display. *WACO UPF-7* N32107 c/n 5739 of 1941. Note—the airworthy machines will probably be seen at Flying Cloud Airport.

DC-3 (Minneapolis)

MINNESOTA LAKE. *Lockheed T-33A* 51-8814.

MONTEVIDEO. Airfield. *Tiger Moth* N12447 c/n 154 ex A17-153, VH-BLK, VH-BTW, S. T. Reeves.

WATTONA. City Park. *Grumman F9F-5 Panther* 125299.

WEST DULUTH. In small park on main road through town *Lockheed F-94C* 51-13556 mounted.

WINNONA. City Park. *Grumman F9F-5 Panther* 125992.

MISSISSIPPI

CORINTH. *Lockheed T-33A* 51-6838 displayed.

GREENVILLE. *T-33A* 53-554 on show.

GULFPORT. *NA F-86D/L* 51-5908.

HAZELHURST. *NA F-86D/L* 53-1061 displayed.

JACKSON. Municipal Airport. *Douglas B-26B Invader* 0-4345. *Tiger Moth* N5984 c/n 86501, ex NM193, F-BGCK, G-AXWM, A. Williams.

JONESTOWN. Airfield. *Piper J-4A* of 1939 N23211 c/n 4/555; Rod Garrison.

KEESLER. AFB. *NA YF-100A Super Sabre* 52-5755 on show.

MERIDAN. *T-33A* 52-9311 displayed on plinth.

VICKSBURG. Airport. *Douglas A-20G Boston* N22M c/n 21356; should be saved!

WEST POINT. *NA F-86D/L* 53-658 displayed.

MISSOURI

CARROLLTON. *T-33A* 51-9021 on show.

CARUTHERSVILLE. *Lockheed T-33A* 53-5044 displayed.

CLARKSDALE. Airport. *Chance Vought (Goodyear) FG-1 Corsair* N4719C ex 92081; James T. Lambert.

FLAT RIVER. *T-33A* 55-4349 displayed.

INDEPENDENCE. Airfield. *T-33A* 52-9469 displayed. *Ercoupe 415C* N93624 c/n 947 is owned and flown by Lee Brown.

JACKSON. *T-33A* 52-9249 displayed.

KANSAS CITY. *NA F-86D/L* 52-4181 on show. Public enclosure has *Grumman F9F-8B Cougar*, blue overall, unserialled, for children. Condition and serial please. *Northrop Delta 1D* N13777 c/n 28 reported dismantled here; Owned by Richard Davis. *WACO YPF-7* N29904 c/n 5401 flies with George Hefflinger. *Fairchild 24 Argus* N81208 c/n R46-109; with Robert Blann. *Beech D17S Staggerwing* N46431 c/n 4893 with Shelly Stafford.

KENNETT. Airfield. *T-33A* 52-9821 displayed. *Stinson SM6000B* N11153 c/n 5021 of 1931 is owned and flown by Dick and Nell Rice, one of the finest trimotors we have recorded—and the best-kept.

LA PLATA. *NA F-86D/L* 52-1983.

MANSFIELD. Louis Anderson's Farm. Said to store 28 vintage machines in and around six buildings, some airworthy, including *American Eagle 101* N4289 c/n 100 of 1928, flown by Andy Anderson. Can someone PLEASE send a listing—our contacts having failed to obtain details.

POPLAR BLUFF. *F-86D/L* 53-946 on show.

RAYTOWN. Airstrip. *Piper J-3C* N70237 c/n 17213 of Don Browett.

RICHMOND. *T-33A* 53-5990 on show.

ST. LOUIS. Airport. *Monocoupe 90-AL* N974 c/n 115; James "Snappy" Harvey. *Douglas DC-3A* N133D c/n 1499, the 6th built, of Ozark Airlines; is this still operating—flown Santa Monica 10 July 1936 and 60,000 hrs by end of 1965—up-dated details please. Is it the oldest airworthy? Originally NC 16005 of American Airlines, subsequently 42-56092 during War II. The National Museum of Transport, Barretts Station Rd., Missouri 63122, Mr. John Roberts, curator (write for opening hours) said to hold:—*Douglas C-47A-80-DL* 43-15331; *DC-7B* N339AA c/n 45236 of American Airlines "Flag-ship Wyoming". *Lambert 145 Monocoupe* NX211—built for Lindbergh. *Gyrodyne XRON-1* helicopter. *Lockheed T-33A* 52-9446. *Goodyear ZPG-2* Bu 141561, non-rigid airship (blimp). At Lambert Field, American Legion Post, displayed, *Republic F-84F Thunderstreak* 51-9422, built by General Motors, ex 131st TFG, Missouri ANG.

TRENTON. *T-33A* 52-9709 on show.

WASHINGTON. *NA F-86D/L* 52-3837 (or 3887) displayed.

MONTANA

BOZEMAN. Gallatin Field. *Travel Air 4000* N9952.

GREAT FALLS. Airport. *Northrop F-89J Scorpion* 53-2547 ex Montana ANG. Only Scorpion to fire nuclear weapon. *NA F-86H* also mounted as wind-tee —serial? In Lions Club Park *F-102 Delta Dagger* 0-61105 (56-1105) ex Montana Air Guard 120th FG on pedestals.

HELENA. School Board. Training Aids, *F-86H* 53-396 ex Maryland ANG, 175 Tactical. *Northrop F-89* 0-32453 ex 186 FIS Montana ANG. *Convair F-102* 0-53417 ex 186 FIS. *Convair F-102* 0-6116 presented to Helena Parks Dept for mounting in local park.

MISSOULA. Municipal Airport. *Lockheed T-33A* 51-4399. Flying from here *Douglas DC-2* N4867V c/n 1368 of Johnson Air Services, used for cargo and for fire-fighting parachutists. This a/c was delivered by Douglas to Pan American as NC14296 in 1935 sold to Mexico as XA-BJL and to Aviateca Guatemala as LG-ACA/TG-ACA, before coming to Missoula. Let us hope it is preserved. *Ford 4-AT-E Trimotor* N7861 c/n 46 and *N9612* c/n 55. *Curtiss Robin* N447W c/n 6B-2040 and N9084 c/u 865. *Douglas B-26* N3246G. (3246G) c/n 90/25 *Grummman TBM-3 Avengers* on water-bombing or spraying:—N7157C, *N7014C* ex 85836, *N3869A, N3249G* ex 91159, *N9010C* ex 53200. *Beech AT-11 Kansan* N6949C, *N6950C* ex 43-10338, *N75189* c/n 998, *N8069H* ex 42-37024.

Stinson SM6000B (Kennet)

NEBRASKA

BEATRICE. *Lockheed T-33A* 51-880 displayed.

BOYS TOWN. *T-33A* 53-5173 is on display.

BURWELL. Airfield. *Arrow A2-100K Sport* N8181 c/n 432 of 1930; Roy Cram.

FORT CALHOUA. *Curtiss Robin* NC363K c/n 477 was being restored by John P. Rathjen—state and photo welcomed.

FRANKLIN. *T-33A* 52-9205 displayed.

HOLDREGE. Airfield. *SC-1 Cirigliano* N775W; the only example known.

SC-1 Cirigliano (Holdrege)

HUMBOLT. *T-33A* 51-9111 displayed. (51-9111)

LINCOLN. AFB. *Boeing B-47B Stratojet* 51-2207. *KC-97F-18-BO* 51-0388 and *NA F-86D* 51-11380 on show. *NA F-86D/L* 53-831 may also be displayed here. *Piper J-3C* N28113 c/n 4588 of 1940 is owned and flown by Allen Graves.

McCOOK. *NA F-86H* 53-1503 displayed.

MINDEN. The Harold Warp Pioneer Village. Harold Warp was an early US pilot and after going solo in a JN-4 he taught his brother John to fly. The following historic machines are here, though not all may be on display, some being stored for rebuilding:—*Bunce CIN2* (Curtiss Pusher of 1912). *Bell P-59 Airacomet* 44-22656 c/n 2656, first jet type produced by USA, with Whittle-type engines. The museum literature states "this was the second P-59 built and, the first having crashed, this is the oldest." Many of my helpers dispute this and as the USAF Museum have 44-22650, there would seem to be doubt. The P-59 was the only jet fighter delivered to USAAF during WW II but did *not* become operational; 20 P-59As and 30 P-59Bs were built, some issued to the 412th Fighter Group, others used as research, drone director and engine development machines. *Cessna A Model* of 1929 c/n 8141, built by Clyde Cessna who had flown his first monoplane in 1910 at Enid, Oklahoma. After barnstorming for years he built his first Cessna for sale in 1927 and by 1959 his was the largest-selling private machine. *Curtiss JN-4 Jenny* 1350 of 1917, 90 hp OX-5 engine. *de Havilland DH.60 Gipsy Moth* of 1929—reg'n wanted. *Hartman monoplane* N286Y of 1910, a single-wing stunt plane used by Art Hartman until 1920 for barnstorming. *Lincoln-Page* of 1928—under rebuild—reg'n wanted. *Pitcairn Autogiro* of 1930 NC11638, last flown at Fort Lauderdale 16 Jan 1954. The US rights to the rotary wing were granted to Pitcairn in 1930 and he built about a hundred during the thirties. *Sikorsky R-4 (VS-316) Hoverfly* N75378 of 1944. *Standard J 1* of 1918—serial please. *Stinson SM-1 Detroiter* N903W of 1930 c/n 4080, ATC194, flown to Minden from Ohio November 1959 for display. "Doughnut" tyres have been substituted for original wheels/tyres, otherwise it is the original 4-place powered by 220 hp Lycoming. *Swallow biplane* of 1926 NC5070 c/n 2656 which on 6 April 1926 flew from Pasco, Idaho, to Elko, Nevada, piloted by Leon Cuddleback, for Mr. Varney who later consolidated with other airline operators to form United Airlines. *Taylor J-2 Cub* N19250 of 1937. *Wright Brothers 1903 Flyer* (replica). A fascinating museum with many other items of great interest to the aviation enthusiast. Do visit.

Swallow biplane (Minden)

Harold Warp Museum (Minden)

OFFUTT AFB. On the North Side, directly adjacent to the City of Bellevue, open to the public until 1600 hrs but now, known as the *Nebraska Aerospace Museum,* owned by the State of Nebraska, is likely to extend the viewing. *Boeing B-17G-85-DL* (converted to DB-17P) 44-83559 c/n 32200, ex ARDC and APGC machine. *Boeing B-29-60-BA Superfortress* 44-84076. *NA B-25J Mitchell* 44-30363. *Convair B-36J Peacemaker* 52-2217 ex 28th BW. *NA RB-45C-NA Tornado* 48-0017 "BE-017" modified bomb-bay. *Boeing B-47E-35-DT Stratojet* 52-1417 ex 301st BW. *Boeing B-52B-15-BO Stratofortress* 52-8711 c/n 16839 ex 22nd BW the first with SAC—

flew 4,000 hrs. *Convair B-58A-1-CF Hustler* 61-2059 "Greased Lightning" which flew Tokyo-London 8,028 miles in 8 hrs 35 mins, ex 305th BW. *Boeing KC-97G Stratotanker* 53-0198 "The Goer". *Douglas C-133B-DL Cargomaster* 59-536A ex 60th MAW. *Republic F-84F-25-RE* 51-1714, in Vietnam-type camouflage. —*McDonnell XF-85 Bantam* 46-523, first prototype. *Sikorsky H-19B-SI Chickasaw* 53-4426 ex SAC. *Vertol H-21B-PH Workhorse* 52-8676, ex ADC; Weapons Centre, *Northrop SM-62A Snark* 57-0005. *Convair SM-65 Atlas D.* SAC's first fully-operational IBM. *SM-75 Thor. HGM-25 Titan I* 60-3699 (Convair-General Dynamics) *LV-1B Blue Scout* (made up from) 12589/12591. *GAM-68 (AGM-28A) Hound Dog* 60-2102. The above are all loaned from USAFM Program. In addition there are also the following:—*Douglas C-54D Skymaster* 42-72724 "Peace through Strength". *Douglas VB-26B Invader* 44-34665 ex VIP a/c ANG Bureau. *Douglas C-47B Dakota* 43-48098. *Douglas C-124A Globemaster* 49-0258 ex 911th MAG, CONAC. *Fairchild C-119G Flying Boxcar* 51-8024 433rd TCW, CONAC. *McDonnell F-101B Voodoo* 59-0462, ASD of AFSC. *Convair F-102A Delta Dagger* 54-1405, ex Wisconsin ANG. *NA F-86H Sabre* 53-1375 ex Maryland ANG. *Grumman HU-16B (SA-16A-GR) Albatross* 51-0006. *Lockheed T-33A-15-LO* (Shooting Star or T-Bird). *Convair T-29A-CO* 50-0190A. *Boeing CIM-99 Bomarc* 54-3074 or 3079. It has also been reported that *Douglas C-133B-DL Cargomaster* 59-0536 ex 60th MAW, *Martin B-57B Canberra* 55-4244 and *Republic F-84F-30-RE* 52-6385 are now here—confirmation please. In front of SAC HQs here stands a *Boeing LGM-30A Minuteman* missile which replaced the Atlas in SAC's inventory.

Boeing B-29 (Offutt)

DH.90 Dragonfly (Omaha)

Lockheed Orion (Omaha)

OMAHA. Airport. *Funk B-85C* N81186 c/n 316; Dean Krueger. It is reported that Rosen-Novak Autos do not now hold any of the ex-Tallmantz machines and that the *Lockheed Orion* NC12222 and *de Havilland DH.90 Dragonfly* N2034 c/n 7508 ex G-AEDT, VH-AAD, are elsewhere in USA—can a reader help?

NEVADA

LAS VEGAS. McCarron Airport. *T-33A* 52-9755 *Douglas B-23 Dragon* N61666 named "Dragonfly" said to fly here. At the Air Facility of South Nevada Vocational Technical Centre *Beech RC-45J* 29583 ex Quonset Point and *T-33A* 19302.

RENO. Harrah's Automobile Collection, P.O. Box 10. *Aeronca C-3* N16277 c/n A658 of 1937, stored. *Arrow F Sport* N18722 c/n 85 of 1936. *Curtiss JN-4D Jenny* N5162 ex 278-508 of 1918. *Curtiss N2C-1 Fledgling* 12264 of 1929, stored. *Curtiss CW-1 Junior* 1052 of 1931, stored *Curtiss Robin* N7145 c/n 6 of 1928, stored. *Curtiss P-40M Kittyhawk III* N1232N c/n 27483, ex AK845, RCAF. *Ford 5-AT-B Trimotor* N58996 c/n 5-AT-8, ex NC9645. *Lockheed P-38L Lightning* N505MH ex 44-53186. *Monocoupe 90A* N11735 c/n 662A of 1934, in store. *Travel Air S6000B* N411N c/n 6B-2024 of 1929, stored. At the airport *NA-86D/L* 53-994 displayed. Flying:—*NA P-51D Mustang* N332 ex 45-11471; Wayne Adams. *Aero C.104* (Czech-built Bucker Bu 131) N121U c/n 215 ex HB-USK; Mira Slovak.

NEW HAMPSHIRE

ANTRIM. *T-33A* 53-9333 displayed.

DUBLIN. Airfield. *DH.Tiger Moth* N82DH c/n 83152 **ex** T540, VH-AOY; J. A. Meath.

EAST KINGSTON. Geert E. Frank, a Northeast Airlines captain, deals extensively in Tiger Moths but whether to teach trainees or to re-sell is not known. The following have been registered to him in recent times:—*N41DH* c/n 84734 ex T6319, G-AIJB, PH-UDB. *N90406* c/n 86553 ex PG644, F-BGDG. *N42DH* c/n 85988, ex EM771, PH-ALG, PH-UAE. *N4942* c/n 82958 ex R5063, A-43, OO-JEU. *N4977* c/n 86514 ex NM206, F-BGCQ. *N8872* c/n 86534 ex PG625, F-BGDC. *N28680* c/n 86378 ex NL935, F-BGJJ. *N28681* c/n 86530 ex PG621, F-BDOK. Can a reader please up-date owners and locations if any have moved on. *Fieseler Storch* N43FS also here.

HOLLIS. Airfield. *Tiger Moth* N9410 c/n 8512 ex DE941, G-ALSE, PH-UDZ.

WEARE. Airport. *WACO C. Custom* N57824; Robert Fargo.

NEW JERSEY

ATCE. *Lockheed T-33A* 52-9367 displayed.

BERLIN. *T-33A* 53-5307 displayed.

BRIGANTINE. *T-33A* 53-5907 displayed.

BRIDGETON/FLEMINGTON. *Republic F-84F* 52-6447 (or 6647) confirmation and exact location requested.

CAMDEN. *Lockheed T-33A* 51-6949 displayed.

DOVER. Airfield. *Piper J-3C* N41172 c/n 7788 of 1941 *WACO UPF-7* N32149 c/n 5781; Lowell Miller. *Piper J-4A* N27879 c/n 4/1102; Ed Mann.

ENGLEWOOD CLIFFS. *T-33A* 52-9284 displayed.

FLEMINGTON. *Lockheed F-94C Starfire* 51-5645 on show.

FORT DIX. Army Training Centre Museum of Missiles etc. *Firestone M-2 Corporal. Martin XM-2 La Crosse. Western Electric M-1 Nike Ajax. Douglas M-31 Honest John.*

FORT MONMOUTH. *Grumman G-134 (YOV-1A) Mohawk* 57-6463.

GLENDOLA. Playground. *Grumman AF9J Cougar* 141117.

HANOVER. *Stearman PT-17 Kaydet* N9298H c/n 75-8387; Joe Haydo. *PT-17* N60398 c/n 75-6559; Al Minor. *Beechcraft Staggerwing* NC15845; Fred Morris.

HAZLET. Diner on Route 35. *Emigh Trojan A-2*, no reg'n.

LAKEHURST. NAS. (site of "Hindenburg" accident) *Grumman F-11A Tiger* 141851 ex "Blue Four" of "Blue Angels", flown from Pensacola 31 Dec 1968. Built 1958 and assigned to VF-191, Comfair Alameda; flew as **carrier** a/c to 1960, then 5 years NAS Litchfield **Park** Arizona "graveyard". To VT-26 1965/7, then Chase Field 1967/8.

MARLTON. Airstrip. *Stearman E75* N939W c/n 75-5231; Willard Z. Wells Jnr.

MILLVILLE. *Lockheed T-33A* 49-919 displayed.

Flying Bomb (Morgan)

MORGAN. Route 35 Lumber Yard. *Fieseler Fi 103 (V1)* taken down but reported as being in yard—available for a museum!

MORRISTOWN. Airport. *Stinson V-77 Reliant* N91037, c/n 77-379. *Spartan Executive* N34SE. *Ryan PT-22* N56535, c/n 2146.

MOUNT HOLLY. Flying W Ranch Airpark (said to be closed to fliers) but believed still to store the following:—*FG-1 Corsair* ex 88303 now Wm C. Whitesell N700G; *Curtiss A-22 Falcon* N500G c/n A22-1; Leroy Skelly. *Lamier Paraplane* N4157A—static. *Grumman FM-2 Wildcat* N90523 ex 74560. *Grumman F9F-8P Cougar* 141708 "VFP 62/951" is in Ironworks Park.

NEWARK. Teterboro Airport. *B-25 Mitchell* N32T ex 45-8882 and *N39E* c/n 108-34379; R. Irving.

OCEAN CITY. *Lockheed T-33A* 15-6703.

OCEAN COUNTY. Robt. J. Miller Airport. *North American F-1C Fury* 135868, painted red and white "Navy 48".

Travel Air D4D (Solberg)

PARAMUS. Airstrip. *Tiger Moth* N5562 c/n 865 ex A17-635, DX833, VH-WON; D. McMillan.

PITTSTOWN. Sky Manor Airport. Tony Tirri and his Group:— *Leopoldoff L-55 Colibri* N10LC quoted as ex F-BHIT, in WW I German markings (sic). This was a small 1937 designed French two-seater biplane. Possibly c/n 2 ex F-BHGT. *Morane 500* (French-built Storch), painted in WW II Luftwaffe markings, airworthy but no reg'n yet. *Two other Storch* fuselages and wings (presumably *Moranes*) awaiting assembly. Details please. *Stampe* N12SV; Sal Labate. *Nord 1101* N1101 ex F-BLTU c/n 107 and one other allegedly to be flown as Messerschmitt Bf 108s. *Caudron C635 Simoun* N85E c/n 7863 ex F-BDXY, sent to England and Algeria for film "Little Prince" but understood owned by Tony Tirri. *WACO SRE* NC58785 c/n 5155; Jack Gugler.

RINGWOOD. Airfield. *Tiger Moth* N5560 c/n 83280 ex T5561, VH-ALX, VH-SSD, VH-AMT; Roger Kemple.

SOLBERG. Airport. New Jersey Aeronautical Historical Society forming Collection with *Travel Air D4D* N434N c/n 1340 of 1929 loaned by Andy Stinnis and with engines etc. Details of registrations and serials with photos of complete a/c will be valued.

STANHOPE. B. O'Keefe is said to have a damaged *Messerschmitt 208* under restoration (also reported as Me 210) and details would be appreciated.

WEST CALDWELL. Caldwell Wright Airport. *NA B-25* N6578D ex 44-31508 which filmed "Battle of Britain" film said to be here in poor condition. *Beech T-34 Mentor* N12289 c/n G-305; A. Meltopse.

WOOD CLIFF LAKE. Airfield. *Buhl LA-1 Bull Pup* N368Y c/n 157; J. Goebel Jnr.
NOTES (i) In the 3rd V. and V. I appealed for news of Pitcairn Autogyro NX11609 "Miss Champion" listed as at Museum of Science & Industry, Chicago, but said to have left for New Jersey. Did it ever get to the museum—can someone please enlighten us all?
(ii) All aircraft obtained for the projected Aeroflex Museum at Newton NJ, are currently at Santee, South Carolina where they are listed in this edition.

NEW MEXICO

ALAMOGORDO. City Park. *Lockheed F-80C Shooting Star* 49-710. In USAF Museum. *Douglas Nike-Cajun. Martin TM-61 Matador. Northrop Q-4 Ryan Q-2 Firebee* (fired 12 times). *Rocket Sled.*

ALBUQUERQUE. Kirkland AFB. *NA F-100* 53-1532 on plinth; ANG HQ's. *Tiger Moth* N5676 c/n 84529 ex T8256, G-AOFG, VH-AWI, VH-WPK; A. Powers. *McDonnell 119* executive aircraft reported here (for museum?) *Rose F-2* N18252 c/n 107 of 1937; Pete Ettinger. At Coronado Airport, Albuquerque, *Douglas B.18 Bolo* N56847, c/n 2469. *Douglas B.23 Dragon* N52327 c/n 2722. *Lockheed 10 Electra* N4886V and *NA B-25 Mitchell* N122B c/n 87-7949 reported flying. *Boeing XC-97 Stratofreighter* 43-27470 prototype c/n 8481 nearby; for preservation?

CANNON. AFB. *NA F-100* on pedestal—serial wanted.

CLAYTON. Fort Jordan Museum. *Northrop SM-62 Snark; Republic F-84F* 51-9312; *NA F-86D/L* 50-459.

CLOVIS. *NA F-100 Super Sabre* 53-1576 displayed.

FARMINGTON. Sandia Atomic Museum. *SM-62 Snark; Boeing B-52B* 52-013. *CGM-13 Mace B* 56-726. These loaned by USAFM Program. The ˙ ˙˗ now also *Boeing B-29-BW* 44-69983 c/n 10848, on display. *Rose A-1 Parakeet* NC14881 c/n 105 is here, flown by Doug Rhinhart.

HOBBS. Airfield. *Messerschmitt Bf108* NX2231 c/n 3059; Confederate Air Force. Also *NAP-51* N542 8V ex 44-73264; *Ryan PT-22* N48747. *PT-17* N727E c/n 75-2362.

HOLLOMAN. AFB. Air Force Missile Development Centre. Officer Mr. Lloyd H. Cornett Jnr., New Mexico 88330 for opening hours to see:—*Bell GAM-63 Rascal; Douglas AAM-N-7 Sidewinder; Douglas MB-1 Genie; Ford JB-2 (US V1) HTV Test Vehicle. Hughes GAR-1D Falcon; Lockheed X-7; Martin TM-61 Matador; North American MX-773 NATIV; Northrop GAM-67 Crossbow; Oerlikon Missile; Parachute Test Vehicle; Q-1 Target Drone; Ryan Q-2 Firebee; Tarzon Guided Bomb.*

ROSWELL. Roswell Museum. *NA F-86D/L* 52-3646: *Fieseler Fi 103 (V1); Rheintochter R-3. A-4(V2)*; Also many early Goddard rockets and other exhibits. Officer —Mr. Eugene Smith.

SANTA FE. Museum of New Mexico. *Lockheed F-80C* 45-8490 ex NM ANG. *NA F-100A* 53-1600. Flying from the local airport *Stinson SM-8* of 1930; 1937 *Fairchild 24G* and *Cessna Airmaster* of 1939—details and pics please.

SOCORRO. New Mexico Institute of Mining and Technology. *Douglas XBT 2D-1 Skyraider* 09102; *Martin A7-1 Mauler* 22260; *Vought F6U Pirate* 122479; *Chance Vought F7U Cutlass,* serial wanted. Owned by Naval Air Systems Command, Washington DC.

TRUTH AND CONSEQUENCES. In Park by Rio Grande. *Lockheed T-33A-5-LO* 51-9022.

WHITE SANDS. Missile Park, Missile Range. Officer Mr. Jack McAhon for details of viewing:—*A-4 Rocket* (V-2) two examples. *Chrysler XSSM-A-14 Redstone. Dart* —anti-tank missile. *Douglas AAM-N-7 Sidewinder. Douglas M-30 Honest John. Douglas MB-1 Genie. Douglas Nike-Zeus. Douglas XM-47 Little John. Douglas XSAM-A-7 Nike-Ajax. Douglas XSAM-A-25 Nike-Hercules Fairchild Lark. Firestone XM4E1 Corporal. Hughes GAR 1-D. Loki missile. Loon missile. Martin SSM-A-12 La Crosse. Martin TM-76 Mace. McDonnell SAM-N-6 Talos. Missile "A" component development vehicle. Northrop GAM-67 Crossbow. Northrop RP-76. Northrop XM-3 Hawk. Pogo Hi. Shavetail. Space General Aerobee Hi. Sperry FAGMS-S Sergeant. SS-10. Waco Corporal XM-21. XQ-4 Drone.*

NEW YORK

BINGHAMPTON. *Republic F-84C Thunderjet* 47-1454.

BROOKLYN. Bayside. Fort Totten. *Douglas XSAM-A-*

25 *Nike Hercules* with booster. *Tiger Moth* N17565 c/n 1000 ex A-17-565, VH-FBR of R. Milligi flies from Bayshore.

BUFFALO. Cornell Institute of Aviation (airworthy) *Douglas A-26 Invader* N9416H and *N9417H* ex 44-34653. *Lockheed F-94A* 49-250 static here. At Burgard Vocational High School is *Standard J 1* c/n 22797, serialled 5957.

CLAY. *NA F-86A Sabre* 48-200 displayed.

ELMIRA. Schweizer Aircraft Factory. *Schweizer E-313* N3840A c/n 1, example of their only powered a/c.

FABIUS. *T-33A* 53-6149 displayed.

FLOYD BENNET FIELD. NAS. *Grumman F-11A* 13623 "7 R".

HAMMONDSPORT. Glenn H. Curtiss Museum of Local History. *Curtiss Pusher,* recently listed as 1911 original but believed N2120 (replica). Confirmation please. *Curtiss JN-4D* (fuselage) of 1917, understood being restored. Serial wanted. *Curtiss Oriole* (fuselage) for restoration, 1919 model. *Curtiss Robin* of 1929— reg'n wanted. *Mercury Chick* of 1928—reg'n please. *Long's Midget Mustang* N6H. *Ohm & Stoppelbein Special Formula One Racer* No 15, last raced 1967—is this still here? Reg'n please.

HARLEM. Corner 118th St/Fifth Avenue. *NA F-86* 53-1272 "272" ex Korea and Floyd Bennet Field.

HEMPSTEAD. *F-94C Starfire* 51-13562.

ISLIP. *F-86D/L* 51-2986.

LIVERPOOL. *Tiger Moth* N8233 ex EM729, PH-UAO, also N3529 c/n 86556 ex PG647, F-BGDH; R. Forger.

LONG ISLAND. Aviation High School 35th St and 47th Ave. *Beech C-45* N56708. *Lockheed T-Bird* (serial wanted) *NA SNJ Texan* Bu 51776.
Hughes GAR-4 Falcon 57-RO 10697 c/n 201-013 is at USAF Recruiting Detachment, Roosevelt Field. Maxson Electric Corpn display *Maxson ASM-7 Bullpup.*

SUFFOLK COUNTY AFB. *NA F-86 Sabre* 53-1306 (may have moved to Central Square). ex NY ANG; Col. Gabreski's a/c.

ZHANS AIRFIELD. *Arrow A2-L60 Sports* N9325 c/n 341. *Tiger Moth* N45TM c/n 86621 ex PG735, F-BGEG, G-AYVH; F. Abrams. *N40DH* c/n 82335 ex N9240, G-ANDI; M. Kenin. *N675 LF* c/n 86572 ex PG675 G-AMLF R. L. Gardner, (currently in England but expected here in late 1973) *N82RD* c/n 86243 ex NL772, CR-AGL; R. Dikovics. *Fiat G-46B-3* N46FM ex MM 53091, 1-AEHX c/n 141; Dr. Frank Marici, painted in Italian Air Force "Sand & Spinach".

MELVILLE. Gene Thomas has *Alexander Eaglerock*—reg'n wanted.

MONROE/WATERLOO. Crane Park. *F-86D/L* 52-10052.

NEWBURG. Stewart AFB. *NA F-86L Sabre* 52-3702.

Mustang (Nyack)

Tiger Moth (Nyack)

NEW YORK. La Guardia Airport. *Douglas XSAM-A-7 Nike-Ajax*. On top of No 7 Water Street *Sopwith Camel* (replica) built from 3 tons of scrap by artist Wm Tarr and hauled up for exhibition. *de Havilland DH.60M Moth* N1510V c/n 506 quoted but in reality is c/n 1322 ex CF-APA. This was owned and flown by Leyland Hayward of Madison Ave—up-dated report please. May now be at Merced, California with Harlam Gurney.

NIAGARA FALLS. Airport. *NA F-1 Fury* 143610 "7W", from Willow Grove NAS.

NYACK. Vintage A/c International—E. A. Jurist. *NA P-51 Mustang* N6356T ex 44-74494. Well-known in Britain as former mount of Charles Masefield and winner of Kings Cup Air Race in 1967. May have a *P-47* ex Peru. *Tiger Moth* N40DH c/n 82335 ex N9240, G-ANDI; M. Kenin believed here.

NORTH SYRACUSE. *F-86A* 49-1301.

PHILMONT. Emil S. Yandik, Upper Main St. *WACO BSO* N914V c/n 4004. *Parks P1* N91H c/n 219. *WACO GXE-10* N5780 and N5764. *WACO Taperwing ATO* N767E c/n A-124 and several others being relicensed.

PLATTSBURG. Park near SAC base. *B-47E* 0-32385 "Pride of the Adirondacks".

POTSDAM. *Fleet 16B* N1328V c/n 325 with Harold B. Franklin.

QUEENS. Site of 1964 World's Fair. Museum of Science & Technology. *Vertol UH 25C Retriever*—serial please. *Thor-Delta. Atlas D (109D). Titan. Agena 5.* Plus many mock-ups of missiles.

RHINEBECK. Old Rhinebeck Aerodrome. Off Route 1; 90 miles from NY City. Cole Palen—engineer and pilot—regarded by many as today's "Phineas Pinkham" the WW I hero-mechanic for whom everything was possible. Certainly over the last thirteen years Cole Palen has made history and we are all in his debt. Viewable normally every day May to October (with flying displays on Sundays May-October) this "Shuttleworth of the USA" is a MUST and, since Cole and his associates are up to the ears in work with little writing-time, it is advisable—and certainly more rewarding all round—if you pay a visit; to see the aircraft :— *Aeromarine Klemm* of 1930, N320N c/n 2-59 (airworthy) *Fairchild 24-C8F Ranger* N19129 c/n 3224 (airworthy) *de Havilland DH.80A Puss Moth. Spartan C-3* with Wright J-5. *Fokker DR-1 Triplane* (replica) N3221, static 110 hp Le Rhone. *Nieuport 28C-1* serial 10 (Doug Campbell's a/c) in "Hat in Ring" Sqdn colours, static, 160 hp Gnome. *Albree Pidgeon Frazer* of 1917 with 160 Gnome, under rebuild. *Sopwith Snipe 7F* E8100 c/n 9262 with 220 hp Clerget, airworthy. *Aeronca C-3* N17447 c/n A-754 (airworthy) *Velie Monocoupe 113* c/n 332 of 1929. *Thomas Pusher* of 1912 airworthy and *Thomas Pusher* of 1911 static. *Curtiss 1910 Pusher* (replica). *Sopwith Camel F.1* (replica) being built. *Bassett 1910 Ornithopter* (replica) from "Magnificent Men" film.

Kept on or near the flying field:—*Avro 504* A2939 (replica from Booker-Blackbushe) with 110 hp Le Rhone—about to fly. *Bleriot XI* of 1910 N60059 c/n 56 and *XI* of 1911 N60094 c/n 153. *Santos Dumont Demoiselle (replica)* airworthy. *SPAD XIII* N2030P serial 16541 in "Indian Head" colours *Fokker DVII* 286/18 flown by Bert Acosta, now N10408 with 160 hp Mercedes. *Curtiss JN-4H* N3918 c/n 38262. airworthy. 160 Hisso engine. *Sopwith Pup (replica)* serialled N5139 "4" owner Dick King. *Bird CK* N850W c/n 4012 with 125 hp Kinner.

WACO 9 N2574; *WACO 10* N5781; *Fleet 16B Finch* N66 6J. *Curtiss-Wright Junior*—reg'n wanted. *DH. Tiger Moth* N8731R c/n 1847 ex RCAF 9690, painted "Royal Navy" tail R8731. *Fokker DR.1 (replica)* N8582. *DH. Tiger Moth N24SS* c/n 1660 ex RCAF 3939, CF-CLB, N7990; of Stanley Segalla *Funk Model B-85C* N943JH of 1938 with 65 Continental. Most of the above, owned by Cole or his friends, are to be seen flying as indicated. Also here, undergoing restoration or in store:—*Short S.29 (replica)* "7" from "Magnificent Men". *1908 Voisin*

Cole Palen (left) and Short S.29—replica (Rhinebeck)

Fleet Finch landing (Rhinebeck)

Fokker DR-1 Triplane—replica (Rhinebeck)

(original) built for Norvin Rinek Rope Co, Easton, Pa, by Frenchmen. Reputedly flown once then hung in factory. *Breguet* of 1911 (stored) *Standard J 1* of 1918 (stored) *Siemens-Schuckert DIII* 1917 (replica) being rebuilt. *Rabkaatsenstein 1921 primary glider,* under rebuild. *R.A/c Factory F.E.8* (replica) airframe being assembled from original drawings. *Taylorcraft BC65* of 1939 with 65 hp Continental. *Aeromarine 39B* of 1918 347N c/n 55923 ex Roosevelt Field. *WACO UPF-7 biplane* N32144 c/n 5776 in blue & yellow, privately owned, flies here. Will readers please up-date the information to relieve Cole's work-load. Do make a point of seeing this fabulous airfield—to which, as we know, many V. and V. readers have gone already.

Nieuport 28C-1 (Rhinebeck)

Bleriot XI N60094 (Rhinebeck)

Fokker D VII (Rhinebeck)

Sopwith Snipe 7F (Rhinebeck)

Aeronca C-3 (Rhinebeck)

Bleriot XI N60059 and Thomas Pusher (Rhinebeck)

Curtiss-Wright Junior (Rhinebeck)

Tiger Moth (Rhinebeck)

WACO UPF-7 (Rhinebeck)

Siemens–Schuckert D III—replica (Rhinebeck)

SANBORN. Airfield. *Monocoupe 90A* N19423 c/n A-775 of 1938; Curtiss C. Whitehead.

SHORTSVILLE. *NA F-86* 53-1337 at American Legion Hall.

SLINGERLANDS. Blessing Road; *Vultee BT-13B* 42-89867 under rebuild.

STATEN ISLAND. *S.E.5a (replica)* being built by N. Thomas at Drumgoole Boulevard. Report please.

SYRACUSE. Airfield. *Fleet N2Y-T* N649M marked "Navy 4-S-1", owner Darrell H. Badore. At Hancock Field, SAGE building, *Bomarc* missile and *Convair F-102 Delta Dagger* 61219 ex Bradley Field, Conn 118th FIS.

SYRACUSE (NORTH) *NA F-86A* 49-1301.

TOWANDA. Corner of Colvin & Brighton. *Grumman F9F-8 Cougar*—serial wanted.

WALDEN. Caldwell Airport. *Ryan PT-22* N61883 c/n 1774. *Stearman PT-17* N1395V c/n 75-5222, N52282.

WHITE PLAINS. *F-86H* 53-1348 displayed.

NORTH CAROLINA

NEW BERN. Route 17 *Grumman F-11A Tiger* 141802 ex Cherry Point.

CHARLOTTE. Airport. *Travel Air 2000* N9004; Ernest Webb. *NA P-51D Mustang* N5551D; Stan Hoke. *NA F-86E Sabre* 50-600 displayed in Charlotte.

CHERRY POINT. MCAS. *NA FJ-3 Fury* 6119 "Marines". *Bell P-63 King Cobra* ex Edwards AFB said to be here; confirmation, also serial of *Hawker P.1127 Kestrel* here, understood for preservation.

ELKIN. *T-33A* 51-8548, on display.

FAYETTEVILLE. Picnic Area, one mile North, Route 301. *Lockheed F-94C Starfire* 51-5576.

FORT BRAGG. Airborne Museum. *Curtiss C-46 Commando* 44-78573 (became N1685M). *WACO CG-15A* 45-5276 c/n 7401, first production model, being rebuilt.

GASTONIA. Airport. *NA P-51D Mustang* N6523D ex 44-74483 and *F-51D* N6325T—owners and histories wanted.

GRIFTON. City Park. *NA FJ-3B Fury*—serial please.

JACKSONVILLE. Post Office. *NA FJ-3 Fury* unserialled.

KITTYHAWK. Wright Brothers National Memorial. Manteo P.O. Box 457. *Wright Brothers 1902 glider (replica)* built 1959. *Wright Brothers 1903 Flyer (replica)* built 1963.

MAXTON. *NA F-86D/L* 53-919 displayed.

MAYODAN. *T-33A* 53-5169 displayed.

OTEEN. Children's Park. *McDonnell F2H Banshee* 6417.

RALEIGH. Bensen Aircraft Corporation. Dr. Igor Bensen, Raleigh-Durham Box 2746, NC 27602, should be contacted to check exhibits available for public viewing:—*Bensen B-5* mid-jet helicopter. *Bensen B-8 Gyroboat. Bensen B-9* "Little Zipster". *B-11 Gyroglider. Bensen B-11M* "Kopter Kart"—still flying. *Bensen B-12 Skymat. Bensen B-13.*

REEDSVILLE. *Lockheed T-33A* 53-6095 displayed.

RICH SQUARE. *T-33A* 51-4505 displayed.

ROCKY MOUNT. Park. *Grumman F9F-8P Cougar*—serial?

SOUTHERN PINES. *T-33A* 53-6024 displayed.

Borate Bombers (Wilmington)

WILMINGTON. New Hanover County Airport. *Grumman F-11A Tiger* 138619 in front of terminal building as memorial. Lifted by CH-53A from Cherry Point. Boeing B-17Gs and Consolidated PB4Y-2s sometimes here but possibly seasonal—details of any permanently based, wanted. *Lockheed T-33A* 52-9766 displayed locally and *F-86D* 53-1007 at the AFB. On the fantail of the battleship USS "North Carolina" *Vought-Sikorsky OS2U Kingfisher* painted 3073 "55" (serial of one of three delivered to ship 1941, when ship known as BB-55). It has been suggested that this a/c, which crashed in thick fog into a mountainside on Calvert Island, Canada, en route to Alaska, could be serial 5917. It may be of interest that whereas the original Kingfisher cost about 39,000 dollars, it is believed it cost Vought Aeronautics Co 100,000 dollars to restore this fine example. Therefore; unless some other funds are forthcoming, the battleship "Texas" at Houston, may find difficulty in securing—and restoring—another Kingfisher for their own ship.

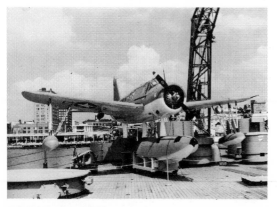

OS2U Kingfisher (Wilmington)

NORTH DAKOTA

BISMARCK. Museum of State Historical Society. *Fokker FVIIa* "The Alaskan" c/n 4909 of the Wilkins 1926 Arctic Expedition (see Brisbane, Queensland, Australia) *Douglas C-47A* 42-93800 also preserved here or nearby. *Grumman F9F-5* 126053 in small city park.

DICKINSON. *T-33A* 53-5078 displayed.

FARGO. Hector Field. *NA P-51D Mustang* 44-74407 in colours of North Dakota ANG, 178 FIS, displayed with *F-102* 56-1502. *Northrop F-89J Scorpion* 53-2465, of ANG, is at Kundert A & P School.

GRAND FORKS. *NA F-86L-55-NA Sabre* 53-719 displayed on pylon.

HATTON. Park, Highway 18, South of town, Carl Ben Eilson Memorial; *Lockheed T-33A* 51-6721.

JAMESTOWN. *F-86H* 53-1253 in Maryland ANG marks.

MINOT. Airstrip. *Funk B-85C* N77719 c/n 349; Doug Hjermstad.

VELVA. *Lockheed T-33A* 51-9100 displayed.

OHIO

AKRON. Airport. *NA AT-6C* CF-JXJ c/n 88-12858; B. G. Willison.

ALLIANCE. Airport. *Mignet Pou-du-Ciel "Flying Flea"* of 1937, built Chicago by Henri Mignet, believed owned by F. Easton and reputedly airworthy—registration and condition please.

BRADNER/RISING SUN. *NA F-86D/L* 53-1023 displayed

CINCINATTI. Lunkin Airport. *Meyers MAC*-145 N3479; M. Bricker In children's playground *NA F-86H* 53-1528N ex ANG. Flying from Blue Ash Field *Aeronca C-3* N16553; *Howard DGA-15* N5450N; *WACO UPF-7* N29309 c/n 5336.

CLEVELAND. Auto-Aviation Museum of Western Reserve Historical Society, 10825 East Boulevard (Ohio 44106). *Curtiss E A-1 Bumble Bee,* USN A-1, A607004 of 1910, flown from battleship 1911 converted to seaplane 1912. *Curtiss MF Seagull* biplane flying boat NC-903 c/n 5543, *Curtiss XP519 Oriole* NC1660 c/n 189 built 1919, Curtiss K6 engine 150 hp, 6 cyl. International orange fuselage, silver wings and tail, license number black "I'm a 1920 Curtiss Oriole" on rudder. *Fleet 16B* trainer NC230H c/n 272 of 1929. *NA P-51K-10-NA Mustang* N79161 ex 44-12116 "Second Fiddle", flown by Bob Swanson to 5th place in the 1946 Thompson Trophy Race. Unpainted natural finish with black lettering including race number "80". *Thomas-Morse S4C* 5452 c/n 633, restored example of "Tommy" Scout of WW I, with 100 hp Gnome Monosoupape, Formerly in Jarrett Museum, NJ. Olive drab with red cowling, star & circle insignia on wings, red and white blue vertical stripes on rudder. *Wedell-Williams "Special" Racer* NX-61Y c/n 109 of 1932 in which he won 1934 Thompson Trophy Race; 825 hp P. & W. Hornet. Also

many speed records. Gold with red license numbers, black "25" aft fuselage. May go to NASM, Washington D.C.

DAYTON. USAF Museum, on a 200-acre tract of land just east of city, on western edge of Wright-Patterson AFB. Open every day except Christmas, 0900 to 1700 weekdays, 1000 to 1800 weekends and holidays, extended hours during summer. Admission free. The original museum was founded 1923 at McCook Field, closed during WW II and re-opened 1954 when 10,000 visited. By 1953 the annual attendance was 592,000 and in the nineteen-seventies, expected to top a million people per year. The magnificent new building, specially designed to house the largest number of historical military aircraft ever gathered together for display, shows the history of the United States Air Force from a replica 1909 Wright Military Flyer right through to space "hardware". The Air Force Museum Foundation, Inc., a non-profit organization, campaigned for funds to finance the construction, housing exhibits valued, very conservatively, at over one hundred million dollars. This wonderful new museum is a lasting tribute and memorial to the men and women who have served in USAF. Apart from the aircraft and missiles, engines etc, there is a 500,000 document library and unique display items such as the original Glen Miller trombone and the carcass of the "Little Boy" atomic bomb. Here, though, we can only list aircraft, missiles: some of which may be outside and some away on loan for, in the writer's

USAF Museum (Dayton)

Aircraft dispersed outside (Dayton)

experience, no organization is more generous with help to others. Those out on loan are listed at present locations. As this is compiled the museum site holds:— *Wright Brothers 1909 Military Flyer* (replica), with engine donated by Orville Wright and chains, sprockets, propellers etc from heirs of Wright estate. Original was Signal Corps Airplane No 1 (NASM). *Bleriot of 1909*, donated by Ernie Hall, Ohio, used until 1918. *Modified Wright "B"* trainer used 1911-1916, at Mineola, NY. It last flew October 1924 at Dayton's International Air Races. Placed on exhibition by Eugene W. Kettering, Chairman, Board of Trustees, Air Force Museum Foundation, in 1962. *Standard J-1* serial 1141, used WW I for primary flight instruction. With Hall-Scott 100 hp. Donated by Robert Grieger, Oakharbor, Ohio. *Curtiss JN4-D Jenny* 2805; America's most famous WW I airplane, more than 6,000 delivered when production ceased after Armistice. Used mainly for flight training but some equipped with guns and bomb racks for advanced training. The mainstay of "Barnstormers" of 1920s and some still flying in 1930s. This example obtained from Robert Pfiel of Taylor, Texas. *SPAD VII* A.S.94099, French designed fighter of Societe Pour Aviation et ses Derives. Equipped the Lafayette Escadrille which became 103rd Aero Sqdn, A.E.F. Obtained from Museum of Science & Industry, Chicago and restored *and flown* by 1st Fighter Wing, Selfridge AFB, Michigan, 1962-66. *Sopwith F.1 Camel fighter (replica)* under construction for display. *Thomas-Morse S4B Scout* c/n 153, AF7077, SC36248, now N74W, is airworthy and, currently on loan from Mrs. Woodard, is understood for sale. *Thomas-Morse S4C* c/n 160, SC38944, slightly modified version of S4B, 497 being produced to supplement the 100 S4B models. Used as advance pursuit trainer. *Dayton-Wright DH.4* N-489, bombing-observation, 1917-1928. *Standard E-1* 49128 fighter-trainer, 100 mph, with 2-hr endurance; indefinite loan from J. B. Petty, Gastonia, NC. *Dayton-Wright Kettering "Bug" (replica)* of the Kettering Aerial Torpedo, the world's first "guided missile", 1918. Speed 55 mph, total weight 530 lbs including 180 lbs explosive, range 40 miles. *Sperry M-1 Messenger* of 1921-25, serial unknown, loaned by NASM. *Douglas World Cruiser "New Orleans"* 23-1232, based on DT-2 torpedo airplane used by US Navy, designed and purchased for circumnavigation of the earth by air—to be built for pontoons or wheels. Following successful testing of first, four more built. The flight left Seattle, Washington 6 April 1924, westward round the earth. "Seattle" crashed in Alaska, "Boston" sank north of Scotland. "New Orleans" and "Chicago" joined at Nova Scotia by "Boston II" (the original DWC), for rest of flight and on 23 September 1924 they returned safely to Seattle, completing the 26,345 mile trip. This exhibit is loaned by Los Angeles County Museum ("Chicago" is at NASM—what happened to "Boston II"?) *Loening OA-1A "San Francisco"* 26-431 observation a/c; loaned by NASM. *Curtiss R3C-2* A6979 c/n 26-33, "43" 1925 Schneider Racer, on loan from NASM, Doolittle's machine. *Consolidated PT-1 Husky* 26-233, the first airplane purchased in substantial quantities following WW I, 221 being delivered from 1925. Developed from Dayton-Wright TW-3. Obtained 1957 from Ohio State University. *Keystone LB-7* bomber 1929-35, serials 29-13 and 29-16 (parts of—for building of one machine). *Thomas-Morse 0-19B* 30-127 observation a/c, parts secured for restoration. *Curtiss P-6E Hawk* 32-261 (restored as 32-240) the last fighter biplane built in

quantity for AAC. Originally Y1P-22, re-designated P-6E. In markings of 17th Pursuit Sqdn. Donated by Edward S. Perkins, Alabama. *Douglas 0-38F* 33-234 observation a/c. *CASA 352* (Junkers Ju 52/3m) T.2B-244 transport from Spain. The type was nicknamed "Iron Annie". *Boeing P-26A* 33-135, a type still in use over Luzon December 1941 where all were lost to enemy or accidents. This example was with 94th Pursuit Sqdn, Selfridge Field, then to Panama Canal Zone but, in 1942, presented to Guatemala. Returned 1958 it is in colours of 34th Attack Sqdn; loaned from NASM. *Martin B-10* bomber used 1934-44, unknown serial, donated by Argentine Navy 1970, after 6 years' negotiations. This is the only known example—which led to B-17 and B-24 monoplane designs. It is believed to have been exported to Dutch East Indies and possibly used against the Japs and then flown to Argentina where it was found stored in a hangar. *Douglas 0-46A* 35-179 observation of 1936, being restored. *Stearman PT-13D Kaydet* 42-17800 with Lycoming R-680 of 220 hp (with Continental it is PT-17, with Jacobs PT-18; with canopy, PT-27). Of 10,346 Kaydets for USA and Allies, 2,141 were PT-13s, AAF. Donated by Boeing Airplane Co (which purchased Stearman Co 1938) it was the very last Kaydet produced. *CASA C-2111* (Spanish-built Heinkel He 111) serial awaited. *Boeing B-17G Flying Fortress* 42-32076 "Shoo Shoo Baby"; *B-17G* 44-83624, ex 3205th Drone Sqdn, brought to director-plane configuration. By time production halted in favour of B-29, 12,726 Flying Fortresses built. *Douglas B-18A Bolo* 37-469, bomber version of DC-3 but used for training. This one seized Florida 1958 when hauling guns to Cuba. *Curtiss P-36A Hawk* 38-001, still in use by AAF Alaska and Pearl Harbor 1941. This example, first to AAC, is in the "desert sand and spinach" of 27th Pursuit Sqdn. Donated by Edward S. Perkins of Anniston, Alabama. *Hispano HA-1112-MIL* (Spanish-built Messerschmitt Bf 109) serial C4K-64, listed as Bf 109 G-2 version. *Curtiss P-40E Warhawk* AK987, from RAF or RCAF (more than 14,000 P-40s produced and this serial quoted as Kittyhawk I elsewhere). *Douglas C-39* 38-515 transport of 1939-45. *Junkers Ju-88 D-1*, serial quoted as 0880430650 but this, from German sources, said to be spare-part number on a fuselage plate. Same source also queries "Zerstörer" which, he says, was only used for Bf 110, Me 210 and Me 410. This particular example is a long-range photo-recce version nicknamed "Baksheesh" and claimed the best-known of the 15,000 built. On 22 July 1943 it was flown into Cyprus by a defecting Rumanian Air Force pilot. Then flown across Atlantic by US pilots to be tested at Wright Field as FE-1598, Werk-Nr quoted as 430650. Can a reader give us the correct serial for this splendid exhibit. *Seversky P-35A (Swedish EP-106)* 282-11; fighter Swedish Air Force quote 2126 as serial. *Curtiss 0-52 Owl* 40-2763, ordered in quantity 1940 for observation duties, was relegated to courier work when USA entered WW II. "L" for liaison-type replaced the "O" designation after Pearl Harbor. This example came from U.S. Federal Reformatory, Chillicothe, Ohio. *Fairchild PT-19 Cornell* 42-191659, trainer. *Vultee BT-13B Valiant* 42-90629, used until 1945. *Bell P39Q Airacobra* 44-3887, initial flight of type April 1939 at Wright Field; 9,584 built. This one from Hardwick A/c Co, El Monte, California. *Stinson L-1 Vigilant* 40-291, liaison a/c. *Mitsubishi A6M2 (Model 21) "Zero"* 11593—obtained from Tom King of Australia who bought it from the Papua-New Guinea War Memorial Trust. It was disabled at Kavieng, New

Thomas-Morse S4B (Dayton)

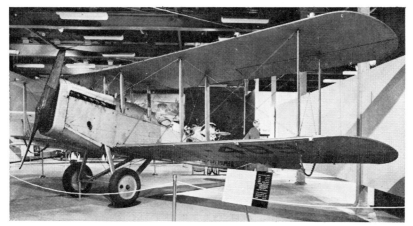

Dayton-Wright DH.4 (Dayton)

Standard E-1 (Dayton)

Curtiss R3C-2 (Dayton)

World Cruiser "New Orleans" (Dayton)

Standard E-1 (Dayton)

Curtiss O-52 (Dayton)

Ju 88 D-1 (Dayton)

PT-1 Husky (Dayton)

Focke-Wulf Fw 190 D-9 (Dayton)

Kettering "Bug" (Dayton)

Boeing B-29 "Bockscar" (Dayton)

Twin Mustang (Dayton)

Douglas Skyraider (Dayton)

Ireland. *Supermarine Spitfire XVI* TE330, donated by RAF and formerly flown by No 601 (County of London) Sqdn, RAuxAF. Later with serial 7449M. Arrived via USAF Academy, Colorado Springs. *North American T-6G Texan* 50-1279, one of the best-known trainers of AAF, purchased as the BC-1 (Basic Combat). More than 10,000 purchased by AAF prior to end of WW II and many thousands for Navy as SNJ, and for 30 Allied nations. Korea gave T-6 new lease of life and many were used for spotting enemy positions with smoke rockets. This example from Pennsylvania ANG. *North American B-25B Mitchell* 40-2344, the type used on the famous Tokyo Raid 18 April 1942 led by (General) Doolittle. More than 9,800 built and this example re-built by North American to the configuration of the Tokyo Raiders and flown to museum April 1958. *Focke Wulf Fw 190 D-9* Werk-Nr 601088 HPS, serial 9053Z01 also quoted (by NASM from where on loan). This was FE-120 received Wright Field 1 August 1945 for evalua-tion. *Ryan PT-22 Recruit* 41-15721. *Douglas A-20G Havoc* 43-22200, the USA's main attack bomber in December 1941. Already used in combat by RAF and French, early in July 1942 six, flown by American crews, ac-companied six RAF on low-altitude mission against four Dutch airfields. This marked the beginning of American daylight experience in Europe. Donated by Bankers Life & Casualty Co. *Radioplane OQ-2A Target Drone* 43-46499 and *unserialled example*. *Beech C-45H Expeditor* 52-10893; type used 1941-1965. c/n AF-823. *Schweitzer XTG-3 Training Glider* 42-14704, also fuselage only of 42-52988. *WACO CG-4A Troop/Cargo Glider* 45-27948. *Martin B-26G Marauder* 43-34581, first flight of type 25 November 1940 design showing such pro-mise that 1,131 ordered September 1940. Combat missions SW Pacific early 1942 but majority sent to England and Mediterranean. Lowest loss rate claimed of any Allied bomber—less than a half of one per cent. At end of production 5,266 built. Example from Air France training school near Paris, June 1965. *Lockheed P-38L Lightning* 44-53232. Public debut of XP-38 11 February 1939, flying California-NY in 7 hours. Nick-named by Germans "Der Gabelschwanz Teufel"—"The Forked-Tail Devil". By end of production 1945, a total of 9,923 built. This one donated by Bob Bean A/c Corpn, Hawthorne, Cal and Kaufman Foundation, Philadelphia, in markings of 55th Fighter Sqdn, England. *Consolidated B-24D-CO Liberator* 42-72843 "Strawberry Bitch". More than 18,000 produced for every combat area. This example flew combat missions from North Africa 1943-44 with 512th Bomb Sqdn and was flown to museum May 1959. *Taylorcraft L-2M Grasshopper*—no serial yet (civilian machine). *Piper L-4 Grasshopper* N42050 c/n 9100, to be given military marks. *Beech AT-11 Kansas* 42-37493 (known as Kansan by many owners.) *Sikorsky R-4B Hoverfly* 43-46506. The R-4 was world's first production helicopter and first service AF heli-copter, developed from the 1940 VS-300 as the XR-4 of 1942. First used in combat in Burma May 1944 when it was reported "Today the 'egg-beater' went into action and the damn thing acted like it had good sense". This example donated by University of Illinois, 1967. *Curtiss C-46D Commando* 44-78018—no history quoted. *Focke Achgelis Fa 330*, unserialled, rotary wing kite. *Republic P-47D-15-RA Thunderbolt* (Razorback) 42-23278 ex N 5087V, N347D, "HV-P". More than 15,600 built. First combat mission of type 8 April 1943 from England. This one donated November 1964 by Republic Aviation Corp-oration after visit to Europe 1963. Known as "T" bolt

Douglas Havoc (Dayton)

P-47D Thunderbolt (Bubble) 45-49458. Nicknamed "7-ton milk bottle", "The Jug" etc. *North American P-51D Mustang* 44-74936, type designed and built at request of British Govt in 1940 and initially had limited high-altitude performance. In 1942, however, with a Rolls-Royce Merlin, performance was greatly improved and 14,000 built for AAF, mainly with Packard Merlin 1,200 hp V-1710-81 engines. For the loss of 2,520 P-51s in combat USAAF claimed destruction, by this type, of 4,950 e/a in the air and 4,131 on the ground—a better ratio than any other US fighter. This example obtained from West Virginia ANG, Jan 1957. It was the last USAF propeller-driven fighter in operation. *Sikorsky YH-5A* 43-46620 (originally the R5-R for rotocraft then H for helicopter). *Ford JB-2*. U.S. built version of V1 flying (buzz) bomb, two examples. *Messerschmitt Me 262 A-1a* "Schwalbe" (Swallow) Werk No. 121442, nicknamed "Screaming Meenie" by US servicemen. Is this FE-107, received Wright Field for evaluation 21 May 1945? *V2* (A4 ballistic missile) from Germany. *Bell P-59B Airacomet* 44-22650. Initial test-flight of type 1 October 1942 at Muroc Dry Lake (now Edwards AFB) Calif. A year later production was ordered and 66 were built. It did not get into combat but provided invaluable data and training. Example came from Kirtland AFB, New Mexico, February 1956. *Northrop P-61C Black Widow* 43-8353 was America's first specific night-fighter, flight-tested 1942 for production 1943. Opera-tional debut Europe with 9th AF as night intruder and interceptor. In Pacific not one was lost in over a year of combat. About 700 built. This one was given to Boy Scouts of America, kept at Grimes Airport, Urbana, Ohio, and was presented to museum by Tecumseh Council, BSA, Springfield, Ohio. *Bell P-63E King Cobra* 43-11728 many to USSR or Free French and mainly used in USA as a trainer. *Douglas A-26C Invader* 44-35733 designed as follow-on to A-20 and known as A-26 and changed to B-26 in 1948. (Not to be confused with Martin B-26). Combat debut 19 November 1944, Europe and by "VJ" Day over 2,500 built. During Korean con-flict Douglas B-26 used as night intruder and early in Vietnam war the Invader again went into action and 40 modified B-26Bs ordered, known as B-26K. In 1966 re-designated A-26A. Example appears in markings and colors used in Korean campaign. *Boeing B-29 Super-fortress* "Bockscar" 44-27297, the machine from which was dropped the second of the atomic bombs on Japan —9 August 1945 on Nagasaki, which brought about the end of WW II. First flown 21 September 1942, it was decided in December 1943 not to use the type in Europe and it began operating in November 1944 from Sapian, Guam, and Tinian against Japan. Used by the RAF and called "Washington" 1950/54. *Lockheed F-80C Shooting Star* 49-696. America's first quantity jet of which about 1,700 built. Initial flight January 1944 as P-80 (re-designated F-80 in 1948). Used extensively in Korean conflict for low-level ground target attacks. Served as basic design for T-33 and F-94. *North American F-82B Twin Mustang* "Betty Jo" 44-65168 developed 1945 by marrying two P-51 airframes with centre wing section. This exhibit flew Hawaii-NY non-stop, 5051 miles, the longest then by a fighter. First three North Korean planes shot down in air combat fell to guns of F-82s. *Radioplane OQ-19* of 1945, serial unknown; target drone. *Kawanishi NIK2J "George"* (NIK2-J Shiden-Kai "George 21"). Produced during last year of WW II, only 428 built because of production problems and part shortage due to B29 raids. One of best "all-round" fighters in Pacific but insufficient altitude performance against B-29 raids. Donated by City of San Diego, through San Diego Sqdn, Air Force Association. *Fuji Kokuki K.K. (Fuji Hikoki) MXY7 Ohka* ("Baka" suicide bomb.) Brought to USA for evaluation, designed primarily for use against ships, particularly effective during invasion of Okinawa. Max Speed 615 mph in attack dive with rocket power, glide speed 229 mph, range 55 miles from release at 27,000 ft. Span 16 ft 5 ins length 19 ft 10 ins weight loaded 4,530 lbs with 2,645 lbs of high-explosive warhead. Three-barrel solid-propellant rocket of 1,500 lbs thrust. *Lockheed P-80R Shooting Star* 44-85200. A specially-modified racer with smaller canopy, shorter wing and re-designed air intakes. Flown by Col Albert Boyd 19 June 1947 to new world speed record of 623.8 mph. Shipped to museum from Griffis AFB, NY. *McDonnell XH-20 Little Henry* 46-689. *Boeing B-50D Superfortress* 49-310 c/n 16086. *KB-50J Superfortress* 49-389 c/n 16165. *Douglas VC-118B Liftmaster* 46-505 "Independence". *Northrop X-4* 46-677 tailless research a/c. *North American* B-45C Tornado 48-010. *Republic F-84E Thunderjet* 50-1143 USAF's first post-war fighter, initial flight 28 February 1946, production from June 1947 and up to 1953 4,450 "straight-wing" (in contrast to F-84F swept-wing) built. First USAF jet fighter able to carry tactical atomic weapon. From Robins AFB. *Convair XF-92A* 46-682, delta-fighter. *North American F-86A Sabre* 49-1067. USAF's first swept-wing jet fighter, initial flight 1 October 1947. On 15 September 1948 an F-86A set new world speed record of 670.9 mph. Over Korea 800 MiGs shot down for 58 Sabres, ratio 14 to 1. *Convair B-36J* (Very Heavy Bomber) 52-2220, type maiden flight 8 August 1946 and on 26 June 1948 SAC received first for operations. When production ceased 1954 more than 380 built. Last flight ever was museum's machine from Arizona to Wright Field. *Lockheed T-33A Shooting Star* 53-5974 (also called

Spitfire XVI (Dayton)

Bell X-5 (Dayton)

T-Bird), jet trainer. *Boeing B-47E Stratojet* 53-2280, world's first swept-wing jet bomber. First flight 17 December 1947. More than 1,200 in SAC when production ended 1957. *Fairchild C-119J Flying Boxcar* 51-8037; type used from 1949 *Northrop F-89J Scorpion* 52-1911, twin-engined two-place all-weather fighter-interceptor, pilot in front cockpit, observer in rear. *Republic XF-91 Thunderceptor* 46-680; prototype-type in service 1949-50. *Lockheed F-94A Starfire* 49-2498, developed from T-33; radar-equipped to locate enemy. *Bell X-5* (Variable Sweep Wing) 50-1838; research aircraft based on Me F1101. *North American X-10* serial 19307; Navaho test vehicle, radio-controlled. *Mikoyan-Gurevich MiG-15 "Fagot"* 2015357, USSR jet fighter. *Douglas X-3 Stiletto* 49-2892, twin turbojet, one of two built. Designed to obtain aerodynamic, power plant, structural and other flight research data at speeds above Mach 2. First flight 20 October 1952 at subsonic and June 1953 first supersonic. From Edwards AFB

Douglas X-3 (Dayton)

MiG-15 (Dayton)

YRF-84F Thunderstreak (Dayton)

where it took off from ground, unlike X-1, X-2, X-15 which were mid-air released. *Cessna O-1E Bird Dog* 51-11917. *North American T-28A Trojan* 49-1494. *Sikorsky UH-19B Chickasaw* 52-7587; *UH-19D* 55-03228. *Aerojet General RTV-A-1 Aerobee,* unserialled. *Boeing CQM-1Q Bomarc* 57-2730, service to present day. *North American F-86D Sabre* 50-477; *F-86H* 53-1352. *American Helicopter XH-26 Jet Jeep,* serial unknown. *Northrop SM-62 Snark* N3290, in use 1953-63. *Republic YRF-84F Thunderstreak* (FICON) 49-2430. *F-84F Thunderstreak* 52-6526 donated by 178th TFG, Ohio and flown by Col Andrew C. Lucy from Springfield to W-P AFB for Lt-Col (Ret) Royal D. Frey ex Cdr 178th CAM Sqdn. *Vertol CH-21B Workhorse* 51-15857, and 52-8685. *Douglas A-1E Skyraider* Bu.132649, used by Major Fisher in Vietnam on mission for which awarded Medal of Honor. *Lockheed EC-121H Constellation* 53-0555 c/n 4370 and *VC-121E "Columbine III"* 53-7885, c/n 4151. Special US Presidential conversion of Naval RTV-1 Bu.131650. Donated Museum 20 April 1966. *Martin RB-57A Canberra* 52-1492, licence-built, debut in Vietnam, 403 produced. *Boeing B-52B Stratofortress* "Lucky Lady III" 53-394. *Douglas RB-66B Destroyer* 53-475. *Douglas C-133A Cargomaster* 56-2008. *McDonnell F-101A Voodoo* 56-235. *Convair F-102A Delta Dagger* 56-1416. *Ryan X-13 Vertijet* 54-1620, for testing VTOL. This particular example made history when on 11 April 1957 it took off vertically from its mobile trailer, nosed into level attitude, then reversed to vertical flight and descended to its trailer for a safe landing. This is one of two built. Engine Rolls-Royce Avon, max speed 350 mph. *North American F-107A,* originally designated F-100B. Three built, first making maiden flight 10 September 1956 and subsequently flew near Mach 2, twice speed of sound. No production owing to lack of funds but valuable for high-speed research data. Pratt & Whitney J75; four 20 mm cannon.

Bell GAM-63 Rascal 52-10985; ground-air missile. *CREE Supersonic parachute test vehicle. Bell UH-13J Sioux* 57-2728. Presidential aircraft. *Douglas PGM-17 Thor* 58-2261—also supplied to RAF. *Chrysler PGM-19 Jupiter* 58-5285. *McDonnell ADM-20 Quail* 59-2245. *Bell XV-3A* 54-148, VTOL. *Convair F-106A Delta Dart* 56-451, development of F-102, first flight 26 December 1956. All-weather interceptor with Hughes MA-1 fire control system and electronic guidance. *Convair HGM-16F Atlas* 61-2554, intercontinental ballistic missile. Flight testing began June 1957 with full-range 6,000-mile flight November 1958. In addition to ICBM role Atlas has been "workhorse" of America's space effort, including Project Mercury, the placing of astronauts in orbit. The Atlas carries the Mercury capsule or other type payload at upper end where ICBM carries nuclear warhead. *Lockheed Agena "A"* 2205-1025 space satellite. *Agena "B"* 1502. *North American X-15A-2* 56-6671 research aircraft. *Convair B-58A Hustler* 59-2458, winner of Bendix Trophy for Los Angeles-NY and return, 5 March 1962, 4,900 miles with three air refuellings at 50,000 ft, time 4 hrs 41 mins, 11.3 secs, average 1,044.96 mph including turnabout time. Pilot Capt. Robt G. Sowers. *Martin CGM-13B Mace "B"* missile 60-5392. *Lockheed Discoverer XIV,* space satellite. *Martin HGM-25 Titan I* 61-4498. *Boeing LGM-30A Minuteman I* 63-180. *Lockheed Agena "D" Snap 10A* C-05282, space satellite. *North American AGM-28A Hound Dog* 60-2097 and 60-2110. *Cessna YA-37A Attack* a/c 62-5951. *McDonnell ASV-3 "ASSET" Lifting Body,* unserialled, of 1964. *Hawker XV-6A P.1127 Kestrel* XS688 now 64-18262, tripartite evaluation a/c leading to the Hawker Siddeley Harrier now flown by USMC. *North American XB-70 Valkyrie* 62-001, claimed the world's most exotic airplane, conceived for SAC as high-altitude bomber three times speed of sound (Mach 3). Only two built, through fund limitations, as research a/c for advanced study of aerodynamics etc. No 1 flew 21 September 1964, achieving Mach 3 12 October 1965. No 2 crashed 8 June 1966 following mid-air collision. No 1 continued the programme until flown to museum 4 February 1969. *Ling-Temco-Vought XC-142A* 62-5924, V/STOL tilt-wing a/c. *Northrop YF-5A Freedom Fighter* 59-4989, c/n N6003. *McDonnell Gemini III "Molly Brown"* 52-00001-3, manned spacecraft. *Martin X-23A (SV-5D/FV-3) "PRIME" Lifting Body,* unserialled. *Bensen X-25A (B-8M) Gyro-Copter* 68-10770 and *X-25B* 68-10771. *Ilyushin Il-10* T2-3000 ex Korea and *Yak-9P* T2-3002 said to be coming. The listing is arranged, as is the museum's, in approximate years of use of the basic model. Not all of the above will be on display as some are being restored and others awaiting rebuild. Do, though, make this your priority if residing in or visiting the USA. With the 17th Bomb Wing (SAC) at Wright-Patterson AFB, on loan from museum are *Boeing B-47E* 53-6244 and *NA B-25J* 44-30649. With the USAF Orientation Group on the base, also loaned, is *Ryan SV-5J (X-24)* VZ-11, direct-lift "Fan-in-Wing". In Dayton's Carillon Park a *Wright Brothers 1903 (replica)* is said to be exhibited and *NA F-86D/L Sabre* 52-3831; *Republic F-84F* 51-9408, *Lockheed F-94C* 51-13526, and *Lockheed T-33A* 51-6857, are also reported in Dayton. Exact locations please. Flying from Dayton Airport:—*Aeronca C-3* N17404 c/n A717 of Erwin Eshelman; *Meyers OTW* N26476 c/n 29 and *WACO UMF3* N14041 c/n 3836 with Harold L. Johnson. *WACO UPF7* N32065 c/n 5697 with E. Heins.

DONNELSVILLE. *T-33A* 51-8623 exhibited.

EVANDALE. Community Centre. *Republic F-84C* 51-1225 and *NA F-86D/L* 53-1060 reported—confirmation wanted.

FAIRBORN. School Yard. *Convair YF-102* 52-7995.

FRANKLIN. *F-86D/L* 53-1058 displayed.

GRAFTON. *T-33A* 51-9184 on show.

HAMILTON. Airport. *NA P-51D Mustang* N6341T ex 44-74774. *Cessna T-50 Bobcat* N58147. c/n 5932. *Beechcraft 17S* N67421.

HASKINS. *T-33A* 52-9756 on show.

KETTERING. *T-33A* 52-9788 displayed.

LUNKIN. *NA F-86H* 53-1528 on display.

MANSFIELD. Airport. *Perth-Amboy CK Bird* NC769Y c/n 2058-33 of Earl Dekker. *Stearman PT-17C* N10Q c/n 75-301 of Dr. H. Morkel. *Stearman PT-17* N104H c/n 75-2820; Chas Hellinger.

MARENGO. *Republic F-84F* 52-6444 displayed.

MARIETTA, *T-33A* 52-9785 on show.

MASSILLEN. *Lockheed F-94C* 51-5610 on show.

MEDINA. Airfield. *Dart GC* N31695 c/n 69 of 1946; Fred Leidig.

MIAMISBURG. Airfield. *NA F-51H* N551H ex 44-64314.

MIDDLETOWN. *Lockheed T-33A* 51-8911 displayed.

NEWARK. *T-33A* 51-9173 displayed.

NEWBURY. The Walter Soplata "Collection". Walter writes (1973) that he has now given up all hope of a real museum but that his place is open free to the public seven days a week to view the many aircraft pieces he owns. As he admits many are beyond restoration. Not all of his aircraft are listed here but enthusiasts will obviously enjoy seeing the fuselages etc of many others:—*Chance Vought F7U-3 Cutlass* 129645, silver with blue rudders. *Cessna T-50* NC60145 c/n 5173. *Goodyear FG-1D Corsair* 88026 "OO" complete, Naval colors. *Lockheed P-80A-1-60* 1260 with Point Mugo marks 689. *NA B-25J,* Air Force configuration marked 80-708 —serial please. *NA T-28A Trojan* c/n quoted as 4021800 —serial wanted. *Lockheed P-82E Twin Mustang* serial given as 46255, with c/n 144-38142, also parts of 4483887. Confirmation of serials appreciated. *Vultee BT-15 Valiant* 42-41597; *BT-13A* 41-9642. *Grumman TBM-3* "8" on cowl "H" on fin one side "S" on other. Obtained from farm in Maryland and painted dark blue—can anyone produce serial or Bu number? *Douglas B-26 On-Mark 4* N919P, engineless, ex Lake Michigan crash—all survived as plane floated for awhile. *Douglas XBT2D (AD-1) Skyraider* (with AD-7 outboard wings) 09103, mainly from Fairless Hills, Penna junkyard. *Bell P-63 King Cobra* 8895 on fin, from Buffalo NY, poor state. Walter will understand why I am not listing incomplete

a/c (including the RB-36E-111-CF 42-13571 from W-P AFB) as he states there is little or no chance of restoration, except of those shown above, some of which are displayable. We take off our hats to Walter and his wife and other helpers for what they have saved from the melting-pots.

ORRVILLE. *T-33A* 51-6546.

PAINSVILLE. *Lockheed P-38L Lightning,* once on top of a local garage, was said to be under restoration by (or for) "Chuck" Lydford—confirmation and serial please.

PARMA HEIGHTS. *T-33A* 51-6816.

PARMA/NEWBURY. *F-86D/L* 53-959 displayed.

Ford Trimotor (Port Clinton)

PORT CLINTON. Airport. Island Airways operate *Ford 4-AT Trimotor* N7684 and N7584 on round-trips to Lake Erie. *Dart GC* N20994 c/n G-12 of 1938 owned by Lloyd Washburn.

SEMINOLE. Dale & Doana Wallace have 1940 *Piper J-5 Cub Cruiser* N28142 c/n 5-115 and *WACO CJC Custom* of 1934—reg'n please.

SHARONVILLE. General Electric Plant. *NA F-86D Sabre* serial and confirmation wanted.

SOUTH DAYTON. Airport. *Luton Minor* N4762T, c/n PAL/11; R. Wagner. *Stinson 10A* N34698 c/n 7998. *WACO F-3, WACO YMF-3*—reg'ns and owners' names wanted.

STRUTHERS. *NA F-86D/L* 52-3719 displayed.

TIFFIN. *NA F-86D/L* 51-3048 on show.

TOLEDO. Express Airport. *Lockheed F-94B Starfire* in Ohio ANG colors painted 0-180.

TOLEDO/SYLVANIA. *F-86H* 52-2059 displayed.

UHRICHSVILLE. *NA F-86D/L* 52-3814 displayed.

URBANA. Airport. *NA T-28A Trojan* N8391H ex 49-1584 of Grimes Mnfg Co. *NA F-86D/L* 53-724 and *T-33A* 51-6682 reported displayed. *Vought F4U-7 Corsair* N33714 ex French Navy 965; Dean Ortner.

VANDALIA. *Lockheed T-33A* 53-5895 displayed.

VAN WERT. *NA F-86D/L* 53-944 displayed.

WAPAKONETA. Armstrong Museum. Honouring Neil Armstrong, astronaut, first on the moon, a million-dollar air and space museum recording his life and the stories of other Ohioans who have pioneered in flight. Included will be the *Aeronca C-2* in which Neil first soloed and the *Douglas F5D-1 Skylancer* prototype serial 139208 flown by Armstrong to study winged scapecraft emergencies. This development of the Skyray did not enter production phase. Confirmation of reg'n and serial please, with photos.

OKLAHOMA

ALTUS. Park. *Boeing B-47E Stratojet* 51-7071 "City of Altus".

BARTLESVILLE. Woolaroc Museum. *Travel Air* "Woolaroc", winner of 1927 Dole Flight.

CLAREMONT. Airfield. *New Standard D-25* of 1929 N149M c/n 156 of Encel Kleier.

DEL CITY. Park. *T-33A* 52-9762.

ELK CITY. *T-33A* 51-8896 displayed.

ENID. *T-33A* 51-4301 displayed.

EL RENO. V.F.W. Post 382, Route 66. *Douglas A-26B Invader* 44-34746 reported.

INOLA. Airfield. *Travel Air D-4000* N688K c/n 1323 of 1929; Herb Karkcom.

KINGFISHER. *NA F-86D/L* 53-773 displayed.

McALESTER. *NA F-86D/L* 52-10142 displayed.

OKLAHOMA CITY. Downtown Airport. *P-51D Mustang* N167F ex 44-73877; Paul Finefrock. It is reported that an Airport Museum is forming; with a *Curtiss Pusher* (replica) built by Billy Parker, donated to Tulsa but transferred here. Details of other exhibits, with photos, welcomed.

SPERRY. *Lockheed T-33A* 51-9183 displayed.

STROUD. *NA F-86D/L* 51-8277 displayed.

TULSA. Brown Field. *NA F-86 Sabre* 51-849 at ANG base. *Ford 5-AT-C Trimotor* N414H c/n 5-AT-74, once on floats with USN, later Pan American and now American Airlines, reported near American Airlines hangars. Also believed to house *Ford 5-AT-B* N9683, said to be promised to NASM when flying ends. N414H also said to be going to California—details please. *Curtiss JN-4* on display in terminal—serial? *NA O-47 Owl*—two examples have been reported—details valued. Flying from here Riverside Airport *Church Midwing* X9167 of 1928 owned by Gene Chase. *Davis D-1W* N848H c/n 106; Fred Tray. *Piper J-3L* N32710 c/n 5542 of 1940; Sherman Elder. *Interstate S-1A* N37241 c/n 84 of 1941; William Griffin. *Andover-Kent-Langley* N51706; John Pierce. *Stearman PT-17* N57949 c/n 75-1668; John Horeth. *Grumman FM-2* N90523 ex Bu 74560; Morris Hudson. At the NA Rockwell Corporation Plant is the first (L-3805) *Aero Commander* N1946 c/n 1; on display outside. In the City Fairground. *Boeing B-47* 0-12387 and three missiles—details please and photos. The South-East Oklahoma State College is said to have "Blue Angels" *Grumman F-11A (F11F-1) Tiger* 141859—location please.

OREGON

ALBANY. Municipal Airport. Route 99E. *NA F-86D/L Sabre* 51-6055 "FU 055" on plinth. *Martin TM-61 Matador* (two on display).

ASTORIA. *F-86D/L* 51-3024 displayed.

ATHENA. Barrett Field. *Naval A/c Factory N3N-3* N1120 c/n 2613; Barrett Tillman. *Stearman C-3R Business Speedster* N794H; J. H. Tillman (see also PASCO, Wash.)

AURORA. State Airfield. *Grumman F6F-3 Hellcat* being rebuilt (1973) by Bill Compton—details please. *NA SNJ-4* flown here by Floyd Goodat & Dennis Polen, reg'n wanted.

BEAVERTON. Airfield. *NA FJ-2 Fury* displayed—serial please.

Ford Trimotor (Tulsa)

CORVALLIS. *NA F-86D/L* 51-8467 displayed.

CRESSWELL. Airport. *Travel Air 4000* N9072, *N379M*. *Stinson SM-8A* N11159, c/n 4302. *Kinner Sportster* N14288 c/n 166 of 1935; Melvin Frers.

ECHO. Private ranch airfield. *Waco UPF-7* of K. Coppinger.

ESTACADA. Airfield. *Student Prince* being restored by W. Dessert.

EUGENE. Mahlon Sweet Airport. *Northrop F-89J* 53-2524 ex Oregon ANG. *Grumman F4F Wildcat* N4629V ex 86564 from Tallmantz still under restoration.

HUBBARD. Lenhardt Field. *Grumman (General Motors) FM-2 Wildcat; NA SNJ-5*, both owned and flown by J. Lenhardt. Also flying nearby *Brunner-Winkle BK Bird* N1116M c/n 2001-52 of 1929 of Walter C. Wright.

JUNCTION CITY. Henry Strauch has a *Waco UBF* N13075 c/n 3692 of 1933, on floats, undergoing rebuild.

KLAMATH FALLS. Airport. *Cessna T-50 Bobcat* N52390. *Vultee BT-13 Valiant* N57248 c/n 2365; Klamath Aircraft.

LAKE OSWEGO. Walter Wright is restoring his *Spartan NP-1* registration and photo appreciated.

MADRAS. *Sopwith Pup (replica)* with B54 Kinner of Harold Bevins, reported for sale.

MEDFORD. Airport. *Consolidated PB4Y-2 Privateer* N3191G ex 59754; Rosendalm Avn. (N6884C used now for spares). *Lockheed P.2E Neptune* N126Z ex 124904; both for borate bombing.

NEWPORT. Airfield. *Stearman PT-17* of Henry Ross, reg'n?

OAK GROVE. Route 99E. On top of a service station *Boeing B-17G-105-VE Flying Fortress* 44-85790.

PORTLAND. Airport. *Northrop F-89J* 54-0332 at ANG base, ex Oregon ANG, at their HQs is *Convair F-102 Delta Dagger* 57-833. *NA P-51D Mustang* N6339T ex 44-64005 flies here, owner unknown. In the Oregon

Museum of Science & Technology, 4015 SW Canyon Rd *Douglas C-47A/DC-3 Dakota* N56589 ex 43-15512. *Northrop F-89J Scorpion* 54-0267. *Grumman HU-16B Albatross* 51-7244 (loaned from USAFM). *NA Sabre* 53-838 also reported in Portland. Is there also an *FJ-2 Fury* in store?

REDMOND. Airport. *Boeing PB-1W Fortress* N5237V ex 77233, 44-83868. *Douglas A-26* N5457V ex 44-34313, N9159Z ex 43-22673; US Forestry Service borate bombers operated by Butler Aircraft.

SALEM. Airport. *T-33A* 51-4038 and *52-9620* displayed. *Stearman PT-17* N63555 flying. *N3N-3* N51H c/n 2660 of 1940 and *Curtiss Robin* N6394T c/n 405 of 1929 owned by Vic Zerbs.

TROUTDALE. Bob Sturges, Cherry Park Rd, restoring *Curtiss P-40 Warhawk; BT-13 Valiant; F-86L Sabre; Stinson L-5 Sentinel* (believed airworthy) *B-25J;* and *Beech AT-11 Kansan.* Details and photos please for V. and V. No 5. From the local airport *NA B-25 Mitchell* N7674 c/n 5272 said to fly.

VALE. *NA F-86D/L* 53-781 displayed.

WOODBURN. State Boys' Home, Route 99E, *Lockheed T-33A T-Bird* 51-6653.

PENNSYLVANIA

AVON. *NA F-86H* 52-2065 displayed.

CAMP HILL. *Lockheed F-94C Starfire* 51-13577.

CARLISLE. *F-94C* 51-5620 displayed.

CORRY. *F-94C* 51-5671 displayed.

DALLASTOWN. *T-33A* 52-9405 displayed.

DELMONT. Newhouse Park. *T-33A-5-10* 51-6742.

DILLISBURG. Vogelsong Private Airstrip. *Bucker Bu 133 Jungmeister* N4970 c/n 2004; Dr. Champe C. Pool.

ERIE. Beside Interstate 90 between exits 5 and 6, two miles south of town, *F-94C Starfire*. Serial please. At International Airport. *F-86H* 53-1338 displayed.

DH.60M (Gettysburg)

FREDERICKSBURG. Farmer's Pride Airport. *DH. Tiger Moth* quoted as G-AOGI fuselage, wings from unknown Tiger—details please. Note G-AOGI became OO-SOA in 1955 and may still be current in Belgium.

FREEPORT. *NA F-86H* 52-2043 displayed.

GETTYSBURG. Airport. *DH.60M Moth* N585M c/n 86, owned and flown by L. Parrish, American-built, history wanted. *Hamilton Helicopter* NC41970 is displayed at airport entrance and *Ganda Helicospeeder* NX61954 is in open storage under polythene.

GREENSBURG. Lynch Field (sports ground) *T-33A-5-LO* 53-5251.

HARRISBURG. William Penn Memorial Museum, Box 232, Mr. Duncan Campbell in charge. *Piper J-3C Cub* NC98629 with Continental 65 hp engine. Was formerly owned by Willis Reiffenberg, based Hazelton Airport. The Piper A/c Co, Lock Haven, re-processed it to meet all "specs" of their 1946 production type.

HIGHSPIRE. *Lockheed F-94C* 51-5622 displayed.

IMPERIAL. Route 22. *NA F-86D/L Sabre* 53-0665, as ANG Memorial.

IRWIN VFW Post 781. *Lockheed T-33A-5-LO* 49-955.

McADOE. *Lockheed F-94C* 51-5998 displayed.

MACUNGIE. Paul Knepper Collection. *Waco 9* NC116 "Miss McKeesport" formerly mailplane of the Pittsburgh-Cleveland route. *Fairchild KR-31* N7744 c/n 219 (airworthy) with *N7780* c/n 223 and *N3615* c/n 119 in store.

MECHANICSBURG. *F-94C* 51-13555 displayed.

MIDDLETOWN. *F-94C* 51-13545 displayed—confirm.

MOUNT JOY. *F-94C Starfire* 51-5593 displayed.

MUSTIN FIELD. Naval Engineering Centre. Displayed *Douglas XA3D-1 Skywarrior* 125413; 2nd prototype.

NEW KENSINGTON. Memorial Park. *T-33A* 51-8513.

NEWVILLE. *F-94C* 51-13537 displayed.

PENDELL. Flannery's Restaurant, as 72-seat cocktail bar *Lockheed L.1049E Constellation* N1005C c/n 4557 "Geneva Trader" ex Capitol Airlines. Originally with Cubana as CU-P-573, later to Seaboard and Western.

Lockheed T-33A (Philadelphia)

PHILADELPHIA. The Franklin Institute, 20th St & Parkway. Hall of Aviation offers *Wright Bros Model "B" Biplane* of 1911 NR14333, with 30 hp 4-cyl in-line Wright Bros engine. Believed the 13th plane built by the Wrights it last flew 14 December 1934 during celebration of the 31st anniversary of the Wright Brothers after restoration by Camdem County Vocational School. Gift of Grover Cleveland Bergdall, the original owner. *Budd Amphibian Model BB-1* NR749N "The Pioneer" amphibian biplane, with 210 hp Kinner radial, built 1931 by Edward G. Budd Mfg Co of Philadelphia to demonstrate practicability of shot weld process with stainless steel. It flew over 1,000 hrs in USA and Europe. Presented by the Budd Co it has been on exhibit outdoors uncovered and exposed to weather since 1934, proving durability of its construction. *Lockheed T-33A T-Bird* 53-6038, jet trainer. Two Link Trainers, for those under eighteen—those showing aptitude qualifying for an hour's flying tuition. Also many engines—Philip Allen is exhibits' engineer, to whom enquiries should be directed. Outside the Piasecki factory stand *Piasecki HRP-2* N961 and *111829*.

PHILIPSBURGH. *NA F-86H* 53-1316 displayed.

PITTSBURGH. Greater Pittsburgh Airport. Pennsylvania ANG Display. *Republic P-47N Thunderbolt* 44-89444; loaned by USAFM. *NA F-86L-60-NA Sabre* 53-0894. *NA P-51D* 44-84900; tail-fin of "H" model. *Convair F-102A* 56-1415. *Republic F-84F* 51-1508; Ricks Trophy winner. Flying here is *Fairchild PT-19* N60109 c/n 741-1271 of 1941; P. C. Brubaker.

READING. Dutch Colony Inn. Antique Aeroplane Restaurant. *Monocoupe 70* N6731 c/n 134 suspended from ceiling.

RED LION. Airport. *Taylorcraft BC-12D-I* N44352 c/n 10152; Richard Wood. *Navion A* N4990K c/n NAV-4-1990; Don Warner.

SADSBURYVILLE. *NA F-86D/L* 52-10046 displayed.

SKYPORT. Airfield. *Howard DGA-15P* N4675N c/n 973.

TOUGHKENAMON. New Garden Flying Field. Colonial Flying Corps Museum:—*General Motors FM-2 Wildcat* N315E ex 47030 of Alexis I. du Pont, airport owner. *NA SNJ-5* N3673F ex 90907. *Ryan ST-3KR* N47082 c/n 1443. *Stinson L-5* N9315H ex 42-15060 (tows sailplanes). *Waco UPF-7* N169V. *Stearman E-75* N9077H. All these flyable. Being readied to fly:—*Stinson L-2* N46149 c/n 5808. Static display but to fly later:—*Lockheed P-38L* "Droop Snoot" CF-NMW ex "Age of Flight" Niagara Falls, Ontario. Under restoration:—*F4F Wildcat* N18 Bu 1931. *Aeronca C-3* N13002, c/n A-217. *Aeronca Chief* of 1938, reg'n unknown. A *Tiger Moth*, registration as yet unknown, is being rebuilt. Also based at this field:—*Aeronca 4-BCM* N2713A c/n 338; Hooper. Clemens, Twyford. *Taylorcraft BC-65* N24375 c/n 1711; E. Smith. *Stinson L-5G* N2581B ex 41-20473; W. Collins. *Fleet 80 Canuck* CF-DZZ is stored here during the winter months. There are also many antique autos and motorcycles.

TULLEYTOWN. In a Junk Yard. The full-scale mock-up of the *Douglas D-558-II*.

TURNER. Airport. Near Lansdale. *Lockheed 12A* N228M.

VALLEY FORGE. Mainline Helioport. *Piasecki UH-25C* 147610 marked "10A/UP", Sqdn HU-1. In store *Haig HK-1* experimental helicopter of 1950, N9065H.

VAN SANT. Airpark, near Erwinna. *Miller Y-1S* N15525 c/n 310, static. *Howard DGA-15P* N9126H c/n 1766, tricycle gear. *Waco RNF* N139Y c/n 3313. *Parks Speedwing* N965X c/n 479. *Ansaldo SVA-9* (Italian WWI fighter) N13148, c/n 89. *Navy N3N-3* N93162. *Stearman Hammond* of 1937 N15525. *Stearman PT-17* N720Y c/n 75-1912; N60398 c/n 75-6559. *Culver Cadet* N34797 c/n 258. *Ryan PT-22* N46501. Being restored here:— *Pitcairn Mailwing*; *Aeronca C-2*; *Aeronca C-3* and *Curtiss JN-4 Jenny*. Details of progress and reg'ns/serials please.

WARMINSTER. NAS. *Douglas NRA-3A Skywarrior* 130358.

WARREN. In Town Centre. *Lockheed F-94C* 51-13524. Also nearby is *F-94C Starfire* 51-13565.

WESTMINSTER FIELD. *Boeing YL-15* N4210A ex 47-429 (dismantled).

WILLIAMSPORT. Lycoming Co Airfield. Area Community College. *Lockheed L-18* N38BF and *Bell 47B*—serial wanted.

WILLOW GROVE. NAS. Main Highway Pa 309. *Arado Ar 196 A-3* "T3-HK" from "Prinz Eugen" German battle cruiser, twin-float scoutplane. *Kawanishi NIK2J Shiden Kai "George"* coded "91" ("111" on tail) bombs under wings. *NA AF-1E Fury* 143568 from USMC, painted also "27" "7W/3568". *Chance-Vought F7U-3 Cutlass* 129642. *Kawanishi NIKI Kyofu "Rex"*. *Nakajima B6N2 Tenzan "Jill 12"*. *Messerschmitt Me 262 B-la/U1* Werk-Nr 110639, FE-610. *Lockheed TV-1 Shooting Star* 33824 "28". *Convair XF2Y-1 Sea-Dart,* the original aircraft, now, alas, drably overpainted and incorrectly marked, proper serial 137634 but this is not shown. The unique Sea-Ski fighter. Let us hope this rare assembly can be given *covered* accommodation at one of the permanent museums.

Me 262 B-1a/U1 (Willow Grove)

YORK. Airport. *Waco UPF-7* NC30165 c/n 5562 of 1941 (immaculate) and *Waco GXE* (being rebuilt) both of John Shue.

Arado Ar 196 A-3 (Willow Grove)

Kawanishi "George" (Willow Grove)

Kawanishi "Rex" (Willow Grove)

Nakajima "Jill 12" (Willow Grove)

Convair Sea-Dart (Willow Grove)

SOUTH CAROLINA

AIKEN. HQs 9301st RR Sqdn. *Lockheed T-33A* 51-9664A.

BEAUFORT. MCAS. *NA F-1C Fury* 135841 mounted as in flight.

CAMDEN. The "Wings & Wheels" store of exhibits to be rotated at Santee (apply Santee for viewing possibilities).

CHARLESTON. Parade Ground of the Citial. *Republic RF-84*, details of serial and exact location wanted.

COLUMBIA. Metropolitan Airport. *Lockheed T-33A* 51-6915 and *51-9169*.

Douglas Dolphin (Edmund)

EDMUND. Colgate W. Darden III's Grass Strip; housing *Douglas Dolphin N26K* c/n 1280 of 1934. *Douglas DC-2 N39165* c/n 1404 of 1935 ex R2D-1 Bu 9993, USN, 1935. *Lockheed 12A N18125* c/n 1222 of 1937. *Spartan 7W N17633* c/n 21 of 1939. *Meyers OTW N26491* c/n 68 of 1941. Interesting notes are that the DC-2 is fitted with the Wright 1820-52. It was never an airliner in the usual sense, leaving the US Navy for North American Aviation, then to Mercer Airlines who did manage to get 23 seats into it. The Lockheed was with Continental Airlines, later to RCAF then Texaco and Noble Drilling (for 20 years). The Spartan Executive has been with Colgate Darden since 1964 and he has flown it more than 600 hrs. Spartan Aircraft completely

overhauled the interior in 1970—their last job before going out of business. The Meyers has been with him since 1962, the Warner 145 now replaced by Warner 165. It must be stressed that this is a *private* Collection, not available except by the owner's personal invitation.

FLORENCE. Florence Air & Missile Museum. US Highway 301 at entrance to Florence Municipal Airport just east of city limits. Open during daylight; adults 50c, under 12s 25c. The first plane was put on display in December 1964 after 14 months of preparatory work as a project of the Greater Florence Chamber of Commerce, since when 23 aircraft and missiles have been donated or loaned by USAF or USN, flown to Florence Airport and de-militarized by special crews from Shaw AFB, Sumter, SC. Visitors are allowed into the larger planes and twice this museum has received awards for being an outstanding tourist attraction. Displayed (1973) are *Boeing B-47B Stratojet* 50-062 (it was a B-47 which accidentally dropped a nuclear device on Florence SC). *CIM-10A Bomarc* missile AF59-1914. *Douglas RB-66B-DL Destroyer* 53-431, from Shaw AFB. *Fairchild C-119C-18-FA Flying Boxcar* 50-128 ex 302nd TCW. *Boeing C-97K-24-BO Stratofreighter* 52-2624, from Offutt, Nebraska. *NA F-86H Sabre* 52-5737 from McGuire AFB, NY. *Northrop F-89D/J Scorpion* 52-2646, 176th FIS. *Kaman HH-43A-KA Huskie* 58-1833 ex WP AFB. *Lockheed T-33A* 53-6089A, ex Langley, Va. *Douglas C-124C-DL Globemaster II* 52-1072 used during Korean conflict, ex USAFM. *Grumman HU-16B Albatross* 51-7212, from USAFM. *Hiller OH-23C Raven* 56-4021, from USAFM. *Vertol H-21B Workhorse*, from the Presidential fleet, serial? *Douglas A-26*, used in Vietnam and flown by Capt. Tim Black, son of Powell Black, Florence City. Serial wanted. *Martin TM-61 Matador* and *NA P-51K Mustang* 44-11807, from Franklin Institute, Philadelphia. *Titan I*, ICBM, missile, 103ft long, 10ft diameter, range 6,300 miles, weight 330,000 lbs. Two-stage weapon with 430,000 lbs of rock-thrust in basic stage and 100,000 lbs in upper stage. *Martin RB-57A Canberra* 52-1459 from Michigan ANG.

McENTIRE. Airfield. South Carolina ANG Display of aircraft formerly flown by the 157th FIS:— *F-86H Sabre* 53-1386. *F-86L Sabre* 53-1064. *Lockheed T-33A*

Air and Missile Museum (Florence)

51-6519. *NA.P-51K Mustang* 44-11807 (presumably loaned from Florence as Franklin Institute say they sent it to Air & Missile Museum). *Convair F-102A* 53-1788 (modified from YF-102A). Photos would be appreciated for 5th edition.

GREENVILLE. *NA F-86H Sabre* 52-1976 displayed.

SANTEE. Wings & Wheels of Santee Exhibitions Inc. P.O. Box 93, Santee. SC 29142. Open seven days a week 0900 to 1800 hrs winter and to 2100 hrs summer. Admission 2 dollars adults, one dollar children 6-12, under 6 free. Opened 17 December 1968 to mark Wright Brothers' anniversary, Dolph Overton's magnificent museum now includes aircraft secured for the Aeroflex (New Jersey) museum which are presently displayed here. There are also *Ford Trimotors* N9612 c/n 4-AT-55

and *N9637* c/n 5-AT-11 ex Pan Am; which give flights as and when required. Other exhibits include (date-order) *Chanute Hang Glider (replica). Wright 1902 Glider (replica). Wright 1903 Flyer (replica). Wright 1909 Model B (replica) Military Flyer. Wright 1911 "Vinn Fizz"* N12A (replica). *Bleriot XI (replica). Curtiss Pusher (replica)* painted as 1105. *Bleriot XII (replica)* 33622. *1915 Bleriot Penguin Ground Trainer* serial 33622. *Curtiss JN-4D Jenny* N6898C ex 34135 and *JN-4D (replica)* with OX-5, N1104 painted A-6. *Fokker Triplane (replica)* N5505. *F1-102/17*, 7/8ths scale, also 7/8ths scale *Fokker DR.1 Triplane* N78001 (Aeroflex). *Sopwith 1F.1 Camel* of 1917 N6254 ex Tallmantz (Aeroflex). *Nieuport II* of 1915. History please. *Nieuport 28 (replica)* N4728V c/n 512 ex Tallmantz. *Depedussin Type Militaire* of 1911, ex Jean Salis (and Aeroflex). *Caudron G-III* of 1914 from France (and Aeroflex). *Maurice Farman M-11* of

Ford Trimotor (Santee)

Wright Flyer—replica (Santee)

Sopwith Camel (Santee)

Depedussin Militaire (Santee)

1914, later N96452 of Tallmantz (Aeroflex). *SPAD XIII* S.4523 of "Hat in Ring" Sqdn. (SPAD VII loaned to NASM). *Pfalz D XII* 7511/18, N43C, the last airworthy example, from Col Jarrett's Collection, then Tallmantz (Aeroflex). *Alexander Eaglerock* serial 86 of 1929. *DH.4* A2169 built by Airco, later NX3258, from Tallmantz (Aeroflex). *SE.5a (Eberhardt)* AS22-296 of 1917, NX4488, from Tallmantz (Aeroflex). *Curtiss Robin* N389K c/n 550 of 1929. *Waco 9* N139E c/n 218 of 1927. *Keane Ace* N69097 c/n 1 of 1918. *Morane Saulnier A-1* (fuselage) for rebuild. *Waco 10* NC5273 of 1928 c/n 1470 (plus Waco 10 fuselage) *Brunner Winkle Bird* N831W c/n 2025-196 of 1929. *Travel Air 2000* N529D c/n 490 of 1928. *Kreider-Reisner KR-21* N362N c/n 1017 of 1930. *Fleet 2* N7629B c/n 157 of 1929. *Command Aire 3C-3A* N970E c/n W-108 of 1930. *American Eaglet* N6855D c/n 1103 of 1930. *Taylor E-2 Cub* N12664 c/n 32 of 1932. *Piper J-2 Cub* N16315 c/n 548 of 1936. *Piper J-3C Cub* N7319H c/n 20579. *Piper J-4 Cub Coupe* N3042 c/n 4-1209 of 1939. *Curtiss Wright Travel-Air 12Q* N417W c/n 12Q-2030 of 1931. *Heath LNB-4 Parasol*

N15792 c/n 1006. *Curtiss Wright F6C-4 Gulfhawk* N982V c/n 1, ex Movieland of the Air, used by USN to perfect dive-bombing techniques. *Aeronca C-3* N11293 c/n A125 of 1931. *Aeronca K Scout* N18844 c/n K110 of 1937. *Aeronca C-3* of 1936 N16529 c/n A673. This a/c holds record for non-stop distance in light a/c. *Pietenpol Air Camper* N1858, c/n A7-1968. *Inland W-500 Sport* N8088 c/n W505 of 1930. *Curtiss CW-1 Junior* N665V of of 1931, also *N11878* c/n 1248. *Aeronca 65-TC Defender* N34414 c/n 9871T of 1941. *Arrow Sport "F"* N18759 c/n 100 of 1937. *Stinson SM8-A* N416Y c/n 4251 of 1930. *Travel Air 6000* N8112 c/n 884 of 1929. *Clemson Aero Club "Little 372"* c/n 1. A one-off a/c built by a college club, patterned after Heath Parasol but no metal was used. Lumber Yard wood was used and the wings are the bottom panels of a Thomas-Morse Scout modified to take ailerons and new drag bracings. Engine is 20 hp 2-cyl Lawrence with single-throw crank. All (except one) of those concerned with the building, entered the aviation business. *Anderson "Scampy"* a

SE.5a (Santee)

Keane Ace (Santee)

homebuilt of 1969 N11H c/n 1. Other aircraft are based here and fly as needed:— *Piper J-3C-65* N78518 c/n 23003 owned and flown by Wings & Wheels PRO, Michael J. Kullenberg who won it in a raffle sponsored by EAA at Rockford, Ill. *Great Lakes 2T-1A* N11326 c/n 243 of 1931 with Warner 165, owned by Rudy Rustin and restored at Camden by Bill Grant. On loan to Wings & Wheels:— *Curtiss Wright Travel Air 16K* of 1939 N422W c/n 16K-2004. *Waco ASO* N9500 c/n 26, *Waco UPF-7* N32199 c/n 5831. A friend who visited says the museum is well-lit for photography with exhibits (including many rare cars etc) spaced conveniently. A wide-angle lens is, of course useful, as in most museums. We wish Dolph Overton, a jet ace of the Korean conflict, every success with his project. We wonder if the *Fokker D.VII* 7748/18, later N6268, Udet's "LO", is at Camden or still at Aeroflex Field, Newton NJ, in store?

SUMTER. Shaw AFB. *Douglas WB-66D Destroyer* 55-392 on display.

SOUTH DAKOTA

BISMARCK. Playground. *Grumman F9F-5 Panther*—serial please.

BRIDGEWATER. *Lockheed T-33A* 51-6926 on show.

CANISTOTA. *T-33A* 53-6093 displayed.

CARTHAGE. *T-33A* 51-8629 on display.

HURON. *T-33A* 53-6100 displayed.

LAKE NORDEN. *T-33A* 51-8665 displayed.

MARION. *Lockheed F-94C Starfire* 51-13563 displayed.

SIOUX FALLS. City Park. *Northrop F-89D Scorpion* 51-11443 ex South Dakota ANG.

STURGIS. *NA F-86D/L Sabre* 51-6071 displayed.

VIBORG. *T-33A* 52-9632 displayed.

TENNESSEE

CROSSVILLE. *Lockheed T-33A* 51-6756 displayed.

DAYTON. *T-33A* 51-6861 on display.

JACKSON. *T-33A* 51-16989 displayed.

JOHNSON CITY. *T-33A* 53-6009 displayed.

KNOXVILLE. *NA F-86D/L Sabre* 52-3679 displayed.

LOOKOUT MOUNTAIN. *NA F-86D/L* 52-3840 displayed.

MEMPHIS. National Guard Armouries in colours of 324th BS *Boeing B-17F-10-BO Flying Fortress* 41-24485 "Memphis Belle", first Fortress to fly 25 missions over Europe. At the airport is *NA F-86D/L* 53-0635 "FU-635" and at the Technical School *Sikorsky UH-19C* 51-14295 and *Bell HTL-6* 143157. Memphis NAS has *Grumman TBF-1 Avenger* 85717; *Douglas A-1 (AD-3) Skyraider*; *Douglas A-1E (AD-5) Skyraider*; *Grumman F9F-6T Cougar*; *McDonnell F3H-2N Demon*; *Sikorsky S-55 (UH-19F) Chickasaw* (two examples); *Sikorsky S-58 (XHSS-1) Choctaw*, all owned by the Naval Air Systems Command, Washington DC. Serials please. Also *Lockheed P2V-3C Neptune* 122947 "001" and, it is thought *Grumman F-11F-1 Tiger*—serial wanted.

NASHVILLE. City Park. *NA F-86L Sabre* 53-0668. Airport:— *P-51D Mustang* N11636 ex 45-11636. *Fleet 21* N939V c/n 503.

PULASKI. *Lockheed T-33A* 51-8775 on display.

TULLAHOMA. William Northern Field. It is reported there are *three Brewster Bermudas* in Dutch East Indies marks. Let us hope one, at least, is preserved. News and serials, please.

Brewster Bermuda (possibly at Tullahoma)

TEXAS

ABILENE. Municipal Airport. *Boeing B-17G Flying Fortress* 44-85599A, dedicated to the city by 96th BG Black Hawk insignia on nose. Reports say a/c neglected —alas!

AMARILLO. Municipal Airport (former AFB). *McDonnell F-101A-1-MC Voodoo* 53-2418 on plinth.

AUSTIN. University of Texas. *NA F-86D.* At Camp Mabry entrance, serial?

BEEVILLE. Airfield. *Grumman F9F-2 Panther* 122563.

BIG SPRINGS. Airport. *F-86D/L* 53-4035 and *T-33A* 51-4300 displayed. *Spitfire LFIXB* N415MH ex MH415 (RAF) c/n CBAF5542, H-65 RNethAF, B.12, SM40 Belgian AF, and OO-ARD, Cogea, then G-AVDJ, Gp Cpt Mahaddie. Now "Col" W. C. Edwards, CAF:— "Col" Edwards, who flew in the "B. of B." film, also has *12 Spanish-built Bf 109s (HA-1112-MIL)* one airworthy to date as N4109G (c/n 220 ex C4K-152, G-AWHR), plus *P-51D Mustang* N150U, ex 44-64122.

BISHOP. City Park. *Grumman F9F-6 Cougar*—serial?

BOWIE. *Lockheed T-33A* 51-6639 displayed.

BRECKENRIDGE. *NA F-86D/L* 53-3693 displayed.

BROWNWOOD. Airport. A base for many CAF a/c (which are listed as at Harlingen). In addition *Stearman PT-17 Cropdusters* N61302; *N61419*; *N49943* c/n 75-4645 and *N65228*.

CHILDRESS. *Northrop F-89H Scorpion* 54-298 displayed.

CLAUDE. *Republic F-84F* 51-1617 displayed.

CLEAR LAKE CITY. American Legion Post. *F-84F* 0-26455 of Texas ANG.

COLLEYVILLE. *Tiger Moth* N10LW c/n 855 ex DX812, A17-723, VH-CJH; L. S. Wright.

CONNELLEY. AFB. *Northrop F-89D/J* 52-1868 displayed.

CORPUS CHRISTI. Park. *Grumman F9F-6 Cougar* "711964" ex "Blue Angels".

CRANE. *Lockheed T-33A* 53-6086 displayed.

DALLAS. Addison Airport. "Col" Dale Milford, CAF, has *Temco TE-1A Buckaroo* N6040 c/n 2, airworthy, with another being restored—details please. It is believed that the *DC-2* VH-CDZ ex Bankstown, NSW, Australia, may come here, owner, Capt. Richad M. Rosser, TWA pilot. Confirmation wanted. *Douglas B-26* N202R c/n 28880, *Lockheed Lodestars* N208S c/n 5694 and N260H c/n 2039, *P-51D Mustang* N469P ex 44-73240 and *NA B-25 Mitchell* N5865V c/n 108-34263 seen flying here. At Hensley Field NAS *Lockheed P-80B* 45-8607; *NA F-86D/L* 53-1030 and *Chance-Vought XF8U-2 Crusader* 140448 are mounted near main gate at north, near highway. *Chance Vought F7U-3M Cutlass*

139908 is said to be under restoration—details of progress please. Is *Republic F-84* still at Dallas University's Engineering Bldg? Serial, please, if so.

DEL RIO. Airport. *NA F-86D-60-NA Sabre* 52-3749 and *Lockheed T-33A* 53-6124 displayed.

DENNISON. American Legion Hut. *F-86L-30-NA Sabre* 51-6144 displayed.

DENNISON/PARIS. *NA F-86D/L* 52-4239 displayed.

DENTON. *Spitfire HFIXC* N1882 ex MK297 once "GW-O" 340 (Ile de France) Sqdn, H-55 R.NethAF, "B15", SM43, OO-ARB, Belgium, then G-ASSD, Swanton Morley, Norfolk (with parts of MH434). Owner R. Smith.

EAGLE MOUNTAIN. Army airfield. *C-47* 66-8836 ex R4D-5 c/n 13105, Bu 17205; was N5541A.

EAGLE PASS. *Lockheed T-33A* 53-6102 displayed.

ECTOR. County Airport. *Bücker Jungmeister* said to be flying here—reg'n please and owner.

EL PASO. Fort Bliss. *A-4 (V2) rockets*, two, at Logan Heights and Pershing/Smith Rd.

FARMERS BRANCH. Valwood Parkway. *T-33A* 53-5011 displayed.

FORT WORTH. Greater South-West Airport. *Grumman F9F Cougar* N7993A c/n 15; John Johnston. *Convair B-36J-CF* 52-2827. Last of the 385 Convair-built "Peacemakers". Maintained by Convair employees. Formerly at Biggs AFB and the Amon G. Carter Foundation. It is stated that this may be made airworthy. At the Pate Museum of Transportation, Highway 377 just north of Cresson (3½ miles). Open 0900-1700 daily, admission free, to see:— *Douglas C-47* 42-108866, donated by USAF. *Vertol H-21B* 53-4324 ex Eglin AFB Rescue Training. *Grumman HU-16B Albatross* 51-7176, loaned from USAFM. *Grumman F9F-6P Cougar* 131063, ex USN. *Republic RF-84F Thunderflash* 53-7595. *Fairchild C-119G Flying Boxcar* 51-2675. *McDonnell F-101B Voodoo* 59-471. *Lockheed T-33A* 58-621. *NA F-86H Sabre* 53-1239. *Hiller OH-23B Raven* 51-16386 and *16387*. *Mock-up Mercury capsule,* vintage cars, tanks etc, make this museum another great Texas attraction. Flying in this area is *Tiger Moth* N12731 c/n 914 ex T.246, A17-491, VH-BAI; M. H. Spinks.

McDonnell Voodoo (Fort Worth)

FREDERICKSBURG. Admiral Nimitz Foundation. *Douglas SBD-6 Dauntless* being restored. Serial wanted.

GOODFELLOW. AFB. *NA F-100A Super Sabre* 53-1573.

GRAND PRAIRIE. Texas ANG Base. *T-33A* 52-9490. *Vultee BT-13* N58423 ex 41-2244.

GRAYSON COUNTY. *NA F-86L* 51-6091, from USAFM Programm.

GREENVILLE. *Douglas C-54D* 43-17248 displayed.

HARLINGEN. Rebel Field. The Confederate Air Force Museum and Flying Field. Two hangars provided by City of Harlingen, a fighter hangar by CAF members. It is one of few "museums" which provide indoor housing for 4-engined bombers. A brief background to this unique "Air Force" is that in the mid-fifties a group of ex-Service pilots in the Lower Grande Valley bought a Mustang for the sheer pleasure of flying one for fun and not under combat conditions. Other pilots became keen and a Bearcat was added. When it was discovered that the U.S. authorities had not preserved at least one of each of the great WW II a/c (as in U.K. also) these enthusiasts decided that if it were still possible they *would* be found and, where practicable, be restored to fly. Thus was organized the Confederate Air Force with "Colonel" Jethro E. Culpepper as mythical leader and with all pilots given the rank of "Colonel" at Rebel Field, Mercedes, (though now moved over to Harlingen because of the larger a/c

acquired). By 1965 the CAF had 170 "officer" members and by December 1971 four "Wings" had formed—two in Texas, one in New Mexico and one in Minnesota. Known everywhere in USA as "The Ghost Squadron" it is estimated that more than three million people saw the CAF in action during 1972 at "Transpo" Washington and at other shows. Non-fliers can also help keep this magnificent force flying—write to "Colonel" Lloyd P. Nolen, CAF, Rebel Field, Harlingen, Texas 78550 for information. We in Europe hope very much to see some of "The Ghost Squadron" aircraft cross the Atlantic— what about the 30th anniversary of "VE" Day—in 1975? Here, though, is the current listing, in itself an un-surpassed achievement of voluntary effort:— *Boeing B-17G Flying Fortress* N7227C ex 44-83872 c/n 77235, acquired in Philadelphia where it was on high-altitude photo work. *Consolidated B-24 (LB-30) Liberator* N12905 c/n 18, the oldest existing, converted, in 1941 to C-87 and used by RAF as AM927. Post-war in Mexico as XC-CAY, acquired by CAF, 1967. *Boeing B-29 Super-fortress* N4249 ex 44-62070 from Naval Weapons Center, China Lake, Cal. Flown to Harlingen by CAF members. *Douglas A-26 B-50-DT Invader* N320 ex 44-35870 c/n 29149 also *A-26B-66-DL* N6101C ex 44-24624 c/n 27903, colours of 552nd Sqdn, 386th BG 9th AF. *Martin B-26 Marauder* N5546N c/n 2253, serial wanted. *NA B-25J Mitchell* N3676G ex 44-29835; donated by "Col" Fred Rowsey. *B-25N* N3161G ex 44-30324 (maintained by Southern Minnesota Wing). *B-25N* N201L ex 44-30606 (maintained by New Mexico Wing) both in 15th AF colours. *Douglas A-20 Havoc* N2217 c/n 21857 in colours and markings of 664th Sqdn, 410th BG, 9th AF. Serial/

B-17G (Harlingen)

Liberator (Harlingen)

B-29 and Mustang (Harlingen)

B-29 (Harlingen)

Douglas Invader N6101C (Harlingen)

Marauder (Harlingen)

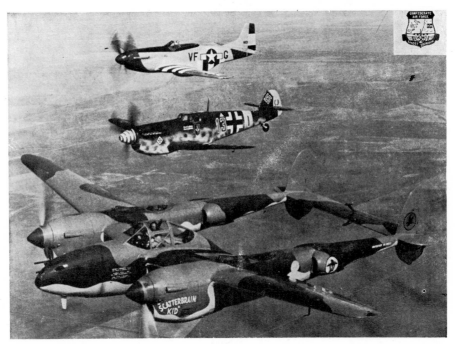

Lightning, HA-1112, Mustang N10601 (Harlingen)

Warhawk and Wildcat (Harlingen)

history please. *Beech C-45J Expeditor* N79AG c/n A-806 (including AT-11 and AT-7 versions over 5,000 produced during WWII for bombadier, navigator or light personnel transports). This aircraft a post war civil production machine built in 1952. *Lockheed L-18 Lodestar* N30N c/n 2274, donated by ''Col'' Tyson Searcy, painted in colours and markings of a Hudson of 224 Sqdn, RAF Coastal Command, to represent one of 2,522 Hudsons delivered. *Bell P-39 Airacobra* N6968 c/n 19597, donated as ''pieces'' by Mr. Joe Brown of Hobbs, New Mexico; believed the only flyable Airacobra. *Bell P-63 King Cobra* N191H c/n 33-11, was on static display Love Field, Dallas, for 15 years then restored by ''Col'' Don Hull of Sugarland. Flying since 1965 it is fully sponsored by ''Cols'' Buck Rodgers and Dudley Johnson. *Lockheed P-38L Lightning* N25Y ex 44-53254 c/n 8342, this example found in high grass outside Yukon, Oklahoma and a CAF photo-version was traded for this which has machine-gun nose. *P-38L* N345 c/n 8057, donated by ''Col'' Gary Levitz, formerly used to gain weather data from Dallas for the U.S. Weather Bureau. *P-38* N38LL ex 43-50281 ''Scatterbrain Kid'', the result of a private project by ''Cols'' Revis Sirmon and Paul Fournet, Lafayette, Louisiana. History appreciated. *Curtiss P-40N Warhawk* N1226N c/n 29629 ''26'' in colours of American Volunteer Group ''Flying Tigers'' in China as tribute to General Claire Chennault's men. History and serial please. *P-51D Mustang* N10601 ex 44-73843, the original CAF machine,

Mustang—old markings (Harlingen)

purchased 1957 in San Antonio and used in movies. It saw service with RCAF and c/n and other deails appreciated. *P-51C Mustang* 42-103655, obtained from Billings, Montana, to be restored—reg'n, colours and markings not yet known. Note:— P-51 N5428V ex 44-73264 often at Harlingen is kept at Hobbs, New Mexico (where listed), maintained by the New Mexico Wing. *Grumman FM-2 (F4F) Wildcat* N681S c/n J55585— the only USN fighter which served with the fleet from start to end of WW II, seeing action in every major Pacific battle. This one in colours and markings of VF-41 ''Red Rippers'' Sqdn USS ''Ranger'' 1940. *Grumman F6F Hellcat* N1078Z c/n ''27354801-66'' coded ''78''. First operational squadron VF9 on 16 January 1943. USN serial please. *Grumman F8F-2 Bearcat* N7825C ex 122674 c/n D-1227. Too late to see WW II combat, but operated with French in Indo-China at Dien-Bien-Phu. *North American F-82B Twin Mustang* N12102 ex 44-65162 c/n 12317-3, world's only flyable example. *Grumman TBM-3E Avenger* N6583D ex 53503, one of almost 10,000 built (7,000 by General Motors). *Douglas SBD-3 Dauntless* N54532 ex 54532, purchased from Californian museum; earlier photo-platform a/c in Mexico. *Curtiss SB2C-5 Helldiver* N92879 ex 83589, also from a Californian museum and still in original paint of WW II. CAF (and V. and V.) are anxious to have a/c history. Can YOU help? *Hispano HA-1112-MIL* (Bf 109s built in Spain) N9939 c/n 234 ex C4K-169, G-AWHT; *N9938* c/n 172 ex C4K-102, G-AWHK; *N8575* c/n 208 ex C4K-144, G-AWHP; *N109ME* c/n 67 ex C4K-31, G-AWHE—from ''Battle of Britain'' filming, in which they were flown by CAF pilots. Now restored and flying in Luftwaffe colours and markings. *Republic P-47N Thunderbolt* N47TB ex 44-53436, from Nicaragua, flown non-stop Nanagua to Brownsville, Texas by ''Col'' Dick Disney 7 February 1963 and fully restored by ''Col'' Tom Homan of Vero Beach, Florida. Of the 15,684 built, all but about three had been exported or destroyed when CAF began its search and eventually ''Col'' Ed Jurist of Nyack, NY, located six in Peru and, after months of negotiation, they arrived at Brownsville, Texas aboard the s.s. ''Rosaldina'' with 50,000 lbs of spares. They are:— *P-47D N47DE* c/n 39955744, Peruvian AF 122; *N47DA* c/n 38595616, ex 114; *N47DB* c/n 39955706 ex 116; *N47DC* c/n 39955720 ex 115; *N47DD* c/n 39955731 ex 119; *N47DF* c/n 39955924 ex 127. Surely the CAF ''T-Bolt'' Sqdn is the pride of the USA—let

Grumman Avenger (Harlingen)

Douglas Dauntless (Harlingen)

Curtiss Helldiver (Harlingen)

Thunderbolt (Harlingen)

Mosquito B/TT.35 (Harlingen)

FG-1D Corsair (Harlingen)

us hope Europe (and East Anglia in particular) will see a "Jug" overhead, once more. *de Havilland Mosquito B/TT.35* N9797 ex RS709, G-ASKA ex Skyfame Museum, Staverton, Glos, and "633 Squadron" film, flown from Luton to Harlingen, one of two airworthy examples in the world; with a third being restored to fly. *Goodyear FG-1D Corsair* N9964Z ex 92468 in colour and markings of an F4U of VMF 124, USMC, carrier "Essex". This example was actually from Buckeye, Arizona, 1960, and came there from Litchfield Park NAS outside Phoenix. *Ryan PT-22 Recruit* N22AL c/n 1831 ex 41-20622, two-place monoplane trainer of Army Air Corps. *Fairchild PT-26 Cornell* N4732G ex 43-36843, type built by both Fairchild and Fleet (in Canada), production ended May, 1944. Sliding canopy and instrumentation for blind flying. *Boeing PT-17 (Stearman) Kaydet* N66004 c/n 75-2294, used for primary training by both Army and Navy (as N2S-3 Kaydet). Production completed February 1945 when 10,346 built in various configurations. *Fairchild PT-19 Cornell*—airworthy example being obtained to honour simple-to-fly training a/c of which production ceased late 1943—used particularly in Canada. *North American AT-6A Texan* N9790Z c/n 3048 (serial wanted); *AT-6-5 Texan* N6298C ex 44-11236; *SNJ-7B Texan* N6463C ex 27850. Flown by more military pilots, worldwide, than any other a/c; first produced as advanced trainer 1938, used in USAF until 1956. More than 10,000 built and 193,444 pilots graduated on this type from USAAF flying schools. SNJ was the Navy version. *Vultee BT-15 Valiant* N75004 c/n 6720 ex 42-1779 (Navy SNV-1) used 1940s

for second-phase training for pilots from civilian schools, to give "feel" of combat planes. That lists the present (1973) airworthy machines, to which must be added the Spitfires owned by individual "Colonels" listed at Big Springs, Denton and Sugarland (Texas) and Fort Collins, Colorado. The static display comprises:— *Douglas C-124C Globemaster* 51-089; *Boeing C-97G Stratofreighter* 53-332; *Douglas C-54D Skymaster* 42-72675 c/n 10780; *Martin RB-57A Canberra* 52-1456; *Grumman HU-16B Albatross* 51-7186 and *7193*; all from USAFM Programm. *Fairchild C-119 Flying Boxcar* 0-12566; *Beech GB-2 Traveller* 23774. *Douglas A-1E Skyraider* 132443 c/n 9460; *Convair F-102 Delta Dagger* 57-0906; *Northrop F-89J Scorpion* 53-2677; *Republic F-84F* 52-8860; *Boeing B-47 Stratojet* 0-34257; *Douglas C-47 Skytrain* 9355; Remains of *DH. Mosquito B.20* N9871F ex RG300 c/n 983157; for possible rebuild. This aircraft was ferried to US January 1957. It is also understood that four of the "Tora, Tora, Tora" film machines, three converted AT-6 Texans to be "*Kate*" and "*Zero*" replicas and a BT-13 (N-11FW?) converted to be a "*Val*", are now flying with CAF, donated to them by Gerald D. Weeks of Nashville, Tennessee N3239G and N11171 quoted; other reg'ns please. The CAF Indoor Museum covers the 1939-45 period in great and authentic equipment and pictorial detail and is well worth a visit. Do go and do remember that the Confederate Air Force will value your practical support to maintain "The Ghost Squadron" as a flying heritage for, as they say "In the glory of America's past lies the dedication to the future".

HOUSTON. Airport. *NA F-86 Sabre* 53-900 displayed. *NA P-51D* N51JB ex N713DW, 44-11553; Jesse Baker.

IOWA PARK. *Lockheed T-33A* 51-8892 displayed.

KERRVILLE. Shriner Field. *Mooney Mk 22 prototype* N3422X (only one with T-tail) displayed at terminal.

LACKLAND. AFB (near San Antonio) Air Training Center. The following machines on loan from USAF Museum Programm:— *Curtiss JN-4D Jenny*, serial unknown. *Boeing B-17G* 44-83512 "FF". *Consolidated B-24M-21-FO Liberator* 44-51228, last of 18,000, this one from Ford, Dearborn, last flown 1954. *Fairchild C-119C* 51-2567. *Lockheed F-80A* 44-85123. *F-80A-1-LO* 44-85125. *NA F-82A Twin Mustang* 46-462A "FQ-262". *(F-82B-I-NA* 44-65162 in store.) *Republic F-84C* 47-1486. *Republic F-84E* 51-505. *NA F-86A Sabre* 47-605, 4th FG ex Korea. *Northrop F-89B Scorpion* 49-2434 (the F-89B prototype). *Lockheed YF-94 Starfire* 48-356 (conversion of Lockheed T-33A; c/n 5001). *NA F-100C Super Sabre* 53-11712. *Republic F-105B Thunderchief* 54-105 and 54-107. *Republic P-47N-25-RE Thunderbolt* 44-89348. *NA P-51H-5-NA Mustang* 44-64376. *Bell RP-63G-1-BE King Cobra* 45-57295, "5572" on fin. *Lockheed T-33A* 52-9497. *Cessna XT-37* 54-718. *Ford JB-2 (V1)* two examples. *Martin TM-61A Matador* 11086. *Boeing YIM-99A Bomarc* 56-0432. *Douglas XSM-75 Thor* 56-732. *Martin MQM-13 Mace* 81464. *Ryan Firebird*—no serial. *VB-10 Roc*, serial unknown. *Republic Thunderstreak F-84F-46-GK* 52-8889 and 52-8973; *F-84F-51-GK* 52-9089, all built by General Motors are thought now to be here at what is known as the "History & Traditions" Museum. Apply to Officer Commanding for viewing details.

LAKE JACKSON. Park. *T-33A-5-10* 52-9463.

LAREDO. AFB. *T-33 T-Bird* 51-6739.

LUBBOCK. Reese AFB. *NA B-25J Mitchell* 44-86880 and *T-33A* 52-9658 on plinths just inside main gate.

McLEAN. *McDonnell F-101A Voodoo* 53-2442.

MARSHALL. *Republic F-84B Thunderjet*—serial?

MERCEDES. Airfield. It is thought that the following may still be displayed at or nearby the old Rebel Field:— *NA F-86D/L* 51-2968. *Sikorsky H-19B-SI Chickasaw* 51-3948. *Vertol H-21B-VL Workhorse* 53-4328; *53-4354; 53-4390.*

MIDLAND. Midland/Odessa Regional Airport has the rare flown *Pliska Biplane* of 1911 (adapted from Curtiss Pusher). First a/c in area. *Bücker Jungmeister* (replica) N713S c/n 11, with 165 hp Warner; R. Satterfield. *Ryan SCW* N147W c/n 210 (one of twelve built). *Douglas A-26* 43-22696. *Mooney Mk 22 prototype* twin-engined design is in airport's junkyard—worth preserving? Nearby the *Nieuport 28* N12237 c/n 3 serial 512 of 1918, later NX10415 of Tallmantz Museum, is with James Hall.

MIDLOTHIAN. Airfield. *Tiger Moth* N6037 c/n 84233 ex T6037, G-ANNB, D-EGYN; J. S. Obarr.

MOUNT PLEASANT. *Lockheed T-33A* 53-6103 displayed.

NOCOMA. *T-33A* 53-5535 displayed.

ODESSA. In Park. *B-25J Mitchell* 44-30779 also *Douglas B-26C Invader*—serial wanted.

PARIS. Airfield. Highway 82. Junior Burchinall & Son operate "Flying Tigers" Air Museum with "How to fly Warbirds" school. Basic course around 1,800 dollars with 10 hrs on Kaydet, 10 on Texan, 2 on Mustang, 2 on Bearcat and 2 on Mitchell. Fleet:— *NA B-25 Mitchell* N453VT; *P-51D Mustang* N12066 ex 44-72773. *Vought FG-1D Corsair* N3440G ex 92433; from Movieland, California. *Grumman F8F Bearcat* N9885C (ex Reno) ex 121751. *Lockheed P-38L Lightning; Grumman FM-2 Wildcat; B-17G Fortress; Boeing-Stearman PT-17 Kaydet* N61194 c/n 75-7602; *NA SNJ-5 Texan* N8203F; *Douglas A-26 Invader* N9421Z ex 44-35224; *NA F-86D Sabre* 52-4239; *Grumman F9F Panther* 123078 (and *F9F-2* unserialled) and *J2F Duck* also reported but as museum does not answer V. and V. letters, can a reader confirm, with missing serials, and photos, please. *Lockheed T-33A* 52-9491 also reported in Paris on show.

PLAINVIEW. Municipal Airport. *T-33A* 51-6753 on plinth.

RICHARDSON. Airfield. *P-51D* N6173C ex 44-73142; Vern Peterson.

RUNGE. *T-33A* 53-6117 on display.

SAN ANTONIO. Kelly AFB. *Convair XC-99* 43-52436, world's largest landplane when constructed, wingspan 232 ft, length 187½ ft (transport version of B-36). Carried

Convair XC-99 (San Antonio)

400 fully-equipped men or 300 litter-patients (or 100,000 lbs freight). Now in care of Disabled American Veterans Inc. and on display. Also *Convair YF-102C Delta Dagger* 53-1797. At the Newell Salvage Co. *Grumman F9F-5 Panther* 126205 believed exhibited. *Curtiss JN-4D Jenny* (serial wanted) reported at Witte Memorial Museum 3801 Broadway, San Antonio (Brackenridge Park). At the Brooks AFB a World War I airplane hangar restored as a museum in honour of the late Edward White, first man to walk in space (he died in the spacecraft fire at Cape Kennedy, January 1967). The USAF Museum have loaned a *Standard J-1* (serial unknown) and *NA P-51A Apache Mustang* 43-6251 ex North Africa, Sicily and Ed Maloney's Museum, are so far displayed with other air and space exhibits. Details please for 5th V. and V. At Stinson Field is the *Alon XA-4* N6399V (only one built) also the prototype *Palomino*—reg'n please.

SHEPPARD. AFB. *Sikorsky H-19B Chickasaw* 56-6674.

SHERMAN. Perrin AFB. *P-47N-RE Thunderbolt* 44-89425 ex "V" now "S-AF" O.D. finish with yellow and black checkered tail, said to be colours of Col. Vermont Garrison. From Puerto Rican ANG and Stewart AFB, NY. *NA-F-86D Sabre* 51-6091 ex 4780th ADW. At Municipal Airport here *Cessna UC-78 Bobcat* N59315 c/n 6620 and *Porterfield Standard* N25492. *NA Sabre* 51-6144 also said to be displayed in this district—details please.

SUGARLAND. *Spitfire IX* N238V ex NH238 RAF painted "JE-J" as tribute to Air Vice-Marshal "Johnnie" Johnson, the RAF's top-scoring pilot in WW II (with no disputed 1940 claims to reduce his tally of 38 confirmed victories, plus many others "probable" or "damaged"). Now with Ed Jurist and Bruce Farens and flying with CAF, earlier with Belgian Air Force as SM36, 00-ARE; damaged in London-Cardiff Air Race 1961 and subsequently displayed at Taskers (Transport) Museum near Andover, then purchased by T. H. Pasteur and kept at Newark until re-sold to USA. Long may it fly to remind us of "J.E.J." who flew with 616, commanded 610, and then the RCAF Wing.

SWEETWATER. *Lockheed T-33A* 51-4380 displayed.

TEXARKANA. *T-33A* 51-4025 displayed.

TULIA. *NA F-86E Sabre* 50-593 on show.

WACO. *Lockheed T-33A* 52-9237 exhibited, also *NA Sabre* 51-2991 and *51-3116*. *Northrop F-89J Scorpion* 52-2147 displayed. At the Texas State Technical Institute is a *Northrop F-89* ex Connelley (or Connally) AFB. Is this 52-1868, or another aircraft? From Waco Airport flies *Vultee BT-13 (or 15)* N62571, owned by Frank Price, fitted to take skis. Now known as Price Viceroy.

WEBB. AFB. *Northrop F-89D/J Scorpion* 51-436.

WHITESBORO. *Lockheed T-33A* 51-8885 displayed.

WICHITA FALLS. *Convair F-102A* 57-826 displayed. Note:— It is thought that *Chance Vought FG-1 Corsair* NZ5648, Bu 92844 "Josephine" incorrectly painted NZ5611 and displayed at Hamilton and Auckland, New

FG1 Corsair (Texas)

Zealand, is en route to Texas, off-loaded at Vancouver BC during a strike. Whether for Confederate Air Force or a private owner, unknown as this is written. New registration and location please.

UTAH

LOGAN. Airport. *NA F-100A Super Sabre* 52-5777.

PROVO. Airport. *F-86L Sabre* 53-0809 ex Iowa ANG—is this still displayed?

SALT LAKE CITY. Airport. *Grumman TBM-3 Avengers* N9592C ex 53256; *N7858C* ex 91171; *N8397H* ex 69459; *N4172A* c/n 6180; *N7029C* ex 53914; *N8398H* ex 53607; Aerial Applicators Inc. Confirmation please of whether airworthy or static. On roof of Evans Welding & Fabrication, 2200W. North Temple St., *Vultee BT-13 Valiant* is displayed—serial and history please.

VERMONT

MANCHESTER. *Tiger Moth* N9393 c/n 82461 ex N9391 (RAF), A-40, PH-NGM; R. Fowler.

NEWFANE. *Nieuport 27 (replica)* from original plans but with steel-tube fuselage and Warner Scarab 165 hp radial; Theodore Corbett, RFD 1.

SWANTON. *Travel Air 4000* of 1927, NC3823 c/n 306 with 220 hp Continental; Floyd E. Handy.

VIRGINIA

ANNANDALE. *DH.82A Tiger Moth* N9279 c/n 61 ex A17-64, VH-AQR; J. R. Frizzell.

BEALETON. Route 17, 12 miles south of Warrenton, The Flying Circus Aerodrome. Flying every Sunday mid-May to end-October from 1400 hrs when professional pilots fly replica WW I types in dog-fights, aerobatics, formations, parachuting displays and races. Static displays (also open on weekdays). This is arranged as a typical aerodrome of the 1914-18 war —telephone 439-8661 for details. Aircraft:— *Beachey 1911 Little Looper (replica)*. *de Havilland DH.2 (replica)*, reg'n please. *Fokker E.III Eindecker (monoplane) (replica)* N1915F, c/n 3-68. *Fokker DR.1 Triplane (replica)* N1917. *Raven S-50A Hot-Air Balloon* N1934R c/n 140. *R.A/c Factory BE.2c (replica)* N1914B serialled 2984; ex G-AWYI. *Rumpler C.IV (replica)* N1915E and *N1916E*. *Sopwith Camel (replica)* N1917H. *Nieuport 24Bis (replica)* N1895. Also *Boeing-Stearman N2S-5* N17811 c/n 75-8648;

N53414 c/n 75-773; N9486H; *Stearman A75-N1* N58212 c/n 75-762; *Fairchild PT-23* N11113 c/n 59FE; *PT-17* N69CB c/n 75-5302; *Brewster Fleet Model 1* N1980M c/n 40. A commendable project, deserving of your support. Check before visiting, though.

CHARLOTTESVILLE. Air & Space Museum. Was due to open 1970 with *FG-1D Corsair* 92246; *F4U-7 Corsair* 133710. Can anyone up-date the information, with location, opening times, admission and other exhibits, please?

CHATHAM. On display. *T-33A* 51-9119.

FORT EUSTIS. US Army Transportation Museum. Virginia, 23604. *Avro Mark II VZ-9 Avrocar* 58-7055 built by Avro Division, Toronto, Canada, powered by three Continental J69 turbojets. Nicknamed "Saucer" the project abandoned 1961. *Bell H-13B Sioux 46-234* engine 17378, MAA plate 185229, built at Fort Worth Texas. The Army obtained its first "B" model February, 1949 and the most ever carried on Army Aviation inventory was a total of 59 in June, 1959. *Bell H-13E* 51-14010. First obtained by the Army, February, 1952, highest number on inventory was 406 in December, 1953. Seats 3 side-by-side, overall length 41 ft 2½ inches width over torsion bar 8 ft 6 inches. Weight empty, 1,380 lbs. *Air Car Gem 2X.* Purchased by the Army from Curtiss-Wright Inc., it is a ground-effects vehicle, Model 2500 Air Car, 360 hp 4-passenger vehicle, speeds up to 60 mph at height of about 10 inches with maximum gradient of 6 per cent. Power plant two 180 hp Lycoming VO 360-A1A engines, producing air-cushion pressure of approx. 1/10 lbs per square inch under the vehicle to support it clear of ground. Weight 2,770 lbs, length 21 ft, width 8 ft. Carries three passengers or 1,000 lbs. *De Lackner Aerocycle DH-4.* One-man flying platform, developed for the Army 1955, by De Lackner Helicopters Inc. Tested by Army 1956/7. Powered by 43 hp Kickhaefer Mercury Mk 55 engine. Cruising speed about 75 mph, weight approx. 400 lbs. Tubular skid landing gear with track of 7 ft 4 inches. *Hiller H-23B Raven* helicopter, 51-16168 coded "III-II". Used primarily for air evacuation and type saw extensive use in Korea. Engine 200 hp Franklin model 6V4-200-C33, air cooled. Craft is 28 ft 6 inches long, 7 ft 1 inch wide, weight 1,998 lbs. *Vertol H-21C Shawnee* helicopter serial 56-2077 used by Army as troop carrier and re-supply vehicle. Engine 1,425 hp Wright R-1820-103; carries crew of two and accommodation for 12 stretchers or troops. In January, 1962 Army had 283 *H-21c's. H-21* went into service with Army 1954 and has seen limited use in Vietnam. *Piasecki HUP-2 (UH-25B) Retriever helicopter.* Bu 130043. Single-engined tandem-rotored. All-metal soundproof fuselage, crew of two and 4 passengers or three stretchers. With blades folded. 32 ft long, 12 ft 11 inches wide and 12 ft 6 inches high First to the Army in February, 1953, most on inventory 63 in June, 1955, 55 hp engine. *Piasecki VZ-8P1* 58-5510 "*Flying Jeep*" developed under contract with USA-TRECOM by Piasecki and first flown May, 1958, completing test flight programme 1959. The project sought to provide the US Army with versatility of conventional jeep as well as capability of hovering and propelling itself above ground. Commercial designation was Model *59K, Sky Car.* Originally used two 180 hp Lycomings but was re-designed with 425 hp Turbomeca Artouste IIB engine. Weight 2,375 lns, length 21 ft,

Piasecki Airgeep II (Fort Eustis)

width 10 ft, height 7 ft 3 inches. Model number interpretation is V-vertical takeoff and land; Z-Research and Experimental; 8-8th vehicle in series; P-Piasecki; 1-first one built by Piasecki for project series *Piasecki VZ-8P-B Airgeep II* 58-5511 Model PA-59H, developed as improved *59K (VZ83).* Second prototype of previous aircraft. Ground and flight tested 1961/62, two three-bladed ducted rotors; two 400 hp Turbomeca Artouste 11C shaft-turbines. Designed to fly at more than 150 hp, stay airborne several hours and carry up to 1,000 lbs cargo. Wheels arranged as tricycle landing gear with size 500 x 5 tyres and Goodyear brakes. *Piper L-21* military version of Super Cub; identical to *L-18* except for 135 hp Lycoming 0-290-D and wing flaps. Most on Army inventory 150 "A" models 31st December, 1951, 69 "B" models 31st December, 1953. *L-21A* used primarily for training, L-21B used in Far East. Maximum speed 110 mph—metal airscrew. *X-2 Air Scooter* built by Princeton University 1959. Round saucer shape with engine cowling and intake on the top protruding from the centre. A bicycle seat and handle bars atop the cowling support the operator. Aluminium frame covered with fabric. 15 hp engine kinesthetically controlled; payload capacity 250 lbs. Weight less engine 65 lbs, 9 ft 5 inches diameter, 4 ft high *Sikorsky R4 Hoverfly* "007". *Sikorsky H-19C Chickasaw* 51-14275; military version of *S-55.* Twelve-seat utility suitable for passenger, airmail or other cargo. Prototype flew 9th November, 1949. This particular example was used extensively in Korea, 1952 with 6th Transportation Helicopter Company near Chongchon. Later participated in "Little Switch" and "Big Switch" POW exchanges and earned several campaign ribbons. *DHC U-6A Beaver* 58-1997. Can anyone add to this listing, please?

FREDERICKSBURG. Shannon Airport. Air/Shannon Co. *Standard E-1* B-123, found in barn 1952, winning prize in 1965 for best-restored a/c. *Pitcairn PA-5 Mailwing* NC3835 c/n 9, bearing notice "Do not exceed Mach 7 inverted before closing relief tube". Built 1927 for airmail contract route flying. *Aeronca C-2N* N11417 c/n A151. *Curtiss Robin J-1* N532N c/n 773.

HAMPTON. Aerospace Park, Mercury Boulevard. *NA F-86D/L* 51-3064; *Northrop F-89H/J* 52-2129; *Sikorsky H-19D Chickasaw* 56-1522 ex U.S. Army (Electronics Command). *Vertol CH-21C-PH Shawnee* 56-2146 from U.S. Army. *Lockheed T-33A* 51-9086. *McDonnell F-101B Voodoo* 0-60246. *Republic F-84F* 0-11786. *Douglas XSAM-A-7 Nike-Ajax. Firestone XM4E1 Corporal. North*

Neptune "Truculent Turtle" (Norfolk Va.)

Kawanishi "Emily" (Norfolk Va.)

American Little Joe (Mercury capsule) launched twice 1961 to demonstrate structural integrity. *Polaris. A-2 (V1).*

LANGLEY. AFB. It is understood that no aircraft are currently on public display but that the *Bell P-63 King Cobra* once at Edwards AFB, Calif., and *F-80C* 49-749 may be under restoration here. *Hawker XV-6A (P1127) Kestrel* 64-18266 probably ex XS694, is with NASA here, with *Sikorsky SH-3A Sea King* 149723, both on occasional exhibition.

NEWPORT. War Memorial Museum. *Vought F4U Corsair*, believed 22811 "7-BF.6". NACA rockets *F.23* and *RM-10.*

NORFOLK. NAS. *Lockheed XP2V-1 Neptune* 89082 c/n 26-1003 "Truculent Turtle" the 1946 world-long-distance record-breaker, 11,236 miles non-stop from Perth, Australia to Columbus, Ohio, in 55 hrs 17 mins. This Neptune is earmarked for eventual transfer to NASM, Washington DC and the very last Neptune was flown to Norfolk by Rear Admiral Thomas D. Davies (pilot of "Truculent Turtle" in 1946). Serial wanted if, as seems likely, this is to replace the NASM a/c when it leaves. Other machines here appear to be the NASM stored:— *Consolidated PBY-5 Catalina* 08317; *Convair XF2Y-1 Sea Dart* 135764; *Convair XFY-1 Pogo* 138649; *Kawanishi NIKI Kyofu "Rex"* c/n 514; *Martin P5M-2 Marlin*—serial wanted; *McDonnell XHJH-1 Whirlaway* 44318 of 1947; *NA FJ-1 Fury* 120351. Also here the cocooned *Kawanishi H8K2 "Emily"* flying boat; *Kawanishi NIKI Kyofu "Rex"* c/n 562; *Kawanishi NIK2J Shiden Kai "George"*; *Culver TD2C-1*

Cadet drone 120082; *Curtiss XF15C-1* 01215; *Douglas BTD-1 Destroyer* 04959; *Douglas XF3D-1 (F-3D) Skyknight* 121458; *Grumman JRF-5G Goose* 37782; *Grumman TBM-3E Avenger* 23602; *McCullogh HUM-1 (MC-4C)* 133817; *Sikorsky S-55 (HO4S-1)* 125506; *Vertol XHJP-1*, serial unknown. All owned by Naval Air Systems Command, Washington. *Grumman F8F-2 Bearcat* N7827C. Bu 121752, thought here with Capt Walter Olrich.

OCEANA. NAS. It is understood aircraft now displayed:— *McDonnell F-4B Phantom II* 148261, silver with "AG" in star on fin, "200" and "Fly Navy" on fuselage. In the Picnic Area:— *Chance Vought F8U-1 Crusader* 145322 "J" with "00" on nose, all-over mid-grey. *Grumman F9F-8 Panther* 123456 "9" all-over light-blue. *Douglas F-6A Skyray* 134950 of AF/VF 64 Sqdn.

PORTSMOUTH. Naval Shipyard Museum. *Polaris* missile in centre of fountain.

QUANTICO. United States Marine Corps Museum, MCAS. In and around hangar at Officers Training School:— *Douglas EA-1E Skyraider* 135178 from Pensacola. *Grumman F8F-2 Bearcat* 121707, ex Kaman Helicopters, where used for tail-rotor testing, as windmachine; Bu *121776* in store. *Hiller OH-23F Raven* 62-12509 and *12510* (ex U.S. Army). *Sikorsky VH-34D Seahorse* 147161 of FMFLANT. *Douglas D558-1 Skyrocket* 37972, "142". *Lockheed F-80C* 49-432, on loan from USAFM, secured from Uruguayan AF, ex serial 218 of No 2 Gruppo Caza. Nearby:— *Grumman F7F-3N Tigercat* 80375 and *80382* ex Anacostia NAS; these were airlifted by CH-53A from Naval Weapons Labora-

Model 22 Ohka "Baka" (Quantico)

tory, Dahlgren, Va (each F7F weighing in excess of 16,000 lbs). *Grumman F4F-4 Wildcat* 12114 (may be in store). *Douglas F3D-2 Skyknight* 124618 ex VMCJ-3. *Beech UC-45J Expeditor* 51178. *Bell (HTL-7) TH-13N Sioux* 145840. *NA FJ-3 Fury* 136119 ex VMF-122 Sqdn. in colours of Brigadier General, USMC. *McDonnell F-2D (F2H-4) Banshee* Bu 127693. *McDonnell FH-1 Phantom* N4283A c/n 456 Bu 111768 civil-registered. *Grumman F9F-5 Panther* 125301 (may be in store). *Douglas SBD-6 Dauntless* Bu 54605, from NASM. *Douglas A-24 (SBD) Dauntless* 42-60817 recovered from Portland, Oregon—was supposed to fly in "Tora, Tora, Tora" and then go to Pensacola—news please. *Sikorsky CH-19E Chickasaw (HRS-3)* Bu 130252, from Korea and to be restored in Korean colours. *Vought F2G-1D Corsair* 88454. *Gyrodyne YRON-1 Rotocycle* 4012, experimental one-man helicopter, powered by Porsche auto engine; tested for possible use by Forward Air Controllers in battle zones. Torpedo-carrying version believed tested. *Grumman F6F-3 Hellcat* 41476 and *F6F-5K* 94263 believed airworthy again and delighting crowds at displays. Undergoing restoration:— *Bleriot* (believed *XI*) of 1911, bought from private source in Boston. *Mitsubishi A6M5 Zero-Sen "Zeke"*, from NASM (earlier at Willow Grove, Pennsylvania). *Model 22 Ohka "Baka"*. A *de Havilland DH.4 (replica)* is being constructed as A-3295, by members of the staff. *Goodyear FG-1D* N448AG ex 92399, wrecked on take-off at NAS Norfolk, has been presented to the museum by Mr. A. T. George of Atlanta, Georgia, and may be restored as a monument to all USMC pilots of this type. *Grumman F6F-5K Hellcat* 80141, donated from Mustin Field, Philadelphia, is thought to be used for static displays. A "Crossbow" missile is crated. The curator, Mr. Clyde Gillespie, will advise on visiting days and times. At Camp Barrett, about 6 miles west of Quantico, the museum at Quantico has on display:— *Grumman F-11A Tiger* 141872 in "Blue Angels" colours. *Douglas F-5A Skyray* 139177 ("Navy" painted over!). *Chance-Vought (Goodyear-built) Corsair* believed FG-1D 92013. *Douglas AD-4B Skyraider* 132261 from USN Weapons, Dahlgren, a Navy advanced trainer, in red/white colour scheme.

RICHMOND. Travelland Park. *Grumman F9F-8 Cougar* 144276. At Byrd Airport, in the Virginia ANG Compound. *F-84F* 52-8837, built by General Motors.

ROANOKE. Transportation Museum. *T-33A* 53-5386. *Grumman F9F-8P Cougar* in patrol-blue—serial wanted. *Piasecki UH-25B Retriever*—serial please. *Atlas* missile.

SOUTH NORFOLK. Airport. *Funk B85C* N81138 c/n 262 and *Vultee Vibrator* said to fly here—further

details appreciated. There is also a *Grumman F-11A Tiger* in the Schoolyard—serial wanted.

SURREY. Town Centre. *NA F-86H-1-NH Sabre* 52-2005.

TAPPAHANNOCK. Airport. *T-33A* 51-6690 of Virginia ANG.

WARRENTON. Fauquier Airfield. *Douglas C-47B* as Gate Guardian in USAF marks—serial please. A *Curtiss JN-4D* is being restored here by Ken Hyde, RFD.1. Serial and history wanted with photo, please.

WESTPOINT. Airfield. *NA B-25J Mitchell* N9090Z (9090Z) ex 44-86734.

WEST VIRGINIA

BELLWOOD. Defense Supply Center. *McDonnell GAM-72-10-MC Quail* 59-2240.

CHARLESTON. Kanawha County Airport. *NA P-51D-25-NA Mustang* 44-72948 "Wham Bang".

MARTINSBURG. Airport. *Spartan 7W* N17614 c/n 13 based here, confirmation and photo please.

WASHINGTON STATE

ARLINGTON. Airport. *Stinson SR-6* N15170 c/n 9647; *Vultee BT-13* N56985 c/n 8557; N60828 c/n 2935. *Monocoupe 90A* N262JL c/n A-802. Owners please.

AUBURN. Municipal Airport. *Beechcraft 17S* N40E c/n 6685. *Fairchild 24-C.8F* N81204 c/n R46-105. Owners please.

CURTISS. E. J. Gothard's Farm. *Auster T.7* HKG-5 and *AOP.9* HKG-6, from Hong Kong Auxiliary Air Force. New reg'ns?

ELLENSBURG. Airfield. *Waco UPF-7* of 1940 N32232; Bedford Hertel. He is also restoring a 1928 *Travel Air 3000*.

EVERETT. Paine Field. *NA P-51D Mustang* N2869D ex 44-84390 and *Lockheed P-38 Lightning* N74883 ex 42-2691 from Ontario Air Museum, California, both owned by "Chuck" (Chas. A.) Lydford III of Bellevue, Wash. Also flying here *Tiger Moth* N3301T c/n 1636 ex RCAF 3975, CF-CKW; Richland Flying Services Inc.

LYNDEN. Airfield. *Arrow Sport* of 1929 N3079 c/n 337; owner?

PASCO. Airfield. *Douglas A-24B Dauntless* N17421 ex N4488N c/n 17421, Navy 54582 but to Army as 42-54582; restored to SBD5 status by four members the "Scarf & Goggles" Club, Barrett Tillman, his father, and two friends. The machine had been used in Portland, Oregon, as a mosquito sprayer. When parked the Dauntless displays a "scoreboard" showing that 6 Japanese carriers, 1 battleship, 3 cruisers, 4 destroyers and 15 transports/merchantmen were sunk entirely or partially by the SBDs between May-November 1942. It is the intention that this Dauntless will be preserved in a flying condition in USA or elsewhere.

PROSSER. Ranch Airfield. *Stearman C3B* NC656K c/n 5007 of 1929 and *C3B* of 1928 N7550 c/n 166 owned by R. J. McWhorter; also a *Stearman PT-13D.*

PULLMAN. Airport. *Zenith Biplane* N392V c/n 3 as cropduster (only 12 built). *Stearman PT-17* cropdusters N9082H c/n 75-8564, *N1729B* c/n 75-5849, *N56628* c/n 5-023, *N58987* c/n 75-5495, *N68480* c/n 75-7225.

PUYALLUP. Thun Field. *Fleet 7* N794V; *Fairchild 22 C7D* NC9480 c/n 910. *Curtiss Pusher (replica)* built by W. Bullock 1947 and flown by Pete Bowers, engineer-pilot of Boeing Co. Reg'n please.

B.&W. Floatplane—replica (Seattle)

Boeing B-1 (Seattle)

SEATTLE. Museum of History and Industry, Boeing Wing. *Boeing B-1* N-ABNA of 1919, used by Eddie Hubbard to fly the nation's first privately-contracted airmail over the world's first international airmail route—between Victoria, British Columbia, Canada—and Seattle. This *B-1* was retired after 10 years of service and 350,000 flying miles, during which it wore out 6 engines. The Edison Technical School has a *Republic F-84F Thunderstreak* serial wanted.

SEATTLE CENTER. Pacific Northwest Aviation Historical Foundation. The PNAHF Museum now has the *Boeing B. and W. Floatplane (replica)* N1916L, a reproduction of the 1916 type which has delighted many crowds during flights over the State. *Boeing WB-47E Stratojet* 51-7066 was flown into Boeing Field, Seattle in November, 1969, for the museum, the gift of USAF. The a/c had served its last days with the 57th Weather Reconnaissance Sqdn, Hickam AFB, Hawaii, the last operational B-47. It had flown 6,393 hrs, from leaving the Wichita factory 26 Oct 1953. In all 2,040 were built (including some by Douglas at Tulsa, Oklahoma and by Lockheed at Marietta, Georgia. The a/c went on show at the airfield pending accommodation in the museum. It was the world's first multi-jet swept-back bomber.

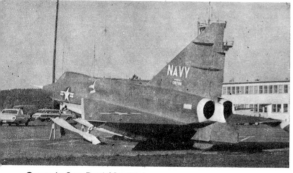

Convair Sea-Dart (Seattle)

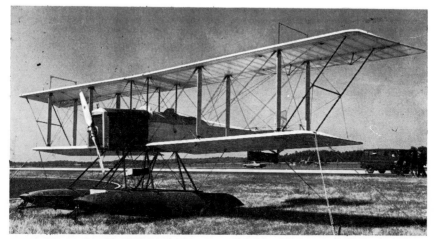

B.&W. Floatplane—replica (Seattle)

Boeing 247D NC3977C ex NC13347 c/n 1729, Pacific Air Transport July 1933, CF-BID with RCAF, plus roundels and serial 7839. Re-registered and used as sprayer USA and Costa Rica to 1955. Flown from Bakersfield, Cal 1966 by Captain Jack Leffler, United Airlines and Ray Pepka of Renton Avn. Re-registered NC13347. *Boeing 80A Trimotor* NC224M found 1960 city dump Anchorage, Alaska; used 1941-6 to haul supplies for the Northway military airstrip. Captain Leffler bought it for 50 dollars and, thanks to USAF, got it to Seattle in a Globemaster. To be restored as United Airlines' 1929 a/c. The world's first air stewardess service was in this type—with Boeing Air Transport. (Restoration at King County Airport.) *Grumman F4 Wildcat* (serial wanted) from White Center? *Bowlus Sailplane. Sorrell "Flying Bathtub"* homebuilt. *Lockheed TV-1* (serial please). *Grumman F9F Cougar* 131232, from King County Park. *"Yakima Clipper"* 1929 sailplane. Curtiss Robin C.1 *"Newsboy"* donated by Capts. Bob van Ausdell & Perry A. Schreffier of TWA; reg'n? Engines etc. Let us look forward to getting an up-dated listing with photos for V. and V. Mk V. *Convair XF2Y-1 Sea-Dart* 135765 is reported at Renton, perhaps to be loaned o the PNAHF Museum for display (from Sandpoint NAS.) Flying from King County Airport (Boeing Field) *Navy N3N-3* N44920 c/n 3061; *Vultee BT-15A* N513L ex 11630; *Cessna T-50 Bobcat* N54302 c/n 5547; *Stearman PT-17* N1193N c/n 75-1218; *Pietenpol B-4* of 1932 N688Y c/n 68-1 of Peter M. Bowers; *CAC CA-18 Mustang* VH-BOW ex A68-100 with Jim Ausland, believed now airworthy again—new reg'n please. *NA (Canadair) Sabre 5* 23096 c/n 286, Boeing chase-plane; *Douglas A-26* 44-35945 "HL-NG"—confirmation of serial please. *NA T-28 Trojan* N3320G; Ray Karrels; *P-51 Mustang* N5482V ex 44-73343 "Seattle Miss" of Ben Hall; *P-51D* N7715C ex 44-84961 of "Chuck" Hale; *Great Lakes 2T* N312Y of Jim Moss normally fly from here.

SPOKANE. Municipal Airport. *Lockheed T-33A* 51-4259 on plinth in Washington ANG colours. Flying from E. D. "Skeet" Carlson's strip at Oxe Madows, a *Stearman C3C* of 1928; *Thomas-Morse S4C* of 1918; *Cessna AW* of 1928; *DH. Puss Moth*; *Student Prince* and *Curtiss JN-4D* are being restored. These are part of the "Scarf & Goggles" Club. The *Great Lakes 2T* of W. Duncan flies nearby.

SUNNYSIDE. Airfield. *NA B-25* (*two examples*) of Max Hanks; details?

TACOMA. Airport. *Davis D-1W* N15785 c/n 801; Major C. E. Seige. *Great Lakes 2T* NC822K c/n 83; "Hank" Dyson. *American Pilgrim 100* N709Y c/n 6605 (first plane used by Alaskan Airlines); *Grumman F6F Hellcat* N4965V ex 08825; owned by President, Alaskan Airlines.

TEKOA. *Great Lakes* (*replica*) with Ranger engine; W. Redfern. Registration wanted.

VANCOUVER. Evergreen Field. *Waco YQC* N46290 c/n 4387; *Waco UPF-7* N29949 c/n 5446 of 1940; W. Olson. *Fleet 7C* of W. Swanson 1929 vintage; *Waco ASO* of 1929, D. Detour; *Fairchild 24* N16899; *Curtiss-Wright Travelair 12Q. Ryan PT-22* N58651 c/n 1426, both Paul Lawrence. *Beechcraft D-17* of 1934 N12592 c/n 12 was with David L. Setler—up-to-date information wanted. Neil Rose, a 29-year-old Scot from Aberdalgie, Perth-shire, son of a pre-WW II and wartime Bomber Command airman, owns a *Hurricane IIB* serial 65022 ex Canadian Car & Foundry, Swift Current, Sask, and also flies a *Harvard IIA*, RCAF 3131, restored to 1942 European colours. Neil has been flying since 16 and we look forward to hearing that his Hurricane is airworthy and in what markings.

WAPATO. Airfield. *Waco V1C* of 1933 N13427 c/n 3783; Greg Babcock.

WENATCHEE. Airport. *Ryan PT-22* N57426 c/n 1301; Vergil Letnes.

YAKIMA. Airport. *Grumman TBM-3 Avenger* N7031C was here, with *Stearman PT-17* cropdusters N1145N c/n 75-2157, *N4762N* c/n 75-6630, *N4814N, N57120, N66617* c/n 75-1515, *N58622* c/n 75-863. Details of owners and present status, please.

WISCONSIN

APPLETON. American Legion Home. *NA F-86H-10-NH* 51-5938 displayed.

CAMP DOUGLAS. Volk Field. *NA P-51D Mustang* (serial wanted) and *NA F-86* (serial wanted) both on poles. *Republic F-84F* 51-9365 also displayed.

GREEN BAY. Airport. *Meyers OTW* N34311 c/n 55; Dick Martin. *Piper J-5 Cub Cruiser* N30368 c/n 5-183; Mark Baldwin.

GREYBULL. Airfield. Hawkins & Powers Aviation. *Consolidated PB4Y Privateers* ex U.S. Coast Guard Service:— N2870G ex 66304 "B22", N2871G ex 66302 "B21", N7962C "B26" ex Bu 59882—any further details, histories, etc., welcomed. These a/c go to Canada for fire-fighting in the summer season.

HALES CORNERS. A Milwaukee suburb. The EAA Air Museum. The Experimental Aircraft Association (Box 229, Hales Corners, Wis. 53130) open their magnificent museum every day to view:—Outside—*Lockheed GF-80C* 48-868; *Lockheed T-33A* 51-8627 and 53-5250; *North American F-86H* 52-1993; *Northrop F-89J* 53-2530; *Republic F-84C* 47-1498—all donated by USAF, with *Republic F-84F* 51-9456 on loan from USAFM Program. Also the *NA P-51 Mustang* N335 ex 44-72902, the late Ed Weiner's transcontinental racer, painted bright-red "14", flown from Los Angeles by W. S. Halfhill of EAA. *NA P-51D* N335J ex 44-74506, Ed Weiner's clipwing racer "49" "Miss Bardahl" (also on indefinite loan from Weiner's estate) was flown from Reno by Jack Huismann, Pewaukee, Wis., past President, Warbirds of America. Bob Hoover had flown a lap of honour at Reno as a tribute to Ed Weiner who died of a heart attack following the Reno Races, 1969. This is painted yellow and black checkerboard pattern. Currently flying aircraft include:— *EAA "Acro Sport"* N-IAC; *Grumman J2F-6* N1186N, loaned by Carl Mies; *Meyers "Little Toot"* N217J c/n JD17-3 from James Mahoney; *NA P-64* N840 ex NA-68 N68622 c/n 68-3061. The last remaining example of seven built for Siam (Thailand) 1939; six taken over by USAAF 1941 as P-64s, serialled 41-19082-87. Jack Canary obtained this post-war, thought ex XB-KUU, paying 800 dollars for it. Used for

EAA Air Museum (Hales Corners)

NA P-64 (Hales Corners)

rain-making as NX37498 and then stored until Paul Poberezny and Art Kilps acquired it 1963 as EAA flying a/c. It appeared Rockford in 1965 as N840—a phoney reg'n. Original 870 hp Wright replaced after WW II by Wright 1820-60 with two-stage blower developing 1350 hp. Fantastic climb and aerobatic performance. *NA SNJ-5* N7986C ex 51698 painted as "Zero"—donors Paul H. Poberezny, Ray Scholler John Stickling. *Vultee BT-13B* N63697 c/n 79-1293 donor John Louck. *Waco CTO* N7527 c/n A-33 donor Fred Grothe. On display, 1973:— Antique and Classic Aircraft—*Aeronca C-3 (Razorback)* N13094 c/n A258 donor Paul Poberezny. *Aeronca C-3* N16291 c/n A668 donor Ken Cook. *Baumann B-290 Brigadier* N90616 c/n 102 a 5-place, twin-engined mid-wing pusher, designed as light and economical executive transport. Built 1952 as follow-on to original B-250 but with Continental C-145s of 145 hp. Span 41 ft, length 27 ft 5 ins, height 10 ft 4 ins. Top speed 190 mph, cruising 165 mph. It was donated by Bill Baumann, Phoenix A/c Mnfg Corp, Northridge, Calif. *Boeing Stearman*

PT-17 Kaydet N11BY c/n 75-5337; loaned by Bernard Yocke. *Curtiss 1912 A-1 Sweetheart* N24034 c/n 12; donated by Dale Critea. *Curtiss C-1 Robin* N9223 c/n 296; donated by Lee Weber. *DH.82C Tiger Moth* CF-IVO c/n 1667 donor, Rev. John MacGillivray. *Fairchild FC-2* N3569 c/n 35; donor Herbert M. Harkom. *Fairchild 22-C7A* N1923F loaned by Don Coleman. *Goodyear GA-22 Drake* N5516M c/n 115; donor Goodyear Aerospace Corpn. *Monocoupe 113* NC7808 c/n 247; donated by John Hatz. *Nicholas-Beazley NB8* N576Y c/n K-18 of 1931; donor John van Andel. *Pheasant H-10* NC151N; donor Philip Stier. *Rearwin 7000 Sportster* N14485 c/n 403; donor L. O. Rupe. *Ryan NYP* (replica) NX211, loaned by David Jameson. *Ryan ST-3KR* N48588, loaned by Don Harrell. *Spartan C.2-60* NC11908 loaned by George E. Goodhead Jr. *Taylor E-2 Cub* N15676 c/n 341, loaned by Gene Chase. Aerobatic and Air Show Aircraft:— *Bücker Bü 133 Jungmeister* N258H c/n 1; donor Sam Burgess, who built the replica in 1967. *Grumman G-22 Gulfhawk II* NR1050—loaned from NASM. *Pitts Special* N58J loaned by Tom Poberezny. *Travel Air D4D* NC606K c/n 1282; loaned by Nick Rezich. Military Aircraft on indoor display:— *Bell P-39Q-15-BE Airacobra* N57591 ex 44-32533, loaned from NASM. (EAA list shows *44-2433*—are there two examples?) *Curtiss 0-52 Owl* 40-2769 donors Glen Courtwright and M. Foose. *Nakajima Ki-43 Hayabusa "Oscar"* c/n Ki 43-2 serial K1A-43, loaned from NASM. *NA P-51D* N6329T ex 44-74582; loaned by Landon Cullum Jr. *Radioplane OQ-19 (drone)* donated by Fred Flood. Amateur-Built Aircraft displayed:— *Beecraft Honey Bee* N90859 c/n 1; donated Walt Mooney. *Bowers Fly Baby* N1340 c/n 67-33; donor Helen Dettman. *Breezy* N59Y c/n 5537; loaned by Carl Unger. Also known as Roloff RLW-1. *Corben C-1*

Baby Ace N9050C c/n 101C; donor Ray Scholler. *Cvjetvokic CA-61 Mini-Ace* N94283 c/n 1; donor Mark Shoen. *Driggers A Sunshine Girl* 891H, donated W. A. Driggers. *EAA Biplane* N6077V, donated by EAA. *Folkerts Henderson* 8902, donor Mrs. Clayton Folkerts. *Foster Taperwing "Aerodyne"* N827Z, donor Henry Foster. *Hoynik 2 "Butch"* N11021, donor Steve Hoynik. *Pitts Special* N58P c/n 6P; loaned by Bonnie Poberezny. *Player Homebuilt* N21778, donor William Earl Player. *Pober P-5 Sport* N51G c/n 105; donated K. G. Bride. *Smith Termite* N377T c/n 1T; donor James D. Clarke. *Stits Sky Baby* N5K c/n 2; donor Ray Stits; also *Stits SA11A Playmate* N5K (correct reg'n?). *Unruh Pretty Prairie Special III* N1473V c/n 1; donor Russell Brown. *Walker Little Toot* N12G c/n 1; donor Ab Walker. *Wittman Tailwind* N11985 c/n 133; loaned by Joseph Hamilton. Racer Aircraft displayed:— *Keith Rider R-5 Jackrabbit* NX264Y c/n A-1; donor James Garvin. *Loving-Wayne "Love"* N351C donor Neal V. Loving. *Pettit Special* N5715N, donor George Pettit. *Wittman Bonzo* NX13688, donor S. J. Wittman. Miscellaneous Aircraft displayed:— *Bede XBD-2* N327BD, donor James Bede. *Nelson GEM* donated by Charles Rgodes. *Tessier Biplane* donated by Rene Tessier. *Woods-Wolfe GEM* donors Harris Woods, George Wolfe. World War I replica aircraft:— *Fokker D.VIII*; E. O. Swearingen; with 145 hp Warner Scarab; flown 17 hours. *Bowers JN2D1 Jenny* N1005Z, donor Frank Murray. *R.A/c Factory S.E.5E* 22-325 of 1922 serial 325 (on loan from NASM, but not shown as *replica* on their listing). *Sorrel DR.1 Fokker* N58P donated by Ron Conrad. *Fokker D.VII* (quarter-scale) donated by West Allis Flying Club. Rotary Wing Aircraft:— *Goodyear GA-400R "Gizmo"* N69N, donated by Goodyear Aerospace Corpn. *Voland V-1 Gyrocopter* N840 donor Donald Voland. Gliders on display:— *Chanute Hang Glider* donated by EAA Chapter 29. *Cessna Primary Glider* N186V, donors C. M. Van Airesdale and Leland Hanselman. *Cleave EPB-1A "Plank"* N19C, donor Al Cleave. *Explorer PG-1 Aqua-Glider* N6498D and *Haufe "Dale-Hawk"* N18278; donor C. M. Van Airesdale. *Helisoar HP-10* N319Y, donor Richard du Pont. *Parasev I* N9765C donated by NASA Flight Research Center. Construction Display Aircraft:— *Fike C* 13390 c/n 4, donor William Fike, *Folkerts (Bamboo fuselage)* donor Mrs. Clayton Folkerts *Heath Parasol*, donor W. H. Nieman. *Hoynik Racer* (fuselage) donated by Steve Hoynik. *Rearwin 7000 Sportster* N17002, donor Paul H. Poberezny. *Rezich Racer*, donor Nick Rezich. *Thorp T-18*, donated by EAA. Aircraft under Construction or Restoration:— *Aeronca K* NC22157 donor Cliff Ernst. *Akron Funk* N24119 c/n 45; donated by Gus Limbach. *Heath Parasol*, donors EAA. *Junkers Ju 87B-2 Trop "Stuka"* painted "A5-HL" on loan from Chicago Museum of Science & Industry, ex Luftwaffe's 1/St.G.2, captured by RAF in Libya. Was damaged during cleaning in Chicago Museum. The remains of the *Grumman G-32A* from St. Charles, Illinois may come here for possible rebuild. *Monocoupe 90-A* N19330 donated by Cliff Ernst. *Pfalz D.XII* of 1918 (loan from NASM). *Taylorcraft BC-12D* N5218M, donor Paul H. Poberezny. *Travel Air E-4000* N648H c/n 1224; donated by John Chesney. Aircraft in Temporary Storage:— *American Flea* N60001V, donor L. A. Kraemer. *Culver PQ-14B* N10146, donated by USAF. *Hartman Self-Propelled Balloon* N209A, donor Art Hartman. *Heath fuselage and tail group* (flatback), donor Hurley Boehler. *Hill and Kemman HK-1* N6831D, donors Keith Hill and Rye Kemman. *Jodel D-9* N7702G, donor Mrs.

Karl Kurbjun. *Lewis Original Design*, donor Mrs. Sevryn A. Lewis. *Lincoln Standard fuselage*, donor Bill Dodd. *Marinac "Flying Mercury"*, donated by EAA Chapter 25. *Mignet HM-360 Pou du Ciel "Flying Flea"* N360HM c/n 001, donor Ralph Wefel. *Mong NS-2K "Sport"* N72411 c/n 0001JBK; donor John Krupp. *Monocoupe 90-A* N11783 c/n A-708, donor Dick Wagner. *Stits SA3B "Playboy"* N4648G c/n P-371; donor Mrs. Wm Brown. *Stits "Skeeto"* donated by Ray Stits. *Thompson-Curtiss Pusher*, donated by Neil K. Carr. *Thorp T-18* N1947 c/n 6; donated by John Foy. *Waco ASO* N6930, donor Gerard Bebeau. *Woody Pusher* N232MB c/n 3; donated by Mrs. Mel Lamb. It is reported that a *Curtiss P-40 Warhawk* (or mock-up?) is coming here from the "Tora, Tora, Tora" film—details of this and any other additions—registrations of those unidentified etc. appreciated. We wish the EAA members, everywhere, good fortune in their work and congratulate them on their successes to date. Flying from Hales Corner Airport is said to be *Cessna 196* N3878V c/n 7346; a modified 195 with P. & W. 985-450 hp engine and two camera-holes. Six of the type converted by Falls City Flying Services, Louisville, Kentucky. Take-off in 300 feet.

JANESVILLE. Airfield. *Aeronca K* N18896 c/n K165; of Ed Schubert.

MEQUAH. Airstrip. *Piper J-3C* of 1939 N32920 c/n 5702 of Al Kelch.

MILWAUKEE. General Mitchell Airport. *NA TB-25M-20-NC Mitchell* 44-30444. A Museum of Military Air Power (Patrick J. O'Hare) is forming at 5354 South Eighth St. and may have *NA F-86H Sabre*, serial? *Fokker DR.1* (*replica*) EI-APY—from Ireland. Further details appreciated.

OSHKOSH. Winnebago County Airport. David Jameson Collection includes:— *Snyder "Baby Bomber"* of 1922/3. *Monocoupe Model 90* N170K c/n 504 of 1930— was flying—the world's oldest. *Waco CTO Taperwing* NR7527 c/n A-33—Transcontinental Air Race Winner. *Monocoupe Model 113* NG5874 c/n 54. *Lockheed Vega* of 1929 (reg'n?) (*Ryan NX211* (replica) bought for 17,500 dollars from Tallmantz is loaned to EAA, Hales Corners.)

PLYMOUTH. Airfield. *Spartan C-3* of 1929 N705N c/n 149; Ed Wegner.

POPLAR. Richard Bong Memorial, near school, on plinth—*Lockheed P-38J-15-LO Lightning* 42-103993, honouring one of USA's greatest fighter pilots of WW II.

PORTAGE. Airfield. *Rearwin 8135 Cloudster prototype* N25451 c/n 809 of George Williams.

STOUGHTON. Truax AFB (near Madison). Air National Guard Display *NA F-86H Sabre* 53-1359; *Convair F-102A* 55-3456. *Northrop F-89D Scorpion* 51-400, the first production 89D; also reported at Truax Field.

WYOMING

CASPER. Airport. *NA F-86E-10-NA Sabre* 51-2826.

CENTRAL AMERICA

COSTA RICA

SAN JOSE. El Coco International Airport. *Curtiss C-46A* TI-1007C c/n 30374 ex 42-96712; *TI-1024C* c/n 180 ex 43-47109 and *C-46D* TI-1008C c/n 33379 ex 44-77983, all with Lineas Areas Costarricenses SA (LACSA). *Curtiss C-46D* TI-1010C c/n 33348 ex 44-77952, with Expreso Aereo Costarricenses SA (EXACO). *Beech C-45G* TI-1027C with Coopesa and *TI-1028C* with Aerovias Cariari. *Douglas B-26* TI-1040L, with Frank Marshall Jnr. *Boeing-Stearman PT-17* (cropdusters) TI-409F, *TI-271P*, *TI-348F*, *TI-356F* and *TI-364F*, with Aviación Agricola and Servicio Aereo Fumigacion. *Luscombe Silvaire 8E* TI-369L with R. Law and TI-259P *Model 8F* with Ernesto Lohrengel S.

EL SALVADOR

SAN SALVADOR. Airport. *NA P-51D Mustang* N13410C ex Dave Forrest "Warbirds of America".

MEXICO

GUADALAJARA. Aviation Military School (Colegio del Aire) *Boeing-Stearman PT-17*—serial and history please.

MAZATLAN. West Coast. *Ford 4-AT* reported static—details of reg'n and condition wanted.

MEXICO CITY. International Airport. *Davis D-1K* XB-AEI c/n 506 of 1929; Senor Augustin Pelaez. *Douglas B-26* XB-PEX, ex N1144, airworthy when reported. *DH.98 Mosquito B.35* XB-TOX—news please of condition—ought to be preserved! *Douglas DC-4M* XB-JVG in use here as coffee-bar. *Fleet 16B* (ex RCAF Finch) owned and flown by M. A. Garcia—*XB-BII* c/n 279, was RCAF 4412; R. S. V. de Romero—*XB-GOD* ex 4614; Cia. Fumigadara de la Huasteca—*XB-KUK* ex 4777; L. G. Hernandez—*XB-TUJ* ex 4725; F. L. Tejeda—*XB-WEJ* ex 4603; A. E. Lopez—*XB-WEM* ex 4804. Photos please. The Museo de Talleres de la Fuerza Aerea Mexicana, Federal District 9 offers:—*Government A/c Factory Parasol Type "H"* of 1919; *Azcatate* 1929 prototype; *Pinocho* of 1936, built by Mexican mechanic. It is thought that a *Douglas B-26* and *Consolidated PBY-5A*, from Mexican Air Force and Naval Air Force, are stored at the airport for the museum. Details wanted. *Northrop N-23 Pioneer* also reported—reg'n please and status.

SAN LUIS POTOSI. El Abane Military HQs Museum. *Latino America* of 1916 on display—photo and details wanted.

SANTA LUCIA. Mexican Air Force Base. On display *Biplane Type "A"* of 1916 built by Government A/c Factory. *Gee-Bee Q.E.D.R-6H* XB-AKM "Conquistador del Cielo" which set record of 10 hrs 47 mins for Mexico City-NY flight in May 1939, piloted by Francisco Sarabia. This aircraft was the last of the Gee-Bee racers and was

Grumman Duck (Santa Lucia)

built in 1934. Registered NX 14307 and powered by one 700 hp P. & W. Hornet, it had a top speed of 240 mph. It was entered in the 1934 MacRobertson Race to Australia but was forced to retire at Bucharest, which fate followed it through most of its racing career in the USA in the middle 30's. Its one record flight was made at 16,000 ft. and ended with a fast down wind landing with only one gallon of fuel left. Its survival is strange for it is reported to have crashed and killed Capt. Sarabia only a few days after the record flight. Confirmation therefore that the aircraft is original would be welcome. *NA AT-6*: and *Republic P-47D-30-RE Thunderbolt,* which operated in Philippines, said to be stored for eventual display—histories, serials, photos, please. *Grumman J2F-6 Duck* MV-08 was flying here.

VERACRUZ. Naval Aviation School. On display *Grumman J2F-6 Duck; Stearman A-75* ME-008, *010*, and *011*, yellow overall, Escadre de Aviacion Naval markings. *Vultee Stinson Sentinel* MU-03, painted blue, in same marks.

PANAMA

PANAMA CITY. Airport. *Douglas B-23 Dragon* N1755 c/n 2748 reported static here—let us hope for preservation. Details of other vintage types, flying or static, please.

PUERTO RICO

ISLA VERDE. Muñiz Air Base at the airport. *Republic P-47N-25-RE Thunderbolt* N345GP c/n 539/C1537 ex 44-89320. Puerto Rico ANG, painted in colours and numbers of Colonel Mihiel Gilorminic, 156 Tactical Fighter Group commander and one of founders of P.R.ANG.; who flew 51 combat missions in P-47s. A/c actually from 198 Technical Flying School, then donated to Miguel Such Vocational School, 1954. Recovered and restored airworthy in 1972 after five years' work. Long may this "Jug" fly.

THE WEST INDIES

ANGUILLA

WALL BLAKE. Airport. *Beech D18S* VP-LLA c/n A-937 operated by Valley Air Services.

BARBADOS

SEAWELL. Airport. *Beech G18S* 8P-ECA c/n BA-562 ex N263V, Eastern Caribbean Airlines.

TRINIDAD & TOBAGO

PORT OF SPAIN. Piarco International Airport. *Percival Proctor 5* 9Y-TBR ex VP-TBR c/n Ae 82, ex G-AHWZ; E. G. F. Lyder. VP-TBP *Slingsby T.31B* hanging in roof, wings stacked below. *Douglas Dakota 3* 9Y-TBJ c/n 16441/33189 ex 44-76857 flying with B. W. I. Airways—history please. On a traffic island on the main road from airport to Port of Spain, the Trinidad & Tobago Flying Club maintain *Cessna 170A* 9Y-TCH/ VP-TCH c/n 19320 as a tribute to Michael Cipriani (1898-1934) Island statesman. White overall with green trim, registration painted over.

VIRGIN ISLANDS

CHARLOTTE AMELIE-ST. THOMAS. *Vought-Sikorsky VS-44A* N41881 c/n 4402 ex USN 12391; the survivor of three ordered 1940 by American Export Airlines, for North Atlantic schedules. Civil variants of the XPBS-1 of USN. In January 1942 the three were taken over by USN, designated JR2S-1 serials 12390-92. NC41881 flew the first NY-Foynes flight 26 May 1942. On 3 October 1942 NC41880 was lost on take-off in Newfoundland but the two others flew 405 crossings of the Atlantic during WW II. NC41882 was lost in South America post-war. NC41881 was rebuilt Baltimore 1950 for a mining company in South America but after delivery flight was abandoned in Peru. In 1957 Dick Probert, Avalon Air Transport, organized recovery and by September 1957 it had been restored and re-fitted as 46-seat transport. It carried 25,000 passengers to and from Catalina Island in its first three seasons. In 1968 it was sold to Antilles Air Boats Inc to fly local Virgin Islands' schedules but has now been reported as static. This historic flying boat MUST be preserved —if not by NASM, Washington, then surely by others. Please advise V. and V. of its future. With Antilles Air Boats, ten *Grumman Goose* and *Grumman Widgeon* are said to be flying including N384 and N703A c/n 1411 (both Goose). Further details please.

VS-44A N41881 "Super Goose" (Virgin Islands)

SOUTH AMERICA

ARGENTINA

BUENOS AIRES. Museo Nacional de Aeronautica, Aeroparque. *Avro Lincoln B.2* B-010 c/n 1414 ex RE408 of 1944. *Beech AT-11 Kansan* E-110 c/n 3495; *Bleriot XI* claimed as 1909 example but earlier reported as reproduction—news please. *Bristol 170 Freighter 1A* TC-330 c/n 12751, ex G-AICH, LV-XIM, LV-AEY. Possibly last surviving example of early marks. *Cierva (Avro) C30A Autogiro* LV-FBL c/n 4435, in store; also stored—*Comper CLA.7 Swift* LV-FBA believed c/n S.30/2 ex G-AAZA. If so, the aircraft is R.222 of the 1931 Trans-Andes Flight. Photo and history appreciated. *I.Ae.D.L.22* of 1944 c/n 728, in store. *Dinfia I.Ae.27 Pulqui I* C-001, prototype jet fighter. *Dinfia I.Ae.33 Pulqui II* jet fighter. *Douglas C-47 Skytrain* TA-05 also reported as TC-32 (on skis). *Fairchild C-82D Packet* LV-FHZ c/n 066; stored. *Henri Farman 1911 (replica)* "El Palomar"—airworthy. *Fiat G-46-5B* Ea. 441 c/n 076. *Gloster G-43 Meteor F.4* C-041 c/n G5/141; Possibly ex EE586 of RAF. *Junkers Ju 52/3m* LV-ZBD Werk-Nr 4043—ex D-ABIS, PP-CAX; —said to be in need of restoration (1972). *Latecoere 25-3-R* LV-EAB c/n 603 in marks of Aeroposta Argentine (was at Lujan) now in store. This was previously F-AIEH of Aeropostale and Air France and R.211 of Aerposta. *Nieuport 28C.1* c/n N6993 of 1918—history please and photo. *North American T-28A Trojan* E-608 ex 51-3574. *Percival T.Mk 1 Prentice* E-390 c/n 091. *SAI-Ambrosini S.1001 Grifo* in store. *Sikorsky S-55 (H-19A-SI) Chickasaw* H-04 ex 51-3886. *Sud Ouest SO.1220 Djinn* LQ-FYY of 1953. *SVA (Ansaldo) Type 10* of 1918 c/n 13164 is in store. There is a *Vickers Viking* fuselage and, it is thought, other types in store—details appreciated. Flying from the Aeroparque said to be *Douglas DC-3* LV-GYP c/n 2108 of the Ford Motor Co, with modified nose containing CCWR, two-green paint and long panoramic windows—a beautiful machine. Built in 1939 as NC21744 for Eastern Airlines, later N80C, N512 and N51D. Flying from Buenos Aires San Fernando Airport is *Focke Wulf Fw 44J Stieglitz* LV-ZAU. From University Airport *Stieglitz* LV-FIC, *Fairchild 24 Argus* LV-NYJ and *Fairchild M 62* LV-NGR. From San Justo Airfield *Douglas DC-2-112* LV-FIF, c/n 1252 ex NC 12726 (TWA), 42-51754, NC12726, PP-AVH, PP-SSE; *NA Harvard* LV-RTN, *Fleet 5* LV-YBC and *Bücker Bü 131 Jungmann* LV-IST.

AT-11 Kansan (Buenos Aires)

Pulqui II (Buenos Aires)

Fiat G-46 (Buenos Aires)

Junkers Ju 52/3m (Buenos Aires)

Pulqui I (Buenos Aires)

NA T-28A Trojan (Buenos Aires)

Photos and any histories valued. Beside the swimming pool at Ezeira International Airport, *Curtiss C-46* of Austral, with Penguin insignia, is reported—registration /serial and history please. In Cieudad Jardin de El Palomar in flying attitude is *Fiat G-46-2B* Ea-434.

LUJAN. Exhibited in museum *Dornier Do J Wal* M-MWAL c/n W-12 "Plus Ultra" which in 1926 flew from Palos de Moguer, Spain to Buenos Aires via Las Palmas, Porto Praia, Noronha, Pernambuco, Montevideo. Crewed by Ramon Franco, Julio Ruiz de Alda, Naval Lt Manuel Duran and mechanic Rada. The flight

Percival Prentice (Buenos Aires)

Dornier Do J Wal (Lujan)

I.Ae.D.L.22 (Moron)

extended from 22 January to 10 February (flying time 59 hrs 35 mins), and cost 400,000 pesetas for the aircraft's costs and 2,500,000 pesetas for the use of cruiser "Blas de Lezo" and destroyer "Alsedo" along the route. King Alfonso XIII gave the machine to the Argentine government, the aviators returning by ship. In 1968 "Plus Ultra" was taken to Madrid for display. *The Golondrina No. 3 (replica)* of a pioneering Argentinian a/c is believed displayed here, from Buenos Aires store.

MORON. Air Force Base. *Gloster Meteor F.4* I-025 ex EE532 displayed. (I for Intercepcion designation, now replaced by C for Combate). When the 3rd V. and V. was issued 40 of the 100 Meteors supplied to this Air Force were still flying—can anyone up-date the figure and say if others are now preserved? Flying from here were Consolidated *PBY-5 Catalina* 1-G-2; *Vickers V.635 Viking* T-90 c/n 294 ex G-AMNS of BEA and ZS-BNI, South African Airways. *Focke-Wulf Fw 44J Stieglitz. I.Ae.D.L.22* serial Ea-701, built Cordoba early post-war, trainer for A.A.F. *Grumman F9F-2 Panther* 3-A-110 and *Grumman TF9-J Cougar* 3-A-151, were based here—updated details appreciated.

RIO PARANA DELTA. Tigre Museum. *Vought F4U-5 Corsair* serialled 3-A-204 exhibited. Details of any other aircraft please.

ROSARIO. Airfield. *Stearman PT-17* LV-GFR. *Lockheed L-414* LV-ITE.

BOLIVIA

LA PAZ. Airport. *Consolidated B-24M Liberator* CP-576 and CP-787. *Boeing B-17G Flying Fortress* CP-753, CP-891. *NA B-25J Mitchell* CP-808, CP-915. *Lockheed PV-2 Harpoon* CP-649. At the military entrance *Republic P-47N* FAB 007 on display with *P-47N* FAB 120 on display inside. Details, with photos, of these and any other vintage types, please. Is *B-17G* CP-162 flying?

BRAZIL

FORTALEZA Air Force Base, Forca Aerea Brasileira. *Republic P-47D Thunderbolt* 4181 erected in flying pose —previous history please. Flying here—*Beech AT-11 Kansan* serial 1529. *Beech C-45* 2821. *North American B-25J Mitchell* 5136. The Esquadrilla da Fumaca aerobatic squadron had six *T-6G Texans*—confirmation please and serials/histories.

Meteor F.4 (Moron)

B-17G Fortress (La Paz)

GOVEMADOR ISLAND. *Gloster Meteor F.8* 4438 of F.A.B.

MINAS GERAIS. Mariano Procopio Museum, Juiz de Fora. *Porterfield CP-50* PP-GAN c/n 619. History please.

Thunderbolt (Recife)

RECIFE. Guararapes Air Force Base. *Republic P-47N Thunderbolt* 42-26450 on display. *Douglas A-26 Invaders* (eight) flying here 1972—serials appreciated. It is said three *Boeing B-17Gs* including 5402 and 5411 are now static, their engines used for the few airworthy examples. *Consolidated PBY-5A* serial CA-10/6509 of 2° Grupo Aviacao may be preserved here, with one Flying Fortress. Confirmation and serials please, with photos.

RIO DE JANEIRO. Santos Dumont Airport. *Curtiss Fledgling* N263H ex K263 believed stored here for museum. *Douglas DC-3* PP-ANU c/n 1545, the first genuine DC-3 (previous machines were DSTs) was here with VARIG, named "Empresa de Viacao" and said to be preserved when flying ends—details of status please. It was originally NC16009 delivered 18 August 1936 to American Airlines, and in 1951 PP-SQH of VASP. *Lockheed 12A* PP-VTA c/n 1278, owned by Luiz Fernando Lucas Campos was also earmarked for museum. At the Naval Base *Grumman TBF-1 Avenger,* on display. Serial and photo helpful. In the Parque do Flamengo's children's playground *Douglas C-47A* PP-VBF c/n 10156 ex 42-24294, ex VARIG.

SAO PAULO. Ibirapuera Park. Museum of Aeronautics of Sao Paulo, Historical Pavilion. Basically a tribute to Alberto Santos-Dumont who flew ballons and

airships early this century and, on 12 November 1906 won the French Aero Club Prize for the first public aeroplane flight in Europe, covering 38 metres at Bagatelle near Paris in a Santos-Dumont canard (tail-first) biplane with 8 hp Antoinette engine. In the museum *1906 Santos-Dumont SD-14bis (replica)* "Tipo No 1" (Type 1); built Brazil, 1956. *Santos-Dumont Demoiselle SD-22 (replica)* from France. *Savoia-Marchetti S.55* flying boat "Genoa" which flew from Italy to Brazil in 1926, commanded by Comdr. Joao Ribeiro de Barros. *Waco CSO* trainer of 1930, the first ever used by Brazil's Air Force. *Curtiss 16W* trainer of 1934. *EAY-210 Ypiranga* prototype PP-TBF which flew from 1935 to 1963. *CAP-4 Paulistinha,* c/n 02 of 1942. *Republic P-47D Thunderbolt* (serial please) ex 1° Grupo de Caca. *Cessna 140A* of 1949 flown by Ada Lêda Rogato. *Muniz M-7* of 1938 is stored, believed undergoing rebuild. The museum office address is Fundacao Santos Dumont, Av. Ipiranga, 84, Sobreloja. S. Paulo and the Director is Cmte. Amadeu da Silveira Saraiva. From Sao Paulo airport at Campo de Mayo (civil/military) *Tiger Moth* PP-DLL c/n 3329 ex Brazil AF 2.1.10; believed the last airworthy in Brazil, believed to fly—photo and confirmation awaited. *Vultee BT-15 Valiant* PP-GUK ex 42-41773 and *Fairchild PT-19 Cornell* PP-GER ex 42-3187; *PP-GLF* c/n 3FG-214; and *PP-GUE* c/n 3FG-451 thought still airworthy. At Sao Paul's Quaratingueta Air Base *Republic P-47D-40-RA Thunderbolt* 45-4151 still in USAF marks "FE-151" is on show. *Douglas A-20 Havoc* A20 6085 and *NA B-25C Mitchell* B-25/5075, ex 41-1288, were thought earmarked for preservation, with *Lockheed 10A Electra* VC-66 2008 still flying. In Sao Paul City *Republic P-47D* serial F-47/4191, coded "C.3" is exhibited in a garden by main road.

QUINTERO. Chilean Air Force, Naval Air Base, 30 miles north of Valparaiso. At the entrance, as monument *Chance-Vought OS-2U-3 Kingfisher* (one of six supplied 1941, Navy Nos 5926-31, VSA nos 2417-2422. Can a reader say correct serial and provide up-to-date photo? Can a reader also please say what happened to the *CAP-1 Planalto* PP-RDW c/n 03 named "Visconde de Carlow" on 20 May 1944 at Santos-Dumont Airport, donated by the British/Canadian Colony and transferred to the Aeroclube da Paraiba by pilot Adail Neves Rodrigues on 5 July 1944. This was a mark of homage to Squadron Leader Viscount Carlow who had commanded No 600 (City of London) Sqdn, Auxiliary Air Force, and who became Air Attache in Brazil, losing his life over England 17 March 1944.

CHILE

SANTIAGO. Museo Aeronautico. *NA Harvard* serial 285. *Miles M.2R Hawk Major* CC-PFB "Saturno" which flew record flight Punta Arenas-Santiago Buenos Aires-Punta Arenas, 1936. *De Havilland DH.60G* "LAN" military serial G.35, which made first flight for Linea Aeropostal Al Norte 5 March 1929. *A Consolidated Catalina* CC-CNF is being restored, at the airport but whether for museum or to fly, is unknown. Details please. The museum also displays a *Grunau SG.9*, a *Minimoa* glider CC-PIA and the wings of an unidentified CC-KSD.

COLUMBIA

BOGOTA. El Dorado Airport. *Junkers Ju 52/3m* 652 built 1934, purchased by Colombian Air Force, later fitted with 640 hp Pratt & Whitney Hornets. Became President's personal transport, then general transport and ambulance. Displayed with nose-mounted P. & W., but with Wright Cyclones port and starboard. *Boeing-Stearman PT-17* FAC-62, personal machine of the Commandant. *Douglas B-26* HK-1247-W. *Fairchild C-82 Packet* HK-426 ex 45-57829. A Museum of the Air Force (FAC) is being established with *Junkers Ju 52/3m* serial 625, *Junkers K.43* (K for Kampfflugzeug —warplane) believed the world's only example, serialled 407—is it floatplane or ski version? *Lockheed F-80* FAC-2061. *Republic P-47* FAC-861. *NA Harvard* 772. *Hiller UH-12B* serial 220. *Beech AT-11* FAC-902. *Douglas B-26* FAC-2023. We shall look forward to up-dated details and illustrations.

EQUADOR

QUITO. Airport. *Douglas B-23 Dragon* HC-APV and *Beech TH-34 Mentor* marked TH344 on display in military area. One Ju 52/3m has been flown to USA and there may be others—details please, also of Noorduyn Norseman a/c believed here.

GUYANA

GEORGETOWN. Airport. Guyana Airways Corpn. *DC-3* 8R-GCF c/n 16448.

PARAGUAY

ASUNCION. Presidente Stroessner Airport. *Consolidated PBY-5A Catalina* ZP-CBA (one at least) flying. *P-38 Lightning* N6190C. *NA B-25 Mitchell* N8194H, N9076Z, N8193H (three at least). *Lockheed Lodestar* (several). *Norseman* ZP-CAZ. Other registrations or serials please, with pictures for V. and V.

PERU

COCHAMBAMBA. Airfield. *Beech 17* CP-613.

COLLIQUE. *Faucett-Stinson F.19* OB-I-140, believed airworthy, ex OB-PAO.

Faucett-Stinson F.19 (Lima)

LIMA. Jorge Chavez Airport. *Faucett-Stinson F.19* OA-BBQ "La Cucaracha" ex OB-R-147 displayed by Faucett. Also here *F.19* OB-R-143, OB-PAJ. *Cessna T-50 Bobcat* OB-T-372 c/n 4021, parked as display a/c, *Douglas DC-3* OB-R581 built as *C-53* 41-20060 c/n 4830, operated here by Servicios Aeros de Transportes Commerciales. Previously N54311, Peru AF 696, 60-314, OB-XAP. *Norduyn Norseman* OB-T-745 ex HC-SNB of Cia Transperuana, said for preservation. *Faucett-Stinson F.19* OB-R-141 said earmarked for USA? In the Parque de las Leyendas, preserved in jungle setting in Peruvian AF markings, *Grumman J2F-5 Duck* ex OB-KAA-164, first a/c used by Instituto Linguistico de Verano in 1946.

URUGUAY

LAGUNA-del-SAUCE. Naval Air Base. *Vought OS2U-3 Kingfisher* painted "752"—full serial and history please.

Vought Kingfisher (Laguna-del-Sauce)

MONTEVIDEO. Carrasco Airport. *NA P-51D Mustang* serialled 270 of Fuerza Aerea Uruguaya, needs restoration. *Lockheed F-80* serialled 210. Is the engineless *Short Sandringham* still in the dock area? Condition, please. A *Martin PBM-5A Mariner* and *Grumman F6F-5 Hellcat* said be readied for exhibition by Aviacion Naval Uruguaya—location and serials wanted.

VENEZUELA

MARACAY. Air Force HQs Museum. *Ryan Flamingo* NC9487 "El Rio Caroni" landed on plateau by Jimmy Angel October 1937 during search for Paul Redfern's a/c lost 1927 flying Georgia-Rio de Janeiro. Also *NA B-25 Mitchell. NA F-86 Sabre* and *NA T-6 Texan*. Serials please and photos.

Index
Part One Aeroplanes, Seaplanes, etc.

Part Two Hovercraft

Part Three Airships, Blimps, Balloons

Part Four Kites, Ornithopters, Man-Powered

Part Five Gliders

Part Six Drones, Piloted Drones Missiles, Missiles, Bombs

Part Seven Rockets (Peaceful) Satellites, Space Capsules, Spacecraft

Part Eight Replicas and Mock-ups: Gliders, Aeroplanes, Missiles, Capsules,

TOTALS:

Aeroplanes, Seaplanes etc.	8,235
Hovercraft	2
Airships, Blimps, Balloons	19
Kites, Ornithopters, Man-Powered	24
Gliders	243
Drones, Piloted Drones & Missiles, Missiles & Bombs	289
Rockets (Peaceful) Satellites, Space Capsules, Spacecraft	39
Replicas & Mock-ups	229
Grand total of entries	9,080

NOTES:

Aircraft built by more than one manufacturer are shown under the best-known, ie, all Mustangs under North American. Only complete aircraft are listed except in cases where the compiler is assured that a full restoration will be completed. Because of space limitations only brief details can be indexed and the compiler will appreciate corrections for any future editions. The figures in brackets after each type indicate the confirmed numbers at time of compilation.